INTRODUCTION TO BUSINESS LAW IN RUSSIA

Markets and the Law

Markets and the Law is concerned with the way the law interacts with the market through regulation, self-regulation and the impact of private law regimes. It looks at the impact of regional and international organizations (e.g. EC and WTO) and many of the works adopt a comparative approach and/or appeal to an international audience. Examples of subjects covered include trade laws, intellectual property, sales law, insurance, consumer law, banking, financial markets, labour law, environmental law and social regulation affecting the market as well as competition law. The series includes texts covering a broad area, monographs on focused issues, and collections of essays dealing with particular themes.

Other titles in the series

China's New Enterprise Bankruptcy Law
Context, Interpretation and Application
Edited by Rebecca Parry, Yongqian Xu, and Haizheng Zhang
ISBN 978 0 7546 7637 9

Product Liability Law in Transition
A Central European Perspective
Magdalena Tulibacka
ISBN 978 0 7546 4710 2

The Yearbook of Consumer Law 2009
Edited by Deborah Parry, Annette Nordhausen, Geraint Howells,
and Christian Twigg-Flesner
ISBN 978 0 7546 7574 7

Statutory Priorities in Corporate Insolvency Law
An Analysis of Preferred Creditor Status
Christopher F. Symes
ISBN 978 0 7546 7519 8

For more information on this series, visit www.ashgate.com

Introduction to Business Law in Russia

VLADIMIR ORLOV
University of Helsinki, Finland

ASHGATE

Published by
Ashgate Publishing Limited
Wey Court East
Union Road
Farnham
Surrey, GU9 7PT
England

Ashgate Publishing Company
Suite 420
101 Cherry Street
Burlington
VT 05401-4405
USA

www.ashgate.com

British Library Cataloguing in Publication Data
Orlov, Vladimir.
Introduction to business law in Russia. -- (Markets and the law)
1. Commercial law--Russia (Federation)
I. Title II. Series
346.4'707-dc22

Library of Congress Cataloging-in-Publication Data
Orlov, Vladimir, 1946-
Introduction to business law in Russia / by Vladimir Orlov.
p. cm. -- (Markets and the law)
Includes bibliographical references and index.
ISBN 978-0-7546-7755-0 (hbk) -- ISBN 978-0-7546-9498-4 (ebk)
1. Business law--Russia (Federation) 2. Commercial law--Russia (Federation) I. Title.
KLB78.B87O75 2010
346.4707--dc22

2010033248

ISBN 9780754677550 (hbk)
ISBN 9780754694984 (ebk)

MIX
Paper from responsible sources
FSC® C013056
FSC www.fsc.org

Printed and bound in Great Britain by
TJ International Ltd, Padstow, Cornwall.

Contents

Preface

This work is a result of my practical experience in Russian entrepreneurial law as a lawyer educated in Russia (Soviet Union) as well as of my studies and teaching at the University of Helsinki. Since I am also fully educated in Finnish law and give lectures and write on Scandinavian law, it is sometimes difficult to avoid the temptation to resort to a simplistic comparison of Russian law with its Western counterpart. Of course, there are issues in respect of which the comparison is productive, as, for instance, those related to the so-called instrumental community. A good example of this is foreign trade regulation. At the level of international trade, it would be pointless to expect that the solutions provided under Russian law to be any different compared with those under Western law. However, the situation is different as soon as one approaches the subject from the point of view of internal (domestic) legal relations, where the question is often of covert differences. At the heart of the matter, especially, are the comparisons between Russian law and common law.

Russian law is still undergoing a process of modernization as it moves ever closer to Western law. However, the systems are still different, regardless of the fact that Russian law originally developed under the influence of the Western legal tradition based on Roman law. In particular, the present Russian societal and cultural environment upon which the legal system stands itself remains different. Moreover, it would be unrealistic to believe that the same legal rules would work in the same way under a different legal system (especially in actual practice). Thus, without prejudice to the process of internationalization and globalization of law, I share with Professor W.E. Butler the idea that any productive study of Russian law requires an *internal* approach. My book therefore emphasizes a basic knowledge of Russian entrepreneurial law. For those who want to enlarge their knowledge of Russian law more generally I recommend Butler's book *Russian Law* (2009).

The legislation presented in this book is up to date at the time of going to press.

Vladimir Orlov
Helsinki

Acknowledgments

I am grateful to Klaus Viitanen, senior lecturer at the University of Helsinki, who made me to believe that a publisher in the United Kingdom could be interested in taking on my book. I am also indebted to Professor Geraint Howells from the University of Manchester, who put forward the idea and gave his support to it. I appreciate the publisher, Ashgate Publishing Ltd, for deciding to publish my book, and I am deeply thankful to the team who have worked on it and helped me to realize my dream. In particular, publisher Alison Kirk, editor Elaine Couper, assistant commissioning editor Sarah Horsley, proofreader Robert Anderson, and editorial administrator Carolyn Court deserve my acknowledgements for editing my work and making it internationally available. I would also like to thank my wife, Vappu, and daughter, Anna, for assisting me in the preparation of this book.

List of Abbreviations

Civil Code	Civil Code of the Russian Federation
Currency Law	Law on Currency Regulation and Currency Control
FTF Law	Fundamentals of State Regulation of Foreign Trade Activities
JSC Law	Joint Stock Company Law
LLC Law	Limited Liability Company Law

To my mother Anastasia Romanovna

Chapter 1
Features of Russian Law

1 Historical Background and Influences

Business law is in general understood as the legal norms regulating enterprise activities, whereas these activities in fact also comprehend the production of products, the performance of works, and the provision of services and transactions subsidiary to them. Business law also concerns personal noncommercial relations relating to business activities as well as state regulation purposed to protect public interests.[1]

The concept of profit-oriented enterprise is expressly enshrined in Russian law.[2] It is a direct reflection of the attempt to continue societal modernization by resorting to market-economy thinking based on the Western model[3] and to discard the socialist economy of the Soviet period when economic activities were based on the principle of planning.[4] Socialist planning was developed to extremes in the Soviet Union, and the concept of Soviet economic law[5] corresponded to it, and this has not yet been fully abandoned in the present Russian law. Hence the concept of economic law is still used alongside a concept of business or commercial law that stresses the regulation of private law. In so far as it stresses the importance of public regulation, economic law is regarded as forming its own branch of law, consolidating the norms of administrative and civil law.[6]

The generally accepted notion is that business law, as commercial legislation, forms the entity of general and special civil law norms. The characteristic feature of civil law regulation is that the parties participating in the relations subject to it are legally equal. Within the scope of application of business law norms which belong to the civil law are the legal relations of persons practicing enterprise activities, including direct relations between entrepreneurs (enterprises) as well as

1 See, for instance, S.E. Zhilinsky, Предпринимательское право [Entrepreneurial Law] (2007): 111–13.

2 According to the Russian Civil Code (Article 2.1), entrepreneurship (business activities) is defined as an independent activity, performed at one's own risk, aimed at systematically deriving a profit from the use of property, sale of goods, performance of work, or provision of services by persons registered in this capacity in conformity with the law-established procedure.

3 The development of the present Russian business law started in the early 1990s when the Russian state became independent and when the aim of creating a market economy in the country was declared.

4 In the Soviet period, the economic activities that state and cooperative enterprises practiced were subject to the general civil law as well as to special economic law norms. The purpose of the economic law norms was to regulate the management and practice of economic activities, or "vertical" legal relations, whereas "horizontal" legal relations between enterprises were regulated mainly by the civil law norms. Thus civil law regulation continued to exist and even developed in the Soviet Union. For more about the Soviet economic system. see V.V. Laptev and S.S. Zankovsky, Предпринимательское (хозяйственное) право [Entrepreneurial (Economic) Law] (2006): 3, the more detailed V. Orlov, *Entrepreneurship in Russia* (1999): 13–29 as well as the literature mentioned in them.

5 The consolidation of private and public law regulation known as *Wirtschaftsrecht* and in France as *droit économique*.

6 See, for instance, Laptev and Zankovsky 2006: iii.

those in which at least one party is an entrepreneur (enterprise).[7] Connected with this concept of business law is also the concept of business law as a legal discipline. In this sense business law as a discipline of studies handles specific features of the public and private law regulation of legal relations related to the practice of enterprise activities including the public organization of these.[8] In that case the scope of consideration includes norms of labor and land as well as administration, finance, tax, and other public law.

Civil law regulation, which covers the main part of the regulation of enterprise activities, was renewed in Russia by its total codification. The purpose of this was to establish new legal conditions for entrepreneurship by strengthening private law regulation. The present Civil Code,[9] composed of four parts, contains all the important civil law rules. Thus, all essential legal rules including definitions and principles can be found in the same statute. Moreover, within the Civil Code the whole body of civil law norms constitutes a solid, methodically structured, logical system of concepts and rules, which is divided into a general part (including basic concepts, principles, and rules) and a special part (including exceptions to, and specifications of, the general rules).[10] In this way, Russian civil law has achieved a relatively good consistency, which means logical (formal dogmatic) uncontradictoriness between legal norms, as well as coherency, which stands for the contentual congruence of the law.[11]

Russian law is grounded in the Roman law tradition.[12] Russian civil law especially is rooted mainly in the Roman–German legal tradition, in which the primary legal source is written law and the legislation is mainly codified. Above all, the roots of the modern civil law of Russia are substantially in Roman–German law, which was influenced by Roman law, and the historical school has had a dominant position in Russian (and, in principle also, Soviet) legal thinking.[13] German civil law influenced the development of Russian law mostly at the time when the doctrine of conceptual jurisprudence (*Begriffsjurisprudenz*) developed in the circle of the historical school. In particular, Russian civil law has been influenced by the German *Pandekt* law doctrine. According to this the legal acts and doctrines of different legal disciplines are divided into a general and a

---

7 V.F. Popondopulo (ed.), Коммерческое (предпринимательское) право [Commercial (Entrepreneurial) Law] 1 (2009): 19; and A.P. Sergeev (ed.), Гражданское право [Civil Law] 1 (2009): 22.

8 Popondopulo 1 2009: 19.

9 The Russian Civil Code represents a unique blend of theory, structure, and norms which collectively represent the transitional era that the Code is intended to both serve and facilitate. See W.E. Butler (ed.), *Civil Code of the Russian Federation,* Parts One, Two and Three (2003): xv.

10 The adoption of the last (fourth) part of the Civil Code signifies that the work on the codification of the Russian law that began at the end of the nineteenth century is now completed. See A.L. Makovsky (2008), “On the Fourth Part of Russia’s Civil Code,” in P.B. Maggs and A.N. Zhiltsov (eds and trans.), *Civil Code of the Russian Federation, Fourth Part*, Parallel Russian and English Texts (2008): 6 and 26.

11 This in practice means that the statute-positivistic approach to law in legal doctrine and practice has always dominated in Russian law and hence that it would be sufficient for a lawyer to read only the Civil Code in order to become acquainted with Russian civil law. In this context, it is worth mentioning that under the Russian legal tradition laws, albeit usually clearly defined, are provided for lawyers’ professional use.

12 The Roman law tradition influenced Russian law not only via Western Europe but was adopted originally, together with the Christian religion, through Byzantium. See, for instance, E.A. Sukhanov and L.L. Kofanov, О роли изучения римского права в России: историко-юридическое исследование [On the Role of Roman Law Studies] (1996): 9 and J.B. Salogubova, Влияние римского права на российское гражданское процессуальное законодательство [Impact of Roman Law on Russian Civil Process Legislation] (1997): 29–37.

13 The development of Soviet civil law was also based on German law regardless of the fact that the Soviet legal system was characterized as a socialist legal system.

special part.[14] However, while its roots are mainly in German law and, through this, in Roman law, Russian civil law should be regarded as relatively original. The explanation for this lies in societal and cultural differences.[15] That said, there are also signs of the influence of Anglo-Saxon common law.[16] [17]

Russian civil law is extensively codified, and written law, in which form not only proper legal rules but also abstract general concepts and general principles are shaped, holds a very strong position.[18] As to praxis and doctrine, they are not (at least officially) regarded as legal sources in Russian law. However, the role of the supreme judicial bodies—the Supreme Court[19] and Supreme Arbitrazh Court[20]—has grown recently in Russia, and their decisions, particularly where they have handed down guiding explanations or interpretive instructions concerning judicial practice, contained in plenum decrees,[21] are followed by the lower courts. These decisions are normative by their nature and thus have a certain generality and binding force.[22] There are also signs that the decisions of the supreme judicial bodies are being recognized as legal sources.[23] [24] One of the reasons for this change in attitude is the important role of Russian courts in verifying the legality of normative acts: if such an act is found to be illegal, it is vacated by the court.[25] Particularly

14 For more on this subject, see W.E. Butler, *Russian Law* (1999): 333–6; T. Giaro, Правовая традиция Восточной Европы: Эпитафия [Legal Tradition of Eastern Europe: Epitaph] (2006): 141–6; V.A. Letyayev, Проблема рецепции римского права в России: историко-юридическое исследование [The Problem of the Reception of Roman Law in Russia: History of the Study of Law] (2000): 61–2, and, in particular, W.E. Butler, *Russian Law* (2009): 388–93, which also contains an illuminating presentation on the comparative and historical aspects of Russian law (3–93).

15 A dependency on its own legal traditions is characteristic of Russia. It is also important to remark that Russian civil law of the Soviet period has not yet been fully abandoned and references to well-known Soviet civil law scholars remain common in the civil law literature.

16 There was an attempt in Russia to implant even trust institution from the common law system. Later on, however, this was modified into the entrusted administration of property.

17 Historical and comparative aspects regarding Russian civil law are presented, for instance, in Sergeev 1 2009: 91–2; Butler 2009: 387–94; C. Osakwe (trans. and comm.), *Russian Civil Code* (2008): 13–38, and V. Orlov, *Entrepreneurship in Russia* (1999): 67 and 359–67.

18 Regarding the contents of the Russian civil law norms, it can be stated that concepts and general rules dominate at the expense of concrete rules.

19 The Supreme Court is the highest instance in the general or ordinary jurisdiction.

20 The Supreme Arbitrazh Court is the highest instance in the system of arbitrazh, or commercial courts. The arbitrazh courts are established to solve entrepreneurial (economic) disputes.

21 *Постановления пленума.*

22 The plenums of the Supreme Court and Supreme Arbitrazh Court in Russia are competent to give not only decisions in concrete appeal cases, but also to generalize judicial practice and pass interpretative rules or guiding explanations on the applicable legal norms obligatory for the courts in the circle of its own system.

23 In respect of the decisions of supreme judicial bodies aimed at bringing judicial practice into uniformity, the opinion is presented in the legal literature that they may be regarded as legal sources that have legal force until a legislative solution can take place. See T.N. Neshataeva, Международное частное право и международный гражданский процесс [International Private Law and International Civil Procedure] (2004): 66–7. However, in Russian legal doctrine it is traditionally considered that judicial institutions do not create norms of law, but merely interpret and apply them. See Butler 2009: 105 and the works cited therein.

24 See Sergeev 1 2009: 61–3, M.N. Marchenko, Источники права [Sources of Law] (2005): 374–402. See also Osakwe 2008: 52–3 and the sources cited therein.

25 See Butler 2009: 103 and the material cited therein.

important are the normative explanations of the Constitutional Court[26] concerning constitutional issues, which are definitive in the Russian legal system. In any case, the role of precedents has grown in Russia, especially in respect of the practice of the Constitutional Court[27] and Supreme Arbitrazh Court. As a matter of fact, precedent is an integral component of Russian law.[28] The Russian legal system is well acquainted with precedents of interpretation and gap-filling, precedents arising out of judicial review, and precedents of discretion. As to the rarity of law-finding precedents,[29] the obvious explanation for it is the high level of codification within Russian law.

The general codification of Russian law, and especially the key position of written law within it, implies that legal discretion is mainly norm-bounded. Russian law in general holds fast to the law-positivistic, or to be exact statute-positivistic, approach.[30] According to classical thinking, the law is held to be a closed system and judicial decisions are deductively (syllogistically) constructed: general rules are applied to the concrete case. However, although legal-dogmatic reasoning still holds a strong position in Russian law, there are also indications of the influence of natural law in legal doctrine,[31] particularly in the practice of the Constitutional Court.[32] In giving its normative explanations concerning constitutional issues, this body is empowered to deviate from the text-

26 The Constitutional Court gives interpretations of the Constitution. It may examine federal laws and other normative acts as well as international treaties of Russia which have not yet entered into force. The Constitutional Court also considers appeals against violations of constitutional rights and inquiries from courts to verify the constitutionality of a law being applied or subject to application in a particular case. See Butler 2009: 174.

27 It is clear that the Constitutional Court, for instance, expects its previous decisions to be followed as *stare decisis*. See Butler 2009: 104–5. Furthermore, the position of judicial power in Russia has been strengthened by Decree no 1-П of 21 January 2010 of the Constitutional Court, by which it empowered the Supreme Court to review cases on the grounds of the appearance of new circumstances, including its new position on the legal question at issue.

28 See Butler 2009: 103–4. See also O.P. Saulyak, Судебная практика как источник российского права [Judicial Practice as the Source of Russian Law], Государство и право [State and Law] 11 (2009): 5–10, and A.A. Ivanov, Речь о прецеденте [Speech on Precedent], published online 19 March 2010, http://www.pravo.ru/review/view/26629/ (accessed 19 May 2010).

29 These four categories of precedents in Russian law are presented in Butler 2009: 104 and in literature mentioned in it.

30 Legal positivism refers to the view that laws must be obeyed, whatever their content. The legal-positivistic approach has been dominant in the Russian law during its modern and contemporary history. In the Soviet Union, the overemphasized role of the state was especially evident in the fact that statute law (in the form of written legal sources) was identified with law. According to this legal-positivistic way of thinking, all statute law was law simply for formal reasons regardless of its contents. This was supported by the principle of socialist legality, according to which legal norms given by the state should be followed exactly and consistently. Even in the 1990s the aim was to build a system of normative acts that totally regulated [*регламенттроватьс максимальной полнотой*] societal life. See, for instance, D.V. Chukhvichev, Кодификационные акты, их специфика и значение в системе права. [Codification Acts, Their Specificity and Significance in the System of Law], Государство и право [State and Law] 8 (2009): 5.

31 See, for instance, D.I. Lukovskaya, Личность и право в истории правовой мысли [Person and Law in the History of Legal Thinking] (2007): 36–8; V.S. Nersesyants, Философия права [Philosophy of Law] (1997): 142, and S.S. Aleksejev, Право: азбука – теория – философия: Опыт комплексного исследования [Law: Alphabet—Theory—Philosophy: Experiment of Complex Study] (1999): 50–51.

32 A good example of the critical attitude of the Constitutional Court to legal dogmatics is presented by its President. He regards a formalistic (that is, rooted in legal positivism) interpretation of law as invalid. See V. Zorkin (2009), "The Global Crisis, Law and Human Rights," *Russia in Global Affairs* 2, published online 7 June 2009, http//eng.globalaffairs.ru/numbers/27/1277.html (accessed 28 August 2009).

bound interpretation of the legal norms and has resorted to using this power in the interpretation of, for instance, tax law.[33] More recently the Constitutional Court has ventured, in its interpretation of the Constitution, to declare that fairness, legal equality, proportionality, and equity are the principles corresponding to the Constitution, and this may be interpreted as a legislative action. There are also other signs that the dogmatic approach is giving way to freer legal thinking, and this concerns the practice of not only the Constitutional Court but also other (federative) courts in which the civil law principles are applied. Under the Civil Code, the principle of fairness is applicable only to certain cases, but there is now a move to enforce fairness as the general principle of the civil law.[34] Thus, the possibilities for the adoption of decisions by using *in casu* discretion look set to be enlarged, and, consequently, the significance of judicial practice will grow.[35]

The Russian legal system is at present in the process of modernization and its civil law is evolving into a functioning system which is still under the influence of Western law. The norms regulating business activities especially are being renewed by following the models of the industrially developed countries. However, the operational environment is quite different and far from the market economy ideal. The position of the state is still strong in Russia, although its direct participation in enterprise is formally minimal. It is still expected that the task of the state is to set the legal norms and that citizens should obey them strictly. Administrative regulation continues to play a significant role in the direction of society, whereas customs and other quasi-legal means have not yet taken firm root in the business culture. However, the impact of the normative regulation on society is far from being effective, and the gap between the nominal values of behavior fixed in law and other normative acts and the real patterns of social and economic behavior, on which the activities of living enterprises are based, is deep.[36] Nonetheless, development continues, particularly on the side of business law, and necessary amendments are being made to the law. Furthermore, the adoption of the "law and economics" approach—the economic analysis of law which focuses on the influence of regulation and legal institutions on the operation of economic systems—is evidently now in process, at least in the doctrine of private law.[37] Irrespective of this, the Russian legal system nonetheless seems to preserve special features,[38] as indeed does the whole of Russian society and culture, the development of which is framed by the conditions imposed not only by world politics but also internal economic, societal, and cultural factors.

---

33 For instance, in its decision no. 11-P(3) of 15 July 1999, the Constitutional Court enforced the principle that any ambiguities of tax legislation shall be interpreted in favor of the taxpayer, whereas in its decision no. 5-P of 17 March 2009 a second tax inspection is regarded, in cases where the tax decision on the previous inspection has become legally final, as contradictory to the Constitution.

34 See V.V. Vitryansky, Обязательственное право: о проекте Концепции [Obligation Law: On Draft of Concept], Хозяйство и право [Economics and Law] 3 (2009): 19–20 and S. Sarbash, Исполнение обязательств [Fulfillment of Obligations], Хозяйство и право [Economics and Law] 3 (2009): 24–8.

35 Significant in this respect is the rule of the Joint Stock Company Law on the rights of shareholders to appeal the decision of the general meeting of the company (Article 49.7). It provides that the appealed decision may remain in force if the vote of the shareholder who appealed would not affect the voting results, if the violations are not essential, and if the decision has not incurred losses to the appellant. Such a rule can be regarded as referring to the consequential approach which belongs to the argumentation theory.

36 In general, the problem of the legitimacy of legislation is still current in Russia.

37 See, for instance, Yu. B. Shubnikov, Об экономических началах частного права [On the Economic Foundations of Private Law], Научные труды РАЮН [Scientific Works of RALS] 9/2 (2009): 893–5; E.A. Sukhanov, Гражданское право России—частное право [*Russian Civil Law—Private Law*] (2008): 14 and 27, and Zhilinsky 2007: 13–16.

38 In particular, it concerns domestic issues.

2 State Regulation of Enterprise Activities[39]

The purpose of the state regulation of enterprise activities in Russia is to secure public interests: among others, to protect the society from the negative consequences possibly connected with its practice as well as to promote conditions for macroeconomic stability and improve competition and consumer protection. The legal basis for the regulation of the Russian economy is formed by the provisions of the Constitution of the Russian Federation[40] on social state (Article 7), freedom of economic activity, protection of different forms of property, guarantees of integrity of the economic space, and support of competition (Article 8) as well as a prohibition on monopolistic activities and unfair competition (Article 34).

The legal basis for the regulation of business activities is provided at the level of the Russian Federation,[41] whose competence includes economic legislation. It is explicitly provided in the Constitution of the Russian Federation that its jurisdiction includes:

- the establishment of the basics of federal policy and federal programs in the sphere of economic development;
- the establishment of the legal grounds for a single market, and
- financial, currency, credit, and customs regulations, monetary issues, and the basics of pricing policy.

The state regulation is performed by state bodies and officials, the competence of which is strictly determined by the law or other normative acts or agreements. In relations with entrepreneurs, the authorities are barred from using power which is not granted by law.[42]

Regulatory Bodies

State regulation is performed in Russia by both generally and specially empowered bodies. Under the Constitution, the generally empowered authorities at the Federation level are the President of the Russian Federation, Federal Assembly, the Government and courts. As the head of state, the President ensures the effective functioning of the state bodies and determines the basic guidelines of the internal and foreign policy of the state (Article 80). The President issues ukases, or edicts,[43] and executive orders[44] (Article 90). The Federal Assembly is a parliament, the representative and legislative body, and is composed of the Council of the Federation and State Duma (Articles 94 and 95). The Government is the executive authority and carries out the tasks vested in it by the Constitution, federal laws, and ukases of the President (Article 114). Among other things, the Government:

39 For more on this subject, see, for instance, Popondopulo 1 2009: 82–103 and Laptev and Zankovsky 2006: 46 and 338–414.

40 See, for instance, *Constitution of the Russian Federation.* Конституция Российской Федерации. *Venäjän federaation perustuslaki* (Helsinki: Finnish Lawyers' Publishing, 1994). See also http://www.constitution.ru/en/10003000-01.htmo (accessed 17 June 2010).

41 Russia is a federative state and the Russian Federation consists of the subjects of the Federation (republics, territories, and regions, cities of federal importance, autonomous regions, and autonomous areas). Russia also has local self-government (administered by municipal bodies).

42 Popondopulo 1 2009: 92.

43 *указ.*

44 *распоряжение.*

- works out and submits the federal budget to the State Duma and ensures its implementation;
- submits to the State Duma a report on the implementation of the federal budget;
- ensures the implementation of a single financial, credit, and monetary policy across the Russian Federation, and
- manages federal property.

The Government also issues decrees[45] and orders or regulations and ensures their implementation.[46]

The Russian judicial system is comprised of the Constitutional Court, general courts, and arbitrazh courts, whose jurisdiction includes the settling of economic disputes.

Specially empowered authorities of the Russian Federation include the Counting Chamber, the Procurator's Office and the Central Bank, the legal status and powers of which are determined by federal laws, ukases of the President and Government decrees. The Counting Chamber executes the state financial control.[47] Among the tasks of the Procurator's Office is general legality control,[48] while the Central Bank controls the system of credits and payments.[49]

The structure of federal executive bodies is determined, according to the Constitution, by the President on the proposal of the Chairman of the Government (Article 112). They comprise, firstly, of ministries, including the Ministry of Trade and Economic Development, whose tasks concern the development of state policy and the normative regulation of the field of activities within the competence of each. Under the federal executive bodies are also services such as the Financial Markets Service which execute control in the field of activities within the competence of each. Besides agencies, such as the Federal State Property Agency there are federal bodies with executive power, and their duties are to provide state services in the field of their competence, to manage state property, and to conduct the administration of justice; supervisory functions, however, are outside their competence. State committees also belong to Russia's federal executive bodies, and their tasks concern the development of state policy and normative regulation, the administration of justice and supervisory functions as well as the provision of state services in the field of activities under the competence of each. By the decision of the Russian Government, federal executive bodies, in order to exercise their powers, may establish their own territorial bodies, as provided by the Constitution (Article 78).

Under federal law, the regulation of enterprise activities can be delegated to subjects of the Russian Federation. Therefore, under the Law on the State Aid for Small- and Medium-sized Entrepreneurship (no 88-FZ of 14 June 1995) some subjects of the Russian Federation have issued their own laws on the promotion of small businesses. Enterprise activities are also indirectly affected at the level of the subjects of the Federation—for instance, by administrative legislation and laws on the exploitation of natural resources, which belong to the joint jurisdiction of the Federation and its subjects. Enterprise activities are also regulated by local autonomous bodies within their authority.[50]

Regulatory Means

In order to protect the public interest, the Russian state offers the following means of regulating enterprise activities:

---

45 *постановление.*

46 For more on this subject, see, for instance, Butler 2009: 93–100.

47 Law on the Counting Chamber no 4-FZ of 11 January 1995.

48 Law on the Prosecution service no 2202-1 of 17 January 1992.

49 Law on the Central Bank no 86-FZ of 10 July 2002.

50 Laptev and Zankovsky 2006: 32–3.

- the state registration of enterprise activities and their licensing;
- the protection of competition;
- state support for small entrepreneurship;
- price and quality regulation;
- bookkeeping and auditing;
- tax and customs regulation;
- privatization and nationalization;
- state regulation of foreign trade activities; and
- a system of currency regulation.

Enterprise activities are in Russia also subject to state control, whose targets include:

- market situation;
- the quality and safety of products;
- prices subject to regulation; and
- the import and use of currency.

Where there are abuses, penalties that may be imposed in Russia include the cancellation of registration and/or licenses as well as monetary fines. Russia's administrative legislation also provides for other administrative sanctions, while the Russian criminal code also contains provisions for criminal sanctions in the case of economic crimes.[51]

3 The Basis for Enterprise Activities in Civil Law

Legal Sources[52]

The legal regulation of entrepreneurship is realized in Russia mainly by civil law norms. The majority of these norms is contained in the Civil Code[53] and other civil laws. In certain cases, international law is also applied to entrepreneurial relations. Business law rules can be included within other normative acts, which are called, in Russian law, normative acts subordinated to laws (substatutory acts). Commercial customs, trade customs, or customs of business turnover are recognized as legal sources, while the use of standard contract conditions and application of analogy[54] are also known in Russian civil law. However, judicial practice is not regarded (at least traditionally) as a proper legal source,[55] although

51 Popondopulo 1 2009: 100–103.

52 For more on this subject, see, for instance, Popondopulo 1 2009: 60–81; Laptev and Zankovsky 2006: 31–40 Sergeev 1 2009: 44–79, and, in particular, M.I. Braginsky, V.V. Vitryansky, Договорное право. Общие положения [Contract Law. General Provisions] (1999): 35–78 and 88–145.

53 The Civil Code is the product of a transitional era in Russian law. It drew upon the prerevolutionary Russian civil law tradition and upon models found in continental Europe, and gives occasional evidence of the influence of common law. The Civil Code also retains many elements of Soviet civil law. It is particularly important for the common law lawyer to understand that the Civil Code is not merely a compilation of particular rules, but rests upon principles and definitions developed in legal doctrine, wherefore the Code constitutes a system of interrelated norms. See Butler 2009: 391–4.

54 See below.

55 According to the opinion presented in Russian legal doctrine, the decrees of the plenums of the supreme judicial bodies aimed at the unification of legal practice can be considered as legal sources, which are in force for a limited time, at least, until the legislative decision solving the problem is made. See Neshataeva 2004: 66–7.

the decrees of supreme judicial bodies are recognized as having precedential value in Russia. On the other hand, by its decisions the Constitutional Court changes and even rescinds normative acts which are in contradiction with the Constitution. Therefore, such decisions could be seen as having legislative effect. In Russia, the regulation of civil law regulation is also realized on the nonnormative level, for instance, by single law application acts and usage, course of dealing and course of performance.

System of civil legislation The term "legislation" is used in Russian law in both the large and narrow sense—in the narrow sense, legislation means only laws (statutes), whereas, in the large sense, it also includes other legal acts. In the narrow sense, the Russian civil legislation comprises the Civil Code and federal laws issued in accordance with it.[56] In the large sense, however, it comprises, in addition to the Civil Code and federal laws issued in accordance with it, other normative acts containing civil law norms. These include other laws and normative acts subordinated to the law (substatutory acts), such as ukases issued by the President and decrees issued by the Government, and normative acts issued by ministries and other executive authorities. The names of legal acts are used rather consistently in the Civil Code and other laws. If the text of a civil law norm mentions "the law," this must be interpreted as meaning the Civil Code and other laws. But "the law and other legal acts" means not only the law but also ukases and decrees (substatutory acts). Sometimes also normative acts are mentioned in the civil law rules, which mean any legal act issued by any state body.[57]

The Constitution of the Russian Federation is used to be mentioned as a source of civil law. The Constitution protects citizens' property rights and their right to use freely their abilities and property for enterprise and other activities not prohibited by law on condition that it is not aimed at monopolization and unfair competition (Articles 34–6). Additionally, the Constitution determines the form of civil legislation and the hierarchy of its norms (Articles 15 and 71).

The normative acts containing the norms of civil law must be published in Russia. According to the Constitution (Article 105.1), federal laws are adopted by the State Duma, and so are regarded as approved from the moment the State Duma has adopted the decision. A federal law adopted by the State Duma is to be submitted within five days for the consideration of the Council of the Federation (Article 105.3), and after this submitted further, also within five days, to the President for signing and making public (Article 107.1). The President must sign the federal law within 14 days (Article 107.2), and thereafter it must be published within seven days.[58] With some exceptions other legal acts must be published within ten days after the adoption. In general, a new law comes into effect ten days after its adoption or immediately on the date of its publication. In some cases the new law or other legal act contains a provision whereby it comes into force at a specified date.[59]

Hierarchy of civil law norms The hierarchy of civil legislative acts is determined directly by the Civil Code (Article 3). Following the provisions of the Constitution, federal law takes absolute priority. Federal law may be used to regulate any issue, unless otherwise indicated in

56 Particularly, their enactment is under the competence of the Russian Federation. See Sergeev 1 2009: 49–50.

57 See, in particular, T.E. Abova, M.M. Boguslavsky, A.Y. Kabalkin, and A.G. Lisicin-Svetlanov (eds), Постатейный комментарий к Гражданскому кодексу Российской Федерации, Частям I, II и III [Article-specific Commentary on the Civil Code of the Russian Federation, Parts I, II and III] (2007): 21–3.

58 Normative acts are published in Russia in the *Российская газета* periodical and *Собрание законодательства Российской Федерации* collection of legislation.

59 The rules on the enactment of laws are contained into the Law no 5-FZ of 14 July 1994. The procedure for the enactment of other legal acts is, in turn, regulated by the Ukase no 763 of 23 May 1996.

the Constitution. According to the Civil Code, civil legislation falls under the Constitution within the jurisdiction of the Russian Federation, and it consists of the Civil Code and other federal laws adopted in accordance with it. In respect of all other laws, the Civil Code requires in principle that the norms they include shall be consistent with it. This means that, in order to impose a new rule, the corresponding amendments must be made in the Civil Code.[60] Furthermore, many norms of the Civil Code contain references only to law, and consequently they contain prohibitions to enact or apply a normative act subordinated to the law.

Other normative acts still form a significant part of Russian civil legislation. However, although the legal acts of the President, Government, ministries, and other Russian executive authorities are regarded as civil law sources, they do not belong to civil legislation proper.

In respect of the presidential ukase, the Civil Code provides that civil law relations may be regulated by them, but only on condition that such ukases do not contradict the Civil Code and other laws (Article 3.3). An ukase may contain guidelines or rules on the application of civil law norms, the purpose of which is to govern relations unregulated by law.[61]

The legal grounds for the power of the Government to issue decrees containing civil law norms can only be, according to the Civil Code, the Civil Code itself and other laws as well as presidential ukases, and is restricted only to the implementation of these (Article 3.4). The Civil Code and other laws sometimes contain direct provisions on the enactment of the Government's decrees. In certain cases, the Civil Code refers directly to the possibility of issuing a law or other legal act, and it also means that the governmental decree may be applied to the legal relation in question.

In respect of the legal acts of federal executive bodies or substatutory acts, the Civil Code provides that these bodies may issue acts containing civil law norms in the cases, and within the limits, provided by the Civil Code, other laws and legal acts (ukases and decrees) (Article 3.7). Thus, the issuance of any administrative normative act must be grounded in the provision of the law or other legal acts.[62]

The priority of the law over normative acts subordinated to the law is directly enforced in the Civil Code. According to Article 3.5, in the event of a conflict between an ukase or decree and the Civil Code or other law, the provisions of the Civil Code or law must be applied. Thus, the ukases and decrees clearly differ by their legal force from the laws and, consequently, in the event that the court discovers a contradiction between the ukase or decree and the Civil Code or other law, it is not only its right but also obligation to leave the contradictory normative acts subordinated to the law inapplicable. As to administrative acts contrary to law, they may be left inapplicable or recognized as invalid by the court.[63]

The rules on the horizontal hierarchy of legal norms are purported to clarify which one of the norms placed at the same level in the vertical hierarchy shall be applied first, and they have usually concerned the question of priority of different laws in Russian law. Traditionally these

60 Abova, Boguslavsky, Kabalkin, and Lisicin-Svetlanov 2007: 22.

61 Abova, Boguslavsky, Kabalkin, and Lisicin-Svetlanov 2007: 22.

62 In Russia, the special order is provided (by Ukase no 763 of 23 May 1996) for the legal acts of federal executive bodies which have the potential to interfere with human and citizens' rights and freedoms as well as obligations, or which determines the legal position of the organization, or for interdepartmental acts. Except where they are secret, such legal acts must be published and registered. As a consequence of noncompliance with these requirements, such a legal act is not regarded as having come into force and thus not considered a legal source. The contract term referring to such an act is also regarded as invalid. Russian judicial practice directly enforces that references to such an act in judicial procedure are ineffective. See Popondopulo 1 2009: 75–6.

63 See further the presentation on legal protection and liability in this chapter.

rules have covered two standards: 1) *lex posterior derogat priori* (or the latter rule shall prevail over the previous one) and 2) *lex specialis derogat legi generali* (the special rule shall prevail over the general rule). The enactment of the Civil Code has additionally presented to the horizontal hierarchy a third dimension, in which the question is of the relationship between the Civil Code and other federal laws.

The standard giving priority to the latter rule is general. Ordinarily, a new law comes into force in Russia ten days after the date of its publication, and other new legal acts seven days after the date of their publication or on the same date. In some cases, a new law or other legal act may contain a provision for it to come into force on a certain day. And so the effective dates for the Civil Code were established in respect of the first part on 1 January 1995, the second on 1 March 1996, the third on 1 March 2002, and the fourth one on 1 January 2008. According to the laws on their enforcement (no 52-FZ of 30 November 1994, no 15-FZ of 26 January 1996, no 147-FZ of 26 November 2001, and no 231-FZ of 18 December 2006), the previous legislative acts were repealed.

The principle giving priority to the latter rule is also clearly present in the rules of the Civil Code on the scope of application in time of civil law norms (Article 4).

The standard prioritization of a special rule is not directly provided in the Civil Code as a general rule,[64] but it is definitely recognized as a general principle in Russian civil law.[65] As a matter of fact, the Civil Code is constructed by using a division between general and special norms. So the general part of the Civil Code, divided itself into general rules regulating obligations and contracts, is placed within the first part of the Civil Code, whereas norms regulating different types of obligations or contracts form the majority of the second part of the Civil Code. The structure of the second part also represents the division into general and special rules. For instance, the norms regulating (purchase and) sale, leases and work also contain, besides the general rules, specific rules on the modifications of these types, such as the supply (of goods), hire and construction work, which in Russian law are regarded as single types of contract.

The enactment of the Civil Code has brought along, as stated above, a third dimension to the horizontal hierarchy of legal norms: the Civil Code includes the provision according to which the civil law norms contained in other laws must be consistent with the Civil Code (Article 3.2). This rule does not cause interpretation problems with respect to ordinary laws, since the Civil Code, as a federal law, prevails in case of conflict. However, the relationship of the Civil Code to other federal law is rather complicated.

Although the Civil Code is a federal law, it is, however, not a constitutional law although its legal force is comparable with that of a constitutional law. In relation to other federal law, the Civil Code is considered as the *primus inter pares*, or the first among equals. According to established opinion in the Russian civil law doctrine, this means that, if there is an intention to adopt a legal act comprising norms deviating from the Civil Code, the respective changes must also be made to

64 The norm prioritizing the special rule occurs only in the norms regulating contracts. According to the rule-defining contract, obligations arising from contracts are subject to the general rules on obligations, unless otherwise specified by the rules on contracts in the Civil Code (Article 420.3).

65 It is supported merely by arguments relating to the legislation technique. Otherwise, the legal system would be comprised merely of general rules and the special rules specifying them, in which case it could be impossible to present the specific nature of certain legal relations in the legislation. The question is also of economy of text, meaning that it is futile to repeat the general rules in the specific norms on types of contract. In addition to considerations of legislation technique, the use of general rules provides for securing the integrity of the legal regulation, and gives help in filling legislative gaps. See Braginsky and Vitryansky 1999: 50.

the Civil Code; otherwise only the norms of the Civil Code shall be applicable. Thus, in the event of conflict between the Civil Code and other federal law norms, the norms of the Civil Code are to prevail. However, it does not mean that the legislator has no power to deviate from the rules of the Civil Code in the new federal law, but, if he does so, the corresponding amendments must be made also to the Civil Code.[66] This rule has been respected in the present legislative practice in Russia: the new laws have included provisions on the necessary amendments to the Civil Code and other law.[67]

Scope of application of civil law norms Regarding time validity of norms, the Civil Code contains both general and special rules. The general rule, according to which civil legislation acts do not have a retroactive effect and are to be applied to relations arising after their entry into force (Article 4), concerns any civil law relations. On the other hand, the general rule contains a provision which directly makes it possible for the effect of a law to extend to relations arising prior to its entry into force, but only in cases directly provided by a law (Article 4.1). However, such an effect may be provided only by the Civil Code or another federal law issued in accordance with it. Furthermore, the general time application norm includes a provision according to which, in respect of relations arising prior to the entry into force of a civil legislation act, that this is applicable only to rights and duties arising after its entry into force (Article 4.2).[68] In respect of contracts, the general time application norm includes the provision that the relations of the parties under a contract concluded prior to the entry into force of a civil legislation act are to be regulated in accordance with the special rules on time validity of the contract law norms (Article 4.2).

The special rules on time validity of the contract law norms (concerning contract and its relationship to the law) are based on the same starting point as the general rule or prohibition on the retroactive application of the law (Article 422). They provide that, if after the conclusion of a contract a law is adopted establishing rules obligatory for the parties other than those that were in effect at the time the contract was concluded, the terms of the concluded contract shall remain in force (Article 422.2). Thus, the special rules of the Civil Code on time application concerning contracts are based on the general principle *pacta sunt servanda*, which means not only the binding effect of a contract but also that the rules of the new law are not applicable to contracts concluded before the law has came into force.

On the other hand, the special rules of the Civil Code on time application concerning contracts also contain exceptions from the rule preventing retroactive effect of the new law. First, the rules are not to be applied to cases when the law specifically provides that its effects extend to relations arising from previously concluded contracts. Second, the same norm provides that a contract must comply with the rules obligatory for the parties established by law as well as by other legal acts (imperative norms) which are in effect at the time of its conclusion (Article 422.1). Thus, only the imperative (mandatory) norms of the law determined to be applied are to be applied to the contract relations arising from contracts concluded before the adoption of the new law. As to the dispositive norms, they are without any legal significance in this instance, since any term of a contract regardless of its content is considered as corresponding to the dispositive norms.[69]

66 See Sergeev 1 2009: 56–7 and Braginsky and Vitryansky 1999: 53–4.

67 See, for instance, the law on the enforcement of the fourth part of the Civil Code no 231-FZ of 18 December 2006.

68 This is an ordinary solution in the rules on the entry into force of a new law.

69 So, in respect of a contract relation, and in cases where the law does not impose retroactive application, the provisions of a new law are also not applicable to the rights and duties related to the relations concluded before the law came into force and which, however, have arisen after it. This is the main difference between

Under the Russian Constitution (Article 71), civil legislation regulating business activities falls, as stated above, within the jurisdiction of the Russian Federation and this rule is repeated in the Civil Code (Article 3.1). This rule indicates that only the Civil Code and federal laws adopted in accordance with it form Russian civil legislation, the norms of which are in force in respect of the whole territory of Russia. Thus, neither the subjects of the Federation nor local self-government bodies may issue their own civil law norms.[70] This does not, however, exclude the situation that a federative body might delegate the adoption of a legislative act to the decision of the subject of the Russian Federation.

On the other hand, the Constitution (Article 72) contains a list of the questions which belong to the joint jurisdiction of the Federation and its subjects. Those questions concern possession, use and prescription of land, subsoil, water, and other natural resources, and housing, land, water, forest, and subsoil legislation. On these issues, the subjects of the Federation are empowered to issue their own legislation, which may not, however, contradict federal laws (Article 76).

Civil law norms are general and they are in principle addressed to every civil law subject. As such subjects, the Civil Code mention citizens or physical persons, including also citizens of foreign countries and stateless persons, Russian and foreign juristic persons,[71] and public law subjects such as the Russian Federation, its subjects, and municipal formations. There are also exclusions to the rule in Russian civil law according to which certain civil law constructions are purported to be used by a certain personnel circle—for instance, entrepreneurs, consumers, banks. There are, for instance, rules the application of which is dependent on whether their subject is a physical or juristic person, or a public law person. Thus different legal regimes are established for them. Differences in the legal status are created in Russian civil law depending on whether an individual entrepreneur or a commercial organization is in question. Also Russian and foreign persons are separated. In many cases the civil law rules are addressed to certain concrete subjects—for instance, to the members of a company or consumers.

Russian contract law regulation, in particular, uses largely person-based classifications. Therefore, the general part of the obligation law of the Civil Code contains in addition to general rules the rules on contracts connected with enterprise activities. Moreover, there are differences in the rules regulating certain types of contracts or modifications thereof depending on which party is in question.[72] In some cases, the participation of an entrepreneur in a contract has, in accordance with the rules on some types of contract, a constitutive effect for it, and some types of contract and modifications thereof require that both parties of a contract are entrepreneurs.

Applicative nature of civil law norms Civil law rules which form norm-based regulation are in general applied voluntarily. Parties to civil law relations comply with them in the first instance. However, the application of legal norms also belongs to the tasks of authorities, and judicial bodies are to apply legal norms particularly in instances where the parties are, for instance, in dispute. The

---

the general rule on time application (Article 4) and the one concerning contracts (Article 422) in the Civil Code. See Braginsky and Vitryansky 1999: 102.

70 The Supreme Arbitrazh Court has therefore stated that any legislative act issued by a subject of the Federation on the obligatory registration of contracts that are not subject to registration under federal laws shall not be applicable since it is contradictory to the Civil Code. See the Informative Letter of the Presidium of the Supreme Arbitrazh Court no 53 of 16 February 2001. Вестник Высшего Арбитражного Суда Российской Федерации [Herald of Supreme Arbitrazh Court of Russian Federation] 4 (2001): 19–33.

71 On the legal status of foreign persons, see the presentation on civil law subjects.

72 Under Soviet civil law, contracts were divided in accordance with their subjects into contracts between socialist corporations or economic law contracts; contracts between citizens, and general civil law contracts.

answer to the question of how obligatory is the application of the norm shall be found by clarifying its applicative nature. The main part of Russian civil law norms are divided into imperative and dispositive norms.

The concepts of imperative and dispositive norms are well-established in Russian law and are used in the Civil Code. According to the rules enforcing the principle of freedom of contract, where a term of contract is provided by a norm which shall be applied as long as the parties have not reached an agreement to the contrary (a dispositive norm), the parties may by their agreement exclude its application or establish a term different from that provided in it, and in the absence of such an agreement the term of the contract shall be determined by the dispositive norm (Article 421.4). In turn, the rules on imperative norms are included within the norm of the Civil Code concerning relations between contract and law according to which a contract must comply with the rules obligatory for the parties established by a law and other legal acts (imperative norms) which are in effect at the time of its conclusion. The dispositiveness of the legal norm is determined in Russian law in a traditional way, which means that the norm itself expresses the application of it, unless otherwise provided by the contract. Such a provision could also cover a number of rules. Therefore, it is clear that in Russian law imperativeness rather than dispositiveness still continues to be presumed.[73]

Civil law regulation is performed in Russia also by facultative norms. These are norms the application of which requires that parties have agreed on their application, and where such an agreement must be expressed in a positive way.[74] Furthermore, reference norms are also known in the Russian civil law. They are used generally in contract regulation, and mean that the rules regulating a certain legal relation (contract) are to be applied to another, usually similar one.

International legal sources Universally recognized principles and norms of international law as well as the international treaties of the Russian Federation are, according to the Russian Constitution (Article 15.4), an integral part of its legal system. Furthermore, the Constitution provides that, if an international treaty to which the Russian Federation is a signatory establishes rules which differ from those provided by law, then the rules of the international treaty are to be applied. These rules are repeated in the general part of the Civil Code (Article 7). Thus, Russian law is subordinated to the general rule that, if Russia signs up to an international treaty, the provisions in it are to prevail in Russian law over those civil law norms applicable to the case. However, international treaties contradictory to the Constitution are not applicable (Article 125.6).

The priority of international principles and norms of international law as well as the international treaties of the Russian Federation are also enforced in many other laws. According to the law on international treaties of the Russian Federation (no 101-FZ of 15 July 1995), the rules of international treaties of the Russian Federation which do not require enactment of an internal legal act for their application are to be directly applied. They are directly in force in Russia, whereas the application of other norms of international law must be provided by an internal legal act.

The question of what international treaties are *directly* applicable is clearly answered in Russian law. According to the Civil Code (Article 7.2), international treaties of the Russian Federation are to be applied to relations regulated by civil legislation directly except in cases where it follows from an international treaty that the adoption of an internal legal act is required for its application. The necessity to adopt an internal legal act, in turn, arises in general owing to a provision included

73 See, for instance, Sukhanov 2007: 85.

74 Thus the legal effect of the facultative norm is based on the direct reference to it in the contract. Such norms grant a large discretion to the parties. For instance, partners may agree, under the rules of the Civil Code (Article 76.1), that their general partnership will not be liquidated but continue its activities.

within the international legal act according to which the member state undertakes to enforce it. In ratifying an international treaty the member state may impose certain reservations on it. In the application of an international treaty whose enforcement requires an internal legal act this provision is also to be observed.[75]

Commercial custom and usage[76] Commercial custom or custom of business turnover and usage are recognized as legal sources in the Civil Code, and they are applicable particularly in the obligation law relations connected with enterprise activities. A commercial custom is a rule of behavior which has evolved and is widely used in any domain of entrepreneurial activities, and is not provided for by legislation, regardless of whether it has been fixed in any document (Article 5.1). Moreover, the Civil Code provides that the applicable custom of trade is not contradictory to the provisions of the law or contract which are obligatory for the participants of in the corresponding relation (Article 5.2).

Commercial custom has an important place among legal sources. Its purpose is to fill gaps which occur in the applicable law, other legal act or contract. According to the general contract law rules of the Civil Code (Article 421.5), if the conditions of a contract are not defined by the parties or the dispositive norms, the respective conditions are to be determined by the commercial custom applicable to the relations of the parties. Thus, the commercial custom is to be applied, unless otherwise provided by the imperative norms of the law or other legal act, the contract or dispositive norms of any normative act.

Usage is referred to in many contract law rules of the Civil Code, and it is expressed by using different terms which mean customary. Commercial custom is distinguished from usage because its application does not require any references to it in the applicable rule of the Civil Code in instances where the subject of regulation is entrepreneurial contract relations, since commercial custom is recognized as a general legal source in respect of such relations. Regarding enterprise activities, commercial customs are always to be used in filling gaps in the legal act or contract. In turn, usage is applicable only where a concrete legal rule refers to it.

Course of dealing is also a known concept in Russian law. It is generally understood to be a sequence of conduct shaped in practice between the parties during prior, usually repeated, transactions in a way that indicates their intentions. In the Civil Code the expression "other generally accepted requirements" (Article 309) and "prior business relations of the parties" (Article 438) are used to mean course of dealing.[77] Owing to the parties having consented to follow such a conduct rule, it can gain legal significance; otherwise, it has no legal force and is not regarded as a legal source. Course of dealing is considered only as a special means by which it is possible to complete the content of the intentions of the parties without resorting to legal sources. Usually a course of dealing is expressed as an implied term of the contract.

Interpretation of civil law norms[78] Rules on the interpretation of civil law norms are absent from Russian civil legislation. These questions are of a general nature and explored in Russia in general legal science or the matter of law and state theory.

---

75 See, for instance, G.K. Dmitrieva (ed.), Международное частное право [International Private Law] (2010): 68–71.

76 For more on this subject, see, for instance, Popondopulo 1 2009: 67–8; Sergeev 1 2009: 63–71 and 75–8, and Braginsky and Vitryansky 1999: 63–78.

77 Sergeev 1 2009: 78.

78 For more on this subject, see, for instance, E.A. Sukhanov (ed.), Гражданское право, Том I [Civil Law, Volume I] (2007): 115–16 and Braginsky and Vitryansky 1999: 136–45.

The main purpose of the interpretation of a norm is to link it to its application and this generally comprises clarifying its content. As a process of clarification, interpretation is executed in different ways. Russian legal science is familiar with the generally known linguistic,[79] logical,[80] systematic,[81] historical, political,[82] and teleological[83] methods of interpretation. Special legal interpretation, which focuses on the analysis of special terms, as well as on the legal techniques and modes of expression of the will of the legislator, is also known in Russia.

Authentic interpretation based on the literal meaning of the text is the main rule in the Russian law. Only where the actual content is different from the text of the norm, is the application of extensive or restrictive interpretation allowed. In these cases, for instance, logical or systematic interpretation take place. Furthermore, the Civil Code includes a number of presumption rules that imply the legislator's will and are purported to facilitate interpretation.[84] However, the hypothetic will of the legislator may not, according to the established opinion in Russian civil law doctrine, supersede the text of the norm, which essentially restricts the possibilities of using the extensive and restrictive interpretation.[85] This clearly reflects the dominance of the statute-positivistic approach in Russian law. The use of extensive and restrictive interpretation is restricted in Russian civil law also on other grounds. Usually it is a question of exception norms or a situation where the legislator's will is clearly expressed in the norm, wherefore the extensive or restrictive interpretation is not allowed. In respect of extensive interpretation, there is also another restriction: it is prohibited if the civil law norm contains an exhaustive list of the grounds for its application.[86]

The official interpretation of the legal norms is the most important one. It is implemented in the form of an official document, and is obligatory for the bodies of administration of justice. It may be passed as a normative or *in casu* explanation. The official interpretation is authentic if it is given by the same body which has issued the legal act, or a legal, if the interpreter is the body empowered to it. Legal interpretation acts may be given in Russia by the Government, by ministries and by other executive bodies.

The official interpretation of legal norms also gets its form through judicial interpretation. The question here is of the interpretive explanations of the Russian supreme judicial bodies, the Supreme Court and the Supreme Arbitrazh Court. In certain cases these judicial bodies—to be precise, their plenums—give interpretive instructions concerning the legislation in force based on generalized practice, which are obligatory for the lower courts, and the aim of which is to secure adequate observance of the law. The interpretive instructions can be joint, in which case they are obligatory for the courts of both general and arbitrazh systems. Owing to the fact that the legal interpretation of the supreme judicial bodies is obligatory, in reality they create new legal norms which have a retroactive effect.[87] Particularly important in Russian law are the

79 By using the rules of grammar.

80 By using the rules of logic and grammar.

81 By identifying the place of the norm in the respective legal act.

82 By clarifying the historical and political background to the issuance of the respective norm.

83 By clarifying the aims of the legislator set out in the norm.

84 See Braginsky and Vitryansky 1999: 326 and n.

85 It has given the reason to suggest that this distinction is groundless. See Sukhanov 2007: 116.

86 Two mutually exclusive methods of interpretation, the conclusion *e contrario* and the *a fortiori* argument, are also presented in Russian legal literature. In applying them, it must be taken into consideration that the result of the interpretation must not be contradictory to the content of the norms regulating the situation which is subject to interpretation. See Braginsky and Vitryansky 1999: 145.

87 In respect of the decisions of the supreme judicial bodies aimed at bringing judicial practice into uniformity, the opinion is presented in the legal literature, as stated above, that they may be regarded as legal

normative explanations of the Constitutional Court concerning constitutional issues. According to the Russian Constitution (Article 125.5), the Constitutional Court must interpret the Constitution of the Russian Federation on request of the supreme state bodies (including the President of the Russian Federation, the Federation Council, State Duma, and the Government as well as legislative bodies of the subjects of the Russian Federation). In giving its normative explanations concerning constitutional issues the Constitutional Court is empowered, as stated above, to deviate from the text-bound interpretation of the legal norms.

The *in casu* interpretation which a court gives in its decision on a concrete case is legally obligatory only for that case. Court decisions are not precedents binding on other courts in Russia, although the decisions of the supreme judicial bodies may in fact serve as a kind of model for the application of norms, particularly in the case of explanatory instructions.

The unofficial interpretation, which comprises legally nonobligatory explanations and comments, plays a relatively minor role in Russian law. Their significance is dependent first and foremost on who has given them, as well as on the correctness and credibility of the interpretation itself. The unofficial interpretation can take the form of doctrinal, special expert and ordinary interpretation. Doctrinal interpretation occurs through legal research and expert opinion, the subject matter of which is practical jurisprudence, and is important in legislative work as well in the administration of justice. Significant also are uninitiated opinions on legal issues which the ordinary interpretation represents, particularly as given by the lay members of the court who participate in the proceedings of certain cases in Russia.

Discretionary norms have become known in Russian law after the enactment of the Civil Code, in which international practice was taken into account. The ratification of the Vienna Convention (on the International Sale of Goods 1980), especially, necessitated the application of discretionary norms and consequently the use of *in casu* discretion in courts. This has not, however, been confined only to the regulation of international contracts, but has become general also in the regulation of internal civil law relations.

Among the discretionary norms known in the Civil Code is one containing the requirements of fairness, reasonableness, and equity (Article 6.2). They are purported to be used generally in analogical application as a frame for the decision based on the general principles and substantive content of the civil legislation. The obligation law norms of the Civil Code contains a number of references to the considerations of reasonableness and equity—for instance, to reasonable time (Article 715), price (Article 738) and expenses (Article 520), sensible management of affairs (Article 72), and disproportionate penalties (Article 333). Also references to "the usual" are used widely in the Civil Code, an example of which is the usual price (Article 424.3). The other expressions used widely in the Civil Code, referring to discretion, include the "necessary," "essential, and "obvious."

The Russian legislator is not used to disclosing the content of the discretionary standards imposed by him, with some exceptions. One of them is the concept of good faith (*bona fide*), which is defined directly in the rules on vindication (Article 302). In accordance with it, the acquirer in good faith (the *bona fide* acquirer) is a person who did not know and could not have known that the assignor did not have the right to alienate the property. This concept may also be used in other cases where the legislator refers to good faith or fairness. Another example of the legislator's attempt to define the discretionary standard imposed by him is the concept of essential breach of contract included in the rules on change and rescission of a contract (Article 450.2). A violation (breach) of

---

sources which are in force for a limited time in case of a legal gap. Such a precedent has legal force until a legislative solution can take place. See Neshataeva 2004: 66–7.

contract is considered essential (fundamental), if it entails, for another party, such damage that he is deprived to a significant degree of that which he has the right to expect in concluding the contract. This definition may also be used in other cases where the law refers to essential breach (violation) of contract. However, in cases where the legislator has left the used discretionary standard undefined, the discretionary power of the judicial authority is enlarged. However, it does not mean that it is unnecessary to ensure the uniformity of interpretation of the discretionary rules, and this is the task in which the role of doctrinal interpretation is considered important in Russia. Moreover, in cases where the legislator has clearly expressed his will, the interpretation corresponding to this requires following the golden rule, according to which the words and expressions contained in the law are to be used in the general (ordinary) sense.[88]

The use of discretionary norms is often connected with the question of burden of proof or the question of who must prove whether the actions under dispute correspond or not with the discretionary standard. Usually a court follows the division of the burden of proof required by the contradictory procedure. In certain cases, however, the rules of the Civil Code concerning the burden of proof are applied. Thus, for instance, in the rules of the Civil Code on the limits of exercise of civil law rights (Article 10.3), the behavior corresponding to the requirements of fairness and good faith is presumed, and this means that the party must prove the unreasonableness and unfairness of the actions of the counterparty.

It seems clear that the significance of judicial practice is growing and that the possibilities for adopting decisions by using *in casu* discretion are becoming greater, as stated above, in Russian law. Significant in this respect is the rule of the Joint Stock Company Law on the rights of shareholders to appeal the decision of the general meeting of the company (Article 49.7). This provides that the appealed decision may remain in force where the vote of the shareholder who appealed would not affect the voting results, where the violations are not essential and where the decision has not incurred losses to the appellant. Such a rule can be regarded as referring to the consequential approach which belongs to the argumentation theory, and, consequently, shows that the dogmatic approach is giving way to freer legal thinking in the interpretation of civil law in Russia.

Analogical application[89] Analogy is known in Russian law as "analogy of the legal rule" and "analogy of the law." Analogy of the legal rule means the application of the rule regulating similar relations. In the case of analogy of the law, the solution to the legal question is found through the general principles and substantive content of the civil legislation and the requirements of fairness, reasonableness, and equity. The rules on the analogical application of the civil law norms are included directly in the Civil Code (Article 6), wherefore they are general rules concerning the whole body of civil legislation in Russia.

There are legality considerations according to which it is expected that certain requirements are to be complied with in the analogy application, and these requirements generally concern every branch of law where analogical application is permitted. A decision based on the analogy application is permitted only in case when the issue to be solved belongs certainly to the circle of civil law regulation, but the norm applicable to it is missing or deficient. Additionally, in the case of analogy of the legal rule, it is required that only the law regulating similar relations, not any other legal act shall be applicable. The application of analogy of the law, in turn, is designated only in the event the application of the legal rule would not lead to satisfactory result.

88 Braginsky and Vitrjansky 1999: 139–42.

89 For more on this subject, see, for instance, Sergeev 1 2009: 71–3; Abova, Boguslavsky, Kabalkin, and Lisicin-Svetlanov 2007: 24–5, and Braginsky and Vitryansky 1999: 129–36.

General Principles of Civil Law[90]

The general principles of Russian civil law, which form its bases, are fixed in the Civil Code.[91] These are understood as the bases of civil law or its principal general rules. They are included directly in the law and are, therefore, normative by nature. Thus, the law requires the general principles to be followed in any legal practice activities. In general, the regulation of civil law in Russia is based on the private law premise which requires a legal system whereby a private person has the right to dispose independently, according to his will, of the legally relevant conditions regarding his behavior.[92] The other starting point of Russian civil law is the rule enforced in the Civil Code according to which goods, services, and financial assets are to move freely throughout the whole territory of the Russian Federation. The aim of this rule is to strengthen the unity of the Russian economic region and reflects the orientation toward the market economy enshrined in the Civil Code.[93]

The general (basic) principles of Russian civil law, as presented in the literature on Russian civil law and grounded in the respective rules of the Civil Code (Article 1), are:

- civil law equality;
- impermissibility of arbitrary interference in private affairs;
- inviolability of ownership;
- freedom of contract;
- dispositiveness;
- unhindered exercise of civil rights;
- prohibition of abuse of rights[94] and fairness requirements, and
- protection of civil rights.

In respect of the application of general principles, exceptions to them are known and provided by the law.

Civil law equality In Russian law the principle of civil law equality is considered as the criterion constituting civil law relations[95] in accordance with which the status of the parties of civil law relations is determined. This states that no subject of Russian civil law, including physical and juristic persons as well as state and municipal bodies, has priority over any other: the parties in civil law relations are equal. Thus, a party to a contract, including a public law subject, has no coercive

---

90 For more on this subject, see, for instance, Sergeev 1 2009: 9–10; Abova, Boguslavsky, Kabalkin, and Lisicin-Svetlanov 2007: 18–19; Popondopulo 1 2009: 24–30, and Butler 2009: 394–6.

91 In contrast to the general view that the principles of business law are expressed in the principles of the civil law, the following principles of business law or the legal regulation of enterprise activities are presented in Russian legal literature: freedom of entrepreneurship, equality of different forms of property, free competition and restriction of monopolistic activities, deriving profit as the main purpose of entrepreneurship, legality in practicing enterprise activities, integration of private and public regulation, and the unity of economic and legal areas as well as state regulation of enterprise activities. See Laptev and Zankovsky 2006: 9–20.

92 See Sergeev 1 2009: 8–9 and Alekseyev 1999: 586.

93 Promoting a market economy is regarded as the most important task of legal regulation. See, for instance, Zhilinskiy 2007: 47–61.

94 The prohibition of abuse of rights is considered in Russian civil law as belonging to the exercise of civil rights. See, for instance, Sergeev 1 2009: 521–5.

95 Sukhanov 2007: 120.

power in respect of another party. On the contrary, their relations are regulated by the same civil law norms. This, however, does not concern issues in which the public law subjects exercise their powers as public authorities (Article 2.3).

According to the Civil Code, the civil legislation rules are also applied to relations in which foreign physical and juristic persons as well as stateless persons participate: under the Constitution (Article 62), the national regime is extended to foreign persons, not including the exemptions that are provided by the (federal) law or by international agreement (Article 2.1).

Legal equality does not, however, purport that subjective civil rights are equal, and the Civil Code includes exceptions to it. The most important exception concerns entrepreneurs who are subject to more than ordinary strict requirements. Moreover, as to the relations between entrepreneurs and consumers, the legal status of a consumer is protected, among others, by the rules of the Civil Code on public contracting (Article 426). An especially noteworthy exception are (state and municipal) Treasury enterprises, the legal capacity of which may be restricted very strictly. Other restrictions known in Russian law include the creditor order in bankruptcy. Restrictions are imposed also in respect of foreign entrepreneurs.

Impermissibility of arbitrary interference in private affairs The prohibition to interfere arbitrarily in private affairs is directly enforced in the Civil Code (Article 1.1) and reflects the private law nature of the civil law. In the first instance, it is addressed to public power. According to this principle, the ability to interfere in private affairs, including the economic activities of civil law subjects, is restricted to cases provided by the law. To secure their obedience to the prohibition, the Civil Code contains the rule according to which a court may, in hearing of the dispute, declare an unlawful act of a state or municipal body invalid or leave it unapplied (Articles 12 and 13).

Inviolability of ownership The principle of inviolability of ownership concerns both private and public property, and purports that the owner may use his property in his interests. No one can be deprived, according to the Constitution (Article 35.3) of his property otherwise than by a court decision and on legal grounds. Furthermore, according to the Civil Code (Article 12), the owner has the right, where his ownership is disturbed or restrained, to demand that the activities which violated his rights, or which threatened to violate them, cease.

Freedom of contract The principle of freedom of contract is characteristic of the exchange relations between independent economic entities and is particularly essential for the regulation of contract law. The principle is directly enforced in the Civil Code rules concerning the basic principles of the civil law legislation and in those regulating contracts. According to it, the subjects of civil law have free power to conclude a contract or choose the contracting party and determine the conditions of the contract (Article 421). A general exception to the principle of freedom of contract are the rules on compulsory (public) contracting by virtue of which contract relations are regulated (Article 426); the Civil Code also provides the possibility of exemption for the purpose of price control, but this requires the enactment of a law (Article 424.1).

Dispositiveness The principle of dispositiveness, or independence and free will in acquisition, exercise, and protection of civil law rights, is closely related to the principle of freedom of contract, and in Russian law is taken to mean above all that the subject of civil law relations is free to form his own will (independently from another subject). According to the Civil Code (Articles 1.2 and 9.1), the subjects of civil law relations acquire and exercise their rights of their own will and in their own interests (and at their own discretion). Thus no one can be obliged by the law to use his rights. Also, a contract which restricts the use of civil rights is invalid and the refusal of a physical or juristic person to exercise his rights does not entail the termination of these rights, unless otherwise provided by the law (Article 9.2).

The principle of dispositiveness is reflected in that the main part of the civil law norms are dispositive. Their application is dependent on the will of the parties. The application of a dispositive legal norm may be excluded or it may be deviated by them.

On the other hand, the principle of dispositiveness also includes restrictions. The general restrictions are first of all the imperative (compulsory) norms of the law—for instance the norms by which the legal status of the civil law subjects, including the legal (act) capacity, and the content of the real rights are to be defined. The basics of the legal order and morality also put limits on the principle of dispositiveness in Russian law. The Civil Code provides directly, based on the Constitution (Article 55.3), that civil law rights may be limited by the (federal) law to the extent to which it is necessary to protect the constitutional order and public morality, to defend the rights and legal interests of citizens and other persons as well as human life and health, and to ensure the national defense and security (Article 1.2). Additionally, the Civil Code (Article 10) directly obliges civil law subjects to act reasonably and fairly and prohibits the abuse of civil rights. The Civil Code also includes cases where the state is empowered, as stated above, to intervene in contract relations.

Unhindered exercise of civil rights The principle of unhindered exercise of civil rights reflects the market economy orientation of Russian civil law and the territorial unity of Russia. It is grounded on the Russian constitutional norms (Article 8) in which the unity of the Russian (Federation) economic region and the free circulation of goods, services, and financial assets, as well as the promotion of competition and freedom to practice economic activities, are guaranteed. Moreover, in accordance with the Civil Code (Article 1.3), goods, services, and financial assets are to move freely throughout the whole territory of the Russian Federation. In turn, the right to practice enterprise activities is enforced in the Civil Code rule regulating such activities by physical persons. Furthermore, in the Civil Code rules on the legal capacity of the juristic person, it is provided in respect of commercial organizations that they should enjoy the civil rights indispensable for the performance of any kinds of activity not prohibited by the law (Article 49.1). On the other hand, the same norm provides that some kinds of activity listed in the law could require a special permit (license). In order to protect public interests, other restrictions can also be imposed by law; such restrictions are included, for instance, in the Competition Law. As to the restrictions in respect of the free circulation of goods, services, and financial assets, they may be imposed, according to the Civil Code (Article 1.3), only by the federal law if this is necessary to ensure safety, the defense of human life and health, or the protection of nature and cultural values.

Prohibition of abuse of rights and fairness requirements The prohibition of abuse of rights can be regarded as a general exception to the basic principles of Russian civil law. In accordance with it, the unrestricted freedom of civil law subjects to exercise civil rights is precluded. The rights granted under Russian law are subject to restrictions in respect of their content and mode of exercise, and their violations are sanctioned. As a general rule it is regarded in the Russian civil law that in exercising rights the other's rights and legal interests shall not be violated.

Prohibition of abuse of rights is expressed directly in the rule of the Civil Code on the limits to the exercise of civil law rights (Article 10), according to which actions of physical and juristic persons made exclusively with the intention of causing harm to another person are not allowed; nor is abuse of a legal right allowed in other forms. The same norm prohibits the direct use of civil law rights for the purpose of restricting competition and the abuse of a dominant position in the market.

Restrictions and prohibitions to use rights are also imposed by other civil law norms. For instance, in the rules on the content of the right of ownership, it is provided that the owner shall have the right at his own discretion to perform with respect to the property in his ownership any actions, not contradicting the law and the other legal acts, and not violating the rights and the law-protected interests of other persons (Article 209.2). In turn, the owner of land and of other natural resources may dispose, under the Civil Code (Article 209.3), of his rights freely, unless this causes harm to the environment or violates the rights and the legal interests of other persons. The obligation law norms of the Civil Code also contain restrictions and prohibitions on the use of rights. The most important of these are the above-mentioned rules on public contracting and competition. Furthermore, the rules on the invalidity of certain transactions found in the Civil Code (Articles 169 and 179) can be regarded as reflecting the prohibition of abuse of rights. This applies to transactions that are purposefully contrary to the bases of the legal order or morality; those made under the influence of fraud, duress, threat, or an agreement made in bad faith, or those made as the result of the concurrence of grave circumstances.[96]

In the rules of the Civil Code on the limits to the exercise of civil law rights (Article 10.3), the requirements of fairness are mentioned. According to them, where the law demands, when granting legal protection, that rights have been exercised reasonably and in good faith, this shall be presumed. The placement of this rule in connection to the norm containing the prohibition of abuse of rights indicates that fraudulent behavior is equated with the abuse of rights. In judicial practice the requirements of fairness were often referred to as a general principle of the civil law,[97] and this view is ready to be accepted in the Civil Code.[98]

As a legal consequence of the abuse of rights, unless another sanction is provided by law, the court may refuse, according to the Civil Code, the person protection of the right he possesses (Article 10.2). Concrete sanctions against abuse of rights may be provided by not only the Civil Code but also other laws.

Protection of civil rights Protection of civil rights as a legal principle refers in Russian law to the possibilities for subjects of civil law relations to defend their rights and legal interests in court procedure; they may also use self-defense and other lawful protection means. In general,

---

96 For more on this subject, see below. The rules on the invalidity of such transactions are distinct from the rule on the prohibition of abuse of rights. The invalidity rules contain objective criteria for invalid transactions, whereas the rule on the prohibition of abuse of rights is constructed so that, where the defendant presents a counterargument, the court is able to use its discretion whether to consider if there has been an abuse of rights or not on the part of the plaintiff. See K.I. Sklovsky, О применении норм о злоупотреблении правом в судебной практике [On the Application of Norms on the Abuse of Rights in Judicial Practice], Вестник Высшего Арбитражного Суда Российской Федерации [Herald of Supreme Arbitrazh Court of Russian Federation] 2 (2001): 45 and 47.

97 The Supreme Arbitrazh Court has rejected, for instance, a claim for abolishing the decision of the general meeting of a joint stock company on the grounds that, due to the fraudulent actions of the plaintiff, the provisions of the charter were violated in the decision making. See Informative Letter of the Presidium of the Supreme Arbitrazh Court no 127 of 24 November 2008, Вестник Высшего Арбитражного Суда Российской Федерации [Herald of Supreme Arbitrazh Court of Russian Federation] 2 (2009): 156–71.

98 See the Concept of development of the general provisions of the Civil Code, Вестник Высшего Арбитражного Суда Российской Федерации [Herald of Supreme Arbitrazh Court of Russian Federation] 4 (2009).

the purpose of the protection means established in the civil law is to restore violated rights, but the Civil Code also contains the rules on the means of security for the performance of obligations (Articles 329–81) which are particularly important in contract law.[99]

Subjects of Entrepreneurship[100]

The subjects of entrepreneurship in Russia are defined in the Civil Code, which also determines their legal status. Such subjects can be divided into individual and collective. Collective subjects practicing business activities or corporations are in general juristic persons, among which are distinct commercial organizations established for business purposes. Noncommercial organizations are also permitted to carry out enterprise activities, although with restrictions. Enterprise activities may also be practiced by subjects who are not juristic persons. They include individual entrepreneurs or physical persons as well as certain collective subjects—for instance farms. Non-juristic persons also include in Russian law representative offices and branches of enterprises. Furthermore, the list of participants in business activities in Russia also includes public law subjects.

Individual entrepreneurs A physical person may engage, according to the Civil Code (Article 18), in business and in any other activities not prohibited by the law. He may practice such activities through the juristic person founded by him independently or jointly with other persons, or without forming a juristic person from the time he is registered as an individual entrepreneur (sole trader) (Article 23.1).[101] Irrespective of this, a person practicing unregistered business activities does not have the right to refer, with respect to transactions concluded by him, to the fact that he is not an entrepreneur and in such a case a court may apply the rules on entrepreneurial obligations (Article 23.4). The main purpose of these rules is to protect the counterparty of a person who is practicing unregistered business activities, and their application signifies, among other things, the prohibition on the inclusion of clauses limiting the amount of liability in contracts with consumers (Article 400.2).

Commercial organizations[102] Commercial organizations act in Russia, according to the Civil Code (Articles 50 and 66), in the form of partnerships and companies regarded as corporations[103] as well as production cooperatives. The Civil Code includes in such partnerships general (full) partnerships[104] and limited (commandite, in commendam) partnerships[105] (Article 66.2), and

---

99 For more on this subject, see Chapter 6.

100 For more on this subject, see, for instance, Popondopulo 1 2009: 104–12; Laptev and Zankovsky 2006: 41–175, and Sergeev 1 2009: 177–214.

101 Where enterprise activities are agricultural in nature, the head of the farm is regarded as the entrepreneur.

102 For more on this subject, see Chapter 2.

103 See Laptev and Zankovsky 2006: 99–101.

104 General (full) partnership is defined, under the Civil Code (Article 69), as a commercial organization (partnership) the participants of which (general partners) are engaged, in conformity with the agreement signed between them, in business activities on behalf of the partnership and bear liability by its obligations with their property, however subsidiary.

105 A limited (special) or commandite (*in commendam*) partnership is defined under the Civil Code (Article 82) as a partnership in which, alongside the general partners (who have the status of the partner in a general partnership), there are also one or several participants-investors (silent partners, or commanditaires).

includes in such companies (so-called capital-based companies) limited-liability companies and additional liability companies (companies with supplementary liability) and (open or closed) joint stock companies (Article 66.3). A partnership is usually an association of physical persons and the number of its participants is small. In turn, in a company the personal qualities and the nature of the relations of the participants are usually without real significance because the question is about a combination of capitals.[106]

In general, as commercial organizations, companies and partnerships in Russia are granted a general legal capacity: they enjoy, according to the Civil Code, civil rights indispensable for the performance of any kinds of activity not prohibited by the law (Article 49.1).

State and municipal unitary enterprises,[107] as independent juristic persons, are also counted among commercial organizations in Russia. A unitary enterprise is defined in the Civil Code as a commercial organization which is not endowed with the right of ownership to the property that the owner (state or municipal) allotted to it. The unitary enterprise always enjoys a special legal (act) capacity (bound to the objects of the activity) and a legal act contradictory to it is null and void.[108]

Production cooperatives are also listed among commercial organizations in Russia. According to the Civil Code (Article 107.1), a production cooperative is a voluntary association of physical persons, based on membership, and established for the purpose of joint production or other economic activity. It is based on the personal labor of its members and other participation, and on combining their share contributions. Production cooperatives are juristic persons and are granted a general legal capacity.

Noncommercial organizations Under the Civil Code, enterprise activity in Russia is also permitted to noncommercial (nonprofit) organizations (Article 50), but such activities must be connected with the objects of the primary activities of the organization. Noncommercial organizations are juristic persons with special legal capacity.[109] According to the Civil Code (Article 50.3), a noncommercial organization may be established as a consumer cooperative, societal or religious organization (association), institution, or other charitable foundation, and also in other forms provided by the law. Furthermore, commercial and/or noncommercial organizations in Russia may establish amalgamations in the form of associations and unions; these are also juristic persons, but their possibilities to practice business activities are restricted (Civil Code, Articles 50.4 and 121–3). An individual entrepreneur may also participate in associations and unions. Special rules are provided for chambers of trade and industry,[110] which are not allowed to distribute their profits between members. Furthermore, noncommercial partnerships are also known in Russia.[111] Financial and industrial groups may also be established, in accordance with the special law regulating them,[112] by juristic persons in Russia and such groups also can be international; financial and industrial groups are not, however, juristic persons. Under a special law the Russian Federation may establish a state corporation

106 Abova, Boguslavsky, Kabalkin, and Lisicin-Svetlanov 2007: 88.

107 For more on this subject, see Laptev and Zankovsky 2006: 124–35 and Popondopulo 1 2009: 155–61.

108 Sergeev 1 2009: 196.

109 For more on this subject, see Sergeev 1 2009: 197–203, and particularly on noncommercial organizations 316–44. See also K.P. Belyayev, Некоммерческие организации в системе юридических лиц [Noncommercial Organizations in the System of Juristic Persons] (2004): 390–405.

110 Law no 5340-I of 7 July 1993.

111 For instance, stock exchanges. Closed to them are advocate offices (bureau, college) and commodity exchanges.

112 Law no 190-FZ of 30 November 1995 as amended on 17 December 1997.

for specified public purposes; as an entity it is close to the state institution, but has property in its ownership.[113] [114]

Public law subjects Besides physical and juristic persons, the state and other public law subjects such as municipal formations may participate in relations regulated by civil legislation, and the rules regulating this are contained in the Civil Code. The state is not, however, a uniform civil law subject but is composed of various subjects of law.[115] They include the Russian Federation and the subjects of the Russian Federation, such as republics, territories, regions, federal cities, autonomous regions, and autonomous areas, which are state formations. Municipal formations represent, in turn, local self-government, and they are comprised of cities and rural settlements and other municipal entities (Article 124.1). Local self-government bodies are not regarded as state bodies, although they also administer public functions.

The state and other public law subjects participate in civil law relations equally with other persons.[116] This means that they are empowered to use public coercive means in respect to other civil law subjects. If a public law subject, however, violates civil law rights or omits its duties, it could become subject to civil law sanctions which are usually imposed in judicial procedure. This implies that, in respect of internal civil law relations, public law subjects are not granted immunity.[117]

Foreign persons The Russian civil legislation rules are also applied, according to the Civil Code (Article 2.1), toward the relations in which foreign physical and juristic persons as well as stateless persons participate. The civil law status and rights to the property situated in Russia of foreign physical and juristic persons are determined in the Russian civil law norms. The national regime is extended, under the Constitution (Article 62), to foreign persons, not including the exemptions that are provided by the (federal) law or international agreement, and this provision is also repeated in the Civil Code (Article 2.1). Foreign persons practicing enterprise activities oriented to Russia must pay particular attention to the regulation of foreign trade activities in the country, including the requirements provided by customs legislation.[118]

Objects of Enterprise Activities[119]

In Russian law the concept of enterprise is connected not only to the forms of juristic persons (civil law subjects) but also to the objects of exchange. In this context, the question is of the assets of

---

113 For instance, the Agency for the Insurance of Deposits under the law on the Insurance of Bank Deposits of Individuals in the Russian Federation no 177-FZ of 23 December 2003.

114 See Abova, Boguslavsky, Kabalkin, and Lisicin-Svetlanov 2007: 143–6, and Sergeev 1 2009: 316–44.

115 See E.A. Sukhanov (ed.), Об ответственности государства по гражданско-правовым обязательствам [On Responsibility of State for Civil Law Obligations] Вестник Высшего Арбитражного Суда Российской Федерации [Herald of Supreme Arbitrazh Court of Russian Federation] 2 (2001): 116.

116 In practice, public law subjects are in a better position than other civil law subjects due, for instance, to the fact that their responsibility is limited by public law legislation. For more on this subject, see Sukhanov 2001: 122–5.

117 In Russian judicial practice, a transaction which exceeds the power of the public body is regarded, in accordance with the Civil Code (Article 168), as null and void. See the Informative Letter of the Presidium of the Supreme Arbitrazh Court no 57 of 23 October 2000. Вестник Высшего Арбитражного Суда Российской Федерации [Herald of Supreme Arbitrazh Court of Russian Federation] 12 (2000).

118 For more on this subject, see Chapter 7.

119 For more on this subject, see, for instance, Sergeev 1 2009: 375–410; Popondopulo 1 2009: 204–84, and Abova, Boguslavsky, Kabalkin, and Lisicin-Svetlanov 2007: 149–74.

enterprise that signify commodities exploited in enterprise activities. As an object of exchange, enterprise is recognized, according to the Civil Code (Article 132.1) as a property complex, used for the performance of business activities. Assets of enterprise include different objects of civil law, which are also separately objects of exchange.

The civil law objects which are also the objects of enterprise activities are explicitly listed in the Civil Code (Article 128), and they are things, including money and securities (commercial papers); other kinds of property such as property rights; works and services; protected results of intellectual activity and means of individualization equated to them (intellectual property); and nonmaterial values.

The civil law objects are divided, according to the Civil Code, into freely alienable, those with restricted alienation, and those which are excluded from circulation. In general, the objects of civil law rights may be freely alienated or transferred from one person to another by way of universal legal succession (inheritance, reorganization of a juristic person), or in another way, unless they are excluded from circulation or limited in this respect (Article 129.1). Among the civil law objects subject to general alienability and explicitly strengthened by the law are, in accordance with the Civil Code, the above-mentioned things; other property, works and services; results of intellectual activity, and nonmaterial values.

In accordance with the Civil Code the restricted alienation of civil law objects means that the objects subject to restrictions can belong only to defined participants in circulation, or whose presence in circulation is allowed only by special permission (Article 129.2). Such objects include, for instance, weapons, the possession of which is restricted with certain exceptions only to defined persons; foreign currency and other currency valuables, the exchange of which requires the special permission of public authorities,[120] artifacts and memorials (of cultural value), the transactions concerning which require notification to public authorities and which are subject to the preemptive right of the state; and natural resources. According to the Civil Code (Article 129.2), objects with restricted alienation are defined in the procedure established by law.

Transactions regarding civil law objects excluded from circulation are directly forbidden. They may not also be subject to changes in ownership. According to the Civil Code (Article 129.2), types of objects of civil law rights that are not allowed to be in circulation must be explicitly indicated by the law.[121] The objects excluded from circulation in Russia include, among others, public objects which are exclusively in state ownership such as roads, buildings, and objects the exchange of which is contrary to the moral basis of society.

The majority of objects of exchange are things and they are divided, according to the Civil Code, into movable and immovable (Article 130). Immovable things (immovable property, immovables) include in Russian law land parcels[122] and natural resources parcels, both separate

120 In Russian law currency valuables include not only foreign currency and securities in foreign currency, but also. with some exceptions, precious metals and stones. According to the Civil Code (Article 141), the order of transactions with currency valuables is defined by the Law on the Currency Regulation and the Currency Control no 173-FZ of 10 December 2003. See Abova, Boguslavsky, Kabalkin, and Lisicin-Svetlanov 2007: 162–3.

121 Such a law has not yet been passed. See Abova, Boguslavsky, Kabalkin, and Lisicin-Svetlanov 2007: 151.

122 Thus, land is included, according to the Civil Code, among the objects of civil law relations. The right of ownership and other rights *in rem* in land are, according to the Civil Code (Articles 260–87), in principle allowed. On the other hand, the rights to land as well as to other natural resources are also restricted in the Civil Code to the extent to which commerce in them is admissible in conformity with the laws relating to the land and other natural resources (Article 129 and 209).

from and firmly connected to land—in other words, objects which cannot be moved without disproportionate harm to their use, including forests, perennial plantings, buildings, and structures as well as unaccomplished constructions. Immovables in Russia also include aircrafts, marine and inland vessels and spacecrafts, inland navigation ships, and space objects which are subject to state registration. Furthermore, as a property complex, an enterprise is also considered as immovable in Russia (Article 132). The Civil Code provides that other property may also be recognized as an immovable (Article 130.1), and so apartments are regarded, in the legislation concerning them, as immovable property.[123] The things which are not categorized as immovables, including money and securities, are considered as movables in Russian law (Article 130.2).

According to the general rule of the Russian civil law enforced in the Civil Code, the rights of ownership to immovable things, as well as the transactions concerning these, are subject to state registration (Article 131). Such registration is regarded as a legal fact by which the public power recognizes and enforces the origin, restrictions, transfer, and termination of the rights concerning immovable things, and it is the only proof that these registered rights exist. As a consequence, these rights are disputable only in judicial litigation. The legal regime provided for immovable property is also extended in some cases to movables. It is directly enacted in the Civil Code that state registration may be established by the law for transactions with movable property of defined types (Article 164.2). Registration may also be required for objects with restricted alienation, such as weapons and vehicles.[124]

Among the objects of civil law in Russia are also property complexes which are purported to be used in whole, and these can consist of immovables and movables. These include enterprises and jointly owned dwellings which are considered as immovable property.

Enterprise as a complex of property used for the performance of business activities comprises, under Article 132.1 of the Civil Code, all property (assets) purported for such activities and includes things usually regarded as immovables: land parcels, buildings, and structures, and as movables: equipment, implements, raw materials, products, choses in action, debts, and also rights to designations individualizing enterprise, its products, works, and services (such as firm name and trade and service marks), as well as other exclusive rights, unless otherwise provided by the law or agreement. An enterprise as a whole but also a part of enterprise may be the object of sale, lease, pledge, or other commercial transaction. Enterprise as a complex of property is considered in Russia as immovable property even where its property does not include land parcel and building.[125]

Things are divided under Russian civil law into individually and group defined. An individually defined thing is unsubstitutable in the legal sense. Only the performance in kind may be claimed in respect of such a thing and compensation for damages if it is destroyed. On the contrary, group defined things are legally substitutable and, if such things are destroyed, the creditor may demand new ones instead. Things are also divided into divisible and indivisible. Complex things are also known, as well as principal things and accessories, consumer and durable goods, receipts as fruits, products and incomes as well as animate and inanimate things.

Money is included in Russian civil legislation as a movable and is regarded as group defined, although its individualization is also possible. According to the Civil Code (Article 140), the ruble is the only legal means of payment within Russian territory. Payments are effected both by cash and non-cash settlements, particularly in relations between enterprises. Non-cash money is

123 Sergeev 1 2009: 377.

124 In such cases, registration has no constitutive effect but is often a requirement for the utilization of the registered object. See Sergeev 1 2009: 481.

125 Popondopulo 1 2009: 226.

considered not as a thing but as an obligation law receivable, and so the term "monetary assets" is used in the civil legislation to refer to it.[126] Non-cash money is not regarded as a general means of payment and in certain cases its exchange to cash money is restricted. Moreover, its use is subject to orders provided by the law.[127] As a receivable, non-cash money is included into assets and belongs correspondingly to the property complex of an enterprise.

Securities or commercial papers,[128] which belong to civil law objects in Russia, are defined in the Civil Code (Article 142) as documents certifying, with the observation of the established form and obligatory requisites, property rights, the exercise or transfer of which are possible only upon their presentation. In Russian legal doctrine, the right to commercial papers and the right arising from them are distinguished. The right to commercial papers as documents usually stands for ownership, whereas the right arising from commercial papers, because their content is regarded mostly as an obligation law right, is considered as some kind of receivable. In principle, the right arising from (or incorporated in) commercial papers follows the right to them.[129]

Commercial papers (securities) as documents are included in movables, and the right incorporated in them can concern movable or immovable things. Commercial papers are traditionally classified in Russia as bearer, named and order ones. Securities may be issued by private persons as well as by the state and municipalities. A commercial paper can incorporate the right to: certain *sums* (money securities), for instance bonds, bills of exchange, checks, deposit and savings certificates; certain *things* (document of title), for instance pledge certificates and bills of lading; or *membership in companies* (corporate securities). Derivatives are known in Russia, while undocumented commercial papers are also familiar to Russian law. However, according to the Civil Code (Article 149), they are not regarded as proper securities since they include the fixation of rights secured by a named or order security in nondocumentary, usually electronic, form. Thus, they may not be presented as the objects of property law or even transactions.[130] Securities in electronic form are widely used in Russia, and shares and other named emission securities, for instance, are found only in electronic form.[131]

Legal Protection and Liability

The legal protection of civil law[132] rights belongs to the general principles of Russian civil law which are enforced directly by law. According to it, the rights and interests of civil law subjects, including entrepreneurs and enterprises, are legally protected. Their rights can be protected by means of judicial procedure, but they have also the right to resort to self-protection and other property law means. The main task of legal protection is to restore a violated right.

Means of protection The means of legal protection of civil law rights in Russia as elsewhere are purported to interrupt, prevent, and cancel the violation of law, restore rights, and/or compensate

126 See Sukhanov 2007: 172.

127 For instance, tax, bookkeeping and bank law regulations.

128 The Civil Code at best attempts to consolidate certain general requirements of securities, including among them examples which modern legal systems do not treat as securities, as for instance, checks and bills of exchange, and recognizes the concept of the paperless security. See Butler 2009: 399–400 and the work mentioned in it.

129 Sergeev 1 2009: 394–5.

130 Sergeev 1 2009: 395.

131 See Abova, Boguslavsky, Kabalkin, and Lisicin-Svetlanov 2007: 172–4.

132 For more on this subject, see, for instance, Sergeev 1 2009: 540–52 and Popondopulo 1 2009: 547–92.

for the damages caused by such violation. The means of legal protection are listed in the Civil Code (Article 12). According to this, the civil rights are protected by way of:

- recognition of a right;
- restoration of a situation which existed before the violation of the right, and restraint on actions violating the right or creating a threat of its violation;
- declaration of a voidable transaction as invalid and application of the consequences of its invalidity, as well as application of the consequences of the invalidity of a (null and) void transaction;
- declaration of the invalidity of an act of the state or local self-government body;
- self-protection of a right;
- a judgment for performance of an obligation in kind;
- compensation for damages;
- recovery of liquidated damages;[133]
- compensation for moral harm;
- termination or modification of a legal relation;
- non-application by a court of an act of the state or local self-government body which contradicts the law, and
- other means of protection provided by law.

The protection of civil law rights in Russia occurs usually in the administration of justice, but it may also be executed by using extrajudicial means. In the administration of justice the protection must be obtained using judicial or administrative procedure. The subject of the violated right must usually use the concrete means of protection specified by law, since the order and limits of each means of protection are determined according to the content of the right to be protected and the nature of its violation. However, in certain cases, the subject of the violated right has an option to choose the means of protection suitable for him, because many of the means of protection can be applied at the same time. Thus, for instance, the retention of things, sometimes regarded in Russian law as a means of self-defense, can be presented side by side with a civil liability for a breach of the main obligation, in which case each of them has its own legal grounds.[134]

Administration of justice The judicial legal protection of civil law rights is the general form in the civil administration of justice.[135] According to the Civil Code (Article 11.1), protection of violated or disputed civil rights are to be provided by the court of general or ordinary jurisdiction,[136]

133 According to Butler (2009: 406) and Osakwe (2008: 104–7), the Anglo-American concept of liquidated damages for nonperformance of a contractual obligation does not exist in Russian law. However, cases of nonperformance and improper performance are distinguished clearly in Russian law. In the event of nonperformance, when the general rule of Article 396 of the Civil Code is to be applied, the payment of the established or agreed amount releases the debtor (contrary to the case of improper performance) from the performance of the obligation in kind. Thus, the debtor is discharged from liability by paying compensation or liquidated damages. Unfortunately, the terms *неустойка*, *штраф*, and *пеня* may signify the same thing, and *неустойка* and *штраф*, in particular, are not distinct in the Civil Code, which is an obvious remnant of Soviet economic law thinking. Thus, it might be helpful to let the term "liquidated damages" stand for an agreed compensation for damages.

134 Sergeev 1 2009: 545–6; Sukhanov 2007: 410–11.

135 On the Russian judicial system, see, for instance, Butler 2009: 167–90.

136 *суд общей юрисдикции.*

the arbitrazh (commercial) court,[137] or the arbitration court,[138] in accordance with jurisdictional rules established by procedural legislation. The courts of general jurisdiction are competent to handle first and foremost civil law disputes in which at least the other party is a physical person as well as other disputes indicated by the law. The arbitrazh (commercial) court procedure is established to resolve in practice any disputes between juristic persons and between juristic persons and individual entrepreneurs. Disputes involving the participation of foreign juristic persons also belong to the jurisdiction of arbitrazh courts. The judicial system of Russia also includes the Constitutional Court, whose main task is to perform constitutional control. A civil dispute may also be handled in an arbitration court or in an arbitral tribunal, which means a (non-state) private court (procedure) of arbitration, and, where a dispute concerns a foreign trade transaction, also using an international arbitration procedure—for instance, in the Russian Court of International Commercial Arbitration.[139] Court proceedings are usually initiated by filing a suit, but in some cases a petition is required. The Constitutional Court is approached with a complaint.

The handling of a dispute may require preliminary proceedings. In the arbitrazh court procedure this is obligatory in those cases indicated by the law.[140] Among these are disputes concerning carriage and postal services. Furthermore, a demand for change or rescission of a contract may be made, according to the Civil Code (Article 452.2), by a party to the court only after proposing it to the other party. Preliminary—for instance reclamation—proceedings may also be provided as obligatory by the contract.[141]

Contrary to judicial legal protection, the administrative (procedural) protection of civil law rights shall be effectuated[142] according to the Civil Code (Article 11.2) only in cases provided by the law. Instead, a decision adopted in administrative proceedings may be appealed in court. Furthermore, a court may, as stated above, recognize as invalid a nonnormative act of the state or local self-government body, and, in cases provided by the law, also a normative act which does not correspond to the law or to other legal acts and which violates the civil rights and protected interests of a physical or juristic person.[143] In any case, an unlawful act of the state or municipal body is to be left unapplied by a court. Moreover, the violated right is subject to restoration or protection by other means (Articles 12 and 13). Moreover, damages caused to a person as a result of the illegal actions of the state or local self-government bodies, or their officials, including the issuance of an act which does not correspond with the law or other legal act, is also subject to compensation by the Russian Federation, the respective subject of the Russian Federation, or the municipal formation (Article 16). In Russian legal doctrine and judicial practice, the rules on the administrative protection rules are regarded as applicable also to other than public administrative actions, for instance, to decisions in corporate governance.[144]

---

137 *арбитражный суд.*

138 *третейский суд.*

139 On arbitration and possible alternatives to arbitration under Russian law, see, for instance, Butler 2009: 228–35.

140 Code of Arbitrazh Procedure (no 95-FZ of 24 July 2002; Art. 4.3).

141 See Popondopulo 1 2009: 548–9.

142 The administrative procedure is initiated in Russia on application.

143 It is explicitly stated in Russian judicial practice that a foreign physical or juristic person may claim for the invalidity of public administration acts. See Joint Decrees of the Plenums of the Supreme Court and Supreme Arbitrazh Court no 6/8 of 1 July 1996. Вестник Высшего Арбитражного Суда Российской Федерации [Herald of Supreme Arbitrazh Court of Russian Federation] 9 (1996).

144 See Sergeev 1 2009: 548–9 and Abova, Boguslavsky, Kabalkin, and Lisicin-Svetlanov 2007: 32–3.

Civil liability[145] Civil liability is understood in Russian law, as elsewhere, as the legal consequences caused by illegal actions by which the rights and interests of other persons are violated. The main purpose of such consequences is to restore the legal position of the injured person to the one which he enjoyed before the violation occurred. Thus, the application of legal consequences is a very important means of legal protection. The characteristic feature of civil liability is that legal consequences are purported to be used in the administration of justice or throughout the public power by applying state coercion, including legal coercion, which does not exclude, however, voluntariness, as, for instance, in the payment of liquidated damages. The concept of civil liability does not, however, concern cases where a party is compelled to fulfill his obligation.

Compensation for damages caused by violation of a right is a general means of legal protection in Russian civil law. According to the general rule on compensation of damages in the Civil Code (Article 15.1), a person whose right has been violated may demand full compensation for the damages suffered. Compensation for damages may be demanded in case of any violation of right unless otherwise provided by the law, whereas the application of other forms of liability are applicable only in cases provided by the law or a contract.

Both material and immaterial damages are known in Russian law. Material damages include material losses—for instance, the reduced value of something damaged—and necessary expenses incurred (actual damages) as well as loss of income, including lost profit. It may be compensated in kind or monetarily. While compensation in kind is favored by the law according to the Civil Code (Article 1082), in practice monetary compensation is the most common form, and this is used in contractual as well as noncontractual legal relations.

Immaterial damages concern personal, physical, or mental sufferings caused by the violation of personal non-property rights or associated with a decrease in personal well-being, including injuries to honor and dignity as well as to bodily integrity and health. Such damages may also concern material losses which shall be compensated as property damages. Otherwise, it is difficult to exactly evaluate immaterial damage, wherefore an estimated or symbolic sum of money may be ordered by the court for its compensation, taking into consideration the requirements of reasonableness and equity as well as personal and other obstacles concerning the injured person (Civil Code, Articles 151 and 1101).

As a rule, civil liability is in Russian law compensatory in nature, and so the amount of the compensation must correspond to the damages occurred. However, in certain cases the amount of the compensation can exceed the damages; such exceptions are known in Russian consumer legislation and in the rules of the Civil Code concerning noncontractual damages (Article 1064). Liability for damages is also restricted, in accordance with the Civil Code (Article 400.1), in certain cases—for instance, in the rules on carriage (Article 796). On the other hand, Russian civil law is also familiar with punitive legal sanctions, such as penalties (fines) and interest, which is recovered from the violator to the injured person irrespective of the damages sustained. Forfeiture of earnest money is also known in Russian civil law, and the rules concerning it are placed in the norms of the Civil Code regulating means of security for performance of obligations (Article 381). Exceptionally, confiscatory sanctions may also be applied and this comprehends that certain property is confiscated from the violator to the state.

The most general forms of civil liability are compensation of damages, including actual damages and unreceived income (lost profit), liquidated damages, and penalty interest. The rules

145 For more on this subject, see Sergeev 1 2009: 939–56; S.S. Zankovsky, Предпринимательские договоры [Entrepreneurial Contracts] (2004): 57–63, and Braginsky and Vitryansky 1999: 607–770.

concerning them are in general dispositive by nature, wherefore the form of liability and its amount can be stipulated by a contract. Exceptional are the rules concerning noncontractual or tort (delict) liability; these are imperative by nature.

Civil liability concerning enterprise activities is regulated not only by general but also by specific rules. According to the Civil Code (Article 401), unless otherwise provided by the law or a contract, a person who has breached his performance obligation is to bear liability if he cannot prove that proper performance was impossible as the result of force majeure (extraordinary and unavoidable circumstances). According to the Civil Code, such circumstances do not include, for instance, contract breaches by contract partners (subcontractors) of the debtor, absence on the market of goods necessary for performance, and the debtor's lack of the necessary monetary assets. Furthermore, the Civil Code provides that the duties of several debtors under an obligation connected with enterprise activities as well as the claims of several creditors under the same obligation are solidary (joint and several), unless otherwise provided by the law, other legal acts, or the obligation terms (Article 322.2).

Limitation of actions Limitation of actions is a question of civil law in Russian law, and the rules on it are included in the Civil Code (Articles 195–208). Limitation of actions is defined in it as the period for protection of a right on suit of the person whose right has been violated (Article 195). With the expiration of the period of limitation, the person whose right is violated forfeits his right to turn to coercive judicial protection, albeit his right remains valid. This arises, for instance, in the case where the performance executed after the expiration of the period of limitation may not be demanded back (Article 206).

The general period of limitation of actions is defined in the Civil Code (Article 196) as three years. In respect of certain types of claims, the law provides special periods of limitation of actions which are shorter than the general period (Article 197).[146] Thus the period of limitation of actions for claims for recognizing a voidable transaction as invalid and for applying the consequences of its invalidity is one year (Article 181).The same period of limitation is known, for instance, in the legislation on carriage (Article 797). The Civil Code also provides claims to which the limitation of actions is not applicable. These include claims concerning nonmaterial values, including personal non-property rights, deposits, and compensation of personal injuries as well as prohibitive demands of an owner and other claims provided by the law (Article 208). The limitation of actions is not applied to demands for the repeal of legal acts, unless otherwise provided by the law.[147]

According to the Civil Code (Article 198), the rules on the periods of limitation of actions may not be changed by agreement of the parties. Such an agreement is considered as void in Russian law. The limitation of actions is applied by a court only at the request of a party to the dispute. The request must be presented before the court adopts its decision, and the expiration of a period of limitation of actions, which the party has requested be applied, is grounds for the court to reject the claim (Article 199).

Self-protection Self-protection belongs in Russian law to the extrajudicial means and is executed by the acts of the right holder without the assistance of authorities. However, self-protection is subject to limitations. According to the Civil Code (Article 14), the means of self-protection must

146 The period of limitation of actions may be determined by the law as longer than the general period.

147 See Sergeev 1 2009: 569 and Joint Decrees of the Plenums of the Supreme Court and Supreme Arbitrazh Court no 15/18 of 2001. Вестник Высшего Арбитражного Суда Российской Федерации [Herald of Supreme Arbitrazh Court of Russian Federation] 1 (2002).

be proportional to the violation and not exceed the bounds of actions necessary for stopping the violation. Damages connected with self-protection are not compensated.

4 Basic Laws Regulating Business

Enterprise activities are regulated in Russia by public and civil law norms. Public law regulation consists of imperative or mandatory norms, whereas the main part of civil regulation forms dispositive norms, albeit it also includes imperative regulation.

Civil Code

The Civil Code of the Russian Federation[148] is the main source of civil law in Russia. Its first part (Articles 1–453; 1994[149])[150] is composed of the general rules of civil law which concern civil legislation, the origin of civil law rights and duties and the exercise and protection of civil law rights; subjects and objects of civil law; transactions and representation; period of time and limitation of actions; the right of ownership and other rights in things, as well as the general provisions of obligation law, which are an important part of civil law regulation. Furthermore, the first part of the Civil Code contains general provisions on contract, including definition of contract and its conditions, conclusion of contract, and its change and rescission. Alongside the civil law norm proper, the Civil Code also includes rules which actually belong to constitutional law, as, for instance, the rules on the legislative power of the Russian Federation (Article 3.1); to administrative law, as, for instance, the rules on the state registration; to process law (the rules on burden of proof) and to other branches of law.[151]

The second part of the Civil Code (Articles 454–1109; 1996[152])[153] contains, in turn, the norms on different types and kinds of obligations or contracts, while its third part (2001[154])[155] includes international private law norms, including conflict-of-laws norms (Articles 1186–224). The fourth part of the Civil Code (articles 1225–551; 2006[156])[157] is entirely devoted to the rules on intellectual property.

Enterprise and Company Laws

The enterprise and company laws contain mainly imperative norms. These include the Joint Stock Company Law 1995, the Law on Limited Liability Companies 1998 and Law on the State and Municipal Unitary Enterprises 2002, the Law on the Protection of Competition (Competition Law) 2006 and Law on Natural Monopolies 1995, the Law on State Registration 2001 and Law on

148 The Civil Code has been translated into English. The translation is excellent in Butler 2003, exact in Maggs and Zhiltsov (2003 and 2008) and adequate in Osakwe 2008.

149 *"Гражданский Кодекс Российской Федерации". Часть 1 от 30.11.1994 N 51-ФЗ.*

150 Last amended by the Law no 352-FZ of 27 December 2009.

151 Sergeev 1 2009: 56–7.

152 *"Гражданский Кодекс Российской Федерации". Часть 2 от 26.01.1996 N 14-ФЗ.*

153 "Last amend by the Law no 145-FZ of 17 July 2009.

154 *"Гражданский Кодекс Российской Федерации". Часть 3 от 26.11.2001 N 146-ФЗ.*

155 Last amended by the Law no 105-FZ of 30 June 2008.

156 *"Гражданский Кодекс Российской Федерации". Часть 4 от 18.12.2006 N 230-ФЗ.*

157 Last amended by the Law no 259-FZ of 4 October 2010.

Licensing of Certain Forms of Activities 2001, as well as the Law on Insolvency (bankruptcy) and Law on the Securities Market 1996. The Land Code 2001, Forest Code 2006, and Water Code also include provisions concerning enterprise activities.

Investment Legislation

Investment legislation is comprised of private and public law norms. It comprises the Law on Foreign Investments (Foreign Investment Law) 1999, the Law on Investment Activities 1999, the Law on Production Sharing Agreements 1995, and the Concession Law 2005.

Taxation Legislation

Legislation on taxation belongs in Russia to public law regulation and it is based on the Tax Code. It is divided into two parts: the first contains general provisions while the second part contains special rules on different taxes.

Foreign Trade Legislation

Foreign trade legislation also belongs to public law regulation in Russia, and the Law on the Fundamentals of State Regulation of Foreign Trade Activities 2003 forms the basis of it. Of significance also are the Law on Currency Regulation and Currency Control (the Currency Law) 2003 and the customs legislation including the Law on Customs Regulation no 311-FZ of 27 November 2010.

Chapter 2
Enterprise and Company Law

The legal regulation of entrepreneurial activities in Russia[1] has been radically changed since the country started its economic, political and societal reforms. The indubitable result of these reforms is that the Russian economy is mainly based on private ownership and the country is officially recognized as a market economy. The Russian company law, especially, has been developing to conform to the requirements of the market economy.

The legal regulation of entrepreneurial activities in Russia is comprised of the enterprise and company norms which are contained, particularly, in the provisions on juristic persons of the Civil Code (Articles 48–123) and other legal normative acts enacted in accordance with it. According to Article 2 of the Civil Code, entrepreneurship, including relations between entrepreneurs, forms part of the civil law relations which are regulated by the norms of the Civil Code and also other legal normative acts. In the Civil Code the Joint Stock Company Law (JSC Law)[2] and the Limited Liability Company Law (LLC Law) are mentioned expressly as such acts. The norms of the JSC Law and the LLC Law are based on the company law norms of the first part of the Civil Code, and they form the main part in the regulation concerning the foundation and activities of companies. Each of these laws could work as an independent legal source in the regulation of companies because they include almost all the rules of the Civil Code concerning them and these are concretized in them.

1 General Rules

The general provisions on juristic persons of the Civil Code include the definitions of entrepreneurship and juristic person as well as the rules concerning legal capacity of juristic persons and their foundation, including capital contributions, reorganization and liquidation. Juristic persons are divided in the Civil Code into commercial (including companies and partnerships) and noncommercial organizations, and the provisions regulating companies and partnerships contain, among other, the rules concerning their participants, and the rights and duties of these, as well as the governing bodies. The Civil Code also provides the liability rules concerning companies and partnerships.

Entrepreneurship

Entrepreneurship (business activities) is defined in the Civil Code (Article 2.1) as an autonomous activity, effectuated at one's own risk, directed toward the systematic obtaining of profit from the use of property, the sale of goods, the fulfillment of work, or the rendering of services by the

---

1 On this subject, see, in particular, V.F. Popondopulo (ed.), Коммерческое (предпринимательское) право, Том I [Commercial (Entrepreneurial) Law, Volume I] (2009): 104–61; W.E. Butler, *Russian Law* (2009): 471–518 as well as Ch. Osakwe (trans. and comm.), *Russian Civil Code* (2008): 321–40 and V. Orlov, *Entrepreneurship in Russia* (1999): 94–175, where comparative aspects are also presented.

2 No 208-FZ of 26 December 1995 as last amended by the Law no 292-FZ of 3 November 2009. See http://www.consultant.ru/popular/stockcomp/ (accessed: 27 November 2010).

person(s) registered in this capacity in conformity with the law-established procedure. The Civil Code also includes the concept of enterprise, and this is recognized as a property complex, used to effectuate business activities; enterprise is regarded, as mentioned above, as an immovable. The concept of enterprise is not, however, included in the enterprise and company law norms of the Civil Code, in which juristic person (legal entity) is used as the basic concept, but it is represented as an object of civil law, which may be transferred by legal acts (transactions) as a whole or a part thereof[3].[4] (Article 132)

Entrepreneurship (business activity) may be practiced by forming or without forming a juristic person (legal entity), but in both cases it requires registration;[5] under the Civil Code (Article 49.1) the activities may also require special permits or licenses and the order of licensing and the list of activities subject to it is established by special law[6].[7] The activities of the enterprise must also conform to the requirements of other legislation.[8] The registration of an enterprise[9] takes place in state registration bodies in the procedure determined by the Registration Law (Article 51)[10] on the grounds of the documents (for instance, the constituent documents and an application).[11] State registration is the last stage in the foundation of an enterprise as a subject of civil law, in which it is examined whether the conditions necessary for the founding of an enterprise have been followed, and, consequently, a decision is made that the organization be recognized as a juristic person with legal capacity. A refusal of state registration is allowed only in the cases established by the law and is subject to appeal.[12] The registration data are included in the unified state register of juristic persons (the Register) and open for general familiarization except those parts (e.g. personal data) the admission to which is restricted.[13]

Juristic Person

The concept of juristic person (legal entity) is essential in the civil law regulation of entrepreneurship in Russian law. The juristic person is defined in the Civil Code as an organization which has solitary

---

3 An enterprise can be sold, leased, or mortgaged; it can be also inherited.

4 See A.P. Sergeev (ed.), Гражданское право [Civil Law] 1 (2009): 695–6.

5 According to the Civil Code, if a physical person intends to engage in entrepreneurship without forming a juristic person, he is obliged to be registered as an individual entrepreneur (sole trader) (Article 23.1).

6 The Law on licensing no 128-FZ of 8 August 2001 as amended 27 July 2010.

7 On this subject, see, for instance, Popondopulo 1 2009: 340–53.

8 Including Tax and Customs Code, laws on competition, and investment activities as well as bookkeeping and technical regulation legislation.

9 As well as the amendments to its charter and termination of its activities through reorganization or liquidation.

10 Special registration rules may be provided by the federal law. Such rules concern organizations practicing credit and insurance activities, and chambers of commerce.

11 The registration of enterprises is executed by the Federal Tax Service and its local bodies on the application submitted at the place of the site of the enterprise. This means that enterprises are also recorded for the purposes of taxation.

12 However, an enterprise which has not submitted taxation documents and executed any operation through its bank account is deemed to have actually finished its activities and is excluded from the Register.

13 For more on this subject, see T.E. Abova, M.M. Boguslavsky, A.Y. Kabalkin, and A.G. Lisicin-Svetlanov (eds), Постатейный комментарий к Гражданскому кодексу Российской Федерации, Частям I, II и III [Article-specific Commentary on the Civil Code of the Russian Federation, Parts I, II and III] (2007): 68–9; M. Yu. Tikhomirov (ed.), Комментарий к Федеральному закону об акционерных обществах [Commentary on the Federal Joint Stock Society Law] (2009): 112–21, and Popondopulo 2009: 327–9.

property in its ownership, economic management, or operative administration,[14] and which is liable for its obligations concomitant to this property, and may in its own name acquire and exercise property and personal non-property rights, as well as bear duties and be a plaintiff or defendant in court[15] (Article 48).[16]

According to the Civil Code, juristic persons in Russian law are distinguished into two kinds: commercial organizations, the list of which is exhaustive (the principle of enumeration), and noncommercial (non-profit) organizations[17] (Article 50), the list of which is not exhaustive but only exemplary. The main purpose of commercial organizations is to practice enterprise activity, and their goal is deriving profits (Article 50); whereas the enterprise activity of non-profit organizations must be connected with the objects of their primary activities.[18]

Under the Civil Code, only (economic) partnerships and companies as well as production cooperatives may act as commercial organizations (Articles 50 and 66). The Civil Code includes to partnerships general (full) partnerships and limited (commandite, *in commendam*) partnerships (Article 66.2), and to companies (so-called capital-based companies) limited liability companies and additional liability companies (companies with supplementary liability) and (open or closed) joint stock companies (Article 66.3). A partnership is usually an association of physical persons and the number of its participants is small. In turn, in a company the personal qualities and the nature of relations of the participants are usually without real significance because the question is about a combination of capitals.[19]

With respect both to partnerships and companies, their participants have, under the Civil Code, only participation rights determined in the special norms regulating these partnership and companies[20] (Article 48.2); the property rights to the assets of the company or partnership rest with these, so the participants (shareholders, members, partners) have no partial property rights to the property of the partnership or company. Contrary to that, the shareholder of a joint stock company has the rights to his shares and the participant of another kind of company or partnership has the rights to his membership's (partner's) share. So usually the company (partnership) has the property rights to the property transferred to it by the participant. However, it could be provided for by the constituent documents that the company has only the possession or use rights to such property.

14 An enterprise may have property also through the other property rights, such as real rights, obligation law rights, and intellectual property rights. See Sergeev 1 2009: 195.

15 The juristic person is characterized in Russian law by four specific features: (1) organizational unity, (2) independent participation in civil law transactions, (3) solitary (separate) property and (4) independent property responsibility. For more on this subject, see Sergeev 1 2009: 187–97.

16 This definition reflects six distinct attributes of legal personality: (1) separate property, (2) independent property responsibility, (3) independent existence from its members, (4) organizational unity, (5) capacity to participate in civil law transactions (substantive dispositive capacity) and (6) capacity to sue and be sued in its own name (procedural dispositive capacity) known in the United States as the attributes of a corporation. Noteworthy is the fact that only de jure legal persons are recognized in Russian law. See Osakwe 2008: 337.

17 Including public and private institutions.

18 For more on this subject, see Sergeev 1 2009: 197–203, and particularly on noncommercial organizations K.P. Belyayev, Некоммерческие организации в системе юридических лиц [Noncommercial Organizations in the System of Juristic Persons] (2004): 390–405.

19 Abova, Boguslavsky, Kabalkin, and Lisicin-Svetlanov 2007: 88.

20 In this case, the use of the term "obligation law rights" in the Civil Code is misleading and has attracted criticism. See Abova, Boguslavsky, Kabalkin, and Lisicin-Svetlanov 2007: 65–6 and particularly V.P. Mozolin and M.N. Maleina (eds), Научно-практический комментарий к гражданскому кодексу РФ, части первой [Scientific-Practical Commentary on the Civil Code of the Russian Federation, Part I] (2004): 99–101.

Furthermore, the obligation law relationship arises between the company or partnership and its participant—for instance, when he demands the payment of determined dividends (profit) or the remaining property of the liquidated company.[21]

As independent juristic persons state and municipal or public unitary enterprises are also included among commercial organizations in Russia,[22] and they are regulated by (in addition to the norms of the Civil Code) the special legislation concerning them.[23] A unitary enterprise is defined in the Civil Code as a commercial organization which is not endowed with the right of ownership to the property that the owner (state or municipal) consolidated to it; the property is entrusted to the unitary enterprise with the so-called right of economic management or operative administration (Articles 113–15).[24] According to the Civil Code, a unitary enterprise may be created in the form of a treasury enterprise which is in federative or municipal ownership, and it has the right of operative administration of the property used by it (Article 115).[25] In addition to that, commercial and/or noncommercial organizations may establish in Russia amalgamations in the form of associations and unions; these are also juristic persons, but their abilities to practice business activities are restricted (Articles 50.4 and 121–3). Also individual entrepreneurs may participate in associations and unions. Special rules are established for chambers of trade and industry,[26] which are not allowed to distribute their profits between their members. Furthermore, noncommercial partnerships are also recognized in Russia.[27] Financial and industrial groups may also be established, in accordance with the special law regulating them,[28] by juristic persons in Russia, and such groups can also be international; financial and industrial groups are not, however, juristic persons. Under a special law, the Russian Federation may establish a state corporation for specified public purposes; this is close to the state institution, but has property in its ownership.[29] [30]

Legal Capacity of Juristic Persons

The norms on legal capacity of the juristic person are incorporated expressly into the Civil Code (Article 49). According to the general rule, the juristic person enjoys (may have) those civil rights (and makes legal acts, transactions) which correspond to the purposes (objects) of its activity

21 Abova, Boguslavsky, Kabalkin, and Lisicin-Svetlanov 2007: 65–6 and Sergeev 1 2009: 197–8.

22 The constituent documents of a unitary enterprise can include some other target than deriving profit—for instance, public utility. See Sergeev 1 2009: 306.

23 Law on State and Municipal Unitary Enterprises no 161-FZ of 14 November 2002.

24 In respect of economic management the restrictions of the rights of the juristic person concern immovable property, whereas in respect of operative administration the restrictions concern all the property entrusted to the enterprise. As to legal capacity, economic management means that *what is not specifically prohibited is allowed,* while operative administration is based on the principle *what is allowed is only that which is specifically permitted.* Furthermore, the owner is not liable for the obligations of the unitary enterprise that is in economic management (except in the case of its bankruptcy), but the state or municipality is liable subsidiarily for the debts of its enterprise that is in operative administration (treasury enterprise). For more on this subject, see Sergeev 1 2009: 305–15 and Popondopulo 2009: 155–61.

25 The right of operative administration is an institution originated in Soviet economic law.

26 Law no 5340-I of 7 July 1993.

27 For example stock exchanges. Advocate offices (bureau, college) and commodity exchanges are special forms of juristic person provided by the law and are not recognized in this way.

28 Law no 190-FZ of 30 November as amended on 17 December 1997.

29 For example the Agency on the Insurance of Deposits under the Law on Insurance of Bank Deposits of Individuals in the Russian Federation no 177-FZ of 23 December 2003.

30 See Abova, Boguslavsky, Kabalkin, and Lisicin-Svetlanov 2007: 143–6 and Sergeev 1 2009: 316–44.

provided in its constituent documents. So special legal (act) capacity is a general principle in Russian law. However, if the objects (purposes) of activity are definitely restricted in the rules of the company,[31] the legal act (transaction) effected in contradiction to (exceeding the limits of) it may be recognized by the court as invalid (Article 49.2 and 173).[32] On the other hand, commercial organizations, with the exception of unitary enterprises and other (types of) organization provided for by the law, enjoy general legal capacity (powers) in Russia: they are not obliged to stipulate in their constituent documents the object of their activity.[33] Thus they may enjoy those civil rights which are indispensable for the performance of any kinds of activity not prohibited by the law (Article 49.1). However, this rule is regarded as an exception to the general principle (of special legal capacity). The unitary enterprise and such organizations whose legal capacity is designated as special by the law as well as noncommercial organizations, always enjoy a special legal (act) capacity (bound to the objects of the activity), and a legal act contradictory to it is absolutely invalid or null and void (Article 168).[34] Some kinds of activity may require in Russia, according to the Civil Code (Article 49.1.3), a special permit (license), and a legal act (transaction) made without a necessary permit is invalid (voidable). On the other hand, it is provided that all restrictions concerning juristic persons are to be based on the law.[35]

The legal capacity of a juristic person arises, under the Civil Code, at the time it is founded (registered) and terminates at the time it is deleted from the State Register (Article 49.3). The recognition of the registration of the juristic person as invalid by the court shall not per se cause invalidity of the transactions concluded by it before that, according to the established judicial practice of Russia.[36]

The Civil Code also includes rules concerning the liability of the juristic person (legal entity); in general, the juristic person other than (public and private) institutions are liable for their obligations with all the property belonging them (Article 56.1).

Participants

According to the Civil Code, the founders as well as participants of a partnership can only be private entrepreneurs and/or commercial organizations (e.g. partnerships and companies), whereas the founders (participants) of a company can in principle be any physical person or other juristic person; these may also participate as silent (limited) partners (investors) in a limited partnership.

31 As stated in Russian judicial practice, this means a closed list of the activities in which the enterprise is allowed to participate. See Joint Decrees of the Plenums of the Supreme Court and Supreme Arbitrazh Court no 6/8 of 1 July 1996. Вестник Высшего Арбитражного Суда Российской Федерации [Herald of Supreme Arbitrazh Court of Russian Federation] 9 (1996) and S.A. Stepanov (ed.), Комментарий к Гражданскому кодексу Российской Федерации [Commentary on the Civil Code of the Russian Federation] (2010): 95.

32 Provided that the other party in the transaction knew or ought to have known of such restrictions.

33 Enterprises are obliged to indicate their fields of activities in the application for registration, which are entered in the Register using the corresponding codes. However, these data are not regarded as restricting legal capacity. See Tikhomirov 2009: 37.

34 Thus, the doctrine of *ultra vires* activities according to which the transactions of a juristic person are void on the grounds that they exceed the authority (legal capacity) granted under their charter, known at common law, is applicable only to these organizations. Osakwe 2008: 325.

35 Abova, Boguslavsky, Kabalkin, and Lisicin-Svetlanov 2007: 66–7; Sergeev 1 2009: 204–7, and Popondopulo 2009: 110–11. See also Osakwe 2008: 325.

36 See the Informative Letter of the Presidium of the Supreme Arbitrazh Court no 54 of 9 June 2000. Вестник Высшего Арбитражного Суда Российской Федерации [Herald of Supreme Arbitrazh Court of Russian Federation] 7 (2000).

A person (private entrepreneur or commercial organization) has the right to be the participant of only one partnership and the general partner of only one limited partnership (Article 69.2 and 82.3). A joint stock company or limited liability company may also be established in Russia by one (any) person, but such a one-man (single company) is not allowed to be in another limited liability company or joint stock company as its sole participant (Article 88.2 and 98.6). The participation of certain physical persons in partnerships and companies, except open joint stock companies, may be prohibited or limited by the law (Article 66.4 and 66.5).[37]

Foundation

The constituent (founding) documents of juristic persons are, under the Civil Code (Article 52), the foundation agreement (contract) and the charter (the Rules). The foundation agreement, concluded by the founders of the enterprise, is regarded in Russian law as a civil law agreement (a simple partnership or cooperation agreement regulated by the norms of the Civil Code[38]), the obligations of which concern the founders and the established enterprise; its main purpose is to regulate the relations of the parties in the process of the foundation of the enterprise and its activities as well as their relations with the enterprise.[39] In turn, the charter, confirmed by the founders of the enterprise, is a local normative act, validated by registration, which specifies the legal status of the established (incorporated) enterprise, and is binding not only for the established enterprise (and its founders) but also third parties. The constituent documents should also meet the general requirements established by law; this means that the name of the juristic person or its trade or firm name,[40] the place of its location (site), the procedure for management and other information specifically required by the law for juristic persons of the corresponding form must be indicated in the constituent documents (Article 52.2). If the founders include stipulations on the objects (purposes) of the enterprise activity in the constituent documents, the enterprise is regarded as enjoying special legal (act) capacity, and, as stated above, the (invalidity) rules concerning the legal acts (transactions) beyond the scope of the charter may be applied according to the Civil Code (Article 173).[41]

Capital Contribution

Under the Civil Code (Article 66.6), the capital contribution to both the company and partnership is to be any property (money, securities, things), including property rights and other rights (including rights *in rem*,[42] rights of claim, and intellectual property rights), which has monetary value; in

37 Such restrictions concern public servants in Russia. See Tikhomirov 2009: 91–4.

38 Articles 1041–54 of the Civil Code.

39 The foundation agreement is outside of corporate law regulation. As a civil law contract, it is regulated by the general rules on legal transactions (contracts), and, consequently, for instance, the question of the validity of the foundation agreement are to be evaluated in accordance with the Civil Code rules on the validity of transactions (Articles 166–81). See Decree of the Plenum of the Supreme Arbitrazh Court no 19 of 18 November 2003. Вестник Высшего Арбитражного Суда Российской Федерации [Herald of Supreme Arbitrazh Court of Russian Federation] 1 (2004).

40 Which is subject to the intellectual property law regulation provided by the norms of the Civil Code (Articles 1473–6).

41 See Abova, Boguslavsky, Kabalkin, and Lisicin-Svetlanov 2007: 69–71, Sergeev 1 2009: 215–17 and Popondopulo 2009: 113–14.

42 However, the right to the permanent use of a plot of land, as provided by the Civil Code (Articles 264 and 268–70), may not be contributed to the company or partnership (Law 25.10.2001/137-FZ). Furthermore,

other words, the criteria for capital contribution is that it must be possible to evaluate it in money. According to judicial practice, the property contributed to the company or partnership is in its ownership, whereas the transfer of property or other rights to the enterprise must be executed by deed or contract of lease.[43]

Rights and Duties

The rights of a participant in a partnership or company are participation rights, and they include, according to the Civil Code (Article 67.1), the right:

- to take part in the administration;[44]
- to get information about the activity (the scope of which is laid down by the constituent documents); and
- to take part in the distribution of profits and receive the remaining property, if the company/partnership is liquidated (the property rights); as well as
- other rights established by the law as well as constituent documents.

The general duty of the participant is, under the Civil Code (Article 67.2), to make a capital contribution and he also has the obligation to maintain secrecy as well as other duties established by the constituent documents—for instance, the prohibition on competition (Article 73.3).[45]

Civil law rights and duties arise in the company, according to the Civil Code (Article 53), through the activity of its governing bodies,[46] including the executive body[47] which represents the company. Moreover, in those instances provided by the law the rights and duties of the juristic person (partnership) arise through the acts of its participants (Article 53.2). The person who by force of the law or of the juristic person's constituent documents comes out on its behalf is expected to act in the interests of the juristic person it represents in good faith and reasonably (Article 53.3); and this is presumed in the Civil Code (Article 10.3).[48]

Liability Rule

The Civil Code also includes the general rule concerning the liability for damages of the representatives of the company (partnership). According to this, if the representative of the company (partnership) causes damages to the company (partnership), he is obliged, upon the demand of the founders (the participants), to compensate the company, unless otherwise provided for by the law

---

a resident in a free economic zone may not participate in the charter capital of the company or partnership by virtue of the lease rights to public property plots (Law 22.6.2005/116-FZ).

43 However, the objects of intellectual property such as patents or know-how are not regarded as capital contributions, whereas the (exclusive) rights to use them—according to the license agreement—are accepted as such. See Abova, Boguslavsky, Kabalkin, and Lisicin-Svetlanov 2007: 87–8; Popondopulo 2009: 113; Tikhomirov 2009: 31, and 83–4 as well as Joint Decrees of the Plenums (1996) 9.

44 This concerns a silent partner in a limited partnership as well as a shareholder in a joint stock company, unless his participation in the administration is restricted by law.

45 Abova, Boguslavsky, Kabalkin, and Lisicin-Svetlanov 2007: 89.

46 The general meeting, the council of directors (supervisory council), the director (the director general), and the board (directorate).

47 The director (the director general) and the board (directorate).

48 Abova, Boguslavsky, Kabalkin, and Lisicin-Svetlanov 2007: 28–9 and 71–2.

or by the agreement (Article 53.3). It is obvious that in this instance the question is initially about negligence liability. Besides the founder (participant), the owner or some other person who has the right to issue the obligatory instructions (orders) for the juristic person, or who may determine its actions in any other way, may, if the insolvency (bankruptcy) of the juristic person has been caused, bear subsidiary liability for the obligations of this (Article 56.3).[49]

Reorganization and Liquidation

According to the Civil Code (Article 57 and 61), the reorganization and liquidation of the juristic person[50] is possible. It could be effected by the decision of its founders (participants) or the body authorized to do this by the constituent documents. The reorganization may be carried out in those cases provided for by the law in the form of a merger (with another juristic person), accession[51] (to another juristic person), division (into many juristic persons), spin-off (separation of a part),[52] or transformation (into another form of juristic person). In those cases provided for by the law the reorganization of the juristic person through its division or separation, or liquidation of it, is to be executed by the decision of the authorized state body or by the decision of a court (Articles 57.3 and 61.2), whereas the merger, accession, or transformation of the juristic person may be effected only upon the consent of the authorized state body (Article 57.3).

The form of the company (partnership) may be, according to the Civil Code, in principle changed to another, and the decision with regard to the transformation is to be made by general meeting (Article 68.1). However, the transformation of the form of the company (partnership) is in some cases restricted in Russia. Such restrictions concern general partnerships (these may not be transformed into a limited partnership or a cooperative if only one participant is left in it; Article 81) and joint stock companies (these may be transformed only into a limited liability company or cooperative as well as into an noncommercial organization (partnership) but not into a general or limited partnership; Article 104). On the other hand, a limited partnership may be transformed into a general partnership, if all the silent (limited) partners have retired from it (Article 86.1). Where the partnership is to be transformed into a company, the Civil Code has a special rule (Article 68.2) concerning the liability of the general partners: the former general partner, who has become the participant (shareholder) of the company, had to bear (for two years) subsidiary liability for the obligations which have passed to the company from the partnership. Even the alienation by the former partner of the participation interests (shares) in his possession does not exempt him from such liability (Article 68).

According to the Civil Code, in the reorganization a general succession takes place; it is regarded that the existing (general or special) legal (act) capacity remains intact. As to the merger, all the rights and duties of the absorbing juristic persons are to pass to the new juristic person, whereas in the accession the rights and duties of the juristic persons are to pass to the existing juristic person with the termination of the absorbed juristic persons. In turn, in the division the reorganizing juristic person is terminated, but remains if only a part of it is separated off, while in the transformation the rights and duties of the reorganizing juristic person passes to the new juristic person (Article 58).[53]

---

49 For more on this subject, see Stepanov 2010: 103–4.

50 See Sergeev 1 2009: 219–35 and Laptev, and Zankovsky 2006: 91–9.

51 Acquisition, affiliation.

52 Without any changes in organizational form in the case of the merger, accession, division, and separation of a joint stock company. As to other companies and partnerships, the restrictions regarding their transformation are to be applied. See Abova, Boguslavsky, Kabalkin, and Lisicin-Svetlanov 2007: 77.

53 Sergeev 1 2009: 221.

Under the Civil Code, the provisions on legal succession in respect of all the obligations of the reorganizing juristic person are to be included in the deed of transfer (in case of the merger, accession, or transformation) or the separation balance sheet (in case of the division or separation) approved by the body which has made the reorganization decision (Article 59).

The juristic person is obliged, under the Civil Code (Article 60), after the adoption of the decision (by its participants or authorized body) to reorganize, (within three days) to inform in writing the registration body on the beginning of the reorganization procedure. After the registration of the reorganization, the reorganizing juristic person must publish notice of the reorganization two times (once per month) in the State Register publication. A creditor of the reorganizing juristic person has the right to demand from it the performance at an earlier date, and, if this is impossible, the termination of any obligation arising from it before the publication of the notice, and compensation for damages connected therewith, unless otherwise provided for by the law. (Article 60.2) The obligations of the reorganizing juristic person to its creditors may be secured by pledge, in which case the creditors may not demand additional securities for the performance (Article 60.5).

The new juristic person(s) are to bear solidary (joint and several) liability on the obligations of the reorganized juristic person where the demands of the creditors are satisfied after the reorganization. The new juristic person(s) are to be solidarily liable, according to the established judicial praxis, if the separation balance sheet does not allow the determination of the legal successor, or is inequitable in respect of the legal successors of the reorganizing juristic person.[54]

A juristic person is regarded, according to the Civil Code (Article 57.4), as reorganized from the moment of the registration of the new juristic person(s) and in the case of the accession from the moment of the registration of the termination of the absorbed juristic person.

A juristic person may be liquidated under the Civil Code by the decision of its founders (participants) or of the juristic person's body authorized for this by the constituent documents, as well as where the term for which it has been created is expired, or the goal for the purpose of which it has been established is achieved. Liquidation will also take place where the court recognizes the registration of the juristic person as invalid because of violations of law or other legal normative acts, committed in its establishment, unless these violations can not be rectified (are of an irremediable nature). A juristic person may be liquidated also by court decision where an activity is practiced without a proper permit (license), or where such activity is prohibited by the law or contradictory to the Constitution, or as a result of repeated or gross violations of the law or other legal (normative) acts (Article 61). The grounds for liquidation can also be the insolvency (bankruptcy) of the juristic person; the juristic person is to be recognized as insolvent by the decision of the court or on the grounds of a voluntary declaration of such (joint decision with its creditors). Where the cost of the net assets of the enterprise is less than its authorized capital, it is to be liquidated as bankrupt following the bankruptcy procedure established by the Law on Insolvency (bankruptcy)[55].[56] (Articles 61.4 and 65) Liquidation of the juristic person means that its rights and duties do not pass to any other person (Article 61.1) in general succession.[57]

Under the Civil Code, a decision on the liquidation of the juristic person must be notified to the state registration body, which duly makes a corresponding entry of such. A liquidation commission must also be appointed, and the order and term of the liquidation procedure laid down;

54 See Decree of the Plenum 19 of 2003 (item 22).

55 Insolvency Law no 127-FZ of 26 October 2002.

56 The list of grounds for liquidation by the court, unlike voluntary liquidation, is exhaustive. See Abova, Boguslavsky, Kabalkin, and Lisicin-Svetlanov 2007: 80–81.

57 This does not exclude the transfer of some rights and duties of the liquidated enterprise by singular succession. See Sergeev 1 2009: 225.

the management of the juristic person's affairs passes to the liquidation commission (Article 62). Information on the liquidation and the order and term for possible claims to be filed by the creditors are to be published; the term for the filing of the claims of creditors is to be at least two months from the publication date. Those creditors which are identified are to be notified in written form. The next stages in the liquidation procedure are the compilation of an intermediary liquidation balance; the organization of the sale of the juristic person's assets at a public auction (if the monetary means are insufficient); the payment of debts to the creditors in accordance with the established order of priority (Article 64);[58] the compilation of the liquidation balance, and the registration of the liquidation. The juristic person is to be regarded as liquidated and its obligations (debts) terminated after the registration of the liquidation (Article 63).[59]

Subsidiary and Dependent Companies

The Civil Code includes general rules on subsidiary companies. The company shall be recognized as subsidiary, if the other (the principal, parent) company (or partnership), on account of its prevalent participation in its charter capital or in conformity with the agreement or in any other way, has the possibility of determining its decisions (Article 105.1). An impact on the decisions of the subsidiary company may be exerted in other ways—for instance by granting a loan, by the right of pledge, or by the appointment of one's own representatives to the board of directors.[60] The subsidiary company may be a joint stock company, limited liability company, or additional liability company, whereas the principal company (partnership) may be any company or partnership (Article 105).[61]

Under the Civil Code (Article 105.2), the subsidiary company is not liable for the debts of the principal company (partnership); whereas the principal company (partnership) bears solidary (joint and several) liability with the subsidiary company by the acts (transactions) effected by the latter in execution of its instructions. However, in case of the insolvency (the bankruptcy) of the subsidiary company due the fault of the principal company (partnership), the latter bears the subsidiary liability for the debts of the subsidiary company. In the first case, it is assumed that the obligatory instructions given to the subsidiary company concern concrete acts (transactions), whereas the liability for falling into bankruptcy does not require any illegality of the acts of the principal company (partnership). In addition to the subsidiary company's right to claim, the participants (shareholders) of the subsidiary company also have the right to claim, under the Civil Code, that the damages caused to it by the fault of the principal company (partnership) be compensated by the latter, unless otherwise provided for by the company laws; this means that such restriction shall not concern the partnership (Article 105.3).

The liability of the principal company (partnership) connected with its relationship to the subsidiary company can be compared with the general rule on the liability of the persons who have caused the insolvency (bankruptcy) of the juristic person according to Article 56.3 of the Civil Code, which is presented above. In both cases there is a question about the use of authority, but the general rule applies to any person using authority, whereas the liability rule concerning the

58 According to it, claims of creditors are arranged into four sequential levels: (1) personal injury claims, (2) wages, (3) obligatory payments to the state budget, and (4) other claims. See Sergeev 1 2009: 227–9. See also Osakwe 2008: 329, where, unfortunately, the amendment to the Article 64.1 of the Civil Code (Law no 231-FZ of 18 December 2006) was ignored.

59 For more on this subject, see Abova, Boguslavsky, Kabalkin, and Lisicin-Svetlanov 2007: 81–5 and Sergeev 1 2009: 226–31.

60 Tikhomirov 2009: 66–67.

61 See Abova, Boguslavsky, Kabalkin, and Lisicin-Svetlanov 2007: 122–4.

subsidiary and principal relation is applicable only to the principal company (partnership). The most significant difference between them is, however, the nature of liability: in the subsidiary and principal relation the use of authority could lead to solidary (joint and several) liability, concerning only the agreements made by the subsidiary company, whereas in the general case the liability is only subsidiary. On the other hand, in the case of insolvency (bankruptcy), the principal company (partnership) could be liable (subsidiarily) merely by its negligence, whereas under the general rule such liability requires the use of authority. Thus, the liability concerning the subsidiary and principal relationship is by nature stricter than the general liability of the persons causing the insolvency (bankruptcy).

The Civil Code also includes general rules on dependent companies. A company is recognized as dependent, under the Civil Code (Article 106), if the other (the prevalent, the participant) company possesses more than 20 percent of its voting shares or charter capital; both the dependent and prevalent companies can only be capital-based companies. The information on the dependent relation must be published without delay when this is in conformity with the order established by the company laws (Article 106.2). However, these requirements do not apply to the foundation of the company. Under the Civil Code, the limits of the mutual participation of the companies and the number of the votes which one company may use at the general meeting of another company is defined by the law (Article 106.3).

2 Companies

Joint Stock Company

The main legal source regulating the establishment, activities, and termination of joint stock companies in Russia is the Joint Stock Company Law (JSC Law).[62] The norms of the JSC Law, the majority of which are imperative, are based on the company law norms of the first part of the Civil Code and form the main part in the regulation of the foundation (formation) and activities of joint stock companies. The JSC Law contains 104 articles and is divided into 15 chapters, in which there are, in addition to the general (Chapter I) and final (Chapter XIV) rules, the rules regulating the foundation, reorganization, and liquidation of the company (Chapter II); the charter capital, shares, and securities of the company (Chapter III) and issuance of them (Chapter IV); the dividends (Chapter V); the shareholders' register (Chapter VI); the general meeting of shareholders (Chapter VII); the board of directors and executive body of the company (Chapter VIII); the acquisition and redemption of issued shares (Chapter IX); large-scale transactions (Chapter X); the interest in conclusion of transactions (Chapter XI); the acquisition of more than 30 percent of the shares (Chapter XI^1),[63] as well as the control over financial and economic activity (Chapter XII) and bookkeeping and other information (Chapter XIII).

Concept A joint stock company is, according to the Civil Code (Article 96) and the JSC Law (Article 2.1), a company whose charter (authorized) capital is divided into a definite number of shares (of stock) certifying rights of obligations of the participants or shareholders (stockholders) to the company (Article 2.1). Shareholders are not to be liable for obligations of the company

62 No 208-FZ of 26 December 1995 as last amended by the Law no 292-FZ of 3 November 2010. See http://www.consultant.ru/popular/stockcomp/ (accessed: 27 November 2010).

63 Chapter XI^1 was added by the Law no 7-FZ of 5 January 2006.

but bear the risk of losses associated with its activity to the extent of the value of shares owned by them. However, the shareholders who have not paid up their shares in full shall be jointly (solidarily) liable for the obligations of the company to the extent of the value of the unpaid part of the contribution of each member. Shareholders may dispose of the shares owned by them without consent of the other shareholders.

A joint stock company is, under the JSC Law, a juristic person, established for an indefinite time unless otherwise is provided for by its charter (Article 2.5). It practices its activities in compliance with the requirements of the charter (rules) approved by the shareholders and has civil rights and bears obligations required to pursue any types of activity not prohibited by the law. However, a joint stock company may not, until 50 percent of the shares distributed among its shareholders is paid, enter into transactions outside of its foundation (Article 2.3). Furthermore, certain types of activity of a joint stock company may require special permits or licenses (Article 2).[64]

According to the JSC Law, the particular aspects of the formation, reorganization, liquidation, and legal status of joint stock companies in the spheres of banking, investment, and insurance activities as well as those practicing activities in agriculture are defined by the (other) laws (Articles 1.3 and 1.4). In addition, the formation and legal status of the Joint Stock Companies originating in privatization must be determined partly in accordance with the federal legislation concerning them (Article 1.5). According to the JSC Law (Article 9.6), the special rules in respect of the foundation of enterprises with foreign investors may be provided by the federal laws.[65]

The joint stock company is to be registered under a trade name. It must have a full name and may also have an abbreviative name. The trade name of a company must contain its name in which the form as well as the type of company must be indicated,[66] as provided for by the Civil Code (Article 96) and JSC Law (Article 4.1). The site of a company is determined by the place of its registration (Article 4.2), which is in general the location of the executive body of the company.[67]

A joint stock company may have, according to the JSC Law, branches and representative offices which are not recognized as juridical persons (Article 5). A joint stock company may have also subsidiary and dependent companies (Article 6) which are juridical persons. In the event the company acquires more than 20 percent of the voting shares of the other company, this principal company is obliged to publish the information thereof in accordance with the requirements of the Security Market and Competition Law (Article 6.4).

A joint stock company may be, according to the Civil Code (Article 97) and JSC Law (Article 7), of two types, open or closed, which must be expressed in its company name (and also in its charter (rules)):

- *Open joint stock company* An open joint stock company has the right to hold open (and also closed) subscriptions to shares (and bonds convertible into shares; Article 39.1) in accordance with the JSC Law and other legal acts. It places and sells such shares without limitations; the right to hold closed subscription may, however, be limited by the charter of the company or legal act of the Russian Federation (Article 7.2).
- *Closed joint stock company* In a closed joint stock company the shares are distributed only among its founders or another previously determined range of persons and the number

64 The Law on Licensing no 128-FZ of 8 August 2001 as amended 27 July 2010.

65 The rules on enterprises with foreign investors are provided by the Law on Foreign Investments no 160-FZ of 9 July 1999. At present, the law grants some legal protection rules. See the presentation on this law in Chapter 7.

66 In Russian (obligatory) and in other languages.

67 According to the Registration Law 2001 (Article 8.2).

of shareholders is not to exceed 50, as provided by the Civil Code (Article 97.2) and the JSC Law (Article 7.3).

It is not allowed to hold open subscriptions to the shares (and bonds convertible into shares; Article 39.1) it places or to offer them in any other way for acquisition to an unlimited circle of persons. Shareholders of the closed joint stock company have a preemptive right (right of first refusal) to acquire the shares offered for sale by the other shareholders of the company proportionally to their stocks, unless otherwise provided for by the charter of the company. This could also contain a stipulation on the company's preferential right to acquire the shares,[68] if the shareholders do not exercise their preferential right to acquire them (Article 7.3). Where the number of the participants of a closed joint stock company exceeds that fixed by the law, such a company must be transformed into an open joint stock company within one year and, upon the expiry of this term, it must be liquidated by judicial procedure (Civil Code Article 97.2).

Participants The participant to the joint stock company may in principle be any physical or juristic person. The joint stock company may, according to Civil Code (Article 98.6), be also established by one person, which means that a single joint stock company is possible, but the information on it must be included in the charter, which must be also registered and published. However, a joint stock company does not have the right to enlist another company consisting of a sole person as its only participant, which means that a single joint stock company is not permitted to be the only participant in another single joint stock company.[69] The joint stock company may be established, according to the JSC Law (Article 7.4), by the Russian Federation, a subject of the Russian Federation, or a municipal formation where permitted by the federal law, and it must be open.[70]

The joint stock company is obliged to ensure the maintenance and storage of the shareholders register, which includes specified information concerning both shareholders and shares. The holder of the register may be the company or a specialized registrar; the latter is obligatory for a company whose shareholders number more than 50 (Article 44). On the basis of the data in the shareholders register, the joint stock company must draw up a list of shareholders for the general meeting of shareholders not later than 45 days before this. This list is to be submitted, however, only to persons possessing not less than 1 percent of the votes at the general meeting; but any interested person has the right to demand information concerning his inclusion in the list of shareholders having the right to participate in the general meeting (Article 51).

Foundation A joint stock company may be founded as a new company or by means of the reorganization of an existing company (partnership), including through a merger, division, or spin-off, as well as by means of the transformation of a commercial organization in another form (Articles 8 and 15, 16, and 18–20).

A joint stock company is founded by the unanimous decision of the founders in the organizational meeting (Article 9), which must include confirmation of the charter and of the monetary valuation

---

68 If a shareholder intends to sell his shares, he must inform other shareholders of his intention. The period for the exercise of the preferential right must not be less than 30 days or more than 60 days from the time of the offer of the shares for sale, as provided by the JSC Law (Article 7.3).

69 This rule, however, may be excepted by the federal law. See Tikhomirov 2009: 94–5.

70 State and municipal bodies are not allowed to participate in joint stock companies, unless otherwise provided in the law, and the participation of an institution in a joint stock company is subject to its owner's permission, as provided by the Civil Code (Article 66.4).

of contributions other than money. The governing bodies of the company must also be elected, and in this case a qualified majority vote (three-quarters) is sufficient.

According to the Civil Code (Article 98) and JSC Law (Article 9.5), the foundation agreement for the foundation of a joint stock company may be made by the founders, and its purpose is to define the order of their performance of a joint activity involved in the establishment of the company, the size of the charter (authorized) capital, the categories of the shares it is going to place and the means of their distribution, as well as the amount and procedure for their paying up, and also the rights and duties of the founders in connection with the formation of the company. The foundation agreement must be made in written form. It is, however, regarded not as a proper constituent document, as stated above (Article 9.5).

As the constituent document of the joint stock company, only the charter is mentioned in both the Civil Code (Article 98.3) and the JSC Law (Articles 11 and 7.3, 27, 31, 32, 35, 37, 52, 66, 85, and 88), and the minimum requirements for it are directly written down in law. It is a local normative act, which is binding for all shareholders as well as for the company and its counterparties.[71]

The charter must contain, according to the JSC Law, the following information:

- the full and abbreviated names of the company and its type;
- the location of the company;
- the categories (also types of the preference shares) and par value of the subscribed (placed) shares as well as their number;
- the amount of the charter capital;
- the rights of the shareholders of each category (or type);
- the composition and authority of the governing bodies of the company and the management procedure, including decisions on matters to be resolved by a qualified majority or unanimous vote;
- data concerning branches and representative offices;

as well as other provisions provided for by the JSC Law (and other federal laws) regarding, for instance, dividends and division of assets to be paid in the event of the liquidation of a company for preference shares (Article 32.2) and the reserve fund (Article 35.1) as well as the securities convertible into preference shares (Article 37.1).[72]

The company's charter as well as the law may impose limits on the quantity and total par value of shares (stock) held or the maximum number of votes cast by one shareholder, as provided for by the Civil Code (Article 99.5) and the JSC Law (Article 11.3). The charter may also include, under the JSC Law, the provisions concerning the cumulative preference shares, according to which the unpaid dividends are to be accumulated and paid subsequently (Article 32.2). It may also include the provisions concerning the converting of shares (into another type of shares); and, if these are convertible preference shares, they may also include the right of vote (Articles 32.3 and 32.5).[73]

71 Abova, Boguslavsky, Kabalkin, and Lisicin-Svetlanov 2007: 113 and V.P Mozolin and A.P. Yudenkov, Комментарий к Федеральному закону об акционерных обществах [Commentary on the Federal Law on Joint Stock Societies] (2003): 58.

72 Tikhomirov 2009: 102–4.

73 In addition to ordinary shares, preference shares (with the rights to cumulative dividends) and convertible preference and (noncumulative) redeemable preference shares are also known in common law. The same concerns the provisions under which the holders of preference shares are not entitled to attend any meeting of the company or vote (non-voting shares) on any resolution of the company unless, for example, the dividend on the preference shares is in arrears, or the company has failed to redeem any preference share.

The charter may also contain other provisions that are not contrary to the law (Article 11.3). The purpose of the charter is to regulate the company's activities. Its provisions are obligatory for all shareholders, bodies, and personnel of the company and for the company itself in its relations both with its participants and third persons.[74] The company is obliged, if so required by a shareholder, auditor, or any interested person, within reasonable periods to provide them with the possibility of familiarizing themselves with the company's charter (Article 11.4).

The joint stock company must be, as mentioned above, registered and is regarded as established (as a juristic person) from the moment of its registration, as provided for by the Civil Code (Article 51) and the JSC Law (Articles 2.4 and 13). The founders of the company are jointly and severally liable, according to the Civil Code (Article 9.2), and the JSC Law (Article 10.3), for obligations associated with the formation of the company and arising prior to its registration; this liability is based on the law, but those obligations may be transferred to the company on the approval of the general meeting of shareholders.[75]

Operating agreement Shareholders have the right, in accordance with Article 32^1 of the JSC Law,[76] to enter into an operating agreement or a shareholders' agreement,[77] which is defined as an agreement on the exercise of rights certified by shares and/or peculiarities of the exercise of rights to shares.

Under the operating agreement, the shareholders undertake to practice and/or refrain from practicing their rights in a determinate way, including:

- voting at general meetings;
- the acquirement and disposal of shares at the price determined by the agreement and/or where conditions determined by the agreement occur;
- refraining from the alienation of shares before the occurrence of determinate conditions, and
- the performance as agreed of other actions relating to the governance of the company as well as its foundation, activities, reorganization, and liquidation.

However, an operating agreement may not contain an obligation on its participant to vote in accordance with the directions of the governing bodies concerning the shares subject to the operating agreement (Article 32^1.1). An operating agreement must concern all the shares belonging to its participant (Article 32^1.3), and it must be concluded in written form by drawing up a single document signed by the parties (Article 32^1.1).[78]

Furthermore, deferred shares which give the holder the right to participate in the residue of the distributed profit are known also in common law.

74 See, for instance, Abova, Boguslavsky, Kabalkin, and Lisicin-Svetlanov 2007: 70 and Tikhomirov 2009: 101.

75 Tikhomirov 2009: 98.

76 Added by the Law no 115-FZ of 3 June 2009.

77 For more on this subject, see Russian Joint Stock Companies Law Finally Recognizes Shareholders' Agreements, *V&E Russia/CIS Legal Update E-communication, June 16, 2009* http://www.vinson-elkins.com/resources/RussianJointStockCompanies.aspx (accessed 15 June 2010) and D. Dmitriev, Некоторые особенности акционерных соглашений (Some Peculiarities of Shareholders' Agreements) (2009), http://www.klerk.ru/law/Articles/161860/ (accessed 15 June 2010).

78 According to the Article 32^1.5 of the JSC Law, where a person has acquired, in accordance with the operating agreement, the right to determine the voting process at the general meeting on shares, the issue of which was accompanied by the registration of the prospectus concerning them, and where, as a result of the

An operating agreement may contain, according to the JSC Law, provisions on the measures securing the performance of the obligations established by it and remedies for their violation, including liquidated damages (Article $32^1.7$). However, an operating agreement is binding only on its participants. A contract violating the provisions of the agreement may be recognized by a court as invalid on the claim of the participant on the condition that he knew or should have known about the restrictions imposed by the agreement. However, a violation of the agreement is not considered as grounds for invalidating the decisions of the company and the consequent transactions concluded by it (Article $32^1.4$).[79]

Assets and shares of the company Under the JSC Law (Article 25), a joint stock company must have common (ordinary) shares and may have preference shares. In a closed joint stock company, fractional shares may also occur where the preemptive right to acquire shares is used as well as in cases of share consolidation (Article 74).[80] Shares are nominal documents in Russia, but a share can be entrusted to a nominal shareholder.[81] As securities, shares can be issued both in documentary and in nondocumentary forms.[82]

The charter capital of the joint stock company comprises, according to the Civil Code (Article 99) and the JSC Law (Article 25), the nominal value of the shares of the company acquired by the shareholders—that is, it is the same as the sum of the nominal value of its shares.[83] The nominal value of all the common (ordinary) shares of a company, which must be placed, must be identical, and the nominal value of the preference shares, which may be placed, must not exceed 25 percent of the charter capital of the company (Article 25). The charter capital of the company determines the minimum amount of the property of a company that guarantees the interests of its creditors, and so the minimum amount of charter capital must not be less than as established by the JSC Law.[84] A reserve fund (not less than 5 percent of the charter capital) must also be created to cover losses; however, it can also be used for the cancellation of company bonds and the purchase of company shares in the event of the absence of other means, as established by the JSC Law (Article 35.1).

When founding a company, according to the JSC Law, all its shares, which must be inscribed, must be placed among the founders (Article 25.2). The company's shares must be paid in full (not less than 50 percent within three months of the registration, and the remaining part within a year of the registration) (Article 34.1).

According to the JSC Law, a joint stock company may have, in addition to the placed shares, also declared (authorized but unissued) shares, the nominal value of which is not counted in the charter capital and which the company may be allowed to place by the decision of the council of directors, if so provided by the charter. The quantity and par value as well as categories of additionally placeable shares, and the rights granted by such additional shares, must be determined

acquisition he alone or with his affiliates acquires the possibility to dispose of 5, 10, 15, 20, 25, 30, 50, or 75 percent of votes, he is obliged to notify the company of this.

79 The operation agreements of Russian joint stock companies governed by foreign law have not been recognized before in Russian judicial practice. See Dmitriev 2009.

80 See below.

81 M.V. Telyukina, Комментарий к Федеральному закону "Об акционерных обществах" [Commentary on the Federal Law on Joint Stock Societies] (2005): 329–30.

82 See Popondopulo 2009: 136.

83 Abova, Boguslavsky, Kabalkin, and Lisicin-Svetlanov 2007: 115.

84 Under the JSC Law, the minimum charter capital of an open joint stock company may not less than a thousand times, and of a closed company not less than a hundred times, the minimum wage on the date of registration of the company (Article 26).

by the charter (Article 27). Additional shares placed by subscription must be paid up in full at the time of their placement (Article 34.1).

The contributions into the charter capital through payment of shares must be, under the JSC Law, things (including money and securities) or rights which have monetary value, including rights to use property; however, the charter may include exclusions for the types of property contributable to the charter capital (Article 34.2). The monetary valuation of the property contributed to pay up shares in the formation of the company is to be agreed among the founders. In turn, the property contributed to pay up additional shares is to be evaluated, according to the rules of the JSC Law (Article 77), by the council of directors, and an independent valuer (or auditor) is to be involved in the monetary valuation (Article 34.3).

The shareholder may not be relieved, according to the Civil Code, from paying for the shares (Article 99.2), but additional shares placed through a closed subscription may be paid for, according to the JSC Law (Article 34.2), by setoff. The share remaining partly unpaid for passes into the ownership of the company. Moreover, the foundation agreement may provide a penalty for failure to pay for the share. The shares passed to the company are voteless, and dividends are not to be credited with regard to them. The company must adopt in such a case a decision on the reduction of the charter capital, or must realize the shares by the decision of the council of directors at a price not lower than their nominal value and no later than one year from the moment of their acquisition by the company;[85] otherwise, the state or local authorities may demand the liquidation of the company in a judicial proceeding (Article 34.1). Furthermore, there is a rule concerning open joint stock companies, according to which the open (public) subscription for the shares is not be admitted until the charter capital is paid up in full, as provided for by the Civil Code (Article 99.3).

A joint stock company may place, according to the JSC Law, the bonds and other emission securities by the decision of the council of directors, unless otherwise provided for by the charter (Article 33). Placement of the bonds is allowed after the charter capital has been paid up in full. The bonds, which can be nominal or negotiable documents, are to have nominal value. Moreover, the nominal value of all the bonds issued by the company is not to exceed the size of the charter capital and/or the amount of the security provided for this purpose by the third persons. In the absence of such security, the bond placement is not permissible until the third year of the company's existence and, additionally, on condition that by this time its two annual balances have been properly approved. These restrictions are not to be applied to mortgage coverings and in other cases provided for by the federal laws on securities. The bonds and other emission securities which a joint stock company is allowed to place can be convertible into shares (but not vise versa; Article 31.3). Their amount must not exceed the amount of the declared shares subject to conversion. The bonds and other emission securities must be paid in money (Article 34.2).

The value of net assets of the company must be valued according to the data of bookkeeping records in the established procedure. If the value of net assets of the company proves to be less than its charter capital at the end of financial year (from the end of the second financial year), the council of directors (supervisory council) of the company is obliged, according to JSC Law (Article 35),[86] to include in the annual report a section on the state of the net assets, including measures for conducting the value of net assets to correspond to the amount of the charter capital. Where the

85 Transactions contradictory to these requirements are, according to the established judicial practice of Russia, null and void. See Decree of the Plenum of the Supreme Arbitrazh Court no 19 of 18 November 2003 (item 7). Вестник Высшего Арбитражного Суда Российской Федерации [Herald of Supreme Arbitrazh Court of Russian Federation] (2004) 1.

86 As amended by the Law no 352-FZ of 27 December 2009. See http://www.consultant.ru/popular/stockcomp/ (accessed: 14 June 2010).

company fails to do this, it must adopt a decision on a corresponding decrease in the charter capital or its liquidation.

Rights and duties of shareholder The rights and duties of the shareholder of the company are defined directly in the general rules concerning companies and partnership of the Civil Code (Article 67), which are presented above. The JSC Law also contains provisions on such rights and duties (Articles 31, 32, 49, 57, and 91).

The holders of common shares have the right:

- to take part in the administration personally or through representatives (Article 57.1) with the restrictions established by the JSC Law (Articles 53 and 55);
- to appeal to a court a decision adopted by the general meeting in violation of the law and the charter (Article 49.7);
- to get information about the activity of the company, the scope of which is laid down by the JSC Law; thus, access to bookkeeping records and minutes of meetings of a collegial executive body of the company is granted only to shareholders owning not less than 25 percent of voting shares (Article 91).

The shareholders have also the right to transfer their shares to third persons, although the sale of shares in a closed joint stock company is restricted by the preemptive right of other shareholders to acquire those shares (Article 7.3). In addition to these non-property rights, the common shareholders have the following property rights:

- to take part in the distribution of profits (to receive dividends), and
- to receive the remaining property (assets) if the company is liquidated (Article 31.2).[87]

Each common share of a company grants an identical amount of rights to the holder thereof (Article 31.1), and the same rule applies to preference shares (within the same type; Article 32.1).

The JSC Law includes special rules on the rights of the shareholders of preference shares (Article 32), and these are limited in general to the right to receive the dividends determined in the charter and the priority right in the distribution of the remaining property of the company.[88] Usually such shares do not grant any right to vote in the general meeting, though the shareholders of preference shares may participate in voting on the reorganization and liquidation of the company. They may also participate in voting at a general meeting of the company deciding the introduction of amendments to the charter which limits their rights; such amendments require the approval of the qualified majority vote (three-quarters) of the preference shareholders. Such shareholders also acquire full voting rights if the determined dividends are not (fully or partly) paid to them. Furthermore, the charter can include the provision that the preference shares are convertible into common shares as well as into another type of preference shares though not into other securities.[89] It should be noted that common shares may not, according to the JSC Law, be converted into preference shares (Article 31.3).

As to fractional shares—which are allowed, according to the JSC Law (Article 25.3), exceptionally in cases where the preemptive right is used by a shareholder to acquire the shares

87 Tikhomirov 2009: 241–6.

88 Tikhomirov 2009: 250.

89 This may also occur under JSC Law in the case of the reorganization of the company (Article 32.3).

offered for sale by the other shareholders (Article 7) or additional shares (Article 40), as well as in share consolidations (Article 74.1)—such a share grants the shareholder the rights granted by a common or preference share, though only in proportion to this. With regard to circulation, fractional shares are equated with full shares.

In addition to the general rule on the duty of the participants of companies and partnerships included in the Civil Code (Article 67.2) to make a capital contribution and to maintain secrecy, which is presented above, the Civil Code as well as the JSC Law also contains special rules on the duties of shareholders of joint stock companies. According to these, the shareholder may not be exempted from the duty to pay for the company's shares, including, according to the Civil Code (Article 99.2) and the JSC Law (Article 34), any exemption from this duty by taking into account his claims against the company. Furthermore, the Civil Code (Article 96.1) and the JSC Law (Article 2.1) provide that shareholders who have not paid up their shares in full are to bear joint responsibility for the obligation of the company regarding the unpaid part of the cost of their shares.

Governing bodies and decision-making procedures The supreme governing body of the joint stock company is, according to the Civil Code (Article 103) and the JSC Law (Article 47.1), the general meeting of its shareholders. In certain cases the personal participation of the shareholders in the general meeting is not required, and so external voting is possible, except, for instance, concerning the election of the council of directors, audit commission (auditor), and the consideration of the annual report as well as the distribution of profits and losses of the company, as provided for by the JSC Law (Articles 50 and 48.1.11). In companies whose number of shareholders exceeds 100, the voting at a general meeting, with regard to matters on its agenda, must be carried out, under the JSC Law, by ballot (Article 60). Moreover in joint stock companies whose number of shareholders is 50 or more, a council of directors (supervisory council) must also be established, and this is also regarded as a governing body (Article 64). The executive power of the joint stock company rests, under the Civil Code (Article 103.3) and the JSC Law (Article 69), with one person (the director, the director general), or it may be collegiate (the board or directorate) together with a one-person executive body. The joint stock company also has, according to the Civil Code (Article 103.5) and the JSC Law (Articles 85–86), an (internal) audit commission or (external) auditor, which is regarded as the body in control of the activities of the company.

The issues falling within the authority of different governing bodies of the joint stock company are generally defined in the Civil Code (Article 103), and they are detailed in the JSC Law (Article 40).

Among the issues which are within the authority of the general meeting of shareholders are:

- changes to the charter, including changes in the amount of the charter capital;
- decisions on the reorganization and liquidation of the company;
- the election of members of the council of directors (supervisory council) and audit commission (auditor) of the company and early termination of their powers;
- determination of the amount, types and par value of the declared shares as well as rights granted by them;
- the formation of the executive body of the company and early termination of its powers, unless such matters fall according to the charter to the authority of the council of directors (supervisory board);
- the approval of annual reports, bookkeeping balance sheets, the profit and loss accounts of the company, and the distribution of its profits and losses;
- the procedure for conducting the general meeting;

- the splitting and consolidation of shares,[90] and
- the approval of bylaws for the regulation of the internal affairs of the company as well as
- decisions concerning certain important transactions of the company.

The general meeting is also authorized to make decisions concerning:

- the acquisition by the company of placed shares and
- participation in financial and industrial groups and other organizations as well as
- other matters provided for by the JSC Law.

The election of members of the council of directors (supervisory council) and auditors as well as the approval of annual reports, bookkeeping balance sheets, and the profit and loss accounts of the company, and the distribution of its profits and losses, are within the authority of the annual meeting; other general meetings than annual meetings are extraordinary, as provided for by the Civil Code (Article 103.1) and the JSC Law (Articles 47 and 48).

The Civil Code (Article 103.1) and the JSC Law (Article 48.2) explicitly forbids the delegation of issues placed within the authority of the general meeting for resolution to the other governing bodies of the company. However, the formation of the executive bodies, mentioned above, and questions concerning amendments to the charter in connection with an increase of the charter capital are not exclusively under the authority of the general meeting and may be also within the authority of the council of directors (Article 48.2). Rather, the general meeting of shareholders has no right to consider and adopt decisions with regard to matters not referred to its authority (Article 48.3), nor any authority to intervene in the authority of the council of directors; thus the authority of the general meeting is, as a matter of fact, strictly restricted by the law.[91] Decisions of the general meeting that exceed its authority are regarded, according to the established judicial practice of Russia, as violating the law, and, consequently, subject to the Civil Code rules on invalid transactions[92] (Articles 166 and 168).[93]

According to the JSC Law, all the shareholders are to be informed about the convocation of the general meeting of shareholders (Article 52),[94] and it is empowered (has a quorum) if shareholders possessing in aggregate more than half of the votes of the placed voting shares of the company have participated in it. As such are regarded shareholders who have registered for participation or submitted their ballots no later than two days before the date of the general meeting. The quorum for a new general meeting convened in place of the unconstituted meeting is at least 30 percent, and even a smaller quorum may be provided for by the charter of the company whose number of shareholders is greater than 500,000 (Article 58). External (absentee) voting is also allowed at general meetings, except on those questions which are within the exclusive authority of the annual meeting (Articles 47.1 and 50), and in such an instance, ballots of the participating shareholder are be submitted before the date of the ending of their acceptance.

---

90 Shares are consolidated where two or more shares are converted into one new share (of the same kind or type) whereas, contrary to this, they are split when a single share is converted into two or more shares (of the same kind or type); such changes also require, under the JSC Law, amendments to the charter (Article 74).

91 See Abova, Boguslavsky, Kabalkin, Lisicin-Svetlanov 2007: 120.

92 See the presentation on invalidity of contract.

93 Tikhomirov 2009: 327 and, in particular, Joint Decrees of the Plenums 6/8 1996.

94 Wrong information about, for instance, the place of the general meeting is regarded violating the rights of the shareholders, and therefore the decision of the general meeting given not in the informed placed may be recognized in the judicial proceedings invalid. See Tikhomirov 2009: 348.

A decision with regard to the:

- reorganization of the company;
- liquidation of the company;
- amendments to the charter of the company;
- determination of the amount, types, and par value of the declared shares as well as rights granted by them;
- acquisition by the company of placed shares; and, in some other cases, concerning, for instance, large-scale transactions, must be adopted according to the JSC Law (Articles 49.4 and 79.3) by the general meeting by a qualified majority (a majority of three-quarters of the votes of the shareholders participating in the general meeting). Decisions concerning other issues shall be adopted by a common majority.

A decision of the general meeting regarding, for instance:

- the reorganization of the company;
- an increase in charter capital by increasing the nominal value of shares or by placing additional shares;
- the splitting and consolidation of shares;
- interested party and large-scale transactions;
- the acquisition by the company of placed shares;
- participation in financial and industrial groups and other organizations, and
- approval of bylaws for the regulation of the internal affairs of the company,

requires under the JSC Law a proposal by the council of directors, unless otherwise provided by the charter (Article 49.3).

Under the JSC Law the general meeting has the authority to adopt decisions concerning the issues included on the agenda of the meeting (Article 49.6). The agenda of the general meeting is usually prepared by the council of directors (Article 54) and the shareholders owning in aggregate not less than 2 percent of voting shares are entitled within a defined period to submit proposals (in writing and substantiated) for the agenda of the annual general meeting, including the nomination of candidates for the governing bodies. The council of directors may refuse the agenda proposals, however, only if the terms for making proposals are not observed or they contain formal mistakes, in which case the decision may be appealed to a court (Article 53). Shareholders owning not less than 10 percent of voting shares as well as the auditors of the company are entitled to require the convocation of an extraordinary general meeting, but the council of directors may refuse it, in which case such a decision may also be appealed to a court (Article 55).

The authority of the council of directors (supervisory council), which is obligatory in a company with a number of shareholders not less than 50,[95] is defined by the law and charter, and issues relegated to it may not be delegated for decision to executive bodies, as provided for by the Civil Code (Article 103.2) and the JSC Law (Articles 64–5). Within the authority of the council of directors is the general direction of the company's activity, except for deciding issues relegated to the authority of the general meeting (Article 64.1). The council of directors makes decisions on the convocation of the annual

95 In a Russian joint stock company whose number of shareholders is fewer than 50 a council of directors is not obligatory but it may be nonetheless established. If the council of directors is not established, the issues of its competence are within the authority of the general meeting. See Tikhomirov 2009: 387–8.

and extraordinary general meeting and on the confirmation of its agenda as well as other questions regarding its conduct. It decides on issue of bonds and other securities and large-scale transactions,[96] and also if, in the conclusion of a transaction, there is a conflict of interest between the company and a person holding office in its governing bodies (interested party transactions).[97] The council of directors also determines the market value of property of the company.[98] (Articles 65 and 81–4) The authority and decision-making of the governing bodies of the company as well as their acting on behalf of the company is defined in detail by the JSC Law and the charter, which may provide for the formation of the executive body of the company. (Articles 48–68)

According to the JSC Law (Article 66), members of the council of directors of a company are elected by the annual general meeting. As a member of the council of directors, only a physical person, not necessarily a shareholder, may be elected. Members of a collegial executive organ of the company can be members of the council of directors, but they may not comprise more than one-quarter of it; however, the person effectuating the functions of a one-man executive organ may not be simultaneously the chairman of the company. Furthermore, the council of directors of a joint stock company must have not fewer than five members. And in a company whose number of shareholders is more than 1,000 at least seven persons must form the council of directors;[99] elections of council members in such a company must be effectuated by cumulative voting.[100] In cumulative voting each share corresponds to as great a number of votes as the number of members on the board of directors, and the votes may be either given to one candidate or divided between several candidates (Article 66.4). This also means that the election of the whole board of directors must be carried out in this way.[101]

The executive body of the joint stock company acts, according to the Civil Code (Article 103.3) and JSC Law (Article 69), on behalf of the company. Within its authority is the current management of the company's activities, and it is responsible to the council of directors (supervisory council) and the general meeting. In other words, the executive body of the company decides on all the issues which are not within the authority of the other governing bodies.

Under the JSC Law the decision on the formation of the executive body may be adopted not only by the general meeting but also by the council of directors, if this is provided for by the charter (Article 65). The executive body of the joint stock company may be collegiate (the board, directorate) and/or one-person (the director, director general). The simultaneous existence of both

96 These are, under the JSC Law (Article 78), transactions involving the acquisition or disposal (including the possibility of such) of assets valued at more than 25 percent of the assets of the company (excluding the ordinary course of business or transactions connected with the issuance of common shares or bonds convertible to these).

97 The interested party may be a director, a member of the governing body, or a shareholder owning 20 percent or more of the voting shares. The transactions of (or with) the interested party are subject to disclosure requirements; otherwise such a transaction may be invalidated and also liability for damages may arise, as provided for by the JSC Law (Articles 81–4).

98 The market value of property of the company is determined by the council of directors (court or some other body), according to the rules of the JSC Law (Article 77), and an independent valuer (or auditor) may and in some cases shall be involved.

99 And in a company with a number of shareholders of more than ten thousands, there must be at least nine members.

100 In a company with fewer than 1,000 shareholders, in the event of elections of members of the council of directors (or supervisory council), cumulative voting may be provided for by the charter.

101 The purpose of the rules on cumulative voting is to protect small shareholders by offering them the possibility to concentrate their ballots in order to elect one or more members of the board. See Mozolin and Yudenkov 2003: 302.

the one-person and collegiate executive body must be provided for by the charter, which must also determine the authority of the latter. In this event, the one-person executive body must also effectuate the functions of chairman of the collegial executive body (Article 69.1). However, the member of the one-person executive body (director) may not, as stated previously, be simultaneously the chairman of the council of directors, whereas the members of a collegial executive body may comprise at most one-quarter of the council of directors (Article 66.2). By decision of the general meeting, the powers of the executive body of the company may be transferred, according to the Civil Code (Article 103.3) and JSC Law (Article 69.1), under a contract to another commercial (managing) organization or even to an individual entrepreneur (manager).

The rights and duties of the executive body (and its members) are defined, in accordance with the JSC Law, by the law and the contract concluded with the each member (Article 69.3).[102] The general meeting or the council of directors, if the authority to form the executive bodies is delegated to it, may decide on the termination of the authorities of the executive body or its members at any time. The general meeting also has the right to terminate the authorities of the managing organization or manager. The charter may provide the council of directors with the power to suspend the authorities of the one-person executive body and delegate them to a provisional body (Article 69.4).

Amendments to charter The company's charter may be amended, under the JSC Law (Articles 12, 48, and 49), in general by a qualified majority vote (of three-quarters) in the general meeting of shareholders. In certain cases, regarding first of all amendments connected with an increase in the charter capital of the company, the amendments are to be made simply with regard to the results of the share subscription by the decision of the general meeting or the council of directors, if so provided for by the charter concerning changes in the charter capital (Article 12.2). In addition, the decision-making procedure in respect of amendments connected with a decrease in charter capital through the acquisition and canceling of the company's own shares is simplified: the decision of the general meeting on such a decrease is sufficient, on the provision that the report regarding the results of such action is approved by the council of directors (Article 12.3).[103] Furthermore, the amendments connected with the establishment of the branch or representative office is simply to be made by the decision of the council of directors (Article 12.5). An amendment of data on the amount of the charter capital is to made in the charter on the results of the share subscription at the moment of the formation of a company through merger by the agreement thereof and the registered report regarding the results of the issue of the shares subscribed in the formation of the company (Article 12.6).

Increase and decrease of charter capital The rules concerning the increase and decrease (reduction) of charter capital of the joint stock company are written down directly in the Civil Code (Articles 100–101) and the JSC Law (Articles 28–30).

Under the JSC Law, the increase in charter capital requires the decision of the general meeting initiated by the proposal of the council of directors, unless otherwise provided by the charter (Article 49.3),[104] and the charter capital may be increased by increasing the nominal value of shares or by placing additional shares, as provided for by the Civil Code (Article 100.1) and the JSC Law (Article 28). The increase in the charter capital is to be admitted after this has been paid in full, as

102 The relations between the company and the executive body (members) fall under the provisions of labor law only in part not contradicting the JSC Law.

103 Amendment (as well as deletion) of the information on the use of the golden share right into the charter shall be executed, according to the JSC Law, by the decision of the (state) governmental body (Article 12.4).

104 The decision on the increase in charter capital may determine the term after the expiration of which the decision is not be executed, as provided for by the JSC Law (Article 49.8).

stated above. The increase in the charter capital by increasing the nominal value of shares is to, and by placing additional shares may, be effected through assets of the company (Article 28.5). In this event, the increased amount of the charter capital must not exceed the difference between the value of net assets and the total amount of the charter capital together with the reserve fund of the company. Where charter capital is increased through assets of the company, additional shares are to be distributed among all the shareholders in correspondence with the categories and types and in proportion to the quantity of shares owned by them. It is also a requirement that such an increase must not result in fractional shares.

Under the JSC Law the decision on the increase in charter capital by placing additional shares can also be adopted by the council of directors, if this is provided for in the charter (concerning the shares declared for issuing);[105] in this event, the decision of the council of directors must be unanimous (Article 28.2). However, the placement of the shares (and emission securities convertible into shares) through closed subscription (Article 39.3), and the placement of the common shares (and emission securities convertible into common shares), the amount of which exceeds 25 percent of the issued common shares, through open subscription requires the general meeting's decision adopted by a majority of three-quarters of the votes of the shareholders participating in the general meeting, unless a greater majority is required by the charter (Article 39.4).

New shares may be placed, according to the JSC Law, by the company only within the limits of the quantity of declared shares specified by the charter; otherwise, simultaneously with the decision on the increase in charter capital by placing additional shares, the decision on the corresponding amendments to the charter is to be adopted (Article 28.3). It is also a requirement that the rights of shareholders of new shares should be determined by the charter of the company (Article 27.1). The paying up of additional shares[106] (as well as other securities) of the company placed by subscription shall be carried out at the market value but not less than their nominal value. The market value, which must be determined by decision of the council of directors, may be undercut by no more than 10 percent only in the event the shareholders use their preemptive rights in acquisition of the additional shares (Articles 36, 38, and 77).[107]

The new shares (as well as other securities) placed by subscription must be paid up in full, under the JSC Law, at the time of their placement (Article 34.1). When paying up additional shares by non-cash means, the monetary valuation of the property contributed to pay them up must be made by the council of directors, and, in the property valuation, an independent valuer (or auditor) is to be involved (Article 34.3).

The JSC Law contains rules which concern the preemptive rights in the increasing of charter capital (Articles 40 and 41). According to them, the shareholders shall have a preemptive right to acquire additional shares and securities convertible into shares in a quantity proportional to the quantity of shares owned by them (pro rata). In the event of the placement of additional shares and securities convertible into shares through closed subscription, also the shareholders who have not taken part in voting or have voted against the adoption of the decision on the placement at the general meeting are to have the same preemptive right. This rule is, however, not applicable to the

---

105 The purpose of such shares is to give to the company after its foundation an opportunity to issue (in addition to the subscribed shares) new shares without changing the charter and breaking the prohibition on the issuance of new shares, as provided for by the JSC Law (Article 27.1).

106 The JSC Law may provide, in accordance with its Article 99.2, a setoff in the payment of placed additional shares.

107 The increase in charter capital by issuing additional shares of the company formed in the process of privatization, if more than 25 percent of its voting shares are in public ownership, is not to result, under the JSC Law, in changes in the publicly owned interest (Article 28.6).

placement of additional shares and securities convertible into shares through closed subscription only among the shareholders, if they have otherwise the right to acquire full shares in proportion to the owned ones.[108] Different to this case, fractional shares may occur when the preemptive right to acquire additional shares is used (Article 25.3).

The decrease of charter capital also requires, under the Civil Code (Article 101) and the JSC Law (Article 29), the decision of the general meeting. The charter capital may be decreased by decreasing the nominal value of shares or by acquiring some of the shares in order to decrease their total quantity. However, in those cases the minimum charter capital of the company may not be decreased (Article 29.1). Furthermore, according to the JSC Law, the decrease of charter capital is not allowed until the charter capital is paid up in full (Article 34), and the obligatory purchase of shares[109] is fulfilled by the company (Article 75.1), as well as if the company is, or could be as a result of the action directed to the decrease, liable by the indicia of insolvency, or if the value of the net assets of the company is, or could be as a result of the action directed to the decrease, less than its charter capital, reserve fund, and excess of the liquidation value of the placed preferred stocks over the par value determined by the charter[110] (Articles 29.4 and 73).

The decision on the decrease of the charter capital by decreasing the nominal value of shares must be initiated, under the JSC Law, by the proposal of the council of directors and adopted by a majority of three-quarters of the votes of the shareholders participating in the general meeting. It may provide payments in money and/or transfer of the securities possessed by the company to all the shareholders. (Article 29.3)

The decrease of the charter capital of the joint stock company by acquiring of a part of its shares for the purpose of reducing the total quantity thereof is permitted, according to the Civil Code (Article 101.2) and the JSC Law (Articles 29.1 and 72.1), only if such a possibility has been provided for in the charter of the company.[111] The shares are to be paid in money, unless otherwise provided by the charter (Article 72.4), and the acquired shares must be canceled (Article 72.3).

The decrease of charter capital can be fulfilled, under the Civil Code (Article 101) and the JSC Law (Article 30), only after the creditors are informed about the decision thereof, and information on this must be published in the state register publication. The creditors have the right to demand from the company the termination or the performance at an earlier date of its obligation and compensation for damages connected therewith.[112] The decrease of the charter capital is to be registered on the condition that the creditors have been duly informed of it.

---

108 See Tikhomirov 2009: 292–4.

109 In case of the reorganization and the conclusion of a large-scale transaction as well as amendments to the charter which limits the rights of shareholders. See below.

110 According to the JSC Law, the decision on the increase in charter capital may determine the term after the expiration of which the decision is not to be executed (Article 49.8).

111 According to the JSC Law, a joint stock company may acquire its own shares for other purposes than to decrease the charter capital, if so provided by the charter. The decision on it must be adopted by the general meeting; the acquisition of the company's own shares may also be, under the charter, within the authority of the council of directors. Also, in this case the minimum charter capital of the company may not be decreased. Furthermore, the acquisition by the company of shares is not allowed if the par value of the stocks of the company in circulation would comprise less than 90 percent of the charter capital of the company (Article 72.2). The acquired shares must be resold by the company at a price not lower than their market value no later than one year after their acquisition; otherwise the charter capital must be decreased by canceling these shares (Article 72.3).

112 According to the JSC Law, the notification on the decrease of the charter capital must be sent to the registration body or tax authorities within three days from the date of adoption of the decision. The company is also obliged to publish the information on the decrease of the charter capital twice, with one

Payment of dividends A joint stock company has the right, under the JSC Law ((Article 42), to adopt a decision on the results of the first quarter, half-year or nine months of the fiscal year, and/or on the results of the fiscal year to pay with regard to placed share dividends, or declare such a decision. The decision to pay dividends constitutes the duty as a debt due to the shareholders, which is transferable and may be recovered in a judicial proceeding.[113]

Under the JSC Law, the company is to pay the dividends declared for each category (or type) of shares in money or by other property, if so provided by the charter. Dividends are to be paid from the net profit of the company (remaining after taxation), and, in the case of the preferred shares, special funds may also be used. Decisions regarding the payment of dividends are to be adopted by the general meeting in accordance with the recommendation of the council of directors, and their amount may not exceed the recommendation (Article 42.3). The dividends must be paid within 60 days of the date of the decision on their payment, unless otherwise provided by the charter or decision of the general meeting (Article 42.4).

The payment of dividends is not, however, allowed, according to the Civil Code (Article 102.3) and JSC Law (Article 43), until the charter capital is paid up in full and the obligatory purchase of shares is fulfilled by the company in accordance with the JSC Law (Articles 75 and 76), as well as if the company is, or can be as a result of the payment of dividends, liable to be deemed insolvent (or bankrupt) or if the value of the net assets of the company is, or can be as a result of the payment of dividends, less than its charter capital, reserve fund, and excess of the liquidation value of the placed preferred stocks over the par value determined by the charter. Furthermore, in paying dividends, the order of priority between different categories of shares is to be complied with. So, for instance, the dividends to common shares are to be paid after the full payment of the dividends to preference shares, including cumulative preference shares.

Large-scale and interested party transactions Large-scale transactions are, under the JSC Law (Article 78), transactions[114] involving the acquisition or disposal (including such a possibility) of assets valued at 25 percent or more of the assets of the company on the date of the last accounting period (excluding ordinary course of business[115] or transactions connected with the issuance of common shares or bonds convertible to these).

The decision on a large-scale transaction is to be adopted, under the JSC Law, unanimously by the council of directors if it concerns property whose value comprises from 25 up to 50 percent of the balance sheet value of the assets of the company. Where unanimity is not achieved, the council of directors may submit the issue for the common majority decision of the general meeting. However, if the value of the property in question exceeds 50 percent of the balance sheet value of the assets, the transaction must be approved by a majority of three-quarters of the votes of

month in between. The creditors of the company may put in their claims within 30 days from the last publishing date. The claim of the creditor may be denied by the court, if the decrease of the charter capital does not violate his rights or if the security provided for the performance of the obligation is considered sufficient (Article 30).

113 See Mozolin and Yudenkov 2003: 204 and Tikhomirov 2009: 303.

114 Including loan and credit as well as pledge and surety. Also transactions connected to the transfer of the debt or right of claim or capital contributions. See Decree of the Plenum no 19 of 2003 (item 30).

115 A transaction connected to the purposes (objects) of the activity of the company may not be regarded, according to the established judicial practice in Russia, as a large-scale transaction. See, for instance, the rulings of the Federal Arbitrazh Court of the Moscow district no KG-A41/7615-06 of 12 September 2006 and of the Northwest district no A21-4740/2006 of 14 December 2007.

the shareholders participating in the general meeting.[116] The application of the rules regulating large-scale transactions is excluded in cases where a large-scale transaction is at the same time an interested party transaction. (Article 79)

In turn, interested party transactions are, under the JSC Law (Article 81), transactions,[117] in the conclusion of which there is a conflict of interest between the company and a person holding office in its governing bodies or a shareholder owning jointly with its affiliates 20 percent and more of voting shares or any other person having otherwise the right to give orders binding for the company. Such persons are regarded as interested parties if they jointly with their relatives and affiliated persons[118] (a) participate in the transaction as an intermediary or representative or are benefactors thereof; (b) possess 20 percent or more of the voting shares (or interests) of a juristic person participating in the transaction, or (c) hold office in the management bodies therein or (d) conform to other cases provided for by the charter. Any person who is liable to be deemed an interested party is obliged to inform the council of directors and auditors of the company thereof. The rules concerning interested party transactions does not, however, apply to single companies, or to transactions in which all the shareholders are interested as well as in cases of the use of the preemptive rights and acquisition and redemption of the shares by the company, and in the merger of the company. Furthermore, transactions of the companies that are obligatory under the law for them (price-controlled transactions) are not placed under the rules on interested party transactions.

Under the JSC Law (Article 83), the decision on the interested party transaction is to be adopted before its execution by a majority vote of the council of directors, excluding those who are interested, in a company whose number of shareholders with voting shares is fewer than 1,000 (Article 83.2), and by a majority vote of the independent directors[119] in a company whose number of shareholders with voting shares is 1,000 or more (Article 83.3). However, if the number of the uninterested or independent directors is not sufficient to make the decision, it is to be adopted by the general meeting.

However, within the exclusive authority of the general meeting of shareholders is the decision on an interested party transaction if the subject thereof is property whose value comprises 2 or more percent of the balance sheet value of the assets of the company. Also a transaction connected with the issuance of common shares or bonds convertible to these, if their number comprises more than 2 percent, is to be adopted before its execution by the general meeting. The decision requires a majority of the votes of the uninterested shareholders. (Article 83.4)

However, an interested party transaction does not require any approval, if its conditions are not essentially exceptional compared to those concluded with the interested party, in the exercising of

---

116 The large-scale transaction may be approved afterwards, according to the ruling of the Federal Arbitrazh Court of the West-Siberia district no F04/3280-713/A46-2004 of 15 June 2004.

117 Including loan and credit as well as pledge and surety. See Decree of the Plenum of the Supreme Arbitrazh Court no 40 of 20 June 2007. Вестник Высшего Арбитражного Суда Российской Федерации [Herald of Supreme Arbitrazh Court of Russian Federation] (2007) 8.

118 Affiliated persons are properly defined in the almost wholly rescinded Competition Law of 1991. They are director general, directors and other officers, founders, and shareholders who own 20 percent or more of the voting shares, or a company in which the other company owns 20 percent or more of the voting shares.

119 According to the JSC Law (Article 83.3), an independent director is a member of the council of directors who is not and has not been during one year before the decision a one-man or a member of the collegial executive body of the company, or a relative or affiliated person to a person holding office in the governing bodies of the company.

the ordinary economic activity of the company before the moment he is deemed to be such. Such an exception is, however, in force before the date of the conducting of the next general meeting (Article 83.5). Furthermore, the general meeting may adopt the decision approving future transactions concluded in the exercising of the ordinary economic activity of the company (Article 83.6).

A large-scale as well as an interested party transaction concluded in violation of the requirements of the law may be deemed to be invalid, in accordance with the JSC Law, by an action brought by a shareholder or the company. In cases of an invalid action in respect of transactions concluded by a joint stock company, the plaintiff must, in order to succeed, prove, according to the established judicial practice of Russia, the violation of his rights at the moment of its conclusion.[120] The interested person shall be liable to the company for the amount of losses caused by him. If several persons are liable, their liability to the company is to be solidary (joint and several).[121] (Articles 79.6 and 84)

Acquisitions of more than 30 percent of shares The acquisition of more than 30 percent of shares of an open joint stock company is under special regulation in Russia,[122] in accordance with the JSC Law (Articles 84^{1}–84^{10}). The special rules are be applied to any acquisition of voting shares resulting in a shareholder having in his, together with his affiliates', possession more than 30 percent of voting shares, including preference shares with voting rights.[123] [124]

A person who intends to acquire more than 30 percent of shares in a company may make an (public) offer on it to the other shareholders (Articles 84^{1}). However, in the event a person has acquired more than 30 percent of shares, he is obliged to make an offer to purchase the remaining shares in the company (Articles 84^{2}).[125] The offer must include information on the identity of the purchaser and his current shareholding, affiliations, and corporate governance, including involvement in any offshore jurisdictions, and the payment obligations of the purchaser must be secured by an irrevocable bank guarantee.[126] [127] The term for the acceptance of the share purchase offer provided thereof is to be no less than 70 and no more, in the case of the voluntary offer, 90, and of the obligatory offer 80, days after the date the offer is received by the company. The offer must be addressed to the company, and its council of directors addresses it further to the

120 See Decrees of the Plenum 19 of 2003 (item 36) and 40 of 2007 (item 2).

121 See Tikhomirov 2009: 453–4 and 470–72.

122 Chapter XII was added by the Law no 7-FZ of 5 January 2006.

123 In case the dividends are not paid, as presented above.

124 The voluntary and obligatory offers as well as redemption offers and demands are, according to the JSC Law, subject to the state control concerning shares traded on stock exchanges (Article 84^{9}).

125 The rules on obligatory offer do not apply, according to the JSC Law, in cases of the acquisition of shares (a) at the founding or reorganization of a company, (b) in exercising the preemptive right to additional shares, or (c) through a voluntary or obligatory offer submitted earlier as well as to the cases of (d) transfer of shares to affiliated persons or as a result of separation of spousal property and inheritance, (e) cancellation of redeemed shares, (f) and in some other cases (Articles 84^{2}.8).

126 The bank guarantee must remain in force for at least six months after the end of the period fixed for the payment of the purchase price of the shares (Articles 84^{1}.5 and 84^{2}.3).

127 The specified purchase price of the shares in the obligatory offer quoted by stock exchanges for a period of more than six months must not be less than their weighted average price for the last six months, and in other cases not less than their market value. However, the offered price must not be in any case less than the maximum price the offerer has paid for the shares earlier (within six months prior the submission of the offer) (Article 84^{8}.4).

shareholders. The offer must be supported with the recommendations of the council of directors, or in lack of such, by the general meeting, in respect of it.[128]

According to the JSC Law (Article 84^6), after the receipt of the share purchase offer, only the general meeting may adopt decisions on the:

- increase of the charter capital by issuing additional shares;
- placement of securities convertible to shares;
- acquisition of shares by the company, or
- increase of remuneration of the members of the governing bodies of the company or modification of their employment termination conditions as well as,
- the approval of transactions in respect of the property worth more than 10 percent of the balance sheet value of the assets of the company (excluding ordinary course of business transactions), or
- interested party transactions.

These restrictions remain in force for 20 days after the end of the expiration of the offer. The transaction concluded in violation of these restriction rules may be deemed to be invalid by the action brought by a shareholder, the company, or the offerer.

If, as a result of the voluntary or obligatory share purchase, a person has acquired more than 95 percent of shares, he, the majority shareholder, is obliged to redeem or buy out the remaining shares (and securities convertible into shares) in the company upon the demand of the minority shareholders; the minority shareholders must be notified on their redemption rights by the majority shareholder within 35 days from the date of his acquisition. The redemption demand is to be presented within six months from the date the minority shareholders are notified by the majority shareholder on his acquisition (Article 84^7). The majority shareholder also has the right to demand redemption of the remaining shares from the minority shareholders (a squeeze-out right). He must inform the company of his demand within six months of the date the (voluntary or obligatory) share purchase offer expired, if as a result of the offer he has acquired not less than 10 percent of the shares of the company.[129] (Article 84^8)

The acquisition of shares of open joint stock companies is also under state control in accordance with the JSC Law (Article 84^9). The voluntary and obligatory offer as well as the majority shareholder's redemption rights notification and demand concerning securities traded on organized stock exchanges is to be submitted for review to the federal security market authorities before their presentation to the company. The authorities may order the applicant to make corrections to the submitted documents to bring them in line with the law and such an order may be appealed to a (arbitrazh) court.

Reorganization and liquidation A joint stock company may be reorganized or liquidated, according to the Civil Code (Article 104) and the JSC Law (Article 15–24), voluntarily, by the decision of the general meeting or in other cases where its grounds and procedure are established by the law.[130] According to the general rules of the Civil Code on reorganization of the juristic person presented above (Articles 57–60 and 68) and corresponding special rules of the JSC Law

---

128 These rules are applied, under the JSC Law (Articles 84^2.7), to acquisitions of more than 50 and 75 percent of shares in an open joint stock company.

129 In the determination of the redemption price, the rules on the obligatory offer purchase price (Article 84^2.4) are to be correspondingly applied (Article 84^2.4).

130 Special rules are provided for the reorganization of natural monopoly companies with more than 25 percent (federal) state participation (Article 15.1). See the Law on Natural Monopolies of 1995.

(Articles 15–20), the reorganization of the joint stock company may be effected in the form of merger with another company, accession to another company, division into several companies, separation from the company or transformation of it.

In general, the purpose of the reorganization of a company is to found a new company (companies) by terminating the existing one(s) with the transfer of its (their) rights and duties to the new company (companies)[131].[132] As a result of the reorganization, the assets of the founded company are to be formed from the property of the reorganized companies. The reorganization of a joint stock company resulting in the merger with or accession to a juristic person of another form, including a limited liability company, is not allowed, according to the instruction of the Supreme Arbitrazh Court. The division and separation of a joint stock company leading to the founding of a juristic person of the other form is also excluded[133].[134]

A joint stock company may be transformed, under the Civil Code (Article 104.2) and JSC Law (Article 20), into a limited liability company or production cooperative[135] as well as into an noncommercial organization (partnership),[136] whereas the reciprocal changes between closed and open joint stock companies may be effected merely by amendments to the charter, inasmuch as those are regarded as being of the same company form.[137] However, an open joint stock company may not be transferred, according to the JSC Law, into a closed joint stock company if, as result of it, the provisions regarding the maximum number of shareholders (Article 7.3) and state and municipal participation (Article 7.4) would be violated. In turn, transformation of a closed joint stock company into an open joint stock company must not contradict the minimum charter capital requirements established for open joint stock companies.[138]

The decision on the reorganization must be adopted by the general meeting on the proposal of the council of directors in the each reorganizing company. The companies participating in the merger as well as in the accession are also to enter into the agreement on it.[139] According to the Civil Code, where provided for by the law, the division of the joint stock company or the spin-off from its structure (separation) may be effected by the decision of the authorized state bodies (such as the antimonopoly committee) or by a court decision (Article 57.2), whereas the merger, accession or transformation may be effected only upon the consent of the authorized state bodies (such as the antimonopoly committee; Article 57.3).[140]

Special rules are established in the JSC Law in respect of the division or separation of the company executed simultaneously with its merger or accession (Article 19^1).[141] According to this, the decision of the company reorganizing through the division or separation may also include the

131 Tikhomirov 2009: 129.

132 However, only the legal statute of the absorbing company is to be changed in case of accession through the transfer of the rights and duties of the absorbed companies. The same concerns the separation of a company where its rights and duties are to pass only partly to the new companies. See Tikhomirov 2009: 153 and 167.

133 See Decree of the Plenum 19 of 2003 (item 20).

134 See Tikhomirov 2009: 134.

135 By a qualified majority (three-quarters') vote of the general meeting of shareholders.

136 In this case by the unanimous decision of the shareholders (Article 20.1).

137 See Decree of the Plenum no 19 of 2004.

138 Tikhomirov 2009: 134–5 and Popondopulo 2009: 138.

139 The conclusion of the agreement is obligatory in these cases, and the law provides the conditions to be included into it (Articles 16 and 17). See also Tikhomirov 2009: 148 and 155.

140 See the Competition Law (Articles 27 and 38).

141 Added by the Law no 146-FZ of 27 July 2006.

decision that the new company resulting from such a reorganization is to be at the same time merged or accessed. The decision may provide a condition on its effect only where general meeting(s) of the company (companies) participating in the merger or accession adopt the decision on it.

After the adoption of the decision on reorganization the company is obliged, under the Civil Code (Article 60), to inform its creditors thereof in writing and publish notice of the reorganization in the state register publication.[142]

The joint stock company is obliged, under the Civil Code (Article 60) and JSC Law (Article 15.6), after the registration of the beginning of its reorganization, to publish notice of the reorganization two times (once per month) in the state register publication. The creditor of the reorganizing juristic person has the right to demand from it the performance at an earlier date, and if this is impossible, the termination of the obligation arisen with it before the publication of the notice and compensation for damages connected therewith, unless otherwise provided by the law (Article 60.2)[143].[144] However, in cases of the reorganization of the open joint stock company through merger, accession or transformation, the creditors have the right, according to the Civil Code (Article 60.3), to demand by judicial procedure the performance at an earlier date or the termination of the obligation and compensation for damages, where the performance of the obligation is not sufficiently secured by the company, its participants or third persons[145].[146]

According to the JSC Law, the companies founded as a result of the reorganization must be registered[147] and the notices of the liquidation of the reorganized companies are to be entered on the condition that the creditors have been duly informed of it (Article 15.6).[148] A company is regarded as reorganized from the moment of the registration of the new company(s) and in case of accession from the moment of the registration of the termination of the absorbed company (Article 15.4). Where the separation balance sheet (in case of the division or separation) or the deed of transfer (in case of the merger, accession or transformation) does not enable the determination of the legal

142 Such a publication does not substitute for the notices to the creditors. See Tikhomirov 2009: 142 and 196.

143 In this case the reorganizing company may not transfer its debt, without the consent of the creditor, to another (e.g. the founding) company. See Decree of the Presidium of the Supreme Arbitrazh Court no 796/00 of 31 October 2000. Вестник Высшего Арбитражного Суда Российской Федерации [Herald of Supreme Arbitrazh Court of Russian Federation] (2001) 1.

144 The merger or accession agreement as well as the decision on reorganization through division, separation or transformation may provide the special order for and even prohibitions on the conclusion of transactions by the reorganizing company. Their nonobservance may result in the invalidity of the transaction, and an invalidity action may be brought by the reorganizing company or its shareholders (Article 15.7).

145 The obligations of the reorganizing joint stock company to its creditors may be secured by pledge, in which case the creditors may not demand additional securities for the performance (GK Article 60.5).

146 The merger or accession agreement as well as the decision on reorganization through division, separation, or transformation may provide the special order and even prohibitions for the conclusion of transactions by the reorganizing company. Their nonobservance may result in the invalidity of the transaction, and an invalidity action may be brought by the reorganizing company or its shareholder (Article 15.7).

147 The decision on the reorganization may determine the term after the expiration of which it may not be executed (Article 49.8). Such a term, however, expires at the moment the result of the reorganization is registered.

148 The reorganization of the company may mean that the shares of those holders dissatisfied with it have to be bought out at the market value, provided the shareholders in question voted against the adoption of the decision concerning the reorganization or did not take part in the voting with regard to the matter (Article 75).

successor, the new company or companies bear solidary (joint and several) liability to the creditors of the reorganized company (Article 15.6).[149]

A joint stock company can also be liquidated voluntarily or by the court decision, according to the general rules of the Civil Code concerning liquidation of the juristic person presented above (Articles 61–5) and the JSC Law (Articles 21–4).[150] It may be liquidated by the decision of the general meeting, for instance, if the term for which it has been created is expired or the goal for the sole purpose of which it has been established is achieved.[151] A joint stock company is to be liquidated by court decision at the demand of the state or local authorities in case of (a) unrectifiable violations of the law committed in the establishment of the company or (b) the practicing of an activity without a proper permit (license) or of an activity prohibited by the law or contradictory to the Constitution or with repeated or gross violations of the law as well as on other grounds provided by the Civil Code (Article 61.2). In addition, if a company is incapable of satisfying the creditors' claims, it may be recognized by court decision as insolvent (bankrupt), and this will entail its liquidation.[152]

The decision on the voluntary liquidation of the joint stock company must be adopted, under the JSC Law, by the general meeting on the proposal of the council of directors (Article 21.2). The registration body must be notified about the decision on liquidation, and the liquidation commission, to which the management of the company's affairs is to pass, shall be appointed, as it is provided by the Civil Code (Article 62). The creditors of the company are to be informed in writing, and the information on the liquidation and the procedure and terms for the claims that may be filed by the company's creditors must be published in the state register publication;[153] the term for the filing of the claims of the creditors can be, according to the Civil Code (Article 63.1), at least two months from the publication date. Where the company has no obligations to creditors, its assets are to be distributed among the shareholders, in accordance with the JSC Law, as follows: first are payments relating to shares which must be redeemed; second, payments to holders of preference shares, and third, payments to holders of common shares (Articles 22.2 and 23). The liquidation of the company is completed with the respective entry by the state registration body (Article 24).

Disclosure and publicity requirements[154] Under the JSC Law, in addition to the general registration requirements (Articles 13 and 14) and disclosure requirements (Articles 15.5, 22.1, and 24) as well as the duty of the major shareholder to submit his offer, notification, and demand concerning his

---

149 See also the Decree of the Plenum 19 of 2003 (item 22).

150 The rules on the liquidation of company are provided for the liquidation of existing companies. If a company has actually finished its activities, the rules on insolvency of the missing creditor are applied (Insolvency Law, Articles 227–30). See Tikhomirov 2009: 183–4.

151 The liquidation of the company with foreign investor requires, according to the judicial practice of Russia, his clear consent. See Informative Letter of the Presidium of the Supreme Arbitrazh Court no 58 of 18 January 2001. Вестник Высшего Арбитражного Суда Российской Федерации [Herald of Supreme Arbitrazh Court of Russian Federation] (2001) 3 and Tikhomirov 2009: 192.

152 The decision on the voluntary liquidation adopted by the general meeting is not to preclude its compulsory liquidation in judicial proceedings, provided by the law, according to the judicial practice of Russia. See Informative Letter of the Presidium of the Supreme Arbitrazh Court no 50 of 13 January 2000. Вестник Высшего Арбитражного Суда Российской Федерации [Herald of Supreme Arbitrazh Court of Russian Federation] (2000) 3 and Tikhomirov 2009: 185–6.

153 Such a publication does not substitute for the notices to creditors. See Tikhomirov 2009: 142 and 196.

154 On this subject, see Tikhomirov 2009: 541–2.

acquisition of shares in the open joint stock company (Article 84.9), and the duty of the principal company to publish the acquisition of more than 20 percent of the shares of another company (Article 6.4) presented above, the Civil Code and JSC Law contain provisions on the control of financial and economic activity and the bookkeeping and other information of the company.

A joint stock company is obliged, under the JSC Law (Article 88), to keep the bookkeeping report and to submit the financial documents (to the public authorities) in accordance with the legal requirements, for which the executive body of the company is responsible. The reliability of the data contained in the financial documents must be confirmed by the audit commission (auditor) of the company. The annual report of the company is subject to preliminary confirmation by the council of directors or, in the absence of this, by the one-person executive body not later than 30 days before the date of conducting the annual general meeting. A company is obliged to store its important documents and grant information concerning it, in accordance with the legal requirements,[155] to the public authorities and third persons as well as shareholders, as presented above (Articles 89–91).

An open joint stock company must publish every year an annual report, a balance sheet, and a statement of the profits and the losses, and also disclose the prospectus concerning the issue of securities and the notices of general meetings of shareholders as well as other information determined by the security market authorities, as provided for by the Civil Code (Article 97.1) and the JSC Law (Article 92.1). In addition, a closed joint stock company can be obliged to publish its annual report and accounting balance in those cases provided for by the JSC Law; and if a closed joint stock company intends to issue publicly traded securities, the information required in such cases must be disclosed (Article 92.2).

The joint stock company which is obliged to publish for general information documents on its activities must draw, under the Civil Code (103.5), upon the services of a professional auditor, not bound up with the company or with its participants by property interests, for checking the correctness of the annual financial reports on the basis of a contract concluded with him,[156] as it is provided by the JSC Law (Article 86). The verification (audit) of the financial–economic activity of the company is to be carried out regardless of its obligation to publish the information on its activities at the request of shareholders owning in aggregate not less than 10 percent of the (voting) shares; the council of directors also has the right to demand an extraordinary auditor's examination, and this is to be carried out at the decision of the general meeting or on the initiative of the auditors (audit commission) as well (Article 85.3). The procedure for carrying out an auditor's examination is defined by the law and the charter, according to the Civil Code (Article 103.5), as well as by the bylaws approved by the general meeting, as provided for by the JSC Law (Article 85.2). The auditor (audit commission) is also entitled to require the convocation of an extraordinary general meeting (Article 85.5).

The disclosure duty of the joint stock company arises not only in connection with the requirements concerning the company's activity information established by the JSC Law but also in accordance with the public law provisions empowering certain authorities to demand certain information from companies. Empowered to demand information are tax, custom, antimonopoly, finance, statistics, and investigation (police) authorities as well as judicial bodies. The disclosure duty is also established by the Law on the Security Market for the public issuance of the company's securities. The violation of the disclosure requirements may cause civil, administrative, and even criminal liability.

---

155 The joint stock company is the subject of the Information Law (2006), and, in principle, has, as an information holder, the right to allow or restrict the entry to its information. See Tikhomirov 2009: 533–4.

156 In certain cases a Russian joint stock company may also have, in addition to an external auditor, an internal auditor [*ревизор*] or audit commission [*ревизионная комиссия*].

Legal protection Among the rules protecting shareholders, including the rules on their property and non-property rights, and on acquisitions of more than 30 percent of shares, presented above, particularly important is the rule established by the JSC Law on the rights of the shareholders to demand the company to redeem their shares according to the JSC Law (Article 75).

Redemption rights are granted, under the JSC Law (Article 75.1), to dissatisfied shareholders (who have not taken part in the adoption of the decision or have voted against it), for cases involving the reorganization of the company and its conclusion of a large-scale transaction, as well as when the amendments to the charter limit the rights of shareholders.[157] Their shares must be bought out at a price not lower than their market value (Article 75.3). It is directly provided by the law that the shareholder in question must vote against the adoption of the decision at issue or not take part in the voting with regard to the matter. However, the company is allowed to use for such purchase no more than 10 percent of the value of the net assets of the company. (Article 76.5)

Under the JSC Law, the redeemed shares are to be, in case of the reorganization of the company, canceled immediately,[158] and in the other cases are to pass to the company. Those redeemed shares are voteless, and dividends must not be credited with regard to them. Moreover, they must be resold by the company at the price not lower than their market value no later than one year after their redemption; otherwise the charter capital must be decreased by canceling these shares.[159] (Article 76)

Where the company is reorganized through its division, it is additionally provided by the JSC Law (Articles 18.3^3) that the dissatisfied shareholder must receive the shares of the each new company in correspondence with his shares in the reorganizing company. Moreover, if this requirement is ignored, the shareholder may demand in the judicial proceeding that the decision of the general meeting is recognized as invalid.[160] A similar rule is also provided for the reorganization of a company through its separation, if the decision on it includes the conversion into or placement of the shares of the new company (Articles 19.3^3).[161]

Also important for the protection of shareholders is the general rule established by the JSC Law on their rights to appeal the decision of the general meeting of the company (Article 49.7). According to it, a shareholder[162] has the right to appeal to a court a decision adopted by the general meeting that is in violation of the law and the charter. If he intends to use this right, he is presumed not to have taken part in that general meeting or to have voted against the adoption of such decision; it is also a requirement that his rights or legal interests were violated by the said decision,[163]

157 Only in such cases may dissatisfied shareholders demand the redemption of all their shares or a part thereof by the company according to the established legal praxis of Russia. See Decree of the Plenum no 19 of 2003 (item 21).

158 See Decree of the Plenum no 19 of 2003 (item 29). For more on this subject, see K.M. Alieva, Право акционера на выкуп акций при реорганизации акционерного общества [Right of Shareholders to the Redemption of Shares in the Reorganization of Joint Stock Societies], *Zakony Rossii: opyt, analiz, praktika* [Laws of Russia: Experience, Analysis, Practice] 8 (2003): 53–8.

159 See Tikhomirov 2009: 130 and 434–5.

160 See Decree of the Plenum no 19 of 2003 (item 21).

161 See Tikhomirov 2009: 163 and 168–71.

162 A person who is not a shareholder at the moment of the convocation of the general meeting may not, according to judicial practice in Russia, appeal against its decision. See N.N. Konnova, Корпоративные споры: обзор арбитражной практики [Corporate Disputes: Survey of Arbitrazh Practice] (2008), http://www.klerk.ru/law/?106820 (accessed 17 June 2010).

163 Thus, in order to succeed, the shareholder must prove that (1) the requirements provided by the law or the charter were violated in the adoption of the decision of the general meeting, (2) he did not take part in

and such a claim may be filed within six months from the date of gaining knowledge of it (Article 49.7). According to the established judicial praxis, at question in such a case are the decisions which have been made in violation of the procedural requirements, such as improper notice of a general meeting (Article 52.1) or issuance of voting ballots (Article 60), or the lack of provision enabling the shareholder to become acquainted with the necessary information on the items on the agenda of the meeting[164] (Article 52.3).[165] However, the appealed decision may remain in force if the vote of the shareholder who appealed would not affect the voting results, if the violations are not essential, and the decision has not incurred losses to the appellant (Article 49.7).[166]

However, the decisions of the general meeting adopted in violation of the rules on its authority, or quorum or agenda, are regarded in judicial practice as null and void under the general Civil Code rules on invalid transactions (Articles 166 and 168), and consequently the court is obliged to intervene in such cases *ex officio* and apply the law[167].[168]

Legal protection for shareholders is also provided in the rules of the JSC Law on large-scale transactions[169] and interested party transactions (Articles 79.6 and 84.1).[170] According to these, a shareholder or the company may, as presented above, bring an invalidity action against such a transaction, if it is concluded in violation of the legal requirements and if, in pursuance thereof, it violated the rights of the shareholder or the company at the moment of its conclusion.[171]

Liability rules The JSC Law contains rules by which the general rules of the Civil Code on liability concerning all forms of companies and partnership, presented above, are detailed. These rules concern:

- the liability which may arise for the principal company (partnership), and
- the liability which a person using authority could fall into, as well as
- the liability of the members of the governing bodies of the company.

In the subsidiary and principal relation the principal company can bear liability, as presented above, on the one hand for the acts (transactions) of the subsidiary company and on the other hand in the case of the insolvency (bankruptcy) of the latter. According to the JSC Law, the liability for the transactions of the subsidiary company presupposes that the principal company has given to it the binding orders, and this right has been established for by the charter of the subsidiary company or in a contract between it and the principal company; this liability is solidary (joint

the general meeting or voted against the decision, and (3) the decision violates his rights or legal interests. See Tikhomirov 2009: 334.

164 See Tikhomirov 2009: 333–8.

165 See Decree of the Plenum no 19 of 2003 (item 24).

166 A similar rule is included in the Limited Liability Company Law (Article 43.2).

167 See Decree of the Plenum no 19 of 2003 (item 26). See also Tikhomirov 2009: 333.

168 The decisions of the council of directors and executive body adopted in violation of the law are also subject to court appeal. See Decree of the Plenum no 19 of 2003 (item 27).

169 Regarding large-scale transactions, the rules of the JSC Law are, contrary to the rules of the LLC Law (Article 46), imperative and may not be excluded by the charter.

170 A similar rule is included in the LLC Law (Articles 45.5 and 46.5).

171 According to the established judicial praxis in Russia, where the other party of the transaction did not and ought not to have known that the transaction at issue was deemed as an invalid transaction as well as that it was not concluded in the proper order, such a transaction may not be recognized by a court as invalid. See the Decree of the Plenum of the Supreme Arbitrazh Court no 40 of 20 June 2007 (item 2).

and several) and strict. Contrary to this, the liability of the principal company for bringing the subsidiary company into bankruptcy is subsidiary[172] and presupposes that the principal company knew in advance that the consequence of its actions (the binding orders given to the subsidiary company) would be the bankruptcy of the subsidiary company. Besides the subsidiary company, its shareholders also have the right to demand that the principal company compensate the damages caused through its faults to the subsidiary company, provided the principal company knew in advance that the subsidiary company would incur losses as consequence of its actions (the binding orders given to the subsidiary company). (Article 6.3) Hence it is obvious that the rules of the Civil Code concerning the liability in subsidiary and principal relations (Articles 105.2 and 105.3) are watered down in the JSC Law in favor of the principal companies; this liability presumes, as a matter of fact, intent (intentional liability) which is quite an unusual solution in Russian law as well as in general[173].[174]

The (subsidiary) liability of the persons in a dominant position in the joint stock company (including the controlling shareholders) for bringing it into bankruptcy provided by the JSC Law is also based on the general company law rules on liability provided by the Civil Code (Article 56.3), but in this case as well as in the subsidiary and principal relation, it is also presumed, according to the JSC Law, that the person in question knew in advance that the consequence of its actions (the binding orders given to the company) would be the bankruptcy of the company (Article 3.3).[175] Furthermore, such a liability presupposes a causal connection between the orders and insolvency.[176]

The liability of the members of the governing bodies of the company provided by the JSC Law is also based on the general company law rules on liability of the Civil Code (Article 53.3) and means in general the liability for negligence. Under Article 71 of the JSC Law, the members of the governing bodies are presupposed to act in good faith and reasonably, but on the other hand, in determining the grounds and extent of their liability, ordinary business practices and other relevant considerations must be taken into account. This liability is personal as well as solidary (joint and several), but the persons who did not take part in the administration (or voted against) is not to bear liability; in this case the company or shareholders owning not less than 1 percent of the common shares of the company have the right to apply to a court with a suit. It seems that in the case of the liability of the members of the governing bodies, including the executives, there is also an attempt to water down the rules of the Civil Code on company law liability.[177]

172 According to the JSC Law (Article 6.3), the principal company is liable for bringing the subsidiary company into bankruptcy.

173 The general construction is, in Russian law, according to the Civil Code (Article 401.1), that the debtor should be released from liability if he proves that he has done his best to perform his obligation (i.e. the liability of the violator is presumed). See Tikhomirov 2009: 350–51.

174 See Stepanov 2010: 158; Sergeev 1 2009: 304, and Orlov 1999: 128–9.

175 According to the JSC Law (Article 3.3), the persons in a dominant position may be liable for bringing the company into bankruptcy, and this means that this question is within a court's discretion (contrary to the above-mentioned rule concerning the liability of the principal company).

176 See Tikhomirov 2009: 53–5.

177 In such a case the claimant must prove that the executive has been dishonest in his dealings, because it is presumed in Russian law, according to the Article 10.3 of the Civil Code, that the executives act in good faith and reasonably; in other words, it must be proved that the person knew or he should have known that his actions would cause damage.

Limited Liability Company

The norms of the Limited Liability Company Law[178] (LLC Law), as for the JSC Law, are based on the company law norms of the first part of the Civil Code, and they form the main part in the regulation concerning the foundation and activities of limited liability companies. Like the JSC Law, the LLC Law may work as an independent legal source in the regulation of limited liability companies because it includes almost all the rules of the Civil Code concerning them and these are concretised in it. The LLC Law contains 59 articles and is divided into seven chapters, in which there are in addition to the general (Chapter I) and final (Chapter VI) rules also the rules which apply to the foundation of the company (Chapter II), the charter capital and assets of the company (Chapter III), listing of the members of the company (Chapter III^1),[179] the management within the company (Chapter IV) and the reorganization and liquidation of the company (Chapter V). A significant part of the norms of it are, contrary to the norms of the JSC Law, dispositive (default rules).[180]

Concept A limited liability company is, under the Civil Code (Article 87) and the LLC Law (Article 2), a company established by one or several persons, the charter capital of which is divided into (ideal) shares (parts) or membership interests or members' ownership interests.[181] [182] Under the LLC Law, a limited liability company is liable for its obligations by its assets, but not answerable for the obligations of its members (Article 3). According to the LLC Law, a limited liability company is a juristic person, established for an indefinite time, unless otherwise provided for by its charter (Article 2.3), and it has civil rights and bears those obligations required to pursue any types of activities not prohibited by the law, provided this is not contradictory to the object and goals of its activities, if these are expressly restricted by the charter (Article 2.2).

According to the LLC Law, certain types of activities may require special permits or licenses,[183] and the particular aspects of the formation (as well as reorganization and liquidation) and the legal status of limited liability companies in the spheres of banking, investment, including the establishment of companies with foreign investors, and insurance activities as well as those practicing activities in agriculture, are defined by (other than the LLC Law) the laws (Articles 1.2, 2.2, and 11.3). Regarding the legal transactions of foreign investors concerning the acquisition of membership interests in limited liability companies of strategic importance for state security and defense and consequently control of them, such transactions are subject to the provisions of the Federal Law on Foreign Investments in Companies of Strategic Importance for State Security and Defense.[184]

The limited liability company must be registered and the trade name of a limited liability company must contain its name and the words "limited liability"; besides the full name a limited

178 For more on this subject, see, in particular, M.Yu. Tikhomirov (ed.), Комментарий к Федеральному закону об обществах с ограниченной ответсвтвенностью [Commentary on the Federal Limited Liability Company Law] (2010).

179 Added by the Law no 312-FZ of 30 December 2008 and last amended by the Law no 227-FZ of 20 July 2010.

180 Tikhomirov 2010: 5–7.

181 Shares of a limited liability company, unlike those of a joint stock company, are not transferable security papers per se.

182 Only the company has ownership rights to the property contributed to its charter capital, and the division of the charter capital into shares does not mean that participants (members) have a share ownership in the property of the company. See Tikhomirov 2010: 21–4.

183 The Law on Licensing no 128-FZ of 8 August 2001 as amended 27 July 2010.

184 No 57-FZ of 29 April 2008.

liability company may have also abbreviative name,[185] as provided for by the Civil Code (Article 87.2) and the LLC Law (Article 4.1). The site of a company is determined by the place of its registration (Article 4.2), which is in general the location of the executive body of the company.[186] According to the LLC Law (Article 6), a limited liability company may have subsidiary and dependent companies, as well as branches and representative offices and the decision on these requires not less than two-thirds of the votes of the members (Article 5.1).

Participants The members of a limited liability company can be, according to the Civil Code (Article 88) and the LLC Law (Article 7), both physical and juristic persons,[187] the number of which is limited by the law to 50.[188] If it is exceeded, the company must be transformed into a joint stock company[189] in the course of a year, or liquidated in a court procedure at the request of a register or some other authorized body. A limited liability company may be established by one person and exists as a single company. It is the minimum requirement, since the LLC Law (Article 26.2) excludes the existence of memberless companies; the single as well as the last member is not allowed to withdraw from the company. Furthermore, a limited liability company may not include under the LLC Law another company consisting of a sole person as a single member (Article 7.2).

The limited liability company is obliged to ensure the keeping and storage of a list of its participants (members) under the LLC Law (Article 31^1). The list includes information concerning each member, the size of his membership interest, and contribution to the charter capital as well as information concerning the membership interests of the company.

Participants (members) of the limited liability company are not, under the Civil Code (Article 87) and the LLC Law (Article 2), answerable for its obligations but bear the risk of the losses in connection with the company's activity within the cost of the interests they have in the charter capital of the company. The members who have not paid up their interests in full are jointly (solidarily) liable for the obligations of the company to the extent of the value of the unpaid part of the contribution of each member. Furthermore, a recovery on the demand of a creditor can be made in regard of an interest or part thereof in a company of a member for his debts, but this requires a court decision and the other members have the right to pay the actual cost of the share, which is determined in accordance with the accounting documents, as provided for by the LLC Law (Article 25).

Foundation A limited liability company is founded, according to the LLC Law (Article 11), by the decision of the founders in their meeting. The decision fixes the results on voting in the meeting regarding the questions required by the law. The decisions on founding the company and approving its charter[190] must be unanimous, and decisions regarding the composition of the governing bodies must be resolved by a qualified majority (of three-quarters of the votes) of the founders.

185 In Russian (obligatory) and also in other languages.

186 According to the Registration Law 2001 (Article 8.2).

187 Under the Civil Code, state and municipal bodies are not allowed to participate in limited liability companies, unless otherwise provided for in the law, while the participation of an institution in a limited liability company is subject to the permission of its owner (Article 66.4).

188 The same limitation is imposed on closed joint stock companies in Russia.

189 More precisely into an open joint stock company, which form allows such an exceeding.

190 Including the evaluation of the (capital) contributions in kind.

For the founding of a limited liability company, the founders enter, under the LLC Law, into a foundation agreement,[191] and its purpose is to define the order of their performance of a joint activity involved in the establishment of the company; the amount of the charter capital and the amount and nominal value of shares of each member or membership interests, and the order and terms of payment of the contributions into the charter capital. The foundation agreement must be made in written form. It is, however, not regarded as a proper constituent document. (Article 11.5)

The constituent document of a limited liability company is the charter, the minimum requirements concerning which are laid down in the Civil Code (Article 89) and the LLC Law (Article 12.2). The charter of a limited liability company must contain:

- the full and abbreviated names of the company;
- the location of the company;
- the composition and authority of the governing bodies of the company, including the issues which are under the exclusive authority of the general meeting, and the management procedure including decisions on matters to be resolved by a qualified majority or unanimous vote;
- the amount of the charter capital;
- the rights and duties of the members;
- information on the consequences and order of the withdrawal of a member and transfer of the membership interest or part thereof to another person, if such a right is established under the charter;
- information on the order of the storage of documents and granting of information to the members and other persons as well as
- other terms provided by the law, for instance, the reserve or other funds, which are not, however, obligatory, as provided by the LLC Law (Article 30).

The charter may also include other provisions which are not contradictory to the law. According to the LLC Law, the company shall be obliged, if so required by a member, auditor, or any interested person, within reasonable periods to provide them with the possibility to familiarize themselves with the company's charter. The charter of the limited liability company may be amended by the decision of the general meeting (Article 12).[192]

The limited liability company must be, as mentioned above, registered and it is deemed established (as a juristic person) from the moment of its registration. According to Article 11.6 of the LLC Law, the founders of the company are (jointly and severally) liable for the obligations associated with the formation of the company and arising prior to its registration; but those obligations may be transferred to the company (only) by the approval of the general meeting. In any case, the liability of the company is not to exceed one-fifth of the contributed charter capital. The amendments to the constituent documents must also be registered to be effective under the LLC Law (Article 2.3 and 12–13). Data on the amount and nominal value of each member's membership interests are also subject to state registration (Article 11.8).

Company assets The charter capital of a limited liability company must comprise the nominal value of the member's interests and not be less than the amount established by the Civil Code

191 An operating agreement may also be concluded by the members in accordance with the LLC Law (Article 8.3). See below.

192 To be effective against third persons the amendments must be, under the LLC Law, registered (Articles 12.4 and 20.4)

(Article 90.1) and LLC Law (Article 14.1).[193] The size of the interest is defined as a percentage or portion of the charter capital. The actual value of an interest is also defined in the LLC Law by reference to the value of the net assets of the company (Article 14.2).

According to Article 14.3 of the LLC Law, the charter may contain provisions on the exceptions from the proportionality of the interests and restrictions on the size (maximum) of the interest of a member and also changes in the proportion of the interests;[194] however, these must not be personal. Changes in respect of such restrictions require the unanimous decision of the members at the general meeting. A person who has acquired the membership interest contrary to the restrictions established by the charter has the right to vote at the general meeting in accordance with the maximum size of the interest established by the charter.

The value of each member's contribution to the charter capital must not be, according to the LLC Law, lower than the nominal value of his membership interest. The contributions are to be things (including money and securities) or rights which have monetary value, including the right to use property,[195] but the charter may include exclusions for the types of property contributable to the charter capital. An in-kind contribution exceeding 20,000 rubles requires an independent valuation. Half of the charter capital must be paid by the date of its registration, and the unpaid portion must be paid within one year, unless an earlier date is specified in the charter.[196] The unpaid part of the membership interest is transferred to the company. (Articles 14–16)

According to Article 20 of the LLC Law, the charter capital can be decreased by reducing the nominal value of the interests of all the members of the company and/or by redeeming the interests belonging to the company. A decrease of the charter capital is obligatory if the value of net assets of the company proves to be less than its charter capital at the end of the financial year (after the end of the second financial year); but if in this case the value of net assets proves to be less than the amount of the minimum charter capital specified in the law, the company must be liquidated. The decrease of charter capital of the company requires that all its creditors be informed in writing thereof, and the creditors have the right to demand from the company the termination or the performance at an earlier date of its obligation and compensation for damages connected therewith. The decision on the decrease of charter capital must be published and its registration requires the evidence of the notification of the creditors. The documents on the amendments of the charter due to the decrease of the charter capital and, consequently, to the reduction of the nominal value of the interests must be presented at the registration within one month of the date of notification of the creditors. Where the company does not adopt the decision concerning the decrease of its charter capital or liquidation, its creditors are also entitled to demand the termination or the performance at an earlier date of its obligation and compensation for damages connected therewith, and in such a case bodies empowered by the state also have the right to demand the liquidation of the company in a judicial proceeding.

The charter capital of a limited liability company may also be increased, according to the LLC Law, after it has been paid in full through assets of the company, additional contributions of

193 The minimum amount of the charter capital of a limited liability company is, according to the LLC law, not less than 10,000 rubles (Article 14.1).

194 Under the LLC Law, unproportionality can be imposed by the charter in respect of the preemptive acquisition of the membership interest by the members (Article 21.4), as well as the additional capital contributions to the assets of the company (Article 27).

195 In case of the anticipatory termination of the right to use the property contributed to the charter capital of the company, this shall be compensated for under the LLC Law (Article 15.3).

196 According to Article 90.2 of the Civil Code, a member of a limited liability company may not be released from the duty to pay his contribution to the charter capital.

members (which may be obligatory), or contributions of new members, unless this is prohibited by the charter. The increase in charter capital through assets of the company or general additional contributions of (all members) requires the decision of the general meeting made by a majority of not less than two-thirds of the members. As to the decision on the increase in charter capital through the acceptance of a new member or an additional contribution of a member (on his application), and the consequent amendments of the charter due to it, it must be made unanimously. General additional contributions[197] shall be paid within two months and single and new member contributions within six months from the date of the decision on the increase of the charter capital. The documents on the amendments of the charter due to the increase of the charter capital and, consequently, the nominal value of the interests, and if necessary, the changes in the sizes of the membership interests, shall be presented at the registration within one month from the date of the decision on enforcement of the results of the contribution procedure. In case of nonobservance of these time-limits, the increase of charter capital is regarded as not taken place. The application for registration of the amendments to the charter shall be signed by the executive body (person who discharges the functions of the one-person executive body) of the company, and it must contain confirmation that all contributions into the charter capital are paid. The members of the company bear jointly (solidarily) subsidiary liability for the obligations of the company to the extent of the value of the unpaid contributions during three years from the date of registration. (Articles 17–19)

A limited liability company can use also other ways to acquire assets. It may issue bonds and other emission securities under the LLC Law (Article 31). Issuance of bonds is allowed after the charter capital has been paid up in full. The bonds have nominal value, and the nominal value of all the bonds issued by the company may not exceed the size of the charter capital and/or the amount of the security provided for this purpose by the third persons. In the absence of such security, the bond issue is not allowed until the third year of the limited liability company's existence and, additionally, on condition that by this time its two annual balances have been properly approved. These restrictions are not to be applied to bonds with mortgage coverings and in other cases established by the federal laws on securities. Furthermore, the charter may impose on the members by decision of the general meeting the duty to make additional capital contributions to the assets of the company, as it provided for by the LLC Law (Article 27). According to the charter, reserve or other funds can also be established by the company, as mentioned above.

Rights and duties of members The rights and duties of the members of a limited liability company are defined explicitly in the general rules concerning companies and partnerships of the Civil Code (Article 67), which are introduced above and are detailed in the LLC Law (Articles 8–9). Members of a limited liability company have the right to:

- participate in the administration in compliance with the law and the charter;
- get information about the activity of the company including accounting books and other documentation in conformity with the procedure provided by the charter;
- appeal to a court a decision adopted by the general meeting in violation of the law and the charter according to the LLC Law (Article 43.1);
- take part in the distribution of profits;

197 According to the Civil Code a setoff in the payment of additional contributions is allowed only in the cases provided for by the law (Article 90.2).

- sell or otherwise transfer their membership interest or part of this to the other member(s) or another person in compliance with the procedure established by the law and the charter;[198]
- withdraw from the company by transferring their membership interest to the company, if such a possibility is provided for under the charter, or demand the company acquire their interest in cases provided by the LLC Law,[199] and
- receive the remaining property (assets), if the company is liquidated.

Members may also have other rights provided by the law and, furthermore, the charter may include so-called additional rights (Article 8).

In addition to the duties of the participants of companies and partnerships imposed in the rules of the Civil Code (Article 67.2)[200] to make capital contribution (or pay duly the membership interests) and to maintain secrecy, which are presented above, the LLC Law may, according to its Article 9, also establish other duties, including the duty to inform the company of any changes in his personal data and membership interests in the company (Article 31^1.3). Furthermore, according to the LLC Law, the charter may impose on the members the duty, for instance, to make additional capital contributions to the assets of the company in proportion to their membership interests, unless otherwise provided for by the charter (Article 27).

Under the LLC Law, additional duties may be imposed and additional rights granted by the charter, and any changes in them require the unanimous decision of the members at the general meeting, if these concern all members. Moreover, if additional rights or duties concern certain members (personal rights or duties), the decision on such rights and duties may be made by a two-thirds' vote, provided they consent. However, the termination of the duties requires the unanimous decision of the general meeting (all the members). Personal additional rights and duties do not go with the transfer of the membership interest; they are not transferable (Articles 8–9).[201]

Operating agreement[202] Members of the limited liability company have the right, in accordance the LLC Law (Article 8.3), to enter into an operating agreement. Under the agreement, they undertake to practice and/or refrain from practicing their rights in a determinate way, including:

- voting at general meetings;
- selling of the membership interest or part thereof at the price and/or in occurrence of the conditions determined by the agreement;
- refraining from selling before the occurrence of determinate conditions, and
- performing as agreed other actions relating to the governance of the company as well as its founding, activities, reorganization, and liquidation.

198 A member of the limited liability company also has the right to put in pledge his partnership interest or part thereof on the consent of the general meeting, unless it is prohibited by the charter. The contract of pledge must be notarially certified (authenticated), and nonobservance of this requirement causes its invalidity, as provided for by the LLC law (Article 22).

199 The withdrawal of a shareholder from a Russian joint stock company is impossible, although this does not prevent him from selling his shares.

200 And also enforced in the LLC Law (Article 9.1).

201 The rules on additional rights are criticized since they contain a risk of unjust privileges and abuses. See, for instance, Tikhomirov 2010: 80–81.

202 On this subject, see Tikhomirov 2010: 81.

An operating agreement must be concluded in written form by drawing up a single document signed by the parties.

Changes in membership interests The membership interest in the charter capital or part thereof can be transferred (and consequently participation in the company ended), according to the Civil Code (Article 93) and the LLC Law (Article 21), to another person through legal transaction or succession or some other legal ground. The sale or some other alienation of the interest or part thereof (that is paid) to another member or other members may require, if it is provided by the charter, the consent of the other members of the company, whereas in case of transfer to a third person or third persons, this can be forbidden by the charter. In these cases, other participants have the preemptive right to acquire the interest or part of it, and the charter may provide the fixed price for the interest as well as the order of the preemptive acquisition (Article 21.4). The charter can contain provisions that the company also have the preemptive right where the members have not used their preemptive right. As to the succession of membership interests (to the heirs and legal successors of juristic persons), the consent of the other members of the company may be required under the charter (Article 21.8). Such consent is explicitly required for the transfer of the membership through sale at a public auction (Article 21.8).

A member of a limited liability company has the right to withdraw from the company through the alienation of his interest to the company, if this is provided for by the charter according to the Civil Code (Article 94) and the LLC Law (Article 26). It is also provided by the LLC Law that a member of a limited liability company who violates his duties or hinders activities of the company may be expelled from it through the court by the demand of the other members holding jointly more than 10 percent of the shares (Article 10).

According to the LLC Law, in cases where the transfer of the membership interest to third persons is forbidden by the charter or the consent of the other members, required by the charter, is not obtained, the company is obliged to acquire it. In cases of decisions of the general meeting regarding large-scale transactions as well as increases of the charter capital, the member who voted against the adoption of the decision or did not take part in the voting has the right to demand the redemption of his membership interest by the company. In all these cases the company must pay the actual value[203] of the membership interest or part of it to the member who has intended to transfer it (or to the heir or legal successor of the member as well to the dissenting or absent member); and the actual value of the interest or its part must be paid from the difference between the value of the net assets of the company and the size of its charter capital.[204] Such a payment may be altered by giving the member in kind the amount of property that would correspond to the actual cost of the interest or part of it. (Article 23) The same payment duty applies to cases of withdrawal under the LLC Law (Article 23.6^{1})[205] and expulsion of members (Article 23.4). However, the property contributed by them to the assets is to remain with the company during the time it has been transferred, unless otherwise provided for by the foundation agreement (Article 15.4).

The membership interests acquired by (or transferred to) the company, where this is allowed by the LLC Law (Article 23), are voteless and grant no rights in the distribution of profits or assets in case of the liquidation of the company, and they are to be distributed by the decision of the general meeting between the members or sold to other members and/or third persons, unless this

203 The actual value of the interest is determined according to the data of the company's accounting over the last reporting period that precedes the date of the respective application or decision.

204 In case of its insufficiency, the company must reduce its charter capital by the deficient amount.

205 The member is not released by his withdrawal from the duty to pay his contribution to the assets of the company (LLC Law, Article 26.4).

is not allowed by the charter, no later than one year after their acquisition, according to the LLC Law (Article 24). The membership interests or part thereof acquired by the company, including those of the withdrawn member, must be sold at a price not lower than that paid for them by the company, and in case of unpaid interest or part of thereof, the minimum price is to be its nominal value (Article 24.4). Unsold interests are to be reimbursed with the corresponding reduction of the charter capital of the company under the LLC Law (Article 24.5). To be effective against third persons the changes in the membership interests must be registered within one month from the date of the transfer of the interest or part thereof (Article 24.6).

Sale transactions of the membership interests (as well as their pledge) must be, under the LLC Law, notarially certified (authenticated), and nonobservance of this requirement causes the invalidity of the transaction (Article 21.11). Notary authentication is not required neither in cases of the distribution of the membership interests between the members nor for their transfer to the company and further realization under the LLC Law (Articles 23 and 24).[206]

A bona fide acquirer is legally protected under the LLC Law[207] (Article 21.17), except in cases of unlawful actions by third persons and other cases of unintended loss of the membership interest. The claim against the bona fide acquirer must be presented no more than three years after the infringement came (or should have come) to his knowledge. As to cases of breach of the preemptive acquisition as well as other rules on the transfer of the membership interests to third persons, the claim must be presented within three months from the date of gaining knowledge of it (Article 21.18).

Governing bodies and decision-making procedures The minimum requirement for a limited liability company is a two-level system of governing bodies consisting of the general meeting and the executive body. However, the charter may provide additionally under the LLC Law (Article 32.2) for the foundation of a council of directors (supervisory council).

The supreme governing body of a limited liability company is, according to the Civil Code (Article 91) and the LLC Law (Article 32.1), the general meeting of its members. Among the issues which are within the authority of the general meeting of members, in accordance with the LLC Law (Article 33.2), are:

- general direction over the activity of the company;
- changes to the charter including changes in the amount of the charter capital;
- formation of the executive bodies or transfer of the executive body powers to an external manager (organization), and
- formation of the audit commission (auditor) of the company;
- approval of annual reports and bookkeeping balance sheets as well as bylaws for the regulation of the company's internal affairs;
- the distribution of its profits;
- the issuing bonds and other emission securities of the company;
- the appointment of the audit, and
- decisions on the reorganization and liquidation of the company as well as
- other decisions provided by the LLC Law, including large-scale transactions (Article 46) and interested party transactions (Article 45).

---

206 See Tikhomirov 2010: 163–4 and 175–6.

207 It is noteworthy in this respect that the general rule on the protection of the bona fide acquirer is included in the Civil Code (Article 302), and that it concerns any compensated transaction except those cases where the owner has lost his property against his will.

Approval of the annual results of the activities of the company is within the authority of the annual meeting; general meetings other than annual meetings are extraordinary (LLC Law, Article 34 and 35). It is explicitly forbidden in Article 91.3 of the Civil Code to delegate those issues placed within the authority of the general meeting for resolution to the executive bodies of the company.

Participation of a member in voting at the general meeting requires his registration under the LLC Law (Article 37.2), and his voting right must correspond, unless otherwise provided for by the charter, to the paid part of the membership interest (Article 16.2). The general meeting is not permitted to adopt decisions with regard to issues not included on the agenda of the meeting unless all the members of the company are present. In general, decisions are adopted by a majority of votes of all members of the company, but decisions with regard to amendments of the charter and in some other cases must be adopted at the general meeting by a qualified majority (a majority of not less than two-thirds of the votes of the members). However, amendments to the charter allowing withdrawal from the company (Article 26.1) and decisions with regard to the reorganization and liquidation of the company must be made, under the LLC Law, by the members unanimously. (Article 37) Unanimous decisions of the general meeting are required also for the monetary valuation of property contributed to the charter capital (15.2 Article). Furthermore, according to the LLC Law, the amendments concerning the additional rights and duties mentioned above and the restrictions on the size of an membership interest or proportion of the interests (as well as votes and dividends) also require unanimous decisions; however, if such a change concerns a certain member, the decision can be made by a vote of two-thirds of the members with the consent of such a person (Articles 21.4 and 27).[208] Amendments to the charter providing a fixed price for the interest as well as the order of the preemptive acquisition requires unanimity of the general meeting; however, the elimination of such provisions may occur by its qualified majority decision (Article 21.4).

A decision of the general meeting may, under the LLC Law (Article 38), be adopted by means of conducting external voting (poll) excepting the approval of annual reports and bookkeeping balance sheet. Cumulative voting with regard to the election of the members of the council of directors, executive body, and audit commission may also be established by the charter (Article 37.9). In a single limited liability company, the decisions of its member in regard of the issues provided for the authority of the general meeting must be completed in writing (Article 39).

An extraordinary general meeting must be held, according to Article 35 of the LLC Law, in those cases provided for by the charter, and also in any other cases if it is necessitated by the interests of the company and its members. The meeting must be convened by the executive body of the company and this also may be required by the council of directors, the auditors as well as members holding not less than 10 percent of the all votes in the company.

Under the LLC Law, the executive body of the company must be elected by the general meeting, and it may be collegiate (the board, directorate) and/or one-person (director general, president).[209] Members of the executive body (including a one-person body) must be physical persons, but not necessarily members of the company; and in this case they as well as members of the council of directors do not have voting rights at the general meeting. A member of the one-person executive body (director general) may not be simultaneously the chairman of the council of directors, whereas the members of a collegial executive body may comprise at most a quarter of the

208 According to the LLC Law, unproportionality can be imposed by the charter in respect of the preemptive acquisition of the membership interest by the members (Article 21.4), as well as the additional capital contributions to the assets of the company (Article 27).

209 The charter may provide that the formation of the collegiate executive body is delegated to the council of directors.

council of directors. The powers of the executive body of the company may be transferred under a contract to an external manager. The charter may also provide the foundation of the internal as well as external audit commission (auditor), and this is obligatory for companies whose number of members exceeds 15. (Articles 32 and 40–42)

The authority and decision-making of the executive bodies of the company as well as their acting on behalf of the company is defined in the LLC Law and they may be detailed by the charter and other internal documents of the company as well as by the contract concluded with the external manager. (Articles 40–42)

In the case of the foundation, under the charter, of the council of directors (supervisory council), many of the issues listed above as those to be within the authority of the general meeting of members may be transferred to its authority in accordance with the LLC Law (Article 32.2^1). Among the issues which are not transferable to the council of directors are:

- changes to the charter including changes in the amount of the charter capital;
- the formation of the audit commission (auditor) of the company;
- the approval of annual reports and bookkeeping balance sheets of the company;
- the distribution of the profits and issuing bonds and other emission securities of the company as well as
- decisions on the reorganization and liquidation of the company.

The charter may provide, in addition to issues transferred from the authority of the general meeting, that decisions on the organization of general meetings are delegated to the council of directors (Article 32.2) and in such a case the executive body of the company is furnished with the right to demand an extraordinary general meeting (Article 32.2^2).

Payment of profits Under the LLC Law, decisions regarding the payment of profits (which must be distributed proportionally or otherwise according to the charter or unanimous decision of the members) may be adopted by the general meeting quarterly, once in six months, or once a year. Such a decision is not allowed until the entire charter capital of the company is paid up in full and until the actual cost of the interest or part thereof to the member leaving the company is paid as well as if the value of net assets of the company is less than its charter capital and the reserve fund or becomes less than the amount thereof, or the company is liable to be deemed otherwise insolvent (bankrupt) as a result of the decision. These are also obstacles to paying profits after the decision on this is made until their termination. (Articles 28–9)

Disclosure and publicity requirements The duty of a limited liability company to keep accounts and records arises from the provisions of the Civil Code (Article 91) and LLC Law (Articles 18, 23, 25, 26, 45 and 46) regulating increases in charter capital through assets of the company, redemption of the membership interest by the company, recovery of the membership interest on the demand of a creditor, and withdrawal from the company as well as interested party and large-scale transactions.

Under the LLC Law, a company whose number of members exceeds 15 must have an auditor (audit commission); otherwise it is voluntary (Article 32.6). The audit commission (auditor) of the company has the right at any time to verify the financial–economic activity of the company and to have access to any documentation concerning it. Any officer or member of the staff of the company is obliged upon the demand of the auditor to give necessary explanations. The annual report of the company must be subject to the audit verification before its approval by the general meeting. The procedure for carrying out an auditor's examination is defined by the charter and bylaws of the company approved by the general meeting. (Article 47) The audit verification of the company may be executed by a professional auditor upon the decision of the general meeting; the auditor must not, however, be bound up with the company or with its participants by property interests. An audit verification may also be carried out at the request of a member by a professional auditor chosen by him. (Article 48)

According to the LLC Law, a limited liability company must publish every year an annual report and a balance sheet and disclose the information on its activities in cases of the public placement of its bonds and other securities. A company is obliged to store its important documents and grant information concerning it, in accordance with the legal requirements, to the public authorities and members of the company, as presented above (Articles 49 and 50).[210]

Reorganization and liquidation A limited liability company can be reorganized or liquidated voluntarily by unanimous consent of its members, as provided for by the Civil Code (Article 92.1) and the LLC Law (Articles 51–58, 33.2.11, and 37.8). The reorganization of a limited liability company may be effected in the form of merger, accession, division, and separation (Articles 51–5). It may also be transformed into a company of another form, partnership, or production cooperative in accordance with Article 92.2 of the Civil Code and Article 56 of the LLC Law. According to the LLC Law, the decision on the reorganization must be published and the reorganization also requires the notification of creditors, evidence of which must be presented at the registration, and they are entitled, as mentioned above, to demand the termination or performance of the company's obligations (Article 51). The decision on the voluntary liquidation and appointment of the liquidation commission must be adopted by the general meeting on the proposal of the council of directors, executive body, or a member of the company (Article 57). A company may be liquidated also by court decision in those cases provided for by the Civil Code (Article 61.2), which are presented above. The assets of the company subject to liquidation remaining after the completion of the settlement of accounts with creditors are to be distributed, under the LLC Law, among the members—first through payment of the unpaid parts of the distributed profits and then the distribution of the assets proportional to the membership interests (Article 58).

Legal protection of members Under the LLC Law, a member of the company may appeal to a court a decision adopted by the general meeting, presuming he has not taken part in voting or has voted against the adoption of the decision at the general meeting; it is also a requirement that his rights or legal interests were violated by the decision (Article 43.1). However, the appealed decision may remain in force if the vote of the member who appealed would not affect the voting results, the violations are not essential and the decision has not incurred losses to the appellant (Article 43.2). A member of the company may appeal to a court also a decision adopted by the executive body of the company, provided his rights or legal interests were violated by the decision (Article 43.3).

Legal protection for the members of the limited liability company is also provided for in the rules of the LLC Law on large-scale transactions (Article 46.5) and interested party transactions (Article 45.5). According to them, a member or the company may bring an invalidity action against such a transaction if it was concluded in violation of the legal requirements and, in pursuance thereof, violated the rights of the shareholder or the company at the moment of its conclusion.

---

210 Under the LLC Law (Article 12), the charter of the limited liability company must include provisions on the order of the storage of documents and granting of information to the members and other persons.

Liability rules The LLC Law contains the rules (Articles 3, 6 and 44) by which the general rules of the Civil Code on liability concerning all forms of companies and partnership (Articles 56 and 105), presented above, are detailed. The rules concern:

- the liability which may arise for the principal company (partnership) and
- the liability which a person using authority could fall into, as well as
- the liability of the members of the governing bodies of the company.

Under the LLC Law, in the subsidiary and principal relation the principal company could bear liability, as presented above, on the one hand for the acts (transactions) of the subsidiary company and on the other hand in the case of the insolvency (bankruptcy) of the latter. The liability for the transactions of the subsidiary company presupposes that the principal company has given to it binding orders; this liability is solidary (joint and several). Contrary to this, the liability of the principal company for bringing the subsidiary company into bankruptcy is subsidiary. In addition to the subsidiary company, its members also have the right to demand that the principal company compensate for the damages caused through its faults to the subsidiary company (Article 6.3). The liability of the members and other persons in a dominant position in the limited liability company guilty for bringing the company into bankruptcy, established by the LLC Law (Article 3.3), is also based on the general company law rules on liability of the Civil Code (Article 56.3) and such a liability is subsidiary.

The liability of the members of the governing bodies of the company established by the LLC Law (Article 44) is also based on the general company law rules on liability of the Civil Code (Article 53.3). The members of the governing bodies are presupposed to act in good faith and reasonably, but, on the other hand, in determining the grounds and extent of their liability, ordinary business practices and other relevant considerations must be taken into account. This liability is personal as well as joint and several (solidary), but the persons who did not take part in (or voted against) the administration do not bear liability. The right to bring an action for damages is held by the company or its members.

Additional liability company The additional liability company (company with supplementary liability) is also known in Russia[211] according to the Civil Code (Article 95). In the additional liability company the members bear liability for the obligations of the company (if its assets would not be sufficient) with their own property in the amount, which is for all of them equally multiplied to the cost of their membership interests according to the charter (for instance twofold, threefold, etc.). The liability of the members in relation to the company is subsidiary, but their mutual liability is solidary (joint and several), and in case of the bankruptcy of one of the members, his liability for the company's obligations is distributed among the rest of the members proportionately to their contributions, unless otherwise provided by the company's constituent documents (Article 95.1). The additional liability company is a juristic person and its trade name must contain the words "additional liability"; the rules on the limited liability company are applied to the additional liability company (Article 95.2–3).

211 This form was known in the Soviet Union in the New Economic Policy period, and the norms on the additional liability company were included into the Civil Code of 1922.

Chapter 3
Tax Law

The shaping of the modern tax system in Russia started in the 1990s, along with the creation of the other legislation oriented toward the development of the country's market economy. The ambition to codify the whole body of the Russian law also extended to tax law rules. Their codification started with the adoption of the first part of Tax Code in 1998 (no 146-FZ of 31 July 1998)[1] containing general provisions and followed by the gradual adoption, until 2004, of the separate chapters of the second part of the Tax Code (no 117-FZ of 5 August 2000)[2] devoted to different taxes. Though codified, the Russian tax law[3] is still subject to changes, additions, and amendments.[4] Nonetheless, the present Russian tax law, developed using Western models, has at least succeeded in creating a taxation system purposed not merely for fiscal interests, but also for the regulation of social policy generally, as well as with regard to regional policies and local self-government, alongside a uniform treatment of enterprises vis-à-vis their tax affairs.[5] However, Russian tax law still has peculiarities.[6]

1 Sources of Tax Law

The constitutional basis of tax law regulation in Russia is expressed in the norms of the Constitution of the Russian Federation. According to Article 57 of the Constitution, each citizen is obliged to pay legally established taxes and charges, and laws establishing new taxes or worsening the position of taxpayers is not to have retroactive force. Article 71 of the Constitution also provides that federal taxes and charges are under the jurisdiction of the Russian Federation. Otherwise tax law regulation forms an independent part of the Russian legislation and its principal legal source is the Tax Code. According to its Article 1, Russian legislation on taxes and charges is comprised of the Tax Code and other federal laws on taxes and charges adopted in accordance therewith.

---

1 *Налоговый Кодекс Российской Федерации. Часть 1 от 31.07.1998 N 146-ФЗ*. See, for instance, http://base.garant.ru/10900200/1/#11111 (accessed 24 August 2010).

2 *Налоговый Кодекс Российской Федерации. Часть 2 от 05.08.2000 N 117-ФЗ*. See, for instance, http://base.garant.ru/10900200/20/#22222 (accessed 24 August 2010).

3 Essentially brief presentations on the subject are presented in V.F. Popondopulo (ed.), Коммерческое (предпринимательское) право, Том I [Commercial (Entrepreneurial) Law, Volume I] (2009): 455–69 and W.E. Butler, *Russian Law* (2009): 567–93. The most recent textbook on Russian tax law is Yu. A. Krokhina, Налоговое право [Tax Law] (2009).

4 The most recent substantial changes to the Tax Code were made by the Law no 229-FZ of 27 July 2010, and they are commented on in, for instance, http://www.buhcenter.net/blog/?p=169 [accessed 24 August 2010]. Changes have been made also by the Law no 242-FZ of 30 July 2010, which contains taxation arrangements concerning the Olympic Games in Sochi in 2014.

5 See Butler 2009: 572–3.

6 The reforms include, for instance, the imposition of tax control tasks on private banks in which taxpayers have accounts, as well as an excessive cultivation of formalistic definitions and rules (in particular, in procedural norms), which may be explained at least partly by the insufficiency of the administrative infrastructure in Russia.

The Tax Code, which consists of two parts, is divided into eleven divisions (I–X added with VIII^{1}). Divisions I–VII form the first or general part of the Code, while the rest comprises the special part devoted to different taxes. Furthermore, the Code is divided into chapters (1–30 added with 25^1, 25^2, 25^3, 26^1, 26^2, 26^3, and 26^4).

Division I (General Provisions) of the Tax Code contains the rules concerning legislation and other legal acts on taxes and charges (Chapter 1, Articles 1–11)[7] and the system of taxes and charges in Russia (Chapter 2, Articles 12–18). The rules on taxpayers and payers of charges and tax agents (Chapter 3, Articles 19–24)[8] and representation in tax law relations (Chapter 4, Articles 26–9) are contained in Division II, while Division III is devoted to the rules on tax, customs, and financial as well as internal affairs authorities and their officials, including the rules on their competence and liability (Chapter 5–6, Articles 30–37[9]).

Division IV is comprised of the general rules on the fulfillment of the obligation to pay taxes and the charges defining the objects of taxation (Chapter 7, Articles 38–43); the fulfillment of the duty to pay taxes and charges (Chapter 8, Articles 44–60), including its arising, change, and termination, the collection of taxes, charges, late-payment interest and penalties; tax assessment procedure, tax base, rates and benefits; tax period and deadlines for paying taxes and charges as well as the obligations of the banks on the execution of orders to remit taxes and charges. Division IV also includes the rules on changes in deadlines for payment of taxes and charges as well as late-payment interest and penalties (Chapter 9, Articles 61–8);[10] tax demands (Chapter 10, Articles 69–71)[11] and the means for securing the performance of obligations to pay taxes and charges (Chapter 11, Articles 72–7); and the offset and refund of overpaid or over-collected amounts (Chapter 12, Articles 78–9).

Division V of the (first part of the) Tax Code includes the rules on tax declarations and tax control (Chapters 13–14, Articles 80–105),[12] Division VI contains the rules on tax law violations and liability for committing them (Chapters 15–18, Articles 106–36),[13] and the rules on appeals against the acts of tax authorities and the actions (or inaction) of their officials are contained in Division VII (Chapters 19–20, Articles 137–42).

The second or special part of the Code contains specific norms regulating different taxes, including rules on taxpayers, objects, and determination of the base, period, rates, and the order of calculation of taxes (charges).[14] Division VIII concerns federal taxes and charges, including value-added tax (Chapter 21, Articles 143–77), excise taxes (Chapter 22, Articles 179–205), personal income tax (Chapter 23, Articles 207–33), uniform social tax (Chapter 24, Articles 235–45),[15] tax on the profits of organizations (Chapter 25, Articles 246–333), charges for the right to use objects of fauna and aquatic biological resources (Chapter 25^1, Articles 333^1–333^7), water tax (Chapter 25^2, Articles 333^8–333^{42}), and tax on the extraction of subsoil resources (Chapter 26, Articles

7 Added with Article 6^1.

8 Article 25 has been deleted.

9 Added with Article 34^2.

10 Added with Article 64^1.

11 Article 65 has been deleted.

12 Added with Articles 93^1, 100^1, 101^2, 101^3 an 101^4.

13 Added with Articles 119^1, 129^1, 129^2 and 135^1; Articles 117, 121, 124, 127, and 130 have been deleted.

14 The norms of the second part of the Tax Code have also been subject to many changes, additions, and amendments.

15 The uniform social tax has been replaced by separate payments to the state pension fund, the national health insurance system, and the national social security fund (compulsory insurance) according to the Law no 212-FZ of 24 July 2009.

334–45). The federal tax system in Russia also includes special tax regimes which are placed into Division VIII^1, and these include the single agricultural tax (Chapter 26^1, Articles 346^1–346^{10}), the simplified system of taxation (Chapter 26^2, Articles 346^{11}–$346^{25.1}$), the single tax on imputed revenue (Chapter 26^3, Articles 346^{26}–346^{33}), and production sharing agreements (Chapter 26^4, Articles 346^{34}–346^{42}).

The rules regulating regional taxes and charges (of the Federation subjects) are contained in Division X, and these comprise transport tax (Chapter 28, Articles 356–363^1), tax on gambling (Chapter 29, Articles 364–371), and tax on the property of organizations (Chapter 30, Articles 372–86^1). Division X of the Tax Code devoted to local taxes (of the local governments) contains only rules on the land tax (Chapter 31, Articles 387–98). However, the local tax system also includes the tax on the property of the physical persons, but this is regulated by the old Law on Personal Property Taxes.[16]

The legislation of the subjects of the Russian Federation on taxes and charges, which is also a part of the Russian legislation on taxes and charges, consists of their laws adopted in accordance with the Tax Code (Article 1.3). Normative legal acts of local self-government bodies on local taxes and charges are also adopted in accordance with the Tax Code (Article 1.4). Thus, the subjects of the Russian Federation and local self-government bodies may introduce and repeal taxes, but only in accordance with the legislation of the Russian Federation. They may also grant greater tax privileges, though only within the amounts of taxes to be credited to their budgets. Thus, not only federal, but also regional and local taxes not provided for by the Tax Code may not be established, and any taxes that are established may be repealed only by the Tax Code.[17]

Legal regulation of taxation in Russia is undertaken by the Government of the Federation, and the federal executive bodies which are empowered with the regulative functions in the domain of taxes, charges, and customs; regional and local executive bodies where provided for by tax legislation may issue normative acts on taxation, though without changing or amending legislation on taxes and charges.[18] However, the federal tax authority empowered with the control and supervisory functions in the domain of taxes and charges and its territorial bodies have no right to enact normative acts concerning taxes and charges (Tax Code, Article 4).

The power to issue normative acts on taxation is granted to the Ministry of Finances of the Russian Federation.[19] In order to be effective, such a normative act must correspond to the following requirements. It must:

- be issued by the proper authority and in the proper order;
- not abolish or restrict the rights of taxpayers and other tax law subjects nor the competence of tax authorities;
- not introduce changes in the content of obligations of tax law subjects established by the Tax Code;
- not prohibit actions of taxpayers and other tax law subjects as well as tax authorities and their officials allowed or imposed by the Tax Code, and

16 No 2003-1 of 9 December 1991 as amended 5 April 2009.

17 Butler 2009: 573 and 592.

18 According to the Tax Code (Article 34^2), the Ministry of Finances of the Russian Federation, and, in the case of the regional or local taxies, the regional or local financial authorities, are obliged to give to taxpayers and tax agents written explanations concerning the application of tax legislation within two months from the date of receiving a request.

19 Customs authorities are also not empowered to issue normative acts regulating taxes and charges.

- not allow actions prohibited by the Tax Code as well as
- not change the grounds, conditions, and order for actions of the participants in tax law relations and
- not change the content of concepts and terms defined in the Tax Code or use them on the basis of other meanings.

A normative act on taxation may not otherwise contradict the general principles and/or literal meaning of the Tax Code rules (Article 6). In the case of noncompliance with any of these requirements, a normative act may be recognized in arbitrazh proceedings[20] as invalid.[21]

International law norms play an important role in the Russian tax law. It is expressly established in the Tax Code (Article 7, following Article 15 of the Constitution) that if an international treaty of the Russian Federation contains rules on taxes and charges which differ from the provisions of the Tax Code, the rules of the international treaty are to apply. The Russian Federation has assumed obligations under tax treaties in force with the former Soviet Union, and a part of these has remained in force. In particular, many double tax treaties of the former Soviet Union are still valid under Russian law, whereas others have been replaced by treaties entered into by Russia.[22]

The subject of tax law regulation is conjoined with the civil law and concerns property relations. However, tax law relations, like other relations based on authoritative subordination of the participants, are excluded, in accordance with the Civil Code (Article 2), from the scope of application of civil law regulation, unless otherwise provided by the law. Thus, tax law norms are prioritized over civil law norms. The Supreme Court and the Supreme Arbitrazh Court stated that civil legislation is applicable to tax law relations only if it is provided for by the law.[23] The civil law rules which are applied to tax law relations include provisions of the Civil Code on the order of priority for debiting funds from an account (Article 855), representation (Articles 182–9), and securities for performance of obligations (Articles 329–79). Moreover, the Tax Code includes many references to civil law in its basic terms and concepts.[24]

2 General Provisions of the Tax Code

Scope of Application

The scope of application of the Tax Code is determined in its Article 2. According to it Russian legislation on taxes and charges regulates public law relations on the establishment, introduction, and collection of taxes and charges in the Russian Federation, and also the relations arising during

20 See, for instance, Decree of the Presidium of the Supreme Arbitrazh Court No 13322/04 of 19 September 2006. Вестник Высшего Арбитражного Суда Российской Федерации [Herald of the Supreme Arbitrazh Court of the Russian Federation] 11 (2006).

21 A demand on recognition of a normative act of the federal executive body shall be filed directly with the Supreme Arbitrazh Court. See Хозяйство и право [Economics and Law] 2 (2008): 125.

22 For more on this subject, see, for instance, Butler 2009: 592–3.

23 Joint decrees of the Plenums of the Supreme Court and Supreme Arbitrazh Court no 6/8 of 1 July 1996. Вестник Высшего Арбитражного Суда Российской Федерации [Herald of the Supreme Arbitrazh Court of the Russian Federation] 9 (1996).

24 For more on this subject, see Krokhina 2009: 53–6.

the exercise of tax control, appeals against the acts of tax bodies, the actions or inaction of their officials, and the imposition of sanctions for tax violations.[25]

The Tax Code also contains rules on the application in time of its norms (Article 5).[26] Federal laws, regional legislative acts, and local normative acts establishing new taxes and/or charges are not to take effect until 1 January of the year following the year of their adoption, but not earlier than one month from the day of their official publication. Furthermore, legislative acts on taxes and charges that worsen the position of taxpayers and other persons participating in tax law relations do not have a retroactive effect and are only applied to relations arising after their entry into force. However, legislative acts abolishing or mitigating tax law sanctions, or providing additional guarantees for the protection of the rights of taxpayers and payers of charges or tax agents and their representatives, are retroactive. Retroactivity may also be provided for legislative acts that abolish taxes or reduce tax rates, eliminate the obligations of taxpayers, payers of charges, tax agents, and their representatives, or otherwise improve their position. It is also possible for the legal act improving the position of taxpayers to enter into force at the date of its publication, if so provided (Article 5.1).

Basic Principles

The basic principles of legislation on taxes and charges are explicitly enforced in Article 3 of the Tax Code. According to them:

- each person shall pay legally established taxes and charges;
- tax legislation must be based on recognition of the universality and equality of taxation and, when establishing taxes, the ability of the taxpayer to pay the tax must be taken into account;
- taxes and charges may not be discriminatory or applied differently depending on political, ideological, ethnic, confessional, or other differences among taxpayers;
- the establishment of differential tax or charge rates and the granting of tax benefits which depend on the form of ownership, citizenship, or origin of capital are not allowed;
- taxes and charges must have an economic basis and may not be arbitrary, and they must not prevent citizens from exercising their constitutional rights
- the establishment of taxes and charges violating the single economic area of the Russian Federation and, in particular, restricting the free movement, either directly or indirectly, of goods, works, services, or financial assets within the Russian Federation, and other restrictions or hindrances on economic activity prohibited by the law of physical persons and organizations, are not allowed;
- no one may be charged with an obligation to pay taxes and charges or other payments which have characteristics of taxes as defined by the Tax Code but are not established by the Tax Code, or are imposed in a way which is different from the one provided by it;
- in establishing taxes, all the elements of taxation must be defined, as stated above, and legislative acts on taxes and charges must be formulated in such a way as to enable each person to know exactly which taxes or charges are to paid, when and in which procedure, and

---

25 The legislation on taxes and charges is applicable to customs payments though only in those cases provided for by the Tax Code (Article 2.3).

26 The rules must also be applied to the normative acts of the federal, regional, and local executive bodies (Article 5.5).

- all ineradicable doubts, contradictions, and ambiguities of the tax legislation are be interpreted in the favor of taxpayers.

3 The Taxation System

A Three-level Tax System

Russia has, as became evident above, a three-level tax system—federal taxes, taxes of the Federation subjects or regional taxes, and local taxes (of the local governments)—and this division is correspondingly reflected in the structure of the tax legislation.

According to the Tax Code (Article 12.1), federal taxes (and charges) are paid to the federal budget and recovered from the entire territory of the Russian Federation, unless otherwise provided for by the Tax Code. The federal taxes are:

- value-added tax;
- excises on goods;
- tax on the income of the physical persons;
- tax on the profits of organizations;
- tax on the extraction of subsoil resources;
- water tax;
- charges for the right to use objects of fauna and aquatic biological resources, and
- state duty (Article 13).

Regional taxes comprise those established by the Tax Code and the laws of the subjects of the Russian Federation, and are subject to obligatory payment in the territories of the respective subjects of the Russian Federation, unless otherwise provided for by the rules of the Tax Code concerning special tax regimes (Article 12.3). Regional taxes come into force and end in accordance with the Tax Code and the laws of the subjects of the Russian Federation. In establishing regional taxes, the tax rates as well as the procedure and the terms of payment of the tax, if they are not established by the Tax Code, must be determined. The legislative bodies of the subjects of the Federation may also establish by their tax laws tax privileges and the grounds and the order of their application within their competence established by the Tax Code. The regional taxes are:

- tax on the property of organizations;
- tax on gambling businesses, and
- transport tax (Article 14).

Local taxes are also established by the Tax Code alongside the normative acts of the representative bodies of local self-government and are subject to obligatory payment in the territories of the respective municipal entities, unless otherwise provided for by the rules of the Tax Code concerning special tax regimes (Article 12.4). Similarly to regional taxes, local taxes come into force and end in accordance with the Tax Code and the normative acts of the representative bodies of local self-government. However, local taxes in the cities of federal importance—Moscow and St Petersburg—are established and come into force under the laws of these subjects of the Federation. Local taxes are:

- land tax and
- tax on the property of physical persons (Article 15).

Federal, regional, and local taxes not provided for by the Tax Code may not be established (Article 12.6), and taxes that are established may be repealed only by the Tax Code (Article 12.5).[27]

Special tax regimes may be established in Russia, according to the Tax Code (Articles 12.7 and 18), by the Tax Code and are applied in the cases and order established by the Code and other tax legislative acts. Special tax regimes may provide new federal taxes, the specific order of determination of the taxation elements or reliefs from individual federal, regional, and local taxes. Special tax regimes are:

- the taxation system for agricultural producers (the single agricultural tax);
- the simplified system of taxation;
- the single tax on imputed revenue, and
- the taxation system concerning the execution of production sharing agreements (Article 18).

Main Taxes on Entrepreneurial Activity

Value-added tax[28] Value-added tax (VAT) is generally defined as a form of recovery to the budget of a part of the added value created at any stage of production and calculated as the difference between the value of the realized goods, works, and services and the value of the material expenses charged to the production and circulation costs. Value-added tax is an indirect tax added to the price of a good.

According to the Tax Code (Article 143), taxpayers of value-added tax are organizations, individual entrepreneurs, and persons recognized as taxpayers of the value-added tax in connection with the transfer of goods across the customs border of Russia as defined according to the Customs Code.

Under the Tax Code (Article 146) the objects of value-added taxation are:

- the realization of goods (works, services) on the territory of the Russian Federation, including the sale of the subjects of a pledge and the transfer of goods (results of performed works, rendered services) under an agreement on compensation for termination of contract[29] or a novation, as well as the transfer of property rights;
- the transfer of goods (performance of works, provision of services) on the territory of the Russian Federation for own purposes, in respect of which expenses are not accepted for offset (in particular, as depreciation deductions) in calculation of the tax on profit of organizations;
- the performance of construction and erection works for own consumption, and
- the importation of goods into the customs territory of the Russian Federation.[30]

According to the Tax Code (Article 163) the value-added tax period is a quarter. The general tax rate is 18 percent and the Tax Code (Article 164) also provides for a 0 percent tax rate, for instance,

27 Popondopulo 1 2009: 469 and Butler 2009: 592.

28 For more on this subject, see Krokhina 2009: 355–69.

29 Article 409 of the Civil Code provides that, by agreement, the contracting parties may terminate an obligation by the presentation, instead of performance, of the termination compensation payment.

30 The Tax Code (Articles 142.2 and 149) also contains a list of operations which are excluded in addition to the general exclusion list (Article 39.3) from the objects of value-add taxation.

on the sale of exported goods and a 10 percent tax rate on the sale, for instance, of food products and goods for social purposes.

Profits tax[31] According to Article 246 of the Tax Code, the taxpayers of tax on profit of organizations, or profits tax, which is a direct tax, are Russian organizations[32] and foreign organizations conducting their activity through permanent establishment. and/or receiving profits from sources, in Russia. As the object of taxation, profit is generally understood as the difference between turnover and expenses. In respect of Russian organizations, profit comprehends received incomes which are reduced by the amount of expenses as defined in the Tax Code (Article 247). As to foreign organizations conducting activity through their permanent establishment, branch, representative office, agency, or another separate subdivision or place of regular activity in Russia, profit comprehends incomes received through the permanent establishment which are reduced by the amount of expenses as defined in the Tax Code. The profit of other foreign organizations is understood, in turn, as incomes received from sources in Russia.[33]

The profit tax base is the monetary expression of the profit defined in accordance with the rules of the Tax Code (Articles 247 and 274). The general profit tax rate is 20 percent, of which 2 percent is entered into the federal budget and 18 percent into the local budget. The local tax rate may be reduced for individual categories of taxpayers by the laws of the subjects of the Federation, though only up to 13.5 percent (Article 284).[34] [35]

Tax on the property of organizations[36] The tax on the property of organizations, or corporate property tax or assets tax, is a regional tax, and its imposition is regulated by the legislation of the relevant subject of the Federation. According to Article 373 of the Tax Code, its taxpayers are Russian organizations and foreign organizations conducting their activity through permanent establishment and/or having in their ownership immovable property in Russia. The objects of corporate property taxation are movable and/or immovable fixed assets owned by the taxpayer in Russia. Land and other natural resources as well as federal property used for the needs of national defense, security, and law and order are not deemed objects of property taxation (Article 374).

The property tax base is defined as the annual value of the property recognized as the object of taxation, and its calculation is based on the depreciated book value of the assets (Article 375). The maximum size of the assets tax rate may not exceed 2.2 percent, and the ultimate size of the assets tax rate is determined by the regional legislative body (Article 380).

---

31 For more on this subject, see Krokhina 2009: 395–400. The presentation is not, however, updated.

32 Russian juristic persons.

33 The Tax Code contains detailed rules on defining those incomes to be included and excluded in defining the tax base (Article 251) expenses (Articles 252–5 and 260–70) as well as depreciation of assets (Articles 256–9).

34 It may be less in the free economic zones. Furthermore, dividends received by Russian organizations are taxed at the rate of 9 and in a certain cases even 0 percent (Article 284.3).

35 Foreign organizations who do not have a permanent establishment in Russia are also subjects to a general profits tax rate of 20 percent, but a 15 percent tax rate applies where a foreign organization has profits in the form of dividends from a Russian organization, and a 10 percent tax rate where the income derives from the use, maintenance, and lease of ship, craft, planes, and other means of transport in international carriage (Article 284).

36 For more on this subject, see Krokhina 2009: 428–30.

Personal income tax[37] The taxpayers of personal income tax, which is a direct tax, are, according to Article 207 of the Tax Code, physical persons,[38] residents of the Russian Federation,[39] and nonresidents of the Russian Federation who receive income from sources in Russia. The objects of personal income taxation are, for the tax residents of Russia, any income received from sources in Russia and abroad, and for nonresidents only income received from sources in Russia (Article 209). A company paying wages and salaries must withhold the income tax and transfer it to the tax authorities; tax agents are also obliged to withhold the tax from amounts paid to taxpayers and remit such taxes to the budget (Article 226). The tax is generally calculated at a flat rate of 13 percent, but incomes of residents in the form of dividends are taxed at the rate of 9 percent (Article 224).[40] If a person receiving income spends less than 183 days in Russia within any 12-month period (and does not fall into the category of having tax residence in Russia) the tax rate is 30 percent, while incomes of nonresidents in the form of dividends are taxed at the rate of 15 percent (Article 224.3).

Tax Privileges

Tax privileges are also recognized in Russian tax law. Tax privileges are, according to the Tax Code (Article 56), benefits which are established by the tax legislation and granted to certain categories of taxpayers. They may concern the right not to pay a tax or to pay a smaller amount of it as compared with other taxpayers. A tax privilege may also occur as an exemption of certain objects from taxation.[41] Privileges are granted and abolished in respect of federal taxes by the Tax Code, in respect of regional taxes by the Tax Code and tax laws of the subjects of the Federation, and in respect of local taxes by the Tax Code and normative acts of municipal bodies.[42] The Tax Code prohibits the granting of tax privileges of an individual character. A taxpayer may refuse to use a privilege, or stop using it for one or more tax periods, unless otherwise provided for by the Tax Code.

A significant tax privilege is the investment tax credit, which is established by the Tax Code (Article 67) for organizations exercising innovative activities. It provides a change of terms in tax payment under which the organization is granted the opportunity during a certain term and to a certain limit to reduce its tax payments with subsequent gradual payment of the sum of the credit and interest. Investment tax credits may be granted with respect to profit tax and regional and local taxes (Article 66).

4 Tax Administration Authorities

The system of taxation in Russia is administered principally by two agencies—the Federal Tax Service and internal affairs bodies[43]—and their duties and rights as well as liabilities are defined in the Tax Code.

37 For more on this subject, see Krokhina 2009: 379–88.

38 Including individual entrepreneurs.

39 A physical person is recognized as a tax resident of the Russian Federation if he/she resides on the territory of the Russian Federation for not less than 183 days within any 12-month period.

40 Certain incomes—for instance, prizes and interest income on bank deposits—are taxed at the rate of 35 percent.

41 Krokhina 2009: 35.

42 In Moscow and St Petersburg by the laws of these subjects of the Federation.

43 Butler 2009: 586.

Tax Authorities

According to the Tax Code (Article 30), the Federal Tax Service[44] is a unified centralized system of control over compliance with legislation on taxes and charges and over the correctness, completeness, and timeliness of payment (transfer) into the budget system of the Russian Federation of taxes and charges and other obligatory payments. The system includes the Federal Tax Service authorized to control and supervise the domain of taxes and charges as well as its territorial bodies.[45] The Tax Code expressly requires that the tax authorities must act within their competence and in accordance with the legislation of the Russian Federation (Article 30.3), and that they must discharge their functions and cooperate with the executive bodies of the Federation and the subjects of the Federation and local self-governmental bodies as well as state non-budget funds through the exercise of their authority as established by the Tax Code and other federal normative acts (Article 30.4).[46]

The obligations of tax authorities are defined in Article 32 of the Tax Code. They are obliged to:

- control the observance of tax legislation;
- keep records of both organizations and physical persons following established procedures;
- inform (also in writing) taxpayers and tax agents free of charge on tax issues;
- adopt decisions on refunding excessive amounts of tax, interest, and fines paid or collected;
- keep tax secrets;
- forward to the taxpayer or tax agent copies of the tax audit acts and decisions of a tax body as well as, where provided for by the Tax Code, the tax notice and the demand to pay a tax;
- give at the request of a taxpayer or tax agent a statement on the balance of tax settlements, and
- conduct a reconciliation of tax settlements with the taxpayer.

The tax authorities are also charged with other duties established by the law (Article 32.2). Furthermore, where taxpayer or tax agent has not paid the arrears within two months of the expiry of the term, and its amount gives reason to suspect a criminal violation of tax legislation, the tax authority is obliged within ten days to submit the materials to the internal affairs body to decide on whether a criminal case should be initiated.

The Tax Code also contains requirements concerning tax officials. They must act in strict compliance with the law, treat duly and courteously taxpayers, their representatives, and other participants in tax relations, and respect their honor and dignity (Article 33).

The rights of tax authorities are also defined in the Tax Code (Article 31). They are empowered to:

- demand from a taxpayer or a tax agent documents in the forms or electronic formats established by state bodies and local self-government bodies necessary for the calculation and payment of taxes and documents confirming the correctness and timeliness of payment;

44 *Федеральная налоговая служба (ФНС).*

45 For more on this subject, see Krokhina 2009: 135–52.

46 In addition to its duties under the Tax Code, the Federal Tax Service is the designated empowered federal executive body carrying out the state registration of juristic persons and individual entrepreneurs; such registration is the concern of the lowest-level tax authority. Registration is a duty of every taxpayer, without which banks will not open accounts. The Federal Tax Service also represents the Russian Federation in bankruptcy cases with regard to obligatory payments and other monetary demands of the Russian Federation; such cases may concern taxpayers but also juristic persons and individual entrepreneurs, among others. Butler 2009: 587.

- carry out tax inspections in the order established by the Tax Code and, if necessary, to seize documents if there are sufficient grounds to suspect that these documents will be destroyed, concealed, changed, or replaced;
- summon in writing taxpayers or tax agents to tax bodies to give explanations on issues relating to the execution of the legislation on taxes and charges;
- suspend transactions on the bank accounts of taxpayers and tax agents and to impose an arrest on the property of taxpayers and tax agents in the order established by the Tax Code;
- examine premises and territories used by taxpayers for deriving revenues or connected with the maintenance of the objects of taxation, regardless of their location, and to execute an inventory of the property belonging to taxpayers;[47]
- determine the amounts of taxes to be paid by taxpayers to the budget calculated on the basis of available information on the taxpayer, and also on the basis of the data on other similar taxpayers, where the taxpayer has refused to allow tax officials to examine his premises and territories, or has failed to submit the documents necessary for the calculation of taxes for more than two months, or in the absence of recordkeeping of revenues and expenses and of the objects of taxation, or where records are in contravention of the established order thereby making the computation of tax impossible;
- demand that taxpayers, tax agents, and their representatives remedy any revealed tax law violations and control the fulfillment of such demands;
- recover tax and charge arrears, as well as penalties, in the order established by the Tax Code;
- demand from banks documents confirming the proper execution of tax payment orders;
- attract specialists, experts, and interpreters for tax control and summon witnesses;
- apply for the cancellation or suspension of licenses for the practicing of activities granted to juristic and physical persons, and
- bring actions in courts of general jurisdiction or in arbitrazh courts.

The tax authorities also have rights of action for the:

- recovery of tax arrears, penalties, and sanctions for tax law violations;
- compensation of damages caused to the state or municipal unity by banks violating the execution of tax payment orders, and
- the rescission of investment tax credit agreements,

as well as in other cases provided for by the Tax Code (Article 31.1.14). The tax authorities may also exercise other rights as provided for by the Tax Code (Article 31.2).[48]

Other Authorities

According to the Tax Code Article 34, the customs authorities and their officials also use the rights and perform the duties of tax authorities in collecting taxes and charges in respect of goods transferred through the customs border.

---

47 In the order established by the Ministry of Finances of the Russian Federation.

48 According to Article 32 of the Tax Code, the superior tax authorities have the right to abolish or change the decisions of inferior bodies that are contradictory to the law.

Furthermore, internal affairs authorities participate in tax administration. According to Article 36 of the Tax Code, internal affairs bodies (the Federal Service for Economic and Tax Crimes[49]), at the request of tax bodies, are to participate, jointly with tax bodies, in on-site tax inspections held by tax bodies.[50] However, in the event of detecting circumstances requiring the commitment of actions attributed by the Tax Code to the authority of tax bodies, internal affairs bodies are obliged within ten days to submit materials to an appropriate tax body for its decision.[51]

Commercial (private) banks in Russia are, in fact, participants in tax relations regulated by the tax legislation, and they have a special status. Banks are not only taxpayers[52] but, in fact, also the third line of tax control in their capacity as the organizations which open and administer bank accounts.[53] According to the Tax Code (Article 86), they must submit the account and other information concerning clients to the tax authorities. Furthermore, banks also deposit tax payments into the account of the Treasury in a timely manner and are prohibited from delaying payment orders issued by taxpayers in favor of the budget or using deposits for this purpose as credit resources. They also execute tax payment demands (Article 60).[54] In some instances banks act as tax agents and accordingly bear the legal rights and duties imposed by the Tax Code in these instances.[55]

5 Duties and Rights of Taxpayers

The rights and duties of taxpayers are expressly defined in the Tax Code by using extensive enumerations. Taxpayers are required under the Tax Code (Article 23.1) to:

- pay legally-established taxes;
- register with tax authorities if the Tax Code so requires;
- keep records of their revenues and expenses and objects of taxation if tax legislation so requires;
- submit to the tax authorities a tax declaration or calculation if it is required by the law;
- submit, unless exempted, bookkeeping records prepared under Russian bookkeeping legislation;
- submit the documents necessary in order to calculate and pay taxes;
- fulfill the legal demands of a tax authority to eliminate violations of tax legislation and not obstruct tax authorities in the performance of their charges;

---

49 *Федеральная служба по экономическим и налоговым преступлениям (ФСЭНП).*

50 For more on this subject, see Krokhina 2009: 152–63.

51 The Tax Code (Article 34²) also contains provisions on the duties of financial authorities. The Ministry of Finances of the Russian Federation, and, in the case of regional or local taxies, the regional or local financial authorities are obliged to give to taxpayers and tax agents written explanations concerning the application of tax legislation within two months from the date of receiving a request.

52 On the taxation of banks and other credit organizations, see Krokhina 2009: 451–5.

53 Enterprises in Russia keep their monetary assets in bank accounts in commercial banks, and their payments are effected, as a rule, by non-cash settlements. A bank account of an organization or individual entrepreneur may be opened only after registration with the tax authorities. Registration is a duty of every taxpayer, without which banks will not open accounts (Article 86.1).

54 Banks execute taxation transactions free of charge (Article 60.2).

55 Butler 2009: 590–91 and Krokhina 2009: 274.

- keep bookkeeping records and other documents necessary for the calculation and payment of taxes for a period of four years, and
- bear other charges established by the tax legislation.

In addition to these general duties, organizations and individual entrepreneurs are required to give notice personally or through a representative, by post or electronically, to their local tax authorities about:

- the opening or closing of an account within seven days;
- participation in Russian and foreign organizations within one month of commencement of such participation;
- all separate subdivisions (except representations and branches) established in Russia within one month of their establishment, and
- reorganization or liquidation within three days of the adoption of such a decision (Article 23.2).

The rights of taxpayers, in turn, include, according to Article 21 of the Tax Code, the right to:

- receive from the tax authorities at the place of registration information free of charge (including in written form) on current taxes and charges, legislation on them, the procedure for calculating and paying taxes, the rights and duties of taxpayers, on the powers of the tax authorities and their officials, the tax declaration and accounting form, and explanations on their fulfillment;
- obtain written explanations concerning the application of tax legislation to them from the Ministry of Finances of the Russian Federation, and, in case of regional or local taxies, from the regional or local financial authorities;
- use tax privileges and exemptions;
- receive a deferral, pay in installments, or benefit from an investment tax credit as provided by the Tax Code;[56]
- set off or receive a refund of taxes, late-payment interest, and penalties paid in excess;[57]
- request a reconciliation of tax settlements;
- represent their interests in tax legal relations in person or act through a representative;
- submit explanations to the tax authorities and their officials on the calculation and payment of taxes;
- be present during a tax audit on site;
- receive copies of tax audit acts and decisions of the tax authorities as well as tax notices and tax payment demands;
- require that tax officials comply in their actions with tax legislation;
- appeal against acts of the tax authorities and actions (or inaction) of their officials;
- demand that tax records be kept secret;
- receive full compensation for losses caused by unlawful decisions of the tax authorities or unlawful actions (or inaction) of their officials, and

56 Thus, tax law regulation includes a dispositive element. A taxpayer has the right to exercise his own tax policy and conclude agreements with tax authorities on investment tax credit as well as to set off his tax law obligations. See Krokhina 2009: 45.

57 Thus, taxpayers have the right to plan and minimize taxes, which actions may not be subject to tax liability according to the Ruling of the Constitution Court No 9-P of 27 May 2003. See, for instance, http://base.consultant.ru/cons/cgi/online.cgi?req=doc;base=LAW;n=42440 (accessed 26 November 2009).

- take part in the process of the consideration of the materials of a tax audit and other acts of the tax authorities as provided for in the Tax Code,

as well as other rights established by the Tax Code and other tax legislation (Article 21.2).

6 Duties and Rights of Tax Agents

Tax agents who are persons obliged under the Tax Code to calculate, withhold from the taxpayer, and remit taxes to the budget system of Russia have the same rights as taxpayers, unless otherwise provided by the Tax Code (Article 24). The duties of tax agents include the requirements to:

- calculate, withhold from amounts paid to taxpayers, and remit taxes to the budget system duly;
- notify the tax authority, in writing, within one month of the impossibility of withholding tax from the taxpayer and inform the tax authority at their place of registration of the amount of arrears;
- keep records of income paid to taxpayers and taxes withheld and remitted to the budgets, including separate records for each taxpayer personally;
- submit to the tax authority at the place of registration documents required to control the correctness of calculation, withholding, and remittance of taxes, and
- keep documents necessary for the calculation, withholding, and remittance of taxes for a period of four years.

7 Fulfillment of Tax Obligations[58]

According to Article 44 of the Tax Code, the grounds for the arising, change, and termination of the obligation to pay taxes (and charges) in Russia are to be established by the Tax Code or other tax legislative act. The obligation to pay a concrete tax is imposed on a taxpayer with the emergence of grounds requiring the payment and usually terminates from the moment the tax is paid. The duty to pay the tax ceases upon the death of the taxpayer or its liquidation, provided that the organization has settled all accounts with the budget system of Russia, or when circumstances arise which the tax legislation links with the termination of the obligation to pay the tax (Article 44.2).

The tax payment duty must be fulfilled by the taxpayer, under the Tax Code (Article 45), unprompted, unless otherwise provided for by the tax legislation. In general, taxes must be paid as lump sum payments (Article 58), and in certain cases preliminary tax payments may be provided. The obligation must be fulfilled within the time limits established by the tax legislation, and a premature performance of the tax duty is allowed. In the event of failure to pay properly a tax, the obligation is to be executed under compulsory proceeding.

A tax obligation is considered fulfilled by the taxpayer, under Article 45.3 of the Tax Code, from the moment:

58 For more on this subject, see Krokhina 2009: 167–75.

- an order to pay the tax is presented to the bank, provided that the monetary balance of the taxpayer's account is sufficient to make the payment; or
- the transfer of the tax payment into the budget is entered into the personal tax account; or
- the tax payment is deposited by a physical person into a bank or with a receiving cashier of a local government authority or a post office for transaction to the budget;

as well as from the day:

- the tax authority has passed a decision on the offset of excessively paid or excessively recovered tax amounts, including late-payment interest and penalties; or
- the tax agent has withheld the tax amount (at source).

In compulsory proceedings, the failed tax obligation will be executed, according to the Tax Code (Article 46), by recovery of the arrears from the bank account of the taxpayer or tax agent. If the tax is due from an organization or individual entrepreneur or tax agent, the arrears will be recovered in an uncontested proceeding[59] under which the tax authority shall send a unilateral decision to the credit organization or bank in which the taxpayer has an account requiring the bank to withdraw the amount due from the accounts of the juristic person and to credit those amounts to the budgets of Russia. If the taxpayer has not sufficient funds to pay arrears, the tax authority has the right to recover them from the other property of the taxpayer. Such a decision must be adopted within one year from the expiration of the tax duty; after it, arrears may be claimed in a court, however, within two years from the expiration of the tax duty (Article 47).

Furthermore, the Tax Code (Article 45.2) establishes that recovery of the arrears by judicial proceeding is to concern:

- the organization for which a personal account is opened, or
- the organization or individual entrepreneur, if its or his obligation is based on a change made by the tax authority in the juridical qualification of the transaction[60] concluded by the taxpayer or of the status and nature of the activities of the taxpayer, and
- the principal company, where the arrears of its dependent or subsidiary company, as defined in the Civil Code (Articles 105 and 106), are overdue for more than three months and where receipts for realized goods (works or services) of the dependent or subsidiary company are entered into the accounts of the principal company, and vice versa.

---

59 However, if the tax is due from physical person, only a judicial proceeding is possible (Articles 45 and 48).

60 According to the Decree of Plenum of the Supreme Arbitrazh Court no 53 of 12 October 2006, in the event of a change in the juridical qualification of the transaction, it must be noted that transactions contradictory to the law (Article 168 of the Civil Code) as well as mock and sham transactions (Article 170 of the Civil Code) are under Article 166 of the Civil Code void per se or independently of their recognition as void by the court. Вестник Высшего Арбитражного Суда Российской Федерации [Herald of the Supreme Arbitrazh Court of the Russian Federation] 12 (2006). On the other hand, the Plenum of the Supreme Arbitrazh Court stated in its Decree No 22 on 10 April 2008 that the rules of Article 169 of the Civil Code nullifying transactions concluded for a purpose contrary to the fundamental principles of public order and morality is not applicable to tax relations. This ruling is, however, criticized as diminishing public interests. See A. Kurbatov, О применении статьи 169 Гражданского кодекса Российской Федерации в налоговых отношениях [On the Application of Article 169 of the Civil Code of the Russian Federation to Tax Relations], Хозяйство и право [Economics and Law] 7 (2008): 112.

8 Securing Measures[61]

Obligations to pay taxes (or charges) may be secured, according to Article 72 of the Tax Code, by pledge of property, suretyship, late-payment interest, suspension of bank account operations, and imposition of arrest on property of the taxpayer. A pledge requires the conclusion of a contract of pledge between the tax authority and the pledgor, who may be not only the taxpayer himself but also a third person (Article 73.2). If the obligation is not performed, the pledged property is levied against in the procedure provided by the Civil Code unless otherwise provided for in the rules of the Tax Code on pledges (Article 73.3). Property pledged under an agreement between the tax authority and pledgor may not be the subject of pledge under another agreement (Article 73.4). Suretyship and late-payment interest under the Tax Code (Articles 74 and 75) are analogous means of securing performance known to the Civil Code (Articles 330 and 361). Suspension of bank account operations, in turn, is taken to mean that no withdrawals are to be made from the account concerned, although deposits will be accepted.[62]

As to arrest of property, this requires the sanction of a procurator and may be resorted to only when there are sufficient grounds to suppose that the taxpayer would take measures to flee or to conceal his property (Article 77). All property of a taxpayer may be subject to arrest; however, only property sufficient to cover the tax liability may be arrested.

9 Tax Control[63]

At registration, each taxpayer is assigned a taxpayer identification number applicable throughout the whole territory of the Russian Federation and with respect to all taxes and charges, including those due in connection with the movement of goods across the customs border of the Russian Federation. The taxpayer identification number must be indicated by the tax authority in all notifications addressed to the taxpayer as well as by the taxpayer on documents submitted to tax authorities (Article 84).

Information about the taxpayer is considered, according to the Tax Code (Article 102), secret except information:

- disclosed by the taxpayer at his own discretion or with his consent;
- on the taxpayer identification number;
- on violations of tax legislation and sanctions for these violations;
- provided to foreign law and order authorities in accordance with international treaties (agreements), and
- provided to the election commission in accordance with the election laws.

Each taxpayer shall file under Article 80 of the Tax Code a tax declaration for every tax due from him, unless otherwise provided for by the tax legislation. This declaration is a written or electronic statement of the taxpayer concerning objects of taxation, generated incomes, and incurred expenses, sources of income, tax privileges, the calculated amount of tax, and/or other data relating to the calculation and payment of tax. The tax declaration must be filed with the tax body at the location of registration of the taxpayer, and it is the basis for tax inspection.

61 For more on this subject, see Krokhina 2009: 175–81.

62 Butler 2009: 579–80.

63 For more on this subject, see Krokhina 2009: 192–202.

The rules on tax inspections are provided in Article 87 of the Tax Code. The tax authorities carry out cameral (or documentary) and on-site (or field) tax inspections of taxpayers.

A cameral tax inspection (audit) is conducted in the office of the tax authority on the base of tax declarations[64] and other documents filed by the taxpayer and documents concerning the activity of the taxpayer which the tax authority has in its possession. It must be conducted within three months of the taxpayer filing a tax declaration. The object of a cameral tax inspection is deemed to be the correctness of the tax declaration and its correspondence with the bookkeeping data.[65] In cases of mistakes or misstatements, the tax authority will demand the taxpayer to amend the tax declaration or provide clarifications within five days. A taxpayer may also submit additional documents to support his clarifications. Where the tax authority establishes, after consideration of presented explanations and documents by a taxpayer, or in the absence of such explanations, that a tax offence or of other violation of the tax legislation has been committed, officials of the tax authority are obliged to draw up a tax inspection report (Article 88).

An on-site tax inspection (audit) must be conducted according to Article 89 of the Tax Code at the location of the taxpayer by the decision of the head of the tax authority or his deputy. However, if a taxpayer has no available premises for conducting an on-site tax inspection, the on-site tax inspection may be conducted at the location of the tax authority. The object of an on-site tax inspection is deemed to be the correctness and timeliness of tax payments. Within the framework of an on-site tax inspection may be checked, unless otherwise provided, the period not exceeding three calendar years preceding the year when a decision was rendered to conduct the on-site tax inspection. According to the Decree of the Presidium of the Supreme Arbitrazh Court,[66] the on-site tax inspection may not concern the fulfillment of duties imposed on banks by the Tax Code:

- to withdraw arrears from the accounts of a taxpayer (Article 46);
- to deposit tax payments (Article 60);
- to suspend bank account operations (Article 76), or
- to provide account and other information,

or the duties connected with the opening of an account for a taxpayer (Article 86).

The tax authorities are not entitled to conduct two or more on-site tax inspections in respect of the same taxes for the same period. Moreover, the tax authorities are not entitled to conduct in respect of one taxpayer more than two on-site tax inspections within a calendar year, except by the decision of the head of the Federal Tax Service (Article 89.5).

The restrictions on the amount of on-site tax inspections are not, however, applicable to the repeated on-site tax inspection,[67] which may be conducted regardless of the time of conducting the previous tax inspection in respect of the same taxes and for the same period. Such an inspection may be conducted by the tax authority which has previously conducted a tax inspection by the decision of its head (or his deputy), if a taxpayer has submitted a specified tax declaration in which a tax amount is lower than previously declared (Article 89.10). If in the repeated tax inspection,

---

64 A cameral tax inspection is conducted only if a tax declaration concerning the tax at issue has been submitted to the tax authorities according to the Decree of the Presidium of the Supreme Arbitrazh Court No 1580/07 of 26 June 2007. Вестник Высшего Арбитражного Суда Российской Федерации [Herald of the Supreme Arbitrazh Court of the Russian Federation] 10 (2007).

65 S. Yadrihinsky, Правовые проблемы защиты законных интересов налогоплательщика [On Legal Problems Regarding the Protection of Taxpayer's Legitimate Interests] (2007): 102–3.

66 No 1176/07 of 2 October 2007. See Хозяйство и право [Economics and Law] 2 (2008).

67 As well as in cases of the reorganization or liquidation of the taxpayer (Article 89.11).

it is detected that a taxpayer has committed a tax offence which was not detected in the initial on-site tax inspection, tax sanctions are not to be applied except for cases when non-detection of a tax offence was the result of collusion between the taxpayer and the tax official. Moreover, if there are sufficient grounds to suppose that the documents detecting the offence may have been eliminated, hidden, changed, or replaced, these documents will be seized in the procedure provided for it by Article 94 of the Tax Code (Article 89.14). On the last day of the inspection, the tax official conducting it will draw up a reference note on the inspection for the taxpayer (Article 89.15).

The rules of the Tax Code on tax inspections contains detailed rules in respect of the participation of witnesses (Article 90), access to the territory or premises of a taxpayer with the exemption of his domicile (Article 91),[68] and the execution of the examination (Article 92) where tax authorities are empowered to demand extradition of documents and information (Articles 93 and 93^1) and seize documents and other objects (Article 94), in which instance the grounded decision of the tax official conducting the inspection is required. If necessary, expert examination will also be executed (Article 95). The Tax Code also includes the rules on the minutes to be recorded in the inspection (Article 99).

According to Article 100 of the Tax Code, the results of the on-site tax inspection and, in case of a violation of the tax legislation, also the results of the cameral tax inspection must be issued in the tax inspection report (tax audit act). The report on the on-site tax inspection must be drawn up within two months from the last day of the inspection; in the case of the cameral tax inspection, the term is ten days. In the event of disagreement with the facts stated in the tax inspection report as well as with its conclusions and proposals, the inspected taxpayer has the right to submit to the tax authority his objections in writing in respect of the report, together with the documents proving his objections (Article 100.6).[69] The tax inspection report and other material will be considered by the head (or his deputy) of the tax body that conducted the inspection in the procedure specified in the Tax Code (Article 101).[70]

Where the tax official detects a tax violation otherwise than in an inspection, he is obliged to draw up the tax violation report in accordance with Article 101^4 of the Tax Code. In the event of disagreement with the facts stated in the tax violation report as well as with its conclusions and proposals, the offender has the right to submit to the tax authority his objections in writing in respect of the report, together with the documents proving his objections[71] (Article 101^4.5). The tax violation report and other material will be considered by the head (or his deputy) of the tax body in the procedure specified in the Tax Code (Article 101^4).

10 Liability for Tax Violation[72]

Violations and Sanctions

The concepts of tax liability and tax violation are linked together in the Tax Code.[73] A tax violation (tax offense) is defined in Article 106 of the Tax Code as an unlawful (in violation of tax legislation)

68 Access to the domicile of a taxpayer may occur only in those cases provided by the law or on the grounds of a judicial decision (Article 91.5).

69 Within 15 days of the date of receiving the report.

70 See below.

71 Within 10 days of the date of receiving the report.

72 For more on this subject, see Krokhina 2009: 203–336.

73 Russian legal doctrine treats them as synonymous. Butler 2009: 582.

act (action or inaction) committed with guilt by a taxpayer, tax agent, or other persons entailing liability under the Tax Code. A tax sanction is also defined in the Tax Code (114) and is a measure of liability for tax violations.

A person guilty of a tax violation may be an organization or physical person (aged 16 or above) who in committing it acted intentionally or with negligence. By intentionality is understood that the offender was aware of the unlawful character of his actions or failure to act and wished or consciously permitted the ensuing harmful consequences of them. In turn, by negligence is understood that the person who committed it was not aware of the unlawful nature of his actions (inaction) or of the harmful nature of consequences of such action (inaction), although he should and could have been aware of it. As to the guilt of an organization in committing a tax violation, this is determined by the guilt of its officials or its representatives whose actions (or inaction) conditioned the committal of the tax violation (Articles 107 and 110). The committal of the tax violation must be established by the decision of the tax authority, which has entered into force (Article 108.3).

In accordance with the general conditions on tax law liability, provided by Article 108 of the Tax Code, no one may be brought to tax law liability for committing a tax violation other than on the grounds and in the procedure provided for by the Tax Code, as well as more than once for the same tax violation. On the other hand, if a taxpayer is brought to liability for committing a tax violation, this does not relieve him from the duty to pay the amount of tax due (Article 108.4).[74]

Moreover, a person may not be brought to liability for committing a tax violation under the Tax Code (Article 109), as in general, if one of the following circumstances is present:

- in the absence of a tax violation;
- in the absence of guilt of the person committing a tax violation;
- where the offender is a minor, and
- where the period of limitations for the committed tax violation has expired.

A taxpayer or tax agent is not obliged under the Tax Code (Article 108.6) to prove his innocence of committing a tax violation. Thus, the burden of proof lies with the tax authorities, who must prove both the fact of the violation and the guilt of the taxpayer in committing such violation. Moreover, it is provided by the Tax Code (Article 3), as presented above, that any ineradicable doubts of the guilt of the taxpayer must be resolved in his favor.[75] As to the period of limitations for tax violation, this is three years after the day following the end of the respective tax period in which the violation was committed (Article 113).[76] The Supreme Court and the Supreme Arbitrazh Court have stated that the period of limitations for tax violations is preclusive, wherefore bringing to liability for a tax violation after its expiry is unlawful.[77]

Furthermore, under the Tax Code (Article 111) the following circumstances preclude the guilt of a person who has committed a tax violation:

---

74 Butler 2009: 582.

75 The presumption of innocence applying to tax violations is formulated identically to that found in the criminal law. Butler 2009: 582. See also Popondopulo 1 2009: 464.

76 Butler 2009: 583.

77 Joint Decree of the Plenums of the Supreme Court and Supreme Arbitrazh Court adopted on 11 June 1999, no 41/9. Вестник Высшего Арбитражного Суда Российской Федерации [Herald of the Supreme Arbitrazh Court of the Russian Federation] 8 (1999).

- the act was committed as a consequence of a natural disaster or other extraordinary and insuperable circumstances, or
- the offender was in a state where he could not understand or control his actions as a result of his illness, or
- the taxpayer or tax agent was acting in compliance with written instructions and explanations given by a tax authority or another authorized state authority or officials thereof within the limits of their competence.

Other circumstances may be recognized by the court or tax authority as excluding the guilt of the taxpayer in committing a tax violation.

The Tax Code also lists circumstances both aggravating and mitigating the liability for committing a tax violation (Article 112). Mitigating circumstances include:

- acting as a result of the confluence of grave personal or family circumstances;
- acting under threat or coercion or by virtue of material, employment, or other dependence, or
- other circumstances recognized by the tax authority or court as mitigating the liability for a tax violation.

Aggravating circumstances, in turn, are the committing of a tax violation by a person who has been held liable for an analogous violation.

Tax violations for which tax law liability may be assessed or a tax law subject sanctioned under the Tax Code include:

- violation of the order of registration with the tax authority (Article 116) and evasion thereof (Article 117);
- violation of the period for submitting information about the opening or closing of a bank account (Article 118);
- violation of the period for submitting a tax declaration (Article 119);
- gross violation of the rules for recording revenues and expenses and objects of taxation (Article 120);
- failure to pay or underpayment of a tax (Article 122);
- failure of a tax agent to fulfill duties to withhold tax (Article 123);
- failure to comply with the procedure for the possession, use, and/or disposition of property, on which arrest has been imposed or which is subjected to pledge (Article 125);
- non-submittal of information necessary for the execution of a tax inspection to a tax authority (Article 126);
- failure of a witness or expert, interpreter, or specialist to perform duties properly (Articles 128 and 129), and
- unlawful non-reporting of information to a tax authority (Article 129^1).[78]

As tax sanctions, the Tax Code provides for fines in the event of a tax violation, applied individually for each violation separately and not cumulated or integrated (Article 114). In the presence of aggravating circumstances, the amount of fine is increased by 100 percent, whereas in the presence of mitigating circumstances, the amount of fine may be reduced to up

78 If a duty to report is imposed by the Tax Code, and in the absence of characteristics of non-submittal of information necessary for the execution of tax inspection (Article 126).

to half. Tax authorities can file a claim in court for collecting a tax sanction not later than six months after the day when the tax violation was discovered and an appropriate act was drawn up (Article 115).[79]

The Tax Code contains the specified rules on tax law violations committed by banks.[80] Banks bear liability for:

- failure to comply with the procedure for opening an account for a taxpayer (Article 132);
- failure to execute the order to remit a tax in the proper time (Article 133);
- failure to comply with a decision of a tax authority to suspend the accounts of a taxpayer or tax agent (Article 134);
- nonfulfillment of the order of a tax authority on the remittance of a tax, preliminary tax payment, charge, late-payment interest, or fine (Article 135),[81] and
- non-submittal to tax authorities of the statements (abstracts) on transactions and accounts (Article 135.1).[82]

Other liability rules are also included in the Tax Code. According to the rules on liability of tax, customs (Article 35), and internal affairs authorities and their officials (Article 37), they are liable for losses caused to taxpayers and tax agents by unlawful actions (decisions), actions or inaction, including those of their employees in performing their duties. Moreover, it is expressly provided by the Tax Code (Article 103) that causing unlawful damage while exercising tax control is prohibited, and that such a damage is subject to full compensation, including the compensation for loss of expected gains (lost profit).

Tax law subjects may also commit actions which are subject to other forms of liability. According to the Tax Code (Article 10), proceedings concerning tax violations containing elements of an administrative violation[83] or crime are to be conducted in accordance with the administrative or criminal procedure, respectively. Furthermore, the Tax Code (Articles 101.15 and 108.4) provides that bringing an organization to liability for committing a tax violation does not relieve its officials from any administrative, criminal, or other liability provided by the law. These persons are not regarded, under the Decree of the Plenum of the Supreme Arbitrazh Court,[84] as subjects of tax law relations, wherefore they are not liable for tax violations sanctioned by the Tax Code. Furthermore, the taxation duties of the officials of taxpayers are defined as dependant on the duties of taxpayers and not subject to enlargement.[85]

79 Thus, the period of limitation for the recovery of sanctions is different to the one for tax violations.

80 The Constitutional Court stated in its ruling no 257-O on 6 December 2001 that violations of such duties are tax law violations. Свод Законов Российской Федерации [Statute Book of Russian Federation] (2002), no 6, item 625.

81 In the case of repeated violations of this duty, the banking license may be invalidated by the Central Bank at the request of the tax authority (Article 60.4^{1}).

82 Fines are graded from 200 to 40,000 rubles and from 10 to 40 percent of the unpaid amount.

83 Tax authorities are empowered to consider designated cases concerning administrative violations relating to taxation. As for criminal liability, this may apply, for instance, to tax evasion. See Butler 2009: 583.

84 No 5 adopted of 28 February 2001. Вестник Высшего Арбитражного Суда Российской Федерации [Herald of the Supreme Arbitrazh Court of the Russian Federation] 7 (2001). See also http://base.consultant.ru/cons/cgi/online.cgi?req=doc;base=LAW;n=30959. (accessed 23 June 2010).

85 Popondopulo 1 2009: 464–5.

Tax Violation Proceedings

The formal basis for applying tax sanctions is the act of the tax authority drawn up on the basis of inspection or some other tax control measure. The decision to apply the sanction is taken by the head of the respective tax body. The Tax Code contains two sets of rules regulating tax violation proceedings. One of them is based on the acts of cameral or on-site inspection (Article 101), and another concerns tax violations detected in other tax control measures (Article 101^4), which, however, is rather similar.

According to Article 101 of the Tax Code concerning the proceedings based on the acts of cameral or on-site inspection, the decision must be rendered within ten days as of the date of expiry of the time period provided for the objections of a taxpayer concerning the tax inspection act, which may be extended but at most by one month. The person in respect of which a tax inspection has been conducted has the right to participate personally and/or through a representative in the consideration of the tax inspection materials, but his nonappearance is not to impede the consideration of the issue, except where his participation is declared obligatory by the head of the tax body (or his deputy). On the results of the consideration of the case, the head of the tax body renders a decision on bringing to liability for committing a tax violation or on the refusal to do so (Article 101.7).[86] The decision enter into force upon the expiry of ten days from the date of its delivery to the person subject to it, and if it is appealed, at the date of the decision of the superior tax authority (Article 101.9).

The execution of the tax authority's decision on tax violation may be secured by precautionary (securing) measures, including:

- a prohibition on alienation of assets;
- the suspension of bank account operations (Article 101.10), which may be replaced by request of the person subject to the decision on tax violation by bank guarantee;
- a pledge of securities, or
- suretyship (Article 101.11),

the rules on which are provided by Article 74 of the Tax Code, mentioned above.

According to Article 104 of the Tax Code, the tax authority, after rendering the decision on bringing an offender to liability for committing a tax violation, makes a proposal to him to pay the amount of the tax sanction voluntarily. Where this fails , the tax authority files the claim against the offender with an arbitrazh court for collecting tax sanctions (from organizations or individual entrepreneurs). The claim will be handled in accordance with the proceedings provided by the Arbitrazh Procedural Code (Article 105).[87]

11 Tax Law Appeals[88]

In addition to the safeguards for the protection of taxpayers and also other tax law subjects provided for in the rules on the basic principles of tax legislation and on the rights of taxpayers presented

86 In the event of detecting of the law violation subject to administrative liability, the act on it shall be drawn up and administrative proceeding shall be applied (Article 101.15).

87 A claim against a physical person who is not an individual entrepreneur is handled in a court of general jurisdiction.

88 For more on this subject, see Krokhina 2009: 337–52.

above, the Tax Code contains special rules for tax law appeals (Articles 137 and 138). The rules provide that taxpayers and other tax law subjects may defend their rights and legitimate interests[89] in both administrative and judicial proceedings in Russia, which is guaranteed in Article 22 of the Tax Code.[90] According to Ruling No 418-O (4.12.2003) of the Constitutional Court, the rules for tax law appeals have the effect of constitutional law, wherefore they are generally binding and preclude any other interpretation in legal practice.[91] [92]

According to Article 137 of the Tax Code every person, not only a taxpayer or tax agent, has the right to appeal the nonnormative acts[93] of tax authorities or actions or inaction of tax officials, if in the view of the person they are violating his rights. Acts of tax authorities and actions or inaction of tax officials can be appealed against to a superior tax authority (higher tax official) or to a court in accordance with the procedure for appealing determined by the Tax Code (Article 138). Appeals must be made in the written form.

Appealing a complaint to or filing a complaint with a superior tax authority (higher tax official) does not rule out the right to a simultaneous or subsequent filing of a similar complaint with a court (Article 138). However, this rule is subject to certain limitations with regard to the committal of a tax violation (Article 101^2.5), according to which a decision on bringing an offender to liability for committing a tax violation or on the refusal to do so may only be appealed against judicially after appealing against this decision with a superior tax authority. Furthermore, it is obvious that, if the judicial decision has entered into force before the administrative decision is made, the judicial decision will prevail, since the act of tax authority may not be contrary to a judicial act.[94]

Judicial appeals against acts (including normative acts[95]) of tax authorities and actions or inaction of tax officials by organizations and individual entrepreneurs are lodged with an arbitrazh court,[96] and they are considered and resolved in accordance with the proceeding provided by the Arbitrazh Procedure Code (Articles 138.2 and 142). The court may suspend the execution of the act or action being appealed (Article 138.3).

Administrative appeal or appeal with a superior tax authority is filed with the higher tax authority if the appeal is lodged against the act of the tax authority, who will be a defendant in the case. However, the appeal is filed with the higher official of the same tax authority, if it is lodged against the action or inaction of a tax official, who will be a defendant in the case (Article 139).[97] In

89 Legitimate interests are not, however, defined in Russian law, although they are even mentioned in the Constitution (Articles 36.2 and 55.3). In respect of tax law relations, legitimate interests of a taxpayer include tax planning and minimization serving reasonable economic purposes. Otherwise, actions of a taxpayer may comprise a tax abuse. See Yadrihinsky 2007: 97–9.

90 Taxpayers may also appeal to the President of the Russian Federation against the decisions of federal authorities. Krokhina 2009: 337.

91 Вестник Конституционного Суда Российской Федерации [Herald of the Constitutional Court of the Russian Federation] 2 (2004).

92 Butler 2009: 586.

93 Normative legal acts of tax authorities can also be appealed in accordance with the procedure provided for by federal legislation (Article 137).

94 Butler 2009: 586.

95 According to the Decree of the Supreme Arbitrazh Court no 7445 of 4 October, a taxpayer may appeal against a normative legal act issued by the tax authority, although he may appeal in judicial procedure against the concrete acts of the tax authorities grounded on such an act. Вестник Высшего Арбитражного Суда Российской Федерации [Herald of the Supreme Arbitrazh Court of the Russian Federation] 2 (2006).

96 Judicial tax appeals by physical persons who are not individual entrepreneurs are filed with a court of general jurisdiction.

97 Butler 2009: 586 and Krokhina 2009: 345 and 351.

the case of administrative appeal, moreover, the execution of the act or action being appealed may be suspended, for which the decision of a superior tax authority is required (Article 138.3).

Unless otherwise provided for by the Tax Code, the appeal must be filed within three months from the date of the violation of the interests coming to the appellant's knowledge (Article 139.2).[98] The appeal may be withdrawn at the written request of the appellant, unless a ruling concerning the appeal has already been rendered. Withdrawal of the appeal will, however, deprive the appellant of the right to file a new appeal based on the same grounds with the same tax authority or the same superior official (Article 139.4).

An appeal against a decision of a tax authority on bringing an offender to liability for committing a tax violation or on the refusal to do it must be filed before the appealed decision has entered into force. Where the decision which has entered into force has not been appealed, it may be appealed within one year from the date of the rendering of the decision (Article 139.2).

Based on the results of consideration of an administrative appeal the superior tax authority (higher official) is entitled, under the Tax Code (Article 140), in respect of the appealed act, to:

- dismiss the appeal;
- cancel the act of the tax authority;
- cancel the decision on and dismiss the tax violation case;
- alter the decision or render a new decision.

Moreover, in respect of the appealed action or inaction of the tax officials, the superior tax authority or higher official is entitled to render a decision on the substance of the case (Article 140.2).

In turn, in respect of the appealed decision, the superior tax authority is entitled to:

- leave the decision unchanged and reject the appeal;
- abolish or change the decision in full or in part and to render a new decision on the case;
- abolish the decision and terminate proceedings on the case (Article 140.2).

A decision in respect of an appeal must be rendered within one month from the date of receiving it. The period may be extended, if necessary, but by no more than 15 days. The appellant must be informed in writing about the rendered decision within three days of its adoption (Article 140.3).

98 The period for appeal may be renewed at the request of the appellant by the head (deputy head) of the tax authority or by a superior tax authority.

Chapter 4
Competition Law

The present Russian competition law, which term encompasses antimonopoly legislation and legislation on the protection (or promotion) of competition used generally in the country,[1] has been adopted, to a great extent, from the legal systems of Western Europe, and particularly from European Union (EU) competition law. It contains the rules regulating monopolistic activities or restrictions of competition, but its principal significance lies in prohibiting monopolistic activity. Russian competition law also contains rules on the control of mergers and acquisitions or state control over economic concentration.[2] While Western European law is the undoubted model, the specific nature of the Russian economy has been taken into account in the competition legislation, which provides possibilities for intervention into acts and actions tending to restrict competition as well as into the monopolistic activities of public (state and municipal) authorities.[3] The acts and actions of public authorities[4] restricting competition are prohibited in the Competition Law.[5] The rules on auction competition or tenders, including the rules on public procurements, on contracting on public property, and the selection of financial organizations as well as public preferences fall under the purview of Russian competition law. The regulation of the activities of natural monopolies and the rules on state monopoly also belong to the field of competition law in Russia.

The majority of the rules of the Russian competition law are contained in the Competition Law (Federal Law on Protection of Competition no 135-FZ of 26 July 2006)[6] enacted in 2006.[7] [8] The new Competition Law has almost entirely replaced the Law on Competition and Limiting Monopolistic Activities on Commodity Markets no 948-I of 22 March 1991 and the Law on

1 A number of books including the term *Конкурентное право* [Competition Law] have been published in Russia recently, as, for instance, A.N. Varlamova, Конкурентное право [Competition Law] (2007). Courses with the same title are also held in Russian universities.

2 V.F. Popondopulo, Коммерческое (предпринимательское) право, Том I [Commercial (Entrepreneurial) Law, Volume I] (2009): 362.

3 Popondopulo 1 2009: 357.

4 Federal bodies of executive authority, state bodies of the subjects of the Russian Federation, bodies of local self-government, other bodies or organizations exercising the functions of the above-mentioned bodies, as well as public off-budget funds and the Central Bank of the Russian Federation.

5 This is regarded as a peculiarity of the Russian competition law. See Popondopulo 1 2009: 366.

6 *Федеральный закон "О защите конкуренции" от 26.7.2006 N 135-ФЗ.* See, for instance, http://docs.kodeks.ru/document/901989534 (accessed 22 June 2010).

7 Last amended by the Law no 40-FZ of 5 April 2010.

8 The content of the Competition Law with commentaries is presented in A.N. Korolev and O.V. Pleshakova, Комментарий к Федеральному закону о защите конкуренции [Commentary on the Federal Law on Protection of Competition] (2007). The provisions of the law are presented also in S.E. Zhilinsky, Предпринимательское право [Entrepreneurial Law]: 548–607 and Popondopulo 1 2009: 357–73. See also R. Chlup and E. Lezheva, *Russian Merger Control: The Framework Is There* (2008): 79–80 and A. Tsarikovsky and D. Aleshin, *Russian Competition Legislation and the Federal Antimonopoly Service* (2008): 63–5.

the Protection of Competition in Financial Services Markets no 117-FZ of 23 June 1999.[9] The main aim of the new Competition Law is to improve the legal regulation of competition law relations in Russia.

The Competition Law is divided into ten parts (chapters). Chapter 1 contains general provisions, which concern the subject and objectives of the law and its application, competition legislation, and basic concepts (Articles 1–9). Chapter 2 includes the rules regulating activity through prohibiting and in certain cases allowing admissibility of it, and the rules on unfair competition (Articles 10–14).

Chapter 3 of the Competition Law contains rules which prohibit acts and actions (inactions) as well as agreements and concerted practices of public authorities that restrict competition (Articles 15–16). Chapter 4 of the Competition Law, in turn, is devoted to the antimonopoly requirements in respect of auction (auctions) (Article 17)[10] and special requirements in respect of contracting on state and municipal property (Article 17^1)[11] as well as to specific rules on the selection of financial organizations (Article 18). Chapter 5 of the law comprises provisions on preferences granted by public (state or municipal) authorities (Articles 19–21).[12]

Chapter 6 of the Competition Law provides the rules concerning the functions and powers of the competition authorities (termed "the antimonopoly authority" in the law).[13] It also includes provisions on the rights of the antimonopoly authority's employees during inspections of observance of the antimonopoly legislation, the general obligation to provide information to the antimonopoly authority, and the obligation of the antimonopoly authority to observe commercial, official, and other legally protected secrets (Articles 22–6).[14]

Chapter 7 of the Competition Law (Articles 27–35) is devoted to the state control over economic concentration, and contains the rules concerning enterprise changes which require the preliminary approval of the competition authorities or which merely require to be notified to them. It also provides for the possibility for the antimonopoly authority to examine on application the correspondence of a draft agreement restricting competition with the requirements of the Competition Law (Article 35).

Chapter 8 of the Competition Law contains the rules on liability for violations of the antimonopoly legislation (Articles 36–8), while the rules on the consideration of such cases are included in Chapter 9 (Articles 39–52). These rules include the initiation of a case of violation, its review commission procedure, and decision making and fulfillment of the prescriptions of the commission as well as the order of appeal against decisions and orders of the antimonopoly authorities. Chapter 9 was added in 2009 and included the rules regulating the period of limitation in respect of demands against competition law violations (Article 41^1), as well as the rules on consolidation and separation of actions (Article 47^1). The Competition Law ends with Chapter

9 Only some concepts have remained in force from the former competition laws.

10 As amended by the Law no 108-FZ of 30 June 2008.

11 Rules on the special requirements concerning the conclusion of contracts in respect of state and municipal property were added by the Law no 173-FZ of 17 July 2009.

12 The title of Chapter 5, "The Granting of State or Municipal Aid," was altered by the Law no 173-FZ of 17 July 2009. Correspondingly, the titles of its articles contained have also been changed and now they provide the concept of the state and municipal preference (Article 19) and the order for granting them (Article 20) as well as the rules on the consequences of violations of the requirements concerning state and municipal preferences (Article 21).

13 The Federal Antimonopoly Service and its territorial bodies (Article 4).

14 Chapter 6 was added by the Law no 164-FZ of 17 July 2009 with the provisions on the execution of the inspections of the competition authorities (Articles 25^1–25^6).

10, which contains concluding provisions and the rule on the coming into force of the law (Articles 53–4).

1 Application Rules

Legislation on the Protection of Competition

Legislation on the protection of competition in Russia comprises, according to the Competition Law (Article 2), the antimonopoly legislation of the Russian Federation, which term is used as a synonym of the Competition Law, and other legal acts. Russian antimonopoly legislation is based on the Constitution (of the Federation) and the Civil Code, and consists of, along with the Competition Law, other federal laws regulating the protection of competition in accordance with the Competition Law (Article 3). Competition law relations may be regulated also by the normative acts subordinated to the law (substatutory acts) such as the decrees of the Government and the normative acts of the Federal Antimonopoly Authority (Service)[15] in cases directly provided for in the antimonopoly legislation. In general, international law norms enjoy priority in Russian law,[16] and this is enforced in Article 2.3 of the Competition Law. According to it, if an international treaty of the Russian Federation establishes different rules than those provided for in the Competition Law, then the rules provided for in the international treaty are to be applied.[17]

Scope of Application

According to Article 3 of the Competition Law, the law is to be applied to those relations which are connected with the protection of competition, including the prevention and restriction of monopolistic activity and unfair competition, and in which, in addition to the public authorities, Russian and foreign juristic persons and organizations, as well as physical persons, including individual entrepreneurs, are involved. They are often called in the Competition Law the economic entity.

The Competition Law also includes the norm on its extraterritorial application (Article 3.2). According to this, the rules of the Competition Law are also to be applied to agreements[18] between Russian and/or foreign persons or organizations and their acts made outside the territory of the Russian Federation. They apply if such an agreement or act concerns production facilities and/or intangible assets located in Russia or shares (or equity interests) of companies or rights, in respect of Russian commercial organizations which are practicing their activities in the territory of the Russian Federation or may otherwise affect competition in Russia.

2 Prohibited Restrictions of Competition

In Russian competition law, prohibited restrictions of competition comprehend monopolistic activities and unfair competition of enterprises.

---

15 The central competition authority in Russia according to the Competition Law (Article 4).

16 See the Russian Constitution (Article 15.4) and Civil Code (Article 7).

17 For more on the Russian antimonopoly legislation, see, for instance, A. Tsarikovsky and D. Aleshin, *Russian Competition Legislation and the Federal Antimonopoly Service* (2008): 63–5.

18 An agreement is, under the provisions of the Competition Law (Article 4), a written understanding contained in a document or several documents, as well as verbal understanding.

Monopolistic Activity

In general, monopolistic activity comprehends acts, actions, agreements, and concerted practices which cause or could cause prevention, restriction, or elimination of competition. Monopolistic activity includes monopolistic pricing, discriminatory conditions, abuse of a dominant position, cartels or monopolistic agreements (including vertical agreements) concerted practices, and other actions prohibited in the Competition Law as such. Based on certain criteria some actions are, however, allowed under the Competition Law.

Prohibited restrictions of competition in the Competition Law are targeted, first of all, at preventing monopolistic activity of enterprises. Monopolistic activity is defined in the Competition Law (Article 4) as the abuse by an economic entity (a group of persons) of its dominant position, agreements or concerted practices prohibited by the antimonopoly legislation, as well as other actions (inaction) recognized as monopolistic activity in accordance with the federal laws. Monopolistic activity is regarded as systematic if it is exposed more than two times in three years under the procedure established by the Competition Law.

Prohibition of monopolistic activity is expressed in the Competition Law through the list of activities which are prohibited as such, including monopolistic pricing and discriminatory contract conditions. Some of the norms containing prohibitions also include exceptions to the rule that grant the possibility of applying equity rules[19].[20] Other exemptions to the norms are admissible where it is possible to prove that the benefits the activities have brought exceed the harm in the market at issue.[21]

Abuse of dominant position The provisions of the Competition Law containing a prohibition on the abuse of dominant position are composed of rules which determine market position mainly through quantitative criteria (of market share) as well as of rules regarding prohibited abusive acts which are constructed by using qualitative characteristics.[22] Prohibited acts and actions include monopolistic pricing or installation and maintenance of monopolistically high and low prices, using discriminatory and unfair contract conditions, and unilateral restrictions of sale and production.

Dominant position at the market is defined under the Competition Law (Article 5) as the position of an economic entity (group of persons) or several economic entities (groups of persons) in the market of a certain commodity giving such economic entity (group of persons) or such economic entities (groups of persons) an opportunity to have a decisive impact on the general conditions of commodity circulation in the commodity market at issue and/or to remove other economic entities from this commodity market and/or to impede access to this commodity market for other economic entities. It is explicitly provided by the Competition Law (Article 5.5) that a natural monopoly enterprise is regarded unconditionally as enjoying a dominant position in the market which is in the state of natural monopoly.[23] An economic entity is presumably in the dominant market position if its share in a certain commodity market exceeds 50 percent, unless

19 These rules are similar to the corresponding rules of EU competition law.

20 Popondopulo 1 2009: 363.

21 Popondopulo 1 2009: 364.

22 Popondopulo 1 2009: 364.

23 The Competition Law (Article 10.3) empowers the Government of the Russian Federation to enact the rules on access to the commodities of the subjects of natural monopolies, aimed at prevention of creating conditions which place one consumer in unequal position in comparison with the other consumers of the same commodities.

in the course of the examination of the case of violation of the antimonopoly legislation or in the course of exercising state control over economic concentration it can be established that it is not dominant in the market.[24] Moreover, even where the share of an enterprise is less than 50 percent the competition authority may establish that, taking into account the situation in the market at issue, it is nonetheless in a dominant position. However, the position of an economic entity (except a financial organization) whose share in the market does not exceed 35 percent can be recognized as dominant only in exceptional cases. According to the Competition Law (Article 5.6[1]), dominance may be recognized where the competition authority discovers in its examination that the market share of the enterprise exceeds the market shares of other enterprises in the same market, and that this may potentially affect decisively the functioning conditions in the market. Additionally market dominance may be recognized where, in aggregate, the following conditions are fulfilled:

- the economic entity has an opportunity to determine unilaterally the price level of the commodity and impact decisively the general conditions of realization of the commodity in the market;
- the access of new competitors into the market is impeded owing to economical, technological, administrative, or other restrictions;
- the commodity sold or purchased by economic entities cannot be substituted with another commodity in the process of consumption (including consumption for production purposes);
- the growth of the commodity price does not cause a corresponding reduction in the demand for this commodity.[25]

The provisions on collective dominant position are contained in the Competition Law (Article 5.3). According to them, the position of each of several economic entities (except financial organizations) is recognized as dominant, if, in aggregate, the following conditions are fulfilled:

- the aggregate share of not more than three economic entities[26] exceeds 50 percent, or the aggregate share of not more than five economic entities[27] exceeds 70 percent;[28]
- where during a long period[29] the sizes of the shares of these economic entities are stable or subjected to insignificant changes, as well as where access of new competitors to the market at issue is impeded;

---

24 An economic entity has the right, according to the Competition Law (Article 5.4), to present evidence before the court or antimonopoly authority that its position in the commodity market cannot be recognized as dominant.

25 Thus, the 35 percent threshold used in defining dominant position is actually abolished. However, the burden of proof is on the competition authorities in such cases. For more on this subject, see Popondopulo 1 2009: 364 and Вестник Высшего Арбитражного Суда Российской Федерации [Herald of Supreme Arbitrazh Court of Russian Federation] 5 (1998): 88.

26 Provided that the share of each of these exceeds the shares of the other economic entities in the market at issue.

27 Also with the proviso that the share of each of these exceeds the shares of the other economic entities in the market at issue.

28 However, this provision does not apply if the share of at least one of the aforementioned economic entities is less than 8 percent.

29 During a period not less than a year or where this period is less than a year during the period of the existence of the commodity market at issue.

- the commodity sold or purchased by economic entities cannot be substituted with another commodity in the process of consumption (including consumption for production purposes), the growth of the commodity price does not cause a corresponding reduction in the demand for this commodity, and the information about the price, conditions of selling, or purchasing of this commodity in the market at issue is available to an indefinite group of persons.

Prohibition on the abuse of dominant position is explicitly provided by the Competition Law (Article 10). According to this, acts and actions (inactions) of an economic entity occupying a dominant position which result or can result in the prevention, restriction, or elimination of competition and/or infringement of the interests of other persons are prohibited. The provisions contain the list of prohibited acts and actions (inactions) which include monopolistic pricing, discriminatory and unfair contract conditions, as well as unilateral restrictions of sale and production.[30] In respect of these prohibitions, it is important to take into consideration that they are not applicable in certain cases provided by the law. It is explicitly enacted in the Competition Law (Article 10.4) that the rules on abuse of dominant position do not apply to acts pertaining to the use of exclusive rights to the results of intellectual activity as well as the means of individualization of juristic persons, performed works, and provided services (intellectual property rights).[31]

Monopolistic pricing is presented in two forms: monopolistically high and monopolistically low pricing. Monopolistically high prices are the usual characteristic of monopolistic activity. However, monopolistically low prices are also used by enterprises in order to achieve or maintain a monopoly position in the market.

The concepts of monopolistically high and monopolistically low commodity prices are contained in the Competition Law. The concepts, however, do not concern financial services (Articles 6 and 7). In both instances the question is of a price established by an economic entity occupying a dominant position at the market, corresponding to the criteria defined in the law. In the definition of both high and low monopolistic prices two equally important methods are used: one is based on cost accounting of the price and the other using the market comparison approach.[32] In any case, however, the commodity price is not to be recognized as monopolistically high or low if it is not higher or correspondingly lower than the price established in the competitive conditions of a comparable commodity market (Article 6.4).

A price is regarded as monopolistically high, according to the Competition Law (Article 6.1), if it exceeds the sum of expenses and returns necessary for the production and realization of such a commodity as well as the price established in the competitive conditions of a commodity market which is comparable in respect of qualitative structure of customers or sellers of the commodity, conditions of its circulation and access to the market, state regulation, including taxation and customs tariff regulation, if such a market exists in the Russian Federation or abroad.

A high monopolistic price may be imposed by increasing the previously installed price provided that, in aggregate, the following conditions are fulfilled:

- the necessary costs of production and realization of a commodity remain unchanged or their changes are not equivalent to the price increase;

30 In order to impose sanctions, the abuse of a dominant position must be proved by the competition authority.

31 See the cases provided by the Competition Law (Article 13.1) presented below.

32 Popondopulo 1 2009: 360.

- the qualitative structure of customers or sellers remains unchanged or its changes are insignificant, and
- the conditions of circulation of the commodity, including those consequent to state regulation, taxation, and customs tariff regulations included, remain unchanged or their changes are not equivalent to the price increase.

A high monopolistic price may also become evident, if the previously installed price remains the same or undecreased, provided that, in aggregate, the following conditions are fulfilled:

- the necessary costs of production and realization of a commodity are significantly decreased;
- the qualitative structure of customers or sellers gives opportunity to decrease the price, and
- the conditions of circulation of the commodity, including those consequent to the state regulation, taxation, and customs tariff regulation included, makes price decrease possible.

However, the price of a commodity is not regarded, according to the Competition Law (Article 6.2), as monopolistically high if such a commodity is a result of innovative activities, and it is a new commodity which is unsubstitutable or substitutable if the production cost of it decreases and/or its quality is improved, provided that the rules of the Competition Law on allowed restrictions of competition are observed (Article 13.1). The same concerns the price imposed by a subject of the natural monopoly within the limits of the tariff for such commodity determined by the authority regulating physical monopolies (Article 6.4).

A price is regarded as monopolistically low, according to the Competition Law (Article 7.1), if it lower than the sum of expenses and returns necessary for production and realization of such a commodity and also the price established under competitive conditions in a comparable commodity market, if such market exists in the Russian Federation or abroad.

Low monopolistic price may be imposed by decreasing the previously installed price provided that, in aggregate, the following conditions are fulfilled:

- the necessary costs of production and realization of a commodity remain unchanged or their changes are not equivalent to the price increase;
- the qualitative structure of customers or sellers remains unchanged or its changes are insignificant, and
- the conditions of circulation of the commodity, including those consequent to state regulation, taxation, and customs tariff regulation included, remain unchanged or their changes are not equivalent to the price increase.

Low monopolistic price may also become evident if the previously installed price remains the same or unincreased provided that, in aggregate, the following conditions are fulfilled:

- the necessary costs of production and realization of a commodity are significantly increased;
- the qualitative structure of customers or sellers gives opportunity to increase the price, and
- the conditions of circulation of the commodity, including those consequent to state regulation, taxation, and customs tariff regulation included, makes price increase possible.

As in the case of high monopolistic price, the price of a commodity is not regarded, according to the Competition Law (Article 7.2), as monopolistically high if:

- the price is imposed by a subject of the natural monopoly within the limits of the tariff for such commodity determined by the authority regulating natural monopolies;
- the price is not lower the price established in the competitive conditions at the comparable commodity market, and
- its imposition has not resulted in the restriction of competition because of a reduction in the number of economic entities which are not included in one and the same group of persons with the purchasers or sellers of the commodity in the commodity market at issue.

As prohibited acts, imposition and maintenance of high and low monopolistic prices are directly mentioned in the rules on abuse of dominant position in the market (Article 10). Prohibited also is the establishment of unjustifiably high or unjustifiably low prices for a financial service by a financial organization.

Discriminatory contract conditions are also regarded as monopolistic acts, and they are explicitly mentioned in the rules on abuse of dominant position at the market (Article 10). Discriminatory conditions are, according to the Competition Law (Article 4), conditions of access to a commodity market, conditions of production, exchange, consumption, purchase, sale, or other alienation of goods when an economic entity or several economic entities are placed at a competitive disadvantage in comparison with another economic entity or other economic entities[33].[34] Furthermore, the Competition Law prohibits economically, technologically, or in any other way unjustified imposition of different prices (tariffs) for one and the same commodity (Article 10.1).

Unfair contract conditions are also mentioned in the rules on abuse of market dominant position (Article 10). According to these, prohibited is the imposition on a counterparty of contract conditions which are disadvantageous for the latter or not connected with the object of the contract. The question here is of conditions which are economically or technologically unjustified and/or requirements on the alienation of financial assets, other property, including property rights which are not provided for explicitly by the federal laws, other legal acts, or judicial acts. Prohibition also concerns the consent to conclude a contract on conditions that these include provisions concerning the commodity in which the counterparty is not interested and other corresponding requirements.

The Competition Law also contains a list of unilateral restrictions of sale and production which are prohibited as abuses of dominant position by enterprises (Article 10). The list includes:

- withdrawal of a commodity from circulation, if the result of such withdrawal is an increase in its price;
- the economically or technologically unjustified reduction or suspension of production of a commodity if there is demand for the commodity or if orders for its delivery are placed and there is nonetheless the possibility of its profitable production, as well as if such reduction

---

33 Exceptions to this rule are explicitly provided for by the Competition Law (Article 13.1).

34 However, it is provided by the Competition Law (Article 10.2) that an economic entity has the right to provide evidence that its actions (inactions) concerning the imposition of discriminatory conditions are to be recognized as eligible in accordance with the requirements provided by the Competition Law (Articles 12 and 13). See below.

or suspension is not explicitly provided for by the federal laws, other legal acts, or judicial acts[35],[36] and
- economically or technologically unjustified refusal to conclude, or evasion of the conclusion of, a contract with individual purchasers (customers) where there are possibilities for the production or delivery of the relevant commodity as well as where such refusal or evasion is not explicitly provided for by the federal laws, other legal acts, or judicial acts.

Other monopolistic acts used by enterprises which are mentioned in the Competition Law as abuses of dominant position include:

- the creation of barriers to entry into the commodity market or exit from the commodity market for other economic entities,[37] and
- the violation of the pricing procedure established by (other) statutory legal acts.

Prohibition of agreements or concerted practices restricting competition Under the general rule provided by the Competition Law (Article 11), agreements between economic entities[38] or their concerted practices (collaborative actions and decisions)[39] or cartels and other restrictive arrangements in the commodity market are prohibited.[40] As in the case of abuse of dominant position, it is unnecessary to prove their negative impact on the market.

At question here are those agreements determined in the Competition Law (Article 4) which can be presented as a written understanding contained in a document or several documents, as well as a verbal understanding. In turn, concerted practices of economic entities comprehend the actions of economic entities in the commodity market that meet both the following conditions:

- the result of such actions meets the interests of each participating economic entity only on the condition that their actions are known to each of them in advance;
- the actions of each participating economic entity are caused by the actions of the other economic entities and are not the consequence of circumstances equally influencing all

35 Exceptions to this rule are explicitly provided by the Competition Law (Article 13.1).

36 However, it is provided by the Competition Law (Article 10.2) that an economic entity has the right to provide evidence for its actions (inactions) concerning the reduction or suspension of production to be recognized as eligible in accordance with the requirements provided by the Competition Law (Articles 12 and 13). See below.

37 Exceptions to this rule are explicitly provided by the law (Article 13.1). Furthermore, it is provided by the Competition Law (Article 10.2) that an economic entity has the right to provide evidence for the creation of barriers to entry into the market or to exit from it to be recognized as eligible in accordance with the requirements provided by the Competition Law (Articles 12 and 13). See below.

38 Defined in the Competition Law as agreements which exist in written form as one or several documents or in verbal form (Article 4).

39 Defined as actions other than those agreed in writing or verbally; this corresponds with international practice, EU competition law included. See Popondopulo 1 2009: 358 and Korolev and Pleshakova 2007: 43–4.

40 This list includes generally per se prohibited price and tender cartels, restrictions of production and divisions of the market, as well as other cartel agreements, all of whose negative effects it is unnecessary to prove. The Competition Law (Article 11) also prohibits other agreements or concerted practices that restrict competition. However, the Competition Law also contains exceptions from the prohibition, thereby allowing an economic unity to prove that an agreement or concerted practice at issue is permitted.

> economic entities in the commodity market at issue. Such circumstances, in particular, can include a change in the regulated tariffs, a change in the prices for raw materials used in the production of the commodity, a change in the price of the commodity on the world commodity markets, a significant change in demand for the commodity within a period of not less than a year or within the period of existence of the commodity market at issue if it has existed for less than a year.

However, the performance of actions under agreement by economic entities is not deemed to be a concerted practice (Article 8.2).[41]

In respect of concerted practices, the Supreme Arbitrazh Court in its plenary session of 30 June 2008/30 presented an interpretative rule for the arbitrazh courts, according to which concerted practice or coordination of actions may be established even in the absence of documentary evidence confirming the agreement about such concerted actions. Thus, a conclusion on the existence of the above-presented condition—that a concert of actions is known to each of the participants in advance—may be made on the basis of the factual circumstances of the case. Concerted actions can be proved, for instance, by the fact that different market participants have acted in a uniform and synchronous manner without any objective grounds.[42]

Prohibited are such agreements and concerted practices if they lead or might lead to:

- the establishment or maintaining of prices (tariffs), discounts, markups (extra charges), or margins (price cartels);
- the raising, lowering, or maintaining of prices at auction (tender cartels);
- the division of the commodity market according to a territorial principle, the volume of sales, or purchases of commodities, the range of sold products, or the composition of sellers or purchasers or customers (division of markets);
- economically or technologically unjustified refusal to conclude contracts with certain sellers or purchasers (customers) if such refusal is not explicitly provided for by the federal laws or (other) statutory legal acts (collective boycotts);
- the imposition on a counterparty of contract conditions which are disadvantageous to the latter or are not connected with the object of agreement (unjustified requirements of alienation of finance assets, other property, including property rights, as well as consent to conclude a contract on condition of including in it provisions concerning the commodity in which the counterparty is not interested and other requirements);
- the economically, technologically or in any other way unjustified imposition of different prices (tariffs) for one and the same commodity;
- the reduction or suspension of the production of commodities for which there is a demand or where the orders for their delivery are placed and there is a possibility that they may be profitably produced (production restrictions);
- the creation of barriers to entry into the market or exit from the market for other economic entities and establishment of conditions for the membership (participation) in professional

---

41 Defined as actions other than those agreed in writing or verbally; this corresponds with international practice, EU competition law included. See Popondopulo 1 2009: 358 and Korolev and Pleshakova 2007: 43–4.

42 See Вестник Высшего Арбитражного Суда Российской Федерации [Herald of the Supreme Arbitrazh Court of the Russian Federation] 8 (2008) and http: www.arbitr.ru as pract post_plenum 19343. html (accessed: 1 October 2009).

and other associations provided that such conditions lead or could lead to prevention, restriction or elimination of competition,[43] as well as
- the establishment of unjustified membership criteria which prevent participation in payment or other systems without which competing financial organizations may not be able to provide the necessary financial services (Article 11.1).[44]

Also prohibited under the Competition Law (Article 11.2) are other agreements between economic entities (except vertical agreements which are recognized permissible in accordance with Article 12 of the Competition Law) or concerted practices of economic entities if they lead or can lead to restriction of competition.[45]

The Competition Law (Article 11.3) also includes a prohibition on the coordination of economic activity between physical persons, commercial organizations, and noncommercial organizations[46] if such leads or might lead to the same consequences of agreements and concerted practices restricting competition outlined above.

Exceptions concerning vertical agreements and other arrangements A vertical agreement is defined in the Competition Law (Article 4) as an agreement between economic entities which are not competing with each other, one of which purchases the commodity at issue or is its potential purchaser, while the other provides the commodity or is its potential seller. Vertical agreements are not subject to the prohibitions imposed in the above-presented general provisions (Article 11), which mainly concern horizontal restrictions of competition (Article 11.1^{1}). However, vertical agreements are also prohibited under the Competition Law (Article 11.1^{2}) where:

- they lead or might lead to the imposition of resale prices or
- under such an agreement the seller of a commodity imposes on the buyer a requirement not to introduce the commodities of its competitor; this excludes agreements for organizing the resale of branded commodities (provided with the trademark or firm name).

The specific nature of vertical agreements is also taken into account in those rules of the Competition Law directly regulating them (Article 12). According to these rules, vertical agreements concluded in written form[47] are permitted if these agreements concern commercial concession. Furthermore, the Competition Law (Article 12.2) includes the *de minimis* rule, according to which vertical agreements between economic entities are permitted where the share of each economic entity in any commodity market does not exceed 20 percent.[48]

---

43 This prohibition, however, does not concern market promotion activities. See Popondopulo 1 2009: 358.

44 See below for the exceptions provided by the law.

45 However, it is provided by the Competition Law (Article 11.4) that an economic entity has the right to provide evidence for agreements reached by it or concerted practices fulfilled by it to be recognized as eligible in accordance with the requirements provided by the Competition Law (Articles 12 and 13). See below.

46 Coordination of economic activity is defined in the Competition Law (Article 4) as concerting of actions of economic entities exercised by a third person who is not included in any group of persons with these. Actions of a self-regulated organization on establishing conditions for access of its members to a commodity market or withdrawal from the commodity market, which are exercised in accordance with the federal laws, shall not be regarded as coordination of economic activity.

47 except vertical agreements between financial organizations.

48 Except vertical agreements between financial organizations.

The Competition Law (Article 13.1) also provides cases where other actions (arrangements) subject to the above-presented prohibitions (including cartel agreements) may be allowed; indeed such provisions correspond to the rules on allowed restrictions of competition provided under EU law.[49] At question here are reasonable restrictions in consideration of which the circumstances enacted in the law or criteria[50] must be taken into account.[51]

This concerns cases provided by the Competition Law (Article 10.2) in which the question is of:

- the economically or technologically unjustified reduction or suspension of production;
- the imposition of discriminatory contract conditions, and
- the creation of barriers for entrance into the market and for exit from it, as well as
- competition-restrictive agreements or concerted practices (Article 11.2)[52].[53]

Such actions may be allowed where:

- they do not create, for particular persons, opportunities to eliminate competition in the commodity market at issue (preservation of competition) and
- they do not impose restrictions superfluous to the achievement of the goal of these actions (inaction), agreements, and concerted practices, transactions, and other actions on participants or third persons (principle of relativity).

Additionally, it is required that they result or may result in:

- the perfection of production, sale of goods or stimulation of technical or economic progress, or the raising of the competitive capacity of Russian goods in the world market (principle of efficiency) or
- the obtaining by consumers of benefits (advantages) which are proportionate to the benefits (advantages) obtained by the economic entities as the result of actions (inaction), agreements, and concerted practices, transactions, and other actions (transfer of benefits)[54].[55]

---

49 Popondopulo 1 2009: 363.

50 The preservation of competition and the principles of relativity, efficiency, and transfer of benefits (see below).

51 Foremost the arrangement must promote economic efficiency or technological development, and the main part of its benefits must be transferred to the consumers. Secondly, the arrangement must not contain additional unnecessary restrictions, and prevent competition in the relevant market.

52 As well as actions subject to the state control of economic concentration (Articles 27–30), which will be presented later.

53 Furthermore, the price of a commodity is not regarded, as stated above, as monopolistically high if such a commodity is the result of innovative activities, and matches with the requirements of the rules of the Competition Law on allowable restrictions of competition (Article 13.1).

54 The Competition Law (Article 13.2) empowers the Government of the Russian Federation to determine those instances where the agreements and concerted practices are allowable as corresponding with the conditions or general exceptions (Article 13.1) presented above. According to the Competition Law (Article 13.3), the general exceptions may also include in addition to the above-mentioned (Article 13.2) conditions other requirements concerning agreements and concerted practices.

55 In these cases the burden of proof is reversed. Thus the economic unity must present evidence that its agreement or action is in accordance with the provisions of the Competition Law (Article 13.1).

The Competition Law (Article 35) provides possibilities for the antimonopoly authority to examine on application whether the conditions of a draft agreement restricting competition corresponds or not to the requirements of the Competition Law. A written application enclosing the necessary documents and information must be submitted to the antimonopoly authority (Article 35.2).[56] The antimonopoly authority is to adopt a decision on whether the draft agreement in written form complies with the antimonopoly law or not within 30 days of the applicant having submitted all the required information necessary for the examination of the application (Article 35.3).[57]

A decision of the antimonopoly authority stating the compliance of the draft agreement with the antimonopoly law may be attached with the prescription aimed at ensuring competition (Article 35.7). Such a positive decision of the antimonopoly authority may be, however, abolished where:

- it is established after the decision has been adopted that the information presented for examination by the economic entity intending to conclude an agreement was unreliable, or
- the economic entities intending to conclude an agreement fail to fulfill the prescription imposed by the antimonopoly authority (Article 35.8).

Among the conditions to the granting of approval by the federal antimonopoly body (FAS) are provisions:

- to provide the companies which are not members of the relevant group of persons with equal access either to a certain product or a service;
- not to unjustifiably reject contracts offered by third parties;
- not to impose different prices for the same product while selling it wholesale to third parties;
- not to reject sales to third parties if the volume of production decreases;
- to submit reports from time to time on compliance with the directions of the FAS;
- to continue performing already concluded short-term and long-term contracts;
- not to decrease the volume of production or stop manufacturing;
- to treat all customers equally (long-arm contracts);
- to update the FAS on the price policy, and
- to update the FAS on changes in the structure of group of persons.

The production of socially important products for basic needs are also within the purview of the FAS.[58]

Prohibition of Unfair Competition

Unfair competition is, under the Competition Law (Article 14), prohibited. Unfair competition is defined in the Competition Law (Article 4) as any actions of an economic entity (groups of persons) aimed at gaining benefits while exercising economic activity not in accordance with the legislation of the Russian Federation, commercial customs (customs of trade) as well as the requirements of

56 The list of such documents is enforced by the federal antimonopoly body (FAS).

57 If necessary, the time of handling of the application may be prolonged but for no longer than 20 days.

58 Chlup and Lezheva 2008: 83–4.

fairness, reasonableness, and equity.[59] Additionally, it is required that such actions should have caused or could cause damage to other competitive economic entities, including harm to their business reputation.[60]

According to the rules of the Competition Law (Article 14), unfair competition is prohibited, including cases of:

- dissemination of false, inaccurate, or distorted information which could inflict losses on an economic entity or cause damage to its business reputation;
- misrepresentation concerning the nature, method, and place of manufacture, consumer characteristics, quality and quantity of a commodity or concerning its producers;
- incorrect comparison by an economic entity of the products manufactured or sold by it with the products manufactured or sold by other economic entities;
- sale, exchange, or other way of input of a commodity into circulation if there was illegal use of the results of intellectual activity and means of individualization equated to them;
- illegal receipt, use, and disclosure of information constituting a commercial, official, or other secret protected by law.

Furthermore, it is directly enacted in the Competition Law (Article 14.2) that unfair competition connected with the acquisition and use of exclusive rights for the means of individualization of a juristic person as well as of products, works, and services is not permitted.[61]

Actions of Public Authorities Restricting Competition

The provisions of the Competition Law regulating the competition-restrictive activities of public authorities, in which their competition-restrictive acts, actions, and decision are prohibited, is a special characteristic of Russian competition law.[62] A part of the rules provided in the Competition Law to regulate the competition-restrictive actions of public authorities are dispositive by nature in the sense that the prohibition they contain is subject to exclusions provided by the law or even other legal act.

Competition restrictive decisions and actions The Competition Law (Article 15) explicitly prohibits competition-restrictive acts and actions (inactions) of public authorities which cause or could cause prevention, restriction, or elimination of competition. The prohibition concerns namely federal bodies with executive authority, bodies of the subjects of the Russian Federation with state power, bodies of local self-government, and other bodies or organizations exercising the

---

59 These general requirements of Russian civil law enacted in the Civil Code (Article 6.2) are presented in Chapter 1.

60 Unfair competition comprehends dissemination of false, inaccurate, or distorted information capable of causing losses to another economic entity. Furthermore, the Competition Law (Article 14.2) explicitly provides that unfair competition connected with the acquisition and use of exclusive rights for the means of individualization is not permitted.

61 Moreover, the Competition Law (Article 14.3) provides that the decision of the Federal Antimonopoly Authority concerning violation of the rules on the acquisition and use of exclusive rights concerning trademarks presented above (for the purposes of unfair competition) may be submitted by an interested party to the federal executive authority for intellectual property who may subsequently recognize the legal protection granted to this trademark as invalid.

62 Popondopulo 1 2009: 366.

functions of the above-mentioned bodies, as well as public off-budget funds and the Central Bank of the Russian Federation.

The list of the actions of public bodies is contained in the Competition Law (Article 15.1), and it includes:

- the introduction of restrictions concerning the foundation of economic entities in any sphere of activity as well as the imposition of bans or introduction of restrictions concerning the exercise of specific activities or production of certain types of products;
- the unjustified prevention of an economic entity from exercising its activities, including the imposition of requirements concerning commodities which are not provided by the law;
- the imposition of bans or introduction of restrictions concerning the free movement of products on the territory of the Russian Federation, as well as other restrictions on the rights of economic entities to the sale, purchase, and other acquisition or exchange of commodities;
- the issuing of orders to economic entities for prioritized supply of products to a certain category of purchasers (customers) or to conclude the contract in prioritized order, and
- the imposition of restrictions for purchasers of products on the choice of economic entities which provide such products;
- granting privileged access to information, or
- granting the state or municipality preference in contradiction to requirements provided in the Competition Law (Articles 19–21).

Furthermore, the Competition Law (Article 15.2) prohibits the investment of public authorities of the subjects of the Russian Federation and bodies of local self-government with powers whose execution leads or could lead to the prevention, restriction, or elimination of competition, except in cases provided for by federal laws. Also prohibited is the combining of the functions of public bodies[63] as well as the granting to economic entities of the functions and rights properly belonging to public bodies, including the functions and the rights of the bodies of state control and supervision.

Competition restrictive agreements and concerted practices The Competition Law (Article 16) contains prohibitions concerning restrictive agreements and concerted practices of public authorities which cause or could cause prevention, restriction, or elimination of competition. Such cases include:

- the increase, decrease, or maintaining of prices (tariffs) except the cases when such agreements are provided for by the federal laws or other legal acts;
- economically, technologically or in any other way unjustified establishment of different prices (tariffs) for one and the same commodity;
- division of the commodity market according to the territorial principle, volume of sale or purchase of commodities, range of sold products or composition of sellers or purchasers (customers), and
- restriction of entry into a commodity market or exit from it, or removal of economic entities from the market.

---

63 The exceptions to this rule may be provided for by the federal law, ukases of the President of the Russian Federation, or decrees of the Government of the Russian Federation.

3 Requirements on Public Preferences

The inclusion of the provisions regulating public preferences in the Competition Law may be regarded, as in the case of the rules on competition-restrictive activities of public authorities, as a particularity of Russian competition law. The provisions contain the general prohibition rule as well as the exception rules, which determine cases when preferences can be granted and the order concerning this.

The rules on public preferences of the Competition Law (Articles 19–21) concern state or municipal preferences. State or municipal preferences are defined in the Competition Law (Article 4) as the provision of advantages by federal bodies with executive authority, bodies of the subjects of the Russian Federation with state power, bodies of local self-government, other bodies or organizations exercising the functions of the above-mentioned bodies to economic entities ensuring for them more favorable conditions of activity in the commodity market at issue in comparison with other market participants (potential market participants) by means of the disposal of state or municipal property or other objects of civil rights, or by granting material privileges.

A state or municipal preference can be granted, under the Competition Law (Article 19.1), by the legal act of the federal body with executive authority, body of the subject of the Russian Federation with state power, body of local self-government, or body or organization exercising the functions of the above-mentioned bodies only with the aim of:

- ensuring vital services for the population in the regions of the remote north and territories equated with it;
- developing education and science;
- carrying out research works;
- protecting the environment;
- developing culture and art, and conserving cultural heritage;
- developing physical culture and sport;
- securing national defense and security of the state;
- producing agricultural products;
- maintaining the social security of citizens;
- protecting labor;
- protecting the health of citizens;
- supporting the subjects of small- and middle-sized entrepreneurship, or
- achieving other aims determined by the laws or other legal acts.

State or municipal preferences are to be granted, according to the Competition Law (Article 19.3), on the written preliminary approval of the antimonopoly authority, excluding cases where the preference is granted:

- by the budget law of the Russian Federation or its subject or by the budget normative act of the body of local self-government which includes or determines the order for defining the quantity of the preference and its concrete receiver;
- by transferring assets of the reserve fund for the covering of unforeseen expenditures in accordance with federal budget legislation, or
- for an amount which does not exceed the maximum amount of cash payments in respect of one transaction between enterprises determined by the Central Bank of the Russian

Federation on the provision that such a preference is granted to one person no more than once per year.

On the other hand, the following cases are not regarded under the Competition Law (Article 19.4) as a state or municipal preference:

- the provision of property and/or other objects of civil law rights as a result of the auction competition organized in the cases determined by the legislation of the Russian Federation, as well as other procedures provided by the legislation of the Russian Federation concerning placement of orders for goods, works, and services for state and municipal needs;
- the alienation, granting, and distribution of state or municipal property to separate persons for the purposes of the liquidation of the consequences of emergency situations, military operations, and conducting counterterrorist operations;
- the assignment of state or municipal property to the economic administration or operative management of economic entities, and
- the provision of property and/or other objects of civil law rights on the grounds of federal law or a court decision that has entered into legal force.

The Competition Law (Article 20) contains the procedural rules for granting state or municipal preferences. According to these, the public body which intends to grant a preference must submit an application to the antimonopoly authority together with the necessary documents for its approval (Article 20.1). The antimonopoly authority will then give its grounded decision on the issue within a period of no longer than one month after the date of receipt of the application and documents (Article 20.2).[64]

Having examined the application for granting the state or municipal preference the antimonopoly authority may adopt one of the following decisions:

- to satisfy the application if the state or municipal preference is considered to comply with the aims stated in the law (Article 19.1) and its granting can not lead to the elimination or prevention of competition;
- to prolong the term of examination of the application if in the course of its examination the antimonopoly authority comes to the conclusion that granting of such preferences may lead to elimination or prevention of competition as well as possible noncompliance of the preference with the aims indicated in the law (Article 19.1) and that additional information is required for making a decision. The term of the examination can be prolonged for a period of not more than two months;
- to refuse to satisfy the application if the state or municipal preference do not comply with the aims indicated in the law (Article 19.1) or if its granting can lead to elimination or prevention of competition.[65]

---

64 The time of handling of the application may, if necessary, be prolonged but for no longer than two months (Article 20.3).

65 Where the antimonopoly authority establishes that the actions which are the object of the application do not correspond with the characteristics of public preference, the applicant must be notified by the antimonopoly authority, within ten days of the date of receipt of the application, that the execution of such actions does not require approval (Article 20.2).

The positive decision of the antimonopoly authority can include provisions which impose restrictions in respect of granting of state or municipal preference. Such a decision is to be taken by the antimonopoly authority for ensuring conformity of the preference with the aims stated in the Competition Law (Article 19.1) which are presented above, as well as to reduce any negative impact of the preference on competition. Restrictions may include:

- the deadline for granting the preference;
- the circle of persons to whom it can be granted;
- its amount and concrete aims, as well as
- other restrictions which may affect the state of competition.[66]

The Competition Law (Article 19.2) explicitly provides a prohibition on using a public preference for purposes other than those corresponding with the aims indicated in the approved application.[67]

4 Requirements for Auction Competitions

The requirements concerning auction competitions or tenders are provided by Articles 17–17^{1} of the Competition Law. According to the Competition Law (Article 17.1), actions in the execution of auctions (auction) which cause or could cause the prevention, restriction, or elimination of competition are prohibited, including:

- the coordination of the activities of the participants in the auction by the organizers of the auction or customers;
- the provision of preferential conditions for participation in the tender for one or several participants, including by means of access to information, unless otherwise provided by federal law;
- the violation of the order of procedure of estimation of a winner or winners of the auction, and
- participation in the auction of the organizers of the auction or of the customers and/or of their employees.

Particular attention is paid in the Competition Law (Articles 17.2–3) to the auction competitions which public authorities[68] organize in respect of public procurements (on placement of orders for goods, works, and services for state and municipal needs). The rules regulating them prohibit restrictions concerning access to participation in auction.[69] The prohibited restrictions include incorporation into the lots of auction of the products (goods, works, and services) which technologically and functionally are not connected with those subjected to the auction.

66 In these cases, the applicant is obliged to submit documents confirming compliance with the restrictions to the antimonopoly authority within a period not exceeding one month from the date of the granting of the preference (Article 20.4).

67 The Competition Law also contains rules on the legal consequences of violations of the requirements provided for public preferences (Article 21); these will be presented later.

68 Federal bodies with executive authority, executive authorities of the subjects of the Russian Federation, bodies of local self-government, and public off-budget funds.

69 Unless it is based on federal law or another legal act.

5 Contracting on State and Municipal Property

The Competition Law (Article 17^1) contains special rules regulating the order of conclusion of contracts concerning state and municipal property.[70] The rules require the organization of auctions for the rights to conclude contracts on public property. These requirements concern contracts on lease, gratuitous use, and entrusted administration of property as well as other contracts providing for the alienation of the rights of possession and/or use in respect of state or municipal property which is not assigned on the rights of economic administration or operative management.[71]

The rules of the Competition Law requiring auction competition, however, do not concern alienation of the rights on the public property:

- by international treaties, federal law, and other legal acts as well as on the grounds of a court decision entered into legal force;
- to public administration bodies, state off-budget funds, and the Central Bank of the Russian Federation;
- to public institutions, as well as to state corporations and enterprises;
- to noncommercial organizations;
- to advocate and notary offices and chambers of commerce and industry;
- to educational institutions and medical institutions, including those belonging to the private health care system;
- in accordance with the rules provided for public preferences;
- and with other aims connected to communication activities, infrastructure, new construction, and privatization as well as public procurement regarding which the tender has been organized.[72]

The organization of an auction competition is also not required where the public property is alienated for the period of 30 days during six months (Article 17^1.1.11). Furthermore, the order on the conclusion of contracts concerning public property is not to be applied to cases where disposition on it occurs under the provisions of the Russian Land, Water, Forest, and Subsoil Code, as well as in accordance the legislation concerning concession agreements (Article 17^1.2).[73]

6 Economic Concentration[74]

Economic concentration is defined in the Competition Law (Article 4) as transactions and other actions the execution of which affects the state of competition, and they are subject to state control.

70 This rule has been amended by the Law no 173-FZ of 17 July 2009.

71 These rules are also to be applied to cases concerning the alienation of state or municipal real property which is under the economic management or operative administration of the unitary enterprise or autonomous institution as well as of assets which belong to the budget institution on the grounds of operative administration (Article 17^1.3).

72 Article 53 of the Competition Law (as amended by the Law no 173-FZ of 17 July 2009 also allows the conclusion of lease contracts without a tender for certain small- and middle-sized enterprises until 1 July 2015.

73 The building property acquired as the result of auction may be subassigned to third persons on the consent of the owner without an auction competition, though not more than 10 percent of it or more than 20 square meters (Article 17^1.4).

74 For more on this subject, see Popondopulo 1 2009: 369–73.

The provisions on economic concentration included in the Competition Law (Articles 27–35) regulate establishments and reorganizations of large-scale enterprises and large-scale transactions concerning shares (equity interests) and assets of enterprises as well as rights to them, including the acquisition of control over enterprises.[75] The provisions of the Competition Law on economic concentration are specified into two main rules. The first regulates those economic concentration actions which require the permission or preliminary approval of the competition authority, whereas the other rules regulate those economic concentration actions that require only notification. The rules of the Competition Law on economic concentration follow international practice, including the corresponding rules of EU law.

Preliminary Approval

Preliminary approval of the competition authority is required in the case of a merger of commercial organizations[76] where:

- the aggregate value of their assets (assets of their group of persons) in accordance with the accounting balance sheets at the latest reporting date preceding the date of the merger exceeds 3 billion rubles, or
- the aggregate revenues from the sale of commodities of the merging organizations (their group of persons) for the calendar year preceding the merger exceed 6 billion rubles or
- one of the merging organizations is included into the register of economic entities whose share in a particular commodity market exceeds 35 percent (Article 27.1.1).

The same criteria are provided for cases of affiliation of one or several commercial organizations[77] with another commercial organization (Article 27.1.2).

The rules on preliminary approval of the antimonopoly authority also concern the case of establishing a commercial organization the charter capital of which is to be paid by the shares (equity interest) and/or property (excluding money) of another commercial organization or where the establishing commercial organization acquires shares[78] (equity interests[79]) and/or property (excluding money) by deed of assignment or in accordance with the division balance sheet and, in respect of these shares and/or property, acquires those rights provided for in the rules on preliminary approval of such transactions (Article 28).[80] Preliminary approval is required in such cases, according to the Competition Law (Article 27.1.4) in the event that:

- the aggregate value of the assets in accordance with the latest balance sheets of the founders of the organization (their group of persons) and the persons (their groups of persons) whose shares (equity interests) and/or property (excluding money) are contributed to the charter capital, exceeds 7 billion rubles, or
- the aggregate revenues from the sale of commodities of these organizations (their groups of persons) for the last calendar year exceed 10 billion rubles, or

75 Popondopulo 1 2009: 369.
76 With the exception of a financial institution.
77 With the exception of a financial institution.
78 Of the joint stock company.
79 Of the limited liability company.
80 See below.

- the organization whose shares and/or property are contributed to the charter capital is entered in the register (of economic entities whose share in a particular commodity market exceeds 35 percent).

The same criteria, in addition to the case where the assets value of the organization (group of persons) subject to acquisition exceeds 250 million, concern transactions in respect of shares (equity interests) and the property of enterprises as well as the rights thereof; these also require the preliminary approval of the antimonopoly authority according to the Competition Law (Article 28). Subject to such approval are also transactions through which changes in the control position in the organization at issue are to be performed. This stands for the acquisition of more than 25,[81] 50,[82] and 75[83] percent of voting shares in the joint stock company and more than one-third, one-half, and two-thirds of the equity (membership) interest in the limited liability company.[84]

Furthermore, the preliminary approval of the antimonopoly authority is necessary where:

- an economic entity (group of persons) obtains in ownership, use, or possession the basic means of production (excluding land plots and buildings purported for nonproductional functions) of the other economic entity,[85] and/or nonmaterial assets, if the balance value of the object of a transaction or mutually related transactions exceeds 20 percent of the balance value of the basic means of production and nonmaterial assets of the economic entity alienating or transferring the property, or
- a person (group of persons) acquires through one or several transactions including those based on the contract on entrusted administration of property, simple partnership, or delegation, the rights enabling him to determine the conditions of the conduct of enterprise activities of the economic entity[86] or exercise the functions of its executive body.[87]

The right to determine the conditions of the conduct of enterprise activities of the economic entity is frequently referred in Russian legal practice to as "other control." In practice, this stands, for instance, for the right to adopt or influence decisions concerning the main directions of the activity, amendments to the charter, reorganization or liquidation, increase or decrease of the charter capital, payment of dividends, and approval of interested party and large-scale transactions as well as decisions on participations in other organizations, approval of internal documents, acquisition of shares and other securities, use of the reserve fund, and establishment of branches and representative offices. Indirect control over the economic entity through third persons is also mentioned. As to the rights to exercise the functions of the executive body of the economic entity, they concern management companies in Russia.[88]

---

81 The blocking share holding or the power to block decisions in the company.

82 The controlling share holding or the power to control the company.

83 The share holding that excludes the possibility of blocking decisions in the company by third persons or to the possibility of nullifying the power of other persons to block decisions.

84 For more on this subject, see Chlup and Lezheva 2008: 75–7.

85 Except a financial organization.

86 Except a financial organization.

87 In general, the preliminary approval of the competition authorities is not required for transactions inside the group of persons (Article 28.2).

88 See Chlup and Lezheva 2008: 77–8.

Notification

The rules on transactions and other actions subject to notification to the antimonopoly authority are contained in a single article of the Competition Law (Article 30). According to these rules, mere notification is sufficient, and the duty to do so provided, for:

- a commercial organization which is established through the merger of commercial organizations[89] where the aggregate asset value according to the last balance sheet or aggregate revenues from the sale of products for the calendar year preceding the year of merger of commercial organizations whose activity is terminated as the result of merger exceed 400 million rubles;
- a commercial organization to which one or several organizations is affiliated, in which case the same criteria concerning the aggregate asset value and aggregate revenues as above are to be applied, or
- persons who acquire shares (equity interests), rights and/or property, the transactions on which are subject to the above-presented requirements of Article 28 of the Competition Law, in the event the aggregate asset value and aggregate revenues of the acquirer(s) and subjects of acquisition exceed 400 million rubles, and additionally provided that the aggregate asset value of the subject of acquisition (group of persons) exceeds 60 million rubles or one of these persons is entered in the register (of economic entities whose share in a particular commodity market exceeds 35 percent).

Mere notification is required also in cases when the founding and reorganization as well as acquisition of controlling shares of the commercial organization are exercised by the group of persons (Articles 27–9). It is possible where, in aggregate, the following conditions are fulfilled:

- actions are executed by persons who belong to the same group of persons;
- a list of persons included in one group with an indication of the grounds on which these persons were included in the group was submitted by any person (applicant) included in this group to the federal antimonopoly authority in the established form not later than one month before the execution of transactions or other actions;
- and this list has not changed at the moment of the execution of transactions or other actions.

Notification to the competition authorities is, however, unnecessary, according to the Competition Law (Article 30.2), where the antimonopoly authority has given preliminary approval to the transaction or action at issue. The possibility of applying for preliminary approval instead of notification are provided by the rules of the Competition Law (Article 33).

Procedure

The procedural rules concerning the requirements for making applications and notifications in respect of transactions and actions subject to state control, their examination and the decision-making on them are contained in Articles 32–3 of the Competition Law. Applications for preliminary approval are to be submitted by the persons executing the reorganization of the commercial organization or

89 Except the mergers between financial organizations.

adopting the decision on the establishment of the company, and the persons acquiring the shares or other property. In turn, notifications are to be submitted by the persons on whom this duty is imposed under the rules of the Competition Law (Articles 30–32). The necessary documents and information must be included with the application or notification,[90] including bookkeeping documents and particulars on the persons in the interest of whom more than 5 percent of the applicant's shares are entrusted to a nominal holder, including persons who are registered in the tax haven state.[91]

The antimonopoly authority examines and shall give its grounded decision on the issue within a period of one month from the date of receipt of the application and accompanying documents.[92] The applicant must be informed on the decision in written form.

In the case of applications for preliminary approval, the antimonopoly authority adopts one of the following decisions:

- to satisfy the application if the transaction or other action whose approval is applied will not cause restrictions of competition;
- to prolong the term of examination of the application (for a period not more than two months) if it is deemed necessary to acquire additional information for making a decision; where the application concerns the establishment or reorganization of the commercial organisation(s) the subject matter of the additional examination can be conditions[93] which must be fulfilled[94] in order for the application to be satisfied;[95]
- to satisfy the application with the prescription to execute actions aimed at ensuring competition;[96]
- to refuse to satisfy the application if the transaction or other action whose approval is applied will cause restrictions of competition, including the emergence or strengthening of the dominant position of the applicant, or if the information contained in the application documents is wrong or insufficient.

The preliminary approval decision ceases to be effective if the transactions or other actions for which the approval has been obtained are not carried out within a year from the date of the decision approval (Article 33.8).

Where actions which are subject to the provisions of the Competition Law cause or could cause competition restrictions, the person who has submitted the application for approval or notification provided by the rules on the state control of economic concentration is obliged to execute actions ensuring competition in accordance with the prescription issued by the antimonopoly authority.[97]

90 The Competition Law (Article 32) provides detailed requirements on these.

91 Or offshore zones.

92 The time of handling of the application may, if necessary, be prolonged but for not longer than two months.

93 The rules on the content of the conditions ensuring competition are enacted in the Competition Law (Article 33.5). They may concern, for instance, the right to access to production and information and the right to use industrial property objects.

94 The period for fulfillment of theses conditions is not to exceed nine months (Article 33.2.3).

95 The Competition Law contains detailed rules concerning the continued handling of the issue in such a case (Article 33.6).

96 Thus, in this instance it will have been established that the action subject to the application causes restrictions of competition (Article 33.7).

97 The rules on it are provided in Article 23.1.2 of the Competition Law.

7 Competition Authorities: Organization, Functions, and Power

The competition or antimonopoly or antitrust authorities in Russia comprehend, under the Competition Law (Article 4), the Federal Antimonopoly Service (FAS), which belongs among the federal or central bodies of executive authorities, as well as its territorial bodies. The functions of the competition authorities, according to the Competition Law (Article 22), include:

- to ensure state control over the observance of antimonopoly legislation by public authorities, economic entities, and physical persons, including the use of land, subsoil, water, and other resources;[98]
- to reveal violations of antimonopoly legislation, to take measures to stop such violations, and call the violaters to account;
- to prevent monopolistic activity, unfair competition, and other violations of antimonopoly legislation by public bodies, economic entities, and physical persons;
- to implement state control over economic concentration in the sphere of land, subsoil, water, and other natural resource use, including control over auction competition in cases provided for by the federal laws.

The antimonopoly authorities are empowered under the Competition Law (Article 23) to:

- initiate and examines cases of violation of the antimonopoly law and
- issue binding prescriptions to economic entities in cases indicated in the Competition Law.

In its prescription the antimonopoly authority may order that the economic entity:

- terminates use of agreements and/or concerted practices restricting competition and executes actions aimed at ensuring competition;
- terminates abuses of dominant position and executes actions aimed at ensuring competition;
- terminates violation of rules of nondiscriminative access to products;
- terminates unfair competition;
- forbear from actions which may prevent the arising of competition and/or may cause restriction or elimination of competition and violation of antimonopoly legislation;
- eliminates the consequences of violations of antimonopoly legislation;
- terminates other violations of antimonopoly legislation;
- restores the situation that existed prior to the violation of antimonopoly legislation;
- concludes the contract, changes the contractual conditions, or rescinds the contract, if in the course of examination by the antimonopoly authority of a case of violation of antimonopoly legislation the persons whose rights were violated or might be violated have applied for such a prescription, or where the antimonopoly authority exercises state control over economic concentration;
- transfers the profit gained as a result of breaches of antimonopoly legislation to the federal budget;
- changes or restricts the use of a brand name, if in the course of examination by the antimonopoly authority of the case of violation of the antimonopoly legislation the persons

98 As amended by the Law no 164-FZ of 17 July 2009.

whose rights were violated or can be violated have applied for such a prescription, or where the antimonopoly authority exercises state control over economic concentration;
- fulfills economic, technical, informational, and other requirements on the elimination of discriminative conditions and prevents their creation;
- executes actions aimed at ensuring competition—these may include actions ensuring access to production facilities or information and granting rights to the objects of industrial property in accordance with the order established by the federal law or other (statutory) legal acts. The prescriptions may also concern the transfer of rights to property or prohibition of such a transfer and preliminary notification of the antimonopoly authority about the intention to execute actions ordered for in its prescription. The antimonopoly authority may also prescribe the sale of a certain amount of products in the commodity market and the preliminary consent of the antimonopoly authority in respect of specific rules concerning the formation of a starting price for the products intended to be sold in the commodity market in accordance with the order established by the Government of the Russian Federation (Article 23.1.2).[99]

Furthermore, the antimonopoly authorities are empowered to issue binding prescriptions to public authorities and their officials demanding them to:

- cancel or change acts violating antimonopoly legislation;
- rescind or change agreements violating antimonopoly legislation;
- terminate other violations of antimonopoly legislation, including resorting to actions for the return of property and other objects of civil law rights granted as the state or municipal preference;[100]
- execute actions aimed at ensuring competition (Article 23.1.3).

However, in respect of the Central Bank of the Russian Federation and Financial Markets Service, the FAS has the authority only to submit its proposals regarding their acts and actions violating the antimonopoly legislation (Article 23.1.4).

The antimonopoly authorities are also empowered to bring to liability organizations, public authorities, and their officials as well as physical persons, including individual entrepreneurs, for violations of antimonopoly legislation, in the cases and in the order established by the law (Article 23.1.5) and apply to arbitrazh court with claims and applications concerning violations of antimonopoly legislation, including claims and applications demanding:

- recognition of statutory legal acts or nonnormative acts, including those causing unreasonable obstacles for practicing entrepreneurship,[101] which contradict antimonopoly legislation as fully or partially invalid;
- recognition of contracts not in conformity with the requirements of antimonopoly legislation as fully or partially invalid;
- obligatory conclusion of contracts;
- changing or rescinding of contracts;
- liquidation of juristic persons in the cases provided by antimonopoly legislation;

99 As amended by the Law no 164-FZ of 17 July 2009.
100 As amended by the Law no 164-FZ of 17 July 2009.
101 As amended by the Law no 164-FZ of 17 July 2009.

- recovery of the profits gained as a result of violations of antimonopoly legislation to the federal budget;
- bringing to liability for violations of antimonopoly law persons that allowed such violations;
- recognition of auction competitions as invalid, and
- enforcement of the execution of decisions and prescriptions of the antimonopoly authority (Article 23.1.6).

Furthermore, the antimonopoly authority, according to the Competition Law (Article 23.1):

- participates in the examination by the court or arbitrazh court of cases connected with applications under and/or violations of the antimonopoly legislation;
- keeps the register of economic unities[102] holding more than a 35 percent share in certain commodity markets;[103]
- posts on the website of the antimonopoly authority its decisions and prescriptions concerning personal interests in general;
- establishes the dominant position of economic unities during examination of cases of violation of antimonopoly legislation and while exercising control over economic concentration;
- executes inspections of organizations, public authorities, and physical persons to ensure that they observe the requirements of antimonopoly legislation, obtains from them the necessary documents and information, explanations in written and verbal form, and, in accordance with the procedure established by the legislation of the Russian Federation, applies to the authorities discharging operative investigatory activities with requests to carry out operative investigations;
- exercises control over the activity of economic unities ensuring the organization of trade in the markets of certain products, for example the electrical energy (capacity) market, where the state regulation of prices (tariffs) for such products has finished, and
- exercises other authorities provided for by the Competition Law, other federal laws, ukases of the Present of the Russian Federation and Decrees of the Government of the Russian Federation.

According to the Competition Law (Article 23.2), other authorities under the competence of the antimonopoly body include the approval of the forms of presenting data to the antimonopoly authority on the conclusion of transactions and regulations as well as, in cases provided for by the law, issuing legal statutory acts and interpretative rules on the application of legislation, and giving necessary statements in respect of the impact of foreign trade law measures on the state of Russian markets. Furthermore, the antimonopoly authority submits proposals to licensing authorities on the cancellation or revocation of licenses of economic unities in violation of the antimonopoly legislation or, on suspension of such licenses, cooperates with international organizations and competition authorities of other countries and otherwise participates in international cooperation, analyzes the practice of application of antimonopoly legislation, and develops recommendations on its application as well as submits report on the state of competition in the Russian Federation to the Government and posts it on the website of the antimonopoly authority.[104]

102 Except financial organizations.

103 The order for the creation and keeping of the register is established by the Government of the Russian Federation under its Decree no 896 of 19 December 2007.

104 See, for instance, the last report on the state of competition in Russia (in 2008): http: www.fas.gov.ru competition goods 20916.shtml (accessed 21 September 2009).

The antimonopoly authorities exercise inspections on the observance of the antimonopoly legislation, in accordance with the Competition Law (Article 25^1),[105] and these are classified as regular and extraordinary by the decision of the head of the antimonopoly body. Regular inspections are to be executed no more than once every three years, whereas an extraordinary inspection is to be initiated on the grounds of:

- receipt of materials from judicial authorities, other state bodies, or bodies of local self-government or societal organizations indicating the characteristics of a violation of antimonopoly legislation;
- notices and applications from physical and juristic persons, and information published in the public means of communication, indicating the characteristics of a violation of antimonopoly legislation, and
- expiry of the term of execution of a prescription issued by the antimonopoly authority in respect of a violation of antimonopoly legislation.

The person who is the subject of the inspection is to be informed of it, in the case of a regular inspection not later than three days and in the case of an extraordinary inspection not later than 24 hours before it starts.

The Competition Law (Articles 25^1–25^6)[106] also contains other detailed rules in respect of the execution of examinations, including those concerning the decisions on them, the rights of the competition authorities to access the territory and location subject to the examination, excluding the domicile of the examined person, as well as the visual survey executed during the inspection, extradition of documents and information, the minutes to be recorded in the inspection, and the final act concerning its results to be executed.

The officials of the antimonopoly bodies have the right in executing their control functions on the observance of the antimonopoly legislation to unimpeded access to public bodies and organizations for obtaining necessary documents and information (Article 24). The law obliges directly commercial and noncommercial organizations, federal bodies of executive authority, bodies of the state power of the subjects of the Russian Federation, bodies of local self-government, other bodies or organizations exercising the functions of the above-mentioned bodies, and public off-budget funds as well as physical persons, including individual entrepreneurs, to provide the antimonopoly authority on its motivated request with documents, explanations in written or verbal form, and information (including information constituting a commercial, official, or other legally protected secret) necessary to investigation of the antimonopoly authority, including correspondence in digital form (Article 25).[107] Information constituting a commercial, official, or other legally protected official secret is to be provided to the antimonopoly authority in accordance with the requirements established by the federal laws (Article 25.3). The Competition Law also imposes strict rules on the observance of commercial, official, and other legally protected secrets, the violation of which can cause civil, administrative, and even criminal liability. Furthermore, the Competition Law provides that the damages caused to the physical or juristic person through violation of secrecy obligations are to be compensated from the Russian Federation treasury (Article 26).

105 The rules have been added by the Law no 164-FZ of 17 July 2009.

106 These rules have also been added by the Law no 164-FZ of 17 July 2009.

107 As amended by the Law no 164-FZ of 17 July 2009.

8 Liability Rules

The Competition Law (Article 37) provides that violations of the antimonopoly legislation cause liability established by the law.[108] As the consequence of a violation of the requirements of the Competition Law, officials of public bodies as well as commercial and noncommercial organizations and their officials and physical persons, including individual entrepreneurs, may bear criminal (the maximum punishment is seven years' imprisonment) or civil (indemnification) liability[109].[110] The general consequence of violations of the Competition Law rules is provided by the rules on administrative liability and it is a penalty;[111] up to the amount equivalent to the 5,000 minimum wage. The rules of the Code on Administrative Violations 2001 concerning administrative liability was amended in 2007 by rules enabling the resort to turnover-based penalties (from 1 to 15 percent) in the case of abuse of dominant position and 4 percent in the case of cartel agreements. Actual punishment rules are, however, incorporated into the Competition Law and these concern abuses of dominant position in the market and violations of the procedural rules concerning public preferences and auction competitions. The Competition Law also includes special rules on violations concerning requirements for economic concentration actions. Furthermore, there are rules on the consequences in cases where prescriptions of the competition authorities are left unobserved.

The penal measures provided by the Competition Law include the compulsory division or separation of a commercial organization as well as noncommercial organization exercising income-bearing activities (Article 38). This is possible if such an organization has a dominant market position and systematically practices monopolistic activity. A decision on the compulsory division of a commercial organization or separation of one or several organizations from it is be adopted, on the application of the antimonopoly authority, by the court.[112] The decision requires that, in aggregate, the following conditions are fulfilled:

- the structural units of the commercial organization are separable;
- there is no technological interdependence between the structural units,[113] and
- the juristic persons created as a result of the reorganization are capable of practicing their activities in the market at issue (Article 38.2).

---

108 Furthermore, it is provided that imposing liability on persons who have violated the competition law requirements does not exempt them from the duty to fulfill the decision and prescription of the antimonopoly authority to submit to the antimonopoly authority application or notices for examination, or to carry out other actions provided for by the antimonopoly legislation (Article 37.2).

109 The Criminal Law has been amended by the Law no 216-FZ of 29 July 2009. The amendments concern criminal liability for prohibited restrictions of competition, and liability has been tightened. Criminal violations of the competition may be punished with up to seven years' imprisonment, and a fine of 500,000 rubles or two years' wages. Furthermore, court may also impose a three-year prohibition of practice on the offender. Moreover, the Criminal Law now includes the leniency rule, which allow authorities to refrain partially or totally from imposing sanctions on the economic unity which is contributing to the discovery and/or clearance of the competition law violation; this rule is used in the practice of the competition authorities.

110 Popondopulo 1 2009: 362.

111 According to Russian arbitrazh court practice, the penalty must be imposed on each offender. See Informative Letter of the Presidium of the Supreme Arbitrazh Court no 32 of 30 March 1998. Вестник Высшего Арбитражного Суда Российской Федерации [Herald of the Supreme Arbitrazh Court of the Russian Federation] 5 (1998).

112 The organization arising in this way may not belong to the same group of persons.

113 For instance, if only 30 or less percent of the overall volume of products (works, services) produced by one structural unit is consumed by the other one.

The court decision on the compulsory reorganization in the form of a division or separation is to be performed in the term determined by the decision, which can not be less than six months (Article 38.3).

The rules on the violation of the procedural rules concerning public (state and municipal) preferences are placed in their own provisions (Article 21). According to these, if the competition authorities establish in executing their control functions concerning the granting of public preferences, in accordance with the order determined by the federal antimonopoly body (the FAS), that the preference is used with aims which do not correspond with the aims indicated in the application on approval for granting the preference, they are to issue to the economic entity which has received the preference, as well as to the federal body of executive authority, body of executive authority of the subject of the Russian Federation, body of local self-government, or other body or organization exercising the functions of the above-mentioned bodies who has granted the state or municipal aid a prescription to take measures to return the property that was allied while allocating the state or municipal aid, if the state or municipal aid was granted through the transfer of state or municipal property or other civil law objects. Moreover, in cases where the preference has been granted in other forms, the competition authorities are to issue a prescription on taking measures for stopping the use of the preference.

Rules on the consequences of violations of the requirements concerning auction competition are also provided in the Competition Law (Article 17.4). According to this, a violation of the rules established for auction competitions is a ground for the court to recognize the auction at issue and the transactions concluded as a result of it as invalid. Such a suit may be filed by the antimonopoly authority.

Furthermore, the Competition Law contains special rules on violations of procedural rules concerning preliminary approvals and notifications provided for cases of economic concentration (Article 34). A commercial organization founded without the preliminary consent of the antimonopoly authority is to be liquidated or reorganized, while a transaction on shares executed without the preliminary consent of the antimonopoly authority is to be recognized, on the application of the antimonopoly authority, as invalid by the court. The same consequences are provided for violations of the rules concerning notifications on economic concentration actions. In all these cases, it is, however, required that the foundation or transaction at issue cause or could cause restrictions of competition, including the emergence or strengthening of dominant position. In cases of nonobservance of the prescriptions of the antimonopoly authority, issued in accordance with the established procedure, a transaction may also be recognized, on the application of the antimonopoly authority, as invalid by the court (Article 34.5). Furthermore, the Competition Law (Article 34.6) provides administrative liability for violations of the requirements concerning state control over economic concentration.

9 Procedure in Cases of Competition Law Violations

Cases of violations of the competition law are to be handled in Russia under the procedures of administrative law. They are considered by the competition authorities according to the procedures established by the law. The courts, in turn, exercise control over activities of the competition authorities by considering appeals against their decisions.[114]

114 Popondopulo 1 2009: 362.

According to the Competition Law (Article 39.1), the antimonopoly authority initiates and reviews the cases of violation of the antimonopoly legislation, adopts decisions on these cases, and issues prescriptions based on these decisions within the limits of its competence. Competition Law violations are subject to a three-year limitation of action period (Article 41^{1}).

A case of violation of the antimonopoly legislation may be initiated, under the Competition Law (Article 39.2), on the following grounds:

- receipt of materials from state bodies or bodies of local self-government indicating the characteristics of a violation of antimonopoly legislation;
- an application from a juristic or physical person;
- detection by the antimonopoly authority of the characteristics of a violation of antimonopoly legislation;
- information published in the public means of communication indicating the characteristics of a violation of antimonopoly legislation, or
- the results of an inspection in which a violation of antimonopoly legislation is detected.

It is explicitly enacted in the Competition Law that the antimonopoly authority is obliged to initiate a case of administrative violation if, in the course of examination of a case of violation of antimonopoly legislation, it reveals circumstances indicating the presence of an administrative violation (Article 39.5).

The rights to participate in a case of a Competition Law violation are provided, under the Competition Law (Article 42), to the:

- applicant who is the person who submitted an application or the state body or body of the local self-government which sent the documents;
- defendant or the person in respect of whom the application was submitted and documents were submitted, or in whose actions (inaction) the antimonopoly authority found the characteristics of the antimonopoly law violation,[115] and
- interested persons or the persons whose rights and legitimate interests the examination of the case of violation of the antimonopoly legislation concerns.

Other persons may also participate in the Competition Law proceedings, including the representatives of the participator, experts, translators, and witnesses. The rights of these persons to participate in the case proceedings are determined by the Competition Law (Article 43), and these rules correspond with the process law rules.

A case of competition law violation may be considered by the antimonopoly authority at the place where the offence was committed or at the location (residence) of the person against whom the complaint on the violation is lodged. The Federal Antimonopoly Authority (FAS) has the right to consider the case in other venues.[116]

For an examination of a case of Competition Law violation, the antimonopoly authority establishes a commission ad hoc, and the proceedings in it are collegial. The commission is represented by the name of the antimonopoly authority and it consists of employees of the antimonopoly authority. The number of commission members must be not less than three. The

115 These persons are recognized as defendants in cases of violations of antimonopoly legislation from the moment the proceedings are initiated.

116 As amended by the Law no 164-FZ of 17 July 2009.

head of the antimonopoly authority or his deputy can be a chairman of the commission. The chairman and the members of the commission are to be approved by the antimonopoly authority. (Article 40)

The antimonopoly authority examines an application or documents concerning the Competition Law violation within the period of one month from the date of their submission. If necessary, the term may be prolonged for not more than two months. On the results of the examination of the application or the submitted material, the antimonopoly authority adopts the decision to initiate the case or to refuse to initiate it (Article 44).

Actual proceedings of the case of the Competition Law violation are to occur within a three-month period from the date of issuing the order to initiate them. If necessary, the term may be prolonged for not more than six months. The persons participating in the case should be duly notified about the time and place of the examination session, but their absence is not an obstacle for the proceedings. On the application of the persons participating in the case or on its own initiative, the commission has the right to announce a recess in the proceedings for a period not exceeding seven days; a postponement and suspension of the hearing are also possible. (Articles 46 and 47) Furthermore, a consolidation and division of actions in the case of the Competition Law violation may be demanded (Article 47^1). The commission adopts in actual proceedings decrees or interim decision, which are purported to determine preparatory actions necessary for the examination of the case, as well as decisions and prescriptions[117] at its session (Article 41).

The actual decision on the case of the competition law violation contains conclusions:

- on the presence or lack of grounds for the dismissal of the case;
- on the presence or lack of a violation of the antimonopoly legislation in the actions (inaction) of the defendant;
- on the presence or lack of grounds for issuing a prescription and a list of obligatory actions to be included in the prescription, and
- on the presence or lack of grounds for taking other measures for preventing and/or removing the consequences of the Competition Law violation and ensuring competition, including initiating a judicial procedure and submitting recommendations on measures to ensure competition to the public authorities (Article 41)[118].[119]

The Commission may also terminate the legal proceedings of the case of the competition law violation in the event of:

- the voluntary elimination of the violation and its consequences by the person who has committed the violation;[120]
- the absence of a violation in the examined actions (inaction);
- the liquidation of the juristic person who is the only onc respondent in the case;
- the death of the physical person who is the only one respondent in the case;

117 Forms of the decision acts are enforced by the federal antimonopoly body or Federal Antimonopoly Service (Article 41.6). The Competition Law also contains detailed regulations on the content of the decision acts.

118 The conclusions of the antimonopoly authorities on the Competition Law violations detected in their examinations are in general nonobligatory.

119 As amended by the Law no 164-FZ of 17 July 2009.

120 The decision must, however, state that the violation of the antimonopoly legislation has occurred. This amendment has been made by the Law no 164-FZ of 17 July 2009.

- the presence of a judicial act entered into legal force containing conclusions on the presence or absence of the Competition Law violation in the actions to be examined by the commission.

The decision on the case of the Competition Law violation adopted by (or only the resolution part of it) is to be declared after the examination of the case is completed. The decision must be formulated in full and sent to the persons participating in the case within the period not exceeding ten working days from the moment of the declaration of the resolution part of the decision. In giving its positive decision, the commission may decide on the prescriptions and their content as well on the necessity of other measures for preventing and/or removing the consequences of the Competition Law violation and ensuring competition, including initiating a judicial procedure and submitting recommendations on measures to ensure competition to the public authorities (Article 49).

The prescription given to the defender simultaneously with the decision on the Competition Law violation is to be fulfilled within the period specified in it. The failure to fulfill the prescription of the antimonopoly authorities in time entails administrative liability. Furthermore, the person whose actions (inaction) are recognized in the procedures established in the Competition Law as monopolistic activity or unfair competition and are impermissible according to the antimonopoly legislation, is obliged, under the prescription of the antimonopoly authority, to transfer to the federal budget the revenue received from these actions (inaction). In the case of failure to fulfill the prescription, the revenue received from the monopolistic activity or unfair competition is to be collected into the budget at the suit of the antimonopoly authority (Articles 50 and 51).

The decision or prescription of the antimonopoly authority may be appealed against within three months from the date of the adoption of the decision and the issuance of the prescription. The appeal to the court or arbitrazh court entails the suspension of the fulfillment of the antimonopoly authority's prescriptions for the period of its examination until the court decision enters into legal force (Article 52).

Chapter 5
Contract Law

In Russia contract, as in other countries with a developed private law regulation, is the main means of organization of civil law relations, particularly between enterprises. Contract law is the most developed part of Russian civil law and now forms the core of private law relations in the country. The Russian contract law regulation is influenced in particular by German law based on Roman law and Roman law is otherwise known in Russia. Such terms, concepts, and institutions in Russian law as *obligatio*, imperative (compulsory) and dispositive norms and customs, freedom and binding force of contract as well as the basic concept of contract have analogues in German law. As to the regulation of contract in common law, Russian contract law differs essentially from it; in particular, grasping the concept of consideration is difficult for an ordinary Russian lawyer.

The general contract law rules of Russia regulating entrepreneurship are concentrated in the first part of the Civil Code. This contains the general rules (provisions) on contracts; those include the norms in which the concept (definition) of contract and conditions (terms) of contract (Chapter 27) and the rules on conclusion of contract (Chapter 28), as well as on change and rescission of contract are enacted (Chapter 29). In turn, the second part of the Civil Code includes the norms regulating different types of contracts, and their provisions usually contain the rules which detail and often make exceptions to the general contract law rules contained in the first part of the Civil Code.

1 General Rules

Concept of Contract[1]

Contract is considered in Russia at present as the most important ground for undertaking obligations. It is the most common ground for the origin of obligations.[2] The leading idea of contract is that the state allows the regulation of contracting and recognizes its legal force.[3] Contract is understood in Russian legal literature, as elsewhere, to mean not only:

---

1 For this subject, see, among others, M.I. Braginsky and V.V. Vitryansky,, Договорное право. Общие положения [Contract Law. General Provisions] (1999): 13–20 and 146–152; A.P. Sergeev (ed.), Гражданское право [Civil Law] 1 (2009): 832–39; E.A. Suhanov (ed.), Гражданское право, Том III [Civil Law, Volume III] (2008): 171–8, and Ch. Osakwe (trans. & comm.), *The Russian Civil Code* (2008): 56.

2 In addition to contracts, the Russian Civil Code indicates as a ground for the origin of obligations tort (delict liability) and other grounds provided by the Civil Code, as for instance, unjustified enrichment. The significance of contract in modern Russian contract law is demonstrated in Russian judicial practice, where it is stated that there is no obligation to pay for work which is performed without a contract based merely on the administrative act and which has not been accepted by the customer. See Informative Letter of the Presidium of the Supreme Arbitrazh Court no 51 of 24 January 2000. Хозяйство и право [Economy and Law] 5 (2000): 79.

3 According to the general principles of civil law confirmed in the definition of obligation contained in the Civil Code (Article 307), the person has the right to demand from the other person a certain behavior (performance) on the grounds of the contract concluded between them or according to the direct provision in the law.

- a legal fact which acts as the grounds for an obligation, but also
- a contracting obligation itself and
- a document in which the contracting obligation is reinforced.

As a legal fact which forms the grounds for the obligation law relation, contract is understood as an integration of the expressions of the wills of the parties, alias an agreement on establishing, changing, or terminating civil law relations, together with the rights and duties of their participants. It is expressly provided in the rule of the Civil Code defining obligation and grounds for its origin that obligations arise from contract (Article 307). As a legal fact contract comprehends a transaction[4] on which obligations are based. In the rule of the Civil Code containing the definition of transaction, it is expressly provided that contract is a bilateral or multilateral transaction (Article 154). Since the concept of contract rests on the concept of transaction, contract is, according to Article 420.2 of the Civil Code, subject to the application of the rules regulating bilateral or multilateral transactions, including the provisions on form and validity of transaction.

As a contracting obligation itself, contract stands for the obligation law relation which arises as a result of the conclusion of the contract (transaction). The question is of the civil law obligations based on the agreement and it is a continuous and relative relation between the debtor and creditor in which the (subjective) rights and duties of the contracting parties exist and are fulfilled. In this sense contract comprehends contract obligations including the contract relation itself and performance of the contract.[5] Contract in this sense comprises the obligations arising from it, and is subject, in accordance with the Civil Code (Article 420.3), to the application of the general rules regulating obligations.

In Russian contract law, it is considered important to distinguish contract in its meaning of transaction from its meaning as contract obligations arising as a result of the conclusion of the contract. Considering the lifespan of a contract, its transaction part has very limited significance. It is dated to the stage of contracting when the rights and duties of the parties—that is, the contract conditions—are determined in order to be legally valid. Therefore, the significance of the rules regulating contracts as transactions is to answer the questions, how contracts shall be concluded, and they contain form requirements for the conclusion of a valid contract. It is only the valid contract which establishes a binding force of contract and binds its parties, and must therefore be performed according to the general contract law *pacta sunt servanda* principle.

In turn, the contentual part of a contract—that is, the content of the rights and duties of the parties—defines what is to be done on the ground of the contract or how obligations are to be performed. The contentual part of a contract is determined by the contract conditions agreed at the transaction stage. These conditions comprise not only the conditions the contracting parties have agreed on and which are ordinarily written into the contract text, but also the imperative or mandatory norms which must be applied and dispositive or discretionary norms applicable to the contract at issue, which contain the rules on obligations. These norms are contained for the most part in the Civil Code and also in other civil legislation acts.

As a document in which the contracting obligation is reinforced, contract stands for the form of agreement or transaction, in other words a document into which the rights and duties of the parties are written. This concept is, however, rather relative, since the parties' agreement does not

4 On the matter of contract as a transaction, see Braginsky and Vitrjansky 1999: 146–52.

5 On the matter of contract as a legal relation, see I.V. Beklenischeva, Гражданско-правовой договор: классическая традиция и современные тенденции [Civil Law Contract: Classical Tradition and Current Tendencies] (2006): 65.

necessarily require a single document. However, if such a document is prepared, and in certain cases it *must* be prepared, it is always named as a contract. In the form of a document, a contract serves as evidence that it has arisen, and at the same as a fixation of its content, in which case the observance of the form requirements is important.[6]

The legal definition of contract is contained in Article 420.1 of the Civil Code. It is recognized as an agreement of two or several persons on establishing, changing, or terminating civil law rights and duties. Thus the legal definition of a contract in the Russian contract law is based on the concept of transaction and comprehends that the contract arises upon the consent of the contracting parties, and that there are actions mutually agreed by the parties in which their reciprocal and congruent expressions of the will have transpired.[7] Furthermore, it is required in accordance with the legal definition of contract in Russian contract law that the purport of these actions or expressions of the wills is to establish, change, or terminate the civil law rights and duties of the parties. The main legal significance of the contract is to bind the contracting parties to their obligation law relation.

Freedom of Contract and Binding Force of Contract[8]

Freedom of contract and its limitations The recognition of contract as the primary ground for the origin of obligations is based on the notion that contractual self-regulation or realization of the autonomy of intention is allowed and its legal force is recognized by the state. In that case the economic content of a commodity exchange act or transaction obtains the necessary legal form for it and its confirmation as well.[9] The allowing of contracting regulation also means the acceptance of the principle of freedom of contract, which transpires in sanctifying that the rights and duties are determined by contract in which the contracting parties have realized their dispositive powers. Freedom of contract is expressly confirmed as a starting point of the civil legislation in the Civil Code (Article 1.1) and belongs therefore to the general principles of Russian contract law. Furthermore, Article 421 of the Civil Code contains the rules directly devoted to freedom of contract in which the concept is clarified. According to the definition of freedom of contract included in Article 421, it comprehends freedom to:

- conclude contract;
- determine the character of the contract to be concluded, and
- determine its conditions or content.[10]

According to Article 421.1 of the Civil Code, physical persons and juristic persons are recognized as free to conclude contracts. In the first place, this means that both physical persons and juristic persons choose themselves the party with whom they enter into a contract, which means freedom

6 Sergeev 1 2009: 838–9.

7 In Russian law, it is presumed that the will and its expression correspond to each other. However, in the event of their inconsistency the legislator has made his choice to protect either the will or its expression depending on the legal policy reasons. The expression of will in the Russian contract law is protected foremost, wherefore in the rules on interpretation of contract its objective or literal interpretation is imposed as the basic rule. For more on this subject, see Sergeev 1 2009: 457–8 and Braginsky and Vitryansky 1999: 266–74.

8 For more on this subject, see, for instance, Braginsky and Vitrjansky 1999: 153–67 and 417–33; Sergeev 1 2009: 839–41, and Suhanov 2008: 174–9.

9 Suhanov 2008: 174–8.

10 The concept of contract in the Civil Code may be regarded as based on the freedom of choice and decision as well as the freedom of type and content.

of choice. It also means that compulsion to conclude a contract is not allowed, except in those cases where the obligation to conclude a contract is established in law or by agreement of the parties. The question is of freedom of decision, according to which the contracting parties make their decisions independently of each other if they establish the contract relation between themselves or not. Freedom of decision is confirmed in Russia in the rules of the Civil Code regulating legal capacity of physical persons (Article 18), which contain the list of the civil law rights belonging to them.[11] In respect of juristic persons, and particularly those who practice commercial activity, freedom of decision is presumed without any conditions.

Freedom of contract transpires, according to the Civil Code (Article 421.2), also in that the parties are free to determine the character of the contract they conclude or to conclude any contract which is provided by the law or not. This means freedom of content and includes freedom of type. Thus, the contracting parties may use any contract model as well as create a new one provided that it is not contrary to the law.

According to the legal definition of freedom of contract contained in the Civil Code, the contracting parties are also free to determine the conditions of the contract they conclude. Hence the conditions of the contract are to be defined at the discretion of the contracting parties. This rule is also extended to concern a contract which is based on the model prescribed by the law as well as a mixed contract or mixed-type contract containing the elements of different types of contract.[12] The rule according to which the content of the contract conditions is to be defined at the discretion of the contracting parties is extended to the extent that the application of the dispositive (discretionary) legal norm may be excluded or deviated, as well as that the legal force of the contract could be extended to concern the relations before the conclusion of it. The only limitation to freedom of content imposed in Russian contract law is that the condition which the contracting parties have chosen or defined may not be contrary to the law or other legal act. Thus, the discretion of the contracting parties in respect of the contract conditions is excluded where the content of the respective condition is determined as obligatory in the law or other legal acts (Article 421.4).

Contracts related to entrepreneurship have their own peculiarities in Russian law. They are have a freedom of contract which is larger than that of common contracts, and this finds expression in the enlarged possibilities of the contracting parties to determine the contract conditions. In respect of the obligations connected with entrepreneurial activity, the parties may provide by their contract, according to Article 310 of the Civil Code, the cases when withdrawal from the obligation and change of its conditions is to be permitted unless otherwise follows from the law or the nature of the obligation.

In Russian civil law freedom of contract is not, as it is stated above, unlimited. Restrictions to it are imposed by the interests of other subjects of law and of society. In addition, the protection of security as well as natural and cultural objects also provide necessary reasons for such limitations. Freedom of contract is restricted in Russia in the provisions contained in the general rules of the

11 They include the right of ownership, the right to inherit and bequeath property, the right run business or any other activity not forbidden by the law, and the right to establish a juristic person, to conclude transactions not contrary to the law and participate in obligations as well as intellectual property and other property and personal non-property rights.

12 Depending on the question at issue, such a contract is governed by the rules of the type of contract which most properly corresponds with the element at issue. Thus, it is regarded in Russian judicial practice that a mixed contract containing elements of the supply and work contract is to be governed, in respect of the consequences of the delivery of defective goods, by the provisions of the Civil Code regulating sale (Article 475.1). This rule provides the buyer with the right to demand compensation for the expenditures for elimination of the defects of the goods. See Вестник Высшего Арбитражного Суда Российской Федерации [Herald of the Supreme Arbitrazh Court of the Russian Federation] 5 (1999): 46.

Civil Code (Articles 1, 10, and 422). The limitations to freedom of contract are also included in the rules of the Civil Code regulating different types of contract. In accordance with the Civil Code, freedom of contract is restricted by prohibitions of certain acts as well as legally prescribed conditions and obligation to contract which may be based on the law or merely agreement. In general, limitations of freedom of contract transpire in the mandatory or imperative norms; the imperative norms known in the Civil Code are the antimonopoly legislation and the norms on consumer protection and price control.[13]

The general limits of freedom of contract are contained in the rules of the Civil Code on freedom of contract (Article 421), public contract (Article 426), and contract of adhesion (Article 428). These limitations restrict freedom to conclude a contract (freedom of decision and freedom of choice) and determine its content (freedom of content, including freedom of type).

The limits of freedom of contract are also implied by the rules of the Civil Code on restrictions of use of the civil law rights (Article 10). According to them civil law protection is dependent on the civil rights being exercised reasonably and in good faith. The rules also include the prohibition of the abuse of civil law rights (prohibition of chicanery). In case of failure to observe these requirements the court may, according to the Civil Code (Article 10.2) refuse to give legal protection.

Russian contract law is also acquainted with subjective restrictions of freedom of contract. For instance, certain species of contract require that the other party or both parties are entrepreneurs, as, for instance, in retail and supply, or that the other party is a physical person as in the rental of housing premises. Subjective restrictions also transpire where certain juristic persons, predominantly noncommercial organizations, are subjected to the rules on special legal capacity which restrict their possibilities to practice enterprise activities (Article 50.3). The rules on special legal capacity also concern bank and insurance activities. Subjective restrictions are also established in the license order in which certain forms of activity are subject to permission.

Binding force of contract The recognition of the legal force of the contractual regulation means the acceptance of the principle not only of freedom of contract, but also of binding force of contract, which comprehends the binding effect of contract or the principle *pacta sunt servanda*. In Russian contract law, this principle transpires in the first place in the rules of the Civil Code regulating the performance of obligations, including the means for safeguarding obligations and the obligation to compensate for damages, as well as in the rules on change and rescission of contract, the purport of which is to compel the contractual parties to observe the contract. Binding force of contract is confirmed in the general rule of the Civil Code concerning the performance of obligations, including contract obligation (Article 309), by the requirements that obligations must be performed in a proper manner in accordance with their conditions and the requirements of the law and other legal acts. It is also confirmed in Article 310 of the Civil Code regulating performance of obligations, by the rule according to which unilateral refusal to perform an obligation and unilateral change of its conditions is not in principle allowed. In the event the obligation of contract is not performed properly, or in the case the breach of contract has occurred, the means for safeguarding of obligations may be applied to the violator of the contract. In Russian obligation law, they include securing measures for fulfilling obligations, operative safeguards, such as withholding right, real performance, including contracting out, as well as price reduction, premature performance, change, and rescission of contract and compensation for damages as well.

The significance of the binding force of contract transpires, in particular, in that contract conditions are purported to stand unchanged. So, according to the Civil Code, changes in the

13 Braginsky and Vitrjansky 1999: 157–9.

civil legislation after the parties have concluded the contract, even if they are mandatory, do not have a direct effect on their contract unless it is provided by the law that its effect extends to relations arising from the previously concluded contracts (Article 422.2). Russian contract law is also otherwise based on a particularly high threshold for the change of the contract (Articles 450–53), considering it as exceptional measure.

Conditions of Contract with Regard to Its Contents[14]

The conditions (terms) agreed between the contracting parties in which their rights and duties are determined constitute the content of the contract. Contract conditions are understood in Russian contract law as a way to fix the mutual rights and duties of the contracting parties which in turn constitute the content of the obligation law relation based on the contract. Therefore, the examination of the contract conditions is linked to the stage of conclusion of contract, when they are considered as legal facts forming the contract. Thus contract is examined as a transaction, and such examination is concentrated on the relation of the conditions contained in the contract to the requirements established in the law. Hence it is usual in Russian law to divide contract conditions into essential, ordinary, and occasional conditions. However, contract conditions may also be understood in a large sense, in which case the central question is what provisions constitute the contentual part of the concluded contract or the content of the contract obligations.

Essential conditions In the Russian rules on conclusion of contract, the concept of essential condition has a basic significance. In the rules of the Civil Code regulating conclusion of contract, it is expressly provided that a contract is to be considered concluded if an agreement has been reached between the parties on all the essential conditions of the contract (Article 432.1). Thus, the reached agreement on essential conditions means that the contract has arisen, and that, on the contrary, if the other contracting party has failed to accept even one of them, a contract is not regarded as having been concluded.[15] Furthermore, it requires that the essential condition is present in the contract during the whole of its term, otherwise the contract is invalid.[16] Thus the question is of the conditions which constitute the contract in general and each type of contract singly. In other words, as essentials are considered in general the conditions which are necessary and sufficient prerequisites for the contract to be considered concluded and the rights and duties of its parties have arisen on the ground of it. However, a contract left unconcluded is not considered invalid in Russian contract law. As a consequence, as it is general in the case of undone transaction, the obligation to return unjust enrichment shall arise.[17] The reason why certain conditions are regarded as necessary to include in the contract as essential conditions is to ensure the stability of

14 For more on this subject, see, for instance, Braginsky and Vitrjansky 1999: 295–339; Sergeev 1 2009: 853–84, and Suhanov 2008: 188–93.

15 This viewpoint is also enforced in Russian judicial practice where it has been stated in respect of a certain type of contract that if the contracting parties had not achieved unanimity even in respect of only one condition indicated in the law, the contract could not be considered concluded. See Вестник Высшего Арбитражного Суда Российской Федерации [Herald of the Supreme Arbitrazh Court of the Russian Federation] 9 (1999): 15. On the other hand, Russian judicial practice states that a contract may be regarded as concluded, even though the contracting parties disagree on a contract condition considered to be nonessential and practically insignificant. See Хозяйство и право [Economy and Law] 7 (2000): 118 and 121–2.

16 Sergeev 1 2009: 853.

17 Braginsky and Vitryansky 1999: 310.

the contractual relations for the parties, which is also important for civil exchange. In that case, the question is often of the legal protection of the interests of the other contracting party, for instance, the weaker party, or of society directly.

The concept of essential conditions is defined in the contract law rules of the Civil Code. According to the general rule on conclusion of contract (Article 432.1), essential are conditions on the object of the contract; the conditions defined as essential or necessary for contracts of the given type in the law or in other legal normative acts; and also all the conditions about which agreement must be reached according to the statement of one of the parties.

The question as to which conditions are regarded in Russian contract law as essential does not cause, in principle, particular dissent in interpretation. The answer to the question of which conditions are to be regarded as essential is usually found in the law (legal normative act) where it does not concern a condition which is necessary for a contract of the given type—for instance, the definition of the price in certain compensated contracts. In certain cases, however, although the condition is established as essential for the contract, it is unnecessary to include it in the contract because its content is defined in accordance with the dispositive norm provided by the law. So, if the parties have not included the condition on price into their contract, then the general rules on price contained in Article 424.3 of the Civil Code are applied. The essentiality of such conditions is, however, evident, since if the parties have not reached the agreement on it, the contract is considered unconcluded. The essentiality of a condition may also be determined discretionarily, in which case the question is about any condition which the other party demands to be included in the contract. The individualization of the work, service, or thing to be transferred—that is, the declaration on its item and number—are regarded in Russian law as the minimum requirement for the essentiality of a condition.[18] [19]

Essential conditions which are always considered necessary for conclusion of the contract are called in the Russian legal literature law-based, or statutory, conditions. If it is expressly indicated in the general rule of the Civil Code that, for instance, the condition on the contract object is essential, then the contract may not arise if such is undetermined. Thus, a contract of sale remains unconcluded if the seller and the buyer do not reach agreement on what things are to be sold, just as a delegation contract is regarded as unconcluded if it lacks the conditions on the tasks the delegate is to perform. The conditions which are not, in principle, necessary for the origin of the contract, but have to be included into the contract on the demand of the other contracting party, are named, in turn, discretionary conditions.

There are not many cases where certain conditions are expressly indicated as essential in the Civil Code or other legal act. Besides the above-presented general rule (Article 432.1), which mentions the condition on the contract object as essential, it is expressly indicated in the rule concerning preliminary contract that this must contain terms enabling the establishment of the object and also other essential conditions of the basic contract (Article 429.3). Essential conditions are also indicated in the norms regulating the sale of residential accommodation (Article 558.1). Essential conditions are also meant in the norm regulating sale of goods on credit with a condition on payment by installment (Article 489.1), according to which such a contract is considered

18 These rules resemble the rules regulating offers in the Vienna Convention (1980), in which the words "sufficiently definite" are used; the provisions determining the quantity and the price are regarded as such.

19 In Russian judicial practice, the contract, although it lacked the terms on price and quality of the goods, was regarded as concluded where the other party had performed his obligation but the other party had alleged that the contract was not concluded. See Вестник Высшего Арбитражного Суда Российской Федерации [Herald of the Supreme Arbitrazh Court of the Russian Federation] (1993) 6: 115.

concluded if it, in addition to other essential conditions for sale, specifies the price of the goods as well as the procedure, the times, and the amounts of payments. These conditions are undoubtedly essentials, although they are not defined as such.

In certain rules of the Civil Code the term "essential conditions" is used in the titles of the norms. Thus, the rules on entrusted administration of property and insurance include the norms concerning essential conditions of the contract of entrusted administration of property (Article 1016) and correspondingly of the insurance contract (Article 942). The contract of entrusted administration of property must indicate, according to the Civil Code, among other things, the composition of the transferred property, the designation or name of the founder or the beneficiary, and the duration of the contract (Article 1016.1). In turn, the insurance contract (both with regard to property and personal insurance) requires under the Civil Code the achieved agreement, among other things, on the insured event, size of the insured amount, and the duration of the contract (Article 942). The conditions listed in these norms are to be considered essential particularly taking into account that there is no contradiction between the title and content of these norms.[20]

There are cases where certain conditions are determined in the Civil Code as having to be agreed. The conditions requiring agreement and which are therefore essential include, in the state or municipal contract, provisions on the amount and price of the work to be performed, the times for its beginning and completion, the amount and procedure for financing and payment for the work, and the securing measures for fulfilling the obligations of the parties (Article 766.1). As another example of the condition requiring agreement and therefore essential may be regarded the rules of the Civil Code on pledge contract according to which a contract of pledge must specify the object of pledge and its valuation and the nature, amount, and time of performance of the obligation secured by the pledge. It also must contain an indication of with which of the parties the pledged property will be kept (Article 339.1).

In the rules of the Civil Code regulating types of contract, the absence of an essential contract condition is considered very often to mean explicitly that the contract has not arisen. Thus, the lease contract on a building or structure is to be, in the absence of a condition agreed upon by the parties in written form on the amount of the lease payment, considered unconcluded (Article 654). The corresponding rule is contained in the rule of the Civil Code concerning the object of the lease (Article 607.3). According to this, a lease contract must contain data that enabled the express identification of the property subject to transfer to the lessee as the object of the lease. Moreover, in the absence of such data, the term on the object of lease is to be considered not agreed by the parties, and the respective contract is to be considered unconcluded (Article 607.3). A similar rule is included into Article 554 of the Civil Code regulating real estate sale contract, and it concerns data enabling defining the immovable property subject to transfer. Also the general rule of the Civil Code on sale contains the provision according to which, if the contract of sale does not make possible the determination of the quantity of the goods subject to transfer, the contract shall be considered unconcluded (Article 465.2).

In the rules regulating different types of contract of the Civil Code, it is often required in order to protect the weaker party that certain conditions must be agreed, and sometimes these conditions are expressly indicated as essential. As an example may be regarded the rules regulating annuity contracts (Article 587.2), in which it is indicated that an essential condition is the term establishing the obligation of the payor of rent to provide security for the

20 Where such a contradiction occurs the priority is to be given, in accordance with the interpretation rules of Russian contract law, to the content of the respective norm.

performance or to insure in favor of the recipient of rent the risk of liability for nonperformance or improper performance of his duty.[21] It is always a question of an essential condition when the purport of the law is the legal protection of the other contractual party or societal interests, and certain conditions are determined to be included into the contract. On the other hand, there are certain cases where the Civil Code or other legal act mentions merely that given conditions are included into the contract and this does not necessarily mean that in the absence of such conditions the contract is to be considered unconcluded. In particular, this concerns situations where such conditions are neither regarded as necessary for the given contract nor have been demanded by the other party to be agreed. Hence, the final decision on the essentiality of a condition mentioned in the law as subject to agreement is made by the court, taking into account, however, the presumption that the condition mentioned as to be included into the contract is essential.[22]

The circumstance that, in the rules of the Civil Code and special legal acts regulating different types of contract, essential conditions may be mentioned but this is not regarded as necessary is of great significance in respect of other than enumerate contracts or contracts which are not regulated by the law. In these cases, the actual question arises regarding what should be considered essential contract conditions in those instances where the law does not provide a clear answer. It is evident that in such cases the condition on the object of contract may be regarded as an essential condition because the object of contract is expressly indicated as such a condition in the general rule of the Civil Code on essential conditions presented above (Article 432.1). Additionally, according to the Civil Code, in respect of contracts unregulated by the law, conditions necessary for the contract at issue and conditions agreed upon at the demand of the other contracting party may also be regarded as essential conditions.

As conditions which are necessary for contracts of the given type and therefore essential are considered in Russian law conditions from which transpires the nature of the contract, and in the absence of which the contract of the given type may not exist. So, for instance, a contract on simple partnership (Article 1041) is without legal significance if the contracting parties do not define the economic or other objective for their intended joint contributions and activities. Similarly, an insurance contract may not arise if the insured event is left undefined in it.

The provisions of the Civil Code that conditions agreed upon at the demand of one of the parties (Article 432.1) are also considered as essential conditions of contract means that, by virtue of the will of the other contracting party, a condition, otherwise not regarded as essential, will become essential. So, for instance, conditions concerning the package of goods are not stipulated in the law as essential for contract of sale; however, if the buyer purchasing, for instance, giftware considers their packing important, he may demand agreement on it, in which case a contract without the condition on packing is considered unconcluded.

According to the provisions of the Civil Code, on conclusion of contract, the terms included in the offer and in the response given to it, if this is regarded as the counteroffer, are considered essential conditions. Therefore, if the offeree makes, in accordance with the rule of the Civil Code on obligatory conclusion of contract (Article 445), a protocol of disagreements, the contract is considered concluded only if the offeror notifies within 30 days from the day of receipt of the

---

21 The general part of the Civil Code also contains the requirements on compulsory conditions, as, for instance, the requirement concerning the content of the founding documents of juristic persons (Articles 52.2, 70.2, 83.2, 89.2, and 122.2), which are purported to protect the creditors and societal interests.

22 Braginsky and Vitrjansky 1999: 313–14.

protocol of disagreements that he has accepted the contract[23] (Article 445.2). This shows clearly that conditions contained in a protocol of disagreements are also essential.[24]

The conditions which became essential because the other contracting party demands them to be agreed also include conditions concerning form of contract. Therefore, if according to the declaration of the contracting party the contract must be made in a special form, and, although such a demand may be stricter than the law requires, the nonobservance of the demanded special form causes the contract to be regarded as unconcluded. It is expressly provided in the rules of the Civil Code on form of contract that, if the parties have agreed to conclude a contract in a defined form, it is considered concluded after giving it the agreed form. This also applies where such a form has not been required by the law for contracts of the given type.

Ordinary and occasional conditions The concepts of ordinary and occasional conditions are used in Russia only in civil law doctrine, since only the concept of essential contract conditions is used in Russian contract law legislation. As ordinary conditions are generally regarded provisions contained in the dispositive or discretionary norms which are to be applied automatically to the contract relation, if the contract has arisen; it is unnecessary for contracting parties to agree upon them. It is presupposed that, if the contracting parties have agreed to enter into a certain contract, they also accept at the same time the conditions included in the law concerning such a contract. Otherwise they must incorporate into the contract the conditions deviating from the dispositive norms. Ordinary conditions also include commercial customs and established practice, and they are to be applied to entrepreneurial contract relations in the event some contract condition has been left undetermined or there is no dispositive norm to be applied to it.

An automatically applicable dispositive norm may be set aside, as it has been stated recently, only by replacing the rule it contains with a contract term. Contracting parties may also exclude entirely the application of the dispositive norm, except, however, where the rule contained in the dispositive norm is essential by its nature. Furthermore, the dispositive norm will remain unapplied in the event it is connected with the condition which is absent from the contract. In that case the question is of a facultative norm. An example of this is the rule of the Civil Code regulating sale (Article 470.2), according to which, in the event a sale contract provides that the seller is to guarantee the quality of the goods, the seller is obliged to transfer to the buyer the goods which must meet the requirements provided by the Civil Code for the course of a determined a period of time established by the contract (guarantee period).

In turn, as occasional conditions are regarded general conditions which are not characteristic for the given type of contract. As such, they do not have any influence on the conclusion of the contract. The inclusion of occasional conditions into the contract depends completely on the will of the contracting parties. In doing so they execute their dispositive powers grounded on the principle of freedom of contract to include any conditions in the contract. The occasional condition, otherwise than the ordinary condition, becomes legally effective only in the event it is contained in the contract. After being agreed, an occasional condition becomes essential.

23 For more on this subject, see below.

24 However, in Russian judicial practice, it is noticed that, if the signed contract is attached with the protocol of disagreements and this concerns the conditions which could not be considered essential, the contract is to be regarded as concluded without such conditions. Also in the event that the contracting parties have not settled their disagreements on the liability issue, the contract is considered concluded without that condition and the price for the delivered goods must be paid. See Survey of the Decrees of the Presidium of the Supreme Arbitrazh Court. Хозяйство и право [Economy and Law] 6 (2000): 118 and 121–2.

Contract conditions in a large sense Contract conditions in a large sense refer to those rules which constitute the contentual part of the concluded contract or the content of the contract obligations in which the mutual rights and duties of the contractual parties are determined[25].[26]

The content of the contractural obligations is determined in Russian law through the contractural conditions agreed as the result of the transactions of the contracting parties. They comprehend not only the terms the contracting parties have reached agreement upon as such, and which are ordinarily written into the text of the contract, but also the conditions to be applied to the given contract as provided by the Civil Code and other civil law acts. These stand for the imperative or mandatory and dispositive or discretionary legal norms which contain the rules concerning obligations.

According to the rule of the Civil Code on the application of the imperative norms, a contract must comply with the rules obligatory for the parties established by the law and other legal acts (imperative norms) in effect at the time of its conclusion (Article 422.1). As to the case where the law, after the conclusion of a contract, establishes rules obligatory for the parties other than those which were in effect upon conclusion of the contract is adopted, the conditions of the concluded contract are to remain in force, with the exception of cases when its retroactive effect is established in the law (Article 422.2).

With respect to the dispositive norms, the Civil Code provides that in cases where a condition of a contract is provided by a norm which applies to the extent not provided otherwise by agreement of the parties (dispositive norm), the parties may by their agreement exclude its application or establish a term different from that provided in it. However, in the absence of such an agreement, the condition of the contract is to be determined by the dispositive norm (Article 421.4).

In certain cases the content of the obligation may also be determined through facultative (optional) norms, by which in Russian law are understood norms the application of which requires that parties have agreed on their application, and such an agreement must be expressed in a positive way; the legal effect of the facultative norm is based ordinarily on the direct reference to it in the contract. Furthermore, reference norms are also known in Russian civil law. By using them generally in contract regulation, the rules regulating certain legal relations (contracts) are to be applied to other, usually similar ones. Commercial customs also have significance in the legal regulation of contract obligations, particularly in respect of the contract relations related to entrepreneurial activity. According to the rule of the Civil Code concerning commercial customs (Article 421.5), if a condition of a contract is not determined by the parties or a dispositive norm, the respective conditions are to be determined by the customs of trade applicable to the relations of the parties. In certain cases the content of the contract obligations may also be determined in Russian law through the application of analogy of the legal rule or analogy of the law.

Understood in a large sense, contract conditions in Russian contract law may generally be placed in the following hierarchy:

---

25 See Sergeev 1 2009: 73–9 and Braginsky, Vitrjansky 1999: 295–315.

26 In a large sense, the contract law regulation is based not only on incorporated or directly written or expressed conditions but also on implied conditions. These are known in particular in the international business practice which is reflected in the UNIDROIT Principles of International Commercial Contracts. The UNIDROIT Principles are known in Russian law as *lex mercatoria* and sometimes even applied directly as international commercial customs. See Braginsky and Vitrjansky 1999: 48 and, in particular, N.G. Vilkova, Договорное право в международном обороте [Contract Law in International Exchange] (2004): 210–14.

1. the imperative norms of the law;
2. the imperative norms of the other legal (normative) acts which are absolutely obligatory for the contractual parties;
3. the terms of the contract agreed upon by the contracting parties;
4. the dispositive norms to be applied in default of the contractual terms;
5. the commercial customs (customs of trade) which are applied in default of both contractual terms and dispositive norms;[27]
6. in default of all the above, the analogy of the legal rule; and, finally,
7. the analogy of the law which, in turn, enables consideration based on good faith, reasonableness, and justice.

In respect of the hierarchy of contract conditions, important is the rule provided by the Russian Constitution (Article 15) and the Civil Code (Article 7) according to which, if Russia joins some international treaty, the provisions of it are to prevail in Russian law over its civil law norms applicable to the case. As to the applicable commercial customs, they must not be contradictory to the law or a contract (Article 5.2). Furthermore, in the rules of the Civil Code concerning the performance of obligations (Articles 311 and 312) there is an exception to the general rule prioritizing a dispositive norm in relation to commercial custom: commercial custom takes priority in those rules. The Russian contract law rules also contain the exclusion to the general rules on the hierarchy of contract conditions concerning imperative norms. In accordance with Article 422.2 of the Civil Code, the terms of contract may take priority over the imperative norms if these are enacted after the conclusion of the contract. And it is only the law (not any other normative act) which may include a provision which supersedes the term of contract.

Classification of Contracts[28]

Contracts are distinguished in Russian civil law in many different ways depending on the aims of classification or on what features of contract are to be clarified. A part of the criteria for classification of contracts is linked to its content, whereas the other part is concentrated on its formal aspects. Formal aspects are important in considering a contract in the capacity of a transaction, in which case the main question is to clarify whether the valid contract is concluded or not. In turn, the content of a contract, or the questions of what the object of a contract is and of what the rights and duties of the parties thereof are, is the focus of attention where contracts are analyzed and are respectively classified as obligations. A significant part of the contract classification reflects the classification of transactions. The most general method of classification is to use a dichotomy based on a certain criterion, some comparative feature. In such a case, contracts may be distinguished into those containing or missing the feature. The other method of classification is based on using certain grounds for constructing an undefined amount of groups in each of which these grounds are identified. The classification of contracts different to the one based on dichotomy is, however, problematic with respect to the achievement of a coherent classification, because it is difficult to find for it uniform criteria. The only solution in such a case is to use a classification based on multifarious criteria. In any case, the classification of contracts may not ignore the norms of the

27 In the event a commercial custom or dispositive norm is included in the terms of the contract, it is regarded as a condition of this.

28 For this subject, see, for instance, Braginsky and Vitrjansky 1999: 383–416; Sergeev 1 2009: 439–45, and 842c53; Suhanov 2008: 179–87; Y.V. Romanets, Система договоров в гражданском праве России [The System of Contracts in Civil Law] (2003): 12–45.

Civil Code, which includes a division of contracts and in which certain contracts are named, usually with their definitions. Important, too, are the rules on the attitude to contracts which are mentioned neither in the Civil Code nor in any other normative act, since this circumstance imposes limits to contract classification.

Contracts as transactions In their capacity as transactions, contracts may be distinguished into real and consensual and compensated and non-compensated contracts as well as causal and abstract ones. Compensated contracts may be divided, in turn, into exchange and risk, or aleatory, ones. Distinct as transactions are also fiduciary contracts which are often regarded in Russian legal doctrine as a *sui generis* group. In this connection, noteworthy is that the classification of contracts does not always correspond unambiguously with the reality. So, for instance, a storage, loan, and delegation contract may be, depending on its conditions, compensated or non-compensated, whereas gift and storage contracts as well as contracts of uncompensated use may occur both as real and consensual.

The distinction between consensual and real contracts is based in Russian civil law on the law, although these kind of contracts are not directly mentioned or defined in the Civil Code. This distinction is grounded on the rules of the Civil Code defining the moment of the conclusion of a contract (Article 433) consisting of the general rule concerning consensual contracts and the special one purposed for real contracts. According to the rule on consensual contracts (Article 433.1), a contract is to be considered as concluded at the moment when the person who has sent an offer has received its acceptance. In turn, the special rule concerning real contracts provides that where the conclusion of a contract also requires under the law the transfer of property, the contract is to be considered as concluded at the moment of transfer of the property at issue (Article 433.2). Thus as consensual is considered a contract which becomes effective at the moment the parties have achieved consensus, and it is just from this moment that the rights and duties are considered arisen for the contracting parties. The consequence of the generalizing consensual contracts in the rules on conclusion of contracts is that consensuality of a contract is presumed in Russian law, wherefore contracts are regarded usually as consensual.

In turn, a real contract is not, in accordance with the same rules on conclusion of contracts, considered as concluded merely on the consensus of the parties. In order to be concluded such a contract requires that the other contracting party transfer the agreed property to its counterparty, and property is understood in this connection in a large sense including also the transfer of rights.[29] Real contracts include, in Russian contract law, loan, storage, and carriage contracts as well as contracts of entrusted administration. There is a particular question connected to a real contract which requires both the expression of intent and transfer of property. What are the consequences in the event the contracting party does not transfer the agreed property, since, in such a case, a contract is regarded as unconcluded? The obligations and corresponding rights may be considered as arisen in such a case only on the condition that the real contract is preceded by a consensual contract existing between the parties, when such a contract may be considered as a preliminary contract.[30]

The distinction between compensated and non-compensated contracts is understood in Russian contract law similarly to the previous distinction. The rules on them are explicitly expressed in the Civil Code. According to the Code (Article 423.1), as compensated is defined a contract under which a party is to receive a payment or other counter-performance in return for the performance

29 If a contract is unconcluded, unjust enrichment is the only remedy in Russia.

30 Braginsky and Vitryansky 1999: 393.

of its obligations. A non-compensated contract is, in turn, a contract under which one party is obligated to provide something to the other party without receiving payment or anything else in return (Article 423.2).

Compensated contracts are characteristic of exchange and they form the majority of contracts. In general, a contract is presumed, according to the Civil Code (Article 423.3), to be compensated, unless it otherwise follows from the law, other legal act, or the content or nature of the contract. Contracts concluded by juristic persons are usually compensated; they may be present as non-compensated only in the event they are not contradictory to the requirements of the law. The presumption that contracts are compensated goes so far that, according to provisions of the Civil Code on price (Article 424.3), in cases where, in a compensated contract, a price is not stipulated and may not be determined proceeding from the terms of the contract, performance of the contract is to be paid for at the price which is usually paid under comparable conditions for analogous goods, work, or services. This rule is, however, applicable only in the event the contract is regarded as concluded—in other words, if the parties had not any disagreement in respect of the price.[31]

The compensated nature of contracts does not mean or require as a general rule the equality of performances of the parties in Russian contract law. However, some limits to that direction are imposed in the rules of the Civil Code on invalidity of transactions, namely in those concerning unconscionable contracts or contracts under duress (Article 179.1). They provides that a transaction which a person was compelled to make on the extremely unfavorable conditions for him that the other party used may be declared invalid by a court on suit of the victim.

Purely non-compensated transactions are in Russian contract law gift and contract of uncompensated use. There are also transactions or contracts which are presumed to be non-compensated, as, for instance, delegation (Article 972.1) or storage in cloakrooms of organizations (Article 924.1), which may also be presented as compensated.

The distinction between compensated and non-compensated transactions or contracts is important in certain cases for defining the ground of liability of the contracting party. According to the Civil Code, if a storage contract is compensated, the bailee is obligated to take all measures provided by the contract to ensure the preservation of the stored thing, whereas in the case of non-compensated contract his responsibility is limited to the duty of care for the thing not less than for his own things (Article 891).[32] The distinction between compensated and non-compensated transactions is also important outside the obligation law rules. So, for instance, the approval of the vindication claim against the *bona fide* (in good faith) acquirer is dependent on whether the contract entitling to possession has been compensated or non-compensated. According to the Civil Code (Article 302.2), the owner always has the right to recover the property which was acquired without compensation from a person who did not have the right to alienate it.

The distinction of contracts into consensual and real ones presented above is also attributed by their division into causal and abstract contracts, which is known to Russian legal doctrine as well. Causal contract stands for a contract in which the aim of the contracting parties is obvious and its validity depends on the presence of the ground for concluding it (*causa*), which means the existence of a legally acceptable and achievable aim. Abstract contract comprehends a contract which is independent of its ground or contractual aim, such as, for instance, a bill of exchange.

---

31 See Joint Decrees of the Plenums of the Supreme Court and Supreme Arbitrazh Court 6/8 of 1 July 1996. Вестник Высшего Арбитражного Суда Российской Федерации [Herald of the Supreme Arbitrazh Court of the Russian Federation] 9 (1996).

32 However, in the case of the above-mentioned storage in a cloakroom, the bailee is obligated to take all measures provided by the contract to ensure the preservation of the stored thing regardless of whether the storage is done for compensation or without it (Article 924.1).

In many cases, the distinction between consensual and real contracts helps to solve the problem considered to pertain to abstract and causal contracts. So, for instance, a loan and storage contract under which the thing is not conveyed may be disputed merely on the ground that a real contract requires the conveyance of the thing, otherwise it is not considered as concluded. On the other hand, Russian contract law is acquainted with contracts in which the legal aim is their indispensable part. In their case, the unattainability of the aim or deviation from it are regarded as a sufficient ground to consider the contract as unconcluded. So, for instance, if a borrower uses credit contrary to the purposes defined in the contract, the creditor has the right to refuse him further credit (Article 814 and 821.3). This is an evident example of a causal contract.[33]

The division of compensated contracts into exchange and risk, or aleatory, contracts is based on the Civil Code rules on the organization of games and wagers (Articles 1062–3). Contracts governing the latter are regarded as risk contracts. Otherwise than ordinary compensated contracts or exchange contracts, risk contracts are constructed on the ground that the aim of the contracting parties to achieve the result accordant with the contract is dependent on coincidental or merely probable circumstances in such a way that it is unknown at the moment of the conclusion of the contract which of the contracting parties will finally win or gain benefit. In a certain sense, aleatory contracts may be regarded as a modification of conditional transactions. However, specific for aleatory contracts in Russia is that, according to the Civil Code (Article 1062), claims connected with the organization of games and wagers, or with participation in them, are not subject to judicial protection except in cases of fraud, duress, threats, or bad faith of the representative as well as in games organized by public bodies or by their permission (Article 1063).

Fiduciary contracts are sometimes regarded in Russian contract law as forming a separate category. Such contracts are based on the special relations requiring personal confidence, and in failure of it, each of the contracting parties has the right to withdraw from the contract performance. An example of such relations is stipulated in the rules of the Civil Code concerning delegation (Article 977.2), according to which the delegant has the right to cancel the delegated task and the delegate to refuse it at any time.

Contracts as obligations In the aspect of obligations, contracts are differentiated multi-levelly. Practically speaking, the most important classification is based on the law and is contained in the special part of the Civil Code in which contracts are divided into different types of contract in accordance with their aims or orientations.[34] This includes such types of contract as purchase–sale, annuity and life estate, lease, work, loan, and credit as well as storage, which are further divided into particular types.[35] The list must be enlarged by a significant number of contract types provided in legal acts other than in the Civil Code. The types of contract are grouped in the Civil Code and, although the groups are not headlined, it is regarded in legal doctrine as clear that the aimed results of contracts are used as grouping principles in it. The grouping is founded on the legal object or basic acts the obligated person is to perform. Additionally other criteria are also used in the

33 It is obvious that causal contracts are recognized, or, at least, the aim of the contracting parties has been subject to consideration, in Russian judicial practice. So the Supreme Arbitrazh Court has stated that a forward contract, particularly if there is no commercial aim connected with it such as insurance against currency or investment risks, is to be regarded as a bet which does not enjoy legal protection in accordance with the provisions of the Civil Code on games and wagers (Article 1062). See Вестник Высшего Арбитражного Суда Российской Федерации [Herald of the Supreme Arbitrazh Court of the Russian Federation] 9 (1999): 40–41.

34 Sergeev 1 2009: 843.

35 The Civil Code contains 26 main types and about 30 particular types of contract.

classification of types of contract in the Civil Code such as the object of contract and the subject part of the contract relation.[36] [37]

According to the legal object or basic acts the obligated person is to perform, contracts are divided into:

- contracts aimed at the transfer of property;
- contracts the object of which is a work performance, and
- contracts the object of which is a service performance, as well as
- founding contracts (agreements) of different corporations.[38]

Contracts on transfer of property[39] include in Russian law first and foremost what are among the commonest contracts, purchase–sale and lease, as well as some other types of contract. Contracts on transfer of property may be divided further into compensated and non-compensated contracts by using as a criterion the legal ground of the transfer. Moreover, if, additionally, the extent of the transferred rights is used as a criterion, all transfer of property contracts may be distinguished into four different groups. The first group is comprised of the compensated contracts on transfer of property into ownership (economic management or operative administration) and includes sale (Articles 454–66), barter (Articles 567–71), annuity, and life estate (Articles 583–605), loan and credit (Articles 807–23), bank deposit (Articles 834–44), and bank account (Articles 845–60). The second group is formed of compensated contracts on transfer of property into use, including lease (Articles 606–70) and lease of residential accommodation (Articles 671–88) as well as franchise (Articles 1027–40). Non-compensated contracts on transfer of property into ownership (economic management or operative administration) comprise the third group and they include gift (Article 572–82). Finally, the fourth group is comprised of a non-compensated contract on transfer of property into use which is represented by a contract of non-compensated use (Articles 689–701).

The specific feature of contracts the object of which are work performances[40] is that the acts of the party performing the contract obligation are aimed at the result. The result is separable from the acts and forms the primary object of the contract. Work performance contracts comprehend in Russian law contracts for (independent contractor) work (Articles 702–68), consumer work (Articles 730–39), and construction work (Articles 740–57), design and exploratory work (Articles 758–62, and work for state needs (Articles 763–8), as well as contracts for performance of scientific research, experimental design, and technological work (Articles 769–78). As a criterion in the division of work performance contracts, the question of who bears the risk of the impossibility of achieving the results is used in Russian legal doctrine. According to it, a contract where such a risk is imposed on the contractor (performer) is evidently considered as a work contract (Articles

36 An example of the contract distinguished by the subject part of the contract relation is the sale of agricultural products provided by Articles 535–8 of the Civil Code. Its contractual parties are agricultural producers and procurers.

37 Y.V. Romanets, Некоторые проблемы квалификации гражданских договоров [Some Problems with the Classification of Civil Contracts] (2000): 53–5.

38 See, for instance, Braginsky and Vitrjansky 1999: 399–403 and Suhanov 2008: 179–87.

39 Contracts on transfer of property are presented minutely in M.I. Braginsky and V.V. Vitryansky, Договорное право. Книга вторая: Договоры о передаче имущества [Contract Law. Book Two: Contracts on Transfer of Property] (2006).

40 For more on work performances contracts, see, in particular, M.I. Braginsky, Договор подряда и подобные ему договоры [The Work Contract and Other Similar Contracts] (1999): 3–217.

702–68). In turn, contracts for performance of scientific research, experimental design, and technological work (Articles 769–78) impose the risks of the impossibility of achieving the results on the customer.

Contracts the object of which are service performances[41] represent a large group in Russian contract law. Some of these form certain types of contract which are regulated separately under their own rules such as carriage (Articles 784–800), freight forwarding (Articles 801–6), factoring (Articles 824–33), storage (Articles 886–926), insurance (Articles 927–70), delegation (Articles 971–9), commission agency (Articles 990–1004), and agency (Articles 1005–11) as well as entrusted administration (Articles 1012–26). Other service performance contracts are, in turn, governed by the rules of the Civil Code on compensable services (Articles 779–83). Service performance contracts are often very close to work contracts. This is reflected, for instance, in the rules regulating compensable services containing references to subsidiary application of the rules regulating work contracts (Articles 783). However, a service usually means more intangible acts than materialized results, and it distinguishes a service from a work. Service performance contracts may be divided the same way as transfer of property contracts into compensated and non-compensated. Almost all service performance contracts are compensated; only delegation contracts may be met as non-compensated.

Founding contracts, which are also called in Russian civil law joint objective agreements,[42] are clearly distinguished from other aim-oriented contracts.[43] It is general for contracts on transfer of property as well as work and service performance that the interests of their parties are opposite. In contrast to this, it is characteristic for founding contracts that their parties have a joint aim. However, it does not mean that the economic and legal results the parties pursue are fully identical. At question is, to be exact, the intent of contracting parties who have a joint objective to organize their joint activities. Consequently, founding contracts like other joint objective agreements mainly regulate the internal relations between the parties. On the other hand, it may be rather difficult in practice to demarcate the difference between joint objective agreements and other agreements. So, for instance, the contribution to joint activities may take the form of a transfer of property into joint ownership or intermediary use or a performance of work, and it is natural that, in these cases, it is impossible to exclude at least partially the application of the norms regulating, for instance, sale, lease, and work.[44]

In the division of founding contracts attention is paid in Russian civil law to the aim of the joint organization of the parties. In other cases, the question is of the establishment of a juristic person (general or limited partnership, joint stock company, limited liability company or association) whereas in other cases the actual purport of the founding contract is to organize joint economic activities without establishing a juristic person (simple partnership; Articles 1041–54).

The rules on the founding contracts of juristic persons are provided in the Civil Code in its general norm (Article 52) and in the norms concerning each corporation form respectively (Articles 70, 83, 89, and 95). The specific feature of such a founding contract is that its signing is a prerequisite

---

41 Service performance contracts are presented in Braginsky 1999: 218–53.

42 Общецелевой договор.

43 See D.V. Lomakin, Договоры о создании и реорганизации юридических лиц: значение и место в структуре Гражданского кодекса РФ [Agreements on Founding and Reorganization of Juristic Persons: Significance and Place in the Structure of the Civil Code of RF] (2004) and T.V. Lamm, Общецелевой договор: понятие и сущность [Joint Objective Agreement: Concept and Essence] (2006): 111–16.

44 Y.V. Romanets, Договор простого товарищества и и подобные ему договоры (вопросы теории и судебной практики) [The Simple Partnership Contract and Other Similar Contracts (Questions of Theory and Judicial Practice)] (1999): 96–7.

for establishing the juristic person. Thus, its aim is the founding of a certain organization, and, for this purpose, the contract defines the joint activities of the parties and their contributions as well as their participation in the activities of the organization. Where the founding contract is the only foundation document, as is the case for partnerships, its content may be very large.

The rules on founding contracts aimed to organize joint economic activities without establishing a juristic person or on founding simple partnership are provided in the norm of the Civil Code regulating contracts of simple partnership (Article 1041). According to this, under a contract of simple partnership (or a contract on joint activity) two or more persons (the partners) are obligated to join their contributions and act together without the formation of a juristic person to derive profits or achieve another goal not contrary to the law.

Other contracts The above-presented classifications do not cover all contracts mentioned in the Civil Code or otherwise known in Russian civil law. Their classification is difficult because of the lack of consistent criteria. Hence, contracts are divided in Russian civil law doctrine into unilateral, bilateral, and multilateral contracts, contracts for the benefit of contracting parties and third parties, real right and obligation law contracts, property law and organizer contracts, main or basic contract and supplementary contract, preliminary and basic contracts, as well as mutually agreed contracts and contracts of adhesion. Furthermore, duty to contract and public contracts are distinct from freely agreed contracts in the Russian contract law. Also fixed-term contracts and contracts with undetermined term (or for the time being) and conditional contracts are known in Russian contract law. Furthermore, contracts for enterprise activities or commercial contracts are ruled by specific rules while consumer contracts are also subject to special regulation. Also innominate contracts, represented, for instance, in the form of the mixed contract or complex contract, are taken into account in the Civil Code in the division of contracts into different types.

Contracts are divided in Russia, according to the distribution of the rights and duties between the parties, into unilateral and bilateral ones. A unilateral contract is obligatory only on one party, whereas the other party has only the rights. A unilateral contract is figured as a loan under which the lender has only the right to demand the return of the loan but no obligation to the borrower, whereas the borrower has no rights but only the obligation to return the loan (Articles 807). Other examples of unilateral contracts are delegation and gift.

Bilateral or reciprocal, or synallagmatic, contracts are contracts imposing reciprocal obligations upon the parties. Both parties have in such a contract both the rights and the duties. It is provided for bilateral contracts that the obligations of the parties are mutual and should enjoy the same fate. Hence, if a sold individualized thing is destroyed before its assignment to the buyer owing to an unexpected event making the performance impossible, the seller's obligation to transfer the thing as well as the buyer's obligation to accept it and pay the price thereof is terminated in accordance with Article 416.1 of the Civil Code. The impossibility of performance may also be caused by an export prohibition issued by the Government which invalidates the entire contract concerning the obligations of both parties.

Bilateral contract often provides reciprocity of obligations. Under the general rule of the Civil Code (Article 328.1) the bilateral contract stands for the situation where the performance of an obligation of one of the parties depends upon the performance of the other party. As a general rule, a bilateral contract entitles both the parties to suspend performance of their obligation or even to refuse to perform it until the reciprocal performance is fulfilled, unless a contract or law provides otherwise.

Russian contract law is also acquainted with multilateral transactions and, correspondingly, multilateral contracts, in which more than two parties participate and each of them is an independent participant with his own expression of will. Such an example is represented in a contract on joint activity (or of simple partnership) concluded, for instance, between three parties. A modification of multilateral contract are founding and operation contracts (or agreements) of juristic persons. Multilateral contracts are distinct from bilateral contracts the parties of which are composed of several persons. A contract with the participation of several persons on the side of one or both parties does not differ from a usual bilateral contract because it is based on the aggregation of expressions of will of the parties and the each contracting party is represented by the joint will.[45]

Contracts for the benefit of the other contracting party or both parties are ordinary contracts. As a general rule, it is the contracting party who may demand the performance. However, also contracts for the benefit of a third person are known in Russian contract law. As a contract for the benefit of a third person or in favor of a third party is recognized under the Civil Code (Article 430.1) a contract in which the parties have established that the debtor is obligated to fulfill performance not to the creditor but to a third person indicated or not indicated in the contract, and which has the right to demand performance of the obligation in its favor from the debtor. Contracts for the benefit of a third person are rather rare and exceptional cases in Russian law. They are found in carriage, insurance, and deposit relations.

The distinction between real right and obligation law contracts[46] is based on the ground that legal relations, in Russian civil law as in general, are divided into real right and obligation law ones. In general, the object of the obligation arisen from a contract is an alienation of the thing to the other party, which means the act for performance of the obligation. However, there are also contracts which give rise to the real right, in most cases the ownership right, of the other party, whereas the alienation of the thing occurs in the stage of concluding the contract but not as a result of its performance. Such contracts are called real right contracts in Russian contract law.

The object of the right arisen from a real right contract is the thing itself, and this right is absolute by nature. An example of a real right contract is the gift which is defined in the Civil Code (Article 572.1) as a contract under which one party (the donor) without compensation transfers to the other party (done) a thing in ownership, and it means also that, in principle, cancellation of the gift is inadmissible (Article 578). On the other hand, the concept of gift in the Civil Code includes also the case where the donor is obligated to transfer to the other party (done) a thing in ownership (Article 572.1). In this case, the question is clearly of obligation law contract, or more precisely of consensual and multilateral contract. By their nature, real right contracts are very close to real contracts. However, a real contract, although arising at the moment when the thing is transferred, is an ordinary obligation law contract under which the parties are in the obligation law relation containing their mutual rights and duties. Contrary to this, it is impossible in the case of a real right contract for a contract to be concluded despite the thing not having been transferred, because the right, usually the ownership right to the thing, arises directly on the ground of the real right contract without any execution requirements.

Russian contract law is also acquainted with cases where the real right elements are present in the obligation law relations. Such an example is represented by the rules of the Civil Code on performance of an obligation at the expense of the debtor (Article 397) and on consequences of the nonperformance of an obligation to transfer an individually defined thing (Articles 398). The former rule provides that in case of nonperformance by the debtor of the obligation to manufacture and transfer a thing in ownership, economic management, or operative administration, the creditor

45 E.A. Suhanov (ed.), Гражданское право, Том I [Civil Law, Volume I] (2007): 451–2 and Suhanov 2008: 184.

46 See, in particular, Braginsky and Vitrjansky 1999: 275–95.

is to have the right, within a reasonable time, to entrust the performance of the obligation to a third person for a reasonable price or to perform it by his own efforts. In turn, the latter rule establishes that in case of nonperformance of the obligation to transfer an individually defined thing to ownership, economic management, or operative administration, the creditor has the right to demand removal of the thing from the debtor.

The performance of an obligation at the expense of the debtor and particularly the removal of the thing are to be considered as directed to the thing and thus located to the real right law means of protection. However, the present Russian civil law is, in addition to these cases, familiar with the real right constructions in which the obligation law elements are present. Hence, the ownership right often comprehends the rights not only to the thing itself but also to demand acts from the counterparty. The roots of this phenomenon are founded in the concept of Roman law known as *res incorporales and iura in re aliena*. This figures clearly in the concept of enterprise as a property complex contained in the Civil Code, which may be the object of purchase–sale, where, in addition to proper real property, claims and exclusive rights are also included (Article 132). A clear example of the combination of real property and obligation law elements is represented in the pledge, the location of which merely within the institutions of real property or obligation law causes problems. Securities, and in particular, bearer securities, also contain both real property and obligation law elements; without which the whole construction of commercial paper would be impossible.

The criterion for distinction between property law and organizer contracts is laid down in the nature of the activity regulated by them. A property law contract is considered as a contract regulating acts of the contracting parties concerning certain commodity (property). It is purposed or aimed to acquire the property or commodity as a result of the obligation performance. In turn, an organizer contract is intended to create conditions for a future entrepreneurial or other activity. A modification of organizer contract are main and general contracts. They define the general conditions of the future activity which are concretized further by the contracting parties in their obligation law contracts. Another kind of organizer contract is the founding contract of organizations.

Main or basic contract and supplementary contract are related to each other. Supplementary contract is used in general if it is necessary to secure the performance of obligation by penalty, surety, pledge, or earnest money. Its existence is, in general, dependent on the existence of the main contract, so if the main contract is recognized as invalid, then the supplementary contract has no legal effect. Contrary to this, the main contract is a fully independent one and the invalidity of the supplementary contract has no legal impact on the validity of the main contract. Although the supplementary contract is dependent on the main contract, it is, however, relatively independent. This transpires in that it is regarded as concluded at the moment when its all essential conditions, which may be included in the text of the main contract, are agreed by the parties.

The distinction between preliminary and basic contracts is based in Russian law first of all on their aims. The main contract gives directly birth to obligations and duties of the contracting parties, which concern the transfer of a commodity or performance of work or service. Contrary to this, the preliminary contract, the provisions on which are contained in the rules of the Civil Code regulating contracts, stands for the event when the parties are obligated to conclude in the future a contract on the transfer of the property, on the performance of works, or on rendering services (the basic contract) on the terms provided by the preliminary contract (Article 429.1). However, although the final aim imposed by the contracting parties will be fulfilled in the event of using the preliminary and basic contract construction in the contract relations only when the basic contract is concluded and charged, there is no legally significant difference between them. The problematic connected with the preliminary contract actually concerns the conclusion of contracts and this will be presented later. The contractual practice in Russia is also acquainted with letters of intent which provide the intentions of the agreed parties to establish the contract relation in the future. A letter of intent does not give birth to any rights and duties between the parties, unless otherwise provided.

The division between freely agreed contracts and contracts which are subject to contracting duty or conclusion by obligatory procedure is founded on the basic rules on conclusion of contract in Russian law. Freely agreed contracts are fully dependent on the will of the contracting parties and represent the majority in Russian contract law. In turn, a contract subject to contracting duty or obligatory procedure stands for the situation where the duty to conclude the contract is imposed on the other or on both contracting parties. Such contracts are exceptional in Russian law as elsewhere. The contracting duty is usually established by the law or other legal act. There are also other grounds for obligatory contracting, as, for instance, provisions of the administrative act or a preliminary contract. The most significant part of contracts subject to obligatory contracting is represented by public contracts.

Public contract is defined in Article 426 of the Civil Code as a contract concluded by a commercial organization and establishing its obligations for the sale of goods, performance of works, or rendering of services which this organization by the nature of its activity must exercise with respect to everyone who turns to it (retail trade, carriage by transport for common use, communications services, energy supply, medicine, hotel service, etc.). By the legal regulation containing imperative norms concerning public contracts, public power intervenes in the contract relations in which the other party is usually as an ordinary consumer the weaker party. It concerns, in particular, the rules on conclusion of contract, which will be presented later.

Also the division between mutually agreed contracts and contracts of adhesion is based on the way they are concluded. Mutually agreed contracts mean the same as freely agreed contracts and their content is determined by the contracting parties. Contract of adhesion represents, in turn, the case where the conditions of the contract are determined by the other contracting party; the rules on conclusion of contract of adhesion are provided by Article 428 of the Civil Code and these will be presented later.

Contracts (transactions) may have in Russian civil law either a fixed term or their period of validity may be left undefined, in which case they are regarded as concluded for an undetermined term or for the time being. The term contained in the contract may comprehend its coming into force or expiration. If a contract contains the term for the birth of the rights and duties of the contracting parties, it is considered in Russian contract law as a suspensive term. In turn, if the contract enters into force instantly but contains the determined term after which it is expired, the question is of a resolutory term. The same contract may contain both suspensive and resolutory terms.

As conditional contracts or transactions are understood in Russian law transactions (contracts) in which the birth or expiration of the rights and duties of the contracting parties is imposed dependant on circumstances which may or might not occur in the future. As such a condition may be a certain event or act of physical or juristic persons, which usually means an act of the contracting parties but sometimes also of third persons. The event or act referred to in the conditional contract must be unknown to the contracting parties, but it must be both legally and physically possible. The rules regulating conditional contracts are based on the rules concerning conditional transactions which are contained in Article 157 of the Civil Code and they concern suspensive and resolutory conditions.

A contract (transaction) is regarded as made under the suspensive condition if the parties have made the arising of the rights and duties dependent on the circumstance about which it is unknown whether or not it will occur. Under such a contract, the rights and duties of the contracting parties arise not at the moment of its conclusion but only in the event the condition becomes realized.

Irrespective of this, the parties are considered to be in the contract relation and they may not deviate from the contract conditions, and, in particular, make actions which prevent the realization of the condition. A contract made under the suspensive condition is distinct from the preliminary contract provided by the Civil Code. It does not require, in order to implement the rights and duties, any other legal fact except the realization of the condition.

In turn, as a contract made under the resolutory condition is regarded, according to the Civil Code (Article 157.2), a contract in which the parties have made the termination of the rights and duties dependent upon the circumstance in respect of which it is unknown whether or not it will occur. The rights and duties of the contracting parties arise under such a contract at the moment of its conclusion but they will cease in the event the condition becomes realized.

In respect of conditional contracts, the Civil Code provides special rules the purpose of which is to protect the honest party of the transaction. According to them, if the occurrence of the condition is hindered in bad faith by a party to whom the occurrence of the condition is disadvantageous, then the condition is to be considered as having occurred; whereas in the event the occurrence of the condition is aided in bad faith by a party for whom the occurrence of the condition is advantageous, then the condition is to be considered as not having occurred (Article 157.3).

Contracts for enterprise activities or entrepreneurial contracts[47] are not specifically distinguished in the rules of the Civil Code. However, it does not mean that the specific nature of the entrepreneurial contract is left unobserved in the Civil Code if not in Russian contract law. For the regulation of such contracts, and the obligations connected with enterprise activities, the Civil Code provides specific rules which are placed in its general as well as special part, in which such specific rules are provided within the general civil law division of contracts into different types.

The Russian contract law is also acquainted with consumer contracts in which one party is an entrepreneur and the other party is a physical person who obtains goods or services or works for his personal needs. The Civil Code does not contain specific rules explicitly regulating consumer contracts, but the consumer is subject to the weaker party protection for the purpose of which there are special rules in the Civil Code. These rules concern public contracts (Article 426) and contracts of adhesion (Article 428) as well as such types of contract as retail (Articles 492–505) and consumer work (Articles 730–39). Alongside these, there is consumer protection legislation in Russia, and the consumer is protected not only by the rules on conclusion of contract but also by the rules providing strict liability of entrepreneurs who participate as counterparties in the contracts with consumers.

Practically speaking, the most important classification of contracts in the Russian law is based on the law. It is used in the part of the Civil Code regulating different types of contract where contracts are listed by types and species. Consequently the legal regulation of civil law relations has been traditionally based on the type of contract distinction, together with the general rule that the rules regulating the other type of contract are not applicable to a contract of the other type unless otherwise provided by the law. Irrespective of this, Russian contract law does not, however, recognize the enumeration principle. Following from this, contracts unmentioned in the law or innominate contracts (*contractus innominati*) are also recognized in Russian contract law.

At present, in Russia as elsewhere in countries with developed civil law regulations, individual contracts often break the boundaries between contract types. So, for instance, sale contract may include elements of the work contract such as obligations of installation and maintenance, which is common for contracts on delivery of equipment. Such subsidiary obligations do not, however, change the nature of the principle contract relation according to which the type of contract is usually

47 For more on this subject, see below.

determined, although the subsidiary obligation is usually subject to its own rules. Furthermore, Russian contract law is also acquainted with mixed and complex contracts the regulation of which is subject to the application of the rules regulating different types of contract.

In the rules concerning freedom of contract of the Civil Code (Article 421.2), it is expressly provided that the parties have the right to conclude a contract, both defined and undefined by the law or by other legal acts. In principle, this rule is interpreted broadly, and the parties have almost unlimited right to choose a contract model from the other legal system or develop themselves a new one. In respect of the freedom of contract model only three exceptions limiting it are known in Russian contract law. First, the Civil Code or other legal act requires in some cases that certain contract relations are subject to the application of only particular contract constructions (models) and this concerns, in particular, carriage and rental of housing accommodation. As a second exception can be considered the rule according to which the legislator may impose on the contracting party the duty to conclude the contract. In such cases, the legislator usually also indicates the contract model to be used in the contracting; this concerns, in particular, state contracts (on supply or works for state needs). The third exception from the freedom of contract model transpires in that certain contract models are allowed to be used only by a limited group of civil law subjects; this concerns, in particular, bank deposits, the other party of which may be only a bank or other credit organization. Such an exception can be met also as a prohibition addressed to certain subjects of the use certain contract models.[48]

The principle of the freedom of contract model does not solve the problem of unmentioned contracts and, in particular, the question of which contracts must be regarded as innominate, taking into account that contracts are classified in the Civil Code into types and species of contract and they are regulated additionally by the general contract law and even civil law rules. As an innominate or *sui generis* contract is considered in Russian contract law only a contract the rules applicable to which are not found in the law or other legal act regulating different types and species of contract. Just such contracts may be subject to the application of the rules regulating a similar type of contract, and, in failure of this, the general contract law rules contained in the general part of the obligation law rules of the Civil Code.[49] However, in the event the application of the analogy of rule or of the general obligation law (contract law) norms does not achieve the desired result, then the application of the analogy of law can be used where the solution is based on the general principles and sense of civil legislation and the requirements of good faith, reasonableness, and fairness. Thus, any contract is valid in Russian contract law, even though the rules on it are not found, as long as it does not contradict the legislation (Article 8). Hence, Russian contract practice is acquainted with various kinds of contracts which are not mentioned in the civil legislation, as, for instance, the above-presented organizer contracts.[50]

Mixed contracts or mixed-type contracts are regarded in Russian law as contracts of specific nature, and they are mentioned in the rules concerning freedom of contract of the Civil Code (Article 421.3). They comprehend contracts which contain the elements of different contracts or different

48 Braginsky and Vitrjansky 1999: 406–7.

49 Sergeev 1 2009: 844–5.

50 For more on innominate, mixed, and complex contracts, see M.I. Braginsky and V.V. Vitryansky, Договорное право. Общие положения [Contract Law. General Provisions] (2001): 331–4; Suhanov 2008: 176, and D.V. Ogorodov and M.Yu. Chelyshev, Смешанные договоры в частном праве: отдельные вопросы теории и практики [Mixed Contracts in Private Law: Certain Questions of Theory and Practice], Законодательство и экономика [Legislation and Economics] 10 (2005), available at http://www.lawmix.ru/comm/213/ (accessed 25 May 2010).

types of contracts provided by the law, which, however, are integrated in the joint obligation.[51] It is expressly established in Article 421.3 of the Civil Code the parties have the right to conclude a contract which contains the elements of different types of contract provided by the law or other legal acts (mixed contract). In such a case, the rules on contracts whose elements are contained in the mixed contract are to be applied in the corresponding parts. As a rule a mixed contract may not be a nominate contracts, except in the case, for instance, of commodity credit[52] and hire purchase,[53] [54] but it must contain at the minimum the elements of one of the nominate contracts, the rules on which are to be applied.[55] In the event of collision between the norms of the Civil Code regulating types of contract applicable to the case and the general rules of the obligation law of the Civil Code, the application of the special norms regulating types of contract is prioritized. However, such a solution may be exempted, in accordance with Article 421.3 of the Civil Code, due to the nature of the mixed contract at issue or because of the agreement between the parties.

Close to the concept of mixed contract is the concept of complex contract. The complex contract relation may be constructed as an integration of different types of contract in which case it is impossible to distinguish the main and subsidiary obligation from the contract. A complex contract is distinguished from a mixed contract in that it is constructed not by the contracting parties as a mixed contract but by the legislator, wherefore it is a nominate contract. Examples of the complex contract are the finance lease or leasing, regulated by Articles 665–70 of the Civil Code, and the commercial concession or franchise, regulated by Articles 1027–40 of the Civil Code.

Entrepreneurial Contracts[56]

Contracts used in the enterprise activities or entrepreneurial contracts have their own peculiarities, although they are not, as stated above, specifically distinguished in the rules of the Civil Code. For the regulation of such contracts and obligations connected with enterprise activities, the Civil Code provides specific rules which are placed in its general as well as special part, in which such specific rules are provided within the general civil law division of contracts into different types. In addition to entrepreneurial contracts which may be regarded as modifications of ordinary contracts, Russian law recognizes contracts which are purported to be used only between entrepreneurs.

Entrepreneurial contracts are characterized in Russian civil law as commercial transactions which form the specific group of civil law contracts. They are contracts in which at least one party is a subject of enterprise activities and by which the rights and duties connected with the enterprise activities arise, are changed, or terminated. Such a contract is the civil law contract and is subject

---

51 O.N. Sadikov (ed.), Комментарий к Гражданскому кодексу Российской Федерации, Части первой [Commentary on the Civil Code of the Russian Federation, Part 1] (2005): 945.

52 According to Article 822 of the Civil Code, unless otherwise provided by the contract of commodity credit, the conditions concerning quantity, assortment, completeness, quality, and packaging of the goods provided by the contract are to be performed in accordance with the rules on sale of goods.

53 See below.

54 M.I., Braginsky, Смешанные договоры [Mixed Contracts] (2007): 71.

55 D.V. Ogorodov and M. Yu Chelyshev, Смешанный договор и вопросы теории правового регулирования [Mixed Contract and Questions of Theory of Legal Regulation] (2007): 52.

56 See Sergeev 1 2009: 852–3 and, in particular, V.F. Popondopulo (ed.), Коммерческое (предпринимательское) право, Том I [Commercial (Entrepreneurial) Law, Volume I] (2009): 285–92; V.V. Laptev and S.S. Zankovsky, Предпринимательское (хозяйственное) право [Entrepreneurial (Economic) Law] (2006): 231–337, and S.S. Zankovsky, Предпринимательские договоры [Entrepreneurial Contracts] (2004): 1–43.

to the application of the general principles of civil law regulation. However, its specific nature must be observed, which transpires through the Civil Code norms concerning the subjects, objects, contracting procedure, and content. The specific nature of entrepreneurial activity is also taken into account in the Civil Code by accepting a commercial custom as a general legal source applicable to contract relations connected with entrepreneurship (Article 5). Furthermore, the specific nature of the enterprise activities is also shown in the special proceedings for resolving disputes between the parties of entrepreneurial contracts which are regarded as economic disputes to be handled in the arbitrazh court.

The commercial transaction, by which term a contract used in enterprise activities is characterized, is generally understood as a transaction regarded in law as commercial irrespective of by whom it is made (objective criterion), or as a transaction the party of which is an entrepreneur pursuing or realizing a commercial goal (subjective criterion). It is presumed that any transaction made by a entrepreneur is related to commercial activities. So the starting point is the subjective criterion of the commercial transaction. The actual aim of the transaction is also important and in respect of the commercial transaction this means profit seeking. In general, a commercial transaction is presumed as compensated in Russian contract law.

In commercial transactions, at least one party must be a duly registered individual entrepreneur or a commercial organization regardless of its legal form or a noncommercial organization within the limits of its practice of enterprise activities. On the other hand, a transaction purported to be commercial for the entrepreneur may be usual (noncommercial), for instance, for the consumer, in respect of whom general civil law rules ought to be applied. The contracts which are purported to be used in Russia only between entrepreneurs include supply, agricultural procurement, and supply for state needs. As commercial transactions used between enterprises are also regarded sale and lease of enterprise, leasing, and commercial concession the aim of which is to practice enterprise activities. In turn, the contracts one party of which must be under the law an entrepreneur include retail, energy supply, rental, consumer work, entrusted administration, and credit as well as bank deposits and bank accounts.

In particular, the special nature of contracts used in entrepreneurship finds expression in the provisions of the Civil Code regulating conclusion of contract, performance of obligations, and liability for violation of obligations. Hence, the scope of freedom of contract connected to entrepreneurial contracts is larger than for usual contracts, and this finds expression in the possibilities to determine contract conditions: in the obligations connected to entrepreneurship it is allowed, under the Civil Code (Article 310), to determine cases where the unilateral refusal to perform the obligation or the unilateral amendment of its terms is admissible, unless otherwise following from the law or from the substance of the obligation. On the other hand, early performance of an entrepreneurial obligation is presumed in the Civil Code (Article 315) to be forbidden; it is allowed only in cases when the possibility of performing the obligation early is provided by the law, other legal acts, or the conditions of the obligation or follows from the customs of trade or the nature of the obligation. Furthermore, the obligations connected with entrepreneurship presume, under the Civil Code (Article 322.2), solidarity (of joint debtors and joint creditors), and, in addition to this, they presume strict liability, which only force majeure may exclude or limit (Article 401.3). However, in Russian law this rule is in fact dispositive—that is, the liability may be limited not only by the law but also by the contract, provided that this is not the case of an intentional breach of contract. The Civil Code expressly provides that a contract (contractual provision) excluding the liability for a future intentional breach is null and void (Article 401.4). Additionally, it is noteworthy that entrepreneurial activity may be subject to obligatory contracting, and entrepreneurial contracts can fall into other restrictions of freedom of contract provided in antimonopoly legislation and the norms on consumer protection and price control.

Conclusion of Contract[57]

Form requirements In Russian contract law, the observance of form requirements is traditionally imposed as a precondition for the birth of a contract. According to Article 432 of the Civil Code, which contains the basic rules on conclusion of contract, a contract is to be considered concluded if an agreement has been reached on all essential conditions of the contract among the parties in the form required in appropriate cases (Article 432.1). The rules on the forms of contract are contained in the norms of the Civil Code regulating not only transactions (Articles 158–65) and conclusion of contract (Article 434) but also different types of contract. The rules on the form requirements may be represented also in the other laws concerning the concrete type or species of a contract. The norms regulating forms of contract contain not only form requirements but also the rules on the consequences of nonobservance of them. The form requirements concerning contracts are significantly important in respect of the transactions between enterprises, which must be done, with certain exceptions, in written (and signed) form. In certain cases, contracts (transactions) are in Russian law also subject to registration requirements.

Contracts (transactions) are divided in the Civil Code, on the ground of the form requirements concerning them, into oral and written, and written contracts are divided, in turn, into those which must be concluded in simple written form, and contracts which require notarial authentication or must be done in notarial form. This division reflects the hierarchy of the form requirements concerning contracts in Russian law: the simplest of them is oral, next is the simple written form and the most taxing form is the notarial form of contract.

According to the generic rule of the Civil Code on the forms of contract (Article 434.1), a contract may be concluded in any form provided for the conclusion of transactions, unless the law for contracts of the given type have established a defined form. The form of transaction established by the law is regarded in Russian law as a minimum requirement, and this entails the prohibition of choosing a form which is simpler than the established one. However, the use of a more taxing form depends entirely on the will of the contractual parties. If the parties use this right and choose for their transaction the simple written or notarial form, such a transaction is subject to the application of the rules of the Civil Code on the consequences of nonobservance of the form requirements of transaction (Articles 162 and 165).

Those cases where oral form may be used for transactions are defined in Russian contract law on the residual principle. According to Article 159 of the Civil Code regulating oral transactions, a transaction for which the law or agreement of the parties has not established a written (simple or notarial) form may be concluded orally (Article 159.1). On the other hand, different documents can be used in the execution of an oral contract as evidence of performance, which, however, does not change its character. As a special case may be regarded the possibility provided by the Civil Code (Article 159.3) to conclude an oral contract for the execution of a written contract unless it is not contradictory to the law, other legal acts, and a contract. Contracts executed at the moment of their conclusion may also be made according to the Civil Code (Articles 159.2 and 161.2) orally. However, this does not concern transactions for which notarial form is established and transactions for which nonobservence of simple written form entails their invalidity.

57 For more on this subject, see, for instance, Braginsky and Vitrjansky 1999: 340–55 and Sergeev 1 2009: 470–82 and 854–60.

In certain cases, a contract can also be concluded in Russia concludently. This transpires from the generic rule of the Civil Code on the form requirements of transactions. According to this, a transaction which may be concluded orally is also to be considered made where the conduct of a person makes his will to conclude the transaction apparent (Article 158.2). In certain cases a concludent act may stand under the Civil Code merely for the prolongation of validity of the contract. Such a possibility is provided in the rules on lease, according to which if the lessee continues to use property after the expiration of the term of the contract in the absence of objections on the part of the lessor, the contract is to be considered renewed on the same conditions and for an indefinite term (Article 621.2).

The possibilities to use concludent act in conclusion of contract are expressly provided in the rules of the Civil Code on this, and this concerns the acceptance of an offer by concludent acts (Articles 434.3 and 438.3). This may occur in the way that the offeree executes, within the period established for the acceptance of an offer, the actions relating to the fulfillment of the contractual conditions specified in it (Article 438.3). Such actions concern, among others, shipment of goods, provision of services, and performance of work, as well as payment of the appropriate amount.

Silence is not usually regarded as an expression of the will in Russian civil law and it may be legally significant only exceptionally. It is expressly provided in the generic rule of the Civil Code concerning the form of transactions that silence is to be recognized as an expression of will to conclude a transaction in cases provided by the law or by agreement of the parties (Article 158.3). It is such a silence that occurs in the situation presented above where the lessee continues to use property after the expiration of the term of the contract in the absence of objections on the part of the lessor (Article 621.2). It is just such a silence which has legal significance.

The provisions on contracts which require written form are contained in the Civil Code in Articles 161 and 162 concerning transactions in written form and in Article 434 regulating form of contract, as well as in the norms regulating different types of contract. In accordance with the rules concerning transactions, the following must be made in simple written form, except for transactions requiring notarial authentication:

- transactions of juristic persons with one another and with physical persons;
- transactions of physical persons with one another for an amount over ten times the minimum monthly wage established by the law, and
- in cases provided by the law irrespective of the transaction amount (Article 161).

As a consequence of nonobservance of the simple written form of a transaction, the Civil Code (Article 162.1) provides the prohibition of relying for confirmation of the transaction and its conditions upon the testimony of witnesses. Furthermore, in cases explicitly indicated by the law or on the agreement of the parties, nonobservance of the simple written form of a transaction entails its invalidity (Article 162.2).

Written form is imposed as obligatory for certain types of contract in the rules of the Civil Code regulating different types of contract. This requirement does not depend on the sum of a contract or on the identity of its parties. In written form must be concluded: a contract of franchise (Article 1028.1), a bank deposit contract (Article 836.1), a credit contract (Article 820), and an insurance contract (Article 940.1). Furthermore written form is imposed as obligatory in the Civil Code for contracts on commercial representation (Article 184.3), suretyship (Article 362), and pledge (Article 339.2), as well as for conditions on liquidated damages (penalty) (Article 331). In respect of foreign trade transactions, it is expressly provided in the rules on the consequences for nonobservance of the written form requirements (Article 162) that nonobservance of simple written form of a foreign trade transaction is to entail its invalidity (Article 162.3).

Written contract is to be made in Russia by the preparation of a document expressing its content and signed by the person or persons concluding the transaction, or by persons properly authorized by them (Article 160). Contract documents may be prepared in several copies and each of them is considered as an original with the same legal force. Contract documents must include the necessary data required by the law and agreed by the parties such as the names of the parties, the object of the contract, the amount of the payment, place of the performance, date, and signatures.[58] A contract must be signed on behalf of the juristic person by the person who is authorized by virtue of the law or constituent documents to act as its executive body. A contract may be signed by using fax copies, electronic signature, or other analogues of personal signature, but on the condition that it is allowed by the law or other legal act or agreed between the parties (Article 160.2).

A contract may also be concluded, according to the rules on form of contract of the Civil Code (Article 434), by the exchange of documents by mail, telegraph, teletype, telephone, electronic, or other communications enabling reliable determination of the fact that the document comes from a party to the contract (Article 434.2).[59] A contract may be made also by concludent acts in response to the written offer (Article 434.3). The demand for written form of contract may stand for other requirements in addition to its signing. The above-presented rules of the Civil Code on written form of transactions (Article 160) expressly provides that the law, other legal acts, and agreement of the parties may establish additional requirements to which the form of a transaction must conform. It may mean execution on a defined printed form, confirmation by a seal, etc. (Article 160.1).

The generic rule according to which ways of concluding a contract other than by preparing a single document are allowed recognizes exceptions which are derived from the norms on different types of contract. They concern sale of immovables (Article 550) and enterprise (Article 560.1), lease of buildings and structures (Article 651.1) and enterprise (Article 658.1), as well as contract on entrusted administration of immovable property (Article 1017.2). These contracts must be made in written form by the preparation of a single document signed by the parties.

Notarial authentication is required according to Article 163 of the Civil Code in cases indicated in the law[60] or as provided by agreement of the parties (Article 163.2). Notarial authentication is under the law obligatory in the cases of:

- a mortgage contract (Article 339.2);
- a contract of pledge movable property or of the right to property in security for obligations under a contract which require notarial authentication (Article 339.2);
- an agreement between the pledgee and the pledgor which allows satisfaction of a claim of the pledgee at the expense of pledged immovable property without resort to a court (Article 349.1);
- an assignment of claim and transfer of debt based upon a transaction made in notarial form (Articles 389 and 391), and
- contract of rent (Article 584).

58 If a contract does not contain the necessary data required by the law or agreed by the parties or the document to be attached to it, it is regarded as invalid.

59 The use of electronic contract documents and electronic signatures in Russia is regulated by the Information Law (Law on Information, Information Technology, and Protection of Information no 1-FZ of 27 July 2006.

60 Notarial authentication is also regulated in the Law on the Grounds of Notary Legislation 1993.

As to the requirements for notarial form provided by the agreement of the parties, these are obligatory upon the demand of the other party.

Many transactions, even where made in the proper form, do not give rise to civil law rights and duties before being registered. It is expressly provided in the generic rule of the Civil Code on time of conclusion of contract (Article 433) that a contract subject to state registration is to be considered concluded from the moment of its registration (Article 433.3).[61] Rights to property subject to state registration also arise, according to the rule on grounds for the origin of civil law rights and duties of the Civil Code (Article 8), from the moment of registration of the respective rights to it (Article 8.2). Registration is directly referred to in the rules of the Civil Code on the origin of the right of ownership to newly created immovable property (Article 219) and acquired property if it is subject to state registration (Article 223.2). The moment of registration is considered decisive also for the transfer of a share in the right of common ownership (Article 251).

The requirements on state registration of transactions are contained in Article 164 of the Civil Code. According to it, transactions with land and other immovable property are to be subject to state registration (Article 164.1). This rule is provided with reference to the rules of the Civil Code on state registration of immovable property (Article 131.1), according to which the right of ownership and other real rights to immovable things,[62] restrictions of these rights, their origin, transfer, and termination are to be subject to state registration in the single state register.[63] According to the Civil Code (Article 164.2), transactions concerning certain movable property may also be subjected under the law to state registration.

In the rules of the Civil Code regulating types of contract, state registration is imposed as obligatory in respect of franchise contract (Article 1028.2), contract for sale of residential accommodation (Article 558.2) and of enterprise (Article 560.3), as well as contract under which immovable property is alienated against payment of rent (Article 584) and contract of lease of enterprise (Article 658.2).

Obligatory registration is also imposed for contract on lease of immovable property (Articles 609.2 and 651.2) and on entrusted administration of this (Article 1017.2). State registration is obligatory under the Civil Code (Article 339.3) for mortgage contracts. It is expressly provided in the rules on these contracts that nonobservance of the registration requirements entails the invalidity of the contract. Furthermore, noteworthy are the rules on intellectual property contained in the fourth part of the Civil Code which expressly establish that the exclusive right to the result of intellectual activity or method of individualization is recognized and protected on condition of the state registration of such result or such method. Also contracts on alienation of exclusive rights and license contracts concerning the objects subjected to state registration are subject to registration. This requirement also concerns transfer of exclusive rights and rights of use without a contract.

61 This rule is also enforced in Russian judicial practice where it is stated that a mortgage contract is considered concluded when it is notarially authenticated and registered in the established order. See Хозяйство и право [Economy and Law] 4 (2000): 124.

62 What is regarded as immovable property is determined in Article 130.1 of the Civil Code defining immovable things and it includes aircrafts, marine and inland vessels and spacecrafts, inland navigation ships, and space objects subject to state registration. The Civil Code also provides that other property may be recognized as immovables (Article 130.1).

63 This rule, however, does not directly provide that transactions concerning these consequences are also to be registered. This was stated in Russian arbitrazh practice. See Вестник Высшего Арбитражного Суда Российской Федерации [Herald of the Supreme Arbitrazh Court of the Russian Federation] 11 (1999). See also Abova, Boguslavsky, Kabalkin, and Lisicin-Svetlanov 2007: 188.

In these cases, too, nonobservance of the registration requirements entails the invalidity of the contract or noncontractual transfer.

From the rules concerning the registration requirements for transactions, it is necessary to distinguish the provisions regulating registration of the right grounded on the transaction. So, in Article 550 of the Civil Code concerning the form of the contract for sale of an immovable, it is only provided that such a contract is to be made in written form by the preparation of a single document signed by the parties, whereas the registration requirement is established in Article 551 of the Civil Code which regulates the state registration of the transfer of the right of ownership to an immovable to concern only the transfer of the right of ownership to an immovable under a contract for sale of immovable (Article 551.1). Furthermore, the same article provides that, although the parties have executed the contract for sale of an immovable before the state registration of the transfer of the right of ownership, it is not a ground for changing their relations with third persons (Article 551.2). Thus, all the legal relations of the contractual parties arisen before the registration continue until the registration has occurred. Therefore, for instance, rent is to continue to be paid to the seller, and the seller is further obligated to perform the pledge duties, until the transfer of the right of ownership is registered. Until this moment the seller has the authority to dispose of the object sold by him as well.[64]

In the Civil Code, the case where the registration duty concerns both the contract and the transfer of the right grounded on it is also known. According to the rules of the Civil Code on contract for sale of enterprise (Article 560.3), it is considered concluded from the moment of its registration (Article 560.3), but the right of ownership to the enterprise passes to the buyer from the moment of state registration of this right (Article 564.1). Thus, the contract itself does not, even when registered, constitute the transfer of the right of ownership. However, it is provided with other legal effects which are established in the rules on sale of enterprise. Accordingly, the buyer to whom the enterprise is transferred before the transfer of the ownership has the right, until the ownership has passed to him, to dispose of the property and rights included as part of the transferred enterprise to the extent to which it is necessary for the purposes for which the enterprise was obtained (Article 564.3).[65]

In Russian civil law, it is regarded as a general principle that the observance of the written form requirement depends on the will of the parties. Only where the other contractual party intends to dispute the existence of the contract or certain conditions of it which are not laid out in the obligatory written form, may he bring a suit concerning it. The written form requirement imposed by the law as obligatory merely mean a presumption that, if the written form is not observed, there is no contract at all. The other party who pleads that the agreement exists, although the form requirements are not observed, has to prove it. However, his possibilities in such a case are rather limited since, according to the rule of the Civil Code on consequences of nonobservance of the simple written form for a transaction (Article 162), this entails that, in case of dispute, the parties lose the right to rely for confirmation of the transaction and its conditions upon the testimony of witnesses;[66] however, their right to present written and other evidence is not to be deprived (Article 162.1). Instead, where the written form requirement is based on the agreement of the

---

64 See Abova, Boguslavsky, Kabalkin, and Lisicin-Svetlanov 2007: 456 and, in particular, Sergeev 2 2009: 119–20 where the opinion that the seller has the right of disposition to the sold immovable thing, as also presented by the Supreme Arbitrazh Court (Вестник Высшего Арбитражного Суда Российской Федерации [Herald of the Supreme Arbitrazh Court of the Russian Federation] (1998) 10), is criticized.

65 Sergeev 2 2009: 126–7.

66 In exceptional cases, including storage contract, the testimony of witnesses is, however, allowed under the Civil Code. The question may be, for instance, of a dispute concerning the transfer of a thing for

parties, the consequence of nonobservance of written form is that the contract shall be considered unconcluded.[67]

The nonobservence of the written form requirement for contract or its conclusion orally may in certain cases, subject to public interests, entail its invalidity (or nullity). Such a consequence is often expressly indicated in the rules in which written form is imposed as obligatory for the above-mentioned types of contract. In other cases where written form is imposed as obligatory, the nonobservence of this requirement may also cause nullity of the contract, which is based on the presumption of nullity of the transaction contrary to the law in Russian law. Moreover, the nonobservance of the requirements on state registration and notarial authentication cause, in accordance with the Civil Code (Article 165.1), invalidity of the contract in which case it is null (and void). However, if there is no direct indication in the law that the nonobservence of registration requirements entails invalidity of the contract, then the contract is considered unconcluded until it is registered.[68] [69] Other consequences of nonregistration are known in Russian law, too. Thus the rules of the Civil Code on commercial concession (Article 1028.2) provide that, where the contract is left unregistered, this is not to be referred to in relations with third persons.

Contract conclusion procedure[70] According to the basic rules of the Civil Code on conclusion of contract, a (valid) contract is concluded when the other contracting party sends an offer or proposal to conclude a contract and the other party accepts it or approves the offer (Article 432.2). Russian law is acquainted with two traditional ways of conclusion of contract, and both are based on the offer–acceptance model. One of them is purported for the situation where a contract is concluded between present parties, whereas the other concerns conclusion of contract between absent parties. Although each of these ways of concluding a contract is subject to its own rules, common to both is that, in the conclusion process, the acceptance follows the offer. What is distinctive is that, in the case of contracting between absent parties, they are relatively far from each other wherefore there is a time interruption in their expressions of their wills, whereas present contracting parties are in direct contact with each other. On the other hand, modern technical development has changed this situation, and even where the parties are physically far from each other, they have still possibilities for contracting between themselves without significant time interruptions by using, for instance, telephone, fax, or email.

Ways to conclude a contract other than the traditional way based on the exchange of offer and acceptance are expressly mentioned in the rule of the Civil Code (Article 434.2) on form of contract. It may be concluded, as presented above, by preparing a jointly signed document using, for instance, different communication forms, provided, however, that it is possible to establish reliably that the document originates from a contracting party. Furthermore, a contract, for instance a long-term contract, may directly include a clause that an order confirming the contract is regarded as received unless its addressee conveys his negative answer, in which case the question is of the possibility of using silent acceptance in contracting. Moreover, contracts concluded at auction

---

storage in emergency cases (Article 887.1). In the event a transaction is connected with a crime, it may also be proved by any evidence whose use is regulated by the criminal process law.

67 See Abova, Boguslavsky, Kabalkin, and Lisicin-Svetlanov 2007: 186.

68 See Sergeev 1 2009: 859.

69 This division into cases where a contract becomes invalid or is considered unconcluded has been subject to detailed criticism. See, for instance, Sergeev 1 2009: 482.

70 For more on this subject, see, for instance, Sergeev 1 2009: 861–9; Suhanov 2008: 196–212; Abova, Boguslavsky, Kabalkin, and Lisicin-Svetlanov 2007: 369–83, and Zankovsky 2004: 44–52, as well as Braginsky and Vitrjansky 1999: 193–266.

are subject to the rules of the Civil Code which deviate from the ordinary conclusion of contract procedure. Moreover, the contract of adhesion forms a special case in Russian contract law, and the rules of the Civil Code concerning it are provided for the legal protection of the adhering party of the contract (Article 428). In certain cases, a contract may also arise in Russian law by court decision in the so-called precontractual dispute procedure (Article 446). Such a procedure is provided in the Civil Code to apply to public contracts and preliminary contracts; close to it is the procedure for the conclusion of supply contracts established under the Civil Code.

According to the general rule of the Civil Code, on conclusion of contract, the basic element of a contract is an offer which is accepted. The contracting procedure starts with the presentation of the offer. All circumstances preceding it, including those occurring at the negotiations with the exception of a preliminary contract containing the obligation to conclude the contract, are irrelevant in respect of the conclusion of contract. This concerns the correspondence between the parties, their letters of intent, and other documents showing their intention to conclude the contract, if they do not correspond to the requirements established for the offer and its acceptance in the law. This does not, however, mean that such documents could be without legal significance since they may be used in the interpretation of the contract. Thus the rules of the Civil Code regulating interpretation of contract enable namely that in the determination of the real common will of the parties, the negotiations and correspondence preceding the contract are to be taken into account (Article 431). These are related, however, only to the determination of the content of the contract, and only as evidence without constitutive effect.

The general offer–acceptance model is purposed to be used in Russia as elsewhere in the cases when offered is:

- an act as consideration for the obligation—for instance, where goods or service are offered against the payment of price; or
- an obligation as consideration for the act or inactions—for instance, where a pecuniary compensation is offered for the future performance of the determined act, or
- an obligation as consideration for the obligation, which means the future performances of both the contracting parties.[71]

As an offer is recognized, according to the Civil Code, a proposal addressed to one or several concrete persons, and it must be sufficiently definite and express the intent of the person who has made it for him to consider himself as having concluded a contract with the addressee by whom the proposal is to be accepted (Article 435.1). Hence, the offer must be enough clear for its addressee to be able to make the right conclusion on its ground that the offeror intends to enter into the contract. Therefore, any indefiniteness of the elements of the future contract concerning contracting parties, their rights and duties, and the object of contract as well may cause dissent in interpretations between the parties, in the consequence of which the proposal is to not be considered to be an offer.

As corresponding to the rules of the Civil Code is regarded a proposal containing all the essential conditions of the contract from which the will of the person who made the proposal appears to conclude a contract on the terms specified in the proposal with anyone who responds—this is considered an offer or, to be exact, a public offer in accordance with Article 437.2 of the Civil Code concerning offers.[72] On the other hand, the rules on offers in the Civil Code contain a

71 Abova, Boguslavsky, Kabalkin, and Lisicin-Svetlanov 2007: 370.

72 In addition to the general provisions on the public offer, the norms of the Civil Code regulating types of contracts contain a special rule (Article 494.2) applied in cases of retail sale. According to it,

general presumption that advertising and other proposals addressed to an indeterminate group of persons are to be regarded as an invitation to make offers unless otherwise expressly indicated in the proposal (Article 437.1).[73]

The binding effect (sanctity) of the offer and its irrevocability are regulated in their own rules in the Civil Code (Article 435.2 and 436). The binding effect of the offer comprehends that, if the concrete addressee of the offer informs the offeror that he has accepted the offer or is agree to conclude the contract on the conditions presented in the offer, the contract is to be considered concluded. In turn, the requirement of irrevocability established for the offer (Article 436) means that the offeror may not revoke his offer during the period established for its acceptance. This rule is, however, dispositive, and the offeror may determine in his offer otherwise. The possibility to revoke the offer may follow from the nature of the proposal or the situation in which it was made.

The requirements of binding force and irrevocability of the offer means that, if during the time of the binding force of the offer, the offeror concludes the contract with the other person than the addressee of the offer, this does not preclude the addressee from informing the offeror that he has accepted the offer, wherefore the contract is to be considered concluded. The accordingly arisen contract empowers its party to demand the contract performance and, where this is impossible, compensation for damages caused by the breach of contract[74].[75]

The binding force of the offer starts, according to the rules of the Civil Code on offers, from the moment it is received by the addressee (Article 435.2). Thus, before it, the offer may be revoked by the offeror, and in the event a notice on the revocation of the offer has arrived earlier than or simultaneously with the offer, the offer is considered not to have been received (Article 435.2).

Revocation of the offer may occur in principle also in the case of an above-mentioned long-term contract in the performance of which supply orders are used. Such orders of the buyer are construed in Russia as acceptances of the continuous offer. Thus, if the order is received by the seller, he is obliged to perform it, but in respect of future deliveries, the seller may revoke his offer.[76]

---

exhibiting at the place of sale (at stands, in shop windows, etc.) of goods, demonstration of samples of them, or presentation of information on goods offered for sale (descriptions, catalogs, pictures of goods, etc.) at the place of their sale is considered a public offer irrespective of whether prices and other essential conditions of a retail sale contract are specified, unless the seller has clearly defined that the respective goods are not meant for sale.

73 Whether the question is of a public order or of an invitation to submit offers depends on the nature of a proposal and it is up to the person who has made the proposal to take care that it is understood as an offer. This he may ensure by indicating expressly in his proposal that it is an offer. On the other hand, in Russian doctrine requests which are designated to an undefined group of people and those addressed to each and every person are distinguished. Accordingly, as an offer is regarded a proposal addressed to each and every person intended to be accepted at any moment only by one person and be revoked before the new acceptance has been reached. In turn, a request designated to an undefined group of people is regarded as an invitation to submit offers, unless it clearly follows from the request that its giver intends to enter into the contract with any person who answers his request. See Abova, Boguslavsky, Kabalkin, and Lisicin-Svetlanov 2007: 373–4.

74 Suhanov 2008: 199 and A.N. Kucher, Теория и практика преддоговорного этапа: юридический аспект [Theory and Practice of Precontractual Phase: Juridical Aspect] (2005): 114–21.

75 Thus, the offeror becomes a party in a contractual relation with both, and each of them may demand the contract performance and in default of it compensation for damages covering his positive contract interest.

76 See Abova, Boguslavsky, Kabalkin, and Lisicin-Svetlanov 2007: 373.

It is not only the binding force of the offer but also the period of its acceptance determined by the offeror which starts from the moment when the addressee has received the offer.[77] The offer expires at the moment, when the offeror receives from the addressee the answer which is negative to or deviates from his offer as well as when the period for its acceptance ends.

As an acceptance of the offer (or consent to the contract) is understood, according to Article 438 of the Civil Code, the response of a person to whom an offer is addressed on its acceptance. An acceptance is, to the same extent as an offer, an expression of the will, and it must be comprehensive–in other words, accepting all the conditions contained in the offer, and unqualified or without any additional conditions. However, as for the offer, there is no form requirements concerning acceptance in the Civil Code. The acceptance must occur, according to the Civil Code (Article 440 and 441), within the period established for it in the offer or by the law, or in the absence of it, in the course of time normally necessary for the acceptance, or within a reasonable time, in the case of a written offer, in which the term for the acceptance is not determined (Article 441.1). As reasonable is considered the time which is sufficient for the bidirectional exchange of the corresponding documents by post. As to the case of an oral offer which does not contain the term for its acceptance, the response to it must be given immediately (Article 441.2).

The answer which contains consent to conclude a contract on terms other than those proposed in the offer or on deviating or additional conditions is not considered, under Article 443 of the Civil Code, as an acceptance. However, it may be regarded as a counteroffer on the provision that it corresponds otherwise the characteristics of an offer or contains all the essential conditions of the future contract. If some essential condition is missing from the answer to the offer, however, it is not even considered as a counteroffer. Such an answer may be regarded as a refusal to conclude the contract and at the same time as a proposal to conclude another contract.

The rules of the Civil Code on acceptance are partly similar to the provisions on offer. This concerns in particular the revocation of acceptance. As in the case of the offer, if a notice on the revocation of an acceptance has reached the offeror earlier than the acceptance or simultaneously with it, the acceptance is to be considered not to have been received (Article 439). Thus, the acceptance likewise the offer may be revoked only before the counterparty has received it.[78] Where the acceptance is received by the offeror, the contract is considered concluded. Thus the late revocation of an acceptance which is the same as the acceptance is without legal significance in Russian law.[79]

Silence is not regarded, according to the Civil Code, as acceptance unless it otherwise follows from the law, commercial customs, or previous business relations of the parties or course of dealing (Article 438.2).[80] Accordingly, it may assume, in Russia, legal significance as the acceptance of the offer (but not as the offer) on the basis of the law, commercial custom, or established practice. Silence is understood according to the Civil Code as either a positive or negative answer. As a positive answer it is used very often. So, according to the rules on lease, if the term of the lease is not determined in the contract, and neither of the parties has refused the contract before the

77 This comprehends the adoption of the reception theory in Russian contract law.

78 The acceptance sent by post is considered as having occurred the moment it is left to be posted, wherefore it is not revocable by a later phone call or fax, even though this has occurred before the acceptance has arrived. See Abova, Boguslavsky, Kabalkin, and Lisicin-Svetlanov 2007: 375.

79 The only possible remedy for the contracting party to get released from the contract obligations in this case is the rescission of the contract. See Abova, Boguslavsky, Kabalkin, and Lisicin-Svetlanov 2007: 375.

80 Silence is subject to the general presumption that it is not a legal fact. This follows from the provision of the Civil Code concerning form of transaction (Article 158.3), according to which silence shall be recognized as an expression of will to make a transaction only in cases provided by the law or agreement of the parties.

expiration of the maximum (limit) term established by the law, the lease contract is to be terminated only upon the expiration of the limit term (Article 610.3).

As a negative answer, silence is represented infrequently in Russian civil law regulation. It occurs in the rules of the Civil Code regulating the transfer of immovables through their sale (Article 556), according to which the refusal by either of the parties to sign a document on the transfer of an immovable on the conditions provided by the contract is to be considered a refusal to transfer and respectively to accept the property or, in other words, a refusal to accept the offer.[81]

The general rules of the Civil Code on conclusion of contract enables acceptance of the offer by concludent acts (Article 434.3 and 438.3). This may occur so that the offeree executes, within the period established for the acceptance, the actions in the performance of the terms of a contract indicated in the offer (Article 438.3). Such actions include shipment of goods, performance of work, and provision of services, as well as payment of the appropriate amount, which are executed[82] in the situation where there is as yet no contract. The action must, however, occur within the time determined for the acceptance, and it must also express the unconditional acceptance of the offer.[83] There are also certain requirements concerning the offer in such a case. It must contain the term established for its acceptance. Additionally, a concludent action may be regarded as the acceptance of the offer only where there are no other provisions in the law, other legal acts, or other indications in the offer (Article 438.3). Also taken into account be that, if the requirements of written form are established for the given contract, the recently presented rule is considered observed only where the offer is made in written form (Article 434.3). This also means, on the other hand, that if the written form is not required for the given contract, this may also be concluded by the above-mentioned concludent action in response to the oral offer.[84]

The question of whether it is possible for the contract to arise as a consequence of the concludent actions (silence) of both contracting parties has been considered in the Russian judicial practice. In a one arbitration court decision, it has been ruled that the dispatch of the goods and reception of them does not constitute the contract, since the prerequisite of contract, the agreement on its essential conditions, has not been fulfilled.[85] It seems at least evident that mutual concludent actions may not constitute the contract, if this must be made in written form. It is explicitly provided in the rules of the Civil Code presented above (Article 434.3 and 438.3) that the written form of a contract is to be considered observed if concludent actions are executed in response to the written offer. As to those contracts which can be concluded orally, the contract may arise through the concludent actions of both parties, provided, however, that the concludent actions of the offeror contain the essential conditions of the contract and the concludent actions of his counterparty contain their acceptance.

Belated acceptance is subject to the provisions of Article 442 of the Civil Code. According to them, in cases when a timely dispatched notification of acceptance has been received late, the

81 Sergeev 1 2009: 857–8.

82 Ordinarily for the performance of the received order.

83 It is not necessary that the acceptance become known to the offeror, especially if this is not required in the offer. See Abova, Boguslavsky, Kabalkin, and Lisicin-Svetlanov 2007: 375.

84 It is stated in Russian judicial practice that as the acceptance of an offer is sufficient that the offeree or person who has received a draft contract has started the performance which corresponds with the conditions presented in the offer or draft contract, within the period established for the acceptance. See Joint Decrees of the Plenums 6/8 1996: 19.

85 See Закон [Law] 1 (1997): 110.

acceptance is not be considered late unless the offeror has immediately informed the offeree of the late receipt of the acceptance. Thus, if it transpires from the answer to the offer or otherwise that it has been sent in time, the answer is considered acceptance unless the offeror informs the offeree immediately that it has arrived belatedly. The silence of the offeror effects in this case the conclusion of the contract. However, where the answer has been sent (evidently) belatedly, the contract may also, according to the Civil Code, become concluded, if the offeror informs (in written) the other party immediately of the receipt (approval) of his belated acceptance[86].[87]

Place of conclusion of the contract is defined in the general rule of Article 444 of the Civil Code, which is dispositive by nature. The priority in it is given to the place which is determined in the contract, and only in the absence of this is the contract to be considered concluded in the domicile of the physical person or the site of the juristic person who sent the offer.

According to Article 425 of the Civil Code, a contract enters into force and becomes binding for the parties from the moment of its conclusion. This rule, moreover, is dispositive by nature and the contracting parties have the right to establish that the conditions of a contract concluded by them should be applied to their relations which arose before the conclusion of the contract (Article 425.2). Thus, the place and time of conclusion of the contract is determined after all by the moment when the contract is considered concluded.

A contract is considered concluded, according to Article 433 of the Civil Code, at the moment of receipt by the person who has sent an offer of its acceptance (Article 433.1). The time of conclusion of contract is specified in the rules of the Civil Code, the other of which concerns the conclusion of a contract on the basis of an offer defining a period for acceptance (Article 440), whereas the other is devoted to the conclusion of contract on the basis of an offer not determining the term for acceptance (Article 441). Where the period for acceptance of the offer is defined, the contract is considered concluded if the offeror receives the acceptance within the limits of the period indicated in the offer.

However, if the period for acceptance of the offer is not defined and this is made in written form, the contract is to be considered concluded if the offeror has received the acceptance before the expiration of the time determined in the law or other legal acts, and, in default of this, within a reasonable time (Article 441.1). However, if the offer without a definition of the period for acceptance has been made orally (if this can be made orally), the addressee must declare its acceptance immediately (Article 441.2), and just at this moment the contract arises.

Where the contract arises according to the Civil Code (Article 434.3 and 438.3) as a result of concludent actions accepting the offer, it is considered in Russian law as concluded at the moment when the offeror gains knowledge that the counterparty has started his concludent actions for performance of the contract.

As an exception from the general rule, the time, and correspondingly the place of conclusion of contract, is determined in the case of a real contract and a contract requiring registration. A real contract or contract the conclusion of which requires under the law also the transfer of the property is to be considered concluded from the moment of the transfer of the respective property (Article

86 Where the offeror does not respond to the obviously belated acceptance, this shall be interpreted as the refusal of acceptance.

87 In Russian judicial practice, there is a case in which a court has clarified the situation where the offer included, in addition to the term for his acceptance, the special term for the handling of the offer (the consideration term). If the notification of acceptance is sent, even though the term for acceptance of an offer is expired, within such a consideration term, the offeror has the right to inform the offeree immediately of his refusal to conclude the contract. See Joint Decrees of the Plenums 6/8 1996: 19.

433.2). In turn, a contract subject to state registration is to be considered as concluded from the moment of its registration unless otherwise established by the law (GK 433.3).[88][89]

Obligatory (compulsory) conclusion of contract or obligatory contracting or conclusion of a contract by obligatory procedure is known in Russian contract law as an exception from the general principle of freedom of contract based on the autonomy of the wills of the contracting parties. The rules regulating obligatory contracting are contained in Article 445 of the Civil Code incorporating the general provisions on contract. The article contains only the rules on how a contract is concluded in the obligatory procedure. As to the conditions of a contract to be concluded in the obligatory procedure, their definition is occurred mainly in accordance with the principle of freedom of contract. Obligatory conclusion of contract is to be grounded only on the law or legal act and is purported to be used mainly in making public contracts. The rules on obligatory contracting are also applied to those cases when the obligation to conclude a contract is based on a voluntary undertaking such as a preliminary contract. The rules imposing the obligation to conclude a contract are also found in the other norms of the Civil Code which concern, in particular, norms on supply and work for state needs.

The concept of public contract subject to the obligatory contracting is contained in Article 426 of the Civil Code. According to it, a public contract is defined as a contract concluded by a commercial organization and establishing its obligations for the sale of goods, performance of work, or provision of services which this organization by the character of its activity must exercise with respect to everyone[90] who applies to it. Article 426 also lists the domains to which its rules apply. They include retail trade, carriage by transport of common use, communications services, energy supply, medicine, and hotel services.

The provisions on public contract of the Civil Code contain five rules. According to the first rule (Article 426.3 art.), a commercial organization subject to public contract procedure has not, in general, the right to refuse to conclude a contract (obligation to contract). The second rule (Articles 426.1 and 426.2) provides that such an organization does not have the right to prefer one person to another with respect to the conclusion of a public contract (prohibition of preference) nor to establish the price of goods, works, and services, as well as other conditions of a public contract, that discriminates between consumers (prohibition of discrimination), except in cases provided for by the law or other legal acts. In accordance with the third rule on public contracts (Articles 426.3 and 445.4), in case of an unjustified refusal by a commercial organization to conclude a public contract, the counterparty of a commercial organization has the right to demand the conclusion of the contract in court and compensation for damages caused by the unjustified refusal. The fourth rule (Article 426.5) in turn provides that the conditions of a public contract not meeting the requirements established for public contracts are null and void. And according to the fifth rule on public contracts (Article 426.4) the Government of the Russian Federation may issue, however, only in those cases provided by the law rules obligatory for parties in the conclusion and performance of public contracts (model contracts, regulations, etc.). All these rules regulating public contracts contained in the general norm on them in the Civil Code (Article 426) are imperative.[91]

---

88 Additionally, the norms on types of contract of the Civil Code contain at least one special rule concerning time of conclusion of contract which is divergent from the general rule and this concerns consumer contracts of energy supply. According to Article 540.1 of the Civil Code, the contract is to be considered concluded from the moment of the first actual connection of the subscriber by the established procedure to the connected network.

89 See Sergeev 1 2009: 864.

90 Or any physical or juristic person.

91 See, for instance, Zankovsky 2004: 28–31; Abova, Boguslavsky, Kabalkin, and Lisicin-Svetlanov 2007: 364–6; as well as T.V. Larina, Особенности правового регулирования публичного договора в

Preliminary contract stands, under Article 429 of the Civil Code, for a contract according to which the parties undertake to conclude in the future a contract on the transfer of property, performance of works, or provision of services (basic contract) on the conditions provided for by the preliminary contract (Article 429.1).[92] Examples of preliminary contract are contract for suretyship by which the performance of the obligation arising in the future is secured (Article 361) and credit contract (Article 819).

The preliminary contract must meet, according to the Civil Code (Article 429.2), the same form requirements as the basic contract and, if those are not established, it must be done in written form; nonobservance of the rules on the form of a preliminary contract entails its invalidity (nullity). The Civil Code also has a requirement on the content of a preliminary contract, such as the definition of the subject and also other essential conditions for the basic contract (Article 429.3). In addition, the term within which the basic contract must be concluded must be determined, but, if it is not defined, the basic contract is subject to conclusion in the course of one year from the moment of conclusion of the preliminary contract (Article 429.4). The obligations of the preliminary contract are terminated if the basic contract is not concluded at the stipulated time or if the other party does not send a proposal to conclude the contract (Article 429.6).

Where the party who concluded the preliminary contract refuses to conclude the basic contract, Article 429.5 of the Civil Code provides that the rules on obligatory conclusion of contract are to be applied, wherefore the contracting party may be compelled to conclude the contract in court proceedings. According to the rules on preliminary contract, the conclusion of a contract by obligatory procedure may be demanded by any party, otherwise than in the case of the public contract where the demand to conclude the contract may be presented only by the counterparty of the organization subject to public contract regulation.[93]

Under the Civil Code, the obligatory procedure on conclusion of contract differs depending on whom the obligation to conclude a contract concerns. It recognizes two sets of rules: one concerning the situation where the obligatory contracting is imposed on the addressee (offeree), and the other applicable to the case when it is the offeror who is subject to the duty to conclude a contract (Article 445).

Where the obligation to conclude a contract concerns the recipient of the offer, or the party who has received the draft contract, the question is of the contracting procedure initiated by the customer (of the organizations subject to obligatory contracting) who is represented as the offeror. In this case the customer who is not subject to obligatory contracting but the counterparty of the party who is subject to obligatory contracting has prepared the offer or the draft contract and sent it to this or to the offeree. On receiving the offer or draft contract, the offeree must, according to the Civil Code (Article 445.1), send to the offeror a notification of acceptance or refusal to accept the offer within 30 days from the receipt of the offer. The offeree may notify the offeror of acceptance of the offer on other terms, in which case he prepares a protocol of disagreements with the draft of the contract containing his proposals and sends it to the offeror. After receiving this, in

---

России [Particularities of the Legal Regulation of Public Contract in Russia], available at http://www.lawmix.ru/comm/2994/ (accessed 6 June 2010).

92 The requirements on the form of a preliminary contract are strict in Russian contract law. According to the Civil Code (Article 429.2), a preliminary contract is to be concluded in the form established for the basic contract, and in the absence of the form requirements, in written form. The consequence of nonobservance of the rules on the form of a preliminary contract is, under the Civil Code (Article 429.2), its nullity.

93 The obligation to conclude the basic contract based on the preliminary contract has a time scope. According to the Civil Code (Article 429.4), where the period for conclusion is not indicated, the basic contract is subject to conclusion within one year from the moment of the conclusion of the preliminary contract.

turn, the offeror notifies the other party about the acceptance of the contract or he may bring the disagreements to the consideration of a court within 30 days from the day of receipt of the offeree's response or of the expiration of the period established for acceptance.[94]

In the case where the obligation to conclude a contract concerns the offeror or the contracting party who has prepared the draft contract—for instance, the contracting process initiated by an electric company—the addressee or the recipient of the offer (customer) may, according to the rules of the Civil Code regulating such cases (Article 445.2), notify his acceptance of the offer within 30 days from the receipt of it. He may also notify the offeror of acceptation of the offer on other terms in which case he prepares a protocol of disagreements with the draft of the contract containing his proposals and sends it to the offeror. On receiving the protocol of disagreement, the offeror must, otherwise than in the case when the conclusion of contract is obligatory for the offeree, send the recipient of the offer a notification of acceptance of the contract in the recipient's version or a notification of rejection of the protocol of disagreements. In the case of rejection of the protocol of disagreements or of nonreceipt of notification concerning this in the established time, the recipient of the offer has the right to bring the disagreements on the conclusion of the contract to the consideration of a court. The disagreements must be brought to the court within 30 days from the day of receipt of the negative response of the offeror or of the expiration of the period established for his response.

Thus, the disagreements[95] arising in obligatory contracting in both the above-presented cases may be brought to the consideration of a court only by the counterparty of the contracting party subject to the obligation to contract—in other words, by the customer.

The rules of the Civil Code regulating obligatory contracting contain in addition to the contracting procedure rules the purport of which is to secure the fulfillment of obligation to contract (Article 445.4). They also protect the customer of those organizations subject to obligatory contracting. The rules expressly provide that, if a party for whom in accordance with the Civil Code or other laws the conclusion of a contract is obligatory has refused to conclude it, the other party has the right to apply to a court with a demand for compulsion to conclude a contract. Such claims are handled in Russia in special proceedings concerning precontractual disputes.

The provisions on precontractual disputes are contained in Article 446 of the Civil Code. According to them, such a dispute may be considered by a court in Russia on the ground that the party, who is under the law subject to obligatory conclusion of contract, refuses to do so (Article 445.4). It may also occur upon the agreement of the parties to contract negotiations according to which the contract conditions subjected to their disagreement are to be defined in accordance with a decision of the court (Article 446). In court proceedings, it is possible in Russia to solve disputes concerning the compulsory conclusion of contract and the disputes arising in the process of its conclusion.

94 The term of 30 days imposed for the actions of the obligatory contracting parties is general, and is to be followed, according to Article 445.3 of the Civil Code, only if other periods have not been established by the law or other legal act, or agreed upon by the parties. Thus, it is a dispositive rule.

95 The conditions subject to disagreement must be essential. It is stated in Russian judicial practice that, if the signed contract is attached with the protocol of disagreements and this concerns the condition which may not be regarded as essential, the contract is considered concluded without such a condition. Moreover, in the event the contracting parties have not settled their disagreements on the liability issue, the contract is considered concluded without that condition and the price for the delivered goods must be paid. See Survey of the Decrees of the Presidium of the Supreme Arbitrazh Court. Хозяйство и право [Economy and Law] 6 (2000): 118 and 121–2.

Where the dispute concerns the compulsory conclusion of contract, the court also includes in its decision on compulsion to conclude the contract the conditions on which the contract is concluded. In practice, this means that the draft contract of the party demanding the conclusion of the contract is transformed into the contract by the court decision. The conditions of a contract arisen in this way are defined, according to the provisions of the Civil Code (Article 446) on precontractual disputes, in accordance with a decision of the court. By its decision on obligatory contracting, the court may also oblige the party which has unjustifiably refused to conclude the contract to compensate for the damages caused by this or the negative contract interest (Article 445.4).

Where the court solves the dispute arisen in the process of conclusion of contract concerning its conditions, its decision is to contain the decision on each disputed condition.[96] In this case, too, as for the compulsory conclusion of contract, the disputed conditions of the contract are to be defined, according to the provisions of the Civil Code (Article 446) on precontractual disputes, in accordance with a decision of the court and they constitute a part of the contract.

Close to the rules of the Civil Code on obligatory conclusion of contract offering measures for the conclusion of a contract are the special rules included in the provisions regulating supply contract which concern the solution of disagreements arising in the conclusion of such a contract (Article 507).[97] According to these special rules, if in the process of concluding a supply contract, disagreements among the parties have arisen on individual terms of the contract, the offeror who has received from the offeree a proposal on agreement on these terms is obliged to take measures for agreement on the respective terms of the contract or notify the other party in writing about his refusal to conclude a contract. The offeror must do this within 30 days from the day of receipt of the proposal, unless another period is established by the law or agreed upon by the parties. In default of this obligation, the offeror is obliged to compensate the damages caused by refusal to agree on the terms of the contract[98].[99] It is considered in Russian judicial practice that such damages include the expenses which the offeree who has notified his acceptation to conclude the contract on the conditions deviating from the offer suffered, as a consequence of which he has undertaken to arrange the performance of the contract after the expiry of the 30 days from the day when the offeror received his answer.[100]

Contracts may be concluded in Russia by the conduct of an auction and this may be made according to the Civil Code in the form of bidding or competition (Article 447.4).[101] An auction by bidding and competition may be open, in which case any person may participate in it, or closed, in which case only persons specially invited for this purpose are to participate (Article 448.1). The winner of the auction by bidding is deemed to be the person who has proposed the highest price, and of the competition, the one who, in the conclusion of a competition commission previously

96 According to 173 Article of the Arbitrazh Process Code no 95-FZ of 24 July 2002.

97 Suhanov 2008: 205.

98 Such damages may be caused by an increase in prices. See Abova, Boguslavsky, Kabalkin, and Lisicin-Svetlanov 2007: 431.

99 This provision has been deservedly criticized. The actual problem lies not in that such liability, which is near to delict liability, is imposed as independent from fault, but in that this *culpa in contrahendo* liability rule is applied only to supplies contracts. See, for instance, Beklenischeva 2006: 162–9; Braginsky and Vitrjansky 1999: 244–5, and Orlov 1999: 241.

100 See the Decision of the Plenum of the Supreme Arbitrazh Court no 18 of 22 October 1998. Вестник Высшего Арбитражного Суда Российской Федерации [Herald of the Supreme Arbitrazh Court of the Russian Federation]3 (1998): 23. See also Sergeev 2 2009: 76.

101 For more on this subject, see, for instance, Sergeev 1 2009: 865–6; Abova, Boguslavsky, Kabalkin, and Lisicin-Svetlanov 2007: 379–83; Braginsky and Vitrjansky 1999: 219–29, and Suhanov 2008: 208–11.

appointed by the organizer of the auction, has proposed the best conditions (Article 447.4). According to the Civil Code (Article 447.1), the contract may be concluded with the person who has won the auction, unless it otherwise follows from the nature of the contract (Article 447.1). Certain contracts, in turn, may be concluded only by organizing the auction.[102] The Civil Code (Articles 447–9) contains provisions which regulate the organization of auctions and the procedure for their conduct as well as the consequences of the violation of these rules, and these rules are also to be applied to public auctions which are conducted by way of performance of a decision of a court unless otherwise provided for by procedural legislation (Article 447.6).[103]

Where the object of the auction has been only the right to conclude the contract, the contracting parties must, according to the rule of the Civil Code (Article 448.5) regulating the organization of auctions, sign such a contract not later than 20 days (or the period indicated in the notice on the conduct of the auction) after the completion of the auction and drawing up of the protocol on the results of this. The protocol is considered in such a case as an auxiliary contract which has all the characteristics of a preliminary contract. Thus, if the other party refuses to conclude the basic contract, the other party has the right to apply to a court with a demand for compulsion to conclude a contract and compensation for damages caused by the unjustified refusal.

Contract of adhesion is[104] defined in Article 428.1 of the Civil Code as a contract whose conditions are determined by one of the parties in printed forms or other standard forms and which may be adopted by the other party only by adhering to the proposed contract as a whole. The purport of the legal regulation of contracts of adhesion is to protect the party who has accepted the standard conditions or adhered to the contract. In the rules regulating contracts of adhesion of the Civil Code, it is expressly provided that the party adhering to the contract has the right to demand the rescission or change of the contract (Article 428.2). The application of these measures, however, requires, according to the Civil Code, the circumstances where the contract of adhesion, although it does not contradict the law or other legal acts, deprives the party adhered to the contract of the rights usually granted under contracts of the given type, excludes or limits the liability of the other party for the violation of obligations, or contains other conditions clearly burdensome for the adhered party which he, on the basis of his reasonably understood interests, would not have accepted if he had the possibility of participating in the determination of the conditions of the contract (Article 428.2). Thus, the adhered contracting party is protected according to the Civil Code in that he may, as an exception from the general rule, demand the rescission of the contract or a change of its conditions, if the contract of adhesion is considered unfair.

The provisions of Article 428 of the Civil Code on contract of adhesion contain special rules on contracts in which the adhering party is an entrepreneur. According to them, the demands of the party who adhered to the contract in connection with the exercise of its entrepreneurial activity, on the rescission or change of the contract on the grounds which otherwise correspond with the above-presented prerequisites on the application of the consequences concerning contracts of adhesion, are not subject to satisfaction if the adhering party knew or should have known on what conditions it concluded the contract (Article 428.3). Thus, the entrepreneur must prove not only the fact that the contract conditions are unfair but also his ignorance of the contract conditions. Hence, he is expected to possess a better-than-average competence in the rules regulating contract of adhesion.

102 For instance, the orders on the grounds of which public procurement or state or municipal contracts are to be concluded must be placed mainly by an auction in the form of bidding or competition.

103 Besides the Civil Code, organization of auctions is also regulated by other normative acts concerning, for instance, privatization.

104 For more on this subject, see, for instance, Sergeev 1 2009: 849–50; Suhanov 2008: 186–7, and Braginsky and Vitrjansky 1999: 258–66.

The rules on contract of adhesion are also applicable to cases when, in contracting, model or standard conditions of contract are used, on which there are provisions in Article 427 of the Civil Code. These directly enforce that it may be provided in a contract that its individual conditions are to be determined by model conditions developed for contracts of the respective type and published in the press (Article 427.1). Such conditions are also referred to in the above-presented rules of the Civil Code on contract of adhesion which mention the conditions which are determined by one of the parties in printed forms or other standard forms (Article 428.1). The question whether the standard conditions of a contract are subject to the regulation concerning contracts of adhesion is to be solved by the court in handling a concrete dispute. On the other hand, it is possible that the legal act concerning standard conditions refers directly to the rules on contract of adhesion. However, even in the absence of such a reference, it is evident that, for instance, the provisions on insurance of the Civil Code (Article 940.3) according to which the insurer in concluding the contract of insurance has the right to use standard forms of contract (insurance policy) developed by it or by an association of insurers for individual types of insurance might not mean that the application of the norms regulating contract of adhesion (which are imperative by nature) is excluded. Thus the insuree must have the right to dispute the insurance contract, invoking the rules on contract of adhesion protecting the party adhered to the contract under duress, although the norms on insurance do not mention this. This general rule must also be applied to other contracts in which standard conditions are used.[105]

Related to the rules on contract of adhesion are the provisions of Article 400 of the Civil Code on the limitation of the amount of liability under obligations, according to which an agreement limiting the amount of liability of a debtor under a contact of adhesion or other contract in which the creditor is a physical person acting as a consumer is null (and void) if the amount of liability for such a type of obligations or for such a violation is determined by the law and if the agreement is concluded before the occurrence of the circumstances entailing liability for nonperformance or improper performance of the obligation (Article 400.2). This rule, protecting the ordinary consumer in the event of his contracting party intimidates him into accepting beforehand the limitation of the amount of liability determined by the law, is interpreted in Russian judicial practice such that such a prohibition concerns also the conditions releasing from liability.[106] The rule on limitation of the amount of liability is, in respect of the contracting party using standard conditions, the most onerous: as a consequence it provides the nullity of the contract condition.

Representation and Authorization[107]

Concept of representation Civil law subjects may execute their civil law rights and duties in Russia, as elsewhere, not only personally but also through their representatives. It is common that obligation law rights are exercised by using representatives. However, personal non-obligation law rights—for instance, the application for a patent for an invention—may also be executed through a representative. Transactions, included contracts, are mainly concluded by using representatives. In certain cases it is, however, impossible owing to the stipulation of the law or because of the nature of the rights or duties, in which case the civil law subject must act himself. Such transactions include, for instance, the will and issuance of power of attorney. The rules regulating representation,

105 See Braginsky and Vitrjansky 1999: 264–5.

106 See Joint Decrees of the Plenums 6/8 1996.

107 For more on this subject, see, for instance, Sergeev 1 2009: 526–39; Suhanov 2007: 542–55, and Braginsky and Vitrjansky 1999: 173–85.

including power of attorney, are contained mainly in the norms of the Civil Code directly devoted to them (Articles 182–9) as well as in the rules of the Civil Code concerning physical persons (Articles 28 and 29) and certain juristic persons and their representations and branches (Articles 55, 72, and 84) as well as invalidity of transactions (Articles 174 and 179). The rules on power of attorney are also included in the type of contracts norms of the Civil Code regulating delegation (Articles 974 and 975), freight forwarding (Article 802), and simple partnership (Article 1044).

According to the rules on representation and power of attorney in the Civil Code, in the event of representation a transaction concluded by one person (representative) in the name of another person (representee) by virtue of the power based on the power of attorney, on the stipulation of the law, or on an act issued by a state body or a local self-government body empowered thereto directly creates, changes, or terminates the civil rights and duties of the representee (Article 182.1).

Representation is recognized in Russian civil law as obligatory or voluntary or discretionary. Obligatory representation is grounded, according to the Civil Code, on the law (statutory representation), and is represented in the representation of a minor (Article 28) or incompetent minor or incompetent person (Article 29), or on the administrative act issued by an authorized state body or local self-government or some other body. The grounds for a voluntary representation or authority may be, in turn, a delegation contract (delegation authorization) or power of attorney (power of attorney authorization; Articles 185–9). As a modification of voluntary representation is regarded commercial representation in Russian law, and the rules on it are contained in a special norm of the Civil Code (Article 184). Specific to voluntary representation is that the representation powers of the representative are determined in accordance with the will of the representee.

In a representation relation there are three parties: the representee or principal, the representative and a third person. The specific feature of representation is that the necessary acts are made by the representative, whereas their results arise to the principle. Furthermore, representation concerns transactions or legally significant but not factual acts, wherefore the representative may act only if he has legal capacity as a physical or juristic person. Thus, in order to act as a representative of a representation or branch office of a juristic person, its director needs the power of attorney (Article 55.3). Then, since the representative acts in the name of the principal, his acts give rise to the rights immediately and directly to the principal, and this is a kind of fiction in accordance with which the acts of another person cause to the principal the same consequences as if he could have acted himself. In general, representation stands for that the principal determines by his will the authority of the representative and this concludes by his will the contract.

Parties of representation In representation, as a representee can be a physical or juristic person, in the name and on behalf of which the representative makes transactions. In Russian law, a physical person may be represented from the date of his birth. As to a juristic person, it can be represented from the date it is duly established.

As representative can be, in representation, a physical or juristic person who has the authority to make legally significant acts in the name and on behalf of the principal. In order to act as a representative in Russia a physical person must be legally competent except several cases concerning labor relations or membership in an association or cooperative. Additionally, there are restrictions in Russian civil process legislation concerning the rights of judicial officers and disqualified advocates to participate as representatives in court proceedings. A chief bookkeeper is prohibited from receiving liquid and other assets of the enterprise from the bank through the power of attorney.

Juristic persons who have special legal capacity may act as representatives if it is not contradictory to the objects of their activities determined in the law or their constituent documents. Thus, for instance, a bank as a credit organization is not allowed to act as a representative in a commercial transaction. Commercial juristic persons (commercial organizations) which are generally provided with the general legal capacity may represent physical persons and organizations which do not practice enterprise activity, though there is no particular mention of it in their constituent documents, on the condition, however, that special permission is not required for the representation in the transaction at issue. Such a representation is called noncommercial representation. In turn, commercial representation stands for situations where a commercial juristic person enjoying the general legal capacity practices enterprise activities as representative in the name of other entrepreneurs.

As a third person linked to representation is understood in Russian law a physical or juristic person in respect to whom the rights and duties of the principal are created, changed, or terminated through the acts of the representative. A third person can be any person which enjoys civil law capacity.

In representation, the following legal relations arise between the principal, representative, and third person:

- the relation between the representative and principal;
- the relation between the representative and third person, and
- the relation between the principal and third person.

The relation between the representative and principal is the authorization relation in which the powers of the representative are defined and which has the nature of obligation law. This is considered in Russian civil law as the internal part or relation of the representation. In turn, the relation between the representative and third person in which the powers of the representative occur is regarded as the external part or relation of the representation.[108] As to the relation between the principal and third person, it is not regarded in Russia as properly belonging to the concept of representation because it simply concerns the result of the executed representation.[109]

Boundaries of representation Representation comprehends that the representative makes transactions on behalf of the principal. The transactions made by the representative are his own discretionary acts which at the same create, change, or terminate the civil law rights and duties of the principal. Owing to this feature, the representative is distinct from the governing bodies of juristic persons in Russian law. In accordance with the rules on the bodies of a juristic person of the Civil Code (Article 53), a body of a juristic person stands for a separate part of its structure which is not an independent civil law subject. This is enforced in Russian judicial practice, wherefore the acts made by the body of the juristic person are considered as made by the juristic person itself.[110]

Because the transactions made by the representative are his discretionary acts, the requirements on the legal capacity of the representative are stricter than in general. Furthermore, the invalidity of the transactions made by him is dependent directly on that no mistake has occurred in respect of the formation of his will and that this is expressed properly. Thus, a representative is distinct from a courier who, otherwise than a representative, does not conclude transactions but delivers

108 See Abova, Boguslavsky, Kabalkin, and Lisicin-Svetlanov 2007: 204.

109 Sergeev 1 2009: 527.

110 See Вестник Высшего Арбитражного Суда Российской Федерации [Herald of the Supreme Arbitrazh Court of the Russian Federation] (1999) 5: 66.

the documents, information, or, for instance, the acceptance to conclude the agreement sent by the sender.

A representative is also distinct from persons who act on behalf of others but in their own name, as well as from the persons who are delegated to be present in negotiations concerning the transactions to be possibly concluded in the future. The circle of such persons is very large. It includes commercial and other intermediaries, arbitration administrators in insolvency proceedings, executors of wills, and acceptors of transactions. It is expressly provided in the rules of the Civil Code that persons who operate in the interest of other persons but in their own name (commercial intermediaries, bankruptcy claims administrators, executors, etc.) as well as persons authorized to enter into negotiations with respect to possible future transactions are not regarded as representatives (Article 182.2).

An intermediary acts under Russian law in his own name and contributes to the conclusion of a contract through searching out possible contracting parties or collecting or giving information concerning the contract. Despite his intensive activities, the intermediary does not carry out any legally bound acts which directly create rights and duties for the other persons. Transactions arise in such cases directly through the expression of intent by the parties.

The activities of the commission agent are similar to those of the representative since a commission agent also carries out civil law acts on behalf of the principal. However, a commission agent acts in his own name, and the rights and duties belonging to the buyer or seller arise just to him, which he only later transfers to the principal. The authority of an arbitration administrator in insolvency proceedings also includes the commissioning of legally significant acts, and, although he makes these in his own name, he acts, however, in the favor of not only the bankrupt but also his creditors. An executor of a will also acts in his own name, and his acts have legal impact on third persons.

The person whose approval or permission is required for conclusion of the transaction is not regarded as a representative, since the task of such a person is to make sure that the transaction is reasonable and appropriate. A guardian holds a similar position: his consent is required, for instance, in respect of transactions concluded by his ward. The owner of a treasury enterprise or the state has in Russian law a similar position in the event of alienation of its property which does not belong to its products.

Representation powers The representation powers or authority or capacity of the representative in Russian law stands for his capacity to conclude transactions in the name and on behalf of the principal, and it is determined on the ground of the legal facts which give birth to the representation. By its content, it is the benchmark for the possible behavior of a representative toward the third person. It may be regarded as his subjective right which he realizes in his relation with the third persons by committing transactions in the name and on behalf of the principal, and these may include the conclusion, fulfillment, and termination of the contract. The essence of the representation transpires therefore in the activities of the representative in which he uses his authority in the name and on behalf of the principal. In turn, the relation between the principal and representative may be regarded as the competence relationship characterized as a prerequisite of the representation, in the scope of which the representation powers arise and take shape.[111]

By their origin and legal nature, representation powers comprehend the subjective right derived from the legal capacity of the principal which is delegated to the representative either through the discretionary act of the principal or on the ground of the facts provided by the law. Consequently,

111 See Sergeev 1 2009: 528–9 and Suhanov 2007: 544–6.

the use of the representation powers by the representative must be regarded as legal facts on the grounds of which the rights and duties arise to the principal. However, the acts of the representative create, change, or terminate the civil law rights and duties of the principal only on the condition that the representative acts within the limits of the scope of his representation powers. In the event this is exceeded, the transaction concluded by him with the third person will not, in principle, bind the principal.

In principle, the will of the representative directed to, for instance, the conclusion of the contract does not differ in Russian law from the will of the principal, and where the representative commits an error—for instance, in respect of the object of the contract—the contract is to be regarded invalid regardless of how large the representation powers (capacity) of the representative are. Where the transaction concluded by the representative is within the scope of his representation powers (capacity) but contradicts what has been preliminary agreed between the principal and third person, it may be recognized as invalid on the grounds of the rules on the consequences of the restriction of powers to conclude a transaction provided in Article 174 of the Civil Code. According to them, if the powers of a person to conclude a transaction is restricted by the contract concluded with a third person,[112] or the powers of the body of a juristic person are restricted by its constituent documents,[113] as compared to the way they are defined in the power of attorney or in the law,[114] or how they could be considered evident from the situation in which the transaction is concluded,[115] and if, in concluding this transaction, such a person or body exceeded the boundaries of these restrictions, the transaction may be recognized by a court as invalid upon the claim of the person in whose interest the said restrictions have been imposed, though only in those cases when it is proven that the other party to the transaction knew or clearly should have known of these restrictions. Thus, the principal bears the risks connected with the conclusion of a transaction without authority or by exceeding its limits. It corresponds clearly to the interests of exchange and, in particular, secures the stability of contract relations.[116] In order to dispute the transaction on the grounds of the termination of the power of attorney (Article 189.2) or the exceeding of the limits of the special legal capacity (Article 173), it must be proven under the Civil Code that the other party to the transaction knew or clearly should have known of it. Consequently, it can be regarded as

112 For instance, if the lessee has not been granted under the lease contract the right to conclude sublease contracts, he has no right to issue the power of attorney for conclusion of a sublease contract.

113 For instance, where the director of a limited liability company has entered into a pledge in the name of the company without the decision of its general meeting, even though such a decision was required by the company charter. In Russian judicial practice, restrictions other than those established by the charter are taken into consideration—for instance, the restrictions decided by the general meeting. See Вестник Высшего Арбитражного Суда Российской Федерации [Herald of the Supreme Arbitrazh Court of the Russian Federation] 3 (1996): 88.

114 Such a transaction violates restrictions on competence or other requirements which are clearly imposed by the law—the Civil Code norm on invalidity of transactions not corresponding to the law or other legal acts (Article 168), according to which such a transaction is null and void. Such invalidity does not depend on the awareness of the other party in the transactions. However, it may be ratified directly later in accordance with Article 183 of the Civil Code. The violation of the law is abolished, for instance, by accepting the transaction in the order established by the law. See, for instance, Вестник Высшего Арбитражного Суда Российской Федерации [Herald of the Supreme Arbitrazh Court of the Russian Federation] 6 (1997): 18.

115 Restrictions may also be provided by the special act of the juristic person.

116 This line is clearly in evidence in the Civil Code. The provisions of the Civil Code on transactions of the participants in joint ownership can be regarded as another example of the intention to protect the stability of contract. If it is disputed by referring to the lack of the consent of the other participants, then the fact that the other participant knew or clearly should have known of the transaction must be proved (Article 253.3).

clear that the ignorance of the other party or the third person about the exceeding of the competence and the limits of the special legal capacity by the representative as well as about the termination of the power of attorney is presumed in Russian law, wherefore the burden of proof to refute the presumption is upon the principal.

In the legal evaluation of the acts of the representative in which he executes his representation powers, attention is paid to the mistakes of his will and the will of the principal, since their consequences are different. If a mistake has occurred in the formation of the will of the representative, it may cause the invalidity of the transaction concluded in the name of the principal by the representative. By contrast, a mistake concerning the will of the principal may mean that no contract will arise between the principal and third person; however, this does not preclude that the contract will be validated through the acceptance of the principal. It can be regarded as concluded in the name and on behalf of the person who made it in accordance with the rules of the Civil Code (Article 183.1) on conclusion of a transaction by an unauthorized person. It is regarded as clear in Russian civil law that it requires, however, the approval of the third person, since it is not insignificant for him if the representative becomes the contracting party to him instead of the principal.[117]

In the execution of his representation powers, the representative is obliged to follow the interests of the principal, wherefore he is not allowed to conclude a transaction in the name of the representee in respect of himself personally or a transaction in which he is the other party (self-dealing or self-contracting).[118] He also may not conclude a transaction with respect of another person whose representative he is simultaneously (concurrence of authorities), with the exception of cases of commercial representation (Article 182.3).[119] The loyalty of the representative toward the principal is also secured in the rules of the Civil Code on transactions according to which a transaction made under the influence of a bad-faith agreement may be recognized as invalid by a court (Article 179.1).

Emergence of representation and its forms The relation between the representative and principal arises on the grounds of the legal facts which also have impact on the emergence and extent of the representation powers. In Russian law, these grounds include:

- the expression of will of the principal providing the authority to the representative which transpires either in the contract or power of attorney;
- the act of the state or local self-government body under which a person is empowered to act on behalf of other person as a representative, or
- some other fact which is sufficient provision according to the law to bestow on a person the authority to represent the other person.

In accordance with these legal facts, there is representation grounded on a contract, on an administrative act, and on the law. Additionally, the representation relation may be grounded on the authorization based on the position held.

117 Braginsky and Vitryansky 1999: 175.

118 In Russian law, as in general, the situations in which the other participant is a spouse or near relative are equated with self-contracting.

119 The purpose of the prohibition of the concurrence of authorities is to protect the weaker party, but this is not considered necessary for cases of commercial representation, in which, however, the other rules protecting the principal are to be nonetheless observed.

Contracts on the grounds of which the representation may arise are contained in the Civil Code and include delegation (Articles 971–9) and agency (Articles 1005–11). In respect of delegation, the Civil Code (Article 971.1) provides that under it one party (the delegate) is obligated to perform certain legal actions in the name of and at the expense of the other party (the delegant). In turn, the agency contract is understood in the Civil Code (Article 1005.1) as a contract under which one party (the agent) is obligated for compensation to perform on delegation from the other party (the principal) legal and other actions in the name and at the expense of the principal or in his own name but at the expense of the principal.[120] The power of attorney given by the principal to the representative is regarded as a unilateral transaction which bestows on the representative the representation powers. The representation grounded both on the contract and on the power of attorney or authorization represents discretionary representation and a certain modification of it is a commercial representation. The discretionary or non-mandatory nature of representation comprehends that it arises by the expression of the will of the representee, and he determines not only whom he authorizes as a representative but also the powers of such authority. Moreover, the representative acts in the name of the representee in accordance with his own will.

There is a variety of acts of the state or local self-government body authorizing somebody to act as a representative in Russia. So, for instance, the state is represented in a joint stock company the shares of which are in state ownership by state officers appointed by the decision of the President, Government or some other governing body of the Russian Federation. The representation grounded on the act of public authority is compulsory since it is imposed irrespective of the will of the representative. As authorization grounded on the administrative act is also regarded as representation of the juristic person where the governing body of the juristic person appoints a person to an office which includes certain representation tasks—for instance, concluding contracts. A branch or representative office is not empowered to represent the juristic person, since this task belongs usually to its director, and he is authorized by the juristic person by the power of attorney given by the latter. Administrative representation is also equated to a representation based on membership of a cooperative or societal organization.[121]

Representation grounded on the law or of legal representatives arises in Russian law much as representation grounded on the administrative act: it is irrespective of the will of the representative or it is regarded as compulsory. Such a representation arises directly upon the provision of the law, where the powers of the legal representative are also determined. Legal representatives are known in Russian family law. So, as legal representatives of a minor in the Civil Code are regarded his parents, adoptive parents, or guardians (Article 28). It is expressly provided in the law that parents (Family Code Article 64), adoptive parents (Family Code Article 137.1), and guardians (Article 32) represent the minor. This means that paternity or maternity, adoption, and the establishment of a guardianship is sufficient ground for such a representation.

According to the Civil Code, authority may transpire in circumstances in which the representative acts (Article 182.1) when the question is of authorization based on the position held. Such powers are commonly linked to the acts of sales clerks in retail trade or cashiers, which such persons execute in the name of their employer in a certain place or in a certain order often using certain identification marks. Thus, anybody who turns to such a person is certain that he is in contact with a person who represents the firm. Any person whom the employer has allowed to work—for

120 In this case, however, the rules of the Civil Code regulating commission agency are to be applied (Article 1011), in accordance with which there is no representation relation between the principal and the agent, as stated above.

121 Sergeev 1 2009: 530.

instance, to perform a service in circumstances that clearly indicate the authorization based on the position—must be regarded as the representative of the firm.[122]

Authorization of the power of attorney The rules concerning authorization of the power of attorney are contained in the norms on representation and power of attorney of the Civil Code (Articles 185–9). They also include the concept of power of attorney. This is defined as a written authorization issued by one person to the other person for representation before third persons (Article 185.1). Power of attorney is the document in which the representation powers or capacity to conclude transaction (transactions) and other legal acts as well as their content and limits are defined. Power of attorney is addressed to third persons, and it certifies the representation powers of the representative. In other words, the representation powers of the representative become clear to a third person from the power of attorney. The power of attorney is issued mostly to certify discretionary powers. However, if it is grounded on the contract between the representee and representative, then the issuance of power of attorney is by legal nature an unilateral transaction made by the representee in accordance with his own discretion. Thus, the issuance of power of attorney and its becoming effective do not require the consent of the representative because the representation powers do not concern his own civil law rights, but grant him the right grounded on the power of attorney to act in the name and on behalf of the representee. On the other hand, the power of attorney itself does not give birth to any representation powers of the representative before he accepts voluntarily the power of attorney and in this way agrees to fulfill the authority. The issuance of power of attorney to a representative is not, in Russian law, a precondition for representation, and, according to the Civil Code, the written authorization for conclusion of a transaction by a representative may be given by the representee directly to the respective third person (Article 185.1).

The purpose of a power of attorney, in contrast to a contract regulating the relationship between the representative and representee, is to secure the external effect of the representation or to establish through the acts of the representative the legal relation between the representee and third person. From the power of attorney the third person gains knowledge what representation powers the representative has. By contrast, the contract, or other legal fact, on the ground of which the power of attorney is given does not concern third persons.

Any transaction or other act which is of legal nature and which the representative makes within the limits of the authorization given to him is binding for the representee. This entails that the representee may not refuse the fulfillment of a contract concluded on the ground of the power of attorney by referring to the fact that the representative has broken the authorization contract concluded with him—for instance, by deviating from the instructions given to him unless they are written in both the contract and power of attorney. In other words, in the event of a contradiction between the contract, which defines the internal relations between the representative and representee, and the power of attorney given to the representative, the rights and duties of the representee deriving from the contract concluded by the representative with the third person are to be determined according to the representation powers (capacity) defined in the power of attorney and not to those (competence) written in the representation contract. However, where an essential mistake is made in the formation of the will of the representative, the transaction must be regarded, as stated above, invalid.

As a transaction, the power of attorney must correspond in Russian law to all requirements provided for transactions in the law. Its object must be only lawful acts in respect of which the

122 Suhanov 2007: 547–50.

transaction maker has legal (act) capacity. Furthermore, the formation of the will of the representee must be free and the expression of the will must correspond to this. There are additionally the specific rules concerning power of attorney in the Civil Code (Articles 185–9).

As a general rule, only fully legally competent persons may issue the power of attorney. Physical persons of the age of 14 to 18 years or those limited in dispositive capacity may independently give the power of attorney only within the limits of the rights they may dispose of. These include the right to dispose of their earnings as well as to make deposits in credit organizations and to dispose of them, to exercise intellectual property rights, and to conduct small everyday consumer transactions. In respect of other transactions, a person limited in dispositive capacity may issue the power of attorney only on the written consent of his legal representative.

A juristic person who has special legal capacity may issue the power of attorney for the conclusion of transactions which are not contradictory to the objects of the activities of it imposed by the law. In turn, commercial juristic persons who are provided according to the law with general legal capacity may issue power of attorney for the conclusion of any transaction taking into account the requirements provided by the law and the licensing rules in respect of certain fields of activities as well. However, where the objects of the activities of the commercial juristic person are determined in its constituent documents, and it issues the power of attorney for a transaction which is contradictory to those objects, the power of attorney may be disputed in accordance with rules of the Civil Code concerning invalidity of the transactions exceeding the limits of special legal capacity (Article 173).

A power of attorney is issued in Russia as a named document, and it must indicate the name of the person to whom it is given as well as the name of the person who has issued it. A power of attorney is issued to one or several persons and these persons may represent jointly or separately. The issuance of power of attorney comprehends, as stated above, a unilateral transaction, wherefore it does not require the consent of the representative. His rights include the right to accept the power of attorney or to refuse it. The duty of the delegate or principal to issue to a delegant or representative the power of attorney is established in the rules on delegation of the Civil Code (Article 975.1).

The person who has issued the power of attorney or representee may cancel it at any time, and this also applies to the power of attorney connected with the delegation relation. Moreover, the representative may refuse the power of attorney at any time. The power of attorney may be issued by one or several person simultaneously. As a case in which there are many simultaneous representees may be regarded the situation where joint owners give the power of attorney to a third person for the execution of the sale concerning their whole property. In accordance with the content and extent of the representation powers of the power of attorney given by the representative, they are divided into general and special as well as single powers of attorney. A general power of attorney empowers a representative to conclude different transactions in general, largely connected with the activities of the representee. Such a power of attorney may be issued, for instance, to the director of the branch office of the juristic person. A special power of attorney empowers, in turn, the representative to execute a bulk of similar transactions or the transactions connected with the specified field of the activity of the representee. Such a power of attorney is issued, for instance, for court representation or receipt of cargo from a carrier. As to a single power of attorney, this is issued for a specified transaction—for the signing of a contract, for instance.[123]

The form requirements concerning the power of attorney are provided in the rules of the Civil Code (Article 185.1). As a general requirement, these provide for the written form even where the

123 Sergeev 2009: 535–6.

contract for which the power of attorney is given may be concluded in oral form. By written form is understood a simple written form provided for transactions under the Civil Code (Articles 159–62). In accordance with these rules, a power of attorney may be made by the preparation of a document expressing its content and signed by the representee (Article 160.1); a power of attorney may be made also in the form of a letter, telegram, or telefax or contained in the contract into which the representative authorization is written. In any event, the document must express that the question is of the power of attorney and it must, in addition, contain the defined representative powers and other necessary requisites provided for the power of attorney. On the other hand, the regulation on the unit of the juristic person and its rights to make contracts are considered in Russian judicial practice as equal to the written authorization.[124]

In the event the power of attorney is intended to be used for making a transaction in respect of which notarial form is required (Article 163), the power of attorney mist also be, under the Civil Code, notarially authenticated except in those the cases provided for by the law (Article 185.2). As notarially authenticated powers of attorney are equated, according to the Civil Code (Article 185.3), powers of attorney of military service personnel and inmates of institutions authenticated by the head of the institution. As for the receipt of wages and other payments connected with labor relations, the power of attorney may be authenticated by the employer. In addition, a bank may authenticate the power of attorney of its client for the receipt of monetary funds from his bank account (Article 185.4). In certain cases the power of attorney may be authenticated in Russia by a postal or housing management organization. Russian consulates may also in certain cases authenticate the powers of attorney of Russian citizens.

A power of attorney must also correspond to other form requirements. The power of attorney must be dated (in words): a power of attorney in which the date of its issuance is not indicated is deemed under the Civil Code (Article 186.1) to be null and void. As a consequence of this, not only the relations between the representative and representee but also all the results of the actions made by the representative, including, of course, the transactions concluded with his participation, will be deemed invalid. And, subsequently, the rules on restitution of invalid transactions contained in Article 167 of the Civil Code concerning the consequences of invalidity of transactions can be applied in respect of not only the representative and representee but also the third person and representee.[125]

The term of a power of attorney may not exceed three years, and if the term is not defined in the power of attorney (in words), it remains in force for one year from the date of its issuance. This general rule of the Civil Code regulating the term of a power of attorney has an exception contained in the Civil Code (Article 186.2) which concerns a notarially authenticated power of attorney for making transactions abroad. If such a power of attorney does not contain an indication of its term, it remains in force until its revocation by the person who gave the power of attorney. Thus, the period of validity of a power of attorney of international nature is not limited in the law. Instead, only thosc mentioned powers of attorney equated to notarially authenticated powers of attorney which authorize for transactions abroad and which do not indicate the term are valid only for one year from the date of their issuance or they are subject to the application of the general rule concerning usual powers of attorney (Article 186.1).

Powers of attorney issued by juristic persons are subject to specific rules. A power of attorney in the name of a juristic person must be issued under the signature of its director or other person

124 Вестник Высшего Арбитражного Суда Российской Федерации [Herald of the Supreme Arbitrazh Court of the Russian Federation] 1 (1995): 83 and 6 (1996): 57.

125 See Abova, Boguslavsky, Kabalkin, and Lisicin-Svetlanov 2007: 207.

authorized by the constituent documents thereto with the attachment of the seal of this organization (Article 185.5). A power of attorney in the name of a juristic person which is based on state or municipal property for the receipt or issuance of money and other property valuables must also be signed by the head (senior) bookkeeper of this organization. On the other hand, it should be noted that a power of attorney given by a juristic person does not require any other confirmation and the notarial authentication is imposed only for the delegation of authorization. As to the powers of attorney authorizing for foreign trade and bank transactions, the specific form requirements concerning them are provided in the rules regulating these transactions.[126]

Delegation of authorization is possible in Russian civil law, and the rules on it are contained in the Civil Code (Article 187). Their starting point is that the person to whom a power of attorney was given must personally perform the actions for which he is authorized. He may transfer the power of attorney to perform them to another person only in two cases:

- if he is authorized by the power of attorney to do so, or
- if he is forced to do so by virtue of circumstances in order to protect the interests of the person who issued the power of attorney (Article 187.1).

In principle, it seems obvious that the representee may allow at any moment the delegation of power of attorney by authorizing the representative to do so in answer to the request of the representative or on his own initiative.

In the delegation of authorization, the original representative is replaced by another person who will execute in the name of the representee the actions determined in the power of attorney temporarily or during the entire period of this. Thus, as a consequence of the delegation of authorization arises the authorization relation between the representee and the person to whom the original representative delegated his representative powers. Owing to this, and taking into account the personal nature of authorization, it is provided in the Civil Code in respect of delegation of authorization that the person who transferred the authorization to another person must notify the person who issued the power of attorney thereof and communicate to him the necessary information about the transferee of the powers (Article 187.2). This information includes not only his personal data but also professional competence and moral proprieties if these are required for performing the representation tasks. The notification on the delegation of authorization must be made by the representative as soon as possible, and the representee has the right to revoke the delegation of authorization. The original representative who has pursued the requirements imposed for the delegation of authorization is not liable for the actions of the person to whom he has transferred his powers. However, if the representative does not notify the representee of the delegation of authorization, he is liable according to the Civil Code for the actions of the transferee as for his own actions (Article 187.2).

In accordance with the Civil Code, the term of validity of a power of attorney issued by way of transfer of powers may not exceed the term of the power of attorney on the basis of which it was issued (Article 187.4). Such a power of attorney must be notarially authenticated (Article 187.3). The exception to this rule is formed by the above-mentioned powers of attorney equated to notarially authenticated powers of attorney the requirements on which also concern the powers of attorney issued by way of transfer of powers established by them. In the delegation of authorization all restrictions concerning this remain in force owing to the derivative nature of it. So the general

126 In accordance with the rules of the Russian international private law, the form of a power of attorney is governed by the law of the country where it is issued.

principle of civil law that *no one can give another a better title than he himself has* also concerns delegation of authorization. The power of attorney given to prove the delegation of authorization may cover the acts delegated to the original representative in whole or in part.

The grounds for the termination of authorization granted with a power of attorney are listed in the rule of the Civil Code on it (Article 188). According to it (Article 188.1), the validity of a power of attorney terminates as the result of:

- expiry of the term of the power of attorney, or where the transaction subject of the single power of attorney is performed;
- revocation of the power of attorney by the person who issued it;
- renunciation to execute the mandate by the person to whom the power of attorney was issued;
- termination of the legal person in whose name the power of attorney was issued;
- termination of the juristic person to whom the power of attorney was issued;
- death of the physical person who issued the power of attorney, declaration of him as lacking dispositive capacity, as having limited dispositive capacity, or as missing, and
- death of the physical person to whom the power of attorney was issued, declaration of him as lacking dispositive capacity, as having limited dispositive capacity, or as missing.

These grounds for the termination of a power of attorney are divided in the Russian civil law doctrine into three groups according to which a power of attorney is terminated:

- where the term of its validity or the mandate is expired;
- where it is revoked, or
- where the representative or representee (juristic person) is terminated or (physical person) dies or falls victim to an occurrence comparable with it.[127]

Additionally, it should be noted that the grounds for the termination of a power of attorney also concern the powers of attorney given for the delegation of authorization because of their derivative nature.

The representee may revoke the power of attorney as well as the delegation of authorization, and the representative may withdraw from the mandate at any moment. Any agreement to waive these rights is, according to the Civil Code, null and void. (Article 188.2) This as well as the other grounds for the termination of a power of attorney rest on that the authorization is considered in Russian civil law as a fiduciary transaction which is based on special personal confidential relations. In that case, it is regarded that, if these relations lose their confidential nature, both parties have the right to withdraw from them.[128] Furthermore, there are rules on the cancellation rights of the representative and representee contained in the norms of the Civil Code regulating delegation where it is directly expressed that the delegant has the right to cancel the delegated task and the delegate to refuse it at any time (Article 977.2).

Termination of a power of attorney comprehends the cessation of the representation powers or authorization of the representative wherefore certain duties arise to both representee and representative on which there are provisions in the Civil Code (Article 189). According to them, the representee, where he revokes the power of attorney given by him, must give notice of the

127 Sergeev 1 2009: 536–7.

128 Sergeev 1 2009: 536.

revocation to the representative and third persons known to him and with respect to whom the power of attorney was issued for representation. The same duty is imposed upon the legal successors of the representee in the event the power of attorney is terminated due to the termination of the juristic person or the death of the physical person or declaration of him as lacking dispositive capacity, as having limited dispositive capacity, or as missing (Articles 188.1 and 189.1). On the other hand, it should be noted that the legal successors of the representee may renew the authorization on the consent of the representative by giving him a new power of attorney, and a power of attorney may also be renewed where the term of the validity of the authorization has expired.

In contrast, he rights and duties arisen as a result of the actions of the representative before he knew or should have known about the termination of the authorization are to remain, according to the Civil Code (Article 189.2), in force for the representee and his legal successors with respect to third persons. However, where the third person knew or should have known about the termination of the power of attorney, this rule is not to be applied—that is, the transaction made by the representative is not binding for the representee (Article 189.2). The burden of proof of these facts rests on the person who disputes the invalidity of the concluded transaction, or demands the performance in accordance with it. In the event the representative knew or should have known about the termination of the authorization but regardless of it still continued the actions, these actions are not considered as grounded on the authorization, in which case the rules of the Civil Code on transactions made without authority are to be applicable (Article 183). Upon the termination of a power of attorney the representative or his legal successor is obligated to return the power of attorney immediately (Article 189.3), and this signifies a legal act with which also the destruction of the power of attorney is equated.

Commercial representation Commercial representation is considered in Russian civil law as a modification of a discretionary representation and the rules on it are contained in the norms of the Civil Code regulating representation (Article 184). Additionally, the peculiarities of commercial representation in specific domains of entrepreneurial activity are to be established, according to the Civil Code (Article 184.4), by the law and other legal acts.

Specific for commercial representation is its special subjective part. As a principle, only an entrepreneur may participate in it, and as to a commercial representative, he is, under the Civil Code (Article 184.1), a person who permanently and independently acts as a representative under the name of other entrepreneurs when these conclude contracts in the entrepreneurial sphere—that is, a person who practices permanently and independently representation as an entrepreneur. Therefore a person who is in a labor relation with the representee may not be regarded as a commercial representative.

According to the Civil Code (Article 184.3), commercial representation must be conducted on the basis of a contract regulating internal relations between the representative and representee. It must be concluded in a written form and contain indications of the authority of the representative. The essential conditions of the contract must also include reference to the enterprise activity. In the absence of indications of the authority of the representative in the representation contract, a commercial representative may act also by virtue of a power of attorney. Thus, the representation powers of the commercial representative must be determined in Russia either in the written contract or in a power of attorney which is purposed to be presented to the third persons.[129]

Contrary to the general rules on representation, a commercial representative is allowed under the Civil Code (Article 184.2) to execute the simultaneous commercial representation of different

129 See Abova, Boguslavsky, Kabalkin, and Lisicin-Svetlanov 2007: 205–6

parties to a transaction with the consent of these parties and also in other cases provided for by the law. The simultaneous commercial representation (concurrence of authorities) requires, moreover, the (direct) authorization for it written into his contracts with both the parties of the future transaction or the powers of attorney issued by them.[130] A commercial representative representing simultaneously both parties must be impartial. Moreover, if a commercial representative acts simultaneously as a representative of both parties, he has the right under the Civil Code to demand payment of the agreed remuneration and compensation for costs borne by him in the performance of the task from both parties in equal shares, which is presumed, unless otherwise provided by their agreement (Article 184.2). Unlike the case of concurrence of authorities, the general prohibition of self-dealing contained in the Civil Code (Article 182.3) also concerns commercial representatives. So a commercial representative is not allowed to conclude a transaction in the name of the representee in which he is the other party.

As an entrepreneur, a commercial representative is obligated under the Civil Code to perform the tasks given to him with the care of an ordinary entrepreneur (Article 184.2), as well as to keep secret the information that has become known to him concerning the trade transactions concluded with his participation as a commercial representative (Article 184.3).

Unauthorized representation A prerequisite to representation in Russian law is, as stated above, that the representative has representation powers. However, it sometimes occurs that transactions and other legally significant actions are made in the name and on behalf of other persons by the persons who lack representation powers (unauthorized representation). In such instances it is often the case that there is no agreement of any kind on representation. In most of such cases, the question is, however, of so-called false authorization, in which a person acts as a representative although in reality he has no authorization to do so. Such cases include, for instance, acting by using a faulty or outdated power of attorney. Furthermore, the exceeding of the authorization determined in the power of attorney may also be counted as a case of false authorization.

The rules concerning unauthorized representation or conclusion of a transaction by an unauthorized person are contained in Article 183 of the Civil Code. According to them, in the absence of representation powers to act in the name of another person or where such powers are exceeded, a transaction is to be considered concluded in the name and in the interests of the person who concluded it unless the other person (representee) subsequently expressly approves this transaction (Article 183.1). So even where the representee does not approve such a transaction, it may be considered as concluded but in the name and in the interests of the person who made it being without competence. Thus, the representee may approve the transaction made without authorization, but if he refuses to do so, then the rights and duties grounded on the transaction arise to the person who made it without authorization, and it is possible that he will bear contractual liability if he breaches his contract obligations. This requires, however, that his legal capacity includes the conclusion of such transactions. So, for instance, if a credit contract is made in the name of bank by a physical person who lacks the authorization to it, such a contract would never be regarded as a bank transaction concluded in the name and on behalf of the physical person, since a physical person may not be granted with the legal capacity belonging to credit organizations. Such a contract is regarded n Russian law as contradictory to the law and consequently null and void.[131] Also a transaction made by an employee without authorization can hardly be transferred to him if

130 It is important to note that commercial representation is allowed only in the domain of entrepreneurial activity.

131 Suhanov 2007: 546.

he employer does not approve it.[132] Furthermore, a representative may not become a party to an agreement concluded for changing or amending the main contract. Such an agreement is recognized in Russian judicial practice as null and void, since it must inherently be an inseparable part of the contract and may not exist and be performed separately.[133]

According to the Civil Code (Article 183.2), subsequent approval of a transaction by the representee creates, changes, and terminates civil rights and duties for him under the transaction from the moment of its conclusion.[134] The approval of a transaction made without authorization must be clearly expressed in Russian law either in written or orally or by actions proving it—for instance, concludently.[135] The approval must be addressed to the representative or the third person who made the transaction.[136] Moreover, it must be made in a reasonable time. In the event the representee is a juristic person, the transaction concluded without representation powers must be approved by the governing body of it or by the person authorized to do it. However, in the case of a transaction made by the governing body of a juristic person which exceeds the limits of its legal capacity, the rules of the Civil Code regulating unauthorized representation (Article 183.1) are not to be applicable, since the governing body of the juristic person is not a representative of the latter. In such a case, applicable shall be either Article 174 of the Civil Code devoted to it or the general rule on the invalidity of transactions not corresponding to the law or to other legal acts whereupon the transaction may be recognized as null and void (Article 168). The general rule of the Civil Code (Article 168) standing for the nullity of transaction must definitely be applied to transactions made by a public law subject in which it exceeded its competence.[137]

The term for approval of the transaction concluded without representation powers is of decisive significance. This means that, if the approval of the principal arrives after the person who acted without representation powers and who later approved the transaction as his own or made in his name has executed all preparatory acts for the performance of the transaction or started its performance, such an approval has no more legal significance. In such a case the transfer of the rights grounded on the transaction to the principal (likewise to any other third person) may occur in accordance with the rules of the Civil Code regulating substitution of persons in an obligation (Articles 382–92).[138]

---

132 Sergeev 1 2009: 539.

133 See Informative Letter of the Presidium of the Supreme Arbitrazh Court no 57 of 23 October 2000. Экономика и жизнь [Economics and Life] 47 (2000): 23.

134 Thus, such approval has retroactive effect. See Abova, Boguslavsky, Kabalkin, and Lisicin-Svetlanov 2007: 205.

135 In Russian judicial practice, as such a concludent act has been regarded, for instance, the collection by the claimant of the belated invoice and penalty based on the contract, the validity of which was disputed. Performances executed for a period of two years have also been regarded as acceptance of the existence of the contract concerning them. See Вестник Высшего Арбитражного Суда Российской Федерации [Herald of the Supreme Arbitrazh Court of the Russian Federation] 7 (1996): 94 and 1 (1997): 53. The acceptance of the reclamation and conclusion of a transaction for securing and performing a first transaction has also been regarded by the Supreme Arbitrazh Court as a later ratification of a transaction concluded in the absence of the authority to do so. See Informative Letter of the Presidium of the Supreme Arbitrazh Court no 57 of 23 October. Экономика и жизнь [Economics and Life] 47 (2000): 23.

136 Where the arbitrazh court establishes in the proceedings against the representee concerning performance of the obligation grounded on the transaction that it was concluded by a person without representation powers and the representee has not approved it, then the claim is to be dismissed.

137 See Informative Letter of the Presidium of the Supreme Arbitrazh Court no 57 of 23 October 2000. Экономика и жизнь [Economics and Life] 47 (2000): 23 and Вестник Высшего Арбитражного Суда Российской Федерации [Herald of the Supreme Arbitrazh Court of the Russian Federation] 5 (1999): 66.

138 Suhanov 2007: 546.

The purpose of the rules of the Civil Code according to which the representee may accept the transaction concluded in his name is to protect the representee. As to the third person, with whom the transaction is concluded, it is assumed in Russian civil law that he knew or should have known about the lack of authorization of the representative since he had opportunities to check the power of attorney. Therefore, if the third person has acted negligently or consciously counting on that the transaction has been approved, the transaction is considered as binding on him. Thus, if the representee approves the transaction and consequently it becomes binding, the third person who knew about the lack of authorization may not refuse the obligation he has undertaken by referring to the lack of authorization. It is, however, another situation when the third person did not know or should have known that the representative concluded the transaction not on his own behalf but for a representee, which may occur when the latter's name is left unmentioned. In such a case the rules of the Civil Code regulating quasi-contract relations—more exactly, transactions in the interest of another person or *negotiorum gestio* (Article 986)—are applicable. According to them, the rights and duties arisen from such actions may pass to the person on behalf of whom the transaction was made, provided, however, that the third person does not object to it.[139]

Invalidity of Contract[140]

Invalidity of contract and the consequences thereof are regulated in the Civil Code mainly by the rules concerning transactions. Additionally applicable are the rules of the Civil Code on contracts which are contained in its general part and special part devoted to different types of contract. In certain cases the rules on invalidity of transactions are, in these rules, concretized and sometimes they contain exemptions from the general invalidity rules. In this connection, it is important to note that the application of the invalidity rules concerning different types of contract may in certain cases cause interpretation problems, where the general rules on invalidity of transactions are ignored.[141]

The validity of any transaction depends on the validity of its elements. As valid is regarded in Russian civil law a transaction:

- the content of which corresponds to the law;
- which is made by a legally capable person;
- in which the expressions of the will corresponds with the wills of the parties, and
- the form requirements provided by the law are observed.

In turn, invalid transactions may be divided on the ground of which element the transaction lacks. Accordingly, invalid transactions are divided in the Russian civil law to those in which:

- there is an error in with respect to its parties (error *in persona*);[142]

139 Sergeev 1 2009: 538.

140 For more on this subject, see, for instance, Braginsky and Vitrjansky 1999: 185–93 and Sergeev 1 2009: 445–500. See also S. Budylin, A Comparative Study in the Law of the Non-existent: Contract Invalidity in the U.S. and Russia, in *Currents: International Trade Law Journal* 15/2 (2006): 28–44.

141 The invalidity rules are not applicable in Russia to those instances where a contract is left unconcluded. See Abova, Boguslavsky, Kabalkin, and Lisicin-Svetlanov 2007: 190.

142 The transactions used in entrepreneurial activity in which the error concerns personal characteristics are related to the special legal capacity of juristic persons or the legal position of the governing bodies of

- there is an error concerning the will (error of intent);[143]
- there is a defect in the form (formal error),[144] and
- there is an error in the content (contentual error)[145].[146]

All these kinds of invalid transactions are mentioned in the rules of the Civil Code (Articles 166–79). Additionally, the Civil Code contains the general rule in accordance with which any transaction not corresponding to the requirements of the law or other legal acts is invalid (Article 168). This rule is regarded as referring in fact to transactions with a contentual error.[147]

Nullity and voidableness of transaction[148] A legally erroneous contract would not be valid, as stated above. It is thus invalid. Invalidity of transaction entails, in Russian civil law, that an action made in the form of a transaction lacks the capacity to be a ground for the civil law results pursued by the parties; they would not be achieved.

A transaction may be, according to the Civil Code (Article 166.1), invalid on the grounds defined in the Civil Code if the court recognizes it as such. In this case the question is about a

---

these. The invalidity rules concerning such transactions of juristic persons which contain the error concerning personal characteristics are included in the rules of the Civil Code which regulate (a) transactions exceeding the limits of the legal capacity of the juristic person to which also transactions concluded without a license are equated (Article 173) and (b) transactions of the governing bodies of juristic persons exceeding the limitations of their authority (Article 174). See Abova, Boguslavsky, Kabalkin, and Lisicin-Svetlanov 2007: 195–7.

143 Transactions with the error of intent are divided in Russian law into transactions which are lacking the internal will of its party to make the transaction and those in which the internal will is formed wrongly. Without internal will are made, according to the rules of the Civil Code, transactions (a) concluded under the influence of coercion, threat, or bad-faith agreement between a representative of one party with another party (Article 179) as well as transactions (b) concluded by a physical person incapable of understanding the significance of his actions or of controlling them. The expression of will in such transactions reflects the will not of its maker but the person who has influenced him. In turn, transactions in which the internal will is formed wrongly include, according to the provisions of the Civil Code, those which are made under the influence of a mistake, and concluded under the influence of fraud, or as consequence of the coincidence of grave circumstances (Articles 178 and 179). The internal will in such transactions seems to be faultlessly expressed, but it has been formed under the influence of such circumstances which has misrepresented the real will of the person who expressed it.

144 The invalidity of transactions with a form error depends on what form for the transaction is imposed by the law or the agreement of the parties. Nonobservence of the form requirements is hardly in question in respect of oral transactions, wherefore the question of the invalidity of transaction concerns usually those which require written form. Nonobservence of written form requirements entails invalidity, however, only in those cases established by the law. Contrary to this are the requirements of notarial authentication and registration, since nonobservence of them always entails, as stated before, invalidity of transaction.

145 It is characteristic for transactions with the contentual error that the conditions included in them are in contradiction with the requirements of the law or other legal acts. They include a) transactions which are made with a purpose contrary to the grounds of the legal order or morality (Article 169), and b) mock and sham transactions (Article 170).

146 See, for instance, Sergeev 1 2009: 445.

147 In fact, in Russian law any transaction containing the error may be regarded as not corresponding to the law or other legal acts. Otherwise, the classification of invalid transactions is relative. See Sergeev 1 2009: 446.

148 For the subject see, in particular, D.O. Tuzov, Ничтожность и оспоримость юридической сделки: пандектное учение и современное право [Nullity and Voidability of Juridical Transaction: Pandect Doctrine and Modern Law] (2006): 164–190.

disputable transaction and respectively about the voidableness of transaction. A transaction can be, according to the same rules, invalid also without the decision of a court confirming its invalidity, in which case the question is of the nullity of the transaction or self-acting or absolute invalidity.

Voidableness or relative invalidity of transaction comprehends that the action made in the form of a transaction may be recognized by the court as invalid if there are grounds to do so established by the law. Thus, a voidable transaction is presumed to be valid, but this presumption may be rebutted by the court. In general, voidableness of transaction is referred to in the concrete legal norms by indicating the court proceeding for recognizing it as valid.[149] According to the Civil Code (Article 166.2), a claim for the recognition of a voidable transaction to be invalid may be presented by the persons specified in each case respectively in the Civil Code; usually, it is an interested person. An invalidity claim must be filed within a year (Article 181.2). In failure of such, the voidable transaction is considered valid, and consequently such a transaction gives birth to all the legal consequences purposed by it and they are in force until the court recognizes the transaction as invalid.

Nullity of transaction or its absolute invalidity comprehends that, on the ground of the action made in the form of a transaction, no legal consequences pursued by the parties shall or could be achieved or arise because the transaction does not correspond to the law, and it is invalid as such[150] from the moment of its execution. As an action against the law, a null and void transaction may cause only such consequences which are established by the law as countermeasures against legal offences. This means mainly restitution obligations and confiscatory sanctions.

According to the Civil Code (Article 166.1), a claim for the application of the consequences of the invalidity of a (null and) void transaction may be presented by any interested person. A court also has the right to apply such consequences on its own initiative—that is, regardless of whether such a demand is presented or not. Thus a void transaction is invalid irrespective of the decision of the court. However, this does not prevent the invalidity of the void transaction being considered in the court proceeding. This is clearly referred to in the rules of the Civil Code on the means of protection of civil law rights (Article 12), according to which civil law rights may be protected not only by means of recognizing a disputable (voidable) transaction as invalid and applying the consequences of its invalidity, but also by applying the consequences of the invalidity of a null transaction. This has been interpreted in Russia not only in the legal literature but also in judicial practice to mean that a claim for declaratory judgment in respect of the nullity of transaction is possible. It is expressly stated in Russian judicial practice that a claim on the invalidity of the null transaction may be presented by any interested person, and, moreover, that the court has the right to apply the consequences provided by the law for void transactions irrespective of whether such a demand has been presented or not by the claimant.[151]

In certain cases, only the invalidity of transaction as a consequence of nonobservance of the form requirements is mentioned in the Civil Code. This concerns the form requirements in respect of foreign trade transactions (Article 162.3), pledge contract (Article 339), contract of suretyship (Article 362), sale contract of an immovable (Article 550) and an enterprise (Article 560.2), as well as lease of building and structures (Article 651) and enterprise (Article 658.3). Certain contract conditions are also prescribed as invalid if they are not made in the proper form, as for instance, the condition on liquidated damages (Article 331). Thus, in certain cases the legislator has not

149 See Sergeev 1 2009: 490.

150 Without declaring it as invalid.

151 See Abova, Boguslavsky, Kabalkin, and Lisicin-Svetlanov 2007: 190; the Joint Decrees of the Plenums 6/8 1996: 13, and Вестник Высшего Арбитражного Суда Российской Федерации [Herald of the Supreme Arbitrazh Court of the Russian Federation] 7 (1996): 89–90, 1 (1999): 27 and 47, and 6 (1999): 42.

specified the species of invalidity. It is evident that the distinction between void and voidable transactions is considered in Russian law formal and also partly unnecessary, wherefore room is left for judicial discretion on this question. Furthermore, it should be noted that, in Russian law, cases of unconcluded contract are also known and they are distinguished from invalid contracts by being excluded from the application of the rules on the consequences of invalidity of transaction. This occurs not only where the essential condition is missing but also if the agreed form of the contract is not observed.[152]

In Russian law invalidity or nullity or voidableness may concern the whole transaction or only a part thereof. For instance, the court may recognize only a part of the conditions of transaction or merely some of them as invalid. The invalidity of individual contract conditions may be grounded on their being contradictory to legal requirements or deficiencies concerning their content owing to the error of intent. According to the Civil Code (Article 180), the invalidity of part of a transaction does not entail the invalidity of its other parts if it is possible to suppose that the transaction would have been made without the inclusion of its invalid part.

The Civil Code also contains concrete rules on the invalidity of certain contract conditions. Hence, the condition on liquidated damages is prescribed as invalid if it is not made in the written form (Article 331.1). The same consequence is provided in the rules of the Civil Code on sale concerning the agreement of the parties to release the seller from liability in the event a third person demands the acquired goods from the buyer, or to limit such a liability (Article 461.2). In this context, noteworthy is the rule of the Civil Code concerning means of security for performance of obligations, according to which the invalidity of the principal obligation entails the invalidity of the obligation securing it, unless otherwise provided for in the law (Article 329.3).

The general rule on nullity of transaction is contained in the norm of the Civil Code regulating invalidity of transactions not conforming to the law or other legal acts (Article 168). According to it, a transaction not conforming to the law or other legal acts is null unless the law establishes that such a transaction is voidable or provides other consequences for the violation.[153] The general rule of the Civil Code is purported to be applied in the event the law does not provide the special grounds for considering an invalid transaction as null, or it may be referred to only in the event there is no directly applicable special rule to the case. The question is, in that case, of the violation of the requirements provided in the law or other legal act. This general rule is usually to be applied to the case where the concluded transaction does not correspond to the concrete requirements imposed in the law or other legal act or merely concrete requirements established in a concrete administrative decision. It is also to be applied where the transaction does not correspond to the general civil law principles.[154]

Transactions made for a purpose contradicting the foundations of the law, of legal order, and of morality, which are also considered in Russian civil law as null and void (Article 169), are directed against the laws or other legal acts containing the basics of the legal order. Such transactions indicate not merely nonobservance of the legal requirements which is general for transactions not conforming to the law or other legal acts (Article 168), but represent contrariness to law in the qualified form. Qualifying for them is their subjective part or the aim: they are made against

152 See, for instance, Abova, Boguslavsky, Kabalkin, and Lisicin-Svetlanov 2007: 186, 190, and 370 and Sergeev 1 2009: 491–3.

153 In a concrete legal norm voidableness may be expressly indicated. On the other hand, a legal norm may provide some other consequence of the invalidity of a transaction. See Abova, Boguslavsky, Kabalkin, and Lisicin-Svetlanov 2007: 192.

154 See, for instance, Sergeev 1 2009: 483–6 and Abova, Boguslavsky, Kabalkin, and Lisicin-Svetlanov 2007: 192.

the legal order established in the country. Thus, characteristic of transactions made for a purpose contradicting the foundations of the law, of legal order, and of morality is, in Russian law, their illegal aim. Such transactions are considered as null merely because they are directed against society and threaten the state and societal interests. The question is of intentional acts (at least of one of the party) for which criminal liability is established. The intent must also concern the aim which is evidently contradictory to the basics of the legal order. In making such a transaction the participants understand the consequences of its illegality[155] and pursue them or at least consciously regard them as possible.[156]

Additionally, as null are regarded in the rules of the Civil Code on transactions mock and sham transactions (Article 170), transactions made by a physical person who has been declared lacking dispositive capacity (Article 171), transactions of concluded by minors under 14 years old (Article 172), transactions in whose conclusion form requirements are not observed, if the law provides nullity in such a case (Article 165.1), as well as, in certain cases, transactions in the conclusion of which registration requirements are not observed (Article 165.1).

The special grounds for nullity transactions established in other legal norms than in the rules of the Civil Code concerns in the first place transactions, the purpose of which is to limit the legal capacity and dispositive capacity of a physical person (Article 22.3). The rules on nullity of transaction are also found in the corporation law norms. As null are regarded, for instance, transactions violating the rights of a participant in a general partnership. It includes limitations to (Article 71.3) or withdrawal from the partnership (Article 77.2), or an agreement of the partners limiting or eliminating their liability for the obligations of the partnership (Article 75.3).

The rules on nullity are also contained in certain norms of the Civil Code regulating different types of contract. In some cases the contract law norms of the Civil Code prescribe certain contract conditions as null and void which cause the partial invalidity of the contract. Nullity is provided, under the Civil Code, to concern an agreement according to which:

- the delegant and delegate waives the right to withdraw from the delegation contract (Article 977.2);
- the right of the debtor and a pledgor who is a third person to terminate the levy of execution toward him and the sale of the pledged property by performing the overdue obligation secured by this is limited in the pledge contract (Article 350.7), and
- the right to withdraw from the contract without time limit is limited in the simple partnership contract (Article 1051).

An agreement concluded in advance on limiting the amount of liability of a debtor under a contract adhesion or other contract in which the creditor is an ordinary consumer is void under the Civil Code (Article 400.2), as is an agreement concluded in advance for eliminating or limiting liability for the intentional violation of an obligation (Article 401.4). Furthermore, conditions of a public contract which do not correspond to the requirements established for them are void (Article 426.5). In certain

155 This nullity rule is also applied to cases in which the law is not directly violated, but only evaded. See Sergeev 1 2009: 487–8.

156 Transactions to which this rule is applied include, according to the interpretive instruction of the Russian Supreme Arbitrazh Court, transactions which are connected with the production and alienation of an object excluded from or limited in commerce, the preparation and distribution of publications containing military and discriminatory propaganda, and the preparation and sale of forged documents and securities. See Decree of the Plenum of the Supreme Arbitrazh Court no 22 of 10 April 20008, available at http://www.arbitr.ru/as/pract/post_plenum/19013.html (accessed 8 June 2010).

cases the nonobservance of the form requirements concerning a contract may also cause its nullity. This consequence is applied to preliminary (Article 429), credit (Article 820), and bank deposit contracts (Article 836) as well as to commercial concession contracts (Article 1028).

Relatively invalid or disputable or voidable transactions include in Russia, according to the rules of the Civil Code:

- transactions of juristic persons exceeding the limits of special legal capacity (Article 173);
- transactions exceeding the restrictions of powers (Article 174);
- transactions made by a minor aged between 14 and 18 years (Article 175);
- transactions of physical persons whose dispositive capacity is limited by a court (Article 176);
- transactions of physical persons who are incapable of understanding the purport of his actions and directing them (Article 177);
- transactions concluded under the influence of a mistake (Article 178), and
- transactions concluded under the influence of fraud, coercion, threat, or bad-faith agreement of the representative of one party with the other party or coincidence of grave circumstances (Article 179).[157]

Transactions of juristic persons, including contracts which juristic persons concluded with other juristic and physical persons, exceeding the limits of the special legal capacity comprehend actions made against the objects of the activities imposed expressly in the charter as well as transactions made without a license to practice the respective activities (Article 173).[158] However, the mere fact that a transaction is made by exceeding the limits of the special legal capacity determined in the charter or without the necessary license is not sufficient for its recognition as invalid in the Russian civil law. Additionally, it must be proven that the other party (physical or juristic person) knew or clearly should have known of the illegality of the transaction. A transaction exceeding the limits of the special legal capacity may be recognized by the court as invalid on the claim of the juristic person, its founder (participant), or a state agency exercising control or supervision over the activities of the juristic person (Article 173). The burden of proof is on the claimant. In the cases provided by the law, a transaction exceeding the limits of the special legal capacity or made without the necessary license is null and void.[159] The general rules on invalidity of transactions are not to be applied, for instance, to (state and municipal) unitary enterprises as well as to other enterprises the legal capacity of which is limited by the law or the activity of which is subject to license. In these cases transactions contradictory to the requirements are null and void.[160]

Also transactions made by exceeding the restrictions of powers, including contracts the other party of which may be a physical and juristic person, can be, according to Article 174 of the Civil Code, invalid in certain cases. This provides, as already presented above, that if the powers of

157 In such cases, contrariness to morality can also be seen. This is, however, the ground for invalidity contained in the other norm of the Civil Code (Article 169). The distinction has significance since a transaction concluded under the influence of fraud, coercion, threat, or bad-faith agreement between a representative of one party with another party or as consequence of the coincidence of grave circumstances (Article 179) may be recognized as void, whereas a transaction made for a purpose contradicting the foundations of the law, of legal order, and of morality is considered in Russian civil law as null and void (Article 169).

158 Licenses are regulated by the provisions on legal capacity of juristic persons of the Civil Code (Article 49) and by the law on licensing of certain activities no 128-FZ of 8 August 2001.

159 See Abova, Boguslavsky, Kabalkin, and Lisicin-Svetlanov 2007: 195–6.

160 See Joint Decrees of the Plenums 6/8 1996.

a person to conclude a transaction are restricted by the contract, or the powers of the body of a juristic person are restricted by its constituent documents as compared to the way they are defined in the power of attorney or in the law, or if they could be considered obvious from the situation in which the transaction is concluded, and if, in concluding this transaction, such person or body exceeded the boundaries of these restrictions, the transaction may be recognized by a court as invalid upon the claim of the person in whose interest the said restrictions have been imposed. However, this shall occur only if it is proven that the other party to the transaction knew or clearly should have known of these restrictions.

A transaction concluded under the influence of a mistake (Article 178) and a transaction concluded under influence of fraud, coercion, threat, or bad-faith agreement of representative of one party with other party or coincidence of grave circumstances (Article 179) may also be recognized by a court as invalid upon the claim of a juristic or physical person.[161]

Voidableness is also recognized also in the contract law norms of the Civil Code. This concerns cases where the norms provide that a contractual party has the right to demand recognition of the contract as invalid. An example of this is the rule regulating the sale of enterprise which protects the creditor who has not informed the seller or buyer in writing of his consent to the transfer of the debt (Article 562.2). The right to demand recognition of the contract as invalid is also established in the rule on lease of residential accommodation (Article 684), insurance (Articles 934.2, 944.3, and 951.3), pledge (Article 349.1), and sale (Article 459.2). Voidableness is also provided in the corporation law rules,[162] the application of which may concern interested and large-scale transactions.

Legal consequences of invalidity of transaction According to the rules in the Civil Code on consequences of invalidity of transaction (Article 167.1), an invalid transaction does not entail legal consequences other than those which are connected with its invalidity, and it is invalid from the moment of its conclusion. However, if it follows from the content of a voidable transaction that it may only be terminated for the future, the court, in declaring the transaction to be invalid, is to terminate its validity under the Civil Code (Article 167.3) for the future. The legal consequences of invalidity of transaction do not appear in Russian law until the transaction stated invalid is partly or fully performed. In that case, however, they will be limited to the consequences established by the property law, among which bilateral and unilateral restitution[163] is the most important. There are also other property law consequences of invalidity of transaction.[164] [165]

Other property law consequences following from the invalidity of a transaction are additional by their nature and comprehend the compensation of costs and of the value of the lost or damaged

---

161 For more on these details, see Abova, Boguslavsky, Kabalkin, and Lisicin-Svetlanov 2007: 199–202 and Sergeev 1 2009: 457–70.

162 Articles 79 and 84 of the Joint Stock Company Law, and Articles 45 and 46 of the Law on Limited Liability Companies.

163 For more on restitution concerning invalid transactions in Russian law, see D.O. Tuzov,. Реституция при недействительности сделок и защита добросовестного приобретателя в российском гражданском праве [Restitution concerning the Invalidity of Transactions and Protection of the Good Faith Acquirer in Russian Civil Law] (2007): 89–120.

164 Claims for the return of performances executed under an invalid transaction are to be governed by the rules of the Civil Code on the obligations to return unjust enrichment, unless otherwise following from the law, other legal acts, or the nature of the respective obligation (Article 1103).

165 The restitution rules provided in the provisions on invalidity of transactions are not applicable, in accordance with the ruling of the Constitution Court, to the claims of a plaintiff in which he demands the

property. In general, the invalidity of a transaction does not invalidate the transactions connected with it, unless the question is of an additional contract such as suretyship and pledge.[166] The period of limitation for a claim for the application of the consequences of the invalidity is determined in the Civil Code (Article 181) in respect of a void transaction as three years[167] and in respect of a voidable transaction as one year.[168]

Bilateral restitution is regarded in Russian civil law as the main form of legal consequence of the invalidity of a transaction. According to the rule of the Civil Code (Article 167.2) concerning the consequences of the invalidity of a transaction in case of the invalidity of a transaction, each of the parties is obliged to return to the other everything received under the transaction and, in case of the impossibility of returning in kind what was received (including when the received consisted of the use of property, work performed, or service provided), to compensate for its value in money. The purpose of the bilateral restitution is to return the parties of an invalid transaction to the position they had before the conclusion of the transaction. The rules on bilateral restitution intended to be applied in accordance with the Civil Code (Article 167.2) apply generally to all cases of the invalidity of a transaction, unless other consequences of the invalidity of the transaction are provided by the law.

Unilateral restitution is provided in the rules of the Civil Code on invalidity of transaction as a consequence of the invalid transactions which are made under the influence of fraud, coercion, threat, or bad-faith agreement of the representative of one party with other party or the coincidence of grave circumstances (Article 179.1). The purpose of this, according to the Civil Code (Article 179.2), is that the other party is to return to the victim everything; if it is impossible to return it in kind, its value in money is to be given in compensation instead. Moreover, the dishonest party does not get his performance back because the property received under the transaction by the victim from the other party and also due to him in compensation for that transferred to the other party is to enter, under the Civil Code (Article 179.2), the budget of the Russian Federation. If it is impossible to transfer the property to the budget of the Russian Federation in kind, its value in money will be recovered instead. Thus the party who has acted dishonestly in the conclusion of an invalid transaction is subject in Russian law to confiscatory sanctions.[169]

The restitution is, however, excluded in a certain case under the Civil Code. In such a case everything received by the parties under the invalid transaction is to be recovered to the income of the Russian Federation (Article 169). This is the case of a specific consequence of the invalidity of transaction which is established to be applied only in the event the transaction is declared invalid as a transaction made for a purpose contradicting the foundations of the law, of legal order, and of morality (Article 169).

---

return of his property invoking the bona fide rules of the ownership law, in which case the vindication claim rules must be applied. See Decree of the Constitutional Court of the Russian Federation No 6-P of 21 April 2003, available at http://ksportal.garant.ru:8081/SESSION/S__Y2mBIaVG/PILOT/main.html (accessed 8 June 2010). For more on this subject, see Tuzov 2007: 168–83.

166 Abova, Boguslavsky, Kabalkin, and Lisicin-Svetlanov 2007: 191.

167 Calculated from the day when the performance of the transaction started.

168 Calculated from the day when the coercion or threat under which the transaction was concluded was used or from the day when the claimant became aware or he should have become aware of the other circumstance entailing the invalidity of the transaction.

169 The rule of the Civil Code concerning unilateral restitution is also applied in the case of a transaction made evidently for a purpose contradicting the foundations of the law, of legal order, and of morality (Article 169) but only the other party has committed the illegal action. In both cases the claimant must prove the intent of the defendant. See Sergeev 1 2009: 495–6.

The application of the general rules on the consequences of the invalidity of transaction may be restricted in Russia by the law in order to protect public interests and the substantive interests of the participants of the civil circulation. An example of this is the rule of the Civil Code regulating sale of enterprise (Article 566) which enables the exceptions to the rules on restitution and confiscation (Article 566). This establishes that the rules of the Civil Code on the consequences of invalidity of transactions providing for the return or the recovery in kind of what has been received is to be applied to the contract for sale of an enterprise, if such consequences do not substantially violate the rights and interests protected by the law of creditors of seller and buyer, of other persons, and do not contradict the interests of society.[170]

Improvement of transaction or rectification of its invalidity[171] In certain cases the invalidity of a transaction (contract) is not definitive, and it can, through the actions of the parties or the other party, become valid or improved. Such possibilities concern, according to the rules of the Civil Code, transactions the conclusion of which is subject to strict form requirements, such as transactions requiring notarial authentication and registration.[172] The rule on the rectification of a contract subject to notarial authentication is contained in Article 165.2 of the Civil Code. According to it, if one of the parties has wholly or partially performed a transaction which requires notarial authentication, and the other party refuses such authentication of the transaction, the court has the right to demand that the party who has performed the transaction recognize transaction as valid. In this event, subsequent notarial authentication of the transaction is not required. Since this rule is general and concerns any transaction, it may be applied irrespective of whether there is a reference to it in the special rules of the Civil Code or not. Thus, the court has discretionary power on the issue and may decide after considering all the relevant circumstances of the case if the contract contrary to the legal requirements or left unnotarized by the parties is valid or not. In considering the case, the court must clarify whether the contract is really concluded, in which case it must follow the above-presented rule of the Civil Code which prohibits the use of the testimony of witnesses as evidence (Article 162.1). This means that if the conclusion of the contract may not be proven through evidence other than testimony, such a contract is unrectifiable and remains definitively invalid. In case of a negative decision of the court the only remedy for the party who performed the transaction is a claim for the return of unjust enrichment, as provided for by Article 1103 of the Civil Code.

The rules on rectification of an unregistered contract are provided in Article 165 of the Civil Code. According to them, if a transaction requiring state registration has been concluded in the proper form but one of the parties refuses to register it, the court has the right on demand of the other party to enter a decision on the registration of the transaction (Article 165.3). The registration of a contract may be demanded by the party, otherwise than in the case of notarial authentication, regardless of whether he has performed it or not. However, it is required, in the conclusion of the contract, that all the form requirements are observed. This means that, if neither the form requirements—for instance, notarial authentication—nor registration requirements are observed, the contract is not rectifiable and remains definitively invalid. The decision of the court on the registration does not, however, exclude the necessity of the registration; neither does it constitute the transfer of the right grounded on the transaction. However, the decision is a sufficient ground

170 See Sergeev 2 2009: 128–9 and Abova, Boguslavsky, Kabalkin, and Lisicin-Svetlanov 2007: 465.

171 See, in particular, Tuzov 2006: 190–202.

172 According to the rules presented here, the transaction in which the form requirements are not observed is rectifiable; otherwise it must correspond with the law.

for the transaction to be entered in the register. The transaction is to be registered in accordance with the court decision (Article 165.3).

In respect of both the ratification of the contract requiring notarial authentication and registration alike, it is provided in Article 165.4 of the Civil Code that the party who unjustifiably refuses notarial authentication or state registration of the transaction must compensate the other party for the damages caused by the delay in concluding or registering the transaction, which means real damages.

Interpretation of Contract[173]

The rules on interpretation of contract are included in the Civil Code (Article 431) as the rules guiding the consideration of a court.[174] Their starting point or the basis for their interpretation is the literal meaning of the words and expressions contained in the contract. Only where the literal meaning of a condition of the contract is not clear is this be established by comparison with other conditions and the sense of the contract as a whole. Where the content of the contract may not be determined in accordance with the above rules, then in accordance with the supplementary rule the real common will of the parties must be clarified, taking into account the purpose of the contract. In such a case all surrounding circumstances are to be taken into account, including the negotiations and correspondence preceding the contract, the practice established in the relations of the parties,[175] the commercial customs and the subsequent conduct of the parties, which play an ancillary role.[176] Additionally, it is regarded in Russian legal doctrine that the rule *contra proferentum* must be applied in the interpretation of a contract containing ambiguous terms. Such a term must be construed against the person who prepared such a contract.[177]

Fulfillment of Contract[178]

The rules on fulfillment (performance) of contract[179] are included in the obligation law norms of the Civil Code. The binding effect of contract means generally, as presented above, that its parties are (legally) obligated to fulfill it (perform its obligations) and even the termination of the validity of the contract does not terminate, according to the Civil Code, the obligation until this is fulfilled in conformity with the contract, unless otherwise provided by the law or a contract (Article 425). This principle or the principle of the proper performance is expressly provided in the general rule

173 On this subject, see Suhanov 2008: 193–5; Sergeev 1 2009: 860–61; Braginsky and Vitrjansky 1999: 266–74; Abova, Boguslavsky, Kabalkin, and Lisicin-Svetlanov 2007: 369 and Stepanov 2010: 456–7.

174 Abova, Boguslavsky, Kabalkin, and Lisicin-Svetlanov 2007: 369 and Stepanov 2010: 457.

175 Thus, in Russian civil law, the established (habitual) practice is legally significant with regard to the interpretation of contract.

176 Thus, the real will of the parties is placed at the third stage of interpretation. See Stepanov 2010: 456.

177 Sergeev 1 2009: 861 and Braginsky and Vitrjansky 1999: 268.

178 For more on this subject, see, among others, Sergeev 1 2009: 880–98 and Braginsky and Vitryansky 1999: 417–33.

179 It is regarded as a transaction. There is a special rule concerning the form of such transactions, according to which legal acts in performance of a contract, concluded in written form, may by agreement of the parties be effected orally, unless this contradicts the law or the contract (Article 159.3). As a matter of fact, any transaction in performance of a contract may be executed orally, unless otherwise provided by the law or the agreement of the parties. See Sergeev 1 2009: 880–81.

of the Civil Code concerning the fulfillment (performance) of obligations (Article 309), according to which the obligations must be performed in the proper way in conformity with the conditions of the contract and requirements of the law and other legal normative acts, and in the absence of those, in conformity with the commercial customs or other habitually presented demands. As regards enterprise activity, the (unilateral) refusal to fulfill the obligation and the unilateral amendment to the contract is admissible only in cases provided by the law or a contract, unless otherwise following from the law or the substance (nature) of the obligation (Article 310).[180] The other general rules implying the binding effect of contract and providing for the fulfillment of contractual obligations in the Civil Code are the main rules on the contractual liability and the conditions on the termination of obligation, which are related to the system of legal consequences applicable in case of the breach of contract. Thus, if an obligation is violated, the contracting party has the right to turn against the violator of the contract the contract law consequences such as the demands to recover damages[181] as well as to pay the liquidated damages (penalty) and also interest in the case of the pecuniary obligation. In certain cases it is also possible to demand the performance of the obligation in kind or have the work done at the debtor's expense (Articles 393–8).

The Civil Code includes a considerable number of dispositive norms on the performance of obligations. They contain the rules concerning the term (including a reasonable term) and place, and in which the conditions of contract, legislation, substance of the obligation, commercial customs etc. are important (Articles 314 and 316). An advanced performance of the obligation connected with entrepreneurship is admissible, under the Civil Code (Article 315), only if it is provided in the law or other normative act or condition of contract, or it is implied from the commercial custom or substance of the obligation. On the same conditions, the obligation to accept performance concerns the creditor (Article 406)—that is, his duty to cooperate—and this means the actions without which it is impossible for the debtor to fulfill his obligations. The duty to collaborate must be stipulated by the contract or it may be inferred from the conditions of the contract. Although the principle of cooperation is not expressly enforced in the Civil Code, it is, however, regarded as the general principle of contract law[182] in Russia. Furthermore, fulfillment of obligation is subject also to the principles of reasonableness and fairness, which are regarded as general principles of Russian civil law.[183]

As means of providing the performance (means of security for performance of obligations), liquidated damages (penalty), pledge (mortgage),[184] retention of property (withholding of property

180 Stability of obligations is the general principle of the Russian obligation law and it follows from the principle of proper performance. See Sergeev 1 2009: 881.

181 In Russian law the right to complete compensation for damages is presumed. See Abova, Boguslavsky, Kabalkin, and Lisicin-Svetlanov 2007: 341.

182 According to the UNIDROIT Principles of International Commercial Contracts. The Principles are translated into Russian by A.S. Komarov. See Принципы международных коммерческих договоров 2004 [Principles of International Commercial Contracts 2004] (2006).

183 Sergeev 1 2009: 883.

184 According to Article 334 of the Civil Code, by virtue of a pledge a creditor under an obligation secured by a pledge (pledgee) has the right, in the event the debtor fails to perform the obligation, to obtain satisfaction from the value of the pledged property preferentially before other creditors of the person to whom this property belongs (pledger) with the exceptions established by the law. As to a pledge of land plots, enterprises, buildings, structures, apartments, and other immovables (mortgage), this is regulated by the law on mortgage. Unless otherwise provided by the contract, the pledged property remains with the pledger (Article 338.1). See also the Mortgage Law no 102-FZ of 16 July 1998, the norms of which are applied to the mortgage (of immovables) prior to the norms of the Civil Code regulating pledge, unless otherwise provided by the law.

of the debtor),[185] surety,[186] bank guarantee,[187] earnest money, and other measures provided by the law or a contract are mentioned in the Civil Code (Article 329),[188] and to this list may be added the rule which allows the self-defense of the civil rights mentioned above (Article 14), which seems to be rather large in Russian law.

In the case of an obligation connected with enterprise activity, the refusal of a contract party to perform the obligation is admissible under the Civil Code (Article 310), not only in case of a breach of the contract by the other party but also if it is agreed, unless otherwise follows from the contract or substance of the obligation. On the same conditions, the creditor could refuse to accept the performance of parts of the obligation; however, in such a case attention must also be paid to commercial custom (Article 311). Furthermore, performance in kind may be substituted by pecuniary compensation for damages or liquidated damages. Under the Civil Code, in case of an improper performance of the obligation, performance in kind may be demanded unless otherwise provided by the law or contract; whereas in case of nonperformance, performance in kind requires the provision for this in the law or a contract (Article 396).[189] The nature of entrepreneurial obligations is also represented in the provisions of the Civil Code on early performance of such an obligation (Article 315), according to which it is allowed only in cases when such a possibility is provided for by the law, other legal acts, or the terms of the obligation, or follow from the customs of trade or the nature of the obligation. It is also noteworthy in this connection that the duties of several debtors relating to an obligation connected with entrepreneurial activity, like the claims of several creditors under the same obligation, are solidary or joint and several, unless otherwise provided by the law, other legal acts, or the terms of the obligation.[190]

Contractual Liability

Rules on contractual liability are also included in the Civil Code norms on obligations, which are applied together with the general rules on civil law liability. The forms of civil law liability are divided in Russia into general liability for damages and special liability (for instance, liquidated damages). The general rules on liability for damages are always to be applied in the case of a

185 According to Article 359 of the Civil Code, a creditor who has a thing subject to transfer to a debtor or person specified by the debtor has the right, in the event of nonperformance by costs and other damages connected with it, to withhold it until the obligation is performed.

186 Under a contract of suretyship, the surety is, according to Article 363 of the Civil Code, obligated to the creditor of another person to be liable for the performance by the latter of his obligations in full or in part.

187 Under Article 368 of the Civil Code, by virtue of a bank guarantee the bank, other credit institution, or insurance organization (guarantor) gives at the request of another person (principal) a written obligation to pay a monetary amount to a creditor of the principal (beneficiary) in accordance with the conditions of the obligation given by the guarantor, upon presentation by the beneficiary of a written demand for its payment. In contrast to other security means, the bank guarantee is independent of the basic obligation, in security of which it was issued.

188 For more on the means of security for performance, see Sergeev 1 2009: 899–938.

189 Unfortunately, the terms неустойка and штраф used in Russian law may comprehend the same, whereas пеня usually stands for penalty interest. In particular, неустойка and штраф are not distinct even in the Civil Code, which is an obvious remnant of Soviet economic law thinking. Thus, there are real difficulties in finding the proper equivalent to the term неустойка which is usually translated as liquidated damages but can also stand for contractual penalty. For more on this subject, see Butler (2009: 406) and Osakwe (2008: 104–7) as well as E.A. Suhanov (ed.), Гражданское право, Том I, полутом 1 [Civil Law, Volume II, Subvolume 2] (2000): 56–7.

190 Popondopulo 1 2009: 310.

breach of contract (and in general if a civil right is violated), unless otherwise provided by the law or a contract. Contrary to this, the rules on special liability are to be applied only if this is provided for by the law or a contract.[191]

The rules on contractual liability are specified in the norms of the Civil Code concerning liability for the violation of obligations (Articles 393–406). The debtor is liable for the breach of contract regardless of the expiry of the term of the validity of the contract (Article 425.4). In addition to the liability for damages, the consequence of the debtor's delay is also, according to the Civil Code (Article 405), the transfer of risks. If, because of the debtor's delay, the performance has lost all interest for the creditor, he has the right to refuse to accept the performance and claim compensation for damages. However, in such a case the creditor may refuse to accept only the delayed part of the performance. The delay of the debtor could also give the creditor the right to suspend his counterperformance (Articles 328 and 405). Under the Civil Code (Article 406), the case when the creditor refuses to accept the performance or neglects his duty of cooperation is regarded as a delay. The general legal consequence of the delay of the creditor is compensation for damages; additionally, the right to suspend his counterperformance is also given to the debtor. The suspension of counterperformance is also admissible in case of the existence of circumstances obviously testifying to the fact that the performance will not be effected within the fixed term stipulated by the contract (Articles 328 and 408.2).

According to the general obligation law rule on liability (Article 401.1), the liability for the violation of the obligation is grounded on fault (intent or negligence), unless other grounds are provided by the law or a contract. Generally the guilt (fault) of the debtor is presumed (Article 401.2), but in certain cases the burden of proof could be imposed on the creditor—for instance, in the carriage. Furthermore, a condition (agreement) on eliminating or limiting the liability for an intentional violation of the obligation in advance is null and void (Article 401.4).

An exception to the general obligation law rule on liability is provided for obligations connected with entrepreneurship. The specific feature of the liability for violation of contractual obligations connected with entrepreneurial activities is that its task in cases of a disturbance in the performance of the entrepreneur's obligations is to transfer the risks to the party violating the contract, which is reflected in the strict liability for this.[192] Unless otherwise provided by the law or a contract,[193] a person violating the obligation of performance connected with entrepreneurship is to bear liability, according to the special rule of the Civil Code on the grounds of obligation law liability (Article 401.3), unless he proves that proper performance has been impossible because of force majeure, meaning extraordinary and unavoidable circumstances. To such circumstances are not, however, referred, for instance, violations of obligations on the part of the debtor's counter-agents, the absence on the market of goods indispensable for the performance, or the absence of the necessary means at the debtor's disposal (Article 401.3).

The general rule is, under the rules of the Civil Code on general liability for damages (Articles 15 and 393), that the damages are to be compensated in full. This entails, first, covering the real, actual damages or the compensatory damages; these include only direct damages which are the direct and unavoidable consequence of the violation of the obligation, but not consequential damages.[194] Second, the expenses which the creditor must pay in order to restore the violated right are also

191 Sergeev 1 2009: 946.

192 Popondopulo 1 2009: 322.

193 For instance, the liability of an agricultural producer for the breach of contract presupposes under the Civil Code his fault (Article 538). A similar liability is provided in the rules on the supply of energy (Article 547.2).

194 Abova, Boguslavsky, Kabalkin, and Lisicin-Svetlanov 2007: 342.

taken into account (Article 15.2).[195] Third, full compensation also includes covering the unreceived profits or the lost profit which the injured party would have received under the usual conditions of civil commerce, if his right had not been violated.[196] However, if the violator has received income as a result of the violation, the injured party is entitled to demand compensation for lost profit in an amount not less than such income (Article 15.2). It is also possible that changes in prices may be taken into account. According to Article 393.3 of the Civil Code, the prices that are to be taken into account are those that existed at the place where the obligation was to be performed on the date of voluntary satisfaction by the debtor of the claim of the creditor, and in default of this, on the day of filing the suit, and proceeding from the circumstances, a court may satisfy a claim taking into account the prices existing on the day of making decision. Russian civil law also knows cases of enlarged liability; it is purposed, for instance, to protect consumers.[197] There are also cases when civil liability is restricted; this concerns, for instance, the carrier's and insurer's obligations.

In respect of obligations connected with entrepreneurship, the scope of the liability[198] may be limited by the law or a contract. So, for instance, if obligations under the contract of energy supply have not been performed or have been performed improperly, the party which has violated the obligation is obligated, according to the Civil Code (Article 547.1), to compensate for the actual damage caused by this. As to contractual limitation of liability, this is generally allowed, as stated above, in respect of entrepreneurial contracts. Furthermore, although fault is excluded from the grounds for liability in case of the entrepreneur's obligations, it is, however, significant in the determination of the scope of the liability. So, for instance, the creditor's guilt could cause the scope of the debtor's liability to be reduced (Article 404).

The Civil Code (Articles 330–33, 394, and 396) also includes rules on liquidated damages; as those (penalty, fine) are recognized the sum of money, defined by the law or contract, which the debtor is obliged to pay to the creditor where he will not perform his obligation in accordance with the contract. Liquidated damages may be defined as a destined sum (single payment) or an interest that will be counted according to the duration of the violation of the contract (for instance, daily) or to its value.[199] The creditor is not obliged by the claim for liquidated damages to prove that the damage has actually been inflicted upon him; the fact of the violation is a sufficient ground for compensation. However, the creditor does not have the right to claim the payment of the damages if the debtor is not liable for the nonperformance or improper performance of the obligation (Article 300).

Under the general rule the liquidated damages cover the compensation for damages, but the rules of the Civil Code on liquidated damages make it possible that the damage will be exacted in full above the liquidated damages. This could be provided by the law or a contract; the law or a contract can also determine the alternative or exclusive liquidated damages (Article 394.1).[200] So the amount of the legal liquidated damages may be increased by agreement between the parties, unless it is prohibited by the law (Article 332.2); on the other hand, the moderation (reduction) of the liquidated damages is also possible in a court procedure (Article 333).

195 The injured party must prove the necessity of his expenses and their assumed amount by presenting calculations, as stated in the Joint Decrees of the Plenums 6/8 1996.

196 The amount of the lost profit must be determined by taking into account the reasonable expenses which the debtor would have suffered in the event of the fulfillment of the obligation, as stated in the Joint Decrees of the Plenums 6/8 1996.

197 Sergeev 1 2009: 945.

198 For more on this subject, see Popondopulo 1 2009: 318–23.

199 See Sergeev 1 2009: 902.

200 See Sergeev 1 2009: 905–6.

In general, the payment of the liquidated damages (as well as the compensation of the damages) absolves the debtor from the performance of the obligation in kind in the case of nonperformance, contrary to the case of improper performance, unless otherwise provided by the law or a contract (Article 396).

The Civil Code also includes the rule on interest, the starting point for which is the obligation to pay to the bank interest for the use of the other person's money without justification. However, where the damage exceeds the amount of the bank interest, the creditor has the right to claim that the debtor recompense him for the damages in the part exceeding the amount of the bank interest (Article 395).

Change and Rescission of Contract

According to the Civil Code (Article 450.1), a contract may be changed (amended) or rescinded (dissolved) by (another) agreement as well as in accordance with the provisions of the law. Such an agreement is regarded in Russian judicial practice as a contract which is subject to the same form and registration requirements as the contract it concerns.[201]

An amendment or rescission of a contract is, under the Civil Code (Article 450.2), also admissible upon demand of one of the parties in case of a substantial breach of the contract by the other party. A violation of a contract is considered substantial if it entails for another party such damage that it is to a significant degree deprived of that which it had the right to expect at the conclusion of the contract. In general, the burden of proof of these facts rests on the person who demands the rescission or amendment of the contract. However, regarding the contract of supply, breach of it by the supplier is presumed substantial, as, for instance, in the case of repeated violation of the periods for supply of goods, where the supplier must prove the absence of essentiality in his breach (Article 523.2). Russian judicial practice also knows cases of recognition of failure to repair of the breach of contract as the ground for its rescission.[202] [203]

A substantial change in circumstances, including economic difficulties in terms of the performance, could also be, under the Civil Code (Article 451), grounds for an amendment or rescission of the contract. A change of circumstances is considered substantial if they have changed to the extent that, if the parties could have reasonably foreseen this, the contract would not have been concluded by them at all or it would have been concluded on significantly different conditions.[204] The burden of proof of a substantial change of circumstances rests on the person who demands the rescission or amendment of the contract.[205]

The decision concerning the amendment or rescission of the contract based on a substantial change of circumstances may, under the Civil Code (Article 451.2), also be adopted by a court. In case of the rescission of the contract the court may apply the fairness discretion (Article

201 See Informative Letter of the Presidium of the Supreme Arbitrazh Court (2003) no 75, item 75. Вестник Высшего Арбитражного Суда Российской Федерации [Herald of the Supreme Arbitrazh Court of the Russian Federation] 1 (2004) and Informative Letter of the Presidium of the Supreme Arbitrazh Court (2001) no 59, item 9. Вестник Высшего Арбитражного Суда Российской Федерации [Herald of the Supreme Arbitrazh Court of the Russian Federation] 4 (2001).

202 This follows from the Informative Letter of the Presidium of the Supreme Arbitrazh Court (1997) no 14, item 8. Вестник Высшего Арбитражного Суда Российской Федерации [Herald of the Supreme Arbitrazh Court of the Russian Federation] 7 (1997).

203 For more on this subject, see Sergeev 1 2009: 872–3.

204 This corresponds with the *clausula rebus sic stantibus* doctrine.

205 Sergeev 1 2009: 875.

451.3); contrary to this, the amendment of a contract is regarded as an exceptional measure and, consequently, it is possible only if the rescission of the contract would contradict societal interests or cause harm to the parties significantly exceeding the expenditures necessary for performance of the contract on the conditions changed by the court (Article 451.4).

The claim for an amendment or rescission of the contact may be filed, according to the Civil Code (Article 452.2), by the party with the court only after he has received refusal from the other party in response to his proposal or in case of the nonreceipt of any response within the established time.

In accordance with Article 453 of the Civil Code, if a contract is changed or rescinded, the contracting parties do not have the right to claim the return of what has been performed by them up to the moment of the change or rescission, unless otherwise provided by the law or a contract. However, the claim for damages may be presented if the ground for the amendment or rescission of the contract has been an essential violation of the contract.[206]

The rules of Russian law on the amendment or rescission of contract may be added to by the norm of the Civil Code on the termination of obligations (Article 417),[207] according to which the amendment or rescission of a contract is possible on the grounds of an act issued by the state or self-governmental body. If, as a result of such an act, the performance of the contract becomes impossible, the party suffering damage has the right to claim compensation for it (from the state or self-governmental body). However, if such an act is recognized as invalid, the obligations are to be restored, unless otherwise following from the contract or substance of the obligation, and unless its performance has lost all interest for the creditor (Articles 13, 16, and 417).[208]

A contract may be changed or rescinded in Russian law also through the withdrawal from it or the refusal of the contract party to perform the obligation. So, in sale, if the seller refuses to transfer the sold goods to the buyer, the buyer has the right, under Article 463.1 of the Civil Code, to refuse to perform the contract, and correspondingly in work, if the contractor does not begin the performance on time, the customer has the right to cancel the performance and demand compensation for damages (Article 715.2). The grounds for withdrawal from the contract may be other than breaches of obligations—for instance, lost confidence in the fiduciary relationship on which the contract of delegation is based (Article 977.2). The possibilities to withdraw from contract may also established by a contract. As presented above, in the case of the obligation connected with enterprise activity, the refusal of the contract party to perform the obligation is admissible, unless it otherwise follows from the contract or substance of the obligation.[209]

2 Types and Species of Entrepreneurial Contracts

The norms regulating different types of contract are included in the second part of the Civil Code. This includes rules concerning the types of contracts which are traditionally known in Russia such as sale (Articles 454–566), lease (Articles 606–25), and work and construction work (Articles 702–62), as well as contracts for performance of scientific research, experimental design, and technological work (Articles 769–78). The Civil Code regulates the types of contracts which are new for Russian law such as lease of enterprise (Articles 656–64), leasing

206 Sergeev 1 2009: 874.

207 The obligations are also to be terminated in Russian law, as presented above, in a case where the juristic person is terminated. The provisions on it are contained in Articles 61.1 and 419 of the Civil Code.

208 See Popondopulo 1 2009: 326 and Sergeev 1 2009: 996.

209 For more on this subject, see Sergeev 1 2009: 876–8.

(Articles 665–70) factoring (Articles 824–33), and franchise (Articles 1027–40), as well as agency (Articles 1005–11), and in the regulation of which attention is paid to international examples. In the regulation of traditionally known types of contract there have also been attempts to approach international practice.

The legal regulation of civil law relations in Russia has traditionally been based on the distinction of types of contract supported by the general rule that the norm concerning one type of contract is not to be applied to another type of contract, unless otherwise provided by the law. However, nowadays individual contracts in Russia, as well as in countries with developed civil law regulation, often cross the boundaries between different types of contract. So, for instance, a contract on sale can include elements of a work contract (erection and maintenance obligations), which is usual in contracts on delivery of machinery and equipment. However, such subsidiary obligations do not in Russian law change the character of the primary contractual relation, and the type of contract is usually determined in accordance with the main obligation, although the subsidiary obligation is governed by the rules concerning it.[210]

On the other hand, the conditions of a contract may be so integrated that they establish a unity of obligations, in which case the question is of a mixed contract,[211] which may even be regarded as a new type of contract. In such a case, in accordance with Article 421.3 of the Civil Code, the rules on contracts whose elements are contained in the mixed contract are to be applied in the corresponding parts, unless otherwise agreed or otherwise follows from the nature of the contract. Other contracts deviating from the traditional division of types of contract are also known in Russian law, and a contractual relation may also be based on a combination of different types of contract in which it is impossible to differentiate the main and subsidiary obligations, thereby forming a so-called complex contractual relation; usually their regulation is based mainly on the stipulations of contract. As stated above, in respect of such contracts the principle of enumeration is not known in Russian contract law, and the principle of freedom of contract is expressly confirmed regarding contracts undefined by the law in the first part of the Civil Code (Articles 1 and 421). Therefore, any contract is valid in Russia even if there are no legal norms concerning it, provided it is not contrary to the legislation according to Article 8 of the Civil Code.[212]

Sale

General rules[213] Contract for (purchase and) sale[214] is in Russian law one of a group of obligations concerning transfer of property into ownership. Its purpose is to be the grounds not only for the corresponding obligation but also for the change of ownership. Sale is a general concept for all obligations which mean transfer of the property against the defined price, and the general norms concerning sale are applied to any modifications of it, unless otherwise provided by law. Contract on sale is also regarded in Russian law as the basic type of contract and the rules concerning it form the grounds for the regulation of such types of contract as, for instance,

210 For more on this subject, see Braginsky and Vitryansky 1999: 412–16.

211 Stepanov 2010: 446–7.

212 For more on innominate, mixed, and complex contracts, see Braginsky and Vitryansky 2001: 331–4 and Ogorodov and Chelyshev 2005.

213 For more on this subject, see Sergeev 2009: 5–44, Abova, Boguslavsky, Kabalkin, and Lisicin-Svetlanov 2007: 387–417, and, in particular, M.I. Braginsky and V.V. Vitryansky, Договорное право. Книга вторая: Договоры о передаче имущества [Contract Law. Book Two: Contracts on Transfer of Property] (2006): 10–74.

214 Купля-продажа.

work, the rules on which contain direct references to the norms regulating sale in the Civil Code (Articles 723, 724, and 739).[215]

The concept of contract of sale[216] is defined expressly in the Civil Code, and in Russian law it covers sale of goods and immovables (as well as sale of an enterprise).[217] According to the Civil Code (Article 454), under the contract for (purchase and) sale one party (the seller) is obligated to transfer a thing (the goods) to the ownership of the other party (the buyer),[218] and the buyer is obligated to accept the goods and pay a defined monetary amount (the price). So the sale is a compensated and bilateral or reciprocal, or synallagmatic, contract. The rights and duties of its parties arise at the moment when unanimity on the essential conditions is reached (consensual agreement) and the essential conditions are the terms on the subject of the contract (the name and quantity of the goods).[219]

By property it is understood in the contract on sale to mean individualized or specified (fungibles) things (which are/shall be materially existent) the civil exchange of which is allowed. Property rights may also be under the Civil Code the object of a sale, unless it otherwise follows from their content and nature (Article 454.4); for instance, rights in things, including ownership, economic management, and operative administration as well as servitude may not be the objects of sale, since these rights follow the thing which is their object.[220] Furthermore, exclusive rights to intellectual property are alienable by sale. The general norms concerning contract of sale are also to be applied to the sale of securities, commercial paper, and currency valuables, unless it otherwise follows from the norms concerning them (Article 454.2).[221]

The Civil Code includes general rules (Articles 455–505) which concern basic conditions. They concern:

- the subject, which is regarded as a minimum requirement for the contract or its essential condition (Article 455);
- the transfer of the goods, to which the transfer of risk of accidental loss and also the transfer of ownership are linked[222] (Articles 456–64);
- the acceptance of the goods, which includes also the obligation of the buyer to assist the seller, unless otherwise provided by the law or contract (Article 484);
- the quantity of the goods, which could be specified in measures and money; it is possible also to define only criteria according to which the quantity will be determined (Article 465);
- the quality and completeness of the goods, in which respect attention should also be paid, in additional to the contractual conditions, to the standard requirements often provided as compulsory (Articles 469 and 479);

215 Sergeev 2 2009: 6.

216 For more on the concept of contract of sale, see, in particular, Braginsky and Vitryansky 2006: 15–20.

217 The norms regulating sale of immovables and enterprise are not presented in this work because of their special nature. It can be stated here, however, that the contracts on them are the subject of strict form requirements: the contract must be compiled as a single document signed by both parties and, additionally, the transfer of ownership must be registered. For more, see the rules of the Civil Code (Articles 549–71).

218 Thus, the object of the contract of sale may also be goods which will be made or obtained in the future, something which is expressly provided for in the Civil Code (Article 455.2).

219 The contract of sale differs from other contracts in that it is compensated, the transfer of the ownership according to it is final and irrevocable and the price to be paid according to it is expressed in money. Sergeev 2 2009: 11 and A.P. Sergeev and Y.K. Tolstoy (eds), Гражданское право [Civil Law] 2 (1997): 6–7.

220 The only exception to this rule is the share in the right of common ownership, which may, in accordance with the Civil Code, be sold (Articles 246.2, 250, and 255).

221 Sergeev 2 2009: 16–18.

222 The transfer of ownership occurs usually at the same moment as the transfer of the goods.

- the consequences of errors in the goods in the rules on which the unconditional right for compensation is provided in case the damage is caused by the delivery of defective goods (Article 475).[223] The seller is also liable for defects in the goods if the buyer proves that the defects in the goods arose before their transfer to the buyer or from causes which existed before that time (Article 476);
- the price and its payment, the rules on which establish that, unless otherwise provided by the contract, law, or nature of the obligation, the price is to be paid at the moment of transfer of the goods or immediately after this, and it is to be paid especially if the goods are accepted;[224] a contract may also call for advance payment (Articles 485–9);
- the obligation of the buyer to give notice to the seller about the nonconformity of the goods; the nonobservance of this duty could limit the rights of the buyer to rely on it (Article 483),[225] and
- the insurance of the goods (Article 490).[226]

The rules of the Civil Code on the basic conditions of sale are intended to be applied in the usual situations and mostly to cases when the contracting parties have not determined otherwise in the contract (dispositive provisions). However, this rule does not apply to the provisions of the Civil Code, which concern for instance the requirements on the essential conditions (Article 455.3) and especially those on the definition of the quantity of the goods (Article 465.2) as well as the liability of the seller if the goods are demanded by third persons (Article 461.2); these provisions are enforced by the imperative norms.[227] On the other hand, the rules of the Civil Code on sale also contain provisions which could be regarded as occasional. As an example, the contract can include a stipulation that the seller retain his ownership of the thing until the moment of payment for it or some other event (Article 491). In this case the buyer does not have the right to alienate the goods or dispose on them in another way, unless otherwise provided by the law or a contract or it follows from the purpose and characteristics of the goods. Furthermore, the seller, who remains the owner of the goods, has the right to demand the return of them. In the event the buyer disposes of the goods subject to retention of title, his transaction with the third person is not invalid, but the third person will not become the owner of the goods before the title to them is transferred to his counterparty or the buyer in the initial sale.[228]

---

223 As a general rule, the buyer has the right at his choice to demand a reduction of the price, elimination of the defects, or compensation for his expenditures for elimination of the defects. In the case of essential defects the buyer has the right to dissolve the contract or demand the replacement of the goods. The question is of consumer protection, wherefore the seller bears strict liability. However, if the buyer demands liquidated damages or compensation for damages the seller is released from liability if he proves the absence of his fault. See Sergeev 2 2009: 37–8.

224 However, if the price is not paid and the goods are not accepted by the buyer, the seller has the right to claim the dissolution of the contract and compensation for damages (Article 486.4), which implies the abolition of the principle of real performance (in kind) in such a case.

225 The corresponding rule is included in the Vienna Convention (Articles 39 and 40).

226 The norms of the Civil Code on sale also include the rules concerning the assortment of goods and packing. The rules providing the right to withdraw from the performance, which are applicable in cases when the performance is disturbed (Article 463), are also noteworthy.

227 O.N. Sadikov (ed.), Комментарий к Гражданскому кодексу Российской Федерации, Части второй [Commentary on the Civil Code of the Russian Federation, Part 2] (1997): 2.

228 Sergeev 2 2009: 44.

Retail sale[229] In Russia, as elsewhere, retail sale contract regulation concerns the retailing or selling of merchandise directly to the consumer. According to Article 492 of the Civil Code, under the contract of retail (purchase and) sale,[230] a seller engaged in entrepreneurial activity for the sale of goods at retail is obligated to transfer to the buyer the goods purposed for personal, family, household, or other use not connected with entrepreneurial activity. Retail sale contract is distinguished from other sale contracts by its subjects and objects. Furthermore, retail sale belongs to public contracts. The legal regulation of retail sale contract is secured mainly by imperative norms purported to protect the consumer.[231] [232] In accordance with the Civil Code, consumer protection legislation is applied to relations under a retail contract not regulated by the Civil Code (Article 492.3). The consumer protection norms regarding consumers as the weaker party are contained in the Law on Protection of the Rights of Consumers 1992 and other normative acts.[233]

Only a juristic person may participate in the retail contract as a seller, usually a commercial organization or individual entrepreneur which is specialized in practicing retail enterprise activities. In turn, the buyer in retail sale may be any civil law subject on condition that the purchased goods are not intended for entrepreneurial activities. Thus, the acquisition of office furniture by a juristic person from a furniture shop is regarded as covered by retail sale, although such a transaction is not subject to consumer protection purported to protect physical persons as consumers or the weaker party in a contract.[234] [235]

As a public contract, retail sale is subject to the general provisions of the Civil Code on public contracts (Article 426). Accordingly, a retail seller has not, in general, the right to refuse from concluding a contract. He also does not have the right to prefer one person to another with respect to the conclusion of a contract nor to establish the price of goods as well as other conditions of a contract that discriminates between consumers, except in cases provided for by the law or other legal acts. Furthermore, the conditions of a contract not meeting the requirements established for public contracts are null and void. Additionally, Article 426.4 of the Civil Code provides that the Government of the Russian Federation may issue rules obligatory for parties in the conclusion and performance of public contracts (model contracts, regulations, etc.), though only in those cases provided by the law.

The public character of retail sale corresponds with the rules of the Civil Code on public offer of goods (Article 494). According to it, exhibiting at the place of sale (at stands, in shop windows, etc.) of goods, demonstration of samples of them, or presentation of information on goods offered for sale (descriptions, catalogs, pictures of goods, etc.) at the place of their sale is considered a public offer irrespective of whether prices and other essential conditions of a retail sale contract are specified,

---

229 For more on this subject, see Sergeev 2009: 44–69; Abova, Boguslavsky, Kabalkin, and Lisicin-Svetlanov 2007: 417–29, and, in particular, M.I. Braginsky and V.V. Vitryansky, Договорное право. Книга вторая: Договоры о передаче имущества [Contract Law. Book Two: Contracts on Transfer of Property] (2006): 65–6 and 75–95.

230 Договор розничной купли-продажи.

231 Characteristic for retail sale is also the principle of real performance established by Article 505 whose rule is imperative. According to it, in the event the retail seller fails to perform his contract obligation, neither compensation for damages nor payment of a penalty shall release him from performing the obligation in kind.

232 Braginsky, and Vitryansky 2006: 75.

233 See Sergeev 2 2009: 55–60.

234 On the other hand, consumer protection is extended in Russia to include consumer work and service contracts. See Popondopulo 2 2009: 206.

235 Braginsky and Vitryansky 2006: 76–7.

unless the seller has clearly defined that the respective goods are not meant for sale. The seller is obliged in such a case to conclude the contract with anyone who responds to the public offer.

Retail sale is also subject to the general provisions of the Civil Code on contract of adhesion (Article 428). The buyer may enter into a retail sale contract by adhering to the contract whose conditions are determined by the seller in printed forms or other standard forms. As a general rule, a retail sale contract is considered concluded under the Civil Code (Article 493) from the moment of issue by the seller to the buyer of a cash register or sale receipt or any other document confirming payment for the goods.[236]

According to the general rule provided by Article 500 of the Civil Code, the buyer is obliged in a retail sale to pay for the goods at the price stated by the seller at the moment of concluding the contract, but the contract may provide for advance payment and retail sale may occur on credit. In accordance with the Civil Code, a retail sale contract may also be made with a condition of acceptance of the goods by the buyer within a term determined by the contract (Article 496). A retail sale contract may be made by acquainting the buyer with a sample of goods offered by the seller and exposed at the place of sale of the goods (Article 497). The moment of conclusion of contract and its performance do not coincide in a sale with a condition on the delivery of the goods to the buyer (Article 499). The Civil Code also provides the rules on sale of goods by using vending machines (Article 498) when the seller and buyer are not in direct contact, although the moment of conclusion of contract and its performance usually coincide in such cases.[237] Furthermore, Article 501 of the Civil Code contains provisions on the contract of hire-purchase in which the rules on retention of right of ownership (Article 491) are modified. According to it, the contract may provide that until the right of ownership to the goods has passed to the buyer, the buyer is deemed the renter or lessee of the goods transferred to him, and the buyer becomes the owner of the goods from the moment of payment for the goods, unless otherwise provided by the contract.[238]

Supply contract[239] Supply contract is regarded in Russian law as the most important species of a sale contract regulating relations between (Russian) enterprises,[240] which represents a specific peculiarity in Russian law[241].[242] The object of supply contract regulation are deliveries. They comprehend economic relations between manufacturers and consumers of products, in which products as goods are transferred from one subject of entrepreneurial activities to another.[243]

The concept of contract for supply (of goods) is directly expressed in Article 506 of the Civil Code. According to it, under a contract for supply a supplier or seller engaged in entrepreneurial activity is obligated to transfer at an agreed time or times goods manufactured or purchased by him

---

236 However, the absence of such documents does not deprive the buyer of the right to rely on witness testimony to confirm the conclusion of the contract and its conditions.

237 In Russia the distance sale of goods is known, the rules on which are contained in the Law on Protection of the Rights of Consumers 1992.

238 For more on this subject, see Sergeev 2 2009: 52–5 and Braginsky and Vitryansky 2006: 91–2.

239 For more on this subject, see Sergeev 2 2009: 69–82; Popondopulo 2 2009: 22–8, and, in particular, Braginsky and Vitryansky 2006: 96–110.

240 Sometimes this is called entrepreneurial or commercial sale.

241 The concept of supply contract has been known in Russia since the eighteenth century. Traditionally it was used to regulate economic relations between the Treasury and private persons, but in Soviet law it became the fundamental concept of economic law.

242 Sergeev and Tolstoy 2 1997: 58.

243 Popondopulo 2 2009: 22.

to the buyer for use in entrepreneurial activity or for other purposes not related to personal, family, household, or other similar use.

Supply contract differs from many other contracts by its subjects. The supplier, who may be a commercial organization or individual entrepreneur or noncommercial organization, must be practicing entrepreneurial activity. As to the buyer, he may be not only a commercial organization or individual entrepreneur or noncommercial organization but also a physical person who is not registered as entrepreneur in the event his activity objectively corresponds to the requirements of entrepreneurial activity. Distinctive for supply contract is the aim of the acquisition of the goods. They are purported for further manufacturing or resale use.[244] Furthermore, supply contract usually concerns regular deliveries of goods (movable things). The particularity of the supply contract is also apparent, as it was in Soviet law, in the special rules on the terms (periods) of deliveries and order of delivery, the supply of a deficient delivery (short supply), the separation of the goods at the seller's place, payments, and breaches of contract. The rules on conclusion of contract also still differ, at least partly, from the general procedure for conclusion of contract.[245]

The definition of the terms of delivery is traditionally considered as the essential condition of the supply contract in Russian legal doctrine.[246] However, Article 508 of the Civil Code provides that in the event where the parties have provided for the supply of the goods in separate installments during the term of the contract, but the times or periods of supply are not defined in it, the goods are to be supplied in equal installments monthly, unless it otherwise follows from the law, or other legal acts, the nature of the obligation, or the customs of trade. Furthermore, it is stated in Russian judicial practice that, in the event the moment of conclusion of a supply contract and its performance do not coincide, and the term of delivery is not defined in the contract, the obligation must be performed in accordance with the Civil Code (Article 314) in a reasonable time after its origin.[247] Thus, it is regarded as sufficient for a supply contract that the term of the contract is defined.[248]

The norms of the Civil Code regulating supply contracts also include the rules on the contracting procedure (Article 507), the order of delivery (Article 509), acceptance of the goods (Article 513), and payments (Article 516). Furthermore, the Civil Code includes the provisions on delay and deficient deliveries (Article 511), according to which the shortage must be covered during the term of the contract, unless otherwise stipulated by the contract.[249] The Civil Code also contains the rules on errors in the goods and the consequences of this; it provides for instance liquidated damages for the deficient delivery or the nonperformance of this. Additionally the Civil Code includes the rules on liability for damages and withdrawal from the performance in case of an essential breach of contract, which can mean that the contract is rescinded or changed (Article 523–4).[250] The norms

244 Sergeev 2 2009: 70–71.

245 For more on the particularities of supply contract, see Sergeev 2 2009: 72–82 and Braginsky and Vitryoansky 2006: 101–4.

246 See, for instance, Braginsky and Vitryansky 2006: 103–4 and Popondopulo 2 2009: 25.

247 Decree of the Plenum of the Supreme Arbitrazh Court no 18 (1997), item 7. Вестник Высшего Арбитражного Суда Российской Федерации [Herald of the Supreme Arbitrazh Court of the Russian Federation] 3 (1998).

248 V.V. Vitryansky, Существенные условия договора [Essential Conditions of Contract Law] (1998): 9–10.

249 The principle of summary obligation. See Sergeev and Tolstoy 2 1997: 67.

250 In such a case, contrary to the general rules of the Civil Code on sale (Articles 450 and 452), it is unnecessary to apply to a court to get the contract dissolved or changed; this may occur only by the notification of withdrawal (Article 523); an essential breach of contract is presumed, for example, in cases

regulating the contract for supply in Russian law are complemented where applicable by the rules regulating the sale.

In particular, it is important not only conceptually but also practically to distinguish supply contract from other sale contracts. Although both sale and supply contracts involve the transfer of ownership of the property, the supply contract in Russia is legislatively differentiated from the usual contract of sale, though the norms regulating this are also applied to the supply contract subsidiarily. Furthermore, the concept of the supply contract in Russian law is regarded as best corresponding to the definition of the sale of goods of the Vienna Convention.[251]

The main difference between sale and supply is that the contract of supply usually presupposes regular deliveries of the goods (things) and is purported to regulate the long-term commercial relations (wholesale trade) between enterprises (as a minimum the seller must be an entrepreneur), whereas the objects of the contract for sale are usually existent and very often individualized things, though they can also be securities and property rights. On the other hand, individualized things could also be the object of the supply contract. Additionally, the conclusion of the contract and the deliveries according to this are not coincident, whereas in case of the contract for sale its conclusion and the transfer of the thing occurs usually simultaneously. Furthermore, in case of the contract for sale an offeror is not usually obliged by law to react to a counteroffer, whereas in case of the contract for supply such an obligation, under Article 507 of the Civil Code, exists: the offeror must agree on the possible disagreements concerning the conditions of contract or notify the offeree of his refusal to conclude a contract; the nonobservance of this obligation could lead to liability (*culpa in contrahendo*) for the damages caused by it, which is regarded as a noncontractual liability.[252]

The rules of the Civil Code on errors in the goods, in particular, differ at least partly from each other in the sale and supply contracts. Similar for both is that the buyer has the optional right to demand a price reduction or to have the thing repaired; and in case of an essential breach of contract he also has an option to demand the rescission of the contract. Additionally, the buyer may demand compensation for damages, if other measures will not be sufficient to recover the damage caused to him, or use the right of exchange. The difference is that only in the case of the supply contract has the seller the right to replace defective goods immediately; while, on the other hand, the buyer selling in retail has the right to demand the replacement of the goods returned by consumers, unless otherwise stipulated by the contract. (Articles 475 and 518)

Supply of goods for public needs[253] Supply of goods for public or state or municipal needs, also known as state and municipal procurement, is regarded in Russian law as some kind of modification of the supply contract, supply *sui generis*, the norms regulating which are included in the Civil Code (Articles 525–34).[254] Public procurements are also regulated in Russia by the Law on Placement of Orders for Supply of Goods, Performance of Work, and Rendering Services for State

---

where deficient goods are not repairable, or if delays in the delivery or payment are frequent. See Sergeev 2 2009: 80–81.

251 The only difference is that the public character of retail sale corresponded with the rules of the Civil Code on public offer of goods (Article 494). Vienna Convention does not require that the term of delivery be included in the contract. See M.G. Rozenberg, Контракт международной купли-продажи [The Contract of International Purchase–Sale] (1996): 288.

252 Sergeev 2 2009: 76.

253 For more on this subject, see Sergeev 2 2009: 82–5 and Popondopulo 2 2009: 28–33.

254 As amended by the Law no 19-FZ of 2 February 2006.

and Municipal Needs.[255] According to it, the orders on the grounds of which public procurement or state or municipal contracts are to be concluded must be placed mainly by an auction in the form of bidding or competition.

The public procurement system is intended to be used for procurements financed by the state or municipality, in the implementation of which, in addition to public procurement (or state or municipal) contract (and in accordance with this), the supply contract on goods purposed for state or municipal needs may also be concluded. According to the Civil Code, the public procurement contract must be concluded by acceptance by the performing party of the order on supply of the goods received from the state or municipality. In certain cases determined by the law, the conclusion of the public procurement contract is obligatory not only for the state or municipal customer who placed the order but also for the performer. However, in these cases the rule that the damage caused to the performer by it is to be compensated is applied; this rule is not, however, applied to a Treasury enterprise. The public procurement contract is to be concluded according to the procedure on obligatory contracting (Articles 525–8).

According to the Civil Code, a public procurement contract may provide that the deliveries be executed to a certain buyer (user) who is attached to the supplier (performer) by the state or municipal customer. In such a case, the notice of attachment is to be sent to each party, on the grounds of which the supply contract on the goods for public needs is to be concluded, following, if necessary, the procedure on obligatory contracting (see above). On the other hand, a buyer has the right to refuse to accept in part or in full the goods notified in the notice of attachment and also to conclude a contract. In this case the state or municipal customer must make a decision within 30 days on the attachment of the performer to another buyer. In default of this, the state or municipal customer is obliged to accept himself the ordered goods and pay for those or compensate possible damage caused by it (Articles 529–34).

Lease[256]

The lease contract[257] belongs in Russian law to the obligations according to which the property is transferred to the (temporary) use of another person. According to it, a person allows another person to use his property (thing) on agreed conditions retaining, however, his ownership or other real right to it. The objects of a lease contract are always individualized and nonconsumable things which are returned to their owner when the contract expires. The concept of lease is used in Russian law to mean both the use of a thing and the exploitation of the yield from it.[258] The objects of lease include, according to the Civil Code (Article 607.1), land parcels and other separate natural objects, enterprises and other property complexes, buildings, structures, equipment, means of transport, and other things which do not lose their natural properties in the process of using them (nonconsumable things).

Under a contract of lease (rent of property), according to the Civil Code (Article 606), the lessor or renter undertakes to provide the lessee or rentee property for payment for temporary possession and use or for temporary use. The lessor keeps his ownership of the leased property, and to the lessor he transfers only the right of use; a thing (the property) is usually transferred to exclusive use.

---

255 Law no 94-FZ of 21 July 2005.

256 For more on this subject, see Sergeev 2 2009: 165–261; Popondopulo 2 2009: 75–101, and, in particular, Braginsky and Vitryansky 2006: 428–604.

257 договор аренды.

258 On the concept of lease, see, for instance, Braginsky and Vitryansky 2006: 428–33

The term of lease is used in Russian law as a general concept and the rules on it are divided into the general rules (Articles 606–25) and the rules which concern rental (Articles 626–31),[259] leasing of means of transport (Articles 632–49),[260] lease of buildings and structures (Articles 650–55), lease of enterprise (Articles 656–64),[261] and financial lease (leasing)[262] (Articles 665–70).[263] Lease is regarded in Russian law as a separate type of contract. Furthermore, a lease contract is a compensated and in general consensual[264] as well as reciprocal, or synallagmatic, contract.[265]

The essential condition of lease in its strict sense is its subject-matter. In particular, according to Article 607.3 of the Civil Code, the leased property (object) must be individualized; otherwise it is regarded that a contract is not concluded. Also the rent (rental charge, lease payment) is sometimes regarded in Russian law as the essential condition of the lease contract;[266] but the default of its determination does not cause the invalidity of the contract; in accordance with Article 614.1 of the Civil Code, in such a case the rent usually paid under the same circumstances is to be followed. This rule does not, however, concern lease of building; according to the Civil Code, the rent in such a case must be determined in the contract, otherwise it is regarded unconcluded (Article 654.1).

In general, the contract for lease is to be concluded, according to the Civil Code, in written form if the other party of it is a juristic person (Article 609.1). The lease contract on buildings (and structures), if the duration of it exceeds one year, and the lease contract on enterprise, are to be done by the compilation of a single document signed by the parties; the contract must also be registered, otherwise it is regarded as unconcluded (Articles 651 and 658).

Among the general rules of the Civil Code on lease are also other important provisions. They include the duties of both the lessor and lessee, the rent, the term of the contract, and rescission of this. The Civil Code also includes the norms regulating the condition of the leased property and the liability of the lessor for it, the repair and maintenance of the property, the yield from it and improvements to it, the rent, the sublease, and amendment and rescission of the contract as well as the effect of the transfer of the leased property.

The property must be transferred by the lessor, according to the Civil Code, in the condition which corresponds with the conditions of the contract and its use; he is liable for the deficiencies of the leased property which obstruct the use of this, regardless of the fact that he could not know about those at the moment of the conclusion of the contract, and, unless it otherwise followed from the legislation or contract, the lessor must carry out major repair works of the leased property at his own expense (Articles 611–12). Hence, it can be provided by the law or contract that the lessee

---

259 The property provided under the contract of rental is usually used for consumer purposes. Rental is a public contract and in the event the lessee is a physical person it is subject to consumer protection. See Sergeev 2 2009: 214–15.

260 On the lease of means of transport, see, in particular, Braginsky and Vitryansky 2006: 494–509.

261 On the lease (rent) of buildings and enterprises, see, in particular, Braginsky and Vitryansky 2006: 510–41. According to the Civil Code, the object of both the lease contracts of buildings and enterprises includes, besides the proper object of the lease, also the land parcel on which it is situated or which is necessary for the use of it (Articles 652–3 and 656). See Sergeev 2 2009: 239–40 and 243–4.

262 The rules of the Civil Code on financial lease (leasing) are based on the UNIDROIT Convention on International Financial Leasing (1988), to which Russia is a party. Additionally, leasing relations are regulated by the Leasing Law no 164-FZ of 29 October 1998.

263 The Civil Code also contains the provisions on lease of residential accommodation (Articles 671–88), which are presented in their own chapter.

264 However, leasing of means of transport is a real contract requiring for its conclusion the transfer of the leased object to the lessee. See Sergeev 2 2009: 167.

265 Sergeev 2 2009: 167–8 and Braginsky and Vitryansky 2006: 432–3.

266 Braginsky and Vitryansky 2006: 437.

is charged with the obligation of repair (Article 616). In turn, the duty of the lessee is to use the property in accordance with the contract and its use, to take care of its condition and carry out (current) repair works, unless otherwise provided by the legislation or a contract, and pay rent at the proper time (Articles 614–15). The lessee has the right with the consent of the lessor to sublease the property, unless otherwise is provided by the legislation (Article 615.2); a renewal of the lease contract is also possible (Article 621).

In general, the lease of land parcel and buildings is in Russia a long-term contract, whereas the lease of equipment as well as other movables is presumed to be short-term.[267] According to the Civil Code, a lease contract could be concluded to be in force for an indefinite time (Article 610.2), and such a contract is dissolvable, in which case the term of its renunciation is three months (in case of the immovable property; in other cases one month). At the termination of the contract the duty of the lessee is to return the property in the same condition as it was when he got it, having regard, however, for normal wear, or in the agreed condition (Article 622). A lease contract may include a stipulation on penalty which is to be paid in the case of delay in returning the leased property; in addition to the penalty, damages can also be compensated (penalty in the strict sense), unless otherwise stipulated in the contract.

The change of the conditions of the lease contract and its early termination by the agreement of the parties is allowed in Russia. Upon demand of one of the parties the lease contract may also be changed or rescinded (early), in accordance with the Civil Code, by the decision of a court in the cases determined by the legislation, first of all in case of the breach of contract; the rescission of the contract in such a case by the lessor requires before the court procedure his written warning (Articles 614 and 619–20). A contract may include a stipulation that the other party may demand a change in rent and, if the other party will not accept this, the rescission of the contract; a contract can also include the stipulation about the fixed rent or the terms of its revision (at a minimum once a year).[268]

The transfer of the ownership or the right of economic management or operative administration [269] to the leased property to another person is not regarded under the Civil Code as a ground for the change or rescission of the contract (Article 617). Furthermore, the lessee, as the possessor of the leased property on the contractual ground, is protected, in accordance with Article 305 of the Civil Code, against any violations of his right by third persons and his possession is protected against the owner as well. However, the termination of the lease contract also causes the termination of the contract of sublease (Article 618).

Under the Civil Code, at the termination of the lease contract the lessee who has attended properly to his duties has a preferential right to renew the contract (Article 621). Where the lessee continues to use the property after the termination of the contract and the lessor does not object to it, the contract is regarded as renewed for an indefinite time (Article 621.2); this rule does not apply, however, to the contracts on which there are limitations on the term of lease provided by the law (Article 610).

According to the Civil Code (Article 624), the leased property may be transferred to the ownership of the lessee at the termination of the term of lease or before this on condition that the lessee pays in full the redemption (buyout) price stipulated by the contract. If a contract does not include the provision on redemption, this may be agreed, and it is possible to agree also that

267 The term of a private contract on the lease of residential accommodation must not, under the Civil Code, exceed five years (Article 683).

268 Other minimum terms can also be found in the special legislation concerning some forms of the lease.

269 The institutions inherited from Soviet economic law concerning state and municipal enterprises. For more, see above.

the executed rent payments be included in the redemption price. According to Article 609.3 of the Civil Code, a property lease contract providing for the future transfer of the ownership of this property to the lessee, is to be concluded in the form established for a contract of sale of such property.

Work and Construction Work Contract

Work contract[270] Work contract is in Russian law among the obligations whose subject is the performance of work. The question is of the services which take material form and are the objects of the civil exchange—that is, individualized results of work (performances of work). However, the subject-matter of the regulation in the work contract is not only the result, which could be not only a thing but also some other material performance, but also the activity (process of work) itself.[271] However, the achievement of the result is characteristic of the work and by this it differs from the service contract which is regulated in Russian law by its own norms (Articles 779–83). On the other hand, if a contract does not contain conditions on the performance of work, it is to be defined as sale rather than work.[272]

The general concept of work contract is provided expressly in the Civil Code. Under Article 702, one party or the contractor is obligated to perform (at his own risk) defined work at the order of the other party or the customer (using materials of the customer or his own) and to transfer its result to the customer, while the customer is obligated to accept the result of the work and pay for it. The work contract is a compensated, consensual, and reciprocal, or synallagmatic, contract as well as a long-term contract in which the moment of its conclusion does not coincide with the moment of the performance of work. It is also a causal contract and the aim of the contractor is to receive payment for his work, whereas the aim of the customer is to receive the result of the work.[273]

Work contracts are separated in the Civil Code into the consumer work contract (Articles 730–39),[274] the construction work contract (Articles 740–57), the contract for the performance of design and exploratory work (Articles 758–62), the work contract for public or state or municipal needs (Articles 763–8), and other work contracts. The Civil Code also contains the rules regulating contracts for the performance of scientific research, experimental design, and technological work; these are distinguished from the work contract in that their object is the work rather than the result, in which case the customer is charged with the risk of the occasional impossibility of achieving the result.[275]

The subject-matter of work contract is, in accordance with Article 703 of the Civil Code, the activities of the contractor for the manufacturing or processing (reworking) of a thing or the performance of any other work with the transfer of its result to the customer. The result of the work or the object of a work contract, the condition on which is regarded as essential in Russian law,

270 For more on this subject, see Sergeev 2 2009: 406–49; Popondopulo 2 2009: 176–87, and M.I. Braginsky, Договор подряда и подобные ему договоры [The Work Contract and Other Similar Contracts] (1999): 4–111.

271 The work contract differs from the employment contract in Russia in that its object is the result the customer pays for; additionally, the contractor himself arranges his work. See Popondopulo 2 2009: 183.

272 See Abova, Boguslavsky, Kabalkin, and Lisicin-Svetlanov 2007: 557–8 and Braginsky 1999: 9–10.

273 See Sergeev 2 2009: 407–9.

274 A consumer work contract is a public contract and subject to the consumer protection. See, for instance, Abova, Boguslavsky, Kabalkin, and Lisicin-Svetlanov 2007: 569.

275 See, for instance, Sergeev 2 2009: 494.

always takes material form as a building, repaired and serviced machine, technical documents, report, etc. The work contract must include the initial and final time for performance of the work (Article 708) and this condition is also regarded as essential.

The Civil Code contains, besides the concept of the work contract and the rules on the terms of works, the rules which concern the work, division of risks, subcontracting, price and payments, right of retention (to withhold), and withdrawal from the contract,[276] as well as duties of loyalty and assistance, quality of work, anticipatory breach of contract, liability for the breach of contract, acceptance of work, obligation to inform and confidentiality, etc. (Articles 702–29).

The contractor arranges, according to the Civil Code, the performance of his work at his own discretion (Articles 703–4) and he also has the right to use in the performance of his obligations other persons or subcontractors (Article 706). He is obligated to transfer the results of the work to the customer and, if he has been supplied with materials by the customer, to secure the preservation of them and his other property (Articles 713–14). In turn, the obligation of the customer is to accept the performance (Article 720) and pay its price (Articles 709 and 711). According to the general rule the ownership of the prepared thing does not transfer to the customer until the moment of its acceptance.[277]

The value of the work to be executed under the work contract may be estimated in a firm price or approximately; the general rule is, according to the Civil Code (Article 709), that the estimate is firm and if the value is approximate, this must be mentioned in the contract. If it is necessary for the contractor to exceed essentially the approximate estimate he must notify the customer about it in time; in this case the customer will have the right to cancel the contract, whereupon he may be obligated to compensate the contractor the performed work. Where the contractor does not inform the customer that it is necessary to exceed the approximate estimate he is obligated to perform work without compensation of the additional expenses. On the other hand, the contractor has the right to demand an increase of the price and, if the customer will not agree to this, also the rescission of contract if (and only if) the prices of the materials and equipment or the services of third persons used by him have risen essentially.

The risks of accidental loss of or accidental damage to materials arise, under the Civil Code, before the moment of the acceptance of the work by the party which has supplied the goods—that is, their owner—and after it by the party which has caused the delay, unless otherwise provided by the legislation or a contract (Article 705). The risks of the performance of the work obligations are carried by the contractor until the moment of acceptance of the work, but the breach of the contract by the customer could cause the risks to pass to him (Article 705.2).

In accordance with the Civil Code (Article 719), the contractor has the right to refuse performance until counterperformance of reciprocal obligations is effected by the customer. Furthermore, in case of nonperformance by the customer of the obligation to pay the price or other due amounts, the contractor has the right to withhold the result of the work and other property of the customer until he pays the respective amounts (Article 712).

According to the Civil Code (Article 723), where the contractor deviates from the contract conditions and this causes a reduction in the quality of the work or some other deficiency, the customer has the right of option to demand:

---

276 According to the Civil Code, the customer has the right to withdraw from the contract performance or dissolve the contract (contrary to the general rule) without any grounds at any time before the transfer of the work (Article 310), in which case he must pay to the contractor the part of the price which is equivalent to the performed work as well as the damages caused by the dissolution, unless otherwise stipulated in a contract (Article 717).

277 Abova, Boguslavsky, Kabalkin, and Lisicin-Svetlanov 2007: 558.

- the repairing of the disclosed deficiencies free of charge in reasonable time, or
- the compensation of the expenses caused to him by the repairing of the deficiencies, provided that the right of the customer to do repairs is stipulated by the contract, or
- the corresponding reduction of the price to be paid for the work.

On the other hand, the contractor has the right to reperform the work instead of repairing the deficiencies (Article 723.2). However, if it is an essential deviation from the contract or there are other essential deficiencies in the work, the customer has the right to demand the rescission of the contract and compensation for damages (Article 723.3).[278] The stipulations of the work contract according to which the contractor is not liable for the deficiencies caused by his fault are null and void in Russian law (Article 723.4).[279]

Construction work contract[280] The subject-matter of the construction work contract[281] in Russia is production activity which concerns the construction, renovation, and reconstruction of residential and factory buildings as well as the performance of erection, launching, and other works in stationary objects. Furthermore, the peculiarities of the construction work contract are revealed in that it is a long-term contract (and even the conservation of the project is possible),[282] and requires active interaction and also cooperation of the contracting parties especially in the overcoming of performance obstacles and, if necessary, changes. Additionally, the system of general contract is widely used in construction work relations and there are many rules and technical normative acts to be followed in the performance of works.[283]

In addition to the rules on construction work contract contained in the second part of the Civil Code (Articles 740–57), there are many other legal normative acts, a great part of which are administrative by nature, which regulate construction works, among which the City Building Code of 2004[284] is especially important; the norms of investment legislation are also to be applied to construction work.[285] It is important to mention here that contract work for public, state, or

278 The period of limitation of actions for claims concerning improper quality of the work is, according to the Civil Code (Article 725), one year from the moment of transfer of the work in case of the visible defect and one year from the moment of disclosure of the latent defect (in the course of two years from the transfer of the work, unless otherwise is provided by the law, contract, or commercial customs, or one year from the moment of the notification given in the course of the guarantee period). As to the buildings, the period of limitation is general or three years, which is established in Article 196 of the Civil Code.

279 Not only with intent as in the general rule of the Civil Code on the grounds of liability for the violation of an obligation (Article 401.4).

280 For more on this subject, see Sergeev 2 2009: 449–72; Popondopulo 2 2009: 187–94, and Braginsky 1999: 112–61.

281 In Soviet law the (capital) construction work contract was regarded as a type of contract and it belonged to the group of contracts covered by plans. In the present civil legislation all references to the plans as the grounds for the contractual relations have been abandoned and, therefore, in the construction work contract there are now less specific features than before.

282 According to Article 752 of the Civil Code.

283 Sergeev 2 2009: 449–53 and Popondopulo 2 2009: 188–91.

284 Law no 190-FZ of 29 December 2004.

285 Construction activities are subject to very many administrative and technical norms and standards. For instance, preliminary for construction works are exploratory works for the preparation of the technical documentation, construction planning, and their expert research, on the grounds of which a construction permit is to be granted or denied. The actual construction works are, in turn, subject to construction supervision. Furthermore, the initialization of the constructed object requires a permit in Russia. See Popondopulo 2 2009: 188–91.

municipal needs covers, under the Civil Code, construction works and is subject to the same rules on the obligatory conclusion of contract as the supply of goods for public needs (Articles 763 and 765).

Under the construction work contract the contractor is, according to the Civil Code, obligated in the time determined by the contract to construct, on order of the customer, a defined object or to perform other construction works, and the customer is obligated to arrange for it the necessary conditions for the contractor for the performance of the work, to accept its result, and pay the price for it (Article 740). The essential condition of construction work contract is its object. The term and the price are also regarded as essential in Russian law, without agreement on which a contract is considered unconcluded. Also important for construction work is the obligation of the customer to arrange the necessary conditions for the performance of the contract.[286]

According to the Civil Code, the contractor must follow the technical documentation and obligatory requirements concerning the works, and he is also responsible for ensuring that the capacity defined by the technical documentation is achieved; on the other hand, he is not responsible for slight deviations from the documentation, if he can prove that those have no effect on the quality of the construction object (Article 754). In accordance with the Civil Code, it is possible to use an engineer in the construction work with whom the customer also enters into a contract (Article 749). The parties to a construction work contract must cooperate for the achievement of its result; where the obligation to cooperate in eliminating the obstacles for the performance is violated, the violating party, under the Civil Code, forfeits the right for compensation for the damage incurred owing to the obstacle (Article 750).

Delegation, Commission and Agency Contract

Delegation, commission, and agency contracts belong in Russian law to the group of service contracts; these differ from other contracts in that their objects are services which appear in a nonmaterial form that is inseparable from the actual activity to perform them, although they are nonetheless characterized as goods. A service is consumed at the same time as it is performed, and so no real right to its object arises to the customer.[287] Especially important is the role delegation, commission, and, in particular, agency contracts play in broking activities, which comprehend actions which are connected with the trade of goods.[288]

Delegation contract[289] The general concept of delegation contract[290] is expressly provided by Article 971 of the Civil Code. Under the contract of delegation, one party or the delegate is obligated to perform the defined legal actions in the name and at the expense of the other party, or the delegant. The delegation contract serves as a ground for representation and may be characterized as a representation contract.[291] It is directly provided by the Civil Code that the legal action (transaction) made by the delegate or representative directly gives rise to the rights and duties of the delegant and the term of legal action is used in the broad sense meaning any acts which cause

286 Sergeev 2 2009: 453.

287 For the legal nature of services in Russian law, see, for instance, Sergeev 2 2009: 498–503.

288 For the use of delegation, commission, and agency contracts in brokerage, see Popondopulo 2 2009: 413–39. Services in Russian law see for instance Sergeev 2 2009: 498–503.

289 For more on this subject, see, in particular, Sergeev 2 2009: 696–707.

290 Договор поручения.

291 Sergeev 2 2009: 696.

legal consequences.[292] The delegation contract is a reciprocal and consensual contract, and at the level of general civil law it is presumed as uncompensated, unless otherwise provided by the law or a contract; however, if the delegation contract is connected with entrepreneurship, which means usually commercial representation,[293] it is presumed as compensated, unless otherwise stipulated by a contract (Article 972). In general, the delegation contract is considered usually fiduciary, based on the loyalty of the parties.[294]

In addition to the concept of delegation, the Civil Code contains rules including those regulating the remuneration of the delegate (Article 972), the duties of the delegate and delegant (Articles 974–5), and the execution of the delegated task (Article 973). Additionally, the delegation contract is also governed in Russia by the rules of the Civil Code regulating representation, including commercial representation (Articles 182–9); these include the rules on power of attorney. The purport of the delegation contract is to regulate the internal relations between the delegate (representative) and principal (delegant), whereas the external part of the representation (in the relations with the other persons) transpires from the authority granted to the representative, according to the power of attorney. The power of attorney is regarded as evidence of the existence of the delegation contract and it must be done, in accordance with Articles 185 and 186 of the Civil Code, in written form and dated; the period of its validity must not exceed three years.[295] [296] Contrary to this, it is not necessary in accordance with Article 971.2 of the Civil Code to mention the term of the contract in the delegation contract itself. Such a contract is regarded as being in force for an indefinite time until the power of attorney is in force.[297] The personal and confidential nature of the contractual relations is presumed in the delegation contract;[298] therefore the contracting parties may not waive their rights to dissolve the contract (Article 977).

In general, the termination of the delegation contract does not effect (except the commercial representation) liability for damages, but the expenses of the delegate are to be, according to the Civil Code, compensated; furthermore, a compensation corresponding to the work done is to be paid if the compensated contract is in question (Article 978).

The representative is not allowed, under the Civil Code, to perform acts for the benefit of persons other than the principal, which is based on the rules regulating representation (Article 182.3); however, this rule does not apply to commercial representation in which it is permitted to represent many principals. According to the rule of the Civil Code concerning the remuneration, this is presumed (Article 972) if the delegation concerns entrepreneurial activities; the remuneration is to be paid, although the contract would not include the exact definition of it.[299] In the Civil Code there are also other peculiarities concerning commercial representation, among which is the retention right of the representative (Article 972.3) as well as the obligation to give notice about withdrawal from the contract (Article 977.3).

---

292 Stepanov 2010: 879.

293 See Popondopulo 2 2009: 422.

294 See for instance Sergeev 2 2009: 696–7.

295 This limitation does not concern, under the Civil Code, the notarized power of attorney for use abroad (Article 186.2).

296 Abova, Boguslavsky, Kabalkin, and Lisicin-Svetlanov 2007: 206–7.

297 Sergeev 2 2009: 698.

298 Stepanov 2010: 879.

299 According to Article 972.2 of the Civil Code, the amount of the remuneration in such a case is to be determined in accordance with the general rule of the Civil Code on price (Article 424.3). Thus, the remuneration usually charged for analogous services under comparable circumstances is to be paid.

Commission contract[300] The general concept of commission (agency) contract,[301] the main purpose of which is to regulate the brokerage activities in the performance of commercial transactions concerning legal services,[302] is also directly provided in the Civil Code. According to it, under the contract of commission agency, one party or the commission agent is obligated on delegation of the other party or the commission principal for compensation to conduct one or several transaction in his own name, but at the expense of the principal (Article 990). The commission contract is a reciprocal and consensual contract and it is compensated according to the Civil Code (Article 991); its objects are only commercial transactions.

Likewise in the delegation contract, the relations regulated by the commission contract are internal and external. The internal relations concern the commission agent and the principal, and are regulated by the rules, the main part of which are similar to these regulating delegation. In turn, the external relations are those between the commission agent and the third person, with whom the commission agent concludes transactions to fulfill the task given by the principal. The rights and duties arising in such transactions belong, under the Civil Code (Article 990.1), to the commission agent who transfers all received by him to the principal; the principal has, however, the right of ownership to the things which the commission agent received from or purchased for him (Article 996). There are also modifications of the commission contract, which are the contracts concluded by the owner of the goods with the broker, dealer, and consignee.[303] The commission contract is based on a large freedom of contract and the commission obligation can be defined, in accordance with the Civil Code (Article 990.2), for a determined time or be in force for an indefinite time; it can also include (or not) the conditions defining the area.

The Civil Code contains, in addition to the concept of commission, the other rules regulating it, including the norms concerning the remuneration, execution of the commission, and liability for the breach of contract. The remuneration of the commission agent is to be determined in accordance with the Civil Code by agreement (Article 991); however, the absence of it does not effect the invalidity of the contract, and the remuneration in such a case is determined by the general rule of the Civil Code (Article 424.3), according to which the performance of the contract must be paid for at the price which, under comparable conditions, is usually taken for analogous services.

According to Article 992 of the Civil Code, the received tasks the commission agent must perform follow the directions of the principal and, in default of them, according to the commercial customs and on conditions which are the most advantageous to the principal; where the commission agent enters into a transaction on conditions which are more advantageous than those announced by the principal, the supplementary profit is to be divided equally between the parties, unless otherwise agreed (Article 992). The commission agent may obtain the right to deviate from the directions of the principal, and if it is a question of the commission agent exercising enterprise activities, he may obtain the right to do so without preliminary inquiry; however, the principal must be notified thereof, unless otherwise stipulated by the contract (Article 995).

When the commission agent concludes a contract with a third person, the rights and duties based on it belong, according to the Civil Code, to the commission agent irrespective of whether the principal is mentioned in that contract or not (Article 990). The commission agent may also be obligated by agreement to *del credere* liability (Article 991.1); otherwise the commission agent is not liable for the performance of the third person, provided that he has exercised necessary caution

300 For more on this subject, see, in particular, Sergeev 2 2009: 708–21.

301 Договор комиссии.

302 Sergeev 2 2009: 708.

303 Abova, Boguslavsky, Kabalkin, and Lisicin-Svetlanov 2007: 748.

in choosing him (Article 993). As a security for claim (receivables), the commission agent has, under the Civil Code, the right of retention to the things which are the object of the contract (Article 996); this right, however, ceases in case of the principal's bankruptcy.

Agency contract[304] The Civil Code includes, in addition to the norms on delegation and commission contract, the norms regulating agency contracts.[305] In such a contract the agent is also expected to do, in addition to legal actions (transactions), real acts (actions) and he may act in his own name or in the name of the principal (Article 1005.1). According to Article 1005 of the Civil Code, under the agency contract, one party or the agent is obligated for compensation to perform, on delegation from the other party or the principal, legal or other actions in his own name but at the expense of the principal or in the name and at the expense of the principal.

The relationship between the agent and principal is, in accordance with the Civil Code, entrepreneurial, not confidential by nature (Article 1006), so the agency contract is not dissolvable unilaterally, unless the term of its expiration is undetermined (Article 1010). An agency contract may include the prohibition to enter into corresponding contracts with other persons (Article 1007), and it may also include territorial restrictions, but personal restrictions concerning third persons, providing the agent with the right to sell goods, perform work, or render services exclusively for a defined category of buyers or customers having a place of location or of residence in a territory defined in the contract, are null and void. According to Article 1011 of the Civil Code, the agency contract is to be governed subsidiarily by the rules regulating the delegation or commission contract depending on whether the agent acts in his own name (commission) or in the name of the principal (delegation).[306]

Simple Partnership (Joint Activity Contract)[307]

The simple partnership,[308] or joint activity contract,[309] is purported to be used for the organization and performance of different kinds of contractual joint ventures of enterprises of commercial nature, but it is used in Russia also as a purely civil law contract aimed at noncommercial purposes, in which case the question is of noncommercial simple partnership.[310] In Russian law simple partnership is included into the scope of legal regulation and the joint activity contract or agreement was known in Soviet law as its own type of contract.[311] In the present (second part of the) Civil Code, the term of joint activity contract is used as subsidiary to the term of simple partnership.

Contract of simple partnership is defined in Article 1041 of the Civil Code. Under a contract of simple partnership two or more persons or the partners undertake to join their contributions

304 For more on this subject, see, in particular, Sergeev 2 2009: 722–8.

305 Агентский договор.

306 Thus, the commission contract differs from the delegation contract in that the commission agent acts in his own name—that is, he is not the representative of the principal but the contracting party in the transaction made by him on account of the principal; furthermore, the commission contract is always compensated and its objects are only commercial transactions. In turn, in the agency contract the elements of both commission and delegation are combined.

307 For more on this subject, see Sergeev 2 2009: 816–38 and Popondopulo 2 2009: 592–601.

308 Простое товарищество.

309 Договор о совместной деятельности.

310 See Sergeev 2 2009: 822 and Popondopulo 2 2009: 593.

311 According to Article 434 of the 1964 Civil Code joint activity agreements between physical and juristic persons were forbidden.

(property and resources) and act jointly without establishing a juristic person for obtaining profits or the achievement of another aim which is not contradictory to the law. The aim of the simple partnership contract may be the establishing of the juristic person, and the foundation agreement (contract) of a juristic person is, by its nature, usually a joint activity agreement,[312] though not fully identical with simple partnership[313].

The simple partnership is a consensual, compensated, multilateral, and fiduciary contract.[314] The subject-matter of a simple partnership contract are the joint activities of the partners aimed at the achievement of the common goal, and the content of these activities must be concretized in the contract in order it for it to be regarded as concluded. The condition on the contributions of the partners to joint activity is also regarded as essential.[315] Simple partnership contract is long-term and it can be concluded for an indefinite time. The rules of the Civil Code on simple partnership do not contain any form requirements in respect of the contract, wherefore it may be concluded in any form. However, even joint activity agreements between physical persons in Russia are not concluded in oral form. If a simple partnership contract is intended for enterprise activities (commercial simple partnership), this requires, according to the Civil Code, that its parties are commercial organizations or physical persons registered as entrepreneurs (Article 1041.2).

The Civil Code contains, in addition to the concept of simple partnership, other rules regulating it, including the norms concerning the contributions of the partners and common property (Articles 1042 and 1043), management of common affairs of the partners (Article 1044), and the unconditional right of the partner to obtain information on this (Article 1045),[316] as well as the distribution of expenditures and losses as well as profits in the joint activities (Articles 1046 and 1048).

The common affairs of the partners are to be conducted, in accordance with the Civil Code, by consensus, unless otherwise provided by the contract (Article 1044.5). The simple partnership contract may provide, for instance, that the decisions on the partnership's affairs be adopted by the majority of the partner's votes.[317] According to Article 1044.1 of the Civil Code, the joint activities may be conducted in a partnership in the following ways:

- each partner has the right to act in the name of all partners, which is presumed; or,
- if it is so agreed, the management of affairs may be conducted jointly, in which case each transaction is to be subject to the agreement of all the partners; or
- the management of affairs is conducted by an individual partner or partners.

The person authorized to conduct the joint affairs is to act, according to the Civil Code, on the basis of the power of attorney given by the other partners, or his authority is to be confirmed by the simple partnership contract concluded in writing (Article 1044.2).

The money or other property contributions of the partners as well as products produced as the result of joint activity and fruits and revenues received from such activity is, according to the

312 Sergeev 2 2009: 820–21 and M. Yu. Tihomirov (ed.), Комментарий к Федеральному закону об обществах с ограниченной ответсвтвенностью [Commentary on the Federal Law on Limited Liability Societies] (2010): 92.

313 The foundation agreement is aimed at the establishing of the juristic person, to which the conducting of activities and property are to be transferred. See V.P. Mozolin (ed.), Гражданское право [Civil Law] 2 (2009): 789.

314 Stepanov 2010: 926.

315 Sergeev 2 2009: 824.

316 Any restriction of this right is null and void.

317 Sergeev 2 2009: 831.

Civil Code, in their common share ownership, unless otherwise provided by law or the contract, or follows from the nature of the obligation (Article 1043). According to the Civil Code, the partners are solidarily or jointly and severally liable for the obligations of the partnership, if it is a question of enterprise activities, irrespective of the grounds for their origin (Article 1047.2). The profit and losses and also other results of joint activity are to be divided between the partners in accordance with their agreement; where the agreement does not include stipulations on such, the profit is to be distributed and the joint expenditures and losses be covered in accordance with the value of their contributions. A contract provision according to which the partner is restrained from participation in the division of profits or released from the obligation to cover expenses and losses in full is. under the Civil Code, null and void (Articles 1046 and 1048).[318]

A partner in the simple partnership has the right, in accordance with the Civil Code, to withdraw from the partnership, and this also concerns the contract for a definite term. The term of notice for a non-fixed term contract of simple partnership is not less than three months (Article 1051). In turn, withdrawal from the contract concluded for a fixed term, or with indication of the aim to be achieved, is allowed for compelling reason with compensation of the actual damages caused by the withdrawal or rescission of the partnership (Article 1052). The fact that the simple partnership is based on personal confidentiality[319] is also reflected in that any personal change which restrains a partner from participating in the joint activities causes the termination of the agreement. This does not, however, prevent the other parties from continuing their contractual relations (Articles 1050–52).[320]

In the norms of the Civil Code on simple partnership the silent simple partnership is also mentioned (Article 1054). This is a partnership whose existence is not disclosed. The peculiarity of it is that the common affairs of the partnership are conducted by each partner separately, in which case each partner is also responsible for the acts done by him. In turn, the relations between the partners are based on the rule of joint obligations. Otherwise this modification of the simple partnership is regulated by the norms on this.

---

318 Under Article 401.4 of the Civil Code, an agreement concluded in advance for eliminating or limiting liability for the intentional violation of an obligation is also null and void.

319 Stepanov 2010: 925.

320 Popondopulo 2 2009: 598–9.

Chapter 6
Intellectual Property Law

In Russia the legal regulation of intellectual property is based on international[1] and national norms. International legal norms for protection of intellectual property are purported to secure a minimum level of legal protection with which the national legislation in the member countries must correspond. The binding force of international law norms is confirmed in Russian law in the provisions of the Constitution as well as other laws, according to which the norms of international law have priority over national legal norms. So, if Russia joins an international treaty, its provisions are to prevail in Russian law over the internal legal norms applicable to the case.

The internal legal norms of Russia which primarily regulate legal relations concerning intellectual property are contained in the fourth part of the Civil Code of 2006, which entered into force on 1 January 2008.[2] The Civil Code replaced the separate laws regulating intellectual property issues in the country.[3]

The fourth part of the Civil Code (Division VII) contains rules regulating the rights to the results of intellectual activity and means of individualization. In addition to general rules (Chapter 69), it incorporates provisions concerning authorship rights (Chapter 70) and rights neighboring to author's rights, or neighboring (or related) rights (Chapter 71), patent rights (Chapter 72), rights to achievements of breeding (Chapter 73), rights to topologies of integral microcircuits (Chapter 74), and rights to secrets of production (know-how) (Chapter 75),[4] as well as rights to the means of individualization of juristic persons, goods, work, services, and enterprises (Chapter 76) and rights to use intellectual activity results in the system of unified technology (Chapter 77). Intellectual property relations are also regulated by other legal acts which the executive authorities of the Russian Federation are empowered to issue in those cases provided for in The Civil Code. Such

---

1 International legal sources include the Stockholm Convention establishing the World Intellectual Property Organization (1967), Berne Convention for the Protection of Literary and Artistic Works (1971), Universal (Geneva) Copyright Convention (1952), Rome Convention for the Protection of Performers, Producers of Phonograms, and Broadcasting Organizations (1961), Paris Convention for the Protection of New Varieties of Plants (1961), Convention for the Protection of Producers of Phonograms Against Unauthorized Duplication of Their Phonograms (Geneva 1971), Brussels Convention Relating to the Distribution of Program-Carrying Signals Transmitted by Satellite (1974), Paris Convention for the Protection of Industrial Property (1883), Patent Cooperation Treaty (1970), Budapest Treaty on the International Recognition of the Deposit of Microorganisms for the Purposes of Patent Procedure (1977), and Eurasian Patent Convention (1994) as well as the Madrid Agreement Concerning the International Registration of Marks (1891), Trademark Law Treaty (1994), and Singapore Treaty on the Law of Trademarks (2009). Russia also ratified the World Intellectual Property Organization Copyright Treaty (1996) in 2008 and the Patent Law Treaty (2000) in 2009.

2 The law no 230-FZ of 18 December 2006, last amended by the law no 259 of 4 October 2010. See http://base.consultant.ru/cons/cgi/online.cgi?req=doc;base=LAW;n=105422 (Accessed: 24 October 2010).

3 The Patent Law of 1992, Law on Trademarks, Service Marks, and Appellations or Origin of 1992, Law on Authorship and Related Rights of 1993, Law on the Legal Protection of Integrated Microcircuit Topology of 1992, Law on the Legal Protection of Electronic Computation Devices and Databases of 1992, and Law on Selection Achievements of 1993.

4 The rights to selection achievements, topologies of integrated microcircuits, and secrecy of production are known in Russian law as so-called nontraditional objects of intellectual property.

regulations may concern authorship rights and neighboring rights as well as the rights to industrial property and achievements of breeding. (Article 1246)

The rules concerning intellectual property are also contained in other legislation, including the Constitution. Intellectual property is, according to Article 44 of Russian Constitution, under state protection. Furthermore, Article 44 provides that everyone is guaranteed the freedom of literary, artistic, scientific, technical, and other types of creative activity. According to the rule of the Constitution important for intellectual property, the legal regulation of this is under the jurisdiction of the Russian Federation. This rule means that the norms regulating authorship, patent, trademark, and other intellectual property rights may be enacted only at the level of the Russian Federation (not at the level of subjects of the Federation such as the republics and regions).

The main source of Russian civil law, the Civil Code, contains, in addition to the norms particularly regulating intellectual property, other norms concerning intellectual property rights. So the Civil Code provides that the results of intellectual activities, and, equated to these, the means of individualization, belong to the objects of civil law rights (Article 128). Furthermore, it is provided that the right of authorship and other personal non-property rights (nonmaterial values) are inalienable and nontransferrable by other means (Article 150), and they are protected by civil legislation (Article 2.2). Intellectual property law relations are also subject to the application of other general civil law rules of the Civil Code, including the norms on transactions, limitation of actions, and general provisions on obligations.

The Civil Code norms which regulate, in addition to those presented above, in particular intellectual property rights, including exclusive rights, include the provisions which concern the content of legal capacity of physical persons (Article 18), the name and site of juristic person (Article 54), the object of pledge (Article 336), and contract for sale of enterprise (Article 559). Important rules concerning industrial property are incorporated into Chapter 38 regulating performance of scientific, research, experimental design, and technological work, and Chapter 54 regulating franchise, which are contained in the special part of the Civil Code.

Rules concerning intellectual property are also found in Russian competition legislation. On the other hand, Article 10.4 of the Competition Law (2006) expressly provides that the rules on abuse of dominant position are to not apply to the acts of use of exclusive rights to the results of intellectual activity as well as means of individualization of juristic person, performed works, and provided services (intellectual property rights). However, sale, exchange, or other way of input of a commodity into circulation if there was unlawful use of the results of intellectual activity and, equated to them, of the means of individualization of a juristic person as well as of products, works, and services is prohibited as unfair competition under penalty of administrative, criminal, and civil law liability. As to the liability for violation of intellectual property rights under the criminal law, the provisions on it are contained in Articles 146 and 147 of the Russian Criminal Code (1997).

1 General Provisions on Intellectual Property

Protectable Objects

According to the Civil Code (Article 1225), objects of intellectual property rights or results of intellectual activity (creative work) and means of individualization protectable by the law include scientific, literary, or artistic works, computer programs and databases, performances and phonograms, radio-, television-, and cable broadcasts, inventions, utility models, and industrial designs, achievements of breeding, integrated circuit layouts and secrets of production, as well as firm names, trademarks, and service marks, names of places of origin of goods and commercial designations. Intellectual rights, included in which are exclusive right as a property right as well as, in cases provided for by the Civil Code, also personal non-property and other rights, or moral rights,[5] such as right to access (*droit d'accès*) and right to follow (*droit de suite*), are recognized to apply to these objects in Russia (Article 1226).

Intellectual rights in Russian law, as elsewhere, are independent of the right of ownership to the physical carrier (the object in which the respective result of intellectual activity or means of individualization are expressed). The transfer of the right of ownership to a thing does not usually entail the transfer or granting of the intellectual rights to the result of intellectual activity expressed in the thing (Article 1227). An exception to this rule occurs where the original of a work is alienated by the owner possessing an exclusive right to it but is not the author of it—unless otherwise agreed, the exclusive right to the work passes to the recipient of the original of the work (Article 1291.2).

Authors of Results of Intellectual Activity

The author of a result of intellectual activity is recognized in Russia as the person by whose creative labor the result has been made. Persons who have not made a personal creative contribution in the making of such a result are therefore not recognized as authors of a result of intellectual activity. The Civil Code mentions such persons as being persons who have rendered technical, consulting, organizational, or financial support or otherwise merely assisted the author in the formalization of rights to such a right or its use, as well as persons who have exercised supervision of the performance of the corresponding work (Article 1228.1). However, the rights to a result of intellectual activity, created by the joint creative labor of two or more persons, are to be considered coauthorship, and belong to the coauthors jointly (Article 1228.4).

Moral Rights

The right of authorship and, in cases provided by the Civil Code, the right to the name and other non-property rights, which particularly concerns authorship rights, usually belong to the author of a result of intellectual property. The right of authorship, the right to the name, and other non-property rights are inalienable and nontransferable, and renunciation of these rights is void under Russian law. The right of authorship and the name of the author are protected without limit of time. After the death of the author, protection of his authorship and name may be conducted by any interested person. This does, however, not apply to the case where the author indicates (following the procedure provided for designating an executor of a will) the person who is to protect his right of authorship, right to the name, and inviolability of the work after his death (Articles 1267.2 and 1316.2). (Article 1228.2)

Exclusive Right and Disposition on Exclusive Right

The author (original rightholder) may dispose of his originally arisen exclusive right to a result of intellectual activity to another person (rightholder), who may in turn alienate it by contract (contract for the alienation of an exclusive right) (Article 1233.1). The exclusive right may also pass to another person on other bases established by the law (Article 1228.3). Transfer of an exclusive right to another person is also allowed without the conclusion of a contract with the rightholder in

5 This applies particularly to authorship rights.

the cases and on the bases established by the law, including by way of universal legal succession (inheritance or reorganization of a juristic person) and in the levying of execution on the property of a rightholder (Article 1241).

The rightholder of an exclusive right (a physical or a juristic person) may alienate his right to another person as well as use it at his discretion in any way not contrary to the law; he may, for instance, pledge his exclusive right. The holder of an exclusive right may, unless otherwise provided by the Civil Code, dispose of his right, as long as it does not conflict with the law and the nature of such exclusive right. He may, at his discretion, permit the use of the object or prohibit such use; it is noteworthy in this context that in Russian law absence of a prohibition is not to be considered consent (permission) to the use of the object. (Article 1229)

The right of use of an object is granted by the license contract to the extent determined by it. Conclusion of a license contract does not entail the transfer of the exclusive right to the licensee, and a contract that does not directly provide a complete transfer of the exclusive right to a result of intellectual activity or means of individualization is to be considered a license contract. This does, however, not apply to a contract made on the right of use of a result of intellectual activity created on special order or for inclusion in a complex object. (Article 1233)

Compulsory Licensing

The norms of intellectual property law of the Civil Code also include the provisions concerning compulsory license (Article 1239). In accordance with them, in certain cases, a court may, on demand of an interested person, take a decision to grant this person, on conditions determined in the decision of the court, a right of use of a result of intellectual activity, the exclusive right to which belongs to another person (a compulsory license).

Use of Complex Object

The exclusive right to a result of intellectual activity, with the exception of an exclusive right to a firm name, may belong to more than one person jointly. In this case, each rightholder may use the object at his discretion, unless otherwise provided in the Civil Code or in an agreement between the rightholders, and their mutual relations are determined by their agreement. The income generated by the use of the object of exclusive right is divided equally among all rightholders unless otherwise provided by their mutual agreement. The rightholders are to dispose of their exclusive right to the joint object jointly, unless otherwise provided by the Civil Code. In certain cases, independent exclusive rights to the same result of intellectual activity or means of individualization may belong to several persons simultaneously. This is enacted in respect to an exclusive right to a topology (Article 1454.3), secret of production (Article 1466.2), and designation of an appellation of origin (Article 1519.1), as well as the right to a collective mark (Article 1510.1). (Article 1229.4)

According to the rules of the Civil Code regulating the use of a result of intellectual activity in the composition of a complex object (Article 1240.1), a person who has organized the creation of a complex object including several protected results of intellectual activity (a motion picture, other audiovisual work, theatrical-audience presentation, a multimedia product, or a unified technology) obtains the right of use of these results on the basis of contracts for the alienation of the exclusive rights or license contracts concluded with the holders of exclusive rights. In the case where the person who has organized the creation of a complex object obtains the right of use of a result of intellectual activity specially created for inclusion in such complex object, the corresponding contract is considered a contract for the alienation of the exclusive right unless otherwise stipulated by agreement of the parties. A license contract providing for the use of a result of intellectual activity in the composition of a complex object is to be concluded for the whole time period, and with respect to the whole territory of the validity of the corresponding exclusive right, unless otherwise stipulated by the contract. Terms of the license contract limiting the use of a result of intellectual activity in the composition of a complex object are to be invalid (Article 1240.2). Furthermore, the Civil Code provides that, in the use of the result of intellectual activity in the composition of a complex object, the creator of such a result is to retain the right of authorship and other personal non-property rights to it (Article 1240.3), whereas the person who has organized the creation of the object is to have the right to indicate his name or designation or demand such indication (Article 1240.4). The rules regulating the use of the result of intellectual activity in the composition of a complex object are also to be applied, according to the Civil Code (Article 1240.5), to the right of use of unified technology created with the use of funds from the federal budget, unless otherwise determined by the provisions of the Civil Code concerning the right of use of the results of intellectual activity in the system of unified technology (Chapter 77).

The object of an exclusive right may not be used by other persons without the consent of its holder, except in cases provided by the Civil Code. The use of an object of exclusive right is unlawful and entails the liability established by the law. However, this does not apply to cases where the use of a result of intellectual activity or means of individualization without the consent of the rightholder is allowed in accordance with the Civil Code (Article 1229.1); this concerns those cases where the exclusive rights are subject to limitations. Such limitations may be imposed on the condition that they do not cause unreasonable damage to the ordinary exploitation of the result of intellectual activity or means of individualization and do not unreasonably prejudice the legitimate interests of the rightholders. (Article 1229.5)

Registration Requirements

It is directly provided in the Civil Code (Article 1232) that, in cases established by it, the exclusive right to the result of intellectual activity or means of individualization are to be recognized and protected upon condition of state registration of this. Contracts for the alienation of exclusive right and license contracts concerning the objects subjected to registration are also to be registered. The pledge and transfer without a contract of such objects are also subject to registration.[6] The order and conditions of registration are established by the Government of the Russian Federation. Nonobservance of the registration requirements entail the invalidity of the contract, and the transfer of an exclusive right is regarded as not having taken place.

In certain cases provided by the Civil Code, the state registration of a result of intellectual activity may depend on the will of the rightholder. In such cases, the registered result of intellectual activity and the rights to it are subject to the rules concerning compulsory registration (Article 1232.7).

Validity Rules

According to Article 1230 of the Civil Code containing the rules on the time period of validity of exclusive rights, exclusive right to the result of intellectual activity or means of individualization are to be effective in the course of a defined time period, unless otherwise provided in the Civil

6 In the case of a compulsory license, the court order on it is regarded as the ground for the registration of the right of use.

Code. The length of the time period, the procedure of calculation of it, the bases and procedure for extending it, as well as the bases and procedure for terminating an exclusive right before the expiration of the time period are established as well by the Civil Code.

Legal Protection, Liability, and Disputes Procedure

The general rules on legal protection of the Civil Code deal in the first place with the general protection of intellectual rights. According to Article 1250 of the Civil Code, intellectual rights are protected by means provided by the Civil Code by taking into account the nature of the violated right and the consequences of the infringement of it. These means are applicable on the demand of rightholders, organizations for the administration of rights on a collective basis, as well as other persons indicated in the law. In the protection of intellectual rights, strict liability is assumed. In other words, this means that the absence of fault does not free the violator from the obligation to stop infringement of intellectual rights or exclude him from the application of measures directed to the protection of such rights. So, the publication of a judicial decision on the infringement in question (Article 1252.1) and the termination of activities infringing the exclusive right are to be conducted regardless of the fault of the violator and at his expense (Article 1250).

The general rules on legal protection of the Civil Code also deal with the protection of personal moral rights (Article 1251). The means for the protection of personal moral rights include action for declaratory judgment, application for restitution and an injunction, and action for damages. According to the Civil Code, the protection of personal moral rights is executed by such means as, for instance:

- the recognition of a right;
- reestablishment of the status existing before the infringement of the right;
- termination of activities infringing the right or creating a threat of its infringement;
- compensation for moral harm, and
- publication of the decision of a court on the infringement committed.

The protection of moral rights concerns not only actual authorship rights but also the right of name of a person who has organized the creation of the composition of a complex object (Article 1240.4), publisher of a compiled work (Article 1260.7), producer of an audiovisual work (Article 1263.4), and (in the case of an employment work) employer (Article 1295.3), as well as producer of a phonogram (Article 1323.1), creator of a database (Article 1333.2), and first publisher or divulger (Article 1338.1).

Furthermore, the general rules of the Civil Code handle the legal protection of exclusive rights (Article 1252). In respect of the protection of these, action for declaratory judgment, application for an injunction, and action for damages may be resorted to, and, moreover, demands of seizure and publication of juridical decision can be submitted. It is directly provided in the Civil Code that the protection of exclusive rights to results of intellectual activity or means of individualization is conducted, for instance, by presenting a demand for the:

- recognition of the right—against the person denying the right or otherwise not recognizing it, and thereby infringing the rights of the rightholder and/or
- prevention of actions infringing the exclusive right—against the person performing or preparing to perform such actions and/or
- publication of the judicial decision stating the infringement committed with an indication of the actual rightholder—against the violator of the exclusive right (Article 1252.1).

Furthermore, in order to protect exclusive rights, a demand for compensation of damages may be presented against the person who has unlawfully used a result of intellectual activity or means of individualization without the conclusion of an agreement with the rightholder or otherwise has infringed his exclusive rights and caused damage to him (Article 1252.1). In the cases provided by the Civil Code, the rightholder is entitled, if his exclusive rights are infringed, to demand compensation for the infringement instead of compensation of damages. Such compensation is to be paid if the infringement is proved to have been taken place. Instead, the amount of caused damages is not necessary to prove, since this may be determined by the court within the limits established by the Civil Code, taking into account the nature of the infringement and other circumstances as well as the requirements of reasonableness and fairness.[7] The rightholder has the right to demand such compensation for each case of unlawful use of the object of his exclusive rights, or for the infringement committed as a whole. (Article 1252.3)

To protect exclusive rights, a demand against the manufacturer, importer, keeper, carrier, seller, other distributor or fraudulent recipient for the seizure of the physical carrier of the exclusive right may also be presented (Article 1252.1). This is specified in the other rule of the Civil Code (Article 1252.4) and this concerns the case where the production, distribution, or other use, as well as import, transport, and storage of physical carriers containing the result of intellectual activity or means of individualization leads to the infringement of exclusive rights. These physical carriers are considered counterfeit and, on decision of a court are subject to removal from circulation and destruction without any compensation, unless other consequences are provided by the Civil Code. Equipment and other facilities and materials mainly used or meant for commission of infringement of exclusive rights are also to be, on decision of a court, subject to removal from circulation and destruction at the expense of the infringer, unless the law provides for their transfer to the income of the state (Article 1252.5). Furthermore, the Civil Code provides that, by the procedure for security for a suit in cases of the violation of the exclusive rights, equipment and materials with respect to which suspicion has been raised of the infringement of the exclusive right, the security measures established by procedural legislation may be applied, among which seizure may be applied to physical carriers, equipment, and materials. (Article 1252.2)

The Civil Code also contains special provisions concerning protection of the exclusive right to a means of individualization. If different means of individualization, such as a firm name, trademark, service mark, or commercial designation, prove to be identical or similar to the point of confusion to other such objects and, as a result of such identity or similarity, consumers and/or counterparties may be led into confusion, the means of individualization the exclusive right to which arose earlier are to have priority. The holder of such exclusive right may, in the order established by the Civil Code, demand that the decision granting legal protection to the other trademark or service mark be recognized as invalid or a full or partial prohibition of the use of the firm name or commercial designation be imposed. For these purposes, by partial prohibition of use is meant:

- with respect to a firm name—prohibition of its use in defined types of activity and
- with respect to a commercial designation—prohibition of its use within the limits of a defined territory and/or in defined types of activity. (Article 1252.2)

---

7 It is a specific remedy established by the law. See O. Kozyr, Гражданско-правовая ответственность за нарушение интеллектуальных прав [Civil Liability for Infringement of Intellectual Rights], Хозяйство и право [Economy and Law] 10 (2008): 16 and A.L. Makovsky (ed.). Гражданский кодекс Российской Федерации.Часть 4. Комментарий [Civil Code of the Russian Federation. Part 4. Commentary] (2008): 381.

In the event of an infringement of the exclusive right, the rules of the competition (or antimonopoly) legislation may also be applied. It is explicitly provided in the Civil Code that in cases where an infringement of an exclusive right to a result of intellectual activity or to a means of individualization has been recognized by the established procedure as bad faith competition, protection of the infringed exclusive right may be exercised both by the means provided by the Civil Code and in accordance with antimonopoly legislation (Article 1252.7). In turn, Article 14 of the Competition Law (2006) directly provides, as presented above, that sale, exchange, or other way of input of a commodity into circulation, if there was unlawful use of the results of intellectual activity and means of individualization of a juristic person as well as of products, works, and services which are equated to them, is prohibited as unfair competition under penalty of administrative, criminal, and civil law liability.

The Civil Code also provides rules on the liability of juristic persons and private entrepreneurs for the violation of exclusive rights. According to them, if a juristic person repeatedly or grossly violates exclusive rights to results of intellectual activity or to means of individualization, the court may adopt a decision on the liquidation of such juristic person on demand of a procurator (prosecuting attorney) in accordance with Article 61.2 of the Civil Code. Moreover, the activity of an individual entrepreneur may be terminated in the corresponding case by decision or sentence of a court under the procedure established by the law.

According to Article 1254 of the Civil Code, the licensee also enjoys legal protection. Thus, if third persons violate the exclusive right to a result of intellectual activity or to a means of individualization for use of which an exclusive license has been granted, the licensee also has the right to use, along with other means of protection, the above-presented means provided concerning the general protection of intellectual rights (Article 1250), protection of exclusive rights (Article 1252), and the liability of juristic persons and private entrepreneurs for violation of exclusive rights (Article 1253). Thus, the exclusive licensee also has the right to demand publication of the judicial decision, stating the infringement committed, and the prevention of actions infringing the exclusive right, which is to be conducted regardless of the fault of the violator and at his expense. The licensee may also resort to action for declaratory judgment, application for restitution and injunction, and action for damages as well as present the demand for seizure. Furthermore, the licensee may resort to the rule which enables the liquidation of the juristic person or the termination of the activities of the individual entrepreneur who has grossly violated exclusive rights to intellectual property.

According to the general provisions of the Civil Code on disputes connected with the protection of intellectual rights (Article 1248), such disputes are to be considered and decided by a court. However, the disputes concerning the submission and consideration of applications for the issuance of patents and certificates connected with the objects of industrial property and their registration or the contesting of the granting legal protection for such objects as well as the termination of this are to be conducted in the cases provided by the Civil Code by administrative procedure in the executive bodies indicated in it. The decisions of these bodies are to enter into force on the day of their adoption, but they may be disputed in a court by the procedure established by the law.

Application and Execution Provisions

According to the provisions of the Civil Code regulating the application of exclusive and other intellectual rights (Article 1231), exclusive rights to results of intellectual activity and to means of individualization established by international treaties of the Russian Federation and by the Civil Code are effective on the territory of Russia. As to personal moral rights and other intellectual rights which are not considered as exclusive rights, they are effective on the territory of Russia also with regard to foreign physical and juristic persons as well as stateless persons (Article 2.1).[8] In the event an exclusive right to a result of intellectual activity or to a means of individualization is recognized in accordance with an international treaty of the Russian Federation, the content of the right, its effectiveness, limitations, and the procedure for its realization and protection are to be determined by the Civil Code regardless of the provisions of the legislation of the country of origin of the exclusive right, unless such international treaty or the Civil Code has provided otherwise.

According to the rules of the Civil Code concerning state regulation in the domain of intellectual property (Article 1246.1), the power to issue normative legal acts subordinated to laws concerning authorship and neighboring rights is directly delegated, as stated above, to the authorized federal executive bodies. The issuance of such acts is vested in the Ministry of Culture.[9] The corresponding rule of the Civil Code also concerns inventions, utility models, industrial designs, computer programs, databases, topologies of integral microcircuits, trademarks, service marks, and designations of appellations of origin (Article 1246.2), and the body empowered with the issuance of the normative acts is the federal executive body authorized to exercise legal regulation in the domain of intellectual property, which is the Ministry of Education and Science. Furthermore, the Civil Code provides in Article 1246.3 that designations of appellations of origin, including the receipt and expert examination of the respective applications and the issuance of patents and certificates confirming the exclusive right of their owners to these results of intellectual activity and to means of individualization, and in cases provided by the law also other actions connected with the legal protection of results of intellectual activity and means of individualization, are to be conducted by the federal executive authority for intellectual property. These tasks are vested at present in the federal service for intellectual property, patent, and trademarks, or Rospatent, which functions under the Ministry of Education and Science.[10]

2 Authorship and Neighboring Rights

Authorship Law[11]

Objects of regulation The objects of the authorship law regulation are authorship rights understood to refer to intellectual rights to a scientific, literary, or artistic work. The following rights belong to the author of a work:

- exclusive right to the work;
- right of authorship;
- right of the author to his name, or right to name;

8 Thus, intellectual rights other than the exclusive rights of foreign and stateless persons are always recognized in Russia, unless it is otherwise provided for by the federal law. See E.P. Gavrilov, O.A. Gorodov, S.P. Grishaev, et al., Комментарий к Гражданскому кодексу Российской Федерации (постатейный). Часть четвертая [Commentary on the Civil Code of the Russian Federation (Article-specific), Part Four] (2007): 20–21.

9 Decree on the Russian Ministry of Culture no 406 of 29 May 2008.

10 See Ukase of the President of the Russian Federation on the system and structure of the federal executive bodies no 314 of 9 March 2004 and Decrees of the Government no 299 of 16 June 2004 and no 313 of 8 April 2009.

11 For more on this subject, see A.P. Sergeev (ed.), Гражданское право [Civil Law] 3 (2009): 151–214.

- right to integrity or inviolability of the work, or right to integrity;
- right to making public of the work, or right to release.

In cases provided by the Civil Code, the author may also be entitled to other rights, including the right to remuneration for use of an employment work, the right to review, as well as the right to access (*droit d'accès*) and right to follow (*droit de suite*), which are related to works of figurative art (Article 1255).

Authorship law rights are traditionally divided into personal moral rights and economic or property rights. The latter are distinguished in the Civil Code as exclusive rights which are subject to specific rules and substantially covered by the concept of copyrights at common law. Therefore other rights can be regarded as proper authorship rights which are subject to the legal regulation of general nature concerning almost any object of the authorship law.[12] Thus the proper authorship rights and exclusive rights are presented in this work separately. On the other hand, the Civil Code also contains highly specific rules which due to their nature are best represented separately.

General authorship law provisions Subjects of authorship rights in Russian law include, in the first place, the creators of a work or authors and then their successors under the authorship law among which are employers and other owners or holders of the exclusive rights whose succession is grounded on the law or agreement.

As an author of a work of science, literature, or art is recognized the person who has created it.[13] It is expressly provided in the Civil Code that the person indicated as the author on the original or other copy of a work are to be considered its author, unless it is proved otherwise (presumption of authorship) (Article 1257).

The objects of authorship rights or the works which enjoy authorship law protection are listed in Article 1259 of the Civil Code. They include:

- literary works;
- dramatic and musical-dramatic works and screenplay works;
- choreographic works and pantomimes;
- musical works with or without text;
- audiovisual works;
- paintings, sculpture, graphics, designs, graphic stories, comics, and other works of figurative art;
- works of decorative, applied, and stage-set art;
- works of architecture, urban constructions, and park and garden art, including in the form of plans, drawings, depiction, and models;
- photographic works and works obtained by means analogous to photography;
- geographic, geological, and other maps, plans, sketches, and plastic works related to geography, topography, and other sciences.

Objects of authorship rights also include:

12 These rights are subject to application of the general rule of the Civil Code (Article 2.1). In accordance with it, the rules of the Civil Code or national regime are also to be applied to relations involving the participation of foreign and stateless persons, unless otherwise provided by the federal law.

13 Since 1993 a Russian juristic person has not been able to be recognized as the author of a work. See Sergeev 3 2009: 169.

- computer programs, which are protected as literary works.

Under the authorship law protection also is also given to:

- derivative works, in other words, works that are a reworking of another work and
- compiled works or works representing a selection or arrangement of materials.

Protection under the authorship law is independent of the worth and purpose of the work as well as of the mode of its expression. Authorship rights extend not only to works that have been made public but also to works that have not been made public which are expressed in any objective form. A work can be materialized in written and oral form (in the form of a public speech, public performance, and in any other respective form). Similarly protected are works in the form of a depiction and a sound or video recording, or in volumetric-spatial form.

Authorship law protection extends to part of a work, to its name, and to a character in the work if by their nature they can be recognized as an independent result of the creative work of the author and they are materialized (Article 1259.7).

For the arising, realization, and protection of authorship rights, neither registration of the work nor the observance of any other formalities is required (Article 1259.4). Thus, only the creation of a work is sufficient, but the symbol of protection of the copyright may be used (Article 1271). Furthermore, in respect of computer programs and databases, the rightholder may chose to register a computer program or database, and the rules on this are provided in the Civil Code (Article 1262).

The Civil Code, in its Article 1259, also contains the list of objects which are not subject to protection under authorship law. They include ideas, concepts, principles, methods, processes, systems, means, solutions of technical, organizational or other tasks, discoveries and facts, as well as programming languages (Article 1259.5).[14] Also the following are not objects of authorship rights:

- the official documents of state bodies and bodies of local self-government of municipal formations, including laws, other normative acts, judicial decisions, other materials of a legislative, administrative and judicial nature, official documents of international organizations, and also their official translations;
- state symbols and emblems (flags, seals, insignia, money, and the like) and also symbols and emblems of municipal formations;
- works of folk creativity (folklore) which do not have specific authors;
- reports on events and facts having an exclusively informational nature (reports on the news of the day, program listings for television broadcasts, schedules for the movement of means of transport, and the like).

Proper authorship rights Proper authorship rights or moral rights regulated under the authorship law belong to the creator or author of the work. According to Article 1265 of the Civil Code these rights comprehend first of all the right of authorship or the right of a person who has created the work to be recognized as its author. The author also has the right to use or permit use of a work under his own name, under a false name (pseudonym), or anonymously (the right to name). The right of authorship and the right to name are inalienable and nontransferable, even where the

---

14 The object of protection under the authorship law is the *form* not the *content* of the work. Sergeev 3 2009: 157 and Gavrilov, Gorodov, Grishaev et al. 2007: 126.

exclusive right to or the right to use the work has been transferred to another person by the law or agreement. In the event the work is published in Russia anonymously or under a pseudonym (with the exception of the case where the pseudonym of the author leaves no doubt as to his identity), the publisher whose name or designation was indicated on the work, in the absence of proof to the contrary, is to be considered as the representative of the author. In this capacity, the publisher is to have the right to protect the rights of the author and to ensure their realization. This provision remains effective until the time when the author of the work reveals his identity or declares his authorship (Article 1265.2).

Proper authorship (moral) rights also include the right of the author to protect his work, including its name, from any distortion or other infringement impugning his honor, dignity, or business reputation (right to respect). According to Article 1266 of the Civil Code, the making of changes, abridgements, or additions to a work or the provision of a work in its use with illustrations, a foreword, or an afterword, commentaries or any explanations are not allowed without the consent of the author (right to inviolability of a work). After the death of the author, the person possessing the exclusive right to the work is to have the right to permit the making of changes, abridgements, or additions to the work, on the condition that this does not distort the thought of the author and does not disturb the completeness of the perception of the work and does not contradict the desire of the author specifically expressed by him in a will, letters, diaries, or other written form. Distortion or other change in the work of the author and an attempt at such actions are to give the author the right to demand protection of his honor, dignity, or business reputation by making a defamation claim in accordance with the rules of Article 152 of the Civil Code. On the demand of interested persons, protection is also permitted for the honor and dignity of the author after his death.

According to the Civil Code (Article 1267), authorship, the name of the author and the inviolability of the work are to be protected without limit of time. The author has the right by the procedure provided for designating an executor of a will to indicate the person to whom he entrusts the protection of authorship, name of the author, and inviolability of the work after his death, and this person exercises his powers for life. In the absence of such indications or in the case of refusal of the person designated by the author to exercise the corresponding powers, and also after the death of this person, the protection of authorship, of the name of the author, and of the inviolability of the work are to be exercised by the heirs of the author, their legal successors, and other interested persons.

The right to release or make the author's work public for the first time or to give consent to this, including the right to recall or rescind his decision thereto, also belongs to proper authorship rights. The making of a work public or accessible for general knowledge may occur, according to the Civil Code (Article 1268), by its publication, public display, public performance, communication over the air or by cable, or in any other manner. As publication or release of a work to the world is regarded the release into circulation of copies of the work that are a reproduction of the work in any material form in a number sufficient for the satisfaction of the reasonable needs of the public proceeding from the nature of the work (Article 1268.2). In the event a work is not made public during the life of the author it may be made public, according to the Civil Code (Article 1268.3), after his death by a person holding the exclusive right to the work if the making of the work public does not contradict the desire of the author of the work specifically expressed by him in written form (in a will, in letters, in diaries, and the like).

According to the Civil Code (Article 1269), the author is to have the right to rescind a previously adopted decision to make a work public (right to recall). He may use this right on the condition of compensation for damages caused by such a decision, to the person to whom the exclusive right to the work was alienated or to whom the right of the use of the work was granted. In the event the work has already been made public, the author is obliged to give public notice of its recall. He has also the right to take out of circulation previously released copies of the work, having compensated for damages caused by this. These rules are not applicable, however, to computer programs, to employment works, and to works that have entered into a complex object defined in the Civil Code (Article 1240).

Exclusive right Under Russian law, in accordance with the provisions of the Civil Code (Article 1256), the exclusive right protection (to a scientific, literary and artistic work) is to be applied:

- to a work made public or not made public but existing in some objective form on the territory of the Russian Federation, in which case the exclusive right is to be recognized for an author (or his legal successors) regardless of his citizenship status;
- to a work existing in some objective form beyond the boundaries of the Russian Federation where the author (or his legal successor) is a citizen of the Russian Federation; or
- to a work existing in some objective form beyond the boundaries of the Russian Federation for an author (or his legal successor) who is a citizen of another state or stateless person in accordance with international treaties of the Russian Federation.

In the event of granting protection to a work on the territory of the Russian Federation in accordance with international treaties of the Russian Federation, the author of the work or other initial rightholder is to be determined according to the law of the state on the territory of which the legal fact took place which served as the basis for obtaining authorship rights (Article 1256.3). Additionally, it is required that a work has not passed into the public domain in both the country of origin of the work and Russia. The Civil Code explicitly provides that the time period of validity of the legal protection under international treaties in Russia is not to exceed the time period of validity of the exclusive right established in the country of origin of the work. (Article 1256.4)

As a property right, the exclusive right to a work belongs to its author, and he may transfer it to the other person or rightholder. According to the Civil Code (Article 1270), exclusive right stands for the right to use a work in any form and any manner not contrary to the law in accordance with Article 1229 of the Civil Code. The exclusive rightholder may dispose of his exclusive right to the work. To indicate his exclusive right to a work belonging to him, the rightholder may use the symbol of protection of authorship rights, which is to be placed on each copy of the work and consist of the following elements: the Latin letter C in a circle (©), the name or designation of the rightholder, and the year of first publication of the work (Article 1271).

Irrespective of whether they are used to seek profit or not, the following actions, among others, are regarded under the Civil Code as subject to the exclusive right protection (Article 1270.2):

- the reproduction of the work (right to reproduction) which comprehends the preparation of one or more copies of a work or of part of it in any material form, including in the form of an audio or video recording, preparation in three dimensions of one or more copies of a two-dimensional work and in two dimensions of one or more copies of a three-dimensional work. The recording of the work on an electronic carrier, including recording in the memory of a computer, is also to be considered reproduction, except where such recording is temporary and constitutes an inseparable and essential part of a technological process having the sole purpose of lawful use of the recording or lawful bringing of the work to general knowledge;
- the distribution of a work by sale or other alienation of its original or of copies (right to distribution);

- the public display of a work (right to public display). A work or a copy of it is publicly displayed by showing it directly or on a screen with the aid of a film, transparency, television frame, or other technical means. The exclusive right protection is also extended to the demonstration of individual frames of an audiovisual work without direct observance of their sequence or with the aid of technical means at a place open for free attendance or at a place where a significant number of persons not belonging to the usual circle of a family is present, regardless of whether the work is perceived in the place of its demonstration or in another place simultaneously with the demonstration of a work;
- the import of the original or of copies of a work for the purpose of distribution (right to import);
- the renting out of the original or a copy of the work (except for computer programs, unless they are actual objects for rent[15]);
- the public performance of a work (right to public performance). A work is publicly performed, in accordance with the Civil Code, if it is presented for hearing or watching in live performance or with the aid of technical means (radio, television, and other technical means). As a public performance is also regarded the showing of an audiovisual work (with or without the accompaniment of sound) at a place open for free attendance or at a place where a significant number of persons not belonging to the usual circle of a family is present, regardless of whether or not the work is perceived in the place of its demonstration or showing or in another place simultaneously with the demonstration or showing of a work;
- communication of a work for general knowledge over the air (including showing, performing, and transmitting) by radio or television;
- communication of a work for general knowledge by cable;[16]
- a translation (right to translation) or other reworking of the work (right to rework). By reworking of a work is understood in this context the creation of a derivative work (adaptation, screen version, arrangement, stage version, or the like). In turn, by the reworking (or modification) of a computer program or a database is understood any changes made to them, including the translation of such a computer program or such a database from one language to another with the exception of an adaptation. This stands for making changes solely for the purpose of the functioning of a computer program or database using the technical means of the user or under the management of his programs;
- the practical implementation of an architectural, design, city planning, or park or garden plan. However, the practical application of the propositions constituting the content of a work, including propositions that are a technical, economic, organizational, or other solution is not regarded as the use of a work subject to exclusive right protection, and
- bringing a work to general knowledge in such a way that any person may obtain access to the work from any place and at any time of his own choosing (bringing to general knowledge) (Article 1270.2).[17]

The limitations concerning the exclusive right of the author or rightholder are related, in general, to the initial bringing of the work to general knowledge by his consent, since the authorship rights are subject to the consumption of the distribution right. According to the Civil Code (Article 1272),

15 See Article 1270.4.

16 More detailed rules are contained in Article 1270.2.8 of the Civil Code.

17 For more on this subject, see Gavrilov, Gorodov, Grishaev et al. 2007: 165–77.

where the original or copies of a lawfully published work have been introduced into civil commerce by means of their sale or other alienation, further distribution of the original or copies of the work is to be allowed without the consent of the rightholder and without payment of compensation to him, with the exception of the case of resale of a work of figurative art in accordance with Article 1293 of the Civil Code (right to follow, *droit de suite*, presented below).

The Civil Code allows reproduction for personal purposes of a work without the consent of the author or other rightholder and without the payment of compensation (Article 1273). However, this does not apply to the reproduction of works of architecture in the form of buildings and analogous structures as well as of books (in their entirety) and of sheet music. The general right to free and uncompensated private use also does not extend to databases and computer programs except for the cases provided by Article 1280 of the Civil Code. Also outside the scope of free use are the video recording of an audiovisual work in case of its public performance[18] at a place open for free attendance or at a place where there are a significant number of persons present not belonging to the usual circle of a family as well as reproduction of an audiovisual work with the aid of professional equipment not meant for use in home conditions. (Article 1273)

A work may be used freely, according to the Civil Code (Article 1274), for informational, scientific, educational or cultural purposes. In such a case it is unnecessary to pay compensation to the author but his name and the source of borrowing must be indicated. The right of free use applies to citation and other borrowing (Article 1274.1). According to the Civil Code, the following are allowed: citation in the original and in translation of works lawfully made public. The purpose of citation may be scientific, polemical/critical, or informative and it can be made in an amount justified by the purpose thereof. Indication of the name of the author whose work is used and of the source of the borrowing is obligatory in citation. Furthermore, a work lawfully made public and excerpts from it may be used as illustrations for teaching in an amount justified by the purpose thereof. Moreover, articles lawfully published in newspapers and magazines on current economic, political, social, and religious issues may be reproduced or communicated over the air or by cable in cases when such reproduction or communication was not specially forbidden by the author or other rightholder. Free use also applies to:

- public speeches;
- works seen or heard in surveys of current events in an amount justified by the informational purpose;
- reproduction for the blind of lawfully published works, and
- library borrowings (Article 1274.2).[19]

Also the creation of a work in the genre of a literary, musical, or other parody or in the genre of caricature on the basis of another (original) work lawfully made public, and the use of this parody or caricature, are to be allowed without the consent of the author or other owner of the exclusive right to the original work and without payment of compensation to him (Article 1274.3).

18 In the event of reproduction of an audiovisual work or phonogram exclusively for personal purposes, the rightholders are entitled to compensation under the article 1245 of the Civil Code. Such compensation is paid from funds collected from manufacturers and importers of equipment and physical carriers used for such reproduction.

19 In general, libraries may borrow copies of works lawfully introduced into civil commerce without the consent of the author and without payment of compensation therefor. However, copies of works expressed in digital form may be provided only on the premises of the libraries on the condition of excluding the possibility of making copies of these works in digital form (Article 1274.2).

The Civil Code also allows free use of a lawfully published work by way of reproduction in a single copy. Such right is granted to libraries and archives as related to their activity. Individual articles and short works and short excerpts from written works may be reproduced by libraries and archives on the request of physical persons for use for educational and scientific purposes and also by educational institutions for classroom work (Article 1275).

Other cases when a work may be used without the consent of the author or other rightholder and without the payment of compensation are also recognized in the Civil Code. They include, first, the reproduction, communication over the air or by cable of a photographic work, a work of architecture, or a work of figurative art which is permanently located in a place open for free attendance, with the exception of cases where the depiction of the work by this method is the basic object of the reproduction, communication over the air or by cable, or where the image of the work is used for commercial purposes (Article 1276). Free use also extends to the public performance of a musical work during an official or religious ceremony or funeral in the amount justified by the nature of such a ceremony (Article 1277) and reproduction of a work for the purposes of application of law (Article 1278). Cases when a work may be used freely also include the right of an organization of over-the-air broadcasting to make a recording for the purpose of short-term use of a work in relation to which this organization has obtained the right to communication over the air (Article 1279).

Furthermore, the Civil Code contains the rules on passage of a work into the public domain (Article 1282), according to which upon the expiration of the time period of validity of the exclusive right, a work of science, literature, or art, whether made public or not made public, is to pass into the public domain. This means that a work may be used freely by any person without any consent or permission and without payment of compensation. However, authorship, the name of the author, and the inviolability of the work are to not be infringed.[20] The Civil Code (Article 1280) also provides for the free reproduction of computer programs and databases and decompilation of computer programs.[21]

According to Article 1281 of the Civil Code providing the rule on the general term of validity of the exclusive right to a work, this is to be effective for the whole life of the author plus 70 years, counting from January 1 of the year following the year of death of the author. In the case of a collective work, the term of the exclusive right protection are to be counted from the death of the author outliving the other coauthors. In turn, for a work made public anonymously or under a pseudonym, the term of validity of the exclusive right is to expire after 70 years counting from January 1 of the year following the year of its lawfully being made public (Article 1281.2). Also in the case of a work made public after the death of the author, the same rule is to be applied, on the condition that the work was made public within the course of 70 years after the death of the author (Article 1282.3).

The exclusive right to a work passes, according to the Civil Code (Article 1283), by inheritance.[22] The exclusive right to a work included in the composition of an inheritance considered escheated in accordance with the law of succession rule of the Civil Code (Article 1151) is to pass, in turn, into the public domain, in which case it may be used, as presented above, freely by any person and also published, unless it would thereby contradict the desire of the author specifically expressed by him in written form, for instance in a will, letters and diaries (Article 1282.3).

20 In such a case, the rights of the person who has made the work public are to be determined in accordance with the rules of the Civil Code regulating neighboring rights (Article 1282.3).

21 See below.

22 The inherited authorship rights are not subject to division. See Sergeev 3 2009: 173.

The exclusive right to a work may be alienated according to the Civil Code by a contract. Under a contract for the alienation of the exclusive right to a work the author or other rightholder transfers or becomes obligated to transfer in full an exclusive right to a work belonging to him to the recipient of such right (Article 1285). The author or other rightholder may also grant to the other party the right of use of his work by a license contract (Article 1286). The Civil Code also contains provisions on the authorship contract, or contract of author's order, under which the author is obligated on the order of the customer to create the work of science, literature, or art provided by the contract on a material carrier or in another form (Article 1288).[23] Furthermore, the Civil Code contains rules on the creation of scientific literary and artistic works under a state or municipal contract (Article 1298), where as a general rule it is provided that the exclusive right is to belong, unless otherwise provided, to the author of a work.[24] By contrast, in the provisions on computer programs and databases created on order (Article 1296), the general rule is that the exclusive right belongs, unless otherwise provided, to the customer. This rule does not, however, apply to the case where computer programs or databases are created in performance of a work contract or another corresponding contract as a byproduct; in such a case the exclusive right belongs in general, according to the Civil Code (Article 1297), to the contractor (performer of the work).

The exclusive right to a work when its original[25] is alienated is subject to special provisions in the Civil Code (Article 1291). According to the general rule, in case of alienation by the author of the original of a work (a manuscript, the original of a work of painting, sculpture, and the like), including where alienation of the original of a work is under a contract of author's order, the exclusive right to the work is to be retained by its author, unless the contract provides otherwise.[26] Where the exclusive right to a work has not passed to the recipient of its original, the recipient is to, however, have the right without the consent of the author and without the payment to him of compensation to display the original of the work obtained in ownership and to reproduce it in catalogues of exhibits and in publications dedicated to his collection and also to transfer the original of this work for display at exhibits organized by other persons (Article 1291.1). However, in case of alienation of the original of a work by its owner possessing an exclusive right to the work but who is not the author of the work, the exclusive right to the work is to pass to the recipient of the original of the work unless the contract provides otherwise (Article 1291.2).

Special authorship law rules Persons who have created a work by joint creative labor (collective work) are, under the Civil Code (Article 1258), coauthors regardless of whether such a work forms a single inseparable whole or consists of parts each of which has independent significance. It is to be used by coauthors jointly, unless an agreement among them provides otherwise. In the case when a collective work forms an inseparable whole, none of the coauthors is to have the right to forbid the use of such work without sufficient grounds. However, if the use of a part of the work is possible independently of the other parts, it may be used by its author at his discretion unless an agreement among the coauthors has provided otherwise (Article 1258). Income from the joint use of the collective work is to be distributed among the coauthors equally, unless otherwise provided by an agreement among them. Disposition

23 Intellectual property contracts are handled separately.

24 For details, see Gavrilov, Gorodov, Grishaev et al. 2007: 252–6.

25 The question is of a work of visual art. See Gavrilov, Gorodov, Grishaev et al. 2007: 228.

26 This rule concerning the author is also to be applied to his heirs, however, within the term of validity of the exclusive right (Article 1291.3).

of the exclusive right to the work is to be conducted by the coauthors jointly, unless otherwise provided by the Civil Code (Article 1229.3).

Translations and other derivative works as well as compiled works are also subject to special provisions of the Civil Code (Article 1260). The translator as well as the author of another derivative work (reworking, motion picture version, arrangement, stage version, or other similar work) are to possess the authorship rights corresponding to the translation done by him and to other reworkings of another (original) work (Article 1260.1). The compiler of a collection and the author of another compiled work (anthology, encyclopedia, database, atlas, or other similar work) are to possess the authorship rights to the compilation, meaning the selection or placement of materials made by them (Article 1260.2).

As a compiled work is also regarded a database, by which is understood the totality of independent materials (articles, accounts, normative acts, judicial decisions, and other similar materials) presented in an objective form and systematized in such a manner that these materials may be found and processed with the aid of a computer (Article 1260.2). The rightholder of a database may, during the term of validity of the exclusive right to it, register such database at a state register, in which case the contract for the alienation and the transfer of the exclusive right without a contract to it are also to be subject to state registration (Article 1262).[27]

A translator, compiler, or other author of a derivative or complied work is to exercise his authorship rights on the condition of his observance of the rights of the authors of works used for the creation of the derivative or complied work (Article 1260.3). Their authorship rights are to be protected as the right to an independent object of authorship rights regardless of the protection of the rights of the authors of the works on which the derivative or compiled work is based (Article 1260.4). The author of a work placed in a collection or other complied work has the right to use his work independently of the complied work unless otherwise provided by the contract with the creator of the complied work (Article 1260.5). However, authorship rights to a translation, collection, or other derivative or complied work are not to be deemed as an obstacle for translating or reworking the same original work by other persons, nor for creating their own complied works by another selection or placement of the same materials (Article 1260.6).

Special rules are provided in the Civil Code for encyclopedias, encyclopedic reference works, and periodicals. The right to the use of such publications are to belong to the publisher, and he has the right upon any use of such a publication to indicate its designation or to demand its indication. However, the authors or other holders of exclusive rights to the works included in such publications are to retain these rights independently of the right of the publisher or other persons to the use of such works as a whole, with the exception of the cases when these exclusive rights were transferred to the publisher or other persons or went to the publisher or other persons on other grounds provided by the law (Article 1260.7).

The legal regulation of computer programs is subject to special provisions of the Civil Code incorporated into its Article 1261. According to it, a computer program is a totality of data and commands presented in an objective from and meant for the functioning of a computer or of other computer facilities for the purpose of obtaining a specific result, including preparatory materials obtained in the course of development of a computer program and audiovisual representations generated by it. Authorship rights for all types of computer programs (including operating systems and program combinations), which may be expressed in any language and in any form, including source code and object code, are to be protected in the same way as authorship rights to works of

27 Nonobservance of the registration requirements entails invalidity of the contract and, consequently, the transfer of the exclusive right is to be regarded as not having taken place (Article 1232.6).

literature. The rightholder of a computer program may, during the term of validity of the exclusive right to it, register such program at a state register, in which case the contract for the alienation and the transfer of the exclusive right without a contract to it are also to be subject to state registration (Article 1262).[28]

The Civil Code contains, as stated above, the rules on free reproduction of computer programs and databases and decompilation of computer programs (Article 1280). A person who lawfully possesses a copy of a computer program or a copy of a database (a user) is to have the right without the permission of the author or other rightholder and without the payment of additional compensation:

- to make changes to it exclusively for the purpose of the adequate functioning of the computer program or database (right to adaptation);
- to prepare a copy for archival purposes or for replacement of the lawfully obtained copy in cases when such a copy has been lost, destroyed, or has become unsuitable for use (backup copy right);
- to study, research, or test freely the functioning of the program (Article 1280.2), and
- to decompile the computer program or reproduce and transform the object code into source text where this is necessary for achievement of the capability for interaction of a computer program independently developed with other programs which may interact with the decompiled program on the condition that the information necessary for achieving the capability for interaction previously was not accessible for this person from other sources and decompilation is conducted with respect to only necessary parts as well as that the information obtained as the result of it is not be used for other purposes (Article 1280.3).

It is expressly provided in Article 1280.4 of the Civil Code that the application of the rules on free reproduction of computer programs and databases and decompilation of computer programs is not to cause unreasonable damage to the normal exploitation of a computer program or database and is not to unreasonably prejudice the legitimate interests of the author or other rightholder.

Audiovisual works are also subject to special provisions of the Civil Code and are incorporated into its Article 1263. An audiovisual work is understood as a work consisting of a fixed series of interconnected illustrations (with or without their being accompanied by sound) and meant for visual and aural (in the case of accompanying sound) perception with the aid of appropriate technical devices. Audiovisual works include cinematographic works and also all works expressed by means analogous to cinematographic (television and video films, and other similar works) regardless of the means of their initial or subsequent fixation.

The authors of an audiovisual work are, according to the Civil Code: the director-producer, the author of the script, and the composer who is the author of a musical work (with or without words) specially created for this audiovisual work (Article 1263.2). The composer of an audiovisual work has the right to compensation in case of public performance or communication over the air or by cable of his musical work (Article 1263.3).

The producer of an audiovisual work or the person who organized the creation of it are to obtain, in accordance with Article 1240 of the Civil Code, the right of use of the audiovisual

28 Also in this case, nonobservance of the registration requirements entails invalidity of the contract and, consequently, the transfer of the exclusive right is to be regarded as not having taken place. See S.A. Stepanov (ed.), Комментарий к Гражданскому кодексу Российской Федерации [Commentary on the Civil Code of the Russian Federation] (2010): 1172.

work on the basis of contracts for the alienation of the exclusive right or license contracts and he is to have the right in case of any use of it to indicate his name or designation or to demand such an indication. In the absence of proof to the contrary, the producer of an audiovisual work is to be recognized to be the person whose name or designation is indicated on this work in the usual manner (Article 1263.4). In turn, the authors of works which have entered as a constituent part in an audiovisual work are to keep the exclusive rights to their works with the exception of cases where this exclusive right was transferred to the producer or other persons on other ground established by the law (Article 1263.5).

The right of authorship to a draft of an official document, including to the draft of an official translation of such a document and also to the draft of an official symbol or emblem, is to belong, according to the Civil Code (Article 1264), to the person who created the corresponding draft or to its developer. The developer has the right to make the draft public unless this is forbidden by a body of state, local self-government, or international organization upon whose order the draft was developed. Upon publication of the draft, the developer has the right to indicate his name. The draft of an official document, symbol, or emblem may be used by a body of state, local self-government, or international organization for the preparation of the corresponding official document or the development of a symbol or emblem without the consent of the developer if the draft has been made public by the developer for use by this body or organization or has been sent by the developer to the corresponding body or organization. In the preparation of an official document and in the development of an official symbol or emblem, additions and changes are allowed. After official adoption for consideration of the draft by the body of state, local self-government, or international organization, the draft may be used without an indication of the name of the developer.

According to the Civil Code (Article 1295), the (moral) authorship rights to an employment work or a scientific, literary, or artistic work created within the limits of the employment obligations established for an employee (author)[29] are to belong to the author (Article 1295.1). Instead, the exclusive right to an employment work are to belong to the employer unless otherwise agreed. However, if the employer within the course of three years from the day when the employment work was put at its disposition does not begin the use of this work, does not transfer the exclusive right to it to another person, or does not inform the author that the work is to be kept in secret, the exclusive right to the employment work are to belong to the author. However, in case the employer begins the use of the employment work or transfers the exclusive right to another person, the author is to have the right to compensation. The author is also to obtain the aforesaid right to compensation where the employer has taken the decision to keep the employment work secret. The amount of compensation and the conditions and procedure for its payment by the employer are to be determined by the contract between him and the employee and, in case of dispute, by a court (Article 1295.2).

The employer is to have the right to use the employment work subject to the exclusive right of the author in accordance with the employment task and within the limits deriving from it, and he is to have the right to make the work public unless otherwise agreed. Otherwise, the right of the employer to use his work is to not be limited. In use of an employment work, the employer may indicate his own name or the designation or require such an indication (Article 1295.3).

The Civil Code also contains special rules concerning the authorship rights to certain particular forms of works. So, in the case of a work of figurative art, the author is to have the right to require from the owner of the original of the work the provision of the possibility of exercising the right to

29 For more on this subject, see Gavrilov, Gorodov, Grishaev et al. 2007: 238–47.

reproduction of his work[30] (right of access). And in the case of a work of architecture, the author is to have the right to require from the owner of the original of the work the provision of the possibility of making photographs and video recordings of the work, unless otherwise provided by the contract (Article 1292). Works of figurative art are also subject to the rule (Article 1293) according to which the author is to have the right to receive upon each public resale of the original of his work compensation from the seller in the form of a percentage[31] deducted from the resale price (right to follow or right to resale royalties). The corresponding right is also provided to apply to original manuscripts (those written by the author himself) of literature and musical works. The right to follow is, though evidently an economic right, inalienable, but it is to pass to the heirs of the author for the term of validity of the exclusive right.

The next special rule in the Civil Code concerns works of architecture, city planning, or garden or park art (Article 1294). The exclusive right of the author to such works extends to the projects for their realization, including developing documentation for construction and implementation of the architectural, city planning, or garden or park plan, unless otherwise agreed; the author also has the right to exercise author's control over the development of documentation for construction and the right of author's supervision of the construction of a building or structure or other realization of the respective plan. The plan and documentation made on its basis for construction may be used repeatedly only with the consent of the author of the plan.

Neighboring Rights[32]

The provisions on rights related to authorship, or neighboring rights, are incorporated into Chapter 71 (Articles 1303–43) of the Civil Code. It is divided into the general provisions (§1) and special rules which concern rights to the performance (§2), right to a phonogram (§3), right of organizations of over-the-air or cable broadcasting (§4), right of the preparer of a database (§5), and rights of the first publisher to scientific, literary, and artistic works (§6).

The general provisions on neighboring rights (Articles 1303–12) contain the definition of neighboring rights and their objects. The general rules also deal with the symbol of legal protection of neighboring rights and free use of their objects as well as contract for the alienation of the exclusive right and license contract. Furthermore, they include the rules on technical means of protection and information on a neighboring right as well as on liability for infringement of the exclusive right and security measures.

The provisions on rights to the performance (Articles 1313–21) concern the performer, neighboring rights to a joint performance, and performance created by way of fulfillment of the employment task as well as legal protection of moral rights and exclusive right to a performance, including its validity and levy of execution on it. Corresponding special rules with some exceptions are provided in the Civil Code to also apply to a phonogram (Articles 1322–8), right of organizations of over-the-air or cable broadcasting (Articles 1329–32), and right of the preparer of a database (Articles 1333–6) as well as rights of the first publisher to scientific, literary, and artistic works or publication right (Articles 1337–43.

As neighboring rights are understood, according to the Civil Code (Article 1303), intellectual rights to the results of performing activity (performances), to phonograms, to communication over the air or by cable of radio and television transmissions (broadcasting by organizations of over-the-

30 The owner of the original is not required, however, to deliver the work to the author.

31 According to the decision of the Russian Government.

32 For more on this subject, see Sergeev 3 2009: 214–36.

air and cable broadcasting), to the content of databases, and also to works of science, literature, or art first made public after their passage into the public domain. Neighboring rights comprise the exclusive right and also personal moral rights in cases provided by the Civil Code. Exclusive right may be transferred to another person by a contract for alienation of the exclusive right (Article 1307), and, by a license contract, the right of use of the respective object may be granted to another person (Article 1308).

Objects of neighboring right protection are, according to the Civil Code (Article 1304.1):

- performances of performing artists and conductors, productions of director-producers of shows (performances) if these performances are expressed in a form allowing their reproduction and distribution with the aid of technical means;
- phonograms meaning any exclusively sound recordings of performances or other sounds or representations thereof, with the exception of sound recording included in an audiovisual work;
- communications of transmissions of organizations of over-the-air or cable broadcasting;
- databases—with respect to their protection from unsanctioned extraction and repeated use of the materials constituting their content, and
- works of science, literature, and art which were made public after their passage into the public domain—with respect to the protection of the rights of the first publishers of such works.

Also neighboring rights of foreign persons may be protected in Russia in accordance with the international treaties on the condition that their objects have not passed into the public domain (Article 1304.3).

According to Article 1304.1 of the Civil Code, for the arising, exercise, and protection of neighboring rights neither registration of their object nor the observance of any other formalities are required. However, the producer of a phonogram and the performer, and also another owner of the exclusive right to the phonogram or performance, are to have the right for notification of the exclusive right belonging to him to use the symbol of protection of neighboring rights, which are to be placed on each original or copy of the phonogram and/or on each case containing it and are to consist of three elements—the Latin letter P in a circle (℗), the name or designation of the owner of the exclusive right, and the year of first publication of the phonogram (Article 1305).

The object of neighboring rights may be used, in accordance with Article 1306 of the Civil Code, without the consent of the rightholder and without the payment of compensation in cases of free use of works provided by the rules of the Civil Code concerning authorship rights (Articles 1273, 1274, and 1277–9), presented above, and also in other cases established by the provisions on neighboring rights. So, the Civil Code allows reproduction for personal purposes of a work without the consent of the author or other rightholder and without the payment of compensation (Article 1273). A work may also be used freely for informational, scientific, educational, or cultural purposes (Article 1274). Free use concerns also the public performance of a musical work during an official or religious ceremony or funeral (Article 1277) and reproduction of a work for the purposes of application of law (Article 1278). The cases of free use of work include the right of an organization of over-the-air broadcasting to make a recording for the purpose of short-term use of a work in relation to which this organization has obtained the right to communication over the air (Article 1279). And in the rules of the Civil Code concerning neighboring rights, it is provided that where the original or copies of a lawfully published phonogram have been introduced into the civil commerce by way of their sale or other alienation, the further distribution of the original or copies are to be allowed without the consent of the owner of the exclusive right to the phonogram and without payment of compensation to him (Article 1325). A corresponding rule is provided to apply to original or copies of work protected by the exclusive right of the first publisher (Article 1344).

Rights to performance Rights to performance belong, according to Article 1313 of the Civil Code, to the person whose creative work is protected by the rules on neighboring rights. The performing artist may be an actor, singer, musician, dancer, or other person who plays a role, reads, declaims, sings, plays a musical instrument, or in another way participates in the performance of a work of literature, art, or folk creativity, including a variety, circus, or puppet act. Rights to performance also belong to the director-producer of a show, meaning the person conducing the production of a theatrical, circus, puppet, variety, or other theatrical-viewing presentation, and to the conductor as well.[33]

Neighboring rights to a joint performance are to belong, according to the Civil Code (Article 1314), jointly to the members of the group of performers, including actors participating in a show, orchestra members, and other members of the group of performers who took part in its creation, regardless of whether such a performance forms an indivisible whole or consists of elements each of which has independent significance.[34] Neighboring rights to a joint performance are to be exercised by the head of the group of performers and, in his absence, by the members of the group of performers jointly unless otherwise agreed. In the event a joint performance forms an indivisible whole, none of the members of the group of performers are to have the right to forbid its use without sufficient grounds therefor. However, an element of a joint performance, the use of which is possible independently of other elements, may be used by the performer who created it at his discretion unless an agreement among the members of the group of performers provides otherwise (Article 1314.2). Income from the use of the joint performance is to be distributed among the performer equally, unless otherwise agreed (Articles 1229.3 and 1314.3).

As the rights to performance which belong to the performer (director-producer and conductor) are indicated in the Civil Code:

- the exclusive right to the performance;
- the right of authorship, and
- the right to the indication of his name or pseudonym on copies of the phonogram and in other cases of the use of the performance or right to name, as well as,
- the right to inviolability of the performance, or right to respect.

These moral rights are protected for an unlimited time (Article 1316).[35] Performers are to realize their rights with observance of the rights of the authors of the works performed. However, the rights of the performer are to be recognized and are to remain valid irrespective of the authorship rights. (Article 1315)

33 The rights to the performance created in fulfilling of the employment obligations are to be determined in accordance with the rules of the Civil Code on employment work (Article 1295). (Article 1320).

34 In turn, in order to protect his own rights, each of the members of a collective of performers may take measures independently including where such performance forms an indivisible whole (Article 1314.4).

35 The performer has the right to appoint, by the procedure established for designating an executor of a will, the person to whom he entrusts the protection of his right of authorship, right to the name, and inviolability of the work after his death. The protection of these rights, in the absence of such indications or in the case of refusal of the person designated by the author to exercise the corresponding powers and also after his death, is to be exercised by the heirs of the author, their legal successors, and other interested persons.

The exclusive right to performance related to the performer comprehends the right to use a performance in any manner not contrary to the law and also to dispose of his exclusive right (Article 1317.1). As the use of a performance are to be considered communication over the air and by cable, radio, or television, including by retransmission, as well as recording of a performance and the reproduction, distribution, including renting out of the original or copies, and bringing to general knowledge of a recording. The exclusive right to performance also extends to the public performance of a recording of a performance in a place open for free attendance or in a place where a significant number of persons not belonging to the usual circle of the family are present, regardless of whether the recording is perceived at the place of its communication or in another place simultaneously with its communication (Article 1317.2). The exclusive right to performance is not, however, to extend to the reproduction, communication, or public performance of a recording of a performance, if such a recording was made with the consent of the performer and its reproduction, communication, or public performance was conducted for the same purposes for which the consent of the performer was obtained at the time of the recording of the performance (Article 1317.3). Moreover, where the performer participates under contract in the creation of an audiovisual work, his consent to the use of the performance in the composition of the audiovisual work is to be presumed. However, his consent to the separate use of sound or image fixed in the audiovisual work must be directly expressed in the contract (Article 1317.4).

According to Article 1321 of the Civil Code, the exclusive right to a performance is to be valid on the territory of the Russian Federation in cases where:

- the performer is a citizen of the Russian Federation; or
- the performance first took place on its territory; or
- the performance was fixed in a phonogram, the exclusive right to which is protected in Russia (Article 1328); or
- the performance not fixed in a phonogram was included in a communication over the air or by cable, the exclusive right to which is protected in Russia (Article 1332), as well as
- in other cases provided by international treaties of the Russian Federation.

The exclusive right to a performance is to be valid, according to Article 1318 of the Civil Code, for the whole life of the performer, but for not less than 50 years counting from January 1 of the year following the year in which the performance or recording of a performance or communication of a performance over the air or by cable took place. The exclusive right to a performance passes by inheritance, but upon expiration of the term of validity of the exclusive right this is to pass into the public domain.

Rights to phonogram Neighboring rights to a phonogram belong to its producer. According to the Civil Code (Article 1322), the producer of a phonogram is to be considered to be the person that undertook the initiative and responsibility for the first recording of the sounds of a performance or other sounds or representations of these sounds. In the absence of proof to the contrary, as the producer of the phonogram is to be regarded the person whose name or designation is indicated in the usual manner on a copy of the phonogram and/or on its packaging.

As neighboring rights related to the producer of a phonogram, the Civil Code indicates:

- the exclusive right to the phonogram;
- the right to an indication on copies of the phonogram and/or their packaging of his name or designation or right to name;

- the right to protection of the phonogram from distortion in the course of its use or right to respect, and
- the right to make public the phonogram, meaning an action that for the first time makes the phonogram accessible for general knowledge by way of its publication, public showing, public performance, communication over the air or by cable or in another manner (right to release).

As making public a phonogram is regarded the release into circulation of copies of a phonogram with the consent of the producer in a number sufficient for the satisfaction of the reasonable requirements of the public. (Article 1323.1)

The producer of a phonogram is to exercise his rights with observance of the rights of the authors of the works and the rights of the performers. However, the rights of a producer of a phonogram are to be recognized and are to be valid irrespective of the authorship rights and performers' rights. The right to name and the right to respect related to the producer of the phonogram are to be valid and protected in the course of his whole life, and, where a producer is a juristic person, until its termination. (Article 1323)

The exclusive right of the producer of a phonogram comprehends the right to use it in any manner not contrary to the law and also to dispose of his exclusive right (Article 1324.1). As the use of a phonogram subject to the exclusive right is to be considered the public performance of a phonogram at a place open for free attendance or at a place where a significant number of persons not belonging to the usual circle of a family are present, regardless of whether the phonogram is perceived in the place of its communication or in another place simultaneously with its communication, communication over the air, and by cable, radio, or television, including by retransmission, as well as bringing of a phonogram to general knowledge in such a manner that any person may obtain access to the phonogram from any place and at any time of his own choice. The exclusive right to a phonogram also extends to the reproduction of one or more copies of a phonogram or a part of it. As reproduction is also to be regarded the recording of a phonogram or a part of it on an electronic carrier, except for the case when such a recording is temporary and purposed for the lawful use of the recording. Furthermore, the exclusive right protection extends to the commercial and other distribution of a phonogram, import of the original or copies of a phonogram for the purpose of distribution including copies prepared with the permission of the rightholder and their renting out as well as reworking of a phonogram. (Article 1324)

A lawfully published and lawfully sold original or copy of the phonogram may be further distributed without the consent of the owner of the exclusive right to the phonogram and without payment of compensation to him (Article 1325). Furthermore, a phonogram published for commercial purposes may be, according to the Civil Code (Article 1326), performed publicly and used in communication over the air or by cable freely but with payment of compensation. For this purpose, the organizations for the administration of rights on a collective basis having state accreditation collect from users the compensation and distribute it among the rightholders in the following proportion: 50 percent to the performers and 50 percent to the producers of the phonograms.

According to Article 1328 of the Civil Code, the exclusive right to a phonogram is to be valid on the territory of the Russian Federation in cases where:

- the producer of the phonogram is a citizen of the Russian Federation; or
- the phonogram was made public or copies thereof were first publicly distributed on the territory of the Russian Federation; or
- in other cases provided by international treaties of the Russian Federation.

The Civil Code (Article 1327) provides for the protection of the exclusive right to a phonogram a general term of validity of 50 years counting from January 1 of the year following the year in which the recording was made. Where the phonogram is made public later but within the course of the protection period, the new 50 years' protection term starts from it. The exclusive right to a phonogram is to pass to the heirs and other legal successors of the producer of the phonogram, but upon expiration of the period of validity of the exclusive right this is to pass into the public domain.

Broadcasting rights An organization of over-the-air or cable broadcasting is to possess, according to the Civil Code (Article 1330), the exclusive right to use a lawfully conductible or conducted communication by it over the air or by cable of radio or television transmissions by any means not contrary to the law and also to dispose of his exclusive right. As the use of a communication of a radio or television transmission (of a broadcast) subject to the exclusive right is to be regarded recording of the communication of a radio or television transmission and its reproduction. The exclusive right protection also extends to the commercial and other distribution of the communication of a radio or television transmission and its retransmission and bringing to general knowledge in such a way that any person may obtain access to the communication of the radio or television transmission from any place and at any time of his own choosing as well as public performance of a broadcast at places with paid entrance regardless of whether it is received at the place of communication or at another place simultaneously with communication. The broadcasting organization is to realize its rights with observance of the rights of the authors of the works, the rights of performers and other holders of the rights to a phonogram or communications of radio and television transmissions. However, the rights of the broadcasting organization are to be recognized and are to remain valid irrespective of the rights of the other rightholders.

According to Article 1332 of the Civil Code, the exclusive right to a broadcast is to be valid on the territory of the Russian Federation in cases where the broadcasting organization is located and conducts communication with the aid of transmitters located on the territory of the Russian Federation or in other cases provided by international treaties of the Russian Federation. The Civil Code (Article 1331) provides for the protection of the exclusive right to a broadcast general term of validity of 50 years counting from January 1 of the year following the year in which broadcast took place. The exclusive right to a broadcast is to pass to legal successors but upon expiration of the period of validity of the exclusive right this is to pass into the public domain.

Rights to database The rights to database belong, according to the Civil Code (Article 1333), to the manufacturer or the person who has organized the creation of a database and work for the collection, processing, and placing of the materials constituting it. In the absence of proof to the contrary, the physical or juristic person whose name or designation is indicated in the usual manner on a copy of the database and/or on its packaging is to be considered to be the manufacturer of the database.

The exclusive right to a database is to be recognized, according to the Civil Code (Article 1334), if the creation of it requires substantial financial, material, organizational, and other expenditures; as such is presumed a database containing not less than 10,000 independent information elements (or materials) constituting the content of the database. The exclusive right of the manufacturer of a database comprehends his right to extract materials from a database and to conduct their subsequent use in any form and by any means. He may also dispose of his exclusive right. The exclusive right of the manufacturer of a database is to be recognized and is to be effective regardless of the authorship rights and other exclusive rights of the manufacturer and other persons to the materials constituting the database and also to the database as a whole as a compiled work. A person lawfully using a database is to have the right without the permission of the rightholder to extract materials from such database and to conduct their subsequent use for personal, scientific, educational, and other noncommercial purposes in an amount justified by the aforesaid purposes and to the degree by which such actions do not infringe the authorship rights of the manufacturer of the database and other persons. The use of materials extracted from a database in a way presupposing the receipt of access thereto by an unlimited group of people must be accompanied by an indication of the database from which these materials were extracted.

According to Article 1336 of the Civil Code, the exclusive right of the manufacturer of a database is to be valid on the territory of the Russian Federation in cases:

- where the manufacturer of the database is a citizen of the Russian Federation or a Russian juristic person; or
- where he is a foreign citizen or a foreign juristic person on the condition that the legislation of his state provides protection for the exclusive rights of the Russian manufacturers of databases, as well as
- in other cases provided by international treaties of the Russian Federation.

The Civil Code (Article 1335) provides for the protection of the exclusive right to a database the term of validity of 15 years counting from January 1 of the year following the year of its creation. However, if a database is made public later but within the course of the protection period, the new 15 years protection term starts from it. The protection periods are to be renewed upon each renewal of the database.

Publication right Neighboring rights to a scientific, literary, and artistic work which is lawfully made public[36] after it has passed into the public domain or left without authorship law protection belongs to its first publisher on the condition that the work corresponds with the authorship law criteria established by the Civil Code (Article 1259). This rule does not, however, extend to works that are in state and municipal archives (Article 1337).

According to Article 1338 of the Civil Code, the exclusive right of the first publisher to a work made public by him also stands for the right to indicate his name on copies of a work made public by him and in other cases of its use including in translation or other reworking of a work. Furthermore, the first publisher during the term of validity of his exclusive right is to possess the powers to permit the making of changes, abridgements, or additions to the work, on the condition that this does not distort the thought of the author and does not disturb the completeness of the perception of the work and does not contradict the desire of the author specifically expressed by him in a will, letters, diaries, or other written form (Article 1266.1).

The exclusive right of the first publisher to a work comprehends the right to use it in any manner not contrary to the law and also to dispose of his exclusive right (Article 1339). However, a lawfully published and lawfully sold original or copy of the work may be further distributed without the consent of the owner of the exclusive right to the published work and without payment of compensation to him (Article 1344). Furthermore, the Civil Code provides (Article 1343) that in case of alienation of the original of a work (manuscript, the original of a work of painting, sculpture, or other like work) by its owner holding the exclusive right of the first publisher to the

---

36 However, not, for instance, if it contradicts to the will of the author specifically expressed by him in written form in a testament, letters, or diaries, and the like (Article 1268).

alienated work, this exclusive right is to pass to the recipient of the original of the work unless a contract provides otherwise. However, if the exclusive right of a first publisher to a work has not passed to the recipient of the original of a work, the recipient is to have the right without the consent of the holder of the exclusive right to display the original of the work and to reproduce it in catalogues of exhibits and in publications dedicated to his collection and also to transfer the original of this work for display at exhibits organized by other persons (Article 1291.1).

According to the Civil Code (Article 1341) the exclusive right of a first publisher is to extend to works:

- made public on the territory of the Russian Federation regardless of the citizenship of the first publisher;
- made public beyond the territory of the Russian Federation by a citizen of the Russian Federation;
- made public beyond the territory of the Russian Federation by a foreign citizen (or a person without citizenship) on the condition that the legislation of his state provides protection for the exclusive rights of the Russian first publisher,[37] as well as
- in other cases provided for by international treaties of the Russian Federation.

The exclusive right of the first publisher is protected under the Civil Code (Article 1340) for 25 years and this period of validity is to be counted from January 1 of the year following the year of the work being made public. On the other hand, the exclusive right of a first publisher to a work may be terminated early by judicial procedure on a suit by an interested person if in the course of the use of the work the rightholder is violating the moral rights concerning the work (Article 1342).

Legal Protection of Authorship and Neighboring Rights and Liability

The Civil Code contains special provisions which protect the exclusive right of the author of a work (Article 1284) and the performer (Article 1319). Levy of execution is not allowed on it.[38] However, execution may be levied on the right of claim of the author or performer against other persons under contracts for the alienation of the exclusive right and under license contracts as well as to income received from the use of a performance. Moreover, execution may be levied on an exclusive right belonging not to the author or the performer himself but to another person and also on the right of use of a work belonging to a licensee. The Civil Code also provides that in case of sale of the right of use belonging to the licensee at public auction for the purpose of levying of execution on this right, the author or the performer is to be granted a preferential right to obtain it. (Articles 1284.2 and 1319.2)

The Civil Code also contains provisions which concern infringement of the exclusive right to a work (Article 1301) and to an object of neighboring rights (Article 1311), which are to be applicable in addition to the general liability rules concerning all exclusive rights to intellectual property (Articles 1250, 1252, and 1253). In the event of infringement of exclusive rights, including actions directed at eliminating the limitations on the use of a work established by the application of technical means of protection of authorship rights and preparation and distribution of devices for such a

37 In such a case the term of validity of the exclusive right in Russia may not exceed the term of validity in the state in which the ground for obtaining the exclusive right has arisen.

38 This rule concerning the author is also to be applied to heirs of the author and their heirs, though only within the term of validity of the exclusive right (Article 1284.1).

purpose (Articles 1299 and 1311), as well as removing or changing information about authorship rights without the permission of the author or other rightholder and use of works with respect to which information about authorship rights has been removed or changed without the permission of the author or other rightholder (Articles 1300 and 1310), the author or the rightholder is to have the right in accordance with Article 1252.3 of the Civil Code to demand at his option from the infringer instead of compensation for damages the payment of compensation. The amount—from ten thousand rubles to five million rubles—is to be determined at the discretion of the court. The compensation may also be double the amount of the value of the copies of the object of exclusive rights or twice the amount of the value of the right of the use of it determined proceeding from the price which, in comparable circumstances, is usually taken for the lawful use of such an object. In cases of infringement of the authorship and neighboring rights, the court or other body authorized by the law may impose security measures. The court may impose seizure of counterfeit objects and also of materials and equipment used or meant for their preparation or reproduction as well as forbid a defendant or other person with respect to whom there are sufficient grounds to suppose that he is an infringer of authorship or neighboring rights to take specific actions threatening these. (Articles 1302 and 1312)

3 Industrial Property Law

Patent Law[39]

Scope of application The objects of patent law regulation are, according to the Civil Code (Article 1345), intellectual rights to inventions, utility models, and industrial designs defined as patent rights. The author of an invention, utility model, or industrial design is to have the exclusive right and the right of authorship to it. In cases provided by the Civil Code, other rights also belong to the author of an invention, utility model, or industrial design including the right to receipt of a patent,[40] the right to remuneration for the use of an employment invention, utility model, or industrial design.

The exclusive rights to patent law objects are to be recognized, according to the Civil Code (Article 1346), on the territory of the Russian Federation in respect of inventions, utility models, and industrial designs, the rights to which are certified by patents issued by the federal agency of executive authority for intellectual property, at present Rospatent,[41] or by patents in force on the territory of the Russian Federation in accordance with international treaties of the Russian Federation. The exclusive right to an invention, utility model, or industrial design is to be recognized and protected in Russia on the condition of state registration of it on the ground of which Rospatent is to issue a patent (Article 1353).

Object of patent rights As the objects of patent rights are regarded, according to the Civil Code (Article 1349), the results of intellectual activity in the scientific and technical area that meet the requirements established by the Civil Code for inventions and utility models and the results of

39 For more on this subject, see Sergeev 3 2009: 237–84.

40 The question is of the right of priority of the applicant, in respect to the other applicant, to receive the patent and obtain the exclusive right to it. A patent is an official document certifying the priority of the author of the invention, utility model, or industrial design.

41 The federal service on intellectual property, patent and trademarks. See its website: http://www1.fips.ru/wps/wcm/connect/content_ru/ru (accessed 9 June 2010).

intellectual activity in the area of artistic design that meet the requirements established by the Civil Code for industrial designs. The patent law rules also extend to inventions containing information constituting a state secret (secret inventions), unless otherwise provided by the special rules of the Civil Code (Articles 1401–5) and by legal acts issued in accordance with them (Article 1349.2). However, the rules on patent law protection are to not be granted to utility models and industrial designs containing information constituting a state secret (Article 1349.3).

Excluded from the list of the objects of patent rights in Russia are, under Article 1349.4 of the Civil Code, methods of cloning of a human being, methods of modification of the genetic integrity of cells of the embryonic line of a human being, and use of human embryos for industrial and commercial purposes as well as other solutions contradicting societal interests, principles of humanity, and morality.

The conditions of patentability of an invention,[42] or the legal requirements for granting the patent, are, according to Article 1350.1, that it is a technical solution related to a product or a means. A product may be a structure, substance, microorganism strain, or culture of cells of plants or animals. In turn, as a patentable means the Civil Code indicates a process of conducting actions on a material object with the help of material means. An invention is to be granted legal protection if it is new, has an inventive level, and is industrially applicable.

An invention is considered, under the Civil Code (Article 1350.2), new if it is not known from the present level of technology, and inventive, if for a specialist it does not obviously follow from the present level of technology. The present level of technology, in turn, means any information that has become generally accessible in the world[43] before the priority date of the invention.[44] As a circumstance precluding the recognition of the patentability of the invention is not to be regarded disclosure of information relating to an invention by the author of the invention, applicant, or other person who received this information directly or indirectly from them, as a result of which information on the nature of the invention became generally accessible. A precondition for it is that an application for the issuance of a patent for the invention has been filed with the Patent Office, or Rospatent, within the course of six months from the day of disclosure of the information. The burden of proof that the circumstances have taken place by virtue of which the disclosure of information does not prevent the recognition of the patentability of the invention is to rest on the applicant (Article 1350.3).

An invention is to be regarded, under the Civil Code (Article 1350.4), as industrially applicable if it may be used in industry, agriculture, health care, other branches of the economy, or the social sphere.

The Civil Code contains provisions determining the objects which are to not be regarded as inventions or subjects to patent law protection (Article 1350.5). Unpatentable are:

- discoveries;
- scientific theories and mathematical methods;
- solutions involving only the external form of manufactures and directed at the satisfaction of esthetic needs;
- rules and methods for games and for intellectual or economic activity;
- computer programs, and
- solutions consisting only of the presentation of information.

42 For more on this subject, see Gavrilov, Gorodov, Grishaev et al. 2007: 321–9.

43 The question is of the publicly available information.

44 The priority of the invention, utility model, or industrial design is determined in general by the date of filing of the patent application.

Legal protection as inventions are also not to be granted, according to the Civil Code (Article 1350.6), to:

- varieties of plants, breeds of animals and biological methods of obtaining them,[45] with the exception of microbiological methods and products obtained through the use of such methods, and
- the topology of integrated circuits.[46]

As a utility model[47] is to be protected under the Civil Code (Article 1351) a technical solution relating to a structure. The conditions of patentability of a utility model[48] are its novelty and industrial applicability.[49] A utility model is to be considered new if the totality of its essential characteristics is not known from the present level of technology. The present level of technology includes information published in the world on means for the same purpose as the utility model applied for and information on their application in Russia if such information became generally accessible before the priority date of the utility model. The level of technology also includes, as in the case of inventions, all inventions and utility models patented or to be patented in Russia. Also in respect of industrial applicability of the utility model, the rules are the same as in the case of inventions. The rules on patentability of objects the information relating to which is disclosed before the submission of the patent application are also similar.

As in the case of inventions, legal protection as utility models is not to be granted, under the Civil Code (Article 1351.5), to solutions involving only the external form of manufactures and directed at the satisfaction of esthetic needs, and to the topology of integrated circuits.[50]

As industrial design is to be protected[51] under the Civil Code (Article 1352.1) an artistic design solution of a manufacture of industrial or handicraft production defining its external form. In order to be protected an industrial design must be in its essential characteristics new and original. The essential characteristics of an industrial design are the characteristics determining the esthetic and/or ergonomic features of the external form of the manufacture, including form, configuration, ornamentation, and combination of colors.

An industrial design is considered new if the totality of its essential characteristics reflected in images of the manufacture and included in the list of essential characteristics of the industrial design is not known from information that had become generally accessible in the world before the priority date of the industrial design. Furthermore, in establishing the novelty of an industrial design all industrial designs patented and to be patented in Russia, as in the case of inventions and utility models, are to be taken into account. (Article 1352.2)

An industrial design is considered original if its essential characteristics are determined by the creative nature of the features of the manufacture (Article 1352.3). As in the cases of inventions and utility models, it is possible to receive the patent to an industrial design the information relating to which has been disclosed (Article 1352.4).

---

45 These are regulated in the Civil Code separately (Articles 1408–47).

46 These are regulated in the Civil Code separately (Articles 1448–64).

47 These are often called small inventions.

48 For more on this subject, see Gavrilov, Gorodov, Grishaev et al. 2007: 329–32.

49 The inventive criterion is not regarded as a legal requirement for the patentability of a utility model.

50 Species of plants and breeds of animals are not mentioned in the provisions on utility model patentability. On the other hand, they are subject to the patentability rules specially provided for them in the Civil Code (Articles 1408–47).

51 For more on this subject, see Gavrilov, Gorodov, Grishaev et al. 2007: 332–8.

As objects to which legal protection as an industrial design are to not be granted to, the Civil Code indicates:

- solutions determined exclusively by the technical function of the manufacture;
- objects of architecture (other than small architectural forms), industrial, hydrotechnical, and other stationary structures, and
- objects of instable form produced from liquid, gas, flowing or similar substances (Article 1352.5).

Patent rights The right of authorship belongs, according to the Civil Code (Article 1356), to the author of an invention, utility model, or industrial design. It comprehends the right to be recognized as the author of an invention, utility model, or industrial design, and he is the citizen by whose creative work the corresponding result of intellectual activity has been created. The Civil Code contains a presumption of authorship by providing expressly that the person indicated as the author in an application for the issuance of a patent is to be considered to be the author, unless it is proved otherwise. (Article 1347)

The right of authorship is to be, according to Article 1356 of the Civil Code, inalienable and nontransferable even in the case of transfer to another person or passage to him of the exclusive right to an invention, utility model, or industrial design or granting to another person of the right to its use. A waiver of this right is void in Russian law.

The right to receipt of a patent for an invention, utility model, or industrial design is also to belong, according to the Civil Code (Article 1357), to the author of the invention, utility model, or industrial design. However, he may transfer it to another person by a contract, including labor contract. The right to receipt of a patent may pass to another person also on other grounds established by the law—for instance, legal succession (inheritance and reorganization of a juristic person). A contract on alienating the right to receipt of a patent for an invention, utility model, or industrial design must be concluded, according to the Civil Code (Article 1357.3), in written form; nonobservance of written form is to entail the invalidity of the contract. Unless otherwise established by agreement, the risk of nonpatentability of an invention, utility model, or industrial design is to be borne by the recipient of the right (Article 1357.4).

According to Article 1346 of the Civil Code regulating the application of exclusive rights to inventions, utility models, and industrial designs, on the territory of Russia exclusive rights to inventions, utility models, and industrial designs are to be recognized and legally protected if these rights are certified by patents issued by Rospatent or by patents which are in force on the territory of Russia in accordance with international treaties of the Russian Federation.

According to Article 1358 of the Civil Code, the exclusive right of use of an invention, utility model, or industrial design is to belong to the patent owner, and he may use it by any means not contrary to the law (Article 1229), and also dispose of the exclusive right. The use of an invention, utility model, or industrial design requires the permission of the patent holder; otherwise it is an infringement of the exclusive right.

The exclusive right of the patent holder to use an invention, utility model, or industrial design stands for its industrial and commercial exploitation and, according to Article 1358.2 of the Civil Code, includes, in particular, import onto the territory of Russia, preparation, use, proposal for sale, sale, other introduction into civil commerce or the storage for these purposes of a product containing a patented solution. In respect of a patented method, there is a special rule in the same article, according to which, if the product obtained by the patented method is new, an identical product is to be considered obtained by way of use of the patented method unless proven otherwise. Thus, the production of the new product by way of use of the patented method is presumed in Russian law. The exclusive right of the patent holder to use the patented object also includes such actions as preparation, use, import, and marketing as well as storage for these purposes with respect to a device during the functioning (use) of which in accordance with its purpose the patented method is automatically exercised as well as the realization of a method in which the invention is used, in particular by the application of this method.[52]

It is expressly provided in the rules of the Civil Code on the exclusive rights to inventions, utility models, or industrial designs (Article 1358.3) that an invention or utility model is to be considered used (permitted or unauthorized) in a product or method if the product contains or if in the method there is used each characteristic of the invention or utility model stated in a separate claim contained in the claims for the invention or utility model in the patent, or a characteristic equivalent thereto that has become known as such in the given area of technology before the product or method is taken into industrial and commercial exploitation. In turn, an industrial design is to be considered used in a manufacture if the manufacture contains all the essential characteristics of the industrial design that found expression in the illustrations of the manufacture and that were stated in the list of essential characteristics of the industrial design. Furthermore, the Civil Code provides that if in the use of an invention or utility model there are also used all the characteristics stated in a separate claim of the claims contained in the patent of another invention or another utility model, and in the use of an industrial design, all the characteristics included in the list of essential characteristics of another industrial design, the other invention, the other utility model, or the other industrial design is also to be considered to be used.

The Civil Code also contains a list of cases not considered infringement of the exclusive right of the patent holder (Article 1359). Among these are:

- use of a product containing the patented invention, utility model, or industrial design in the construction, supplementary equipment, or exploitation of means of transport and space technology of foreign states, which is present temporarily or accidentally on the territory of Russia on the principle of reciprocity;
- the conduct of scientific study or an experiment concerning the patented object;
- the utilization of a patented object in extraordinary circumstances (natural disasters, catastrophes, accidents);[53]
- the utilization of a patented object for private use;
- the one-time preparation in pharmacies on physicians' prescriptions of medicinal substances involving the use of the invention, and
- the utilization, including marketing, of a product containing the patented object which was previously introduced into civil commerce.

Additionally, the Civil Code provides that the Government of the Russian Federation is to have the right, in the interests of national security, to permit the use of an invention, utility model, or industrial design without the consent of the patent holder (Article 1360).[54]

The limitation of the exclusive right is also contained in the provision of the Civil Code on the right of prior use (Article 1361). It entitles to use further the same solution as the patented

52 Thus, patent protection in Russian law is also extended to equivalent elements.

53 In this case the patent holder must be notified as soon as possible and the proportionate compensation paid to him.

54 Also, in this case the patent holder must be notified as soon as possible and the proportionate compensation paid to him.

invention, utility models, or industrial design without expanding the volume of such use, if it has been created independently of the author and its use before the priority date in Russia has been in good faith. The right of prior use may be transferred to another person only together with the enterprise at which the use of the same solution took place or on which the necessary preparations had been made.

The patent law exclusive right is additionally, in accordance with the Civil Code, subject to interference in the provisions on compulsory license (Article 1362). This concerns the case where an invention or industrial design is not used or is used insufficiently by the patent holder during the course of four years from date of the issuance of a patent (for a utility model, during the course of three years from the date of issuance of the patent) leading to insufficient offering of the respective goods, work, or services on the market. In such a case, any person wishing and prepared to use such invention, utility model, or industrial design is to have the right to apply to court with a suit against the patent holder for the granting of a compulsory simple (nonexclusive) license for a parallel use, for which the current compensation is to be paid. Also by judicial procedure, the effect of a compulsory license may be terminated if its conditions are expired. The granting of a compulsory license may also be demanded by the holder of another patent if he cannot use the invention to which he has the exclusive right without infringing thereby the rights of the owner of the first patent to an invention or utility model—in particular, if his invention shows that it is an important technical achievement and has a significant economic advantage over the invention or utility model of the owner of the first patent.[55] A right obtained under the license to use the invention protected by the first patent may not be transferred to other persons except in case of alienation of the second patent. (Article 1362.2)[56]

According to Article 1363 of the Civil Code, the time period of validity of the exclusive right to an invention, utility model, or industrial design and of the patent certifying this right is to be calculated from the filing date of the original application for the issuance of a patent upon the condition of observance of the requirements established by the law, and it is to constitute 20 years for inventions, 10 years for utility models, and 15 years for industrial designs. Protection of the exclusive right certified by a patent may be realized only after state registration of the invention, utility model, or industrial design and issuance of the patent to it. In case of an invention relating to a drug, a pesticide, or an agrochemical, for the use of which a special permission is required by the law, and the receipt of this permission has lasted for more than five years, the time period of validity of the exclusive right to the corresponding invention and of the patent certifying this right is to be extended on request by the patent holder. However, the time period of validity of the exclusive right to the corresponding invention and of the patent certifying this right is to be extended on request by the patent holder for not more than for five years. Also the time period of validity of the exclusive right to a utility model and the patent certifying this right may be extended for not more than three years, and of the exclusive right to an industrial design and of the patent certifying this right for not more than ten years (Article 1363.3). Upon the expiration of the time period of validity of the exclusive right, an invention, a utility model, or an industrial design is to pass, according to the Civil Code (Article 1364), into the public domain. The exclusive right also ceases when a patent expires or is held invalid (Articles 1363.5, 1398, and 1399).

Where an invention, utility model, or industrial design is made by the joint creative labor of two or more persons, they obtain, according to Article 1348 of the Civil Code, coauthorship. Each

55 In the event such a compulsory license is granted, the first patent holder also has the right to receive a simple (nonexclusive) license for the use of the invention depended on his patent.

56 Compulsory license is subject to state registration with Rospatent.

of the coauthors is to have the right to use the invention, utility model, or industrial design at his discretion, unless agreed otherwise (Article 1348.2). Income from the use of it is to be distributed among the coauthors, unless agreed otherwise (Article 1229.3 and 1348.3). These rules also applies to joint patent holders (Article 1358.4). The coauthors also dispose jointly of the exclusive right to an invention, utility model, or industrial design, unless the Civil Code requires otherwise (Article 1348.3). The disposition of the right to receipt of a patent is also to be conducted by the authors jointly. However, for the protection of his rights to the invention, utility model, or industrial design, each of the coauthors is to have the right to take measures independently (Article 1348.4).

According to Article 1370 of the Civil Code, an invention, utility model, or industrial design created by an employee in connection with the performance of his employment obligations or of a concrete task from the employer is to be recognized correspondingly as an employment invention, employment utility model, or employment industrial design, and the right of authorship to it is to belong to the author or the employee (Article 1370.2). By contrast, the exclusive right and the right to receipt of a patent are to belong to the employer unless the labor or other contract between the employee and the employer provides otherwise (Article 1370.3). In the absence of such an agreement, the employee must notify the employer in writing of the creation in connection with the performance of his employment obligations or of a concrete task from the employer of such a result with respect to which legal protection is possible. If the employer within four months from the day of the notification does not submit an application for the issuance of a patent or transfer the right to receipt of a patent to another person, or inform the employee that the information on the corresponding result of intellectual activity is to be kept secret, the right to receipt of a patent is to transfer to the employee. Irrespective of this, the employer during the time period of validity of the patent is to have the right to use the employment invention, employment utility model, or employment industrial design in his own production on the conditions of a simple (nonexclusive) license with payment to the patent holder of compensation. Moreover, in the event the employer receives a patent for an employment invention, employment utility model, or employment industrial design, or takes a decision to keep information on it secret and communicates this to the employee or transfers the right to receipt of a patent to another person or does not receive a patent on an application filed by him due to circumstances for which he is responsible, the employee is to have the right to remuneration. (Article 1370.4)

By contrast, an invention, utility model, or industrial design created by an employee with the use of financial, technical, or other material resources of the employer, but not in connection with the performance of his employment obligations or of a concrete task from the employer, is not regarded, according to the Civil Code (Article 1370.5), as an employment invention, utility model, or industrial design. The right to receipt of a patent and the exclusive right to such invention, utility model, or industrial design is to belong to the employee. However, in this case, the employer is to have the right at his option to demand a simple (nonexclusive) license for the use of the created result of intellectual activity for his own needs for the whole time period of validity of the exclusive right or compensation for the expenditures borne by him in connection with the creation of such invention, utility model, or industrial design.

An invention, utility model, or industrial design may be created in the performance of a work contract or a contract for performance of scientific research, experimental design, or technological work[57] which does not directly envision its creation. In such a case, the right to receipt of a patent and the exclusive right is to belong, under the Civil Code (Article 1371), to the contractor (the performer) unless the contract between him and the customer provides

57 These are regulated by rules in the Part II of the Civil Code (Articles 769–78).

otherwise. However, the customer is to have the right, unless otherwise provided by the contract, to use the invention, utility model, or industrial design created in such manner for the purposes for the achievement of which the corresponding contract was concluded on the conditions of a simple (nonexclusive) license during the course of the whole time period of validity of the patent without payment of supplementary compensation for this use. The customer is to retain this right even in the case the contractor transfers his right to receipt of the patent or alienates the patent itself to another person.

Where the right to receipt of a patent or an exclusive right to an invention, utility model, or industrial design has been transferred, in accordance with a contract between a contractor and a customer, to the customer or to a third person designated by him, the contractor is to have the right to use the created invention, utility model, or industrial design for his own needs on the conditions of an uncompensated simple (nonexclusive) license during the course of the whole period of validity of the patent unless otherwise provided by the contract (Article 1371.2).

The Civil Code also contains the provisions concerning an industrial design made on order (Article 1372). Otherwise than in the previous case, the original right to receipt of a patent and the exclusive right to such an industrial design are to belong to the customer, unless the contract between the contractor (performer) and the customer provides otherwise. Nevertheless, the contractor (the performer) is to keep the right, to the extent that the contract does not provide otherwise, to use such industrial model for its own needs on the conditions of an uncompensated simple (nonexclusive) license during the whole time period of validity of the patent. However, if the right to receipt of a patent and the exclusive right to an industrial design belong under the contract to the contractor (the performer), the corresponding right to use belongs to the customer.

The Civil Code also contains the provisions (Article 1373) which concern an invention, utility model, or industrial design created in performance of work under a state or municipal contract for state or municipal needs or public contract. The right to receipt of a patent and the exclusive right are to belong in such a case to the organization performing the state or municipal contract (the performer) unless the state or municipal contract provides otherwise. According to the public contract, the rights may belong to the Russian Federation or the subject of the Russian Federation (the state contract) or to the municipal formation (municipal contract). In such cases the public customer—who is the counterparty of the performer in a public contract—is acting in their name.[58] The right to receipt of a patent and the exclusive right may belong jointly to the performer and public formation. However, the right of a public formation to receipt of a patent may become transferred to the performer if the public customer does not file an application for the issuance of a patent in the course of six months from the day of the written notification by the performer of the receipt of a patentable result of intellectual activity (Article 1373.2). A patent holder who is not the Russia Federation or the subject of this or a municipal formation may be, however, obligated to grant to the person indicated by the public customer an uncompensated simple (nonexclusive) license (Article 1373.4).[59] In turn, in the case of a joint patent the public customer is to have the right to grant a compensated simple (nonexclusive) license for the use of a patented invention, utility model, or industrial design for the purpose of performing work or conducting supply of products for state or municipal needs after having notified the performer of this (Article 1374.5).

58 In such a case the performer (contractor) is obligated to ensure that all rights are transferred to the public customer, and the performer has the right to compensation for the expenditures caused by it (Article 1373.3).

59 In which case both the patent holder and the person indicated by the public customer has the right to use the patented object.

Additionally, it is provided in the Civil Code that, if a performer who has received a patent takes a decision for the early termination of the validity of the patent, he is to be obligated to notify the public customer of this and on its demand to transfer the patent on an uncompensated basis to the Russian Federation, subject of the Russian Federation, or municipal formation (Article 1374.6). A similar obligation is established for the public customer in the event the validity of its patent is terminated.

In all cases concerning inventions, utility models, or industrial designs created under contract, the author of an invention, utility model, or industrial design, if he is not the patent holder, is to be paid, according to the Civil Code, remuneration (Articles 1370.4, 1371.3, 1372.4, and 1373.7).

Patenting rules[60] A patent or an official document certifying the exclusive right to an invention, utility model, or industrial design is to be applied for, in accordance with the Civil Code (Article 1374), by a person holding the right to receipt of a patent or by the author, employer, or legal successor. An application for granting a patent is to be filed with Rospatent or through a patent agent registered with Rospatent. The applicant for a patent, if he is a physical person permanently residing abroad or a foreign juristic person, is to conduct proceedings with Rospatent, unless a treaty of the Russian Federation provides otherwise, through patent agents registered with it. (Article 1247)

An application for granting a patent filed with Rospatent[61] must contain:

- a request
- for the grant of a patent with an indication of the name of the author and of the person in whose name the patent is sought and also of the place of residence or place of location of each of them;
- a description of the patent object in a verbal form, and
- necessary appendices.

In cases of invention and utility model, the application for granting a patent must include:

- claims for the invention or utility model, which expresses its essence and which is fully based on its description as well as
- an abstract.

The application for granting a patent for an industrial design, in turn, must be appended by:

- a set of depictions of the manufacture giving a full, detailed representation of the external form of the manufacture.[62] (Articles 1375–7)

In accordance with Article 1378 of the Civil Code, the patent application may be corrected and clarified, including by way of submission of supplementary materials, until the taking of a

60 For more on this subject, see Gavrilov, Gorodov, Grishaev et al. 2007: 398–416.

61 According to the principle of unity of the industrial property object enforced by the Civil Code (Articles 1375.1, 1376.1, and 1377.1), the patent application must relate to one object or to a group of objects connected with one another to the extent that they form a unified idea.

62 The description of the invention and utility model must be sufficiently thorough to permit its realization. Furthermore, it is to follow the international patent classification (IPC) established by the Strasbourg Agreement 1971. In the case of industrial design, the description is to follow, in turn, the international industrial design classification (ICID) provided by the Locarno Agreement 1968.

decision on the issuance of a patent or on the refusal of it, on the condition that these corrections and clarifications do not change the nature of the invention, utility model, or industrial design at issue. In turn, changes in the documents of an application of information on the applicant and also corrections of obvious and technical mistakes may be made before the registration of the invention, utility model, or industrial design. The Civil Code also provides the possibility to transform an application for an invention into an application for a utility model and vice versa (Article 1379).

According to Article 1381 of the Civil Code, the priority of an invention, utility model, or industrial design is to be established by the date of filing of an application for granting a patent. In the case of the transformation of an application for an invention into an application for a utility model or vice versa, the priority may be established by the date of receipt of the initial application (Article 1379.3).

As a general rule, the exclusive right is to be granted only to one invention, utility model, or industrial design. In the case where different persons have filed applications for identical inventions, utility models, or industrial designs, and their applications have one and the same priority date, the Civil Code contains special provisions (Article 1383). The patent is to be granted in such a case on the application of the person determined by agreement among the applicants, and the patent is to cover the identical inventions, utility models, or industrial designs presented in the other applications. Only one application is also to be accepted in the case where the same person has filed several applications, one of which concerns the invention and the other the utility models, and on one of which applications the patent is issued. In such a case, the issuance of a patent on the other application is only to be possible on the condition of the termination of the effect of the earlier issued patent. (Article 1383.2)

The priority of an invention, utility model, or industrial design may be established, under the Civil Code (Article 1382), also as of the date of the first application for the invention, utility model, or industrial design in the other state which is a participant in the Paris Convention for the Protection of Industrial Property (Convention priority), on the condition of the filing with Rospatent of an application for an invention or a utility model in the course of 12 months from the aforementioned date and an application for an industrial design in the course of six months from the aforementioned date.[63]

According to the Civil Code all patent applications are subject to a formal examination (Articles 1384, 1390.1, and 1391.1). Its purpose is to verify the presence of the necessary documents and their correspondence to the established requirements. In respect of an invention and industrial design the applicant is to be notified of a positive result of formal examination and of the filing date of the application or priority date immediately after the completion of the formal examination. If an application does not meet the established documentary requirements, Rospatent is to send the applicant an inquiry with a proposal to present corrected or missing documents within two months of the date of the receipt by him of the request.[64]

The information on the application for an invention which has undergone formal examination with a positive result is to be published in the official gazette upon the expiration, and on petition of an applicant before the expiration, of 18 months from the day of submission of an application. This information is to be publicly accessible (Article 1385).

On petition of the applicant or of third parties, the substantive examination of the application for an invention is to be conducted during the course of three years; otherwise the application is to be considered withdrawn (Article 1386). As to an industrial design, though a substantive examination

63 This term may be extended, but for no longer than two months.

64 This term may be prolonged by the Russian Government by ten months.

of it ought to be conducted, the information on the application for it is not to be published and the information on the industrial design is not to become publicly accessible until the patent is granted. In turn, in the case of a utility model, the substantive examination is to not be conducted and the information on it not to be published, since for a patent for a utility model to be granted a formal examination is sufficient, in which, however, it must be established whether the decision applied for relates to the technical decisions capable of protection as a utility model[65]. (Articles 1390–91)

Substantive examination of application for invention[66] concerns, according to the Civil Code (Article 1386), its novelty, inventivity, and industrial applicability. Substantive examination of an application for industrial design, in turn, is conducted to verify its novelty and originality (Article 1391).[67] In conducting research, filed by the petition of the applicant and third persons in order to determine the level of technology in comparison with which the evaluation of the novelty and inventive criteria of the invention applied for will be conducted, national and international information sources are to be used. Upon the request of Rospatent, the applicant must present supplementary materials (including amended claims for the invention) without which the conduct of expert examination would be impossible. In this case supplementary materials that nonetheless do not change the essence of the invention must be presented within the course of two months, otherwise the application is to be considered withdrawn (Article 1386.5); this rule is also applied to the conduct of the examination of an application for an industrial design (Article 1391.2). According to Article 1392 of the Civil Code, an invention for which an application has been properly filed is to be granted temporary legal protection, but is to be considered as expired in the event the patent is not granted.

The decision on the granting the patent or refusal of the patent application is to be conducted on the basis of the substantive examination in the case of inventions and industrial designs and merely on the basis of formal examination in the case of utility models. According to Article 1394 of the Civil Code, Rospatent is to publish in the official gazette information on the issuance of a patent, after which any person is to have the right to become acquainted with the documents of the application and the report on the information search. On the basis of a decision on issuance of a patent *Rospatent* is to enter the invention, utility model, or industrial design into the corresponding state register[68] and is to issue a patent for it. State registration is to be conducted and the patent is to be issued on the condition of payment of the corresponding patent fee (Article 1393). A decision of Rospatent on the issuance of a patent or on refusal of this, or on recognition of an application for an invention, utility model, or industrial design as withdrawn, may be contested by the applicant by submitting an objection with the Patent Dispute Chamber of Rospatent, and the decision of this may be appealed to a court (Articles 1387.3, 1390.1, and 1391.2).

A patent for an invention, utility model, or industrial design may be recognized, during the course of its time period of validity upon the demand of a third person, as invalid in whole or in part. As the grounds for its invalidity the Civil Code (Article 1398) indicates:

- failure to correspond to the conditions of patentability;
- presence in the claims for the invention or utility model or in the list of essential characteristics of an industrial design which are contained in the decision on issuance of the patent of characteristics which were absent in the patent application, and

65 Thus, the utility model patent does not guarantee its validity. The validity may be ensured by a novelty examination which may be applied for by the applicant.

For more on this subject, see Gavrilov, Gorodov, Grishaev et al. 2007: 446–52.

66 For more on this subject, see Gavrilov, Gorodov, Grishaev et al. 2007: 434–40.

67 For more on this subject, see Gavrilov, Gorodov, Grishaev et al. 2007: 452–5.

68 In which compulsory licenses are also registered.

- issuance of a patent in the presence of several applications for identical inventions, utility models, or industrial designs having one and the same priority date without an agreement among the applicants.

These demands are to be considered by the Chamber for patent disputes. Furthermore, also issuance of a patent with an indication in it as the author or patent holder of a person who is not such is indicated as a ground for invalidity of a patent, and in this case the invalidity claim are to be considered by a court.[69]

A patent may also be applied for, according to the Civil Code (Article 1395), abroad.[70] An application for the issuance of a patent for an invention or utility model created in Russia may be filed with a foreign state or with an international organization upon the expiration of six months from the day of filing of the corresponding application with Rospatent, unless the applicant has been informed that his application contains information constituting a state secret.[71] Since Russia is a member of the Patent Cooperation Treaty, an international patent application may be filed, in accordance with the Civil Code (Article 1396), with Rospatent, if Russia is indicated in it as a state in which the applicant intended to receive a patent.[72] Rospatent is to commence consideration of an international application upon the expiration of the thirty-first month from the day of the priority requested in the international application, though on request of the applicant the international application is be considered before that.

Patenting of an invention or utility model may also occur, according to the Civil Code (Article 1395.2), by applying for a Eurasian patent, under the terms of the Eurasian Patent Convention to which CIS countries, excluding Ukraine and Georgia,[73] are signatories. A patent application may be filed through the national patent office or with the Eurasian Patent Office, and the patent is applied for through a single application. The Civil Code (Article 1397) contains the rules on resolving collisions between the Eurasian and Russian patents. In the case where a Eurasian patent and a patent of the Russian Federation to identical inventions, or an identical invention and utility model, and having one and the same priority date, belong to different patent holders, they may be used only with the observance of the rights of all their patent holders. However, if the patents belong to one and the same person, then this person may grant any person the right of use under license contracts concluded on the basis of these patents (Article 1397.2).

In accordance with Article 1399 of the Civil Code, the validity of a patent for an invention, utility model, or industrial design may be terminated on the basis of a request filed by the patent holder. Furthermore, for maintaining a patent the patent holder must pay the patent fee, and failure to do so may cause the termination of the patent. However, the validity of a patent may be reinstated on petition of the person to whom the patent belonged, and the petition may be filed during the course of three years from the day of expiration of the time period for payment of the patent fee but before the expiration of the time period of validity of a patent. A person who, in the period between the

69 License contracts concluded on the ground of a patent later recognized as invalid are to be, however, valid to the extent that they were performed before the invalidity decision (Article 1398.4).

70 For more on this subject, see Gavrilov, Gorodov, Grishaev et al. 2007: 463–73.

71 The patent applicant may request a verification of the presence in his patent application of information constituting a state secret, in which case the application may be filed earlier.

72 In the event the international patent application is filed directly with the international patent organization in which the preliminary examination is to be performed, it is regarded as properly filed in the state which is indicated in the patent application as the patent application state.

73 The signatories to the Eurasian Patent Convention are Armenia, Azerbaijan, Belarus, Kazakhstan, Kyrgyzstan, Moldova, Tajikistan, Turkmenistan, and Uzbekistan.

date of termination of the validity of the patent and the date of publication in the official gazette of Rospatent of information on the reinstatement of the patent, began use of the invention, utility model or industrial design, or made the preparations necessary for this, is to keep the right (of later use) to its further uncompensated use, though without broadening the scope of its use. (Article 1400)

According to Article 1406 of the Civil Code, disputes connected with the protection of patent rights are to be considered by a court.[74] Such disputes include in particular, disputes:

- on the authorship of an invention, utility model, or industrial design;
- on establishing the patent holder;
- on infringement of the exclusive right;
- on the conclusion, performance, amendment, and termination of contracts for the transfer of an exclusive right (or alienation of a patent) and license contracts for the use of an invention, utility model, or industrial design;
- on the right of prior use, and
- on the right of later use as well as
- on the amount, time period, and procedure for payment of the patent law remunerations and compensations.

Furthermore, the Civil Code (Article 1406.2) provides that the protection of patent rights related to patent decisions (Articles 1387, 1390, and 1391) and patent invalidity (Article 1398), presented above, are to be conducted by administrative procedure.

Rights to Means of Individualization[75]

Trademark law As a trademark (service mark) is regarded, in accordance with the Civil Code (Article 1477), an indication serving the individualization of goods, performed works, or provided services of juristic persons or individual entrepreneurs. An exclusive right to a trademark is to be recognized, and the holder of it may be a juristic person or an individual entrepreneur (Article 1478). The exclusive right to a trademark is to be effective on the territory of the Russian Federation on the condition that it is registered by Rospatent in the State Register of Trademarks, and also in other cases provided by an international treaty of the Russian Federation (Article 1479 and 1480).

According to Article 1482 of the Civil Code, registered by Rospatent as trademarks may be verbal, pictorial, three-dimensional, and other indications or their combinations. A trademark may be registered in any color or color combination. For a registered trademark a trademark certificate is to be issued and this is to certify the priority of the trademark and the exclusive right to the trademark with respect to the goods indicated in the certificate (Article 1481).

State registration as trademarks is not to be allowed, according to Article 1483 of the Civil Code, for indications not having the capability of distinguishing, or consisting only of, elements:

- which have gone into general use for indication of goods of the specific type;
- which are generally accepted symbols and terms;
- which characterize goods,[76]

74 For more on this subject, see Gavrilov, Gorodov, Grishaev et al. 2007: 500–505.

75 For more on this subject, see Sergeev 3 2009: 285–332.

76 Including indicating their type, quality, quantity, nature, purpose, or value and also the time, place, or means of their production or sale.

- or consisting of the form of goods that is determined exclusively or mainly by the nature or purpose of the goods.

These elements may be, however, included in the trademark as unprotected elements if they do not occupy a dominant position in it.

Furthermore, state registration as trademarks are to not be allowed, in accordance with an international treaty, for indications consisting only of elements which are:

- state coats of arms, flags, or other state symbols and marks;
- abbreviated or full indications of international and intergovernmental organizations, their coats of arms, flags, or other symbols and marks;
- official verification, guaranty, or sample seals, stamps, awards, and other marks of quality, as well as
- indications similar to the point of confusion with the above-indicated elements.

However, such elements may be included in a trademark as unprotected elements in a trademark if there is consent by the corresponding competent authority. (Article 1483.2)

Moreover, state registration as trademarks is not allowed for indications that are or contain elements which are:

- false or capable of leading a consumer into deception concerning goods or their producer, or
- contradictory to societal interests, or to principles of humanity or morality (Article 1483.3).

Furthermore valuable objects of Russian and world cultural heritage (Article 1483.4) and, among others, foreign brands of wine and alcoholic beverage are also protected (Article 1483.5). The registration restrictions are also extended, without the consent of the rightholder, to the use of the names of authors of scientific, literary, and artistic works who are well known in Russia as well as to their content. The same concerns also the use of a name and portrait or image of a person well-known in Russia without the consent of this person or his heir (Article 1483.9). A trademark subject to registration are to not also infringe the rights of other persons with respect to goods of the same type and having earlier priority (Article 1483.6).[77]

The rightholder of a registered trademark are to have, according to the Civil Code (Article 1484), the exclusive right to it. This right may be realized for the individualization of the goods, work, or services with respect to which the trademark is registered, in particular by the placement of the trademark on goods, in performance of work or rendering of services and in documentation connected with them. According to Article 1484.3 of the Civil Code, no one has the right to use, without the permission of the rightholder, indications similar to his trademark with respect to the goods for the individualization of which the trademark was registered or goods of the same type, if as the result of such use a likelihood of confusion will arise. For giving notice of his exclusive right to a trademark, the rightholder is to have the right to use the symbol of protection, which is to be placed alongside the trademark and which consists of the Latin letter R or the Latin letter R in a circle (®) or the verbal indication "trademark" or "registered trademark," which symbol indicates that the indication used is a trademark protected on the territory of the Russian Federation (Article 1485).

77 For more on this subject, see Gavrilov, Gorodov, Grishaev et al. 2007: 652–62.

The rightholder may dispose of the exclusive right to his trademark (Article 1484.1). The exclusive right to a trademark may be alienated to the other party by contract. It may concern all the goods or a part of the goods for the individualization of which the trademark is registered. The alienation is to not be, however, allowed if it can be the cause of bringing the consumer into confusion with respect to the goods or their manufacturer (Article 1488). The holder of the exclusive right to a trademark may also grant to the other party the right of use of a trademark under a license contract within the limits determined by the contract (Article 1489). A contract for alienation of the exclusive right to a trademark, a license contract, and also other contracts by which disposition of the exclusive right to a trademark is exercised must be concluded in written form and are subject to state registration with Rospatent under penalty of invalidity (Article 1490).

The application procedure for registration of a trademark and service mark at Rospatent corresponds to the similar rules provided for other industrial property objects, including formal and substantive examination[78] and priority rules[79].[80] An application for a trademark must indicate the goods (services) with respect to which state registration is requested and these are to be grouped according to the classes of the International Classification of Goods and Services for the Purposes of Registration of Marks.[81] On the registered trademark, Rospatent is to issue a trademark certificate which certifies the priority of the trademark and the exclusive right to use it in the goods with respect to which the trademark has been registered and the certificate is issued (Article 1481). Information relating to state registration is to be published by Rospatent in its official gazette. (Articles 1492–507)

In the course of conduct of the examination of a indication applied for (substantive examination), the correspondence of this to the requirements excluding the registration is to be verified, and the priority of the trademark is to be established. In the verification of novelty, into consideration are to be taken trademarks with respect to similar goods as well as firm names and commercial designations which have been registered in Russia earlier. Furthermore, in verifying novelty, the trademark subjected to registration is to be compared to trademarks protected in Russia in accordance with an international treaty of the Russian Federation (Article 1499). Thus, in Russian trademark law, otherwise than in respect of the patent law objects, the principle of relative novelty is to be applied.

Legal protection, which corresponds with the protection established for trademarks, is extended, according to the Civil Code (Article 1508), to generally known trademarks.[82] As a generally known trademark may be recognized, according to the Civil Code (Article 1508.1), upon request by the decision of Rospatent, a registered trademark, or a non-registered one which is in accordance with an international treaty protected in Russia, or an indication used as a trademark which is not subject to legal protection in Russia. The legal protection of a well-known trademark is to be effective without time limit (Article 1509).

An amalgamation of persons created is to have the right, according to the Civil Code (Articles 1510 and 1511), to register a collective trademark[83] which they are to use in similar goods. The condition for registration is that the creation and activity of the applicant amalgamation does

78 Substantive examination is called in this case examination of the indication applied for as a trademark (the indication applied for).

79 There are also similarities in the provisions concerning the right to contest the registration.

80 For more on this subject, see Gavrilov, Gorodov, Grishaev et al. 2007: 675–96.

81 In accordance with the Nice Classification Agreement (NICE, 1957).

82 For more on this subject, see Gavrilov, Gorodov, Grishaev et al. 2007: 696–701.

83 For more on this subject, see Gavrilov, Gorodov, Grishaev et al. 2007: 701–5.

not contradict the legislation of the state in which it was created. Alongside the collective mark application filed with Rospatent is to be attached a charter containing among other things:

- the name of the applicant amalgamation (the rightholder);
- a list of persons having the right of use of the collective mark, and
- the purpose of its registration, as well as
- a list of the uniform characteristics of quality or other common characteristics of the goods that are to be designated by the collective mark;
- the conditions for its use, and
- provisions on the procedure for supervision of the use of the collective mark.

The right to a collective mark may not be alienated and the object of a license contract (Article 1510.2). The collective mark and a collective mark application may be transformed respectively into a trademark and a trademark application and vice versa (Article 1511).

The exclusive right to a trademark is to be valid, according to the Civil Code (Article 1491), during the course of ten years from the day of filing an application for state registration of it, and may be extended for ten years on the request of the rightholder. However, legal protection of a trademark may be terminated not only as a result of the expiration of the term of its validity, but also early as the result of the uninterrupted nonuse of the trademark without acceptable ground in the course of any three years after its state registration. A request for the early termination may be filed by any person with the Chamber for Patent Disputes of Rospatent (Article 1486). Legal protection of a trademark may also be terminated in other cases, including, in addition to the above-mentioned cases: when the registration of trademark is not allowed according to Article 1483 of the Civil Code; the termination of the activity of the patent holder; abuses of right and unfair competition as well as in the case of the transformation of the trademark into an indication which has gone into general use as the indication of goods of the specific type (Articles 1512 and 1514). In respect of collective marks, termination is also possible in case of the use of the collective mark on goods not possessing the uniform characteristics of their quality or other common characteristics (Article 1511.3).

A decision on the registration of a trademark may be contested and, in accordance with the Civil Code (Article 1512), such a contestation also means appealing against the recognition of the exclusive right as well as the granting of legal protection to it. The registration of the trademark may be contested during the course of the whole time period of validity of the exclusive right to a trademark. This does not, however, concern the granting of legal protection to a trademark which is identical or similar to the point of confusion to trademarks (generally known trademarks and designations of the place of origin) of other persons (Article 1483). Such a decision is to be contested in the course of five years from the date of publication of information on the registration (Article 1512.2). In general, objections against the granting of legal protection to a trademark may be filed by any interested person, and where the legal protection to a trademark has been granted in violation of the requirements of the Paris Convention for the Protection of Industrial Property in one of its member states in the name of an agent or representative of the holder of the exclusive right to the trademark, he is authorized as an interested holder of the exclusive right to file objections against the granting of legal protection to the trademark.[84] An objection to the registration of a trademark is to be filed, in general, with the Chamber for Patent Disputes of Rospatent except for the case where the ground for contest of the registration is an abuse of right or unfair competition (Article 1512.2); in this case an objection is to be filed directly with Rospatent. (Article 1513)

84 The appeal may be filed in the other member state (Article 1513.3).

A designation of place of origin of goods, or an appellation of origin of goods,[85] is subject to legal protection in Russia, and the provisions on it are incorporated in Articles 1516–37 of the Civil Code. They contain the basic provisions in which the designation of place of origin and the validity of the exclusive right to it are defined as well as the rules on state registration of designations of place of origin. There are also provisions on the use of designation of place of origin. The provisions on registration and the granting of exclusive right are detailed in the following rules which concern the application for a designation of place of origin and the examination of it as well as the decision on the application and any contestation of this, the registration procedure and issuance of a certificate and the term of validity, and the rules on publication of information on registration and international registration. Furthermore the provisions of the Civil Code on a designation of place of origin concern legal protection and its termination.

A designation of place of origin of goods is defined in the Civil Code (Article 1516) as an indication which is or contains a modern or historical, official or unofficial, full or abbreviated designation of the country, city, or rural settlement, locality, or other geographic locale and also an indication derived from such a designation or otherwise identifying with the locale, provided it has become known as the result of its use with respect to goods, special characteristics of which are exclusively or mainly determined by natural conditions and/or human factors characteristic for the given geographic locale.

A designation of place of origin of goods, the manufacturers of which may obtain the exclusive right to use it in Russia (Article 1516), are to be registered, on application at Rospatent, in the State Register of Designations after the execution of the formal and substantive (examination of an indication applied for) examination on the results of which a certificate is to be issued. Information relating to registration are to be published by Rospatent in the official gazette (Articles 1518 and 1522–34).[86] For giving notice of his exclusive right to a designation of place of origin, the rightholder may attach the designation with the symbol of protection in the form of the verbal indication "registered designation of place of origin of goods" or "registered DPOG," showing that the indication used is the designation registered in Russia (Article 1520).

A designation of place of origin which is legally protected in a foreign state may also be registered in Russia, and as the holder of the exclusive right to it is to be recognized only the person whose right to the use of the designation is protected in the country of origin of the goods (Article 1517.2). In turn, Russian juristic and physical persons have the right to register a designation of place of origin in foreign states (Article 1534).[87]

Unlike in the case of a trademark, a designation of place of origin may be registered and the exclusive right to use it may be granted to any person[88] who, within the boundaries of the same geographic locale, produces goods having the same special qualities (Article 1518). Thus, the exclusive right to the designation of the place of origin is to not arise to an individual holder, and, consequently, it may not be alienated to another person. Article 1519.4 of the Civil Code expressly provides that disposition of the exclusive right to a designation of place of origin is to not be allowed.

---

85 For more on this subject, see Gavrilov, Gorodov, Grishaev et al. 2007: 714–40.

86 The certificate holder has the right for notification of his exclusive right to place on his goods the symbol "registered designation of place of origin of goods" (Article 1520).

87 In order to register the designation of place of origin abroad a Russian person must register it in Russia first (Article 1534.2).

88 For a physical person to be granted the right to use the designation of place of origin he need not be registered in Russia as an entrepreneur.

The registered designation of the place of origin[89] is to be protected during the whole time of the existence of the possibility of producing the goods, the special qualities of which are exclusively or mainly determined by the natural conditions and/or human factors characteristic for the corresponding geographic locale (Article 1516), though a certificate of an exclusive right to a designation of place of origin is to be valid during the course of ten years. However, the validity term of the certificate may be extended on request of the holder of the certificate for ten years on the condition that the certificate holder further produces, within the boundaries of the corresponding geographic locale, goods possessing the special qualities indicated in the State Register of Designations (Article 1531). However, the legal protection of a designation of place of origin is to be terminated if, for instance, the production of goods possessing the special qualities indicated in the State Register of Appellations has become impossible or a foreign juristic person has lost his right to the given designation of place of origin in the country of origin of the goods (Article 1536).

The registration of the designation of place of origin, as with the trademark, may be contested, according to the Civil Code (Article 1535), during the course of the whole time period of validity of the exclusive right to it, excluding those cases where the use of the designation may confuse consumers with respect the goods and their producer and those connected to a trademark with earlier priority. Such a decision is to be contested within five years of the date of publication of information on the registration.

The Civil Code provides the rules on legal protection of trademarks (Articles 1483 and 1515) and designations of place of origin (Article 1519). As an unlawful use of a trademark, as likewise of a designation of place of origin, or as an infringement of the exclusive right of its holder, is to be regarded in accordance with the Civil Code the unauthorized placement of it or an indication similar to it to the point of confusion on the goods[90] which are or intended to be introduced into commerce on the territory of Russia. This also concerns labels and packaging of goods as well as their marketing, including the use of Internet and commercial documentation (Article 1484). Goods, labels, and packaging of goods on which a trademark or an indication similar to it to the point of confusion are placed unlawfully are considered under Article 1519 of the Civil Code counterfeit. However, as an infringement of the exclusive right are not to be regarded, according to the Civil Code, the use of a trademark by other persons with respect to goods which were introduced into civil commerce on the territory of Russia directly by the rightholder or with his consent (Article 1487).

In addition to the general means of legal protection concerning all objects of intellectual property, including the prohibition by the court of the use and compensation for damages as well as the publication of the decision of a court on the infringement committed in order to restore the reputation of the person suffered from the infringement (Article 1252), the Civil Code (Articles 1515 and 1537) provides means of special protection that are directly applicable to infringements of trademark law. Thus the rightholder is also to have the right to demand removal from commerce and destruction, at the expense of the infringer, of counterfeit goods, labels, and packaging on which there is an unlawfully used trademark or indication similar to it to the point of confusion. Where the introduction of such goods into commerce is necessary in the interests of society, the rightholder is to have the right to demand the removal of the unlawfully used trademark or indication. Furthermore, the Civil Code provides that the rightholder of a trademark as well as of a

89 The legal protection of the designation of place of origin may also be based on international treaty.

90 Also in the provision of work and services.

designation of place of origin is to have the right to demand at his option from the infringer instead of generally provided compensation for damages payment of penal compensation:

- in the amount of 10,000 rubles to 5 million rubles, determined at the discretion of the court proceeding from the nature of the infringement or
- of double the amount of the value of the goods on which the trademark was illegally placed or of double the amount of the value of the rights of the use of the trademark determined proceeding from the price that in comparable circumstances is usually taken for lawful use of the trademark (or designation of place of origin). (Articles 1515.4 and 1537.2)[91]

Firm name and commercial designation According to the Civil Code (Article 1473), a juristic person which is a commercial organization is to act in civil commerce under its firm or trade name, which is defined in its founding documents and is included in the single state register of juristic persons upon state registration of a juristic person. The firm name of a juristic person must contain an indication of its legal form and the actual name of the juristic person, which may not consist solely of words designating the type of activity. A juristic person must have a full name and has the right to have an abbreviated name in the Russian language, and it may also have a full or abbreviated name in a foreign language. The firm name of a juristic person may not include official names with some exceptions nor indications contradictory to societal interests and to principles of humanity and morality, and it must be distinguishable. The registration authorities have the right to compel a change of firm name, if it does not correspond to the established requirements (Article 1473.5).

A registered firm name is subject, according to the Civil Code (Article 1474), to the exclusive right protection in Russia, and the juristic person is to have the right to use its firm name as means of individualization in any manner not contrary to the law (the exclusive right to a firm name) including by its indication on signs, letterheads, bills, and other documentations, in announcements and advertising, and on goods and their packaging. However, disposition of the exclusive right to a firm name (including by its alienation or the granting to another person of the right of use of the firm name) is not allowed (Article 1474.2).

The exclusive right to a firm name is protected in accordance with the Civil Code (Article 1476) as a separate object (independently from the protection of a commercial designation and trademark). In the case of misuse of a firm name, its rightholder may demand that the violator cease the misuse and compensate for damages caused by it (Article 1474.4).

According to Article 1538 of the Civil Code, a juristic person conducting entrepreneurial activity[92] and also an individual entrepreneur may use a commercial indication for individualization of trade, industrial, and other enterprises belonging to them which is not, however, a firm name subjected to obligatory inclusion in the founding documents and registration. A commercial indication may be used by the rightholder for individualization of one or several enterprises. However, two or more commercial indications may not be used simultaneously for the individualization of one enterprise.

The exclusive right to a commercial designation is to belong, according to the Civil Code (Article 1539), to its rightholder who may use it as a means of individualization of an enterprise belonging to him, including by indication of the commercial designation on signs, letterheads, bills,

91 The Civil Code (Articles 1515.5 and 1537.3) also provides liability to a person who produces a warning marking with respect to a trademark or designation of place of origin not registered in Russia.

92 Including noncommercial organizations to which the right to conduct such activity has been granted in accordance with the law by their founding documents.

and other documentation, in announcements and in advertising, and on goods and their packaging, on the condition that such a designation possesses sufficient distinguishing characteristics and its use is known within the boundaries of a specific territory. The exclusive right to a commercial indication may pass to another person (including by contract,[93] by way of universal legal succession, and on other grounds established by the law) only in the composition of an enterprise for the individualization of which such designation is used (Article 1539.4).[94]

According to the Civil Code (Article 1540), the exclusive right to a commercial designation is to be effective on the territory of the Russian Federation, if it is used for individualization of an enterprise located on the territory of Russia. However, the exclusive right is to be terminated if the rightholder does not use his commercial designation continuously in the course of a year.

The exclusive right to a commercial designation is protected in accordance with the Civil Code (Article 1541) as a separate object (independently from the protection of a firm name and trademark). In the case of misuse of a commercial designation, its rightholder may demand from the violater to cease the misuse and compensate for damages caused by it (Article 1474.4).

4 Intellectual Property Contracts

General Rules

The rules on intellectual property contracts are contained into the above-presented general provisions of the fourth part of the Civil Code (Articles 1233–8) as well as the norms on authorship and neighboring rights (Articles 1285–90, 1296–8, and 1307–8), and industrial property rights (Articles 1365–9 and 1488–90). Intellectual property contracts are also regulated by the norms of the Civil Code concerning rights to secret of production (know-how) (Chapter 75) and rights to use the results of the intellectual activity in the system of unified technology[95] (Chapter 77).[96]

In accordance with general intellectual property law provisions the exclusive right may be alienated by contract to another person in whole when the question is of a contract for the alienation of an exclusive right. Also by contract the right to use the object of the intellectual property law may be granted to another person. In this case the question is of a license contract where no transfer of the exclusive right occurs, which is a general presumption in the rules regulating intellectual property contracts.

The term defining the object of a contract is generally considered in Russian civil law an essential condition. The rules of the Civil Code (Article 1235.6) on license contract expressly provide that it must define the object of the contract to which the right to use is granted and the ways of use of

93 The rightholder may grant, according to Article 1539.5 of the Civil Code, the right to use his commercial designation in accordance with the contract of lease of enterprise (Article 656) or commercial concession (Article 1027).

94 Where the commercial designation is used for the individualization of several enterprises, the transfer of it to another person is to entail the loss of the right to use it for the individualization of the remaining enterprise(s) (Article 1539.5).

95 The norms regulating unified technology include the provisions on technology transfer contracts or, to be precise, contracts on the transfer of rights to technology.

96 Intellectual property rights are usually the objects of innovative activities and they are purported to be used in production. In innovative activities, various contracts which merely represent contractual regulation are used.

it. Thus, the terms on object and the ways of its use are regarded as essential conditions, and in the absence of them a contract is to be considered unconcluded.[97]

It is also directly provided in the Civil Code that a contract for the alienation of an exclusive right must be concluded in written form and, in general, subjected to state registration under penalty of its invalidity (Article 1234.2), and a similar rule is provided concerning a license contract (Article 1235.2). In the event the contract is recognized as invalid, the rules of the Civil Code on the restitution order (Article 167) concerning void legal transactions are to be applied. So if a payment has been made under such a contract, the court is to decide on its refund. Additionally, the Civil Code provides that terms of a license contract or a contract of alienation of an exclusive right to intellectual property limiting the right of a person to practice intellectual activity of a defined type or in a defined area or to alienate the exclusive rights to its results,[98] are to be considered invalid (Article 1233.4).[99]

Contract for alienation of exclusive right A contract for the alienation of an exclusive right may be either compensated or uncompensated, and this must be mentioned directly in the contract.[100] In the event a contract for the alienation of an exclusive right is compensated, it must contain the term defining the amount of compensation or the procedure for its determination (Article 1234.3). It is an essential condition, and in the absence of it, the contract is to be considered unconcluded. Hence in this case the general provision on determining a price (in the absence of a corresponding contractual stipulation; Article 424.3) of the Civil Code is not applicable.[101]

In respect of the compensation concerning a contract for the alienation of an exclusive right, the Civil Code additionally provides (Article 1234.5) that if the recipient of the exclusive right substantially breaches his obligation to pay the rightholder within the established time period, it is considered a substantial breach of contract (Article 450.2.1), and in this case the former rightholder is entitled to demand in judicial proceedings the transfer to himself of the rights of the recipient of the exclusive right, as well as a compensation for losses, if the exclusive right has passed to its recipient. In case the exclusive right has not passed to the recipient, the rightholder may unilaterally withdraw from the contract and demand compensation for the losses caused by the dissolution of the contract.[102]

License contract A license contract may also be either compensated or uncompensated, and this must be mentioned directly in the contract.[103] In the event a license contract is compensated, it must

97 In Russian legal practice it is regarded that, if the contract is recognized as unconcluded, then the restitution rules concerning invalid transactions of the Civil Code (Article 167) are not applicable. The only remedy for the party who performed the transaction in such a case is to be the claim for the return of unjust enrichment.

98 Alternatively, the contract may contain the condition by which the rights of the author to conclude license contracts concerning the specified future results of intellectual activity are restricted. See Gavrilov, Gorodov, Grishaev et al. 2007: 28.

99 The question is of absolute invalidity, which must be taken into account, unlike in the case of voidableness, *ex officio*.

100 See Gavrilov, Gorodov, Grishaev et al. 2007: 31.

101 According to Article 424.3 of the Civil Code, in cases where in a compensated contract a price is not stipulated and may not be determined proceeding from the terms of the contract, performance of the contract is to be paid for at the price which is usually paid under comparable conditions for analogous goods, work, or services.

102 It is not necessary for the rightholder to turn to the court in this case. See Gavrilov, Gorodov, Grishaev et al. 2007: 33.

103 See Gavrilov, Gorodov, Grishaev et al. 2007: 31.

contain, as in the case of a contract for the alienation of an exclusive right, the term defining the amount of compensation or the procedure for its determination (Article 1235.5). In this case, too, the question is of an essential condition of the contract in the absence of which the contract is to be considered unconcluded. So, too, in respect of license contracts the general provision on determining a price (in the absence of a corresponding contractual stipulation; Article 424.3) of the Civil Code is not applicable.

Furthermore, in respect of a license contract the Civil Code (Article 1235.4) provides that the time period for which a license contract is concluded may not exceed the time period of validity of the exclusive right to the object. Furthermore, in the absence of the definition of the term for the contract, it is to be regarded as concluded for five years unless otherwise provided by the Civil Code. However, in case of termination of the exclusive right the license contract is also to be terminated. This rule is also applicable to contracts for the alienation of an exclusive right.[104]

According to the general provisions on intellectual property of the Civil Code (Articles 1235–8), the right to use the object may be transferred by:

- simple nonexclusive license, in which case the licensor retains the right of issuance of licenses to other persons,[105] or
- exclusive license, in which he does not have the right to issue licenses to other persons[106] (Article 1236).

The general provisions on intellectual property of the Civil Code also make it possible to use sublicense contracts under which the licensee may (with the written consent of the licensor) grant by contract the right of use to another person (Article 1238). Furthermore, it is directly presumed in the Civil Code that unless otherwise specified in the license contract, the license in question is simple (nonexclusive). On the other hand, the same license contract applying to different uses of the same object may contain different conditions applying to different types of license contract—in other words of both simple and exclusive license contracts.

Under the general provisions of the Civil Code regulating performance of license contract (Article 1237), which firstly concern the licensee, it is determined that, if the license object is used in a way not provided by the license contract, or after the term of validity of the license contract, or is in another way beyond the limits of the rights granted to the licensee under the contract, this is to entail liability for infringement of the exclusive right established by the Civil Code, other laws, or contract (Article 1237.3). The licensee is also obliged to supply the licensor with a report on the course of use of the result of intellectual activity or means of individualization unless otherwise provided by the license contract. If the license contract requiring presentation of reports on the use of the license object does not establish the times and procedure for their presentation, the licensee is obliged to present such reports to the licensor on his demand.

The rules of the Civil Code on performance of license contract (Article 1237) also concern the licensor. Therefore, the licensor is, during the time period of validity of the license contract,

---

104 See, for instance, Gavrilov, Gorodov, Grishaev et al. 2007: 370.

105 This is presumed.

106 In this case the licensee also has the right to resort to other legal remedies which are provided in the Civil Code for the protection of intellectual rights (Article 1250) and exclusive rights in general (Article 1252) as well as to the rule on liability of juristic persons and individual entrepreneurs for the infringement of exclusive rights (Article 1253).

obliged to refrain from any actions capable of hindering the realization by the licensee of the right of use granted to him within the limits established by the contract.[107]

Pledge contract The general provisions on intellectual property contracts also include the rules regulating the case of conclusion of a contract for the pledge of an exclusive right to an object of intellectual property. In this case the pledger has the right to use the object during the period of validity of the contract and to dispose of the exclusive right without the consent of the pledgee, unless otherwise provided by the contract (Article 1233.5).

Application of general civil law rules According to Article 1233.2 of the Civil Code, contracts for the disposition of the exclusive right to intellectual property objects, including contracts for the alienation of the exclusive right and license (or sublicense) contracts, are subject to the application of the general provisions of the Civil Code on obligations (Articles 307–419) and on contract (Articles 420–53), unless otherwise provided by the rules of the Civil Code on intellectual property rights or as follows from the content or nature of the exclusive right at issue.

Among the obligation law norms of the Civil Code applicable to intellectual property contracts are the provisions defining the concept of obligation (Article 307) and the parties thereto (Article 308), as well as the rules regulating the performance of obligation (Articles 309–28) and securing it (Articles 329–81), change of persons in obligation (Articles 382–92), liability for violation of obligations (Article 393–406), and termination of obligations (Articles 407–19).

In turn, the contract law norms of the Civil Code applicable to the intellectual property contracts contain the provisions defining the concept of contract and its conditions (Articles 420–30), including interpretation of contract (Article 431), as well as regulating conclusion of contract (Articles 432–49) and change and rescission of contract (Articles 450–53).

Authorship Law Contracts

Contract for alienation of exclusive right to work The exclusive right to a work may be transferred under Article 1285 of the Civil Code by contract. Under a contract for the alienation of the exclusive right to a work the author or other rightholder transfers or becomes obligated to transfer in full his exclusive right to another person.[108] A contract for the alienation of the exclusive right to a work is subject to the application of the above-presented general provisions of intellectual property law.

Authorship license contracts The authorship law norms of the Civil Code contain the rules which regulate such specific license contracts as a license contract for granting the right to use a work and publication license contract. Otherwise, these contracts are subject to the application of the general provisions regulating intellectual property contracts which are presented above.

Under a license contract for granting the right to use a work regulated by Article 1286 of the Civil Code, one party, the author or other rightholder (the licensor), grants or becomes obligated to grant to the other party (the licensee) the right of use of the work within the limits established by the contract. According to the Civil Code (Article 1235.6), a license contract for granting the right to use a work must define the object of the contract or work the right to use of which is granted

107 On the obligation to maintain secrecy concerning license contract relations, see Sergeev 3 2009: 333–40.

108 However, attention must be paid to the norm of the Civil Code which protects the exclusive right of the author (Article 1284), according to which levy of execution on it is not allowed.

and the ways of its use. The terms on object and the ways of its use are generally considered essential conditions for license contracts, and in the absence of them a contract is to be considered unconcluded.

In general, a license contract must be concluded in written form under penalty of its invalidity, but if a work is intended to be used in a periodical press publication, it may also be concluded in oral form (Article 1286.2). Furthermore, the Civil Code provides for license contracts concerning computer programs and databases the possibility to use the contract of adhesion (Article 428),[109] in which the standard terms of the contract are stated on a copy of such a program or database obtained or on the packaging of such a copy. In these cases the beginning of use of the program or database is regarded as consent to the conclusion of the contract (Article 1286.3).

A compensated license contract for granting the right to use a work must contain the terms on the amount of compensation for the use of the work or the procedure for calculating it (Article 1286.4). In this case, too, the question is of essential conditions in the absence of which a contract is to be considered unconcluded. Compensation may be provided in such a contract as fixed one-time or periodic payments or in the form of interest calculated from income or in another form. The Government of the Russian Federation is empowered to determine minimum rates of compensation for separate types of use of works.

Among the general intellectual property law provisions of the Civil Code regulating license contracts for granting the right to use a work, especially important is the rule according to which if the licensee breaks his obligation to pay to the licensor the compensation for the use of a work within the time established by the contract, the licensor has the right to withdraw from the contract and demand compensation for damages caused by the rescission of the contract (Article 1237.4).

Article 1287 of the Civil Code on publication license contracts contains special rules regulating their basic conditions. The question is of a contract concluded between the author or other rightholder with a publisher or a person who has undertaken the obligation to publish the work. In order to be concluded, a publication license contract, like any other license contract, must define the object of the contract or work the right to use of which is granted and the ways of its use (Article 1235.6).

Under a publication license contract the publisher or licensee is obligated to begin the use of the work within the time indicated in the contract. In default of this the licensor has the right to withdraw from the contract without duty to pay compensation to the licensee of the damages caused by it or to rescind the contract. Where the concrete time for the beginning of the use of the work is not defined in the contract, the use of the work must begin within the time usual for the given type of works and the way of their use. In default of this, the licensor has the right to rescind the contract in accordance with Article 450 of the Civil Code.[110] In both cases of rescission of a publication license contract the licensor is to keep the right to demand payment of the compensation provided by the contract in the full amount (Article 1287.2).

Publication license contracts are also subject to the application of the general intellectual property provision authorizing the licensor to withdraw from the contract and demand compensation for damages caused by the rescission of the contract, in the event the licensee has broken his obligation

109 Contract of adhesion stands in Russian law for a contract the terms of which are determined by one of the parties in printed forms or other standard forms and which may be adopted by the other party only by adhering to the proposed contract as a whole (Article 428.1).

110 This case is subject to application of Article 450.3 of the Civil Code, under which in case of unilateral refusal to perform a contract in whole or in part, when such a refusal is allowed by the law or agreement of the parties, the contract is to be considered respectively changed or canceled. See Gavrilov, Gorodov, Grishaev et al. 2007: 218.

to pay to the licensor the compensation for the use of a work within the time established by the contract (Article 1237.4).

Authorship contract Under an authorship contract, the provisions on which are contained in the Civil Code, the author is obligated on the order of the customer to create the work of science, literature, or art provided by the contract on a material carrier or in another form (Article 1288). The original or material carrier of the work is to be transferred to the ownership of the customer unless the agreement provides for its transfer to the customer for temporary use. Authorship contract is considered compensated, unless otherwise provided by it.

An authorship contract may provide that the exclusive right to a created work is to be alienated to the customer in which case the norms of the Civil Code regulating contracts for the alienation of an exclusive right is to be applied (Articles 1234 and 1285). However, the agreement may merely concern granting the right to use of the work within the limits established by it and in this case it is subject to the application of the norms regulating license contracts (Articles 1235–7 and 1286 and 1287). (Article 1288.2)

According to the provisions of the Civil Code on the term for performance of an authorship contract (Article 1289), a work provided for by the contract must be transferred to the customer within the time established by it. In the absence of the condition on the term for performance a contract is to be considered unconcluded. In the event of acceptable grounds, a supplementary grace term for the performance may be granted. If upon expiration of this, the work is not transferred to the customer, he is to have the right to rescind the agreement. The customer is also allowed to use his rescission right instantly after the end of the term for the performance, if its importance is evident from the contract.

Liability under contracts concluded by authors According to Article 1290 of the Civil Code, the liability of the author under a contract for the alienation of an exclusive right and license contract is limited to the compensation of real damages, unless the contract provides for a lower amount of liability of the author. Where the author is in breach of his contract obligations, he is obligated to return to the customer an advance, and also to pay him liquidated damages provided by the contract. However, the overall amount of these payments is limited to the amount of the actual harm caused to the customer.

Contracts on Neighboring Rights

Contracts for the alienation of an exclusive right and license contracts are recognized in the provisions of the Civil Code regulating neighboring rights. According to its Article 1307, under a contract for alienation of the exclusive right to an object of neighboring rights, one contracting party—the performer, the producer of the phonogram, the organization of over-the-air or cable broadcasting, the manufacturer of the database, the first publisher of a scientific, literary and artistic work, or other rightholder—transfers or is obligated to transfer his exclusive right in full to the other party or the recipient of the exclusive right. In turn, under a license contract, one contracting party—the performer, the producer of the phonogram, the organization of over-the-air or cable broadcasting, the manufacturer of the database, the first publisher of a scientific, literary and artistic work, or other rightholder—who is the licensor grants or is obligated to grant to the other party, or the licensee, the right of use of the object of neighboring rights within the limits established by the contract (Article 1308). Contracts on neighboring rights are otherwise subject to the application of the general intellectual property provisions of the Civil Code regulating contracts for the alienation of an exclusive right (Article 1234) and correspondingly license contracts (Article 1235–8).

Industrial Property Contracts[111]

Patent law contracts The patent law norms of the Civil Code contain the provisions regulating contracts for the alienation of an exclusive right to an invention, utility models, or industrial design, contracts for alienation of the right to receipt of a patent, and license contracts. The Civil Code directly provides that a contract for the alienation of an exclusive right or a patent, license contract, and also other contracts under which the exclusive right to an invention, utility model, or industrial design are to be disposed must be concluded in written form and registered with the federal service for intellectual property, patent, and trademarks, or Rospatent, under penalty of its invalidity (Article 1369).

A contract for the alienation of the right to receipt of a patent must also be concluded, according to the Civil Code (Article 1357.3), in written form under penalty of its invalidity. Furthermore, in respect of contracts for the alienation of the right to receipt of a patent the Civil Code provides that, unless otherwise agreed by the parties, the risk of nonpatentability of an invention, utility model, or industrial design are to be borne by the recipient of the right to receipt of a patent (Article 1357.4).

Under a contract for the alienation of a patent or the exclusive right to an invention, utility models, or industrial design one party, who is the patent owner, transfers or is obligated to transfer, according to the Civil Code (Article 1365), his exclusive right in whole to the other party, or the recipient of the exclusive right (the recipient of the patent).[112] The author of an invention may attach to his patent application, as stated above, a declaration to the effect that in the case of issuance of a patent he is to be obligated to conclude a contract for the alienation of the patent, on conditions corresponding to established practice, with any Russian physical or juristic person who has first declared such a desire to Rospatent. Such a condition is effective within the course of two years from the day of publication of information on the issuance of a patent. After the expiration of this period the patent holder may apply for the withdrawal of his declaration (Article 1366).

The object of a patent alienation contract is the exclusive right to an invention, utility model, or industrial design which is certified by the patent. The extend of the rights certified by the patent is determined in the case of an invention and utility models by the claim for it, and in the case of an industrial design, in accordance with the list of essential characteristics. The term on the object of a patent alienation contract is considered an essential condition, in the absence of which a contract is to be considered unconcluded.[113]

According to the Civil Code (Article 1367), under a license contract granting the right to use an invention, utility model, or industrial design, the patent holder (the licensor) grants or is obligated to grant to the licensee the right of use of an invention, utility model, or industrial design certified by the patent within the limits established by the contract. The patent holder may, as stated above,

111 For more on industrial property contracts, see O.A. Gorodov, Правовая инноватика (правовое регулирование инновационной деятельности [Legal Innovatics (Legal Regulation of Innovation Activities] (2008): 328–53.

112 After the alienation of his exclusive right the patent holder loses all the right to use the aliened object. See Stepanov 2010: 1296; Sergeev 3 2009: 270, and Gorodov 2008: 330.

113 See Gavrilov, Gorodov, Grishaev et al. 2007: 369; and Gorodov (2008): 330. A patent alienation contract is subject to application of the general rules concerning intellectual property law contracts presented above.

attach to his patent application a declaration on an open license or that he is ready to grant the rights of use of an invention, utility model, or industrial design to any person (Article 1368).

As stated above, a license contract must define, according to the Civil Code (Article 1235.6), the object of the contract or the invention, utility model, or industrial design and the ways of its use. These terms are considered for license contracts essential conditions, and in the absence of them a contract is to be considered unconcluded. Furthermore, in the event a license contract is compensated, it must contain the term defining the amount of compensation or the procedure for its determination (Article 1235.5); otherwise the contract is to be considered unconcluded.[114]

Moreover, a license contract must also define, according to the Civil Code (Article 1235.3), the territory upon which the use of the exclusive right is permitted. In the absence of this term, the licensee has the right to use the object on the whole territory of the Russian Federation.[115]

Trademark law contracts The trademark law norms of the Civil Code contain the provisions regulating contracts for the alienation of an exclusive right to a trademark and license contracts concerning the granting of the right to use a trademark. The Civil Code directly provides that a contract for alienation of the exclusive right to a trademark, a license contract, and also other contracts under which the exclusive right to a trademark are to be disposed must be concluded in written form and registered with Rospatent under penalty of its invalidity (Article 1490).[116]

Under a contract for alienation of the exclusive right to a trademark, the rightholder transfers or undertakes to transfer in full scope his exclusive right to the trademark in respect of all or a part of the goods for the individualization of which it is registered to the recipient of the exclusive right (Article 1488). In the event a trademark the exclusive right to which is alienated by the contract includes a designation of the place of origin which, although not covered by the trademark law protection, is, however, protected as such in Russia, the recipient must obtain the exclusive right to use this designation of place of origin (Article 1483.7 and 1488.3).[117] Furthermore, the Civil Code explicitly provides the prohibition of alienation of the exclusive right to a trademark, if this may mislead consumers with respect to the goods or their manufacturer (Article 1488.2).

The object of a trademark alienation contract is the exclusive right to a trademark which is certified by the trademark certificate, and this right must be alienated in whole. The term on the object is considered for trademark alienation contracts essential conditions in the absence of which a contract is to be considered unconcluded.

Under a license contract for granting the right to use a trademark, one party, who is the holder of the exclusive right to it (the licensor), grants or undertakes to grant to the other party (the licensee) the right of use of a trademark within the limits determined by the contract with an indication of the territory on which the use is permitted with respect to the defined domain of entrepreneurial activity or without such an indication (Article 1489).

As stated above, a license contract must define, according to the Civil Code (Article 1235.6), the object of the contract or the trademark the right to use of which is granted by the contract, and the ways of its use. These terms are considered for license contracts essential conditions, and in the absence of them a contract is to be considered unconcluded. Furthermore, in the event a

114 The question is of the essential conditions of the contract.

115 Patent license contract is subject to application of the general rules concerning intellectual property law contracts presented above.

116 Trademark contracts are subject to not only special but also the general rules on intellectual property contracts presented above.

117 The object of the trademark and the designation of place of origin must be the same goods in such a case (Article 1483.7).

license contract is compensated, it must contain the term defining the amount of compensation or the procedure for its determination (Article 1235.5); otherwise the contract is to be considered unconcluded.

According to Article 1489.2 of the Civil Code, the licensee is obligated to ensure the correspondence of the quality of goods produced or sold by him on which he places the licensed trademark to the requirements for quality established by the licensor, and the licensor has the right to supervise the observance of this condition. On claims against the licensee as the manufacturer of the goods, the licensee and the licensor are to bear joint and several liability.

In the event the object of a license contract is a trademark which includes a designation of place of origin which, although not covered by the trademark law protection, is, however, protected as such in Russia, the licensor is also to have the exclusive right it (Articles 1483.7 and 1489.3).

Chapter 7
Regulation of Foreign Trade Transactions

1 Basic Concepts

International commercial transactions, in other words international trade transactions in general, and foreign trade transactions or foreign economic transactions from the viewpoint of an individual state, are regulated in Russian law by the norms of different branches of law. The totality of these norms is usually covered by the concept of international trade law; sometimes it is even regarded as its own either independent or complex branch of law. However, in present-day Russian law the more established is the conception according to which the international trade law belongs, like international private law, to the scope of private or civil law regulation. Traditionally international trade transactions have been placed within the scope of the regulation of international private law.[1] On the other hand, public law regulation has a significant position in the regulation of international trade transactions. It is not restricted only to civil law issues but is extended to concern questions of organization,[2] competition restrictions, customs treatment, and currency control in foreign trade or foreign economic activity. In Russian law the foreign trade legislation comprises both private and public law norms regulating foreign trade transactions.[3]

In Russian law, the concept of foreign economic transaction is generally used in respect of international contracts but is left undefined in the law.[4] It comprehends commercial transactions or entrepreneurial activity of international character conducted by private (physical and juristic) persons. The essential elements of foreign economic transaction in Russian law are that the parties of such a transaction belong to different states (or that it has an international nature) and that it is of a commercial character.[5] As a civil law transaction, a foreign economic transaction establishes, changes, or terminates civil law rights and duties, the objects of which are the creation, exploitation, and distribution of material commodities and other results of human activities.[6]

---

1 For more on this subject, see G.K. Dmitrieva (ed.), Международное частное право [Private Law] (2010): 280–88 and T.N. Neshatayeva, Международное частное право и международный гражданский процесс [International Private Law and International Civil Procedure] (2004): 244–50.

2 These are subject to international economic law regulation—in particular, where they concern international macroeconomic relations.

3 See, for instance, V.F. Popondopulo (ed.), Международное коммерческое право [International Commercia Law] (2006): 11–22.

4 The term "foreign economic transaction" is used in the provisions of the Civil Code concerning the form of transactions (Articles 162.3 and 1209.2).

5 A contract concluded abroad by a branch of the Russian juristic person with another Russian juristic person is regarded in Russian legal practice as a foreign economic transaction. However, a contract concluded in Russia by a branch of the foreign juristic person with a Russian juristic person is not so considered. Hence, an enterprise of the foreign person is recognized as having a site in Russia if it practices its activities directly or through a branch on Russian territory.

6 For more on the concept of foreign economic transactions, see, for instance, Dmitrieva 2010: 273–80, where she has used also the larger concepts of transborder contract obligations and international transactions, and V.A. Kanashevsky, Внешнеэкономические сделки. Материально-правовое и коллизионное

The concept of foreign trade activity is used in Russian foreign trade legislation in its public law part. According to the Law on the Fundamentals of the State Regulation of Foreign Trade Activities (FTF Law; no 164-FZ of 8 December 2003[7]), such activities stand for foreign economic transactions regarding goods, services including works, information, and intellectual property (Article 2.4). So, in this case too, the essential elements of the activities are that the parties belong to different states (international character) and that they are commercial or entrepreneurial nature. The Law on the Fundamentals of the State Regulation of Foreign Trade Activities contains, in its part concerning foreign trade of goods, the third criterion of foreign trade activity: the border crossing of goods or their import into or export from Russian territory (Article 2).[8]

In Russian law, a broader concept than the concept of foreign trade activity is also used. This is the concept of foreign economic activity which is contained, for instance, in the Law on Export Control no 183-FZ of 18 July 1999.[9] It comprehends, in addition to foreign trade activity investment activity and other activity, productional cooperation included, the exchange of goods, information, works, services, and (the rights to) results of intellectual activity (Article 1).

2 System of Legal Regulation[10]

International economic activities, including international transactions, belong, owing to their nature, to the scope of application of international law, the important goal of which is to minimize national differences in the legal regulation of international trade. The subjects the legal relations of which are regulated on the level of international law are states and other subjects of international law.

On the level of international law, the basis of which is the concept of state sovereignty,[11] states undertake to enact in their legislation concerning international economic activities the provisions corresponding to certain requirements. This may be achieved by the state obligating itself to follow directly the international law document (agreement, treaty) by ratifying it and, in pursuance of this, by granting to it by incorporative act priority over internal legislation. International law norms may be also transformed into internal law by enacting the corresponding national legal acts. International law is comprised of the universally obligative norms and of treaties concluded between two or more states as well as of established practice or international custom law.

In its relation to the provisions of international public law agreement, (private law) transactions have an autonomous position. At the conclusion of a contract the parties must take into consideration the provisions of international agreement, but after this their contract law rights and duties are to be determined merely in accordance with the contract conditions. Possible changes in the provisions

регулирование [Foreign Economic Transactions. Material Law and Conflict of Laws Regulation] (2008): 1–33.

7 As amended by Laws no 222-FZ of 22 August 2004, no 117-FZ of 22 July 2005, no 19-FZ of 2 February 2006, and no 285-FZ of 3 November 2010. See http://www,constultant.ru/online/base/?req=doc;base=LAW;n=106400 (accessed: 2 December 2010).

8 See, for instance, V.F. Popondopulo (ed.), Коммерческое (предпринимательское) право, Том I [Commercial (Entrepreneural) Law, Volume I] (2009): 493–6, where the problems connected with the application of this criterion are presented.

9 As amended by the Law no 283-FZ of 29 December 2007.

10 For more on this subject, see, for instance, Dmitrieva 2010: 280–88.

11 The exclusive power of the state to exercise supreme authority or its legal powers within its own territory and its independence in foreign policy relations.

of an international agreement do not have an automatic impact on the content of the contract, wherefore the parties must, if necessary, make changes in their contract conditions to correspond to the provisions of the international agreement. This rule has often been enforced in Russian international arbitration practice.[12]

International transactions are, however, regulated primarily by internal law norms, the object of which are the legal relations between physical and juristic persons of different states. The national or internal law which regulates foreign economic relations is comprised of public law and civil law norms. The public law norms contain imperative or compulsory administrative law rules, which are included into customs, tax, and currency control legislation. The nonobservance of public law (imperative) norms causes the legal impossibility of the fulfillment of the private law transaction.[13]

As to the civil law regulation, its leading principles are freedom of contract and sanctity of contract, which comprehends the binding effect of contract or the principle *pacta sunt servanda*. The norms contained in national civil law regulate the issues which concern among others juristic persons participating in international trade and their legal capacity as well as international transactions or contracts concluded by them. International private law, the norms of which play an important role in the regulation of international transactions, is also a part of the internal law of each of respective states and is included into its civil law. Its norms regulate transnational or cross-border private law relations or these between physical and juristic persons of different states. The object of the international private law is, thus, civil law relations of international character,[14] and it is essentially comprised of the national law norms which concern the general competence of the authorities or their powers in cases of international character and of the law applicable in such cases or choice of law rules which are purported to solve possible collisions between laws or legal orders.

A significant role in the regulation of international transactions is also played by non-state regulation or quasi-legal regulation. Its scope includes contract conditions in which the autonomy of will of the contracting parties or the principle of freedom of contract is realized, as well as international trade customs or *lex mercatoria*[15] *and praxis* or judicial practice, including arbitration practice[16].[17]

In Russian law, international recommendation acts are also known. Among them are the Incoterms, prepared by the International Chamber of Commerce for delivery sale, and the FIDIC[18] Conditions of Contract for Construction as well as the Principles of International Commercial Contracts, developed by UNIDROIT.[19] Such recommendation acts are, however, outside of the

12 G.K. Dmitrieva (ed.), Международное частное право [International Private Law] (2000): 348 and Dmitrieva 2010: 284.

13 Dmitrieva 2010: 282.

14 The international nature of legal relations commonly stands for, in international private law, that the legal solution is to be found by taking into account the legal norms of two or more states.

15 The question is of the norms which are not based on national legislation, the sources of which include recommendations of international organizations, model laws, standard (contract) conditions, and uniform rules. These are often applied directly where the contract did not include the choice of law clause.

16 However, their use may not exclude the application of national legal norms. See Kanashevsky 2008: 67–8.

17 Dmitrieva 2010: 282.

18 International Federation of Consulting Engineers.

19 International Institute for the Unification of Private Law.

Civil Code rules on international norms, though it is nonetheless regarded as possible that they are recognized as commercial customs.[20]

3 International Law Sources

The status of international law norms in Russian law is determined on the constitutional level. According to the Russian Constitution (Article 15.4), universally recognized principles and norms of international law as well as the international treaties of the Russian Federation are an integral part of its legal system. Furthermore, the Constitution provides that, if an international treaty of the Russian Federation establishes rules which differ from those stipulated by law, the rules of the international treaty are to be applied. These rules are repeated in the general part of the Civil Code (Article 7). Thus, Russian law is subordinated to the general rule that, if Russia joins some international treaty, the provisions of it are to prevail in Russian law over its civil law norms applicable to the case. However, international treaties contradictory to the Constitution are not applicable (Article 125.6).

The priority of international principles and norms of international law as well as the international treaties of the Russian Federation is also enforced in many other laws. According to the Law on International Treaties of the Russian Federation no 101-FZ of 15 July 1995, the rules of international treaties of the Russian Federation, which do not require enactment of the internal legal act on their application, are to be directly applied. They are directly in force in Russia, whereas the application of other norms of international law must be provided by an internal legal act.

4 Internal Public Law Regulation

Fundamentals of Foreign Trade Regulation

As a part of public law regulation, foreign trade legislation has been developed in Russia in order to facilitate its membership of the World Trade Organization (WTO) and corresponds with the WTO's requirements concerning legal regulation. In many respects Russian foreign trade legislation is similar to the corresponding regulation in the European Union.

The legal regulation of foreign trade in Russia is based on the (federal) Law on the Fundamentals of the State Regulation of Foreign Trade Activities (FTF Law; no 164-FZ of 8 December 2003), which is a general law and purported to integrate the whole system of regulation of foreign trade in the country. It is supported by the (federal) Law on Special Protective, Antidumping, and Compensatory Measures at Import of Goods (no 165-FZ of 8 December 2003). The Law on Currency Regulation and Currency Control (Currency Law; no 173-FZ of 10 December 2003)[21] is also a very important law concerning foreign trade in Russia. Additionally, the customs legislation and other normative acts regulating foreign trade contain foreign trade legal norms.

20 See, for instance, Popondopulo 1 2009: 67 and M.I. Braginsky and V.V. Vitryansky, Договорное право. Общие положения [Contract Law. General Provisions] (1999): 36–7.

21 As amended by Laws no 58-FZ of 29 June 2004, no 90-FZ of 18 July 2005, no 131-FZ of 26 July 2006, no 267-FZ of 30 December 2006, no 83-FZ of 17 May 2007, and no 127-FZ of 5 July 2007, and 150-FZ of 22 July 2008. In accordance with the amendments, most restrictions were abolished.

The FTF Law is purported to secure favorable conditions for foreign trade activities and protect the economic and political interests of Russia (Article 1). The principles of state regulation of foreign trade activities in Russia include:

- protection of the rights and lawful interests of foreign trade participants as well as Russian producers and consumers;
- equality and nondiscrimination of the participants in foreign trade;
- unity of the custom area of Russia as well as its state regulation system;
- reciprocity in state relations;
- promoting fulfillment of the international obligations;
- proportionality in application of regulative measures as well as their
- transparency, justification, and appealability (Article 4).

Among the rules of the FTF Law, those of importance concern the competence of the Russian Federation and its state power bodies as well as its subjects regarding foreign trade activities, the participating parties of foreign trade activities, and the basic rules of state regulation of foreign trade activities, including its methods and provisions on conclusion of international trade agreements. Additionally, it contains special rules which concern border trade, free economic zones, foreign barter transactions, and trade missions. The law also includes provisions on measures for promoting foreign trade activities as well as on the supervision of foreign trade activities and liability for violation of legal requirements.

According to the FTF Law, the state regulation of foreign trade activities in Russia is based on its Constitution and is realized by federal laws and other normative acts (subordinated to the law). The generally accepted principles and norms of international law as well as the international agreements of Russia are also recognized as sources of legal regulation (Article 3). The shaping of foreign trade policy and protecting public order, as well as the conclusion of international agreements and participation in international organizations, also fall under the competence of the Russian Federation. As to the independent position of the subjects of the Russian Federation (republics, regions, and the cities of Moscow and St Petersburg) regarding foreign trade activities, they are only empowered to negotiate and conclude agreements on international economic relations directly with the corresponding subjects of foreign states (Article 8).

Under the FTF Law, state foreign trade regulation is to be realized in Russia by tariff and non-tariff regulation and trade restrictions on services and intellectual property as well as by economic and administrative measures promoting foreign trade activities. Other methods (means) are forbidden (Article 12).

The participating parties in foreign trade activities are, according to the FTF Law (Article 10), any Russian and foreign (juristic or physical) persons. The right to participate in foreign trade activities can be restricted only in cases stipulated by international agreement or law. Foreign persons are subject to the national regime with the exceptions provided by Russian (federal) law. Participation of the Russian Federation and the subjects of the Russian Federation (republics, regions, and the cities of Moscow and St Petersburg) as well as municipal entities in practicing foreign trade activities is restricted to the cases established by law.

According to the FTF Law, foreign trade activities concern transactions regarding goods, services including works, information, and intellectual property (Article 2). Under the FTF Law, state regulation of foreign trade activities regarding goods includes tariff and non-tariff measures, quantity restrictions, and licensing. There are also rules on the supervision of export and import of certain goods and exclusive rights of export and import of certain goods, as well as special protection measures, antidumping and compensatory measures, and on the freedom of international transit of goods (Articles 19–32). In turn, state regulation of foreign trade activities regarding services embodies the national regime for their renderers and special protective measures for public policy purposes (Articles 33–35), and such measures are also stipulated in the norms regarding intellectual property (Article 36). Special protective measures may include, in accordance with the FTF Law (Articles 37–40), special trade restrictions in case of the balance of payments problems and countermeasures. Rules on special protective measures as well antidumping and compensatory measures are specified in the Law on Special Protective, Antidumping, and Compensatory Measures at Import of Goods mentioned above.

Currency Regulation

Currency regulation connected with foreign trade is realized in Russia by the Law on Currency Regulation and Currency Control (Currency Law) mentioned above. The main objective of the law is to establish unified coherent rules for currency transactions. According to it, currency transactions are regulated in Russia, and the central body regulating them is the Central Bank of the country. Russian legal rules including customs legislation are to be followed in export and import as well as in the transferring from and to the country of not only foreign but also Russian currency.

Under the Currency Law, currency transactions are to be conducted via authorized banks. All currency operations between Russian residents and nonresidents are be conducted freely and without any restrictions or permissions except those directly named in the law. As a general rule, the law prohibits payments in foreign currency between residents (of Russia). However, it states the list of operations which can be carried out without limitations. On the other hand, foreign currency may be purchased and sold on the domestic currency market in Russia; furthermore, Russian physical and juristic persons may also open, according to the established order, foreign currency accounts at banks outside Russia, whereas foreign persons (nonresidents) may open accounts in the Russian currency at Russian (authorized) banks.

The reporting requirements have important practical meaning for Russian foreign trade participants. They include the notification of currency operations to the currency control authorities. For this purpose a passport of transaction must be filled in for almost every international currency transfer made pursuant to loan transactions, export–import contracts for goods, and international service agreements. The requirement that export proceeds must be repatriated is also important for Russian foreign trade participants (although there are certain exemptions).

Customs Regulation

Russia is at present a member of the Customs Union which is formed together with Belarus and Kazakhstan.[22] Customs regulation in Russia[23] is based on the Customs Code of the Customs Union enacted in accordance with the Treaty on the Customs Code of the Customs Union, adopted on 27 November 2009.[24] In addition to the Customs Code, the Russian system of custom legislation includes international agreements of the member states, including the one on unified customs tariffs, as well as the Federal Law on Customs Regulation in the Russian Federation,

22 In accordance with the Treaty on the Establishment of the Common Customs Territory and Formation of the Customs Union of 6 October 2007.

23 As well as in the other member states of the Customs Union.

24 See http://www.customs.ru/ru/tssouz/tssouzbelarus/detail.php?id286=6363&i286=4 (accessed 12 June 2010).

containing provisions on customs offences and procedure for their prosecution, and other legal normative acts.

The Customs Code of the Customs Union[25] contains the uniform conditions and procedures for recognizing persons performing customs activity, the definition and concretization of forms of customs control, the principal requirements for the performing of customs operations by participants in foreign economic activity and customs authorities, as well as the unified rules concerning customs procedures. Provisions of the Customs Code of the Customs Union are aimed at the facilitation of the procedure of customs clearance and customs operations for the participants in foreign economic activity.[26] As to the territories of member states, they constitute a single customs territory or an integral customs zone with no internal customs boundaries between them[27].[28]

The Law on the Customs Regulation in the Russian Federation, which has replaced the Customs Code of the Russian Federation, contains rules which in the Customs Union are submitted to the level of national legislation. The law provides among others rules on:

- the system of customs authorities of the Russian Federation, their duties, competence and responsibility;
- the procedure of appeal against the actions of the customs officers;
- the procedure of maintaining registers of persons performing activity in the field of customs affairs;
- the computation, paying, and recovery of customs duties;
- the peculiarities of performing certain forms of customs control;
- the disposal of goods converted into federal property, and
- the peculiarities of customs declaration, customs procedures, and conveyance of certain types of goods.

Customs regulation rules, established by the Customs Code (Article 150), provide that goods conveyed across the customs border of the Custom Union are to be subject to customs registration and customs control in accordance with the Code. It is also provided (Article 94) that, in conducting customs control measures, the customs authorities proceed from the principle of selectivity and, as a rule, confine themselves to the forms of customs control sufficient for ensuring the observance of the customs legislation of the Russian Federation (relying on the risk management system).

Generally applied customary customs procedures are recognized in the Customs Code, and the customs procedure regime may be freely chosen and changed to another one in accordance with the Code (Article 203). The following customs procedures are applicable in the Customs Union (Article 202):

25 See http://www.customs.ru/ru/tssouz/tssouzbelarus/detail.php?id286=6364&i286=3 (accessed 12 June 2010). The Customs Code is based on the provisions of the Kyoto Convention on the Simplification and Harmonization of Customs Procedures.

26 According to the Customs Code, importation of plant and equipment for an investment project will be exempt from customs duties. Tariff benefits may also be granted with regard to goods imported from third countries as contributions to the charter capital of companies.

27 Thus, goods manufactured or released for free circulation on the territory of any of the member states will circulate within the Customs Union territory: (1) without payment of customs duties, (2) free of any economic restrictions, and (3) with simplified customs formalities.

28 On the content of the Customs Code, see, for instance, http://www.russianlawonline.com/law-firms-publications/baker-mckenzie-customs-union-russia-belarus-kazakhstan and http://www.customs.ru/en/news/index.php?id695=31939 (accessed: 12 June 2010).

- release for domestic consumption;
- export;
- customs transit and customs warehouse;
- inward and outward processing procedures and processing for domestic consumption;
- temporary importation and exportation;
- re-import and re-export;
- duty-free trade, as well as
- disposal and rejection in favor of the state,
- free customs zone, and
- free warehouse, as well as
- special customs procedure for customs purposes.

Under the Customs Code, customs payments include import and export duties, value-added tax, and excise tax levied on goods imported to the customs territory of the Union as well as customs fees. As to the special antidumping and compensational duties established in accordance with international treaties and/or national legislations, they are to be levied in accordance with the rules of the Customs Code with regard to import duties (Article 70).

The rules on customs tariffs in the Customs Union contain the regulations on export and import duties; besides the general customs treatment, most-favored-nation (preferential) treatment is also known. The customs tariffs provisions contains a rule according to which an enterprise with foreign investments may be exceptionally relieved from duties on goods imported as a contribution into its charter capital.

Customs procedures for importing and exporting often include certification requirements, including declarations and certificates of conformity. They are purposed to be the evidence, for instance, that products meet the standards provided for by technical regulations (general and special).[29] Certification is mandatory in Russia only for products included in the list of commodities subject to obligatory certification, whereas products which are not subject to the mandatory attesting of conformity can be imported without declarations or certificates of conformity.

5 Investment Legislation

The promotion of investment activities was the most important economic policy goal in the Russian economic reforms. In particular, foreign investments were regarded as means to improve economic conditions for business activities in the country, though without great success for the Russian economy. Nevertheless, the promotion of foreign investment still plays an important part in Russia's economic policy, although there are also clear indications that the problems caused by them are taken very seriously indeed. To promote investment activities including foreign investments special legislation has been developed in Russia and in some cases it also contains restrictions for foreign investors.[30]

29 According to the Law on Technical Regulation no 184-FZ of 27 December 2002 as amended by laws no 45-FZ of 9 May 2005, no 65-FZ of 1 May 2007, no 309-FZ of 1 December 2007, and no 385-FZ of 30 December 2009, and 243-FZ of 28 September 2010.

30 Investment legislation is regarded in Russia as regulating legal relations which are the object of the investment law. The investment law is, in turn, defined as a complex branch of law, the object of which is the legal norms regulating relations concerning the attraction of investment, their use, and control over

Foreign investments are regulated in Russia by the Law on Foreign Investments in the Russian Federation (Foreign Investments Law; FI Law), which was enacted on 9 July 1999 (no 160-FZ)[31]. The FI Law is aimed, according to its preamble, at giving protection to the rights of foreign investors regarding their investments and income and profits thereof, and defining conditions for their enterprise activities in Russia. Its purpose has been to attract foreign material and financial resources, advanced technology, and management into the country, and to use them in the national economy.

Foreign investment activities are also to be regulated, in accordance with the FI Law, by other federal laws and normative acts as well as international agreements of the Russian Federation. The FI Law also empowers the subject of the Russian Federation to issue laws and normative acts on investment activities in accordance with their competence stipulated by the law (Article 3) and to give preferences and guarantees to foreign investors as well as to participate in the financing of investment activities (Article 17).

The FI Law includes the concepts of investor and foreign investment as well as direct foreign investment; the investment project and the priority investment project are also defined in the law (Article 2). It contains provisions on legal regime and guarantees as well as preferences regarding foreign investments (Articles 4–17). The norms of the law also regulate the establishment and liquidation procedures of commercial organizations with foreign investments and branches of foreign juristic persons (Articles 20–22).

For foreign investments and the investment activities of foreign investors, the national regime—that is, the principle of national treatment—is enforced in the FI Law with the exceptions provided by federal laws (Article 4). Furthermore, it is provided that foreign investors shall enjoy the full and unconditional protection of their rights and interests and shall have the right to reimbursement for damages caused by illegal acts or omissions by federal or local (self-government) bodies or officials in accordance with the law (Article 5). Furthermore, investments must not be nationalized or requisitioned with the exception of those cases provided by the federal law or international agreement. However, where nationalization or expropriation does take place, compensation of the value of the property seized must be paid and also, in case of nationalization, compensation for damages is provided (Article 8). The law also provides guarantees of repatriation or other use of profits, including reinvestment and re-exportation (Articles 11–12), as well as gives the right to settle disputes arising out of investment activities in international arbitration (Article 10). It also permits the purchase of corporate and governmental securities (Article 13) and participation in the privatization process (Article 14) as well as the acquisition of rights to land, natural resources, buildings, and other immovable property (Article 15) in accordance with the law. In addition, the FI Law expressly provides that incentivizing exceptions in the form of privileges for foreign investors may be established by Russian legislation in the interest of the social and economic development of the country. On the other hand, exceptions of a restrictive nature may also be imposed by the federal law in order to maintain public order (Article 4.2).[32]

Exceptions of a restrictive nature are established in Russia by the Federal Law on Foreign Investments in Companies of Strategic Importance for State Security and Defense (no 57-FZ of 29

---

investment activities, as well as issues related to the liability of investors. See, for instance, V.V. Guschin and A.A. Ovchinnikov, Инвестиционное право [Investment Law] (2006): 87.

31 As amended by the laws no 31-FZ of 21 March 2002, no 117-FZ of 25 July 2002, no 169-FZ of 8 December 2003, no 117-FZ of 22 July 2005, no 75-FZ of 3 June 2006, no 118-FZ of 26 June 2007, and no 58-FZ of 29 April 2008.

32 For the protection of fundamental constitutional principles, morality, health, or the rights and legal interests of others, or to provide for the defense of the country and the security of the state.

April 2008). According to it, the acquisition of control of a strategic sector company by a foreign investor requires in certain cases prior approval[33] or notification[34] of the authorized state body. Strategically important activities are listed in the law, and they include activities in sectors such as defense, nuclear, aviation, and space, television and radio broadcasting, printed mass media, and natural monopolies, as well as geological survey and exploration and development of subsoil areas on a large scale.

Foreign investors can be foreign physical and juristic persons, as well as non-juristic entities and stateless persons, which have the right by virtue of the laws of their state to carry out investment activity in Russia. States and, by virtue of a treaty with the Russian Federation, international organizations can also act, according to the FI Law, as foreign investors.

Foreign investments include, according to the FI Law, all kinds of material assets and intellectual property as well as services and information invested by foreign investors into entrepreneurial activities. In turn, direct investments are defined as:

- the acquisition by a foreign investor of at least 10 percent of the shares of a Russian company or partnership;
- the contribution by a foreign investor of at least 10 percent of the charter capital of such an organization;
- investment in the fixed assets of a branch office of a foreign juristic person, or
- the execution as lessor of a leasing contract for certain equipment having a value of at least 1 million rubles.

An investment project comprehends, under the FI Law, a set of detailed business plans, including feasibility studies, for a direct foreign investment, while a priority investment project requires involvement of an aggregate volume of foreign investment of at least 1 billion rubles in value or is an investment project in pursuit of which foreign investors contribute a minimum of 100 million rubles into the charter capital of an enterprise (commercial organisation) with foreign investments; additionally it is provided that such project is included on a list approved by the Russian government (Article 2).

The preferences and guarantees provided by the FI Law are designed not only for foreign investors but also for (established or acquired) enterprises with foreign investments that have at least 10 percent foreign ownership and for branches of foreign juristic persons. Enterprises with foreign investments must register their status and a branch office must be accredited with the authorized state body.

According to the FI Law (Article 9), investors and enterprises with foreign investments are entitled in certain cases to a guarantee of legal stability up to a maximum of seven years. The guarantee applies to investors and enterprises with foreign investments that are implementing a priority investment project. Exceptionally, the seven-year limit may be extended if:

- the priority investment project concerns production or transportation or other infrastructure and
- the total investment is equivalent to at least 1 billion rubles.

33 For instance, the acquisition of control of more than 50, and in some cases 10 and even 5, percent of a strategic company.

34 For instance, acquisition of 5 percent or more of the shares of a strategic company.

6 International Private Law Rules[35]

International or foreign trade transactions are governed, as stated above, by civil law norms. Civil law relations of international character are, in turn, regulated in Russia by the norms of international private law, according to which in addition to domestic law norms, foreign law or rules of an international treaty may have to be applied. The international private law provisions, the main purpose of which is to determine the cases in which the private law of the state where the action is pending or *lex fori*,[36] and where the private law of a foreign state[37] is to be applied, are contained in the third part of the Civil Code.

The international private law rules included in the third part of the Civil Code are intended as basic in nature, and this means that the norms regulating civil law relations of international character may also be contained in other legal acts. Such norms are included in the normative acts concerning leasing and pledge, among others. Furthermore, family and labor law relations of international nature are regulated separately in Russian law. In respect of this, it is also important to note that the international private law norms of the third part of the Civil Code do not contain international civil process law rules, which are not considered in Russian doctrine as belonging to international private law.[38] In the Russian legal system they are included in the civil process law norms[39].[40]

The international private law norms in the third part of the Civil Code contain general provisions (Chapter 66) and choice of law rules concerning legal status of physical and juristic persons (Chapter 67), as well as property law and personal non-property law relations (Chapter 68). The choice of law rules of the Civil Code concern the legal status of physical and juristic persons, and in accordance

35 For more on this subject, see Dmitrieva 2010 and Boguslavsky 2009. The provisions of the international private law are commented upon in Abova, Boguslavsky, and Svetlanov (eds), Комментарий к Гражданскому кодексу Российской Федерации Том 2 [Commentary to the Civil Code of the Russian Federation, Volume 2] (2010): 125–98; S.A. Stepanov (ed.), Комментарий к Гражданскому кодексу Российской Федерации [Commentary on the Civil Code of the Russian Federation] (2010): 1071–97, and T.E. Abova, M.M. Boguslavsky, A.Y. Kabalkin, and A.G. Lisicin-Svetlanov (eds), Постатейный комментарий к Гражданскому кодексу Российской Федерации, Частям I, II и III [Article-specific Commentary on the Civil Code of the Russian Federation, Parts I, II, and III] (2007): 948–1016. As to the legal regulation of international transactions in Russia, see Kanashevsky 2008.

36 The law of the jurisdiction where the action is pending.

37 The governing law is to be determined by applying choice of law or conflict of laws norms.

38 In Russian legal doctrine, Russian international private law is regarded as a separate field of law and is characterized as a system which is comprised of principles, internal and international conflict of laws norms, and uniform material international private law norms. They regulate private law relations complicated by a foreign element through solving collisions of private laws of different states. See Dmitrieva 2010: 37–8.

39 In the settlement of disputes of international nature, the international arbitration procedure plays an important role. It is regulated in Russia by the Law on International Commercial Arbitration of 1993. The law provides among others that, in the absence of a choice of law clause, the arbitration court shall apply the law determined by the conflict of laws rules which it deems appropriate (Article 28.2). The Russian Law on International Commercial Arbitration is otherwise based on the UNCITRAL Model Law on International Commercial Arbitration of 1985. For more on this subject, see, for instance, Dmitrieva 2010: 592–648 and A.S. Komarov, Некоторые актуальные вопросы международного коммерческого арбитража в Российской Федерации [Some Actual Questions of International Commercial Arbitration in the Russian Federation], Международный коммерческий арбитраж. Специальный выпуск [International Commercial Arbitration. Special Edition] (2006).

40 See Abova, Boguslavsky, Kabalkin, and Lisicin-Svetlanov 2007: 948–51.

with them the legal order under which the private law questions closely related to a person are settled is determined. These personal statute provisions contain, besides the rules on personal law of a physical[41] and juristic person, the rules regulating state participation in international civil law relations. In turn, the choice of law provisions of the Civil Code concerning property law and personal non-property law relations contain, firstly, the rules on the law applicable to property rights as well as to the statute of limitations and form of transaction. Secondly, they include the obligation statute rules or the rules determining the applicable law not only to a contract (contract statute) but also to obligations arising from unilateral transactions. These include assignment of a claim and payment of interest as well as obligations arising from causing harm or tort liability and from unjust enrichment or unjustified enrichment. The third part of the Civil Code ends in the rules determining the law applicable to relations arising from succession.

General Provisions

The general international private law provisions of the third part of the Civil Code (Chapter 66), firstly, define the sources of international private law, the scope of application of the international private law norms of the Civil Code, and their relation to the international material law norms. Furthermore, it contains the general choice of law rule, and the rules on qualification or characterization of legal concepts as well as the provisions on the application of foreign (state) law and on public order (*ordre public*) the rules on which impose the limits for the application of foreign law.

Legal sources he Russian international private law rules, under which the law applicable to civil law relations of international character is determined, are comprised, in accordance with Article 1186 of the Civil Code, of the norms of international treaties of the Russian Federation and the Civil Code (Articles 1186–224) as well as of the federal laws adopted in accordance with it (Article 3.2). The position of the norms of international law is enforced in Russian law at the constitutional level (Article 15.4), and, if an international treaty of the Russian Federation establishes rules which differ from those stipulated by law, then the rules of the international treaty are to be applied, and this rule also applies to colliding civil law norms. According to the Civil Code (Article 7.2), international treaties of the Russian Federation are to be applied to relations directly regulated by civil legislation, except in cases where it follows from an international treaty that the adoption of an internal legal act is required for its application. Moreover, Article 1186.3 of the Civil Code determining the law applicable to civil law relations contains the rule prioritizing international law norms, in accordance with which the international material law norms contained in an international

41 The Civil Code provides the rule which is to be applied in determining the legal capacity of a physical person to exercise entrepreneurial activity (Article 1201). It is purposed to regulate the case where a physical person exercises entrepreneurial activity without the founding of a juristic person. In such a case, the law of the country where a physical person is registered as an individual entrepreneur is applicable, and this personal statute follows him everywhere irrespective of the place he practices entrepreneurial activity. In the event the personal statute of the individual entrepreneur may not be determined due to the absence of the obligatory registration, the law of the country where entrepreneurial activity is mainly practiced is to be applied. Thus, the personal statute of a foreign individual entrepreneur acting in Russia is to be determined in accordance with the law of his native country, if he is registered there as an individual entrepreneur, or in accordance with Russian law, if obligatory registration is lacking in his country but his main place of business is in Russia. Practicing of individual entrepreneurial activity in Russia, in turn, requires registration, and the foreign individual entrepreneur registered in Russia is, with some exceptions, subject to the application of its national regime.

treaty of the Russian Federation supersede the application of conflict of laws or choice of law norms to the question at issue (Article 1186.3).

The law applicable to civil law relations is also to be determined, according to the Civil Code (Article 1186.1), on the basis of commercial customs recognized in the Russian Federation. In respect of contract law relations the international private law provisions of the Civil Code include additionally the rule concerning the case when commercial terms generally accepted in international trade, for instance Incoterms, are used in the contract. It is regarded in such a case that, unless otherwise provided by the contract, the parties have agreed on the application of the commercial customs embodied in those terms to their relations.

Scope of application The international private law rules of the Civil Code are applied to civil law relations of international character. These are, according to Article 1186.1 of the Civil Code, relations with the participation of foreign physical and juristic persons or civil law relations complicated by another foreign element, including cases where the object of civil law rights is located abroad.

Although the application of international private law rules of the Civil Code is general, it is nonetheless allowed to deviate from them where a dispute is handled under the international commercial arbitration procedure. The Civil Code directly provides that the peculiarities of determining the applicable law in an international commercial arbitration is to be established by the law on international commercial arbitration (Article 1186.1). Such provisions are contained in the Russian Law on International Commercial Arbitration Procedure (1993). In accordance with it (Article 28.2), in the absence of the choice of law clause, arbitrators of the commercial arbitration court are to decide on the choice of substantive law applicable to the substance of the dispute in accordance with the conflict of laws rules which they find most applicable to the case.

General choice of law rule The international private law rules of the Civil Code determine minutely those cases where a civil law issue of international character is governed by Russian law or foreign law. In respect of the cases where the determination of the applicable law under the Russian international private law norms is impossible, the Civil Code provides a safety valve rule for general application (Article 1186.2). According to it, in such a case the law of the country with which the civil law relation is most closely related or the law of closest connection or the law of the most significant relationship is to be applied.

Qualification Qualification or characterization comprehends usually the legal definition of facts and circumstances relevant for the issue subject to consideration, and the general provisions on it are contained in the Civil Code (Article 1187). They comprise a main and subsidiary rule. According to the main rule, in the determination of the applicable law, the interpretation of legal concepts used in qualification are to be governed by Russian law, unless otherwise provided by the law (Article 1187.1). In turn, the subsidiary rule (Article 1187.2) is purposed for those cases where the legal concepts requiring qualification are not known to Russian law or are known under another verbal designation or with other content and cannot be determined by interpretation under Russian law. In such a case the foreign law may be applied. The qualification rule is provided also in the provisions of the Civil Code on property statute (Article 1205.2), the starting point of which is the law of the country where the property is located (*lex rei sitae*).

Application of foreign law The international private law rules of the Civil Code contain mainly two-sided conflict of laws rules consisting of the principle or rule on the basis of which the applicable law is to be chosen; the question is of the choice between the Russian legal order and that of a foreign state. Conflict of laws rules are, however, merely choice of law rules, and, though they are the legal ground for the application of foreign law,[42] they do not contain the answer to a material question. They indicate only the national legal order on the basis of which the legal question is solvable. Moreover, in the event the applicable law is under the choice of law rule the law of a foreign state, then the question arises as to how the content of a foreign law is to be ascertained.

The international private law norms of the Civil Code include rules aimed at determining the content of a foreign law. The application of a foreign law is also appended with such questions as the application of the law of a country with a multiplicity of legal systems, reverse reference, or *renvoi*, reciprocity, retorsion, and public order, or *ordre public*, the rules on which are provided in the international private law norms of the Civil Code.

Article 1191.1 of the Civil Code regulating the establishment of the content of foreign law contains the basic rule according to which, in the application of foreign law, a court establishes the content of its norms in compliance with the official interpretation, application practices, and doctrine in the respective foreign state. Thus a Russian court must *ex officio* or on its initiative (officially) take into consideration the norm of foreign law and apply it. The general requirement is that the foreign law must be applied with the same content as is applied in the respective foreign state and it must be applied as legal norms or legally peremptory provisions.[43] Under the obligation of a court is also that the content of the foreign law be clarified.[44] In order to establish the content of norms of foreign law the court may apply, according to the Civil Code (Article 1191.2), in due procedure to the Ministry of Justice of the Russian Federation and other competent bodies or organizations, including research institutes, in the Russian Federation and abroad for assistance and clarification. The court may also use the services of experts.

In the process of clarification of the content of foreign law, according to the Civil Code (Article 1191.2), parties to a case may present documents confirming the content of foreign law norms to which they refer in order to justify their claims. The parties may also in other ways assist the court in clarifying the content of such norms. Thus, the parties have only the right to aid in clarification of legal norms applicable to their dispute (or other legal issue), but the legal consideration in the case is under the duty of the court. In the event the claims of the parties are related to enterprise activities, the burden of proof of the content of foreign law may be placed by the court upon the parties (Article 1191.2).

The provisions of the Civil Code on the establishment of the content of foreign law also contain the rule regulating the situation when the content of a foreign law norm cannot be clarified within a reasonable time despite the aforementioned measures (Article 1191.3). In such a case, Russian law is to be applied, and this means that the establishment of the content of foreign law is to be governed by the *lex fori* rules.

In the application of the law of a foreign state, a problem may arise if the state in question has multiple legal orders. Ordinarily, these are states divided into administrative territorial units, such as federative states. With respect to such cases, referred to as an interlocal collision, the Civil

42 The application of foreign law is understood in Russian legal doctrine as that (a) it is to be applied by courts and other bodies of administration of justice, and (b) if it is referred to, then its application is obligatory for authorities, and (c) it comprehends the legal norm system or legal substance. See Dmitrieva 2010: 146.

43 According to the Russian international private law doctrine, in the application of foreign law, its content must be clarified not only on the bases of the legislative texts of the respective state but also by resorting to the official interpretation, legal consciousness, legal doctrine, and legal practice in the country. See Dmitrieva 2010: 147.

44 Thus, the application of foreign law is equated with the application of national law.

Code provides special rules (Article 1188). The provision of the Civil Code on multiplicity of legal systems also contains the safety valve rule as a subsidiary one. According to it, in the event the applicable law is the law of a country where several systems of law are in effect, the legal system of law determined in compliance with the law of that country is to be applied. However, if under the law of that country, it is impossible to determine which of the legal systems is applicable, the legal system with which the relation is most closely connected is to be applied. Thus, in the case of an interlocal collision, subsidiarily or as a safety valve rule, applicable is the law of closest connection or the law of the most significant relationship. The rules on interlocal collisions of the Civil Code are also applicable to cases of interpersonal collisions, where different groups of person are governed by different legal norms.[45]

The main purpose of the conflict of laws norms or choice of law rules is to indicate the law applicable to an individual case or *lex causae*, and it stands for the material norms of the legal order indicated by the choice of law rule. However, the reference to the law of another state may lead to the situation that the choice of law rules of this state may be applicable, and, in turn, these rules may refer to the application of the norms which are not of this state but of the state where the issue is under consideration. As a result, the situation termed *renvoi*, or reverse reference, may arise and this means that the issue returns for settlement to the state the choice of law rules of which have been originally applied. It is possible also that the choice of law rules of the state originally referred to refer forward to the law of some third state, in which case the situation termed forward reference may occur. In respect of these situations the Civil Code contains the rules on reverse reference (Article 1190). The general rule in Russian international private law is that a reference to a foreign law is regarded as a reference to the material law of the respective state but not to its conflict of laws norms (Article 1190.1) or choice of law rules. However, the provisions on reverse reference of the Civil Code contain an exception to the general rule (Article 1190.2), and this concerns the determination of the personal statute of a physical person provided in the Civil Code (Article 1195–200). In such a case, reverse reference to foreign law is applicable in cases of reference to Russian law.

Among the basic rules of Russian international private law is the requirement that the courts and other judicial authorities are under the duty to apply the foreign law indicated by choice of law rules without demands for reciprocity. According to Article 1189.1 of the Civil Code, foreign law is applicable in the Russian Federation irrespective of the applicability of the Russian law to similar relations in the respective foreign state. However, as an exception, it is possible that, in accordance with the Civil Code, the law imposes the requirement of reciprocity for the application of a foreign law. In this case, or if the application of a foreign law depends upon reciprocity, this is to be presumed, unless proved otherwise. Thus, according to the Civil Code, the principle of reciprocity is in such a case in effect until proved to the contrary.[46]

International private law norms of the Civil Code also contain the rules on retorsions (Article 1194), which are countermeasures provided by international law, by of the use of which the state may reply to unfriendly acts of another state. According to the Civil Code, reciprocal limitations (retorsions) may be established by the Government of the Russian Federation. They may concern the property and personal non-property rights of citizens and juristic persons of states in which

45 So-called intertemporal collisions are handled in the same way. These arise owing to the existence of legal norms enacted at different times but regulating the same legal relations. In practice, this means that the implementing provisions of the applicable law must be taken into consideration. For more on this subject, see Dmitrieva 2010: 153–4.

46 Dmitrieva 2010: 155.

there are special limitations on the property and personal non-property rights of Russian citizens and juristic persons.

Ordre public As a concept, *ordre public* is connected with the fact that, in general, the state imposes principled limits on the applicability of foreign law. Equivalent terms such as public order, foundations of the legal order, and principle of absoluteness as well as public policy are commonly used. The basic purpose of the *ordre public* rule is that the applicable foreign law norms must not be contradictory to the foundations of the legal order of state—this is the so-called negative *ordre public* or principle of absoluteness. The *ordre public* or public order also stands for moral and justness, or equity, rules and the basic interests of state and its members, and nowadays it also frequently comprehends generally recognized principles and norms of international law.[47] The application of the *ordre public* rule or principle means that a foreign law chosen through the conflict of laws norm is not to be applied, nor the subjective rights arising by such a foreign law be protected, if such an application or protection are against the public policy of the own country, or *lex fori.*

Often, the concept of *ordre public* also entails that the internal directly imperative or peremptory material legal norms of the country are to be applied irrespective of whether the otherwise material law norms of the legal order of another state chosen through the conflict of laws norm are applicable—in this case the question is of so-called positive *ordre public.* In general, the directly applicable norms comprehend domestic legal norms. On the other hand, they also stand for foreign law norms, which are to be applied irrespective of whether they are contained in the legal order indicated by the choice of law rule or not. In such cases the question is of the application of forcign private law norms, since the *ordre public* rules belong to the private law provisions. However, in considering a question of an international character a court may not often ignore the public law norms of a foreign state. However, the court may only take such norms into consideration since it is allowed to apply only the private law norms of a foreign state. This means that it is, in principle, impossible through the application of the choice of law norm to avoid the legal effect of public law norms.[48]

The international private law norms of the Civil Code contain both negative and positive *ordre public* rules. The negative *ordre public* rule, or principle of absoluteness, is contained in the provision where the reservation of public order is prescribed (Article 1193). According to it, in exceptional cases a norm of applicable foreign law chosen through the international private law rules of the Civil Code is not be applied. However, non-application of a foreign law norm is allowed, according to the rule, only if not only the content of the applicable norm but also the consequences of its application would obviously contradict the foundations of the legal order or public order of the Russian Federation. Thus, the application of the public order reservation requires that the disregarding of a foreign law norm is justified *in casu*, and as justification may be presented merely the observation that the application of it would lead to a result which is against the foundations of the Russian legal order. Additionally, the public order norm of the Civil Code directly provides that a refusal to apply a norm of foreign law may not be based merely on a

---

47 The Russian public order may be regarded as consisting of (1) the basic principles, in the first place, of constitutional law but also of the private law, (2) generally recognized moral principles on which the Russian legal order is based, (3) the legal interests of Russian citizens and juristic persons as well as the legal interests of Russian society and the state, the protection of which is the main aim of the legal system of the country, and (4) generally recognized principles and norms of international law that form a part of the Russian legal system, including the international standards of human rights. See Dmitrieva 2010: 159.

48 See Dmitrieva 2010: 165–6.

difference in the legal, political, or economic systems between the respective country and the Russian Federation.[49] In the event a foreign law norm is disregarded owing to the application of the *ordre public* rule, if necessary, the relevant norm of Russian law (or *lex fori*) is to be applied (Article 1193). On the other hand, a legal norm of a foreign state may also be applied, and is to be determined under the law of the country with which the civil law relation is most closely related, taking into account that the Civil Code provides the safety valve rule for the subsidiary application (Article 1186.2), which is the law of closest connection.

The positive *ordre public* rules are contained in Article 1192 of the Civil Code regulating the application of imperative norms. According to it, the international private law rules of the Civil Code are not to be applicable in the event the imperative norms of the Russian (Federation) legislation, owing to an indication contained in them or in connection with their special significance, govern the respective relations directly, irrespective of the applicable law (Article 1192.1). The question is of directly applicable or absolutely imperative or peremptory (mandatory) material law norms. Prescriptions on mandatory application in Russian civil law are included, firstly, in the provisions on the form of foreign economic transactions; they must be concluded in written form on penalty of nullity (Article 162.3). The provisions of the Civil Code (Article 208) listing the demands to which the limitation of action does not apply also belong to the rules which are to be applied irrespective of the otherwise applicable law indicated by the choice of law rules. Among the legal norms which are to be directly applied because of their special significance, the Civil Code (Article 1192.1) indicates, in particular, the norms purposed for securing the rights and interests of participants in civil law relations.[50]

The provisions of the Civil Code on the application of peremptory norms make it possible for the public order of a foreign state to be also protected in Russia. According to Article 1192.2 of the Civil Code, in the application of a foreign state law determined through the choice of law rules a court may take into consideration the peremptory norms of the country with which the civil law relation is most closely related. The precondition for taking into consideration foreign state imperative norms is that under the law of the respective country such norms must regulate the respective relations irrespective of the applicable law or will be applied instantly. Thus, a Russian court may under its consideration take into account directly applicable imperative or peremptory norms of the legal order of the country which has the closest connection to the legal question at issue. The question of whether the legal norm is of absolutely imperative or peremptory character covered by *ordre public* or not is to be solved in accordance with the conceptions of the respective legal order. For taking into consideration the peremptory material law norms belonging to the foreign state *ordre public* the rules of the Civil Code on the application of imperative norms impose additionally an important requirement: the court must consider the purpose and nature of such norms and also the consequences of their application or non-application (Article 1192.2). This can

49 The application of the *ordre public* rule must be exceptional. See K.B. Yaroshenko and N.I. Marysheva, Комментарий к Гражданскому кодексу Российской Федерации, части третьей (постатейный) [Commentary on the Civil Code of the Russian Federation, Part Three (Article-specific)] 2004: 390 (Komarov). On the other hand, the public order of Russia presumes fairness and the equality of the parties, and a ruling based on forged documents is to be considered as violating the basic principles of Russian law. See A.S. Komarov, S.N. Lebedev, and V.A. Musin, Международный коммерческий арбитраж. Комментарий законодательства [International Commercial Arbitration. Commentary on Legislation] (2007): 367 (Rogozhin).

50 An example of such a norm is the rule provided by the Civil Code according to which the refusal of a physical or juristic person to exercise his rights does not entail the termination of these rights, unless otherwise provided by the law (Article 9.2).

mean also that the Russian court disregards the foreign imperative norm directly applicable to the issue on the ground that the result of its application is contradictory to the Russian *ordre public*.[51] In such a case as well as where the application of a foreign law norm is set aside due to the application of the Russian law *ordre public* rule, the norms of Russian law (*lex fori*) are to be applicable.

Choice of Law Rules

Personal statute The choice of law rules concerning the legal status of juristic persons, according to which the private law issues closely connected to a juristic person or personal statute (*lex personae*) is to be determined, is contained in Article 1202 of the Civil Code regulating the personal law of a juristic person. It contains, besides the choice of law rule, the list of issues which belong, in accordance with the Russian international private law rules, to the personal statute of a juristic person and which are to be determined under the personal law (Article 1202.2). They include:

- the status of the organization as a juristic person;
- the legal form of a juristic person;
- the requirements for the name of a juristic person;
- issues concerning the formation, reorganization, and liquidation of a juristic person, including legal succession;
- the content of the legal capacity of the juristic person;
- the procedure for the acquisition of civil law rights and assumption of civil law duties by the juristic person;
- internal relations, including relations of the juristic person with its participants as well as,
- the capacity of the juristic person to respond for its obligations.

According to the choice of law rules concerning the legal status of a juristic person, the personal law of a juristic person is the law of the country where the juristic person has been founded (Article 1202.1).[52] The foundation of a juristic person generally requires registration, wherefore the law of the state of registration is commonly regarded as the personal statute of a juristic person. Under the law of the state of registration the legal (act) capacity of a juristic person is determined and it arises at the moment of registration. The content of the rights or legal status of a juristic person is determined in accordance with its original foundation documents presented at the registration. The legal status of the juristic person may be subject to the provisions of an international treaty, which may stand for granting a certain regime and reciprocal recognition. It is possible also that the nationality or legal status of a juristic person is determined by an international treaty to be the state of its site.

The provisions of the Civil Code on the personal law of a juristic person also include the rule purported to protect third persons (Article 1202.3). According to it, a foreign legal entity may not refer to a limitation of the powers of its body or representative to enter into a transaction which is not known in the law of the country where the body or the representative has entered into the

51 The application of the *ordre public* of the foreign law is also subject to the contract statute provision of the Civil Code regulating choice of law by contracting parties (Article 1210), which will be presented below. Unlike the general rule on the application of imperative norms (Article 1192), the contract statute rule, in which the free will of the parties is restricted, is formulated as a fixed rule (Article 1210.5). This has the restriction that the contracting parties may not exclude by the choice of law clause the application of the imperative norms of the state to which the contract is most closely connected.

52 Which is regarded as its nationality.

transaction, with the exception of cases when it is proved that the other party knew or should obviously have known of the limitation. Thus, in the event a contract is concluded in Russia, the good faith, or *bona fide*, of the Russian contracting party of a foreign legal entity is protected from the risk that the legal (act) capacity of a foreign legal entity or its representative deviates from the provisions of Russian law on it.

The international private law norms of the Civil Code contain the rules which concern subjects of international private law other than physical persons and juristic persons. They include organizations which are not juristic persons and the state.

According to Article 1203 of the Civil Code, although a foreign organization is not a juristic person under its national law, its personal law is the law of the country where this organization was founded. In the event Russian law is applicable to the activity of such an organization, the corresponding rules of the Civil Code regulating the activities of juristic persons are to be applied, unless it otherwise follows from the law, other legal acts, or the nature of the relation. Such an exception may be provided, for instance, by a bilateral treaty of the Russian state.

The international private law rules of the Civil Code are also applicable, according to its Article 1204, to the participation of the state in civil law relations of international character. In such relations, the state participates in accordance with the general rules of international private law. This means that its legal status in international private law relations is in principle the same as that of other subjects of law. However, the law may provide otherwise, according to the Civil Code, and the most important exception is represented by the rules of state immunity.

Property statute The rules on the property statute determine the legal order of the state the norms of which are to be applied in considering material law questions belonging to property law, and in Russian international private law they are contained in the Civil Code as the general provisions on the law applicable to property rights (Article 1205) as well as the rules on the law applicable to the origin and termination of property rights (Article 1206) and the property rights to ships (crafts) and space objects (Article 1207).

According to the general provisions concerning property rights, the content of a right of ownership and other rights to immovable and movable property as well as their exercise and protection[53] are to be determined according to the law of the country where the property is located (Article 1205.1). Thus, Russian international private law has adopted the *lex rei sitae* rule. The law of the location of the property is also applied to the property law qualification, as stated above, where the classification of property as immovable or movable is to be determined (Article 1205.2). Instead, the applicable law to the ownership and other property rights to aircrafts, sea vessels, inland vessels and space objects which are subject to state registration as well as the exercise and protection of the rights is the law of the country where such object is registered (Article 1207).

According to Article 1206.1 of the Civil Code providing the rules on the applicable law to the origin and termination of property rights, this is determined by the law of the country where such property was located at the time when the legal fact for the arising and termination of the right was present. Thus, the ownership and other property right to the thing once acquired remains constant, or the ownership right to the thing legally transferred to the ownership of another person in the other state remains effective even though the thing is transferred to the other state. However, although the ownership right to the thing acquired abroad remains, its content may change.

53 However, the origin and termination of the right of ownership and other property rights relating to movable property are, under the Civil Code, outside the scope of the property statute (Article 1210.1).

Additionally, the provisions of the Civil Code on the law applicable to the origin and termination of property rights contain the rule (Article 1206.2) which applies to the movable property en route, for instance goods *in transitu*. According to it, the origin and termination of a right of ownership or other property right under transaction concluded in respect of such property is to be determined by the law of the country from which the property was sent, unless otherwise provided by the law. The provisions of the Civil Code on the law applicable to the origin and termination of property rights also contain the rule (Article 1206.3) on the origin of the ownership and other property rights by virtue of acquisitive prescription. This is determined by the law of the country where the property was located at the time of expiry of the acquisitive prescription term. If this occurred on the territory of Russia, Russian law is applied, according to which the acquisitive prescription term is, in respect of immovable property, 15 years and, for other property, five years (Article 234.1). Additionally, Russian law provides that the rights to the property subject to registration are to arise from the moment of their registration (Article 234.2), unless otherwise established by the law (Article 8.2). The registration requirements in Russia concern the ownership right to immovable and, in certain cases, movable property.

Statute of limitations Limitation of action is regarded in Russian law as belonging to civil law, and it is related to questions of property law. According to the international private law rules of the Civil Code, the statute of limitations is determined by the law of the country governing the respective relation (Article 1208). Thus, the law applicable to the statute of limitations depends on what kind of property is in question, where the civil law object is located, and to which country's law it is subordinated. If the question is, for instance, of demands based on a foreign economic transaction and related to the obligation statute, their limitation term is to be determined in accordance with the obligation statute.

Form of transaction[54] In Russian international private law, as in general, the law applicable to the form of a transaction (contract) or form statute is regarded as separate question. The provisions on it in the Civil Code are placed in its own article, which contains besides the general provisions special rules concerning the form of foreign economic transactions concluded by Russian juristic persons and transactions on immovable property. According to the general provisions (Article 1209.1), the form of a transaction is to be governed by the law of the country where it is concluded (*locus regit formam actus*). This is, however, the main rule, since the general provisions of the Civil Code on the transaction form contain additionally, as a subsidiary conflict of laws rule, the provision according to which a transaction concluded abroad may not be recognized as invalid on the grounds of its noncompliance with the form requirements, if those of the Russian law have been observed.[55] Thus, a transaction concluded abroad, according to Russian law, is valid in the event that the requirements of the Russian law or the law of the country where it is concluded are followed. The rules of the general provisions are also to be applied to the form of a power of attorney (Article 1209.1).

According to the special rules of the Civil Code concerning the form of foreign economic transactions concluded by Russian juristic persons, if at least one party of such a transaction is a Russian juristic person, the form requirements of the transaction are to be determined according to Russian law, irrespective of the place of its conclusion. Russian law is also to be applied, according

54 For more on this subject, see, for instance, Dmitrieva 2010: 304–9 and Abova, Boguslavsky and Svetlanov (2010): 166–70.

55 Thus, the facultativeness of the form statute is a general rule in Russian international private law.

to the Civil Code, to the form of a transaction in which at least one party is a physical person practicing entrepreneurial activity, whose personal statute is, according to the Civil Code (Article 1195), Russian law (Article 1209.2). In respect of foreign economic transactions, including a power of attorney for it, Russian law provides an obligatory written form, the nonobservance of which causes invalidity of the transaction (Article 162.3).[56]

According to the special rule of the Civil Code concerning the form of a transaction on immovable property (Article 1209.3), the form of a transaction in respect of immovable property is to be governed by the law of the country where the property is located. However, Russian law is to be applied, according to the Civil Code, in respect of immovable property subject to registration in Russia, including Russian aircrafts, sea vessels, inland vessels, and space objects.

Obligation statute[57] The choice of law rules of the Civil Code on contract statute or the provisions according to which the law applicable to contract obligations is determined are divided into general provisions and special rules, which are applicable to a contract with the participation of a consumer, a contract in respect of immovable property, and an agreement for the foundation of a juristic person with foreign participation. The international private law norms of the Civil Code also contain the rules determining the law applicable to an assignment of a claim which may occur not only by contract but also by unilateral transaction.

The general provisions of the Civil Code on the contract statute contain, firstly, the rules on the scope of application of the law applicable to a contract (Article 1215) or the issues which form the content of the contract statute. The issues to which the applicable law is determined in Russian law according to the rules on contract statute include:

- the interpretation of the contract;
- the rights and duties of the parties to the contract;
- the performance under the contract;
- the consequences of nonperformance or improper performance of the contract;
- the termination of the contract, and
- the consequences of invalidity of the contract.[58]

All these issues are related to the rights and duties of the parties to the contract. Therefore, questions which do not concern the rights and duties of the contracting parties are outside the scope of the obligation statute and subject to other choice of law norms, unless otherwise provided by the law. Such issues include statute of limitations, payment of interest (Article 1218), and assignment of a claim (Article 1216) which, according to the Civil Code, is to be governed by the law of the country which is applicable to the respective obligation.[59]

The basic rule on the law applicable to the issues belonging to the contract statute is contained in Article 1210 of the Civil Code concerning the choice of law clause. According to it, the contracting

56 In turn, if both parties of a contract are foreign persons, then its form is determined in accordance with the general rule. Thus, the contract is valid if it corresponds with the form requirements of the country where it is concluded or the Russian general form requirements on transactions, which do not demand written form for their validity.

57 For more on this subject, see Dmitrieva 2010: 288–91.

58 On the law applicable to the invalidity of foreign economic transactions, see Kanashevsky 2008: 157–62. The choice of law depends on the grounds for invalidity. In general, they concern the issues which belong to the obligation statute.

59 Dmitrieva 2010: 290.

parties may, at the conclusion of the contract or thereafter, choose by their agreement the law that will govern their rights and duties under the contract. This means the enforcement of the principle of the free will, or *lex voluntatis*, in the Russian international private law. It comprehends, firstly, that the contracting parties may, at their discretion, define the content of their contract and determine the law applicable to it by the choice of law clause. Then, in accordance with the same rule, the law chosen by the parties will govern the origin and termination of the right of ownership and other property rights relating to movable property without prejudice to the rights of third persons (Article 1210.1).[60]

According to the Civil Code, the choice of law clause or the agreement of the parties on the applicable law must be directly expressed or must become evident from the terms of the contract or the circumstances of the case (Article 1210.2). In the event the choice of law clause is made after the conclusion of the contract, it has retroactive force and is considered valid, without prejudice to the rights of third persons, from the moment of conclusion of the contract (Article 1210.3). The choice of law clause may concern, in accordance with the Civil Code, the contract as a whole as well as specific parts of it (Article 1210.4), and this means that Russian international private law recognizes the situation where different parts of the contract are governed by different laws (*dépeçage*).

The free will of the contracting parties or their freedom to determine the law applicable to their contract is restricted in the Civil Code by not only the above-presented rules protecting third persons[61] but also the rule on the application of imperative norms. According to it, if from the totality of circumstances at the time of the choice of the applicable law, it is evident that the contract is actually connected with only one country, the parties may not supersede the imperative norms of that country (Article 1210.5).

In the absence of the choice of law clause, the law applicable to a contract is determined under the rules provided in Article 1211.1 of the Civil Code, and this is the law of the country with which the contract has the closest connection. Thus, the principle of closest connection or the proper law principle is established in Russian international private law[62] not only as a general subsidiary rule governing any civil law relation (Article 1186.2) but also as a subsidiary conflict of laws rule applicable to contract obligations in the absence of the choice of law clause.

The law of the country with which the contract has the closest connection is defined in the rules of the Civil Code on the law applicable to a contract in the absence of the choice of law clause (Article 1211.2). According to it, as such is understood, unless it otherwise follows from the law, the terms or the nature of the contract, or the totality of the circumstances of the case, the law of the country where the place of residence or main place of activities of the party, whose performance has decisive significance for the content of the contract, is located. Related to this, the Civil Code provides a group of connections which refer to the law of the party, the obligation of which has decisive significance, and which indicate the law of closest connection.[63]

According to the Civil Code (Article 1211.3), as the party whose performance has decisive significance for the content of the contract is to be regarded, unless it otherwise follows from the

60 This issue is regarded as also belonging to the obligation statute. See Abova, Boguslavsky, and Svetlanov 2010: 186.

61 Outside the scope of free will are also issues which do not belong to the contract statute, including legal (act) capacity, form of contract, ownership relations, and invalidity of contract.

62 For more on the proper law principle in Russian law, see Dmitrieva 2010: 300–304.

63 However, these rules may be dismissed on the presumption of the fair intent of the parties to conclude a valid contract which is also applicable in Russian judicial practice. Thus, the court may not apply a law according to which the contract at issue is invalid. See Kanashevsky 2008: 162–3.

law, the terms or the nature of the contract, or the totality of the circumstances of the case, the party who is, in particular:

- the seller in a contract of sale;
- the donor in a contract of gift;
- the lessor in a contract of lease;
- the lender in a contract of gratuitous use of property;
- the contractor in a work contract;
- the carrier in a contract of carriage;
- the freight forwarder in a contract for freight forwarding;
- the lender (creditor) in a contract of loan (credit contract);
- the finance agent in a contract of financing against assignment of a monetary claim;
- the bank in a contract of bank deposit and a contract of bank account;
- the bailee in a contract of storage;
- the insurer in a contract of insurance;
- the delegate in a contract of delegation;
- the commission agent in a contract of commission agency;
- the agent in an agency contract;
- the franchisor in a contract of franchise;
- the mortgagor in a contract of mortgage;
- the surety in a contract of suretyship, or
- the licensor in a license contract.

In respect of certain contract types, taking into account their specific nature, the provisions of the Civil Code on the law applicable to a contract in the absence of the choice of law clause directly indicate the law of the country with which the contract has the closest connection, unless otherwise follows from the law, the terms or the nature of the contract, or the totality of the circumstances of the case. So, as the law with which the contract has the closest connection is regarded in the case of:

- a construction work contract and a contract for the performance of design and exploratory work—the law of the country where the results stipulated by the contract are mainly created;
- a contract of simple partnership—the law of the country where its activities are mainly practiced, and
- a contract concluded by auction, tender, or at exchange—the law of the country where the auction or tender is held or the exchange is located (Article 1211.4).

The provisions of the Civil Code on the law applicable to a contract in the absence of the choice of law clause also contain the rule concerning a mixed contract (Article 1211.5). According to it, a contract which contains elements of different types of contract is to be governed, unless otherwise follows from the law, or the terms or the nature of the contract, or the totality of the circumstances of the case, by the law of the country with which this contract as a whole has the closest connection.

The provisions of the Civil Code on the law applicable to a consumer contract (Article 1212) are purposed to protect a consumer or a physical person who uses, obtains or orders or intends to use movable things (works, services) for personal, family, household, or other purposes not connected with the practicing of entrepreneurial activity. According to the Civil Code, the choice of the law applicable to a consumer contract must not cause the disregarding of the imperative norms of the consumer law of the country of the place of residence of the consumer, or *lex domicile*, if the contract is objectively connected to this. The *lex domicile* serves also as a subsidiary collision of laws rule in the determination of the law applicable to a consumer contract in the absence of the choice of law clause. The rules of the Civil Code on the law applicable to a consumer contract are not, however, applicable to a contract of carriage and a contract for the performance of work or provision of service fully abroad.

7 International Contracts

Foreign trade is usually practiced by concluding civil law contracts between enterprises which belong to different countries and performing their corresponding obligations. The objects of foreign trade are products existing in material form as well as services and industrial property rights which take the form of goods in civil exchange. The general aim of contracts concerning those objects is to receive a counterperformance: one party is obligated to fulfill a certain action and the other party is obligated to a counterperformance.

Russian law does not directly impose particular restrictions on the autonomy of will of the parties of a foreign economic transaction except with respect to the application of the imperative norms, which may not be excluded by a choice of law clause, as presented above. Contracting parties may not only refer to the law of the country they have chosen but also agree that their contractual relations are to be determined by the principles of international commercial contracts or customs of international trade or general legal principles, or *lex mercatoria.* Parties of a foreign economic transaction also have large possibilities to choose the proceedings for the resolution of their disputes, and international commercial arbitration is very common in international contract relations.[64] On the other hand, in Russian judicial practice—international commercial arbitration practice, to be precise—a list of the issues subjected to an arbitration clause or agreement has been formed. They include interpretation of contract, the rights and duties of contractual parties, fulfillment and termination of contract, as well as the consequences of its invalidity.[65] In arbitration procedure, disputes concerning limitation of action, the origin and termination of the property right to the property subject to transaction, as well as the moment of transfer of risk of unintentional destruction or damage of property have also been handled.

Characteristic for foreign contracts is the use of other than statutory or legislative sources of law, and this also concerns contracts concluded by Russian enterprises. So, in addition to the above-mentioned Incoterms conditions (discussed below), commercial customs and trade usages as well as model or standard conditions of contract are widely known in Russia.

International commercial customs and trade usages are widely applied in international economic exchange.[66] This is based merely on the fact that the legal provisions regulating international trade law disputes refer directly to them. For instance, in accordance with Article VII.1 of the European

64 Dmitrieva 2010: 332–49; Kanashevsky 2008: 119; M.G. Rozenberg, Контракт международной купли-продажи [Contract of International Purchase–Sale] (2003): 30–32 and M.G. Rozenberg, Международный договор и инностранное право в практике Международного коммерческого арбитражного суда [International Contract and Foreign Law in the Practice of the International Commercial Arbitration Tribunal] (1998): 16–17.

65 Rozenberg 1998: 16–17.

66 For more on this subject, see, in particular, N.G. Vilkova, Правила толкования международных торговых терминов [Rules for the Interpretation of International Commercial Terms] (2008): 25–43.

Convention on International Commercial Arbitration 1961, in applying the applicable law, the arbitrators should take account of trade usages. Also the material law provision regulating foreign trade may require the application of trade usages. Moreover, the rules of the Civil Code on customs of trade (Article 5), presented above,[67] make it possible that in some cases, contrary to the rules of the Vienna Convention, a rule of conduct may be recognized as a custom of trade because of its wide application but not of its cognizance.[68]

Standard conditions used in international trade are also known in Russian foreign trade.[69] Such conditions, which are generally regarded as international trade customs, and the model terms of contracts regulated by Article 427 of the Civil Code have both similarities and differences. The similarities lie in that both the model terms of contracts regulated by the Civil Code and standard conditions used in international trade are regarded as related to the offer. In the event of their acceptance by quoting their content or referring to them, they are considered to have become contract conditions, whereas if such conditions or terms are explicitly rejected in a contract, they are not applicable to the contract. Differences between the standard conditions used in international trade and model terms of contracts regulated by the Civil Code occur where they are ignored wholly in the contract. In international transactions, it is common to apply standard conditions, even in the absence of direct reference to them in the contract, and this is based on the irrefutable presumption that, due to the fact that the contracting parties must have known the standard condition, they have implicitly accepted the application of it to their contract. However, the solution concerning model terms of contracts is different in the Civil Code (Article 427.2): there, in the absence of any reference to such terms, they are to be applicable only where the custom of trade corresponds to them. Furthermore, it is noteworthy that the model term of a contract, not included in it, is placed under Russian civil law as a custom of trade in the last position in the hierarchy of legal sources. This means that its content must not contradict neither imperative nor dispositive norms of the Civil Code (Article 421.5).[70]

Forms of Foreign Economic Transactions

Sale of goods (movables)[71] Sale of goods (movables), the objects of which are goods in material form, is the main form (type) of contract in Russia, as well as in general, because the exchange of goods still forms the major part of international economic relations. Many forms of work contract, including performances of work and services which usually follow the supply of machinery and equipment, are also closely connected with the contract for sale of goods. The significance of the norms regulating sale of goods is also important for other forms of trade as well as for the legal regulation of cooperation agreements, because its rules form a general regulative basis for almost

---

67 See Chapter 1.

68 M.I. Braginsky and V.V. Vitryansky, Договорное право. Общие положения [Contract Law. General Provisions] (1999): 72–4 and Vilkova 2008: 41–2.

69 Standard conditions used in international trade are generally distinguished into mutually and unilaterally prepared. Mutually prepared standard conditions arise as a result of the negotiations between the parties, mostly their representatives. In turn, unilaterally prepared standard conditions are represented by contracts of adhesion, the content of which is rarely subject to negotiations. They are made by the other party, entrepreneur, or the organization which represents the area he practices his activities, and the other party may enter into such a contract only by adhering to the proposed contract as a whole.

70 Braginsky and Vitryansky 1999: 82–4.

71 For more on this subject, see, in particular, Popondopulo 2006: 366–401 and M.G. Rozenberg, Международная купля-продажа товаров [International Sale of Goods] (2006).

all compensated contracts.

The contracting parties in the sale of movables are the buyer and seller, and the object of their legal transaction is a thing or goods in material form. The distinctive feature of the sale of movables is the transfer of ownership of the thing or goods from the seller who is the owner to the seller who becomes the owner. Generally, in sale, the basic obligation of the seller is to hand over or deliver the goods, surrender the associated documents, and transfer their ownership, whereas the basic obligation of the buyer is to take delivery of (accept) the goods and pay the price for them. An international contract of sale provides that the seller undertakes to transfer the goods cross the border to the buyer whose enterprise is sited in another state.[72]

Russia is party to the Vienna Convention, whose contracting parties also include many Western countries. The Convention consists of substantive law rules regulating not only the rights and duties of the parties of the contract for sale of goods (in material form) but also rules concerning the conclusion of contract, liability for the breach of contract, and so on. The application of the rules of the Convention is general: they are to be applied unless otherwise (in a different or exceptional way) agreed by the parties. In other words, the rules of the Convention replace to a certain extent the norms of internal law (which regulate the same questions).[73] Thus, a contract for sale of goods concluded between a Russian and foreign enterprise is to be governed primarily by the rules of the Vienna Convention even in the case where the contracting parties have not referred to them; it is not even necessary for the parties to know about the existence of the Convention.

The Vienna Convention provides the material rules regulating the formation, interpretation, and form of a contract for sale of goods, the rights and duties of buyer and the seller, breaches of contract and their legal consequences or remedies, the transfer of risks, compensation for damages, interest and relief from liability, rescission of contract, and preservation of the good. However, outside of the scope of application of the Convention are the general contract law questions, the validity of a contract and its conditions, property law impacts in respect of the sold goods, limitation of action, assignment of a claim, setoff, and personal damages. These questions are to be settled, in accordance with Article 7 of the Convention, by following the general principles it is based on and in conformity with the law applicable by virtue of the rules of private international law. In Russia the UNIDROIT principles are regarded as such general principles[74].[75]

Regarding the cases (Article 3) and questions (Article 4) whose scope is not under the rules of the Vienna Convention, a contract made with a Russian enterprise is to be governed by Russian law and especially its civil law norms contained in the Civil Code. This takes place in the case where the contract includes a reference to Russian law or the applicable law is not determined in it but the buyer is a Russian enterprise, in accordance with Article 1211 of the Civil Code, particularly if a dispute (probably arisen) is to be settled in Russia. However, it should be noted that in cases where a contract is concluded at auction by bidding, exchange, or competition and it does not contain the choice of law clause, the applicable law is, under the Civil Code, the law of the place of their proceedings (Article 1211.4). However, only Russian civil law is to be applied to questions

72 See, for instance, V.F. Popondopulo (ed.), Международное коммерческое право [International Commercial Law] (2006): 227–9.

73 See Articles 1–6 of the Convention and the interpretation of those in the work Венская конвенция [The Vienna Convention] 1 (1994): 6–26.

74 However, the International Commercial Arbitration of Russia (of Russia's Chamber of Commerce) has often resorted in respect of such questions to the subsidiary application of Russian law.

75 On the application of the Vienna Convention in Russia, see, for instance, Boguslavsky 2009: 324–30.

of ownership if the property is situated in Russia (Article 1205);[76] the form of contract is also to be determined under Russian law if one of the contracting parties is a Russian person (Article 1209).

The Incoterms conditions can also be applied to a contract for sale of movables concluded with a Russian enterprise, and these conditions are also regarded in Russia as commercial customs; they include conditions concerning transport and insurance, transfer of goods, ownership, and risks to them, which in Russia are termed as basic conditions. The Incoterms conditions have been applied in the praxis of Russian international commercial arbitration even in a case when a contract did not include any reference to them.[77]

Lease (rental) and leasing In Russia, as in general, the lessor is obligated under the lease contract to transfer a thing (the property) to the temporary and usually exclusive use of the lessee against payment. The lessor retains his ownership of the leased property and to the lessee he transfers only the temporary right of its use. The main points of the contract for lease are the duties of the lessee and lessor as well as the conditions concerning the rent, the term of contract, and the rules on its dissolution.

In case of an international lease contract, the question about the applicable law is usually resolved by applying the rules of international private law (choice of law rules). If a dispute arising from the contract is to be settled in Russia, the Russian rules of international private law, or *lex fori*, contained in the Civil Code is to be naturally applied; and under the Civil Code, if the lease contract does not contain any condition on the choice of law, the proper law in Russia with regard to the rights and duties of the contracting parties is in principle the law of the lessor's country (Article 1211.3). This means that if the lessee is a Russian enterprise and leases equipment from a foreign enterprise, the law of the country of this enterprise is to be applied; whereas in case where the lessor is a Russian enterprise, Russian law or the rules of the Civil Code (Articles 606–89) are to be applied to the contract relations. If the contractual relations are regulated under the Russian law, it is relevant to pay attention to the peculiarities of Russian law which are presented above, specifically the rules concerning re-lease as well as redemption of the leased property and renewing of the lease contract. In turn, if the object of the lease contract is a land, subsoil, or water object or other immovable property located on the territory of the Russian Federation, it is governed exclusively by Russian law or only Russian law is to be applied to the contractual relations[78] (Article 1213.2).[79]

The leasing contract is recognized as a contract according to which the lessor transfers to the lessee the right to use the object of leasing during the agreed term and for the agreed rent. Among leasing contracts, financial leasing in particular is general in contractual practice. Another usual form of leasing which is also known in Russia is operational leasing. The term of leasing in this instance is usually very short and the object of leasing can be leased to many lessees one after another; thus, operational leasing is a modification of the ordinary lease contract.[80]

---

76 However, a contract in respect of immovable property may be governed by the law which the contracting parties has chosen (Article 1213).

77 For more on this subject, see, in particular, Vilkova 2008 (which includes a model contract in Russian on pp. 423–35) and also Popondopulo 2006: 366–401.

78 See, for instance, Abova, Boguslavsky, Svetlanov 2010: 176 and 183.

79 As amended by the Law no 73-FZ of 3 June 2006.

80 See Vitryansky, V.V., Договор аренды и его виды: прокат, фрахтование на время, аренда зданий, сооружений и предприятий, лизинг. [Contract of Lease and Its Species: Rental, Time-charter, Lease of Buildings, Structures and Enterprises, Leasing] (2001): 250 and 256. See also, in particular, Kravchenko,

Financial leasing is subject to the application of the UNIDROIT Convention on international financial leasing of 1988, in which Russia has participated since 1998. In addition, the Civil Code also contains provisions on financial leases or leasing which follow the Convention provisions. According to its Article 665, under a financial lease contract (leasing contract), the lessor undertakes to acquire into ownership the property indicated by the lessee from the seller chosen by him and grant for a compensation to the lessee the temporary possession and use of it for entrepreneurial purposes. The lessor in this case does not bear responsibility for the choice of the leased object and the seller. The recently mentioned UNIDROIT or Ottawa Convention on international financial leasing provides the rules applicable to international financial leasing contracts, which are similar to the provisions of the above-presented Vienna Convention, for cases where the parties of a contract are sited in different states which are the members of the Convention. The application of the rules of the Convention is also general: they are to be applied unless otherwise (in a different or exceptional way) agreed by the parties.[81]

Work and construction work contract Installation and reparation works, technical maintenance of machinery and equipment, research and development work, etc. are usually performed under work contracts. In turn, building works are usually performed on the basis of the construction work contract. Furthermore, construction on a turn-key basis or some other corresponding principle, if it is simplified to the level of the main obligations, can be regarded as covered by the building contract, although it can include in its entirety many other deliveries and performances.[82]

In Russia, as well as in general, the contractor is obligated under the work contract to perform certain work by order of the customer using materials of the customer or his own at his own risk, and the customer is obligated to accept it and pay for the performed work. The object of the work contract or the result of the work always takes the material form of a building, repaired and serviced machine, technical documents, report, etc. The conditions concerning the object, price, and term of performance are regarded as the most important conditions of the work contract. The exact description of the order and payment conditions, as well as questions of liability, in particular, take a central place in the work contract.

A work contract can be governed by the substantive norms of Russian law or the provisions of the Civil Code regulation on work and construction work contracts. They are to be applied in cases where the contract includes reference to Russian law or, in the case of a construction work contract and a contract for the performance of design and exploratory work, if there is no definition of the applicable law in it, and the results stipulated by the contract are mainly created in Russia (Article 1211.4). As to the other work contracts, the law of closest connection, according to the Civil Code (Article 1211.3), is to be the law of the contractor. Thus, the application of Russian law is to be dismissed in those cases where the contractor is a foreign juristic person, and, in particular, if he performs his works on the basis of his technical condition accepted by the Russian customer.[83]

Under Russian law, the work contract concluded by a Russian enterprise with a foreign enterprise is a foreign economic transaction, in which case the party's freedom of contract regarding the content of their obligations is almost unlimited and, hence, especially the use of general conditions is common. At present the FIDIC Conditions of Contract for Works of Civil

S. Виды договора лизинга [Species of Leasing Contract], http://pda.fassko.arbitr.ru/novosti/vestnik/archive/8245.html (accessed 11 June 2010).

81 See, for instance, Neshatayeva 2004: 285–6.

82 On the content of international work contracts, see, for instance, M.M. Boguslavsky, Международное частное право [International Private Law] (2009), 336–40.

83 Boguslavsky (2009): 336–40.

Engineering Construction are recognized and generally used in construction works in Russia. It is usual, however, for the works, particularly construction works, to be performed in the place where their object is situated, and if this occurs in Russia, then it is difficult and sometimes even unnecessary to avoid the application of Russian law, especially in as far as it concerns the technical norms and acceptance of the works.

Service contract In a foreign economic transaction a service performance can be either an independent, separate object (for instance, advertising) or it can be connected with the usual sale of movables when its function is to secure or supply the performance. Such service performances are transport, insurance, payment, credit, etc. As an independent object, the service performance is a characteristic of contracts which concern productional and technical orders—for example, consulting services, researches and development works. These are covered in Russia under the general name of engineering services. Furthermore, management services and so on can be an independent object of trade. Rental and tourist services are also included in the same group, although each of these has its own specific features.

The main point of the contract for service performance is, as in the work contract, the obligations of the performer of the service and especially the exact description of the order. Service obligations are commonly personified. As the service relation can require loyalty from the contracting parties, it is therefore natural that the contract includes the condition according to which the contract may be dissolved even without any justified reason. Service contracts are at present regulated in Russian civil law by the special norms regulating service performances, which form their own group in the second part of the Civil Code. Delegation, commission, and agency as well as the storage, transport, and expedition, in addition to payments and financing, are also often regarded as services in Russia, but they are regulated by their own norms in the Civil Code. The contract relations concerning services are often constructed by using the rules of different types of contract depending on the nature of the service performance, and often the norms regulating work contracts are used as a basis for it. On the other hand, a service usually means nonmaterial activities rather than a result to be achieved in material form, and this is the point by which the service contract is distinguished from the work contract. It is usual that the same contract includes performances of differing nature; a service contract can be a long-term contract which is purported to regulate continuous service performances.[84]

Brokerage Brokerage activities are known in Russian internal entrepreneurial activities and foreign trade in many different forms. These include delegation, commission, and agency, the norms on which are contained in the Civil Code. Also resale, distribution, and consignation contracts are known in Russian contractual practice.

In Russia as in general, brokerage activities comprehend actions which are connected with the trade of goods and which are executed under the orders of producers (exporters) by brokers who are independent from the producers on the basis of a contract or separate orders. The activities can include different kind of services such as searching for a trading partner, preparation and conclusion of transaction, credit granting and credit checking of the customer, transport and expedition, marketing and maintenance, etc. The important reason for the use of a broker in the sale of goods can be the intent of a seller to improve the readiness for delivery and reliability of maintenance on

---

84 For more on this subject, see V.F. Popondopulo (ed.), Коммерческое (предпринимательское) право, Том II [Commercial (Entrepreneural) Law, Volume II] (2009): 205–23; Popondopulo 2006: 296–314, and A.P. Sergeev (ed.), Гражданское право [Civil Law] 2 (2009): 498–510.

the territory of the sale of goods. Therefore, a contract can contain special obligations of the broker (reseller, agent) concerning the storage of goods and installation and maintenance services; storage is an essential element of the consignation contract.

Delegation, in which, in accordance with the Civil Code (Article 971), the delegate undertakes to fulfill legal actions in the name of the delegant or principal and on his account, usually takes, as concerning entrepreneurial activities, the form of commercial representation, which is also regulated by the norms of the Civil Code (Article 184). As stated above, a commercial representative is allowed to execute the simultaneous commercial representation of different parties to a transaction, though only with the consent of these parties or in cases provided for by the law. In turn, commission contract, the rules on which are also purported to regulate the mediation activities in the performance of commercial transactions, is defined in the Civil Code (Article 990) as a contract under which the commission agent undertakes on delegation from the principal to conduct one or several transactions in its own name but at the expense of the principal. As to agency contract, it stands for a contract under which the agent, similarly to the delegant in a representation contract, fulfills legal actions and additionally also other or real actions; the agent may act in his own name or in the name of the principal. Hence, in the agency contract elements of both commission and delegation are combined.

Other forms Among other forms of foreign economic transactions, different joint activity arrangements are well known in Russia. Many of them are contractual obligations based on the rules regulating license and work contracts as well as simple partnership. A franchise contract, the object of which are exclusive rights in complex, is used in organizing joint entrepreneurial activities. The rules on these types of contract are contained in the Civil Code, and they include also choice of law rules (Articles 1235–8, 702–29, 1041–53, and 1027–40 respectively as well as 1211).

Joint activities may also be practiced in corporate form through the establishment of a company. In Russia it may be a joint stock company or a limited liability company. In establishing a company in Russia Russian law is to be followed, and it will be a Russian juristic person. A Russian company may also be acquired through purchase of shares or membership interest in it. Russian law also provides opportunities to purchase a Russian company as a whole or property complex. The most recent amendments to both Joint Stock Company and Limited Liability Company Law have introduced a radical change in the Russian corporate law by providing for the use of operation agreements.[85] They make possible contract law arrangements and consequently the application of foreign law, at least to some extent, to the relations between participants in a Russian company.

85 See Chapter 2.

Index